Image and Video-Based Artistic Stylisation

Computational Imaging and Vision

Managing Editor

MAX VIERGEVER
Utrecht University, Utrecht, The Netherlands

Series Editors

GUNILLA BORGEFORS, *Centre for Image Analysis, SLU, Uppsala, Sweden*
DANIEL CREMERS, *Technische Universität München, München, Germany*
RACHID DERICHE, *INRIA, Sophia Antipolis, France*
KATSUSHI IKEUCHI, *Tokyo University, Tokyo, Japan*
REINHARD KLETTE, *University of Auckland, Auckland, New Zealand*
ALES LEONARDIS, *ViCoS, University of Ljubljana, Ljubljana, Slovenia*
STAN Z. LI, *CASIA, Beijing & CIOTC, Wuxi, China*
DIMITRIS N. METAXAS, *Rutgers University, New Brunswick, NJ, USA*
HEINZ-OTTO PEITGEN, *CeVis, Bremen, Germany*
JOHN K. TSOTSOS, *York University, Toronto, Canada*

This comprehensive book series embraces state-of-the-art expository works and advanced research monographs on any aspect of this interdisciplinary field.

Topics covered by the series fall in the following four main categories:

- Imaging Systems and Image Processing
- Computer Vision and Image Understanding
- Visualization
- Applications of Imaging Technologies

Only monographs or multi-authored books that have a distinct subject area, that is where each chapter has been invited in order to fulfill this purpose, will be considered for the series.

Volume 42

For further volumes:
www.springer.com/series/5754

Paul Rosin · John Collomosse
Editors

Image and Video-Based Artistic Stylisation

Springer

Editors
Paul Rosin
School of Computer Science & Informatics
Cardiff University
Cardiff, UK

John Collomosse
Centre for Vision Speech & Signal Proc.
University of Surrey
Guildford, Surrey, UK

ISSN 1381-6446 Computational Imaging and Vision
ISBN 978-1-4471-4518-9   ISBN 978-1-4471-4519-6 (eBook)
DOI 10.1007/978-1-4471-4519-6
Springer London Heidelberg New York Dordrecht

Library of Congress Control Number: 2012951684

Mathematics Subject Classification: 68U05, 68U10, 65D18

© Springer-Verlag London 2013
This work is subject to copyright. All rights are reserved by the Publisher, whether the whole or part of the material is concerned, specifically the rights of translation, reprinting, reuse of illustrations, recitation, broadcasting, reproduction on microfilms or in any other physical way, and transmission or information storage and retrieval, electronic adaptation, computer software, or by similar or dissimilar methodology now known or hereafter developed. Exempted from this legal reservation are brief excerpts in connection with reviews or scholarly analysis or material supplied specifically for the purpose of being entered and executed on a computer system, for exclusive use by the purchaser of the work. Duplication of this publication or parts thereof is permitted only under the provisions of the Copyright Law of the Publisher's location, in its current version, and permission for use must always be obtained from Springer. Permissions for use may be obtained through RightsLink at the Copyright Clearance Center. Violations are liable to prosecution under the respective Copyright Law.

The use of general descriptive names, registered names, trademarks, service marks, etc. in this publication does not imply, even in the absence of a specific statement, that such names are exempt from the relevant protective laws and regulations and therefore free for general use.

While the advice and information in this book are believed to be true and accurate at the date of publication, neither the authors nor the editors nor the publisher can accept any legal responsibility for any errors or omissions that may be made. The publisher makes no warranty, express or implied, with respect to the material contained herein.

Printed on acid-free paper

Springer is part of Springer Science+Business Media (www.springer.com)

Preface

"Computers are useless. They can only give you answers."
Pablo Picasso, *1881–1973*.

Almost two hundred years ago, the advent of photography was heralded as the beginning of the end for traditional painting. Rather than rendering painting obsolete, the technology instead motivated a new era of abstraction in visual art, delivering—among many other movements—Impressionism, Futurism, and Cubism, which continue to inspire contemporary art. Similarly, the astonishing achievements in visual realism delivered by Computer Graphics have motivated new research into the rendering of non-photorealistic styles. Non-photorealistic Rendering (NPR) is now a firmly established field within Computer Graphics, spanning over two decades of research. With origins in artistic simulation and scientific visualization, NPR has now broadened to intersect computational photography, perceptual modelling and interaction design. NPR research regularly appears in top tier graphics conferences and journals, and has delivered commercial impact through digital photography and mobile applications, and through the creative industries.

This book assembles a catalogue of classical and contemporary techniques capable of transforming 2D footage—i.e. images and video—into synthetic artwork. This sub-discipline within NPR is often referred to in the literature as *Artistic Rendering*, and sometimes by the more specific title *Artistic Stylization*. Even limiting ourselves to the rendering of images and video primarily for aesthetic value, there has been a huge diversification and development of the field over the past decade—approximately the time since the last survey of the field was published.

One significant development has been the emergence of NPR as a truly multi-disciplinary field; a focal point for the convergence of Computer Graphics, Computer Vision, Human Computer Interaction and perceptual Psychology. The convergence with Computer Vision is particularly relevant to this book's topic of 2D artistic stylization. The increasing complexity and diversity in style demanded by techniques demands a correspondingly greater degree of sophistication in the parsing and extraction of information from source footage. In the mid-1990s when automated artistic stylization techniques began to emerge, there was a reliance upon low-level image processing operators to guide the rendering process. In the early 2000s mid-level interpretation of imagery through image segmentation, perceptual salience measures, and more sophisticated filtering operators yielded improved style diversity and the robustness and temporal stability necessary to coherently stylize video. As the field matures it is now common to see a fusion of even more sophisticated image parsing, combined with careful interface design, recognizing the role of artistic stylization as a practical creative tool. Consequently in recent years, this research has begun to deliver commercial impact in major digital image and video manipulation products.

The structure of this book echoes this categorization of artistic stylization research. Part I focuses upon image stylization through the placement of marks (such as strokes, hatches and stipples), or through non-linear filtering operators. This is arguably the largest area of 2D stylization research, and also one of the most active. Part II focuses on region-based techniques that require images to parsed into a visual structure via interactive or automated algorithms. Regions may be shaded using a variety of gradient effects, or packed with rendering primitives such as strokes, space filling curves, tiles and other marks. Furthermore, scene semantics may be derived from regions enabling specialised rendering to be applied e.g. to enable portrait rendering. Part III extends the discussion of both categories of stylization to video, and explores both low-level methods based on optical flow, and mid-level methods based on regions. In addition to processing real video into stylized animation, the issue of processing existing animations into other stylized forms is discussed. Finally, Part IV discusses the matter of evaluating NPR output. As the field of artistic stylization matures, key questions include how to assess the benefits of a new proposed approach, and how to assess the suitability of a particular approach to a particular requirement or scenario. In this book we present complementary perspectives on the matter of evaluating a rendering generated primarily for aesthetics. Finally, we discuss the emerging commercial impact of NPR "in the wild"; that is, the application of NPR to real world scenarios. Crucially this requires consideration of the users of NPR and its creative implications.

Picasso doubted the benefit of computers on the basis that they are merely powerful calculating machines. Yet research in our field has shown that, enabled by such machines, we can begin to ask new questions about art, computing, and their interaction. With advances in Vision, Machine Learning, and Human Factors merging into this maturing sub-discipline with Computer Graphics, this is an exciting time to be working in NPR.

Cardiff University, UK Paul Rosin
University of Surrey, UK John Collomosse

Acknowledgements

We would like to thank Reinhard Klette for encouraging us to start working on this book, and also Jan Eric Kyprianidis whose help and technical expertise enabled us to complete it.

Contents

Part I Strokes, Marks and Filters for Artistic Stylization

1. **Stroke Based Painterly Rendering** 3
   David Vanderhaeghe and John Collomosse

2. **A Brush Stroke Synthesis Toolbox** 23
   Stephen DiVerdi

3. **Halftoning and Stippling** 45
   Oliver Deussen and Tobias Isenberg

4. **Non-photorealistic Shading and Hatching** 63
   Victor Ostromoukhov

5. **Artistic Stylization by Nonlinear Filtering** 77
   Jan Eric Kyprianidis

6. **NPR for Traditional Artistic Genres** 103
   Eugene Zhang

Part II Stylization from Structure

7. **Region-Based Abstraction** 125
   David Mould

8. **Gradient Art: Creation and Vectorization** 149
   Pascal Barla and Adrien Bousseau

9. **Depiction Using Geometric Constraints** 167
   Craig S. Kaplan

10. **Artificial Mosaic Generation** 189
    Giovanni Puglisi and Sebastiano Battiato

11. **Non-photorealistic Rendering with Reduced Colour Palettes** 211
    Yu-Kun Lai and Paul L. Rosin

| 12 | **Artistic Rendering of Portraits** 237
Mingtian Zhao and Song-Chun Zhu

Part III Stylized Animations

| 13 | **Temporally Coherent Video Stylization** 257
Pierre Bénard, Joëlle Thollot, and John Collomosse

| 14 | **Computer-Assisted Repurposing of Existing Animations** 285
Daniel Sýkora and John Dingliana

Part IV Evaluation and Impact of Artistic Stylization

| 15 | **Evaluating and Validating Non-photorealistic and Illustrative Rendering** 311
Tobias Isenberg

| 16 | **Don't Measure—Appreciate! NPR Seen Through the Prism of Art History** 333
Peter Hall and Ann-Sophie Lehmann

| 17 | **NPR in the Wild** 353
Holger Winnemöller

Erratum to: Artistic Rendering of Portraits E1
Mingtian Zhao and Song-Chun Zhu

References 375

Index 395

Contributors

Pascal Barla Inria Bordeaux, Talence Cedex, France

Sebastiano Battiato University of Catania, Catania, Italy

Pierre Bénard University of Toronto, Toronto, ON, Canada

Adrien Bousseau Inria Sophia Antipolis, Sophia Antipolis Cedex, France

John Collomosse Centre for Vision Speech and Signal Processing, University of Surrey, Guildford, Surrey, UK

Oliver Deussen Dept. of Computer and Information Science, University of Konstanz, Konstanz, Germany

John Dingliana Trinity College Dublin, Dublin 2, Ireland

Stephen DiVerdi Adobe Systems Inc., San Francisco, CA, USA

Peter Hall Department of Computer Science, University of Bath, Bath, UK

Tobias Isenberg INRIA Saclay, Orsay, France

Craig S. Kaplan University of Waterloo, Waterloo, Ontario, Canada

Jan Eric Kyprianidis Hasso-Plattner-Institut, University of Potsdam, Potsdam, Germany

Yu-Kun Lai School of Computer Science and Informatics, Cardiff University, Cardiff, UK

Ann-Sophie Lehmann Department of Media and Culture Studies, University of Utrecht, Utrecht, The Netherlands

David Mould Carleton University, Ottawa, Canada

Victor Ostromoukhov CNRS/Université Claude Bernard Lyon 1, Villeurbanne, France

Giovanni Puglisi University of Catania, Catania, Italy

Paul L. Rosin School of Computer Science and Informatics, Cardiff University, Cardiff, UK

Daniel Sýkora FEE, DCGI, CTU in Prague, Praha 2, Czech Republic

Joëlle Thollot LJK, INRIA, Grenoble University, Saint Ismier, France

David Vanderhaeghe IRIT, Université de Toulouse, Toulouse CEDEX 9, France

Holger Winnemöller Adobe Systems, Inc., Seattle, USA

Eugene Zhang School of Electrical Engineering and Computer Science, Oregon State University, Corvallis, OR, USA

Mingtian Zhao University of California, Los Angeles, CA, USA

Song-Chun Zhu University of California, Los Angeles, CA, USA

Part I
Strokes, Marks and Filters for Artistic Stylization

Part I of this book focuses on the generation of synthetic artwork using filtering or other low-level image analysis. In many cases, artistic renderings are produced by placing a multitude of small marks (hatches, stipples, painterly brush strokes) on a virtual canvas. The placement of the marks reacts to the image content via heuristics that seek to emulate the placement of marks by a human artist. In other cases, morphological or anisotropic filtering operators perform edge-preserving simplification of the image to create a stylized appearance.

Stroke based painterly rendering of Annecy, France; regular venue of the ACM/Eurographics Symposium on Non-photorealistic Animation and Rendering (NPAR). Produced using the genetic algorithm described in Sect. 1.3.2

Chapter 1
Stroke Based Painterly Rendering

David Vanderhaeghe and John Collomosse

1.1 Introduction

Stroke based Rendering (SBR) is the process of synthesizing artwork by compositing rendering marks (such as lines, brush strokes, or even larger primitives such as tiles) upon a digital canvas. SBR under-pins many Artistic Rendering (AR) algorithms, especially those algorithms seeking to emulate traditional brush-based artistic styles such as oil painting.

The SBR paradigm was proposed in the early 1990s by Paul Haeberli [8], in the context of his semi-automated 'Paint By Numbers' painting environment that sought to rendering impressionist paintings from photographs. Although this work is now regarded as having catalyzed the field of AR, Haeberli's stated intention was to improve the richness of manually created digital paintings. Such paintings frequently lacked color depth, which Haeberli attributed to a prohibitively paintings lacked lengthy 'time to palette'; the time taken by the user to select a new color.

Haeberli's concept was simple but effective. The user interacts with a canvas of identical size to the source photograph they wish to render in a painterly style. Each time the user clicks to place a brush stroke on the digital canvas, the color of that stroke is sampled from the corresponding position in the source photograph. The strokes are much larger than the pixels from which the color is sampled, and this leads to an abstraction of detail reminiscent of that seen in real paintings. Furthermore, the noise inherent in the sampling of individual pixel color leads to a color variation reminiscent of the impressionist style (this can be further exaggerated by addition of Gaussian noise to the RGB values of the color).

D. Vanderhaeghe (✉)
IRIT, Université de Toulouse, 118 Route de Narbonne, 31062 Toulouse CEDEX 9, France
e-mail: vdh@irit.fr

J. Collomosse
Centre for Vision Speech and Signal Processing, University of Surrey, Guildford, Surrey GU2 7XH, UK
e-mail: j.collomosse@surrey.ac.uk

Fig. 1.1 Stroke based Rendering. *Left*: Impressionist rendering created interactively using Haeberli's Paint by Numbers algorithm [8]. The source image in the *top-right* is rendered as the user clicks upon the canvas with pre-selected stroke sizes. *Right*: Driving the interactive elements of this process using a pseudo-random number generator will cause loss of salient detail [9]

Table 1.1 Haeberli's representation of a painting as an ordered list of strokes underpins many later SBR algorithms

Attribute	Name	Derived
$\mathbf{P} = (x, y)$	stroke seed position	Manually
s	stroke scale	Manually
$\theta = \Theta(x, y)$	stroke orientation	Automatically
$\mathbf{c}$	RGB color	Automatically
o	stroke order	Manually

Haeberli's system not only automates the selection of color, but also drives other stroke attributes such as orientation. In impressionist artwork, strokes are often painting tangential to edges in the scene. This can be emulated by running an edge detector (e.g. the Sobel operator) over the grayscale source photograph $I(x, y)$:

$$\Theta(x, y) = \operatorname{atan}\left(\frac{\delta I}{\delta y} \bigg/ \frac{\delta I}{\delta x}\right) \qquad (1.1)$$

i.e. strokes are painted so that their longest axis is orthogonal to $\Theta(x, y)$. Figure 1.1 illustrates the effect achieved using an open implementation of Haeberli's system.[1]

Note that in Haeberli's system the user selects the size of stroke, the position on the canvas, and the order in which strokes are laid down. The set of stroke attributes are summarized in Table 1.1.

Under Haeberli's framework, strokes behave rather like 'rubber stamps'—an image of a stroke is painted centered at $\mathbf{P}$ and oriented by θ. The texture and visual properties of the stroke (beyond the color) are decoupled from the representation

---

[1] Available at http://kahlan.eps.surrey.ac.uk/EG2011.

of the ordered stroke list. This representation is therefore highly versatile and can be used to represent pastel, crayon, oil paint etc. Later, more sophisticated AR algorithms sought to automate beyond these paint daubs, to produce elegant curved brush strokes [12]. We discuss these approaches later in Sect. 1.2.3.

In this chapter we restrict ourselves solely to the matter of semi-automatic or automatic stroke placement. We briefly consider the simple texturing of strokes, but refer the reader to Chap. 2 for a more detailed discussion of brush and media simulation. In line with most AR research papers, we consider the matters of stroke rendering and stroke placement as decoupled.

1.2 Iterative Approaches to Automatic Painting

Haeberli's interactive systems catalyzed the development of fully automated painterly rendering algorithms, raising research questions such as "can the user be left out of the rendering work-flow?" and if so, "to what degree is it desirable to do so?". As we describe later in Chap. 13, increased automation has also opened up the possibility of video stylization. The issue of user control in discussed further Sect. 1.4.

A trivial adaptation to fully automate Haeberli's pipeline is to drive the values of manually set attributes with a pseudo-random number generator [9]. However, randomizing the order of strokes and their sizes can cause a loss of important ('salient') detail in the image as Fig. 1.1 illustrates.

A human artist will typically over-paint fine strokes, on top of coarser strokes, to depict fine important details in the rendering. Therefore we can link rendering order and stroke size to a simple automated measure of detail derived from the image. Since we already compute first derivative edge information to derive $\Theta(x, y)$ we can also derive a measure of edge magnitude $|\nabla I(x, y)|$:

$$|\nabla I(x, y)| = \left(\frac{\delta I^2}{\delta x} + \frac{\delta I^2}{\delta y}\right)^{\frac{1}{2}} \quad (1.2)$$

Strokes should be scaled size in inverse proportion to $|\nabla I(x, y)|$. The stroke ordering should be modified so as to paint smaller strokes later, over-painting coarser details.

1.2.1 Automated Impressionist Painting

Litwinowicz published the first automated painterly rendering algorithm in 1997 [17]. Litwinowicz' technique not only automated the rendering process, reducing user interaction to parameter setting, but also extended painterly rendering to video. We describe the latter aspects of the algorithm in further detail within Chap. 13.

Fig. 1.2 Stroke detail in impressionist rendering. Comparison of painting via Litwinowicz' method [17] with and without interpolation of orientation gradient. © 1997 ACM, images used by permission

Litwinowicz addresses the stroke placement and ordering problem in a straightforward manner. Pixel locations are sub-sampled in a regular grid, and a stroke generated at each sampled location. In practice, strokes are generated densely typically at every other pixel location. These strokes are rectangular in shape, and rendered in a random order. As performed by Haeberli's system, the color and orientation of each stroke is determined automatically. The latter using the Sobel operator (first derivative of intensity) as per Eq. (1.1).

To prevent loss of detail, each stroke is clipped against strong edges in the image. These are detected via thresholding field $|\nabla I(x, y)|$ at a constant value (Eq. (1.2)). The stroke may be thought of as a rectangle centered upon the initial stroke position, and oriented to align with the local edges in the image. The rectangle extends from the center position outward until a strong edge is met or the stroke exceeds a maximum length. This process prohibits strokes to cross strong image edges, preventing loss of detail through "coloring outside the lines".

Unfortunately the gradient field $\Theta(x, y)$ (Eq. (1.1)) does not offer reliable values over the whole image, and provides a noisy estimate when the source image gradient varies smoothly, or not at all. To provide smooth direction flow and mitigate noise, a more robust direction flow computation is usually required.

Gradient direction is reliable when the magnitude of edge gradient $|\nabla I(x, y)|$ is high, i.e. close to image edges and other high frequency artifacts. A practical approach to obtain a cleaner direction flow is to estimate the gradient direction local to such artifacts and interpolate elsewhere. Litwinowicz proposed the use of thin-plate spline interpolation [17], resulting in an improved aesthetic (Fig. 1.2). The mathematics of this interpolation are covered in more detail within Chap. 8.

Radial basis function are also well adapted to perform directional interpolation, and were explored by Hays and Essa [11] for video painting. But interpolation of vector fields $\frac{\delta I}{\delta x}$ or $\frac{\delta I}{\delta y}$ do not provide results consistent with the fact we only care about orientation angle; considering the direction flow as a tensor field provides better results as described by Kagaya et al. [16]. This extends earlier work exploring the interactive editing of the directional field by Zhang et al. [26].

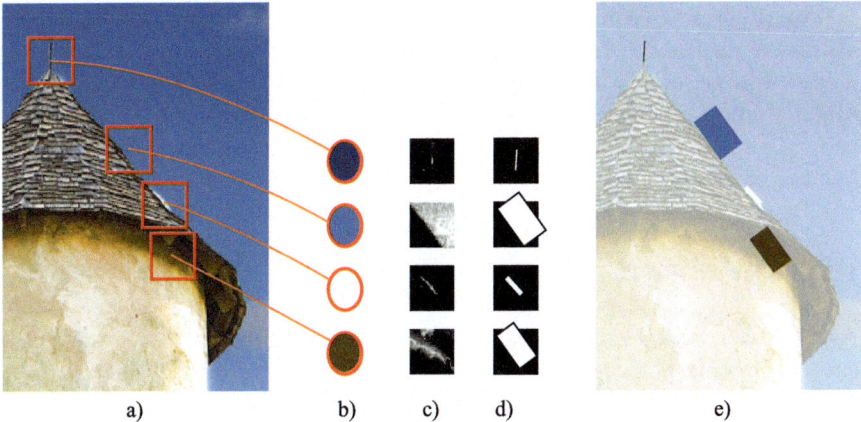

Fig. 1.3 The iterative approach of Shiraishi and Yamaguchi [20]. (**a**) Source image, (**b**) pixel color for four sample pixels, (**c**) difference between the pixel color and surrounding pixel colors is stored in an array, (**d**) moment analysis of the array gives a rectangle with the same moments, (**e**) for each anchor point, the attributes of the rectangle computed for this pixel are read to render the stroke

1.2.2 Painterly Rendering Using Image Moments

Shiraishi and Yamaguchi [20] proposed an alternative mechanism to orient and scale strokes, that does not rely upon edge gradient. Rather, they rely upon 2D statistical moments computed local to each stroke; an approach suggested earlier by Treavett and Chen [23]. Shiraishi and Yamaguchi compute, for each pixel p of the source image, the difference in color between p and pixels around p in a window of user specified scale. The result of each difference is stored in an array A of the same size of the window as indicated in Fig. 1.3.

The system computes the 2D central moments of A to define a rectangular stroke that approximates the region of similar color in the neighborhood of p. Strokes are aligned so that their principal axis is aligned with the principal eigenvector of the difference array. The output image may be over-painted in several passes from coarse scales, to finer scales, reminiscent of Hertzmann's multi-resolution paint process (described shortly in Sect. 1.2.3). As with most painterly rendering algorithms, the stroke color is sampled locally from the source image.

1.2.3 Multi-resolution Painting Using Curved Strokes

Early painterly rendering algorithms [8, 17, 23] were limited to placing simple daubs of paint. Essentially these were 2D sprites (textured rectangles) resembling a brush stroke, that were scaled and oriented by the stroke placement process.

Hertzmann proposed an alternative paradigm for painting in 1998 [12], that progressed painterly rendering with two key innovations. First, the painting process uses long, curved β-spline strokes rather than sprites for painting. This greatly enhances the realism and aesthetics of the resulting renderings. Second, the painting process was performed iteratively over multiple "layers" from coarse to fine. The painting process for each layer was driven by a source image down-sampled to a particular spatial resolution. For this reason this innovation is sometime referred to as multi-resolution painterly rendering.

1.2.3.1 Curved Stroke Formation

As with prior work, Hertzmann's algorithm makes independent decisions for each stroke's placement based on information in the source image local to the stroke position. Execution proceeds in a local, greedy manner with each stroke being rendered in a pre-determined randomized order (after [17]). We first describe how a single layer is painted; this process is summarized in Algorithm 1.1.

Each stroke is generated independently via a process of "hopping" between pixels, reminiscent of Line Integral Convolution (LIC). Given a starting point or "seed" pixel, the stroke by jumping from the current (seed) pixel to another pixel a pre-determined distance away. The direction of jump is derived from the gradient field $\Theta(x, y)$ of Eq. (1.1). Specifically the jump is made orthogonal to this angle in order that the stroke is formed tangential to edge structure in the source image. At each hop there is 180° ambiguity in the hopping direction, the direction of hop that minimize the curvature of the stroke being formed is taken. Stroke growth is terminated when the color of the image pixels departs significantly from the color of the stroke being formed. A minimum and maximum size for strokes is also enforced.

Each pixel visited forms a control point for a spline curve. Thus the eventual shape of the stroke is defined by a path which is built by following the direction flow. In Hertzmann's method these control points are approximated by a β-spline, which helps to smooth noise. However, other closely related painting techniques that perform a similar hopping (e.g. the genetic paint system of Sect. 1.3.2 use an interpolating Catmull–Rom spline for greater accuracy.

1.2.3.2 Coarse to Fine Painting

Hertzmann's algorithm generates layers of paint strokes, from coarse to fine. Prior to painting, a low-pass pyramid is generated by blurring and sub-sampling the source image at a range of decreasing scales. Typically octave intervals are used for each level of the pyramid. For example, a low-pass pyramid of four levels would comprise images {1, 2, 4, 8} times smaller than the original. The coarsest rendering layer is generated from the most heavily sub-sampled image.

The coarsest painting layer is first generated by creating strokes for all pixels, using the algorithm described in Sect. 1.2.3.1. Stroke size (radius) is proportional to the degree of sub-sampling used at the corresponding layer of the low-pass pyramid, and reflects the scale of visual features expected to occur at that level.

Algorithm 1.1 Hertzmann's algorithm for build the list of control point that form a brush stroke, used in Algorithm 1.2. Here the functions $I_{\text{src}}(.)$ and $I_{\text{paint}}(.)$ denote the RGB pixels values in the source image and painting respectively

```
 1: function MAKESTROKE(x, y) return stroke
 2:     d ← Θ(x, y)
 3:     strokeColor ← I_ref(x, y)
 4:     stroke.pushControlPoint(x, y)
 5:     for i: 1 → maxSize − 1 do
 6:         (x, y) ← (x, y) + d
 7:         d' ← Θ(x, y)
 8:         d ← f_dir d + (1 − f_dir)d'
 9:         srcColor = I_src(x, y)
10:         paintColor = I_paint(x, y)
11:         if i >= minimumSize AND |srcColor − strokeColor| > |srcColor − paintColor| then
12:             break
13:         end if
14:         stroke.pushControlPoint(x, y)
15:     end for
16: end function
```

Subsequent layers are then painted by compositing over strokes already laid down in previous layers. However, unlike the first (coarsest) layer, the algorithm does not paint the entire layer (as this would entirely occlude the previously painted layer). Rather, the algorithm selects which areas must be repainted by monitoring differences between the current and previous layers in the low-pass pyramid. This is equivalent to detecting which visual details have been revealed by moving to a higher resolution layer in the low-pass pyramid. Specifically, to trigger the start of a new stroke, Hertzmann's approach computes the sum of squares differences over a cell of size equivalent to the stroke's radius. If this difference is over a user defined threshold, then the stroke is painted. The algorithm is summarized in Algorithm 1.2.

Figure 1.4 illustrates the results of the painting process across successive layers via this multi-resolution algorithm. The main drawback is the repeated over-painting of edges and discontinuities in the scene. Strokes painted at such discontinuities cause large differences between successive layers, so triggering the edge for re-painting at each level of detail. To mitigate against this Huang et al. [15] propose to use multiple brush sizes per layer, rather than a constant size. Huang et al. define a grid with varying cell size (Fig. 1.5) and draw strokes starting in each cell with a radius function of grid size. Cell size is adapted to reflect a pre-supplied importance map. A trivial importance map might be simply the edge magnitude field $|\nabla I(x, y)|$, however, as discussed later, such maps are better derived from automated salience measures. Each cell is divided along the longest axis until the sum of the importance

Algorithm 1.2 Hertzmann's coarse to fine painting algorithm [12]

1: **function** PAINTIMAGE(I_{in})
2:     **for all** R in Radius from largest to smallest **do**
3:         $I_{ref} \leftarrow F(I_{in}, R)$
4:         $GridSize \leftarrow R$
5:         **for all** cell C of the grid spacing $GridSize$ **do**
6:             $A \leftarrow \sum_{(i,j) \in C} |P(i,j) - I_{ref}(i,j)|$
7:             **if** $A > t$ **then**   ▷ t is a user defined threshold
8:                 $(x, y) \leftarrow \text{argmax}_{(i,j) \in C} |P(i,j) - I_{ref}(i,j)|$
9:                 $S \leftarrow makeStroke(x, y)$
10:                paintStroke(P, S)   ▷ paint S onto the virtual canvas P
11:            **end if**
12:        **end for**
13:    **end for**
14: **end function**

---

map it covers is below a user defined threshold, or a minimum size is reached. The axis aligned cutting line position i with

$$\arg\min_{i} \left(\frac{M_i^s + \delta}{M_i^l + \delta} \right) \left(\frac{A_i^s}{A_i^l} \right)$$

M_i^s and M_i^l denote respectively the average importance over respectively the smaller and the larger divisions of the cell, and δ is a small constant to prevent from divide by zero. A_i^s and A_i^l are the respective areas of the smaller and larger divisions of the cell. Cells that are larger than a maximum allowed size are also subdivided (Fig. 1.5). Having selected stroke scale and position using this process, painting proceeds as per Sect. 1.2.3.1.

1.2.4 Transformations on the Source Image

In the algorithms described so far, the raw source image is used to drive the rendering process. However, pre-filtering the source image can improve the painterly result. Basic filters that remove noise and small color variations in the image are good candidates for such a pre-process. Such noise can trigger the generation of strokes with spurious color or inappropriate size. Chapter 5 describes a variety of filters such as Gaussian blur, the bilateral filter and morphological operators that are well suited to filter the source images of a SBR system.

Other transformations include color shift. Zhao and Zhu [27] propose to boost color saturation proportional to the underlying importance map computed for the source image. The SBR process of point sampling color, and generating marks of greater size than one pixel, may be regarding as an integration or low-pass filtering process. Such a process has a propensity to wash out colors, and so this process can help emphasize important details in the final rendering.

Fig. 1.4 Hertzmann's multi-resolution curved brush approach [12]. From *top* to *bottom*, *left* to *right*. The source image, three successive layers of the painterly rendering process demonstrating the over-painting, and the final rendering. Courtesy of chefranden@flickr.com

1.2.5 Texturing Spline Strokes

The curved brush strokes formed by stroke growth algorithm, such as variants of Hertzmann's algorithm [12], are interpolated with smooth (C^1) continuity using a β-spline or Catmull–Rom spline [7]. Chapter 2 describes a number of brush models,

Fig. 1.5 Grids computed using Huang's approach [15]. Importance map (*left*) and the grid derived from the importance map (*middle*) and maximum cell size constraints. The input image as per Fig. 1.4

of increasing sophistication, that may be swept along this curved path to emulate a variety of media types. However, in many SBR implementations a simple texture mapping suffices to produce a reasonable aesthetic.

As the piecewise cubic spline of the stroke is commonly expressed in a parametric form, it is trivial to compute a normalized local coordinate system (u, v) for the purpose of texture mapping. The u coordinate of the texture map spans the total path of the curve, and the v coordinate is expressed along the normal. Note that u should be an arc-length parameterization to ensure smooth texture mapping. The direction of the normal can be obtained via the second derivative of the curve at any point. The spatial extent of the v axis is constant, and relates directly to the stroke radius; i.e. the radius of a circle that would cover the stroke's footprint if swept along the curved path of the stroke. This radius is half the stroke's apparent width when rendered.

Sampling (u, v) at regular intervals yields a simple quad-strip sweeping along the path. A triangular strip may be similarly constructed. Either forms the basis for texture mapping. Usually the texture applied is a digitally scanned brush stroke, with an alpha mask to enable overlapping strokes to be seamlessly rendered. In addition to regular texture mapping, it is also possible to introduce a bump map texture onto the same coordinate system usually with minimal additional implementation com-

Fig. 1.6 Example spline strokes textured along a quad-strip defined from the curved stroke path

plexity in the graphics library (e.g. OpenGL). Figure 1.6 provides some examples of textured strokes.

1.3 Global Optimization for SBR

The algorithms discussed so far place strokes in a local greedy manner according to a set of heuristics. These heuristics encourage aesthetically beneficial behavior, such as painting fine details last with small strokes, or aligning strokes tangential to edges. By designing such heuristics within the algorithm, we aim to guide the output emerging from the process towards a desired aesthetic. However, because rendering decisions are made independently on a per-stroke basis, it may be difficult to ensure the generation of that aesthetic.

An alternative approach, discussed in this section, is to consider rendering as an optimization (search) problem. In SBR our final output is a visualization of an ordered list of strokes (and associated attributes). Finding the rendering that is in some sense exhibits the "optimal" or intended aesthetic for a given image is equivalent to finding the correct sequence of stroke configurations. Quantitatively assessing the optimality of an artistic rendering is neither a trivial nor even a well-defined task, as any art critic might attest! Nevertheless, given a source image, a number of low-level criteria may be expressed by which we may judge the quality of the resulting artistic stylization. For example, measuring the degree to which important details in the source image and depicted within the painting. Or ensuring that where possible, long expressive strokes are used with minimal over-painting.

Defining the optimality of a rendering (i.e. stroke configuration) is one hurdle to overcome when tackling SBR as an optimization problem. The other is to decide how to perform the global optimization over all strokes; a very high dimensional search space. We now discuss two early approaches to painterly rendering that propose solutions to these key problems.

1.3.1 Paint by Relaxation

Although optimization based painting was suggested as early as Haeberli's seminal paper [8], the first algorithmic solution did not appear in the literature until almost ten years later. Hertzmann proposed a *paint by relaxation* process [13] in which his curved stroke algorithm (Sect. 1.2.3) was used to create an initial painting. The strokes comprising that painting were then iteratively modified; either strokes were added or deleted, or strokes were moved to better positions, in order to maximize an "energy" function.

Hertzmann's innovation was to treat each stroke as an active contour or *snake*. Snakes are commonly used in Computer Vision to fit curves to edges in an image. Like brush strokes under Hertzmann's curved brush model, snakes are also typically represented by a piecewise cubic spline whose position is determined by a set of control points. When a snake is fitted to a edge, its control points are iteratively updated to minimize an energy function comprising internal and external terms. This process is known as *relaxation*. The internal term sums the magnitude of the first and second derivatives over the snake. With respect to these quantities, the snake will have high energy if its control points are irregularly spaced or it exhibits high curvature. The external term measures the evidence for an edge based on the portion of the image the snake is currently positioned over. A high value reflects poor alignment with an edge.

Hertzmann adapted this relaxation idea, replacing the classical snake energy function with his own weighted sum of terms. Given a source image $S(x, y)$ and an output painting $O(x, y)$, the energy a particular painting (P) comprising a set of S strokes is

$$E_{app}(P) = \omega_1 \sum_{x=1}^{\text{width}} \sum_{y=1}^{\text{height}} |P(x, y) - M(x, y)| \qquad (1.3)$$

$$E_{area}(P) = \omega_2 \sum_{S \in P} \text{Area}(S) \qquad (1.4)$$

$$E_{nstr}(P) = \omega_3 \cdot |S| (\text{in } P) \qquad (1.5)$$

$$E_{cov}(P) = \omega_4 \cdot (\text{unpainted pixels in } P) \qquad (1.6)$$

The weights $\omega_{1..4}$ control the influence of each quality attribute and are determined empirically. The first term E_{app} is a function of the appropriates of strokes, based on the difference of vector functions $P(x, y)$ and $G(x, y)$. These functions encode the RGB pixel color in the painting and source photograph, respectively. The other subscripted energy terms $E_{...}(P)$ refer to area of strokes (*app*), number of strokes (*nstr*) and coverage of the canvas (*cov*). Expression $S \in P$ refers to all strokes comprising painting P. Summing the areas of strokes in Eq. (1.4) yields a value analogous to the quantity of paint used in the painting. During optimization, the *minimum* of this energy function is sought. A similar model of stroke redundancy was proposed contemporaneously in the global approach of Szirányi et al. [22], though using an alternative form of optimization (Monte Carlo Markov Chain).

The optimization adopted by Hertzmann is an adaptation of Amini et al.'s snake relaxation process [1]. This is a dynamic programming based algorithm that efficiently scans the pixel neighborhood of each control point on the curve, and identified the "move" for a particular control point that will best minimize the energy function. In addition, each stroke is visited in a randomized order to determine in the energy function would be better minimized if the stroke were deleted. A similarly stochastic stroke addition process is also incorporated; further details are given in [13].

Hertzmann's optimization technique dramatically improves stroke accuracy and retention of detail versus the local greedy approach described in Sect. 1.2.3. The technique has a secondary benefit in that a painting optimized for a given image, may be optimized over a slightly different image without incurring major changes to the constituent strokes. This stability to change enables coherent video stylization; the current frame is optimized using the previous frame as an initialization. However, the drawback of the approach is the significant computational expense of the optimization.

1.3.2 Perceptually Based Painting

Paintings are abstractions of photorealistic scenes in which salient elements are emphasized. Artists commonly paint to capture the structure and elements of the scene that they consider to be important; remaining detail is abstracted away in some differential style or level of detail. For example, an artist would not depict every leaf on a tree, or brick in a wall, present in the background of a composition.

The painterly rendering algorithms described so far are guided by intensity gradient magnitude ($|\nabla I(x, y)|$), or similar statistical measures that exhibit responses to high spatial frequencies in the image. They therefore have a tendency to emphasize all high frequency content in the image, rather than the perceptually salient visual content that an artist might depict. To produce renderings that ostensibly represent artwork, it is often necessary to manually doctor this field to reduce fidelity in the painting and enhance the composition [13].

Collomosse et al. proposed a global optimization technique using a Genetic Algorithm (GA) to search the space of possible paintings, so locating the optimal painting for a given source image [6]. Their optimality criterion measures the strength of correlation between the level of detail in a painting and the *salience map* of its source image. A salience map (sometimes referred to as importance map) is an automatically computed 2D field that encodes the perceptual significance of regions within an image. Their optimization technique builds upon an earlier local greedy approach to painting using salience maps [4].

Like most SBR approaches, the technique builds upon Haeberli's abstraction of a painting; an ordered list of strokes [8] (comprising control points, thickness, etc. with color as a data dependent function of these). Under this representation the space of possible paintings for a given source image is very high dimensional, and the aforementioned optimality criterion makes this space extremely turbulent. Stochastic searches that model evolutionary processes, such as GAs, are reasonable search strategies in such situations; large regions of problem space can be covered quickly, and local minima more likely to be avoided [14]. Furthermore the GA approach adopted allows different regions within a painting to be optimized independently, and later combined to produce improved solutions in later generations.

The optimization proceeds as follows. First, a population of several hundred paintings are initialized from the source image using a stochastic variant of Hertzmann's curve stroke algorithm [12] (Sect. 1.2.3). The curved strokes are created by hopping between pixels, with direction sampled from a Gaussian normal variate center upon $\Theta(x, y)$. Brush stroke length and order are also stochastically. The random variates introduced into the stroke generation process generate a diverse population of possible paintings, some of which are better than others.

The entire population is rendered, and edge maps of each painting are produced by convolution with Gaussian derivatives, which serve as a quantitative measure of local fine detail. The generated maps are then compared to a precomputed salience map of the source image. The mean squared error (MSE) between maps is used as the basis for evaluating the fitness quality $F(.)$ of a particular painting; the lower the MSE, the better the painting:

$$F(I, \psi) = 1 - \frac{1}{N} \sum |S(I) - E(\Psi(I, \psi))|^2 \qquad (1.7)$$

The summation is computed over all N pixels in source image I. $\Psi(.)$ is our painterly process, which produces a rendering from I and a particular ordered list of strokes ψ corresponding to an individual in the population. Function $S(.)$ signifies the salience mapping process described in Sect. 2.2.1, and $E(.)$ the process of convolution with Gaussian derivatives.

The population is evaluated according to Eq. (1.7) and individuals are ranked according to fitness. The bottom 10 % are culled, and the best 10 % of the population pass to the next generation. The middle 80 % are used to produce the remainder of the next generation—two individuals are selected stochastically using roulette wheel selection. These individuals are bred via genetic crossover, and subjected to genetic mutation, to produce a novel offspring for the successive generation. Figure 1.7 demonstrates the results of the optimization, showing salient detail being emphasized and non-salient detail being abstracted away over 70 iterations of the optimization. Figure 1.8 shows the abstraction effect of the salience map versus a process drive by intensity gradient.

A further contribution of Collomosse et al.'s system was a user-trainable measure of image salience [10], recognizing the inherently subjective nature of image important. This simultaneously measured salience and classified artifacts into categories such as corner, edge, ridge and so on. This information could also be harnessed to lay down different styles of stroke to depict different image artifacts.

1.4 Creative Control

Early artistic stylization papers broached the topic of impersonating the human artist, or seeking to pass an "artistic Turing Test". However, the major of contemporary techniques tend to now motivate their goal as offering a creative tool for use

Fig. 1.7 Three iterations of refinement in the Genetic Painting process of Collomosse et al. From *left* to *right*, 1st iteration, 30th iteration and 70th iteration. Images courtesy of Collomosse et al. [6], Springer

Fig. 1.8 Global optimization using a Genetic Algorithm. *Left*: Source image, and a painterly rendering produced using Litwinowicz' method [17] based on intensity gradient; all fine details are emphasized in the painting. *Right*: A rendering using the salience adaptive scheme of Collomosse et al., with close-up on the sign (region A). The non-salient trees have been suppressed, but salient detail on the sign is emphasized. In region B the salience map has been artificially suppressed to illustrate the abstraction effect

by artists, rather than removing the artist from the loop completely. An interesting question is then the degree of control a creative has over the artistic rendering process, and how this is expressed.

User control is a trade-off between efficiency, freedom of expression and ease of use, i.e. a system provide a way to obtain the user's desired aesthetic while lessening tedious, automatable tasks.

Currently most artistic rendering systems enable the user to influence the "style" of presentation; using the terminology of Willats and Durand [24]. Willats and Durand refer to the rendering process as a mapping between a scene—a reference image in our case and a set of marks with attributes (color, color gradient, relative depth, etc.). The link between the scene and the marks is the style. Other higher level aspects of the scene such as geometry and composition are typically not manipulated, though there has been some progress in this area [5, 27].

One may consider this control over style to be expressed at either a low, medium of high semantic level.

1.4.1 Low-Level Control

The lowest level of SBR style control is the modification of individual parameters that govern the heuristics on the stroke placement algorithm itself. For example, the thresholds on maximum stroke length during Hertzmann's stroke growth [12], window sizes in Shiraishi and Yamaguchi's method [20], the levels of low-pass filtering in a multi-resolution method, or coefficients on a color transfer function. For an expert user these offer precise control. However, the final rendering is an emergent property of a complex process incorporating many such parameters. This makes them counter-intuitive for non-expert users to set.

1.4.2 Mid-Level Control

Mid-level control enables algorithm parameters to be set at the level of the desired style, for example specifying presets for algorithm parameters that are known to generate output resembling a particular artistic genre. Hertzmann documents four such presets for his curved brush algorithm [12], covering expressionist, impressionist, pointillism and colorist wash. It is also possible to define regions of an image containing specific parameter presets. This is a broader definition of the behavior seen in the "paint by optimization" approach, where differing levels of emphasis may defined for different regions in the image.

Zeng et al. [25] presented a region-based painterly rendering algorithm that splits the scene into a tree of regions, each region being classified by its semantic content. This allowed the users to select different styles for human skin, buildings, vegetation or sky. They also use the decomposition to compute the orientation of strokes. Region based control over stroke orientation is also a feature of interactive painting environments such as AniPaint [18].

1.4.3 High-Level Control

High level control is goal directed, enabling intuitive control at a semantic level. A user might desire a "bright, cheerful" or "dark, gloomy" painting in a particular style, but not have the experience to select the individual parameters necessary to create the effect. This kind of control was first demonstrated by Shugrina et al. in the context of an interactive painting, where the user's facial expression was used to estimate user state within a 2D emotional space. A mapping was established between this space, and a higher dimensional parameter space of an impasto oil painterly algorithm [21] (Fig. 1.9). Another option is to let the painterly rendering system provide some potential paintings and let the user rate them [3]. Then new paintings are generated taking into account the score of each candidates, using an interactive evolutionary algorithm.

1 Stroke Based Painterly Rendering

Fig. 1.9 High-level style control: a face picture is analyzed to define a mood. The mood is linked to middle level strokes attributes to produce the painting using the technique of Shugrina et al. [21]. Image courtesy John Collomosse

1.5 Discussion

We have documented the development of SBR from the semi-automated paint systems of the early 1990s, to automated processes driven by low-level image measures (such as image gradient) and higher level measures such as salience maps.

Many forms of visual art are created through the manual composition of rendering marks, such as brush strokes. Stroke based rendering (SBR) has therefore become a foundation of many early and contemporary automated artistic rendering algorithms. Many of the subsequent chapters in the first part of this book describe more sophisticated algorithms that build upon the SBR concepts presented here.

SBR focuses only on the lowest level of stylization; that of placing individual marks (strokes) in a greedy or global manner. There are many other considerations in the creation artwork, for example geometry, layout and scene composition, that require analysis at a higher conceptual level [19, 24].

Due to their reliance on structural information in the image, a higher level of spatial of temporal analysis is required to access these styles [2]. For example, in the second part of this book we see techniques analyzing the image at the level of the region or performing domain specialized structural analysis (e.g. for portrait painting). Nevertheless these algorithms often incorporate some form of SBR in the final presentation of the processed scene elements.

References

1. Amini, A., Weymouth, T., Jain, T.: Using dynamic programming for solving variational problems in computer vision. IEEE Trans. Pattern Anal. Mach. Intell. **9**(12), 855–867 (1990)
2. Collomosse, J.P.: Higher level techniques for the artistic rendering of images and video. Ph.D. thesis, University of Bath, UK (2004)
3. Collomosse, J.: Supervised genetic search for parameter selection in painterly rendering. In: Proceedings EvoMUSART (LNCS), vol. 3907, pp. 599–610. Springer, Berlin (2006)
4. Collomosse, J., Hall, P.M.: Painterly rendering using image salience. In: Proc. Eurographics UK, pp. 122–128 (2002)
5. Collomosse, J., Hall, P.M.: Cubist style rendering from photographs. IEEE Trans. Vis. Comput. Graph. **4**(9), 443–453 (2003)
6. Collomosse, J.P., Hall, P.M.: Genetic Paint: A Search for Salient Paintings. In: Proceedings of EvoWorkshops. Lecture Notes in Computer Science, vol. 3449, pp. 437–447. Springer, Berlin (2005)
7. Farin, G.: Curves and Surfaces for CAGD: A Practical Guide, 5th edn. Morgan Kaufmann, San Francisco (2002)
8. Haeberli, P.E.: Paint by numbers: abstract image representations. In: Computer Graphics (Proceedings of SIGGRAPH 90), pp. 207–214 (1990)
9. Haggerty, P.: Almost automatic computer painting. IEEE Comput. Graph. Appl. **11**(6), 11–12 (1991)
10. Hall, P.M., Owen, M.J., Collomosse, J.P.: A trainable low-level feature detector. In: Proceedings Intl. Conference on Pattern Recognition (ICPR), vol. 1, pp. 708–711. IEEE Press, New York (2004)
11. Hays, J., Essa, I.: Image and video based painterly animation. In: Proc. NPAR, pp. 113–120 (2004)
12. Hertzmann, A.: Painterly rendering with curved brush strokes of multiple sizes. In: Proceedings of SIGGRAPH 98, Computer Graphics Proceedings. Annual Conference Series, pp. 453–460 (1998)
13. Hertzmann, A., Perlin, K.: Painterly rendering for video and interaction. In: NPAR 2000: First International Symposium on Non Photorealistic Animation and Rendering, pp. 7–12 (2000)
14. Holland, J.: Adaptation in Natural and Artificial Systems. An Introductory Analysis with Applications to Biology, Control and Artificial Intelligence. University of Michigan Press, Ann Arbor (1975)
15. Huang, H., Fu, T.N., Li, C.F.: Painterly rendering with content-dependent natural paint strokes. Vis. Comput. **27**(9), 861–871 (2011). doi:10.1007/s00371-011-0596-5
16. Kagaya, M., Brendel, W., Deng, Q., Kesterson, T., Todorovic, S., Neill, P.J., Zhang, E.: Video painting with space-time-varying style parameters. IEEE Trans. Vis. Comput. Graph. **17**(1), 74–87 (2011)
17. Litwinowicz, P.: Processing images and video for an impressionist effect. In: Proceedings of SIGGRAPH 97, Computer Graphics Proceedings. Annual Conference Series, pp. 407–414 (1997)
18. O'Donovan, P., Hertzmann, A.: AniPaint: interactive painterly animation from video. IEEE Trans. Vis. Comput. Graph. **18**(3), 475–487 (2012)
19. Santella, A., DeCarlo, D.: Visual interest and NPR: an evaluation and manifesto. In: Proc. NPAR, pp. 71–150 (2004)
20. Shiraishi, M., Yamaguchi, Y.: An algorithm for automatic painterly rendering based on local source image approximation. In: NPAR 2000: First International Symposium on Non Photorealistic Animation and Rendering, pp. 53–58 (2000)
21. Shugrina, M., Betke, M., Collomosse, J.P.: Empathic painting: interactive stylization through observed emotional state. In: NPAR 06, pp. 87–96. ACM, New York (2006). doi:10.1145/1124728.1124744
22. Szirányi, T., Tóth, Z., Figueiredo, M., Zerubia, J., Jain, A.: Optimization of paintbrush rendering of images by dynamic MCMC methods. In: Proc. EMMCVPR, pp. 201–215 (2001)

23. Treavett, S.M.F., Chen, M.: Statistical techniques for the automated synthesis of non-photorealistic images. In: Proc. EGUK, pp. 201–210 (1997)
24. Willats, J., Durand, F.: Defining pictorial style: lessons from linguistics and computer graphics. Axiomathes **15**(3), 319–351 (2005)
25. Zeng, K., Zhao, M., Xiong, C., Zhu, S.C.: From image parsing to painterly rendering. ACM Trans. Graph. **29**(1), 2:1–2:11 (2009)
26. Zhang, E., Hays, J., Turk, G.: Interactive tensor field design and visualization on surfaces. IEEE Trans. Vis. Comput. Graph. **13**(1), 94–107 (2007)
27. Zhao, M., Zhu, S.C.: Sisley the abstract painter. In: NPAR'10: Proceedings of the 8th International Symposium on Non-Photorealistic Animation and Rendering, pp. 99–107. ACM, New York (2010). doi:10.1145/1809939.1809951

Chapter 2
A Brush Stroke Synthesis Toolbox

Stephen DiVerdi

2.1 Introduction

Digital painting has progressed by leaps and bounds since its humble beginnings [30]. What some of the original painting applications called "brushes" were really simple line-drawing mechanisms based on the model of a circular tip, swept along a path. Still, within these systems, artists prevailed to make impressive images with the first inklings of a natural media style.

Things have advanced greatly since then. Much of the rest of this book deals with the rise of non-photorealistic rendering, and in some cases specifically painterly rendering, in which 3D models or 2D images and videos are processed automatically to have the appearance of a piece of natural media artwork. On the other hand, traditional media artists who consider moving into the digital media world look for the same level of expressive control and manual interaction that they have mastered with physical brushes. From this perspective, painting engines that aim to replicate or emulate real artistic tools represent the path forward, and there has been a correspondingly large amount of research in the field.

However, it is not the case that brush strokes are only interesting to manual digital painters. For example, in the automatic generation of painterly images from photos or 3D models, many algorithms are based around the idea of stroke-based rendering (SBR) [21], where the composition is broken down into a set of brush strokes that combine to form the target output. The primary distinction between SBR and brush simulation is that SBR assumes realistic brush strokes as an input to the algorithm, whereas brush simulation is concerned with the synthesis of those realistic brush strokes, but clearly the two areas are closely connected. SBR is discussed in detail in Chap. 1.

S. DiVerdi (✉)
Adobe Systems Inc., 601 Townsend St., San Francisco, CA 94107, USA
e-mail: stephen.diverdi@gmail.com

Algorithm 2.1 The swept stroke algorithm

1: **function** BASICSWEEP($\mathbb{S}, d$)
2:     **for** $i \leftarrow [1, n-1]$ **do**
3:         DRAWLINE($d, \mathbf{s}_i, \mathbf{s}_{i+1}$)
4:     **end for**
5: **end function**

Therefore, brush strokes are a sort of atomic unit of non-photorealistic rendering, and brush stroke synthesis is a bread and butter algorithm that underlies the success of many different applications.

The basic and most commonly used algorithm for constructing brush strokes will be described in Sect. 2.2. It is a baseline for creating strokes that are parameterized by some input path and a selected brush tip, and is the core of many commercial applications and research systems. To go beyond this simple model, we will survey the available technologies for more realistic brush stroke synthesis from the research community in Sect. 2.3. In the remaining sections of the chapter, we will show step-by-step how to implement a more complex, physically based model, and discuss the tradeoffs at each stage of the process. By the end of this chapter, we will have collected a set of algorithmic tools that will allow us to tailor a brush stroke synthesis algorithm to satisfy constraints from real-world painting applications.

2.2 The Basic Brush Model

In the simplest case of brush stroke rendering, the user provides an input curve in the form of a 2D trajectory, uniformly sampled in time, from an input device such as a mouse or a tablet. The set $\mathbb{S} = \{\mathbf{s}_1, \ldots, \mathbf{s}_n\}$ is the sequence of these 2D samples. The goal is to make a stroke that follows this trajectory, with a simple circular brush of diameter d. Then, given a function DRAWLINE($w, \mathbf{p}, \mathbf{q}$) that draws a line of width w from $\mathbf{p}$ to $\mathbf{q}$ (found in any 2D graphics package), the pseudocode in Algorithm 2.1 produces the desired result. See Fig. 2.1 for an illustration.

This model is fast and easy to implement, but also has some significant limitations. For example, it does not properly draw transparent strokes, because of the overlapping line endcaps at each sample point. It cannot create any kind of textured brush stroke, such as the smooth falloff of an airbrush or the scratchy appearance of a dry paint brush. It is unable to support variations along the stroke, such as controlling the size of the stroke by the pressure of a tablet stylus.

A straightforward amendment to this simple algorithm will enable a wider variety of brush strokes with a similar level of complexity. Rather than draw a line between consecutive sample points, we will walk along the input trajectory and place stamps of the brush footprint at uniform arc length. Given δ is the distance between stamps (called the "spacing"), INTERPOLATE($\mathbb{S}, a$) is a function that returns the 2D position along trajectory $\mathbb{S}$ at arc length a, Ω is the 2D raster image of the brush footprint, and STAMP($\mathbf{p}, \Omega$) is a function that draws the brush footprint at position $\mathbf{p}$.

Fig. 2.1 A demonstration of the different output possible with the basic model. *Top* to *bottom:* the input trajectory, the output of BASICSWEEP, the output of BASICSTAMP with a circular stamp, with a gaussian blob stamp, and with a "brush" stamp

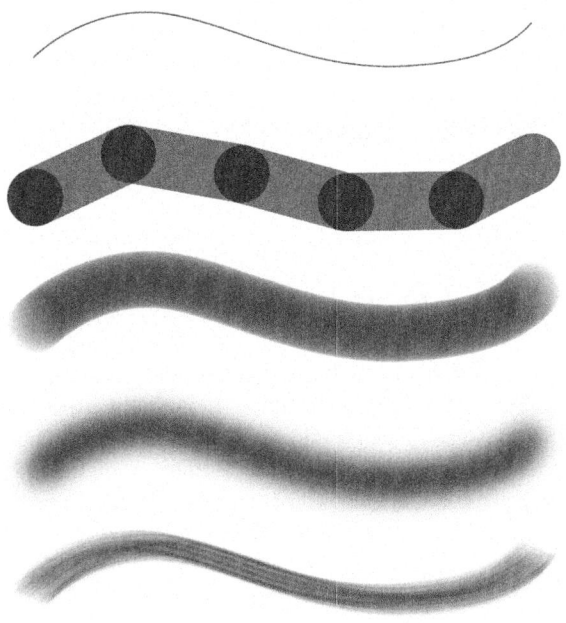

Algorithm 2.2 The stamped stroke algorithm

1: **function** BASICSTAMP($\mathbb{S}, \Omega, \delta$)
2:     $l \leftarrow$ ARCLENGTH($\mathbb{S}$)
3:     $a \leftarrow 0$
4:     **while** $a \leq l$ **do**
5:         $\mathbf{p} \leftarrow$ INTERPOLATE($\mathbb{S}, a$)
6:         STAMP($\mathbf{p}, \Omega$)
7:         $a \leftarrow a + \delta$
8:     **end while**
9: **end function**

Algorithm 2.2 is the core of most digital painting brush engines. Selection of the brush footprint image can create different stroke textures (e.g. a filled circle, a gaussian blob, or a pattern of dots—see Fig. 2.1). Extending the STAMP function to support affine transforms allows the size and distortion of the stamp to be controlled dynamically by tablet parameters such as pressure and tilt. Trajectory smoothing can be handled by modifying INTERPOLATE. Transparency and buildup are correctly handled within STAMP. Finally, dynamic brush footprints are possible by parameterizing Ω by additional parameters, such as the output of a physical simulation.

These two examples, BASICSWEEP and BASICSTAMP, also demonstrate a fundamental difference between stroke synthesis algorithms. "Tweening" is short for "in-betweening", and refers to the generation of intermediate states between sample points. Sweeping and stamping are two ways to address the problem, and roughly correspond to analytical and numerical solutions. Stamping has the limitation that the necessary sampling rate (i.e. spacing) can be high depending on the frequency content of the brush footprint. Sweeping on the other hand, is limited to strokes that can be analytically computed in an efficient manner, which makes effects like textured appearances difficult. This issue will be discussed in more detail in Sect. 2.6.

2.3 Available Technologies

Particularly in the last decade, realistic brush stroke synthesis has been an active area of research. Major contributions in the field are summarized in Table 2.1. Much of this work has been conducted as part of larger agendas around the simulation of paint media as well, such as watercolor or oil paint, but these results are out of the scope of this text and are not considered here. In addition to research work, we also consider some of the most popular commercially available applications for digital painters [2, 3, 16, 18].

To help understand the space of different technologies available, we have categorized the contributions of each work based on common themes. These categories are the output type, the algorithm strategy, the spline model, the brush head model, the solution method by which new states are computed, and the type of tweening used. Each of these categories is discussed in turn.

Output Type The options for the output of a brush stroke synthesis algorithm are raster or vector. Raster is the most common type, and means that the output brush stroke is a 2D grid of pixels. Conversely, vector output represents the brush stroke as a set of filled, Bézier-bounded paths instead of pixels (n.b. vector representations can be more complex, but for the purposes of this text, this definition is sufficient). Adobe Illustrator [2] is a common example of a program that outputs vector brush strokes. Vector representations are desirable because they are resolution independent and sparse (for compactness of storage), but they are limited in terms of the types of appearance they can represent. Soft airbrush strokes or textured dry brush strokes are generally not supported by vector algorithms.

Algorithm Strategy The different strategies for creating brush strokes can be grouped into a few bins: procedural, simulation, acquisition, and data-driven. Procedural strategies include those of commercial painting applications and are based on simple, ad hoc models that can be controlled programmatically to create brush strokes, without modeling a virtual 3D brush head. Alternately, simulation is the approach of computing the dynamics of a physical system that mimics a real brush. Rather than trying to compute the brush footprint shape, the acquisition strategy uses custom hardware to measure the shape of a real brush in real-time. Finally, data-driven approaches record real brushes offline and reproduce their effects via machine learning of some form.

2 A Brush Stroke Synthesis Toolbox

Table 2.1 Overview of existing implementations and their characteristics. *Output:* raster (R) or vector (V). *Strategy:* acquisition of real brush footprints (A), physical simulation (S), data-driven methods (D), or procedural methods (P). *Spline:* for work that models splines, are they discrete (D) or continuous (C). *Brush:* for work that models a brush head, is it a mesh (M), skeleton (S), interpolated geometry (I), or individual bristles (B). *Solution:* systems can be solved via integration (I), energy minimization (M), or data-driven methods (D). *Tween:* short for in-between, intermediate states between simulation steps can be generated by stamping (T) or sweeping (W)

work	output	strategy	spline	brush	solution	tween
Adobe Illustrator [2]	V	P	–	–	–	W
Adobe Photoshop [3]	R	P	–	–	–	T
Ambient Design ArtRage [18]	R	P	–	–	–	TW
Bai et al., 2007 [5]	R	P	–	–	–	T
Baxter at al., 2001 [9]	R	S	D	M	I	T
Baxter and Govindaraju, 2010 [7]	R	D	C	M	D	T
Baxter and Lin, 2004 [8]	R	S	D	MI	M	T
Chu and Tai, 2004 [14]	R	S	D	S	M	T
Chu, 2007 [13]	R	S	D	S	M	W
Corel Painter [16]	R	P	–	–	–	TW
DiVerdi at al., 2010 [19]	RV	S	C	B	I	TW
Lu and Huang, 2007 [25]	R	S	C	B	M	T
Mi et al., 2002 [26]	R	P	–	–	–	W
Okabe et al., 2005 [27]	R	A	–	–	–	T
Pudet, 1994 [28]	V	P	–	–	–	W
Saito and Nakajima, 1999 [29]	R	S	C	M	M	T
Van Laerhoven and Van Reeth, 2007 [32]	R	S	D	MI	M	T
Vandoren et al., 2009 [34]	R	A	–	–	–	T
Vandoren et al., 2008 [33]	R	A	–	–	–	T
Xie et al., 2010 [35]	R	P	–	–	–	W
Xu et al., 2004 [36]	R	D	–	MB	–	T

Spline Model For algorithms that work by creating a virtual brush head, the spline is a basic building block that can deform in bristle-like ways to control the shape of the brush head and thus footprint. These splines can be modeled discretely, as a piecewise linear approximation consisting of sample positions joined by straight line segments. Discrete models lend themselves to easy computation of physical dynamics and collisions, but may require many segments for acceptable quality. Continuous splines are also possible, using e.g. a Bézier or helix, and manipulating the control points to change the shape. Collision and dynamics are more complicated, but the resulting shape will always be smooth.

Brush Head Model Given a spline or set of splines, the brush head model controlled by the spline(s) can be of varying levels of complexity. In the simplest case, the brush head is represented as a single bulk triangle mesh, which is deformed by the shape of a control spline running through it. A more structured brush head can use a skeleton of splines, branching off one another, to provide a way to control the (potentially asymmetric) changes in spread of the brush. To represent the brush head as a collection of bristles, each piece of bristle geometry can be controlled by an individual spline, for maximum fidelity, but at a large computational cost. A faster way to model a collection of bristles is by interpolating the bristle geometry from a few control splines.

Solution Method When computing a physical simulation of spline dynamics, the most straightforward way to update the shape is by integration of the internal and external forces. As brush bristles tend to be stiff systems, implicit integration is necessary. Furthermore, bristles tend to achieve their rest shape very quickly in the presence of changed forces, and so a commonly explored alternative is to compute the quasi-static configuration via energy minimization. Potentially fastest of all, data-driven solutions can determine the rest shape without costly math.

Tweening As discussed in Sect. 2.2, tweening refers to the generation of intermediate states between samples. For brush strokes, there are two options. Stamping is the numerical approach that works by computing many samples, whereas sweeping is the analytical approach that attempts to compute the final result in a single step.

2.4 Spline Modeling

To begin our more realistic brush stroke synthesis, in this section we construct the spline model. Our spline is comprised of a chain of rigid links connected by hinge joints. This is a discrete model, which allows for a simpler formulation of the spline dynamics than a continuous model, at the cost of some fidelity. An illustration of the spline model structure can be seen in Fig. 2.2.

A canvas is necessary to provide a surface for the spline to collide with, to create the characteristic deformations. We will use a simple plane to represent the canvas surface. The canvas will also provide friction forces to cause the bristles to drag appropriately. To control the brush, we attach the base link of the spline to a brush handle cylinder. This handle has a position and orientation that is controlled by the user's input. Ideally, a tablet and stylus with six degrees of freedom (2D position, pressure, 2D tilt, and barrel rotation) is available, which can provide a direct mapping between all the input DOFs and the handles'. Otherwise, some sort of indirect control must be defined.

As bristles are stiff, the spring constants for the spline joints must be high. This creates a stiff system that means we will need to use an implicit integration scheme.

Physical simulation is a complex topic and an active area of research, which has been covered many times in other texts [6]. Getting into the details of how to

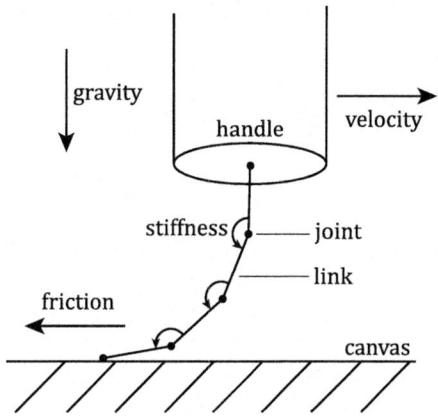

Fig. 2.2 The basic model of a brush spline as a chain of rigid links connected by stiff joints. The user controls the handle's position and velocity, while gravity and the canvas deform the spline

construct and solve a system of equations based on our system design would be quite involved and would distract us from our goal of brush stroke synthesis. However, the purpose of this chapter is to provide the reader with practical tools to achieve the effects we have discussed. Therefore, to implement our brush simulation, we will employ a physics engine.

Free, open source physics engines are available today largely thanks to their rising popularity in the game industry and the maturation of the mathematical techniques to implement fast and robust simulations. Some of the more popular examples include ODE [31], Bullet [17], and Tokamak [23]. There are even efforts to define a common API across all the engines to allow for decoupling of a program's system definition from the underlying engine [11, 12]. Each library emphasizes different aspects of the problem, such as focusing on robustness or on real-time performance. Support for advanced features like soft bodies and fracturing varies. However, the formulation of our spline model is relatively simple and can be supported by any of these engines. Therefore, we will use ODE for the remainder of this section, because of its prioritization of absolute robustness above all else.

A comment on notation: in the algorithm listings in this section, function names that begin with a 'd' and are typeset like `dWorldCreate()` refer to functions in the ODE API. Consult the ODE documentation for the particulars of input arguments, return values, and types.

2.4.1 Creating a Spline

Creating the basic brush and spline geometry in ODE is straightforward, and is addressed in Algorithm 2.3. The CREATEHANDLE function initializes the ODE world and creates the brush handle object. Multiple brush handles could exist in the same world, but we will assume there is one. Then CREATESPLINE can be used multiple times to add individual splines to the brush. ODE's model is such that rigid bodies

Algorithm 2.3 Creating the brush geometry

```
 1: function SETMASS(b)
 2:     M ← dMassSetCapsule(radius, length)
 3:     dMassSetMass(M, mass)
 4:     dBodySetMass(b, M)
 5: end function
 6:
 7: function CREATEHANDLE()
 8:     W ← dWorldCreate()
 9:     dWorldSetGravity(0, 0, g)
10:     H ← dBodyCreate(W)                              ▷ brush handle body
11:     SETMASS(H)
12:     I_body ← dGetInertialTensor(H)                  ▷ store for later
13: end function
14:
15: function CREATESPLINE()
16:     for i ← [1, n] do                               ▷ create each chain link
17:         b_i ← dBodyCreate(W)
18:         dBodySetPosition(b_i, px_i, py_i, pz_i)     ▷ initialize link pose
19:         dBodySetQuaternion(b_i, qx_i, qy_i, qz_i, qw_i)
20:         SETMASS(b_i)
21:     end for
22:     for i ← [1, n] do                               ▷ create joints between links
23:         j_i ← dJointCreateUniversal(W)
24:         if i = 1 then
25:             dJointAttach(j_i, H, b_i)               ▷ attach first link to handle
26:         else
27:             dJointAttach(j_i, b_{i−1}, b_i)
28:         end if
29:         dJointSetUniversalAnchor(j_i, px_i, py_i, pz_i)
30:         dJointSetUniversalAxis1(j_i, 1, 0, 0)        ▷ x-axis hinge
31:         dJointSetUniversalAxis2(j_i, 0, 1, 0)        ▷ y-axis hinge
32:     end for
33: end function
```

are represented as objects that store a position, orientation, and a mass and inertia tensor. Joints are separate objects that define a connection between two bodies. Collision detection is done on separate geometry objects that are associated with bodies, to decouple the dynamics from the collision detection, and is discussed in Sect. 2.4.4.

CREATESPLINE specifically mentions creating "universal" joints, which are a standard concept in mechanical systems that allows two degrees of freedom—rotation about the two axes perpendicular to the major axis. A third DOF is twist about the major axis, which a universal joint restricts. An alternative joint type is

Algorithm 2.4 Animating the brush geometry

```
1: function STEPSIMULATION( )
2:     m ← number of substeps
3:     for i ← [1, m] do
4:         ADDBRUSHFORCEANDTORQUE( )           ▷ see Sect. 2.4.2
5:         dSpaceCollide2(G, S_s, C)            ▷ see Sect. 2.4.4
6:         dWorldStep(Δt)
7:         dJointGroupEmpty(C)
8:     end for
9: end function
```

"ball and socket", which allows all three DOFs and is supported by ODE. Full physical hair simulation, particularly for long hair such as on a virtual character's head, includes twist in its formulation because it has a significant impact on the overall dynamic behavior, but for short, stiff brush bristles, it is generally unnecessary.

Once the handle and spline bodies and joints have been created, animating them is handled by the STEPSIMULATION function in Algorithm 2.4, which should be called once per frame in the application's main loop. Simulation in its most basic form consists of calling dWorldStep, but with gravity as the only force on the spline, its behavior will not be particularly interesting. Next we will see how to add user control for a more interactive simulation.

2.4.2 User Control

Once the virtual brush handle and spline have been constructed, the user input needs to be integrated to allow for control of the brush. We assume that the user has some mechanism of providing the six degrees of freedom (DOF) necessary to position and orient the brush handle. Ideally this would come from directly manipulating the six DOF of a tablet stylus, but other approaches are fine as well.

The instantaneous state of the brush handle is $\Gamma = \langle \mathbf{p}, \mathbf{v}, \mathbf{q}, \omega \rangle$, where $\mathbf{p} = \langle p_x, p_y, p_z \rangle$ is the 3D position, $\mathbf{v} = \langle v_x, v_y, v_z \rangle$ is the 3D velocity, $\mathbf{q} = \langle q_x, q_y, q_z, q_w \rangle$ is the orientation quaternion, and $\omega = \langle \omega_x, \omega_y, \omega_z \rangle$ is the 3D angular velocity.

At time t_0, the state is $\Gamma_0 = \langle \mathbf{p}_0, \mathbf{v}_0, \mathbf{q}_0, \omega_0 \rangle$. User input specifies the position and orientation $\langle \mathbf{p}_1, \mathbf{q}_1 \rangle$ at the end of the timestep, $t_1 = t_0 + \Delta t$. Therefore, we must compute the force and torque to apply to the brush handle to achieve the change in state over the timestep. The relevant equations are

$$\mathbf{f} = \frac{m}{\Delta t^2}(\mathbf{p}_1 - \mathbf{p}_0 - \mathbf{v}_0 \Delta t) \tag{2.1}$$

$$\omega_1 = \frac{2}{\Delta t}(\mathbf{q}_1 - \mathbf{q}_0)\mathbf{q}_0^{-1} \tag{2.2}$$

$$\mathrm{I}_0 = \mathrm{R}(\mathbf{q}_0)\,\mathrm{I}_{\mathrm{body}}\,\mathrm{R}(\mathbf{q}_0)^\mathsf{T} \tag{2.3}$$

$$\tau = \frac{1}{\Delta t} I_0 (\omega_1 - \omega_0) \qquad (2.4)$$

where m is the brush handle's mass, $R(\mathbf{q})$ is the 3×3 rotation matrix corresponding to $\mathbf{q}$, and I_{body} is the brush handle's 3×3 inertia tensor in local coordinates. In Eq. (2.2), the 3D ω_1 is constructed from the 4D quaternion product by omitting the quaternion's w-component. The results of these equations are $\mathbf{f}$, the 3D force vector and τ, the 3D torque vector, which are applied to the brush handle in ODE using dBodyAddForce and dBodyAddTorque.

It is helpful to break this process up into substeps, to improve ODE's stability and convergence (see Algorithm 2.4). If the desired simulation step is $\Delta t = 0.016$ s (corresponding to 60 Hz), then with three substeps, the timestep becomes $\Delta t = 0.005$ s. Furthermore, the user input specifies $\langle \mathbf{p}_3, \mathbf{q}_3 \rangle$, and the force and torque computations must be done three times to compute the three substeps from Γ_0.

With user input-based control of the brush handle, the simulation should be more interesting—changing the position and orientation will result in forces being applied to the spline, so it should swing around like a limp rope. Two problems remain however. First, it does not collide with the canvas, and second, the spline has no stiffness. We will add stiff springs next.

2.4.3 Adding Springs

Because brush bristles are stiff, our spline needs stiff springs at each of the joints to maintain its rest shape. For example, a real brush's bristles do not droop due to gravity, because the strength of the bending stiffness is greater than the effect of gravity on the bristle's mass. Due to the stiff behavior, we must construct the springs in such a way that they are implicitly integrated by ODE.

External body forces in ODE are integrated explicitly, but constraint forces are integrated implicitly. Constraint forces are represented with joints in ODE. As we have universal joints constructed between each consecutive pair of links in the spline, we can modify them to add springs. Specifically, each joint has a notion of "joint limits", which restrict the range of motion the joint allows about its degrees of freedom (think of an elbow and how the forearm cannot bend back past a certain angle). As joint limits are hard constraints, they are implicitly integrated, and so are ideal for our uses.

Algorithm 2.5 contains the SETJOINTSPRINGS function which sets the parameters of a universal joint to have a straight rest shape of some springiness. The low and high stops are both set to $\theta = 0$, which is the rest angle. $f_{\max}$ is the maximum restorative force that can be applied. The CFM and ERP parameters determine the spring and damping coefficients of the constraint. ERP stands for the Error Reduction Parameter, in the range of [0, 1], and represents how much of a constraint violation is corrected in each timestep (for hard contacts, e.g., it would seem a value of 1 would be desired, but this can lead to instability). The CFM is the

Algorithm 2.5 Adding bristle stiffness

1: **function** SETJOINTSPRINGS()
2:     dJointSetUniversalParam(j, dParamLoStop, θ)
3:     dJointSetUniversalParam(j, dParamHiStop, θ)
4:     dJointSetUniversalParam(j, dParamFMax, f_{max})
5:     dJointSetUniversalParam(j, dParamStopERP, ERP)
6:     dJointSetUniversalParam(j, dParamStopCFM, CFM)
7: **end function**

Constraint Force Mixing, in $(0, \infty)$, a measure of how much a constraint is allowed to be violated. These two parameters are fundamentally related to the spring and damping coefficients, k_p and k_d respectively, of the joint, and can be computed by

$$\text{ERP} = \frac{\Delta t k_p}{\Delta t k_p + k_d} \qquad (2.5)$$

$$\text{CFM} = \frac{1}{\Delta t k_p + k_d} \qquad (2.6)$$

After the joint springs have been set, our spline model should be much less rope-like. Without something to collide with, the only way to see the spline bend is by moving the brush quickly, or by increasing gravity (or decreasing the spring coefficient). Finally we will add collisions, to complete the spline model.

2.4.4 Adding Collisions

Collisions in ODE are orthogonal to the dynamics by design, so applications that need collisions but not dynamics (e.g. collision detection to keep players from navigating through walls in virtual environments) can be supported, as well as simulations that have specific collision detection requirements (such as a-priori knowledge about the types of objects that will be colliding with one another).

Creation of the collision objects is shown in Algorithm 2.6's CREATECOLLIDERS function. Geometry objects are contained in spaces for organization, and associated with body objects for bookkeeping. Geometry objects and body objects need not be the same shape or mass (a common optimization is to represent an entire virtual avatar with a single capsule), but for now we will make them the same. Also a ground plane is necessary for the spline to collide with.

For collisions to be detected, dSpaceCollide2 must be called in STEPSIMULATION. This function checks the geometry (in our case the ground plane) against the geometry in the space (containing the spline) for potential collisions by using an approximation such as overlapping bounding boxes. When it detects a potential collision, it calls a callback function DETECTCOLLISION in Algorithm 2.7 that

Algorithm 2.6 Creating brush collision objects

```
 1: function CREATECOLLIDERS()
 2:     C ← dJointGroupCreate()                   ▷ holds contacts
 3:     S_w ← dSimpleSpaceCreate()                ▷ collision space for world
 4:     S_s ← dSimpleSpaceCreate(S_w)             ▷ collision space for spline
 5:     G ← dCreatePlane(S_w, 0, 0, 1, 0)         ▷ x, y ground plane
 6:     for i ← [1, n] do                         ▷ create each link collision object
 7:         g_i ← dCreateCapsule(S_s, r, l)
 8:         dGeomSetBody(b_i, g_i)                ▷ attach collision object to link body
 9:     end for
10: end function
```

Algorithm 2.7 Handling collisions

```
1: function DETECTCOLLISION(g_1, g_2)
2:     if dCollide(g_1, g_2) then
3:         c ← dJointCreateContact(W, C)         ▷ stored in contact group
4:         b_1 ← dGeomGetBody(g_1)
5:         b_2 ← dGeomGetBody(g_2)
6:         dJointAttach(c, b_1, b_2)
7:     end if
8: end function
```

uses dCollide to find a specific contact point, and if it is successful, creates a temporary joint object to represent the contact.

In this manner, collisions are detected and responded to for our spline, and once this functionality is added, we should have a springy spline that we can press into the canvas to cause characteristic bristle-like deformations.

2.5 Brush Head Modeling

A deformable spline is an important building block towards creating a brush stroke, but by itself it is incomplete. Brush heads normally contain hundreds of bristles, but it is not currently feasible to simulate hundreds of splines with high enough fidelity. Therefore, different approaches are used to "bulk up" a simulated brush head, by using a small number of splines to control a larger amount of geometry. We will consider two such approaches. The first creates additional un-simulated bristles by interpolating among splines, which is very fast but still creates a large amount of geometry. The second represents many bristles as a single triangle mesh which is deformed by splines. The mesh is even faster, but is more limited in what types of effect it can reproduce.

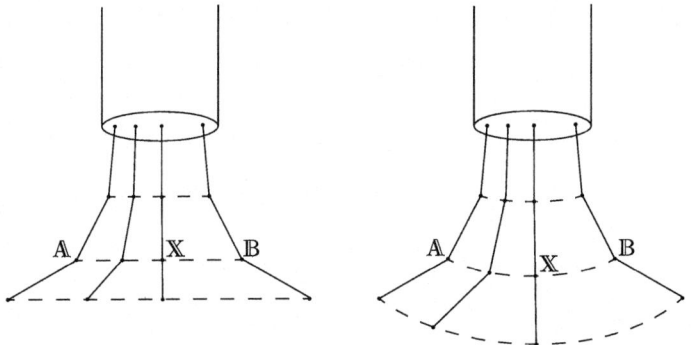

Fig. 2.3 Bristle $\mathbb{X}$ can be linearly interpolated between splines $\mathbb{A}$ and $\mathbb{B}$ either based on the vertex positions (*left*) or on the joint angles (*right*)

2.5.1 Interpolation-Based

Regardless of simulation strategy, the output of a spline-based model is a sequence of 3D positions of points along the spline in its new shape. Call this sequence, $\mathbb{A} = \{\mathbf{a}_1, \ldots, \mathbf{a}_n\}$. Then if there are three splines, $\mathbb{A}$, $\mathbb{B}$, and $\mathbb{C}$, arbitrary linear interpolations can be created from them as

$$\mathbb{X}(\alpha, \beta, \gamma) = \alpha \mathbb{A} + \beta \mathbb{B} + \gamma \mathbb{C} \qquad (2.7)$$

$$\mathbf{x}_i(\alpha, \beta, \gamma) = \alpha \mathbf{a}_i + \beta \mathbf{b}_i + \gamma \mathbf{c}_i, \quad \forall i \in [1, n] \qquad (2.8)$$

This linear interpolation of positions is fast and simple, but has the downside that it can result in interpolated splines that are shorter in length than the simulated splines. See Fig. 2.3 for an illustration. The magnitude of this effect depends on the difference among the splines being interpolated, and so for larger numbers of simulated splines, or for less severe brush head deformations, it may be sufficient.

Rather than interpolating splines' 3D positions $\mathbb{A}$, another option is to interpolate their 2D joint angles instead, $\overline{\mathbb{A}}$. Then after computing $\overline{\mathbb{X}}$ as a linear combination of spline joint angles, the spline positions $\mathbb{X}$ can be constructed with knowledge of the interpolated spline's link lengths. This will ensure interpolated splines have the same length as simulated splines, but has the downside that it could result in splines that penetrate the canvas plane. To compute $\overline{\mathbb{A}}$ from $\mathbb{A}$, each joint is defined by three consecutive points, $\mathbf{a}_{i-1}$, $\mathbf{a}_i$, and $\mathbf{a}_{i+1}$, where $\mathbf{a}_i$ is the joint location, and $\mathbf{u}$ and $\mathbf{v}$ are the joint's local right and up vectors. Then, we define $\mathbf{d}_1$ as the default direction for the joint and $\mathbf{d}_2$ as the deformed direction, such that $\mathbf{d}_1 \cdot \mathbf{u} = \mathbf{d}_1 \cdot \mathbf{v} = 0$. To find the angles about the $\mathbf{u}$ and $\mathbf{v}$ vectors, we can use

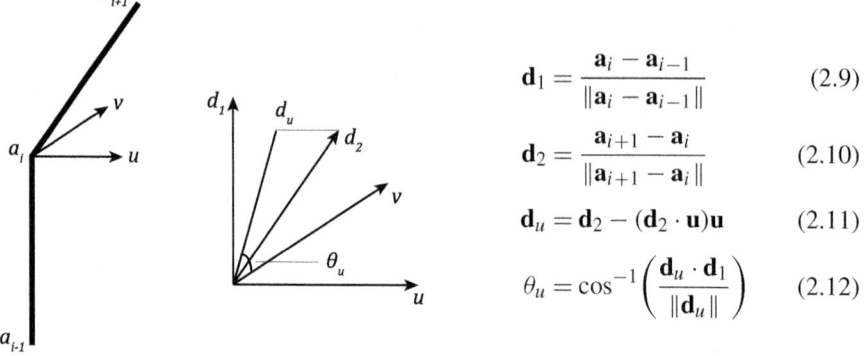

$$\mathbf{d}_1 = \frac{\mathbf{a}_i - \mathbf{a}_{i-1}}{\|\mathbf{a}_i - \mathbf{a}_{i-1}\|} \qquad (2.9)$$

$$\mathbf{d}_2 = \frac{\mathbf{a}_{i+1} - \mathbf{a}_i}{\|\mathbf{a}_{i+1} - \mathbf{a}_i\|} \qquad (2.10)$$

$$\mathbf{d}_u = \mathbf{d}_2 - (\mathbf{d}_2 \cdot \mathbf{u})\mathbf{u} \qquad (2.11)$$

$$\theta_u = \cos^{-1}\left(\frac{\mathbf{d}_u \cdot \mathbf{d}_1}{\|\mathbf{d}_u\|}\right) \qquad (2.12)$$

(with corresponding equations for θ_v). Then θ_u and θ_v are the joint angles, which allows us to construct $\overline{\mathbf{a}_i} = \langle \theta_u, \theta_v \rangle$.

To do the reverse transform and compute $\mathbb{A}$ from $\overline{\mathbb{A}}$, starting at the base of the spline with $\mathbf{d}_1$, the up and right vectors, $\mathbf{u}$ and $\mathbf{v}$ and the joint angles θ_u and θ_v, we can use the equation

$$\mathbf{d}_2 = \mathbf{d}_1 + \mathbf{u}\tan\theta_v + \mathbf{v}\tan\theta_u \qquad (2.13)$$

where $\mathbf{d}_2$ is the direction of the subsequent spline link.

Regardless of the scheme used, interpolation can be used to generate bristles inside the triangle defined by any three splines. Therefore, to produce the best bristles, create as many splines as possible to simulate distribute around the head of the brush, and then triangulate their positions to determine which splines should be interpolated for new bristles at arbitrary locations.

2.5.2 Mesh-Based

Creating interpolated splines can make a nice bristly appearance for scratchy strokes, but for smoother paint application, modeling the brush head as a continuous mesh may be more desirable. In that case, one or more splines can be used to control the deformation of one or more triangle meshes that represent a bulk collection of bristles and wet paint. We will discuss here how to control a single triangle mesh, but a brush head can be modeled by multiple meshes to support a wider range of behaviors. For example, a wide flat brush could benefit from multiple meshes to allow it to support splitting deformation, which a single mesh would not allow.

Deforming a mesh by a collection of splines is a straightforward application of vertex skinning, also known as vertex blending or skeleton-subspace deformation [24], which is a commonly used algorithm in the realtime 3D video games field for character mesh animation based on an animated skeleton of rigid bones. The approach is well-documented in many places [10], which we will summarize here. See Fig. 2.4 for an overview.

The core concept is that each bone's new position defines a transformation matrix that can be applied to any vertex in the mesh. Thus, by assigning a weight to the

Algorithm 2.8 Computing vertex weights

```
 1: function FINDNEARESTNEIGHBORS(v, n, S)
 2:     return indices of n closest points to v in S, sorted by distance
 3: end function
 4: function ASSIGNWEIGHTS(n)
 5:     for all v ∈ V do
 6:         {i₁, ..., i_{n+1}} ← FINDNEARESTNEIGHBORS(v, n + 1, S)
 7:         max ← ‖v − s_{i_{n+1}}‖
 8:         min ← ‖v − s_{i₁}‖
 9:         for j ← [1, n] do
10:             d ← ‖v − s_{i_j}‖
11:             w_j ← 1 − (d − min)/(max − min)
12:         end for
13:         for j ← [1, n] do
14:             w_j ← w_j / ∑_k w_k              ▷ normalize weights
15:         end for
16:     end for
17: end function
```

influence of each bone per-vertex, the new position of the vertex is generated by a linear combination of the bones' transformations. Generally, a vertex has only a small number of non-zero weights, between two and four. In our case, the bones are each link of the spline. Therefore, a mesh vertex position can be computed as

$$\mathbf{v}' = \sum_i w_i \mathbf{M}_i \mathbf{v} \qquad (2.14)$$

where w_i are the bone weights, $\mathbf{M}_i$ are the bone transformation matrices, from model coordinates to world coordinates, and $\mathbf{v}'$ is the output vertex position. This can be efficiently computed inside a vertex shader on modern graphics cards.

Once a triangle mesh and set of splines have been specified, the vertices' bone weights can be specified by hand, though this may be a tedious process. Alternately, they can be computed automatically based on the distance of each vertex to the bones. Consider the pseudocode in Algorithm 2.8, which assigns n weights per-vertex for a mesh of vertices $\mathbb{V}$ and the spline $\mathbb{S}$.

Mesh skinning is still an active area of research, and so as new techniques are developed, they may be applied here, if they are found to have more desirable properties [22].

While mesh-based brush heads have an advantage over bristle-based, in that they can have significantly less geometry and can produce smoother strokes, they have difficulty reproducing some brush head behaviors. Specifically, tip-spreading is a common effect where, for example, the point of a round brush will spread out when it is pressed into the canvas. Using multiple splines to control a single mesh can mimic this behavior, or other workarounds may be employed depending on the quality of result needed.

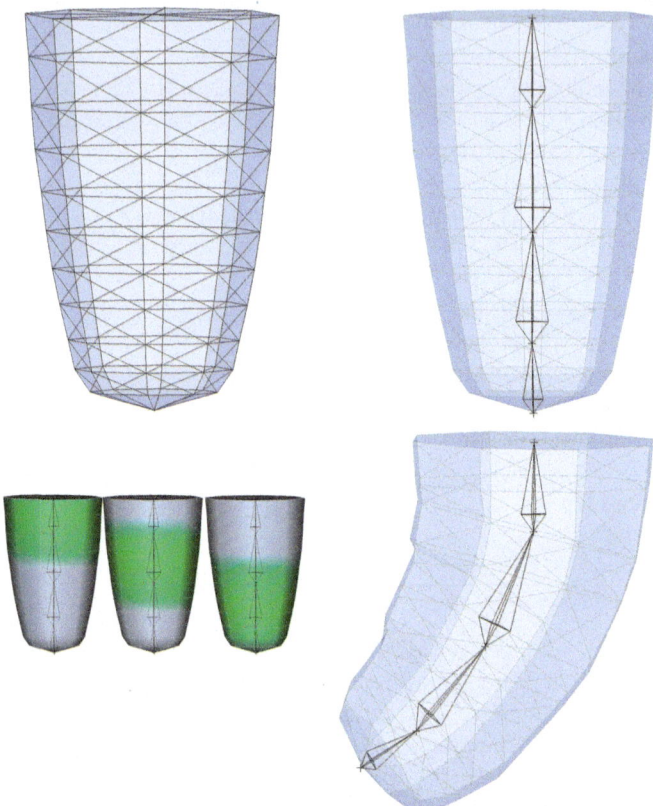

Fig. 2.4 A triangle mesh based brush head modeled in a common 3D modeling application. *Left* to *right*, *top* to *bottom:* The triangle mesh. The bones corresponding to spline links, placed in the mesh. The mesh vertex weights for the first three bones, computed by Art of Illusion [20]. The mesh is deformed based on the position of the bones by Eq. (2.14)

2.6 Stroke Rendering

At this point, our virtual brush has a physically simulated deformable head that is represented either by a set of bristles or as a triangle mesh. Using it to create the brush stroke output is the final step of this chapter. This process is non-trivial for a number of reasons, and the tradeoffs made here have a significant impact on the final output of our algorithm.

The first issue is that physical simulation is expensive to compute. It might be appealing to perform a simulation step for each new position of the brush (perhaps after some number of pixels have been traversed), but realistically, users can move the brush at arbitrary speeds across large canvases, creating a prohibitive computation burden. Furthermore, physics engines in general and ODE in particular, are significantly more stable when they are stepped with uniform time increments. Therefore, our strategy is to compute a constant number of physics steps per update of the application (generally per frame render). As fast strokes mean there will be a significant pixel distance between consecutive steps, the question becomes how to fill in the pixels in between.

As discussed in Sect. 2.2, tweening is the term for generating in-between samples when filling in a sparsely computed system (the source of the term is 2D animation, where smooth transitions are drawn between artists' keyframes). We will consider both the numerical approach of stamping, and the analytical approach of sweeping, from the perspectives of bristle-based and mesh-based brush heads.

It is interesting to note that brush strokes are inherently inexact—that is, it is difficult to quantify a specific desired output for a set of parameters. There is an important question of how much fidelity is necessary to produce a usable painting system, which has been partially answered by the availability of digital painting programs to date. Therefore, the process of generating the output brush stroke from a physical simulation is as much a matter of taste as it is of science, and hence there are many opportunities to tune the particulars of an implementation.

2.6.1 Stamping

Stamping is the numerical approach to generating the continuous output of a brush stroke. Rather than trying to directly compute the value of each pixel covered by a stroke, the instantaneous pose of the brush is computed many times at small increments, and their effect is combined to generate the final output. This has a number of important implications to our algorithm design. Since this is the method of choice for commercial digital painting applications, the design space has been extensively explored already.

First, the instantaneous stamp needs to be computed. For a virtual brush head, we call this the brush's "footprint"—the contact area between the bristles and the canvas, where paint is deposited. The output of our brush head model is some geometry that we could test for actual canvas contact, but that would likely be a very small area and would not reflect the size of the mark we would expect such a brush to make. Realistically, a brush head has wet paint on it which creates a larger contact area with the canvas than just the bristle geometry. Therefore, we use what we call a "deposition threshold" which is a plane slightly offset from the canvas, and state that any geometry in the volume between the deposition threshold and the canvas is considered to be in contact (see Fig. 2.5).

For a triangle mesh brush head, computing the footprint is therefore very easy. The mesh is simply rasterized using a standard rendering library such as OpenGL, with an orthographic projection setup looking down at the canvas and the deposition threshold set as the depth clipping distance (the camera's near or far plane).

With a bristle brush, from interpolation or individual bristles, each bristle can be rendered in the same OpenGL setup as a bent cylinder. This geometry is straightforward to compute on the CPU, or a geometry shader can be used in OpenGL to generate it automatically on the GPU, but either way it results in a significant

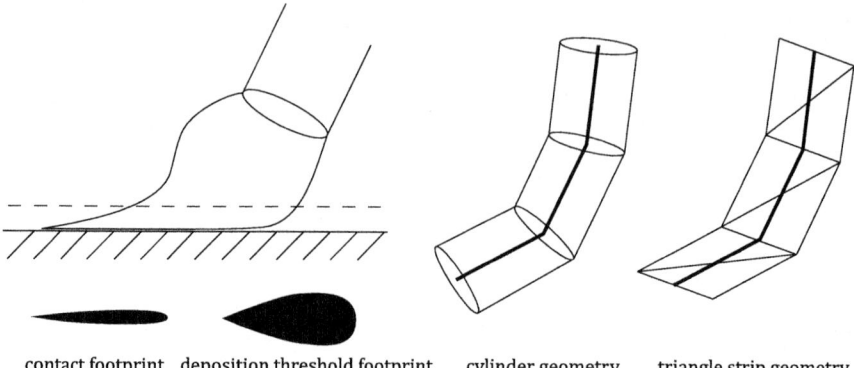

contact footprint   deposition threshold footprint   cylinder geometry   triangle strip geometry

Fig. 2.5 *Left:* The deposition threshold is offset slightly from the canvas surface and results in a significantly larger brush footprint than the exact contact area. *Right:* An individual bristle can be represented as a bent cylinder or as a triangle strip

amount of geometry to be processed. An alternative is to render each bristle as a strip of triangles, oriented perpendicular to the camera view direction. This way the width of the bristle can still be explicitly controlled, but with a significantly smaller geometry burden. These options are illustrated in Fig. 2.5.

The second important consideration for stamping is how frequently to place the stamps, called the brush "spacing". Because each stamp has an associated cost in terms of memory bandwidth and computation, the best performance will come from placing as few stamps as possible. However, the frequency content of the stamp images dictates how closely spaced stamps must be placed to create a stroke without sampling artifacts (see Fig. 2.6). For example, the commonly available gaussian blob brushes in programs like Photoshop [3] have only very low frequencies, and so can generally be used at high spacings of around 25 % of the size of the brush without artifact. On the other hand, hard-edged circular brushes at 25 % create obvious stepping and un-smooth silhouette problems, and require spacings closer to 1–5 %. For our brush heads, thin individual bristles can be as small as a single pixel, and worse, since they are dynamic within the stamp image, even a spacing of 1 pixel may be insufficient. Tricks like using wider bristles and applying a small gaussian blur or a motion blur can help reduce the problem.

The other difficulty of spacing is that it can make proper coverage and cumulative effects difficult to calculate. For example, while it is easy to apply an alpha value to each stamp, the number of overlapping stamps at a single pixel is determined by a combination of the footprint and the spacing rate, and can mean that changing either one alters the final stroke's transparency. This issue is further compounded when bidirectional (brush ↔ canvas) pigment transfer is considered, as discussed by Chu et al. [15].

Finally, the last concern with stamping is how to interpolate all the data to create the intermediate stamps, such as the x, y stamp position and the intermediate brush head configuration. Linear interpolation is straightforward, but creates piecewise linear brush strokes that are immediately apparent and undesirable. Smooth strokes

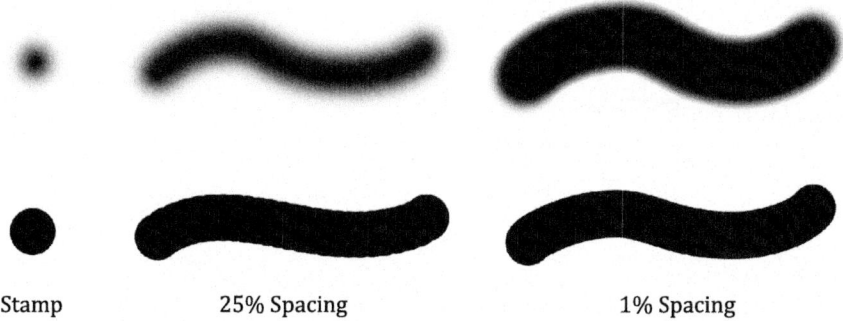

Fig. 2.6 Stamping artifacts depend on the stamp used and the spacing. For a low frequency stamp (*top*), a high spacing produces a smooth stroke while a low spacing causes more alpha accumulation than desired. For a high frequency stamp (*bottom*), a low spacing results in silhouette artifacts

are the result of interpolating the x, y positions with a higher order technique such as cubic interpolation or Bézier fitting [4]. As higher order interpolation can be used for the stamp position, it can also be used for each brush vertex's position as well, but the additional fidelity is not generally noticeable or worth the computational cost.

2.6.2 Sweeping

The alternative to the numerical approach of stamping is the analytical approach of sweeping. Computing swept volumes of 3D models is a much-researched problem for applications like robot motion planning [1]. The same problems arise in the case of 2D swept areas. Many approaches for computing sweeps rely on simplifying assumptions about the nature of the problem, such as translation-only motion, or convex polyhedra (polygon) models only.

In the case of a bristle-based brush head model, we can take advantage of such a simplifying assumption. Specifically, computing a sweep is trivial if the object being swept has fewer dimensions than the space in which it is being swept. Consider a 2D square being swept along a path in 3D—the swept volume can be generated by connecting the corners of the square in consecutive positions. Similarly, for a 1D line segment swept along a 2D path, the swept area can be generated by connecting the end points of the line segment at consecutive positions. See Fig. 2.7 for an illustration. We can use this simplification to create sweeps trivially out of the motion of bristles across the canvas. For each link in each bristle, given its position at the previous simulation step and the current one, use a rasterizer such as OpenGL to render a quad defined by the end points of link at the two timesteps. With the same camera setup as described in Sect. 2.6.1, clipping to the deposition threshold will provide the same approximation of canvas contact.

The main limitation of computing the stroke as the swept area of line primitives is that when the bristle is straight (when looking down from above) and the motion

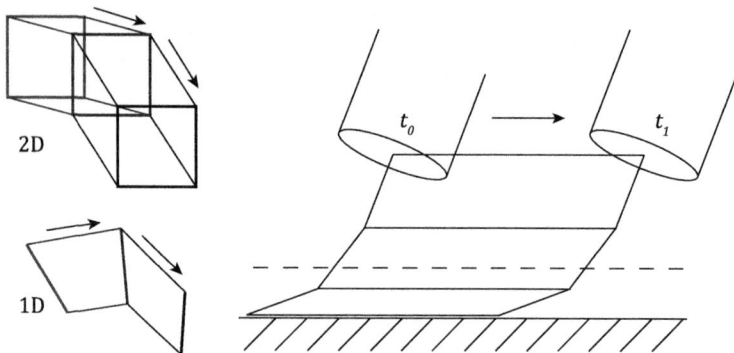

Fig. 2.7 *Left:* Trivial sweeps of a 2D square in 3D, and a 1D line in 2D. *Right:* Since a bristle consists of a set of 1D lines, bristle sweeps can be trivially computed by connecting the vertices of the same bristle at consecutive timesteps

of the bristle is parallel to its contact with the canvas, then the swept area will be zero because a 1D line has zero width. This can be worked around in a number of ways. For example, the bristles could always be made to have a slight curve, or many bristles could be put on the brush at different angles to avoid the case that all the bristles will ever become parallel. Each of these workarounds is an approximation of varying quality, with its own pitfalls that may be significant depending on the specific use case.

Another approach that also supports triangle mesh brush heads is to compute the 2D swept area of a 2D polygon using an algorithm such as that proposed by Pudet [28]. Pudet describes a way to efficiently compute brush strokes generated by sweeping a 2D brush stamp along an input path. An algorithm like this is the basis of the calligraphic brush tool in Adobe Illustrator [2], so it has been demonstrated to be robust. To use Pudet's algorithm, we need the brush footprint represented as a 2D polygon. Given the deformed triangle mesh of the brush head, it is possible to find the intersection between the mesh and the deposition threshold, and to extract the polygon contour of that intersection for use in sweeping. To reduce the number of triangles that need to be considered, only the triangles where two vertices are on opposite sides of the deposition threshold need to be considered.

The downside of creating a swept area from the brush head triangle mesh is that the output of the sweep algorithm is a single contour to which a constant fill gets applied. Therefore, if 50 % gray ink is deposited, the output brush stroke will be a solid 50 % gray, which loses some of the natural media textural quality that is desirable in real brush strokes. To create more variation within the stroke, rather than computing a single sweep from a triangle mesh footprint, re-consider the individual bristle model. Each bristle's contact with the canvas can be considered to be a polygon (e.g. an ellipse for simplicity), dynamically sized based on the bristle thickness and the length of the bristle-canvas contact. Then Pudet's algorithm can be used to compute the swept area of each bristle's contact independently, outputting one flat-filled region per-bristle. The combination of all these swept bristle regions, when given transparent fills, can create the desired variation in shading across the

Fig. 2.8 *Left*: A brush stroke with a single, flat fill. *Right*: One flat fill per bristle adds texture

brush stroke (see Fig. 2.8). This is the algorithm used in Adobe Illustrator's bristle brushes [19].

One of the primary advantages of sweeping is that it can be used, as described above, to generate vector output. The nature of Pudet's algorithm is that it computes the polygonal outline of the swept stroke, and the end-point connecting approach generates triangle vertices as its output. In either case, the final primitives are resolution-independent and can be stored efficiently in vector image formats such as SVG.

2.7 Summary

At this point, we have described the different components necessary to create a physically based virtual brush and to use it to render brush strokes. For each component, we have provided an assessment of the advantages and disadvantages of the available options. Finally, we have summarized the research literature on brush stroke synthesis, so interested readers can pursue a deeper understanding of the material, while implementers interested in a practical understanding of brush stroke synthesis can use this chapter as a guide.

References

1. Abdel-Malek, K., Blackmore, D., Joy, K.: Swept volumes: foundations, perspectives, and applications. Int. J. Shape Model. **12**(1), 87–127 (2006)
2. Adobe: Illustrator (2012). http://www.adobe.com/illustrator/
3. Adobe: Photoshop (2012). http://www.adobe.com/photoshop/
4. Armstrong, J.: Composite Bezier curves (2006). http://www.algorithmist.net/composite.html
5. Bai, B., Wong, K.W., Zhang, Y.: An efficient physically-based model for Chinese brush. In: Proceedings of the International Conference on Frontiers in Algorithmics, pp. 261–270 (2007)
6. Baraff, D., Witkin, A.: Physically based modeling: Principles and practice. In: ACM SIGGRAPH Courses (1997). http://www.cs.cmu.edu/~baraff/sigcourse/
7. Baxter, W., Govindaraju, N.: Simple data-driven modeling of brushes. In: Proceedings of the ACM SIGGRAPH Symposium on Interactive 3D Graphics and Games, pp. 135–142 (2010)
8. Baxter, W., Lin, M.: A versatile interactive 3D brush model. In: Proceedings of the Pacific Conference on Computer Graphics and Applications, pp. 319–328 (2004)
9. Baxter, B., Scheib, V., Lin, M., Manocha, D.D.: Interactive haptic painting with 3D virtual brushes. In: Proceedings of ACM SIGGRAPH, pp. 461–468 (2001)
10. Beeson, C.: Animation in the "Dawn" demo. In: Fernando, R. (ed.) GPU Gems, pp. 223–233. Addison-Wesley, Reading (2004)
11. Boeing, A.: Physics Abstraction Layer (2009). http://pal.sourceforge.net/

12. Boeing, A., Bräunl, T.: Evaluation of real-time physics simulation systems. In: Proceedings of Computer Graphics and Interactive Techniques in Australia and Southeast Asia, pp. 281–288 (2007)
13. Chu, S.H.: Making digital painting organic. Ph.D. thesis, Hong Kong University of Science and Technology (2007)
14. Chu, N., Tai, C.L.: Real-time painting with an expressive virtual Chinese brush. IEEE Comput. Graph. Appl. **24**(5), 76–85 (2004)
15. Chu, N., Baxter, W., Wei, L.Y., Govindaraju, N.: Detail-preserving paint modeling for 3D brushes. In: Proceedings of the International Symposium on Non-photorealistic Animation and Rendering, pp. 27–34 (2010)
16. Corel: Painter (2012). http://www.corel.com/painter/
17. Coumans, E.: Bullet physics library (2010). http://www.bulletphysics.org/
18. Design, A.: ArtRage (2012). http://www.artrage.com/
19. DiVerdi, S., Krishnaswamy, A., Hadap, S.: Industrial-strength painting with a virtual bristle brush. In: Proceedings of the ACM Symposium on Virtual Reality Software and Technology, pp. 119–126 (2010)
20. Eastman, P.: Art of illusion (2012). http://www.artofillusion.org/
21. Hertzmann, A.: A survey of stroke-based rendering. IEEE Comput. Graph. Appl. **23**, 70–81 (2003)
22. Kavan, L., Sloan, P.P., O'Sullivan, C.: Fast and efficient skinning of animated meshes. Comput. Graph. Forum **29**(2), 327–336 (2010)
23. Lam, D.: Tokamak physics engine (2010). http://www.tokamakphysics.com/
24. Lewis, J.P., Cordner, M., Fong, N.: Pose space deformation: a unified approach to shape interpolation and skeleton-driven deformation. In: Proceedings of ACM SIGGRAPH, pp. 165–172 (2000)
25. Lu, T.K., Huang, Z.: A GPU-based method for real-time simulation of Eastern painting. In: Proceedings of the International Conference on Computer Graphics and Interactive Techniques in Australia and Southeast Asia, pp. 111–118 (2007)
26. Mi, X., Xu, J., Tang, M., Dong, J.: The droplet virtual brush for Chinese calligraphic character modeling. In: Proceedings of the IEEE Workshop on Applications of Computer Vision, pp. 330–334 (2002)
27. Okabe, Y., Saito, S., Nakajima, M.: Paintbrush rendering of lines using HMMs. In: Proceedings of the International Conference on Computer Graphics and Interactive Techniques in Australasia and South East Asia, pp. 91–98 (2005)
28. Pudet, T.: Real time fitting of hand-sketched pressure brushstrokes. Comput. Graph. Forum **13**(3), 205–220 (1994)
29. Saito, S., Nakajima, M.: 3D physics-based brush model for painting. In: Proceedings of ACM SIGGRAPH Conference Abstracts and Applications, p. 226 (1999)
30. Smith, A.R.: Digital paint systems: an anecdotal and historical overview. IEEE Ann. Hist. Comput. **23**, 4–30 (2001)
31. Smith, R.: Open Dynamics Engine (2007). http://www.ode.org/
32. Van Laerhoven, T., Van Reeth, F.: Brush up your painting skills: realistic brush design for interactive painting applications. Vis. Comput. **23**(9), 763–771 (2007)
33. Vandoren, P., Van Laerhoven, T., Claesen, L., Taelman, J., Raymaekers, C., Van Reeth, F.: IntuPaint: bridging the gap between physical and digital painting. In: IEEE International Workshop on Horizontal Interactive Human Computer Systems, pp. 65–72 (2008)
34. Vandoren, P., Claesen, L., Van Laerhoven, T., Taelman, J., Van Reeth, F.: FluidPaint: an interactive digital painting system using real wet brushes. In: Proceedings of the IEEE International Workshop on Tabletops and Interactive Surfaces (2009)
35. Xie, N., Laga, H., Saito, S., Nakajima, M.: IR2s: interactive real photo to Sumi-e. In: Proceedings of the International Symposium on Non-Photorealistic Animation and Rendering, pp. 63–71 (2010)
36. Xu, S., Tang, M., Lau, F., Pan, Y.: Virtual hairy brush for painterly rendering. Graph. Models **66**(5), 263–302 (2004)

Chapter 3
Halftoning and Stippling

Oliver Deussen and Tobias Isenberg

3.1 Halftoning

Shortly after photography was invented, images became part of printed newspapers and books. William Fox Talbot, one of the inventors of photography, already mentioned an etching method (intaglio printing) for processing photographic screens which was commercialized in the 1880s.

Georg Meisenbach, a German inventor, developed and patented a halftone process on the basis of sets of parallel lines that were superimposed with the input photograph. He created his pattern by engraving lines in glass and darkened them using asphalt. Two or more such line patterns were superimposed and worked as a filter for the input image that divided it into dots of varying size (see Fig. 3.1).

3.1.1 Digital Halftoning

In digital halftoning, the screening process is implemented by representing the input image by electronically generated dots. Companies such as Linotype in the 1970s developed film recorders where the film was electronically illuminated dot by dot using precision optics.

O. Deussen (✉)
Dept. of Computer and Information Science, University of Konstanz, Konstanz, Germany
e-mail: oliver.deussen@uni-konstanz.de

T. Isenberg
INRIA Saclay, Orsay, France
e-mail: tobias@isenberg.cc

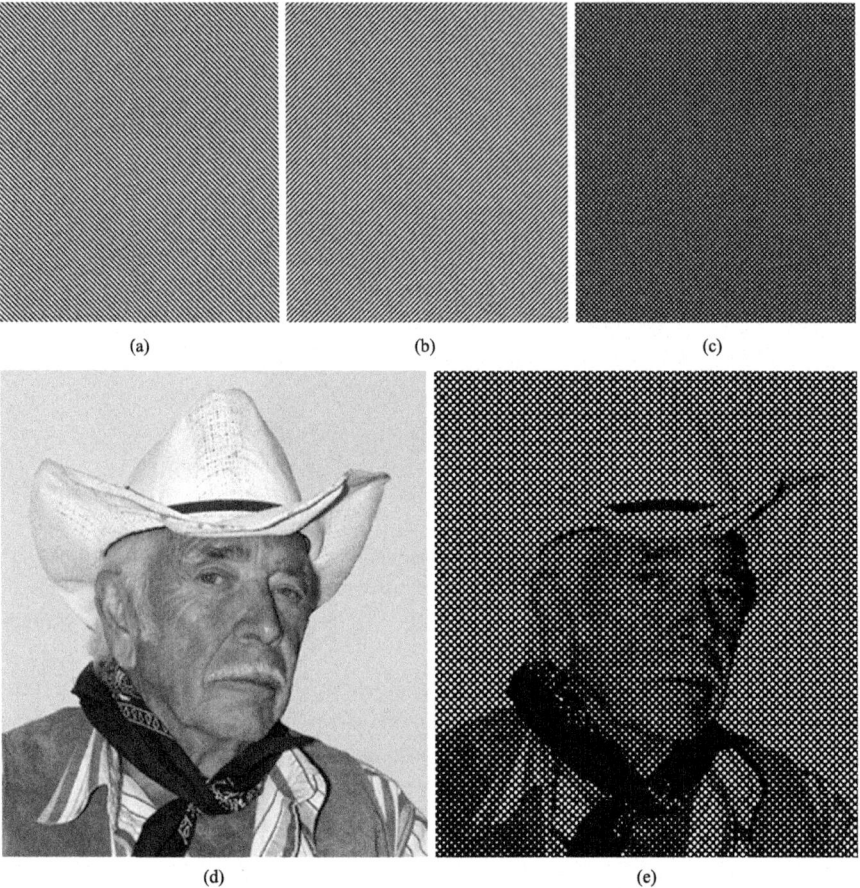

Fig. 3.1 Reproducing a photograph by multiple line patterns. (**a**) First line screen; (**b**) second line screen; (**c**) resulting screening pattern; (**d**) Input Image: Rosemary Ratcliff/FreeDigitalPhotos.net; (**e**) resulting halftoning pattern

When fully digital printing was invented for laser printers, halftoning meant to convert grayscale images into black and white pixels that were directly realized by printers.

3.1.2 Threshold Quantization

The easiest way to convert a given grayscale image into black and white pixels is to use a threshold, typically half of the highest intensity. Doing so, the resulting image shows large black and white areas (cf. Fig. 3.2(a)). A random variation of the threshold avoids such large areas but introduces noise (Fig. 3.2(b)).

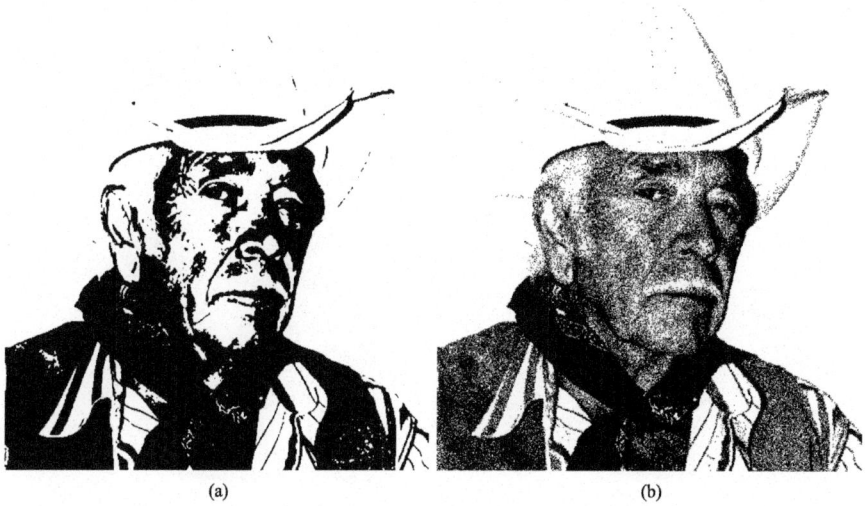

Fig. 3.2 (a) Quantization with fixed threshold; (b) threshold is varied randomly

---
Algorithm 3.1 One-dimensional Error Diffusion

Input: A grayscale image
Output: An image of black and white pixels approximating the input
for $y :=$ height to 0 step 1 {
  for $x := 0$ to width-1 step 1 {
    if (input$[x, y] > 127$)
      $K := 255$;
    else
      $K := 0$;
    error $:=$ input$[x, y] - K$;
    input$[x + 1, y] :=$ input$[x + 1, y] +$ error;
  }
}

Each decision if a pixel is represented in white or in black introduces a visual error. If the threshold is randomly varied, this error statistically averages and the overall image appears in the right tonal values. However, the noise remains and thus better techniques were developed.

Floyd and Steinberg [3] invented error diffusion for halftoning. When representing a pixel in white or black, the error in grayscale is determined and diffused to the neighbor pixels. The simplest case is one dimensional (cf. Algorithm 3.1), here a line of pixels is processed left to right and the error is diffused to the right neighbor.

In Fig. 3.3(a) the result of one-dimensional Floyd Steinberg quantization is shown. Vertical patterns appear since for every line almost the same error is distributed leading to almost the same patterns in every line. The two-dimensional

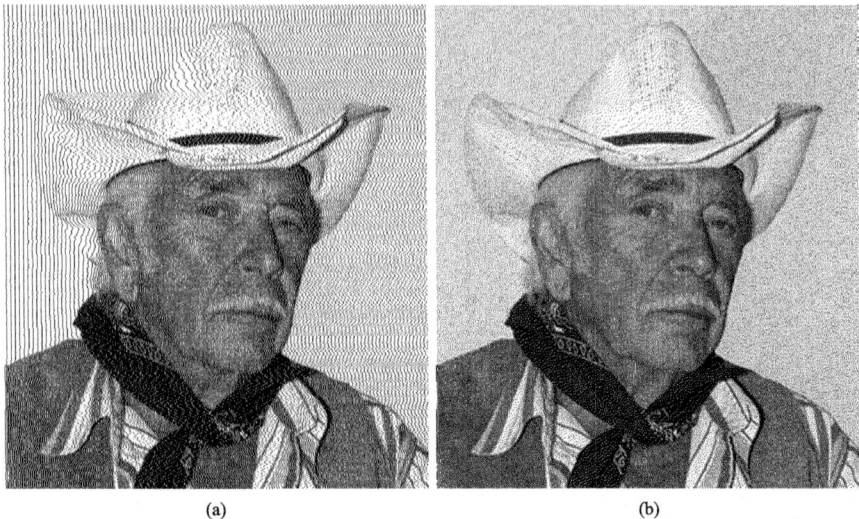

Fig. 3.3 Floyd Steinberg quantization: (**a**) in the one-dimensional version vertical patterns appear; (**b**) the two-dimensional variant avoids this

---

Algorithm 3.2 Floyd Steinberg Error Diffusion

Input: A grayscale image
Output: An image of black and white pixels approximating the input
for $y :=$ height to 0 step 1 {
  for $x := 0$ to width-1 step 1 {
    if (input$[x, y] > 127$)
      $K := 255$;
    else
      $K := 0$;
    error $:=$ input$[x, y] - K$;
    input$[x + 1, y] :=$ input$[x + 1, y] + 7/16 *$ error;
    input$[x - 1, y - 1] :=$ input$[x - 1, y - 1] + 3/16 *$ error;
    input$[x, y - 1] :=$ input$[x, y - 1] + 5/16 *$ error;
    input$[x + 1, y - 1] :=$ input$[x + 1, y - 1] + 1/16 *$ error;
  }
}

---

variant of the algorithm (see Algorithm 3.2) avoids such patterns since here the error is not just distributed to the right neighbor but to the local neighborhood of the pixel.

Here four pixels around the current pixel are updated. The error is distributed with individual weights that were found by experiments. Figure 3.3(b) shows the improvement in the visual output.

3 Halftoning and Stippling

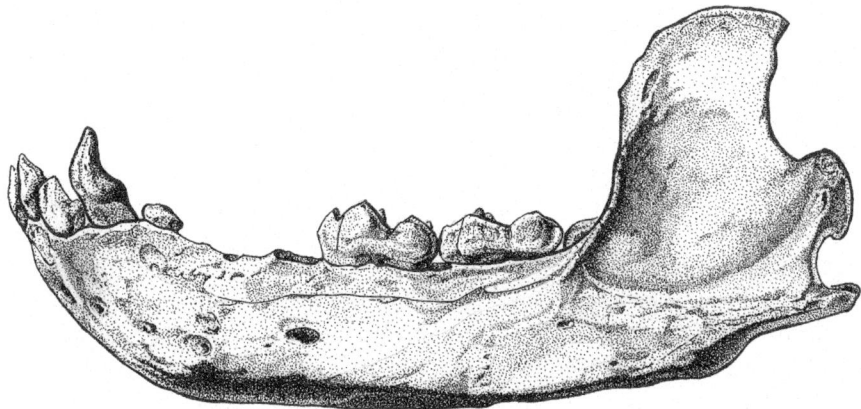

Fig. 3.4 Manually generated stipple drawing. Image courtesy by Brian L. Sidlauskas, Oregon State University

Many other halftoning techniques have been developed. Screening techniques imitate Meisenbach's superposition of an image with a repeating structure of varying width. A dither kernel (a small matrix of threshold values) that is repeatedly placed on the input image. Since the threshold values repeat regularly, the image impression is also more regular than with error diffusion.

3.2 Stippling

Stippling is an illustration technique that relies on dots. In contrast to halftoning methods, dots are distributed manually. The artists tries to set dots randomly but in most cases with almost uniform point-to-point distances.

The technique allows artists to represent tone plus material of an object, thus such techniques are used by scientific illustrators when objects have to be printed in black and white while faithfully representing their surface details. An example from biology is shown in Fig. 3.4, the surface of a bone is represented by the smooth arrangements of the dots, especially in the lighter areas almost uniform point-to-point distances are visible.

While in Fig. 3.4 silhouette lines were also used, in the following we want to concentrate on how to distribute points with the necessary characteristics by means of computers.

So called Centroidal Voronoi Tessellations create dot distributions that arrange points in the desired manner. Du et al. [2] describe them thoroughly, an analysis of different configurations of such tessellations and corresponding energy levels are given in [5, 16].

Centroidal Voronoi Tessellations for creating stipple patterns were introduced in [1, 17]. Other applications for such point sets are sampling [9] and numerical integration [18, 19]. In both cases the spectral characteristics of such sets (Blue Noise characteristics) are the reason for their usage.

3.2.1 Voronoi Tessellations and Lloyd Relaxation

Let us assume that we have n points $S = s_1, \ldots, s_n$ on our paper. The Voronoi cell $V(s_i)$ of a point is the area around s_i for which each additional point on the paper would be closer to s_i than to any other point of the given set S. The regions of all points in S form a tessellation of the plane, meaning that they are pairwise distinct and jointly covering the entire plane.

Such tessellations are called the Voronoi diagrams $VD(S)$ of S. Since a tessellation of the entire plane would have open Voronoi regions for the outer points of S, typically such regions are closed by intersecting them with a (rectangular) frame that encloses the given point set. This frame is our canvas on which the points are distributed.

Ordinary Voronoi Tessellations use the Euclidean metric as a distance function. Many other distance functions can be used. However, for the purpose of Stippling the Euclidean distance is sufficient since it is a "natural" distance function with an intuitive relation between value and perceived distance.

Centroidal Voronoi Tessellations (*CVTs*) are ordinary Voronoi Tessellations with the additional property that every point s_i is placed in the centroid c_i of its Voronoi cell $V(s_i)$. The centroid (xc_i, yc_i) is defined by the moments of the area:

$$m_i^{0,0} = \int_{y_{i1}}^{y_{i2}} \int_{x_{i1}(y)}^{x_{i2}(y)} dx\,dy$$

$$m_i^{1,0} = \int_{y_{i1}}^{y_{i2}} \int_{x_{i1}(y)}^{x_{i2}(y)} x\,dx\,dy \quad (3.1)$$

$$m_i^{0,1} = \int_{y_{i1}}^{y_{i2}} y \int_{x_{i1}(y)}^{x_{i2}(y)} dx\,dy$$

$$xc_i = \frac{m_i^{0,0}}{m_i^{1,0}}, \quad yc_i = \frac{m_i^{0,0}}{m_i^{0,1}} \quad (3.2)$$

with A_i being the area of the Voronoi Cell and $x_{i1}, x_{i2}, y_{i1}, y_{i2}$ the boundary of the cell. Such a Cendroidal Voronoi Tessellation is shown in Fig. 3.5(b). The points are still almost at random but now with much less variance in their point to point distances.

Cendroidal Voronoi Tessellations can be achieved by applying the *Lloyd relaxation* to the points. This algorithm was invented by S. Lloyd in the 1960s at Bell Labs and later published in [11]. Each step of one iteration of this algorithm moves

3 Halftoning and Stippling

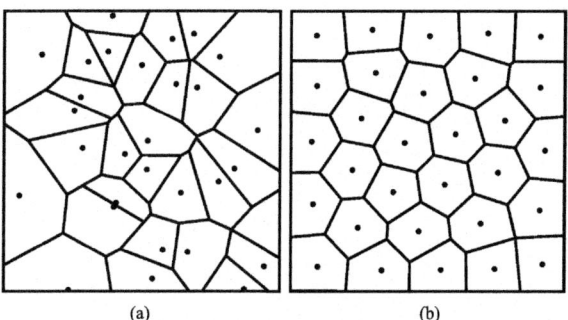

Fig. 3.5 (a) Voronoi Diagram; (b) movement of points during relaxation

each point towards the centroid of its Voronoi Region. If $c_i = (xc_i, yc_i)$ is the centroid of a Voronoi Region the movement can be represented

$$s_i^{(t+1)} = s_i^{(t)} + \alpha \left(c_i^{(t)} - s_i^{(t)} \right) \tag{3.3}$$

where $\alpha \in (0, 1]$ determines the speed of the movement. In the original algorithm α is set to one. The iteration is repeated until the movement of the points is below a given threshold. Figure 3.5(b) visualizes the movement during such a relaxation.

The CVT minimizes the following energy function, which measures the compactness of the Voronoi Regions (see [2]):

$$F_v(S, V(S)) = \sum_{i=1}^{n} \int_{V(S_i)} \|x - s_i\|^2 dx \tag{3.4}$$

This energy function sums up the integral of all quadratic distances of the points in a Voronoi Cell towards the corresponding point s_i. This is minimal for compact regions with almost uniform aspect ratio, thereby approximating hexagons [2]. Furthermore, it implies an almost uniform distribution of point-to-point distances since these distances are maximized for compact regions.

The Lloyd relaxation minimizes Eq. (3.4) and therefore can be used as a local optimization method for F. It moves the points into a distribution with almost uniform point-to-point distance. If continued for too long, it converges to a hexagonal distribution. This is not desired and typically iterating is stopped after a smaller number of steps.

3.2.2 Weighted Voronoi Tessellations

The Lloyd iteration distributes points in a uniform manner. However, for representing an input image we need varying density and thus have to find ways to modify the sizes of the Voronoi cells locally. Secord [17] published a variant of the iteration

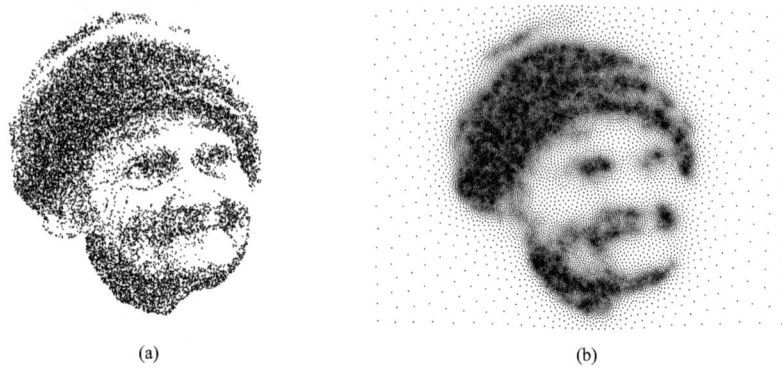

Fig. 3.6 (**a**) Initial Point distribution for a face; (**b**) point distribution after 20 steps of Lloyd's relaxation. The points spread over the entire drawing plane, image details are lost

in which every point on the plane is assigned a weight in proportion to the needed point density (grayscale value).

For doing so, the definition of the moments from Sect. 3.1 is modified in order to encapsulate the weights:

$$
\begin{aligned}
m_i^{0,0} &= \int_{y_{i1}}^{y_{i2}} \int_{x_{i1}(y)}^{x_{i2}(y)} \rho(x,y)\,dx\,dy \\
m_i^{1,0} &= \int_{y_{i1}}^{y_{i2}} \int_{x_{i1}(y)}^{x_{i2}(y)} x\rho(x,y)\,dx\,dy \\
m_i^{0,1} &= \int_{y_{i1}}^{y_{i2}} y \int_{x_{i1}(y)}^{x_{i2}(y)} \rho(x,y)\,dx\,dy
\end{aligned}
\qquad (3.5)
$$

with $\rho(x,y)$ being the density function that reflects the needed point density on the image. Parts of the equations can be precomputed, see [17] for details, and this allows for a fast computation of the integrals.

Let us have a look what can be produced with this simple optimization scheme. Since the method only moves points, an initial set has to be given. Usually one uses one of the above described halftoning methods and for every black pixel one dot is created.

Figure 3.6(a) shows such an initial point distribution for the face of a woman. If we apply the normal Lloyd Iteration for this point set, the points are spread over the entire drawing plane and all the details of the face are lost (cf. Fig. 3.6(b)). In Fig. 3.7(a) a weighted Centroidal Voronoi Tessellation is displayed. Here, in addition to the initial distribution the image itself was given to determine density and weights. Due to the weights the details of the face are captured better. If all points that are placed on white areas are removed the result looks similar to a stipple drawing (cf. Fig. 3.7(b)).

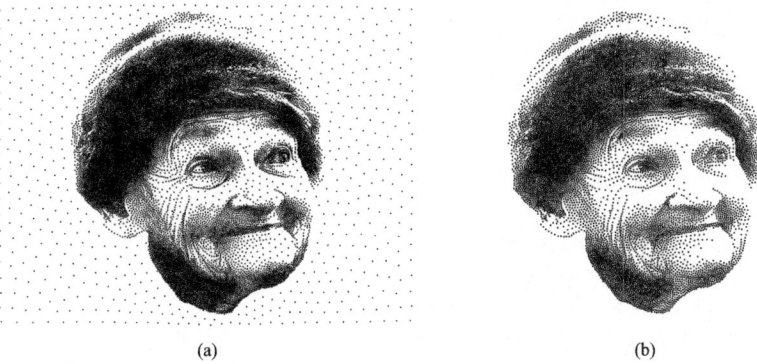

Fig. 3.7 (a) Point distribution in weighted Voronoi Tessellation; (b) point distribution with points in white regions omitted

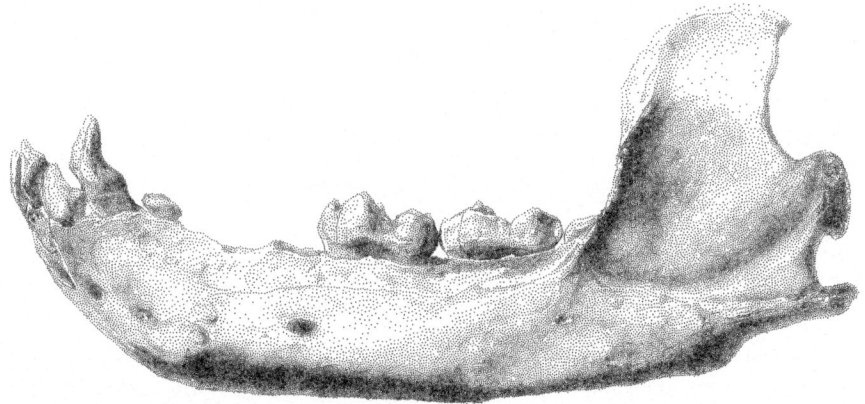

Fig. 3.8 Automatically stipple illustration of the bone from Fig. 3.4

Finally, in Fig. 3.8 the automatically stippled version of the bone of Fig. 3.4 is shown. Please note that this result is entirely automatic and no additional lines are inserted.

3.3 Beyond Stippling

In general, Lloyd's relaxation method can be applied to arbitrary objects, provided that their Voronoi Diagram can be calculated. For each object the center of gravity is determined. During iteration, the object is moved so that its center of gravity lies upon the center of gravity of its Voronoi Region. Additionally, objects can now be rotated (see Algorithm 3.3).

Algorithm 3.3 Modified Lloyd relaxation

Input: A set of objects o_i on the plane and a density function $\rho(x, y)$
Output: A relaxed centroidal Voronoi tessellation and a relaxed object-distribution.
1. Determine the mass centroids and main inertia axes of the objects o_i
   repeat
   2. Determine the Voronoi-Regions $V(o_i)$ of the o_i
   for $i = 1$ **to** n **do begin**
   3. Calculate the mass centroids (xc_i, yc_i) of the Voronoi cell $V(o_i)$
   4. Move the mass centroids of the objects onto the
      mass centroids (xc_i, yc_i) of the Voronoi cells
   5. Rotate the objects main axis so that it matches the main axis φ of $V(o_i)$
   end
   until the object positions converge

To compute the rotations we need to determine the second-order moments of the Voronoi cells:

$$m_i^{1,1} = \int_{y_{i1}}^{y_{i2}} \int_{x_{i1}(y)}^{x_{i2}(y)} xy \, dx \, dy$$

$$m_i^{2,0} = \int_{y_{i1}}^{y_{i2}} \int_{x_{i1}(y)}^{x_{i2}(y)} x^2 \, dx \, dy \qquad (3.6)$$

$$m_i^{0,2} = \int_{y_{i1}}^{y_{i2}} y^2 \int_{x_{i1}(y)}^{x_{i2}(y)} dx \, dy$$

Using these moments and mass centroids one is able to calculate the main inertia axes and the desired rotation angle φ for the object. The two-dimensional inertia tensor is given as

$$\mathbf{J} = \begin{pmatrix} \mu_{2,0} & \mu_{1,1} \\ \mu_{1,1} & \mu_{0,2} \end{pmatrix}$$

The eigenvalues of $\mathbf{J}$ form the maximal and the minimal inertia moments j_1, j_2:

$$j_{1,2} = \frac{1}{2}\left(\mu_{2,0} + \mu_{0,2} \pm \sqrt{(\mu_{2,0} - \mu_{0,2})^2 + 4\mu_{1,1}^2}\right) \qquad (3.7)$$

The angle φ of the main inertia axis is the angle of the eigenvector v_1 of $\mathbf{J}$ which belongs to the eigenvalue j_1:

$$\varphi = \frac{1}{2} \arctan\left(\frac{2\mu_{1,1}}{\mu_{2,0} - \mu_{0,2}}\right) \qquad (3.8)$$

Figure 3.9 shows an object with its main axes (solid arrows), its Voronoi cell and its main axes (dashed arrows). These axes are determined for each iteration and the object is rotated so that the axes match.

3 Halftoning and Stippling

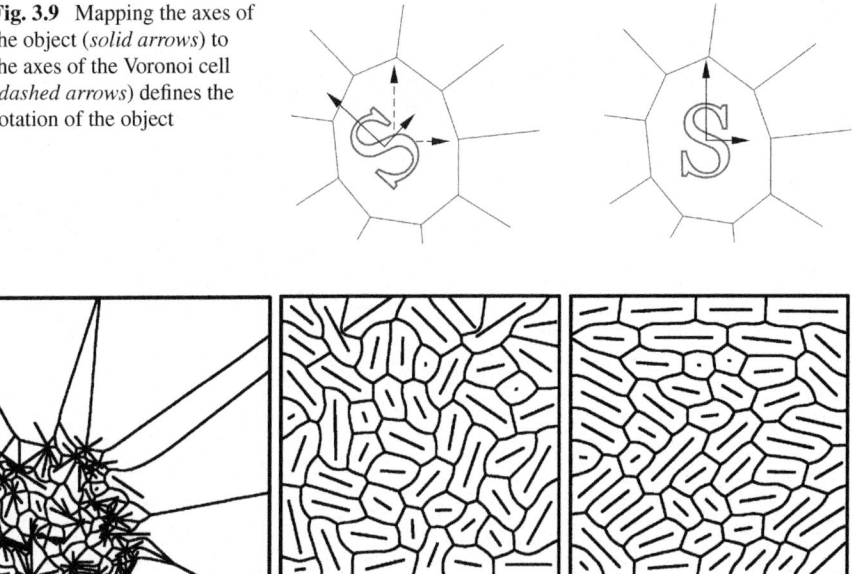

Fig. 3.9 Mapping the axes of the object (*solid arrows*) to the axes of the Voronoi cell (*dashed arrows*) defines the rotation of the object

Fig. 3.10 A set of points and lines are relaxed using the extended relaxation method. © Eurographics Association, used by permission

This allows the user to set up the algorithm for the extension of Lloyd's relaxation that is able to incorporate object rotations. Within the process, it is assumed that first the mass centroid of the object is moved over the mass centroid of the corresponding Voronoi cell, and that the orientation is then adapted.

In Fig. 3.10(a) a set of points and lines is shown. Applying the method an even distribution as shown in Fig. 3.10(b) is achieved. Please note that the iteration works well with the very badly distributed initial set shown in Fig. 3.10(a).

The variants of the iteration can be mixed while working with an object set. Similar to what was proposed earlier [1], an interactive editor was built that allows the user to model sets of objects in various ways. One can move objects, insert or delete them using a number of "brushes". A special variant of the editor allows the user to apply one or more steps of each variant of the iteration.

The editor also enables the user to generate mosaics [4] (for more detail see Chap. 10). Here, small tiles have to be arranged in order to follow important structures in the input image, also the tile size was reduced for important regions such as the eyes to enhance precision. Examples are found in Figs. 3.11 and 3.12.

3.4 Stippling by Example

The techniques described so far create stipple patterns with a single characteristic—despite the fact that artists most often develop variants of such a patterns according

Fig. 3.11 A stipple illustration that uses different small objects as stipple marks. © Eurographics Association, used by permission

Fig. 3.12 Computer-assisted mosaics using the modified Lloyd's relaxation. © Eurographics Association, used by permission

to their own taste and style. It would, therefore, be desirable to create such stipple distribution patterns from examples given by the artists.

Such an approach was presented by Kim et al. [7]. For this work an example of a stipple drawing has to be given that incorporates different tonal values. In a first step patterns for a set of tonal values are extracted and their dot distribution is determined.

Since in hand-made stipple drawings the stipple marks have a variety of forms, such forms are extracted and stored together with the stipple distribution. A statistical analysis of the distribution [12] is used to find parameters for the stipple synthesis done on the basis of a texture synthesis algorithm.

Figure 3.13 shows example results of Kim et al.'s [7] approach. The grayscale image in Fig. 3.13(a) and the artistic stipple distribution in Fig. 3.13(b) is given

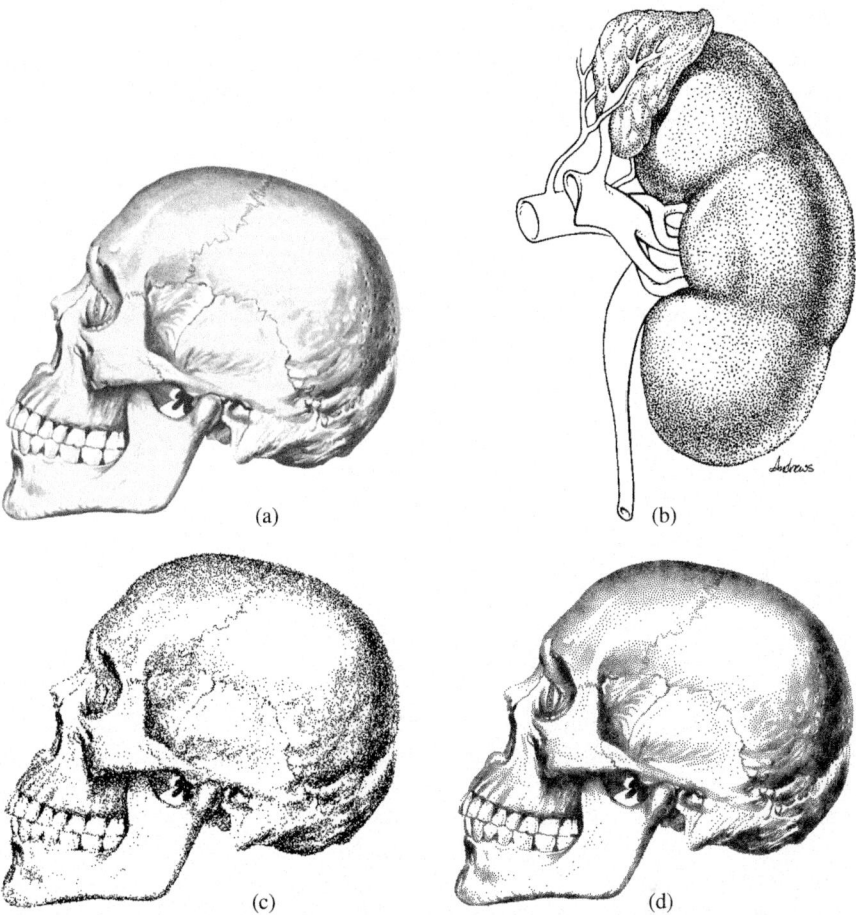

Fig. 3.13 Stippling by example: (**a**) grayscale image; (**b**) artistic stipple example used as the source of the example-based stipple distribution; (**c**) computer-generated pattern by example; (**d**) weighted Voronoi stippling for comparison. (**a**) Copyright © David Darling, used by permission, (**b**) copyright © 2009 William M. Andrews, used by permission, (**c**) copyright © 2009 Kim et al., used by permission

as input. The algorithm produces the new stipple drawing shown in Fig. 3.13(c). In contrast to the standard solution using weighted Voronoi Stippling (see Fig. 3.13(d)), the distribution of dots follows the characteristics of the input.

Another approach of stippling by example by Martín et al. [13, 14] does not look at the statistics of the stipple point distribution but, instead, at the resolution and scale at which the stipple dots are placed as well as the specific shape of the individual points. This technique addresses one of the limitations of the previous one by Kim et al. [7]—namely the inability of Kim et al.'s technique to produce the nice merging of stipple points in medium gray regions.

To address this issue, Martín et al. [13, 14] no longer treat the stipple points as black dots on a white background. Instead, they use grayscale scans of actual stipple points which they distribute based on halftoning. However, they also compute the correct resolution of stipple points on a paper of a given size, and use stipple dot scans of the appropriate pixel size so that the resulting scale-dependent images are produced for a given paper size (e.g., A4 or Letter paper). Moreover, due to the grayscale treatment, the grayscale stipple dots overlap and thus create the merging effects known from hand-made stippling. Interestingly, the randomized halftoning distributions that result from this process exhibit similar statistics as hand-made stippling, confirmed using Maciejewski et al.'s [12] distribution analysis.

Figure 3.14 shows an example of Martín et al.'s [13, 14] technique. Based on the input image in Fig. 3.14(a), a grayscale stipple image was produced at 600 ppi for A5 size (Fig. 3.14(b)), and the same stipple distribution was generated for the 1200 dpi black-and-white image in Fig. 3.14(c). Notice that due to the scale-dependence the same stipple dot scans and the same distribution is used for both images because they were produced for the same paper size—even though they have a different (pixel) resolution.

3.5 Structure-Aware Stippling

One issue raised, among others, also by Martín et al. [13, 14] is that low-level stipple placement is not sufficient for being able to produce high-quality illustrations. While Martín et al. analyze the stipple process by traditional stipple artist including such high-level processing, some authors have tried to incorporate higher-level processing into the NPR stippling pipeline (also compare some of the hatching techniques described in Chap. 4).

For example, Mould [15] transforms the input image into a regular graph whose edges are weighted according to the local gradient magnitude. Then, Mould uses a version of Dijkstra's algorithm to place stipple dots based on the graph. Next, Mould places the dots progressively along the frontiers of growing regions, which preserves the structure of meaningful artifacts such as edges in the images.

A related technique by Kim et al. [6] attempts to re-create the traditional hedcut illustration style which arranges stipples dots along lines for portraits of people. They first extract a line map and a tone map of the input image, then build a distance field and from that offset lines, and then use the extracted maps to optimize the placement of stipple dots. A different group of authors, Kim et al. [8], extend the initial portrait stipple approach by adding perceptual depth cues to the stipple image. Kim et al. [8] extract the image edges as well as a number of isophote lines (i.e., lines of the same brightness) and use these, similar to Kim et al. [6], as means to place stipple points. The isophote lines are extracted by quantizing the input image and extracting edges of identical color value. Based on the edge map and the isophote map, Kim et al. then produce a *weighted distance map* which they use to produce offset lines which, in turn, are used to place stipple points.

3 Halftoning and Stippling

Fig. 3.14 Resolution-dependent stippling by example: (**a**) input image; (**b**) grayscale stipple result; and (**c**) black-and-white thresholded at a higher pixel resolution. (**a**) Copyright © 2012 Domingo Martín, used by permission; (**b**, **c**) copyright © 2012 Martín et al., used by permission

Recently, Li and Mould [10] suggested another way for stipple rendering to take the input image's structure into account using structure-aware error distribution that also permits the user to control how many stipple points are being used. For this purpose, Li and Mould consider one pixel to be one stipple and provide means to reduce the number of stipples by increasing the positive and reducing the negative errors to avoid having to place too many stipples (on a regular grid). Both types of error result in less pixels and, thus, less stipples being placed. This approach results in a high degree of preservation of the structure in the input image, even if only relatively few stipple dots are being used to represent the input image. Moreover, Li and Mould [10] also describe a number of further adjustments that result in different effects such as screening using textures or patterns.

3.6 Conclusion

Stippling is a powerful but cumbersome illustration technique for scientific illustrators since it allows to represent grayscale values and texture at the same time. It is widely used in archeology and biology. Computer-generated stipple drawings allow the production of such illustrations, for example for scientific visualization purposes, much faster since automatic methods exist that mimic what artists do.

Data-driven methods use patterns created by artists. They enable to capture the style of an illustrator quite precisely. Such methods enable the computer to create a much larger variety of patterns with different spatial characteristics; however, the price is that we have to use much more complex methods.

References

1. Deussen, O., Hiller, S., van Overveld, K., Strothotte, T.: Floating points: a method for computing stipple drawings. Comput. Graph. Forum **19**(4), 40–51 (2000). doi:10.1111/1467-8659.00396
2. Du, Q., Faber, V., Gunzburger, M.: Centroidal Voronoi tessellations. SIAM Rev. **41**(4), 637–676 (1999). doi:10.1137/S0036144599352836
3. Floyd, R., Steinberg, L.: An adaptive algorithm for spatial grey scale. Proc. Soc. Inf. Disp. **17**(2), 75–77 (1976)
4. Fritzsche, L.P., Hellwig, H., Hiller, S., Deussen, O.: Interactive design of authentic looking mosaics using Voronoi structures. In: Proc. 2nd International Symposium on Voronoi Diagrams in Science and Engineering 2005, pp. 1–11 (2005)
5. Gersho, A.: Asymptotically optimal block quantization. IEEE Trans. Inf. Theory **25**(4), 373–380 (1979). doi:10.1109/TIT.1979.1056067
6. Kim, D., Son, M., Lee, Y., Kang, H., Lee, S.: Feature-guided image stippling. Comput. Graph. Forum **27**(4), 1209–1216 (2008). doi:10.1111/j.1467-8659.2008.01259.x
7. Kim, S., Maciejewski, R., Isenberg, T., Andrews, W.M., Chen, W., Sousa, M.C., Ebert, D.S.: Stippling by example. In: Proc. NPAR, pp. 41–50. ACM, New York (2009). doi:10.1145/1572614.1572622
8. Kim, S., Woo, I., Maciejewski, R., Ebert, D.S.: Automated hedcut illustration using isophotes. In: Proc. Smart Graphics, pp. 172–183. Springer, Berlin (2010). doi:10.1007/978-3-642-13544-6_17

9. Kopf, J., Cohen-Or, D., Deussen, O., Lischinski, D.: Recursive Wang tiles for real-time blue noise. ACM Trans. Graph. **25**(3), 509–518 (2006). doi:10.1145/1141911.1141916
10. Li, H., Mould, D.: Structure-preserving stippling by priority-based error diffusion. In: Proc. Graphics Interface, pp. 127–134. Canadian Human-Computer Communications Society, School of Computer Science, University of Waterloo, Waterloo (2011)
11. Lloyd, S.P.: Least squares quantization in PCM. IEEE Trans. Inf. Theory **28**(2), 129–137 (1982). doi:10.1109/TIT.1982.1056489
12. Maciejewski, R., Isenberg, T., Andrews, W.M., Ebert, D.S., Sousa, M.C., Chen, W.: Measuring stipple aesthetics in hand-drawn and computer-generated images. IEEE Comput. Graph. Appl. **28**(2), 62–74 (2008). doi:10.1109/MCG.2008.35
13. Martín, D., Arroyo, G., Luzón, M.V., Isenberg, T.: Example-based stippling using a scale-dependent grayscale process. In: Proc. NPAR, pp. 51–61. ACM, New York (2010). doi:10.1145/1809939.1809946
14. Martín, D., Arroyo, G., Luzón, M.V., Isenberg, T.: Scale-dependent and example-based stippling. Comput. Graph. **35**(1), 160–174 (2011). doi:10.1016/j.cag.2010.11.006
15. Mould, D.: Stipple placement using distance in a weighted graph. In: Proc. CAe, pp. 45–52. Eurographics Association, Goslar (2007). doi:10.2312/COMPAESTH/COMPAESTH07/045-052
16. Newman, D.J.: The hexagon theorem. IEEE Trans. Inf. Theory **28**(2), 137–138 (1982). doi:10.1109/TIT.1982.1056492
17. Secord, A.: Weighted Voronoi stippling. In: Proc. NPAR, pp. 37–43. ACM, New York (2002). doi:10.1145/508530.508537
18. Smith, J.: Recent developments in numerical integration. J. Dyn. Syst. Meas. Control **96**(1), 61–70 (1974). doi:10.1115/1.3426777
19. Stoer, J., Bulirsch, R.: Introduction to Numerical Analysis. Springer, Berlin (1980)

Chapter 4
Non-photorealistic Shading and Hatching

Victor Ostromoukhov

4.1 Introduction. Shading and Hatching as Essential Visual Cues in Marr's Model

Seeing the external world is an essential ability of the human being. It ensures the most vital survival functions such as avoiding predators, search of food or reproduction. Our visual system is a fine result of millions of years of evolution and constant improvement. It is not surprising that it is extremely fast and provides to our brain the information about spatial structure of the external world, as well as the information about relative movement of external objects and the observer himself. The science of vision (neuroscience, psychology, computer vision) studies the process of perception of the external world, starting from retinal stimuli and ending up in a complete spatiotemporal internal brain image. According to the most influential Marr computational model of vision, the whole process is divided into several stages: from unstructured retinal image to primal 2.5 sketch, then to object-based categorial model, essential to develop an understanding of the scene. This process is extremely complex, with several feedback loops [19, 26]. To facilitate the task at early stages of the perception process, our vision system uses, as visual cues, various pieces of information available in the scene: variations of tone due to natural distribution of light in the scene, relative size and foreshortening of objects due to the perspective, presence of edges due to particular viewing point, etc. It has been discovered that some of these perception functions are 'wired' (e.g., lateral inhibition in the retinal processing, which facilitates edge detection); others are high-level functions of our brain, which are learned from experience [19, 26].

Artists were always interested in depicting the external world. Early examples of such depictions can be found in Lascaux caves; they are estimated to be 17,300 years

---

V. Ostromoukhov (✉)
CNRS/Université Claude Bernard Lyon 1, 43, bd du 11 novembre 1918, 69622 Villeurbanne, France
e-mail: victor.ostromoukhov@liris.cnrs.fr

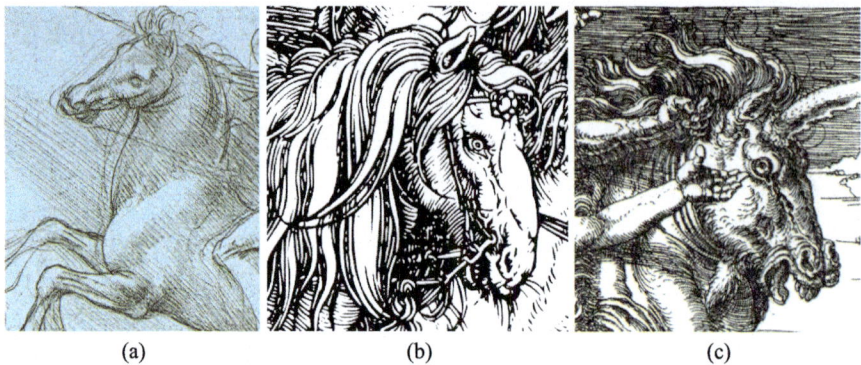

Fig. 4.1 Examples of usage of hatching for the purpose of shading in traditional art: (**a**) pencil drawing by Leonardo da Vinci, (**b**) woodcut by Albrecht Dürer, (**c**) etching by Albrecht Dürer

old. During centuries of constant improvements, the artists were constantly improving the degree of realism in artificial depictions. Until XVII century, the highest possible realism was considered as the ultimate goal of the artificial depiction [11]. Still, many skilled artists struggled with inherent limitations of the media, such as limited dynamic range, flatness or static nature of the depiction, among many others. Also, artists used discrete depiction primitives, marks of finite shape and size, which are very different from continuous distribution of shades in the scene [4, 28]. In order to overcome these limitations, traditional artists often used special technical 'tricks', special rendering techniques which would allow to enhance the perception of the depicted scenes [16]. Unconsciously, the artists pursue a two-fold goal: on the one hand, facilitate the task of visual interpretation of the depicted scene; on the other hand, to provide pure aesthetical and stylistic interpretation of the depicted object, to produce depictions pleasant for our eyes.

Figure 4.1 shows a few examples of usage of hatching for the purpose of shading in traditional art. It is interesting to notice that both irregular and regular repetitive structures of elementary strokes have been traditionally used. In many striking cases of traditional etching and engraving techniques, large patches of almost-parallel strokes were used. The directions of the engraving lines somehow follow the features of the depicted object. This additional visual cue greatly facilitates understanding of 3D scenes and helps object-background separation, clearly visible in Fig. 4.1(c).

In computer graphics, depiction of 3D scenes with artificial elements based on line drawing appeared as early as in 1960s [2, 25]. But the dawn of true full-featured NPR systems, which incorporate sophisticated shading, appeared in the 1990s. In the early days of NPR, researchers were often concentrated on reproducing traditional artistic media with new computerized techniques. Namely, they tried to reproduce traditional shading techniques such as pen-and-ink [21–23, 29], copperplate engraving [17], freehand drawing [6].

There are many different conceptual approaches to generate NPR rendering with shading, according to the nature of the input sources: static unstructured images

Fig. 4.2 Pen-and-ink drawing system, as described in [22]. (**a**) A coherent set of stroke textures produced for various gray tones. (**b**) The resulting pen-and-ink illustration. © 1994 ACM

(photos), video sequence of unstructured images, static images with geometry information, animated sequence of images with geometry information. As the problems of animation and temporal coherence are covered in Chap. 1 and Chap. 13, we shall concentrate our attention on NPR shading of static unstructured images. In many cases, elements of geometric information may enrich unstructured images; this information may come from different sources: from image processing techniques (e.g., edge- and surface-detection algorithms), from video processing techniques (e.g., structure-from-motion algorithms), or simply from a modeler tool. It is important to mention that all shading methods described in this section remain inherently and fundamentally planar: they use the artistic mark metaphor, inspired by traditional artwork on planar support.

4.2 Interactive Pen-and-Ink Illustration

The method described by Salisbury et al. [22] introduces an interactive pen-and-ink drawing system. The system takes various 2D grayscale images as input: scanned photos, or 2D output from an external 3D rendering system. This work introduces the notion of stroke textures—collections of strokes arranged in different patterns— to generate texture and tone of the input image. These stroke textures can be drawn manually by a skilled artist or can be generated algorithmically, as shown in Fig. 4.2. In case of algorithmic generation, the user controls the randomness of the distribution.

The whole dynamic range of gray scales is divided into reduced set of available gray scales, for which stroke textures have been generated. During the process of rendering, the local gray scale of the input image is mapped onto the set of available gray scales, and the corresponding stroke texture is transferred onto the output. As the stroke textures for different tones are mutually coherent, the resulting pen-and-ink rendering looks very nice and seamless—see Fig. 4.2(b).

Later, in [21, 23] the same group of researches considerably improved the initial drawing system described in [22]. Namely, thanks to adaptive treatment of the

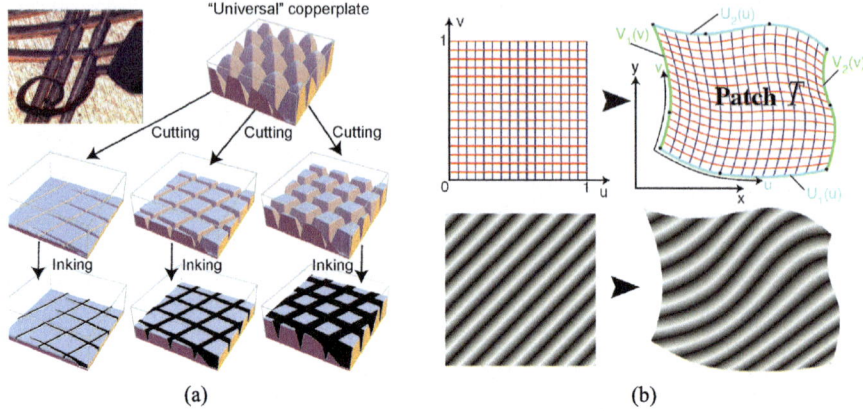

Fig. 4.3 Basic elements used in copperplate engraving technique, as described in [17]: (**a**) *Top-left*: A micro-photography of the graver's tip making a furrow in the copperplate showing a shaving lifted by the bevel. Virtual universal copperplate cut at different heights, producing furrows of different widths. Putting ink into the furrows imitates the true copperplate engraving printing process. (**b**) Parametric grid defined on a unit square in parametric space uv is transformed into a morphed parametric grid inside the patch T, in image space xy (*upper row*). This transformation maps Basic Engraving Layer onto Transformed Layer (*lower row*). © 1999 ACM

scale of the drawing, they were able to produce convincing examples of pen-and-ink illustration which provide almost equivalent appearance at different scales. An interactive tool was used to guide local arrangement of the strokes.

Winkenbach and Salesin [29] use additional geometric information such as depth or orientation of surfaces in the depicted scene. They base their approach on first principles usually applied to hand-drawn illustrations and which can be found in comprehensive guides for graphic artists. During the rendering time, the appropriate pen-and-ink texture is picked up from a set of precomputed textures, according to local lightness of the depicted objects. In order to suppress too dull and impersonal rendering, the user of this system can introduce pseudo-randomness through 'indications'. The resulting rendering appears much more appealing. This paper introduces many clever features that greatly improve artistic appearance of the results: scale-dependent levels of detail in rendering, orientation-based rendering, etc.

4.3 Copperplate Engraving

The system described in [17] imitated copperplate engraving, largely used as traditional support for reproducing grayscale images in bank notes, post stamps, etc. The system is based on the analogy between the process of producing copperplate engraving and digital halftoning (see [27] and Chap. 3). This analogy is illustrated in Fig. 4.3(a). In traditional copperplate engraving, the width of the furrows produced by the tip of the graver influences the engraving line width. The furrows have a specific triangular shape. Based on this observation, one can build a virtual 'universal' copperplate. This 'universal' copperplate can be cut at different heights thus producing furrows of different widths. By putting ink into the furrows we imitate the true copperplate engraving printing process. But at the same time the process described here is nothing other than conventional digital halftoning [27], a well known method in computer graphics. Simply, the term of virtual 'universal' copperplate stands for the threshold matrix (threshold levels corresponding to the height of our 'universal' copperplate), while cutting and inking stand for comparison between the input signal level and the current threshold value, thus producing a black or white output signal. The analogy is so perfect that the art of digital copperplate engraving may be resumed as the art of building appropriate threshold structures looking like the 'universal' copperplate. Once this threshold structure is built, the rendering may be done using conventional dithering software.

The target 'universal' copperplate is composed of separate layers containing warped patches as shown in Fig. 4.3(b). The geometry of the warping is user-defined, according to the features present in the depicted object, as shown in Fig. 4.3(c). Usually only a few layers are needed, even for rather sophisticated geometrical objects (only five layers were needed to produce the engraving shown in Fig. 4.6).

The layers may partially overlap each other. In this case, they can be merged using one of several available merging modes. The superimposition of several layers is performed sequentially, one layer after another. It is important to define a set of basic rules for superimposing two layers, the extension to several layers being straightforward. Each engraving layer, before the superimposition, may undergo two range transformations: it may be scaled (range scale) and raised or lowered (range shift):

$$T'(x, y) = T(x, y) \times S(x, y) + D(x, y)$$

where range scale values $S(x, y)$ and range shift values $D(x, y)$ are two matrices of the same dimensions as the matrix of threshold values $T(x, y)$ which forms the transformed engraving layer.

Superimposing engraving layers consists of consecutively merging the current layer (CL) into the resulting layer (RL). Once merged, the current engraving layer becomes an independent entity. The merging is performed according to the merging mode. Figure 4.4 enumerates some merging modes, among the most important ones. This list in not exhaustive: additional modes may be added if needed.

Figure 4.5 illustrates the use of merging modes. The sample image contains two parts: a uniform gray ramp and four flat patches whose respective intensities are 1/8, 3/8, 5/8 and 7/8. the 'copy' mode serves to initialize the resulting engraving layer for the very first merging operation. The 'smaller' mode produces cross-etching which is very close to traditional cross-etching known in the art. Notice different cross-hatching effects obtained when 'smaller' and 'bigger' merging modes are used: black-line cross-hatching in the former and white-line cross-hatching in the latter.

merging mode	description
.. **copy** CL	$T_{RL}(x,y) = T_{CL}(x,y) * S(x,y) + D(x,y)$
.. **smaller** CL	$T_{RL}(x,y) = \mathrm{MIN}(T_{RL}(x,y), T_{CL}(x,y) * S(x,y) + D(x,y))$
.. **bigger** CL	$T_{RL}(x,y) = \mathrm{MAX}(T_{RL}(x,y), T_{CL}(x,y) * S(x,y) + D(x,y))$
.. **multiply** CL	$T_{RL}(x,y) = T_{RL}(x,y) * (T_{CL}(x,y) * S(x,y) + D(x,y))$
.. **add** CL	$T_{RL}(x,y) = T_{RL}(x,y) + (T_{CL}(x,y) * S(x,y) + D(x,y))$

Fig. 4.4 Merging modes used for generation of different cross-hatching, as described in [17]

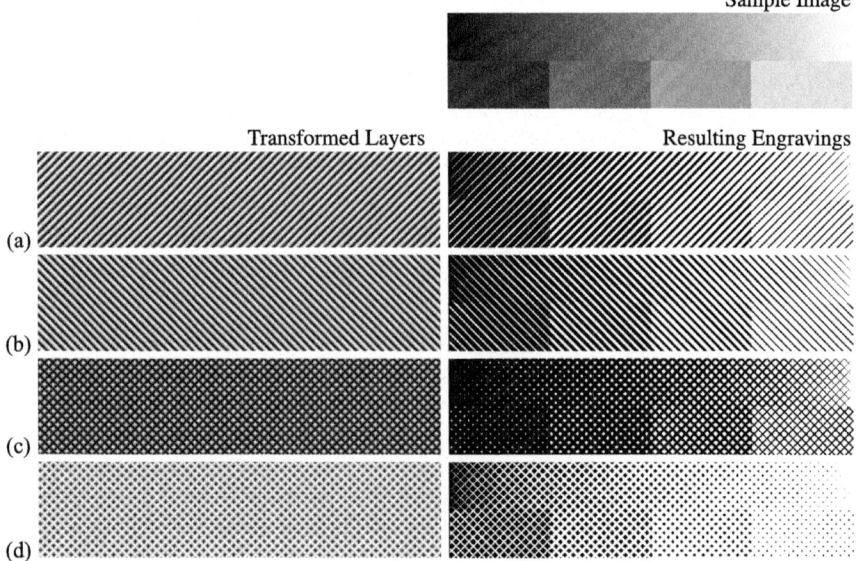

Fig. 4.5 Merging modes used for generating different cross-hatching patterns, as described in [17]. *Left column*: the threshold structure obtained by superimposing threshold structures L1 and L2 using different merging modes. *Right column*: a sample image (the *topmost image*) rendered using the threshold structures shown in the *left column*. Used merging modes were: (**a**) *copy* L1, (**b**) *copy* L2, (**c**) L1 *smaller* L2, (**d**) L1 *bigger* L2. Notice different cross-hatching effects obtained when *smaller* and *bigger* merging modes are used: *black-line* cross-hatching in the former and *white-line* cross-hatching in the latter

In order to locally preserve a linear histogram of threshold levels, required for digital halftoning, the paper suggests the use of local histogram equilibration. Figure 4.6 shows an example of black and white engraving of the head of Michelangelo's Giuliano de Medici using five separate engraving layers. The paper demonstrates successful combination of regular etching with a simulated irregular engrav-

4 Non-photorealistic Shading and Hatching

Fig. 4.6 A copperplate engraving from [17], produced using only five partially overlapping warped patches. © 1999 ACM

ing technique (mezzotint), as well as an extension of this engraving technique to full-color imaging, as shown in Fig. 4.7.

A simple yet efficient technique has been proposed to extend black-and-white copperplate engraving to color. For a given RGB input color image, three separate Red–Green–Blue (or Cyan–Magenta–Yellow) separations use the same warped patches to produce Red–Green–Blue engraved separations. Red and blue engraving lines follow u parameter, whereas green engraving lines follow v parameter of Fig. 4.3.

Durand et al. [5] extended the initial engraving system described in [17]. Namely, this paper extends the notion of patch of regular engraving lines to more general patches of irregular drawing elements such as pencil or charcoal strokes, dry point strokes, or even more abstract arbitrary strokes. These drawing elements can be scanned from physical support or generated algorithmically. The procedure for fine tonal adjustment follows the guideline introduced in [17], with one notice-

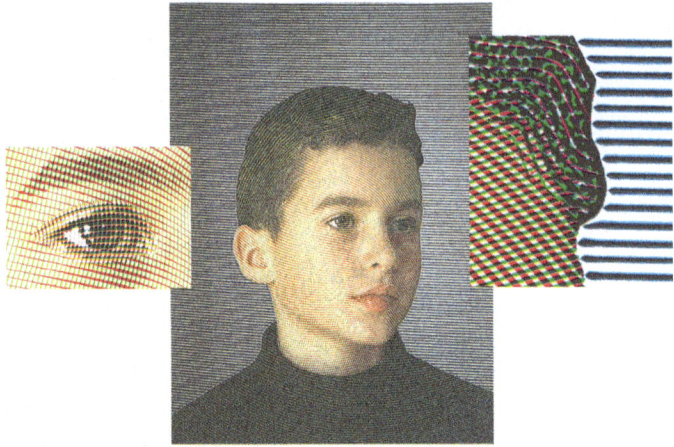

Fig. 4.7 Color copperplate engraving. In this case, the same warped patches were used to produce Red–Green–Blue separations. *Red* and *blue* engraving lines follow the *u* parameter, whereas *green* engraving lines follow the *v* parameter of Fig. 4.3. © 1999 ACM

Fig. 4.8 A few examples produced by a drawing system which imitates traditional artistic shading, as described in [5]. (**a**) Charcoal shading, (**b**) sanguine shading. In both cases, the input image was an unstructured photograph. © 2001 Eurographics Association

able exception: the local histogram equilibration is performed based on statistical basis, taking into account the number of overlapping strokes at each point—see Fig. 4.8.

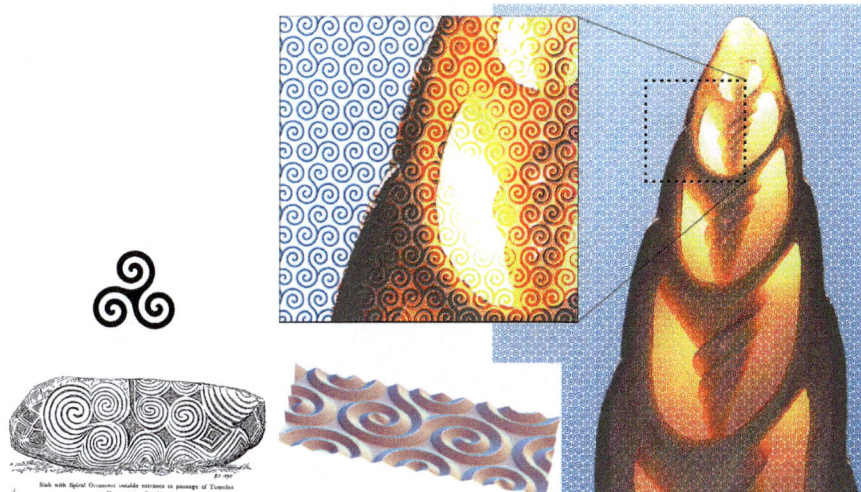

Fig. 4.9 Multi-color and artistic dithering, as described in [18]. *Left*: the source is a celtic motif taken from the book by J. Romilly Allen [1]. *Middle*: a 3D view of the threshold structure built for the purpose of multi-color and artistic dithering. *Right*: the resulting artistic dithered image which incorporates the celtic motif. © 1999 ACM

4.4 Multi-color and Artistic Dithering

Multi-color and artistic dithering [18] is a natural extension of the method for copperplate engraving that we have seen in the previous section. Both methods share several mutual principles and techniques: both are tightly related to digital halftoning, both are matrix-based, both use local histogram equilibration to ensure high fidelity in tone reproduction. The main difference between the two methods consists of the way of preparation of the dither matrices: copperplate engraving uses warped patches of regular sine waves, whereas multi-color and artistic dithering allows building sophisticated dither matrices from arbitrary images of from mathematical functions.

Figure 4.9 gives a typical example of the NPR rendering using multi-color and artistic dithering. A source celtic motif is taken from an influential textbook on the history of celtic culture by J. Romilly Allen [1]. This motif is converted into a threshold matrix structure, using various image-processing tools (the threshold matrix structure is shown in Fig. 4.9 as a 3D surface). Then, local histogram equilibration is applied on the threshold matrix, to ensure a locally linear histogram of threshold levels, required for digital halftoning. The equilibrated matrix is used to produce the image shown in Fig. 4.9(right). Notice that multi-color and artistic dithering preserves tonal fidelity of the original input image, while using artistic marks of arbitrary complexity (celtic motif in this case; many other examples are shown in [18], including a highly professional bank note design expressly produced for Swiss notes manufacturer Oriel Füssli).

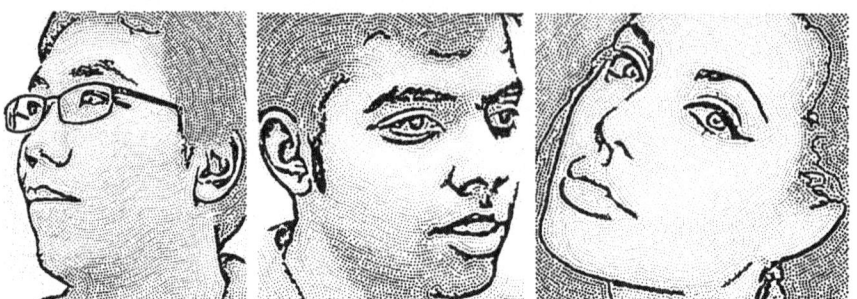

Fig. 4.10 Some results of automated hedcut illustration using isophotes, as described in [15] © 2010 Springer

4.5 Automated Hedcut Illustration

Hedcut illustration shares many common features with copperplate engraving described in Sect. 4.3. Nevertheless, the method described in [15] does not explicitly use digital halftoning as in [17]. Instead, it uses standard image processing tools in order to extract useful information from the input images. First, edges are extracted, and the luminance of the input image is quantized. From the latter, an isophote map is built. A feature map is built from isophote and edge maps. This feature map is used to guide the process of optimization in of the distribution of individual marks. The final result is a combination of the extracted features and individual marks (stipples). The produced results are visually appealing. The paper explicitly uses shading visual cues in order to enhance visual impact of NPR images, as shown in Fig. 4.10.

4.6 Other Geometry-Based Hatching Techniques

From the early days of computer graphics, people started to use simple line models to represent edges and contours of the depicted objects. In the early 1990s, Saito and Takahashi [20] introduced hatching based on isoparametric and planar curves. Several papers introduced NPR shading, which take into account 3D geometry, with lines whose directions follow principal curvature of the surface to render [6, 7, 12]. This approach, very powerful mathematically, was sometimes judged as being too mechanical. In fact, artists represent shading more intuitively. Hertzmann and Zorin [10] proposed a more sophisticated distribution of hatching lines based on principal curvature directions. More recently, Singh and Schaefer [24] proposed a considerable improvement over this family of techniques. They construct a gradient field of the diffuse intensity of the surface to guide a set of adaptively spaced lines. The shape of these lines reflect the lighting under which the object is being viewed and its shape. When the light source is placed at the viewer's location, these lines emanate from silhouettes and naturally extend suggestive contours.

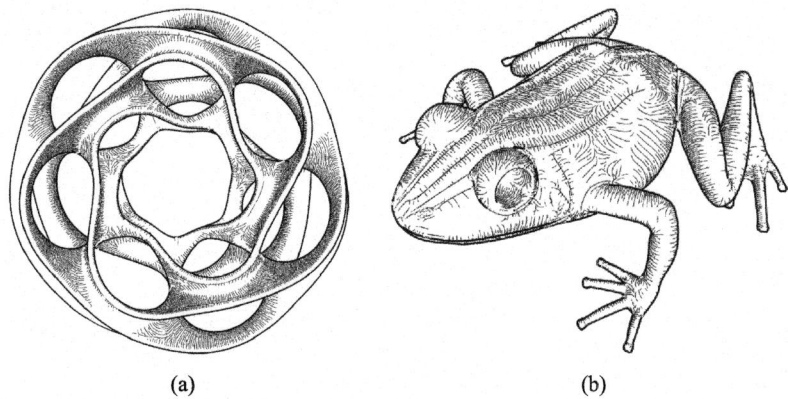

Fig. 4.11 Suggestive hatching as described in [24]. © 2010 Eurographics Association

The results produced with their technique produce very satisfactory results in many cases of sophisticated geometry, as can be seen in Fig. 4.11.

Very recently, Kalogerakis et al. [14] proposed a more advanced technique for pen-and-ink illustration. Their key idea is to learn the quality of distribution of hatching strokes from examples provided by skilled artists. The artists' work is analyzed following several criteria: the nature of hatching (simple hatching, cross-hatching or no hatching), stroke orientation, spacing, intensity, length, and thickness. The result of such context-dependent analysis is applied to a concrete scene using standard computer learning techniques. A user study shows very satisfactory levels of quality produced with this method. Some results produced with these automatic methods are hardly distinguishable from the artwork produced by the skilled artists.

4.7 Automatic Generation of Distributions of Primitives

As mentioned in the previous sections, most applications for NPR shading place drawing primitives either interactively, or by taking geometrical considerations (curvature, projection, boundary) into account. Several researchers have tried to generate distributions of strokes, including their 'look and feel', from given examples. Jodoin et al. [13] model relative locations of strokes based on a statistical analysis of the distribution of the input (example) distribution. Barla et al. [3] propose a powerful method for the generation of shading primitives from examples. Their method is based on texture synthesis techniques, which require the following steps: first, an analysis of the given pattern properties is performed in order to extract meaningful pattern elements. Then, a synthesis algorithm based on similarities in the detected stroke clusters produces output distributions of strokes of arbitrary size, which look very much similar to the original distributions. The results of this technique look very convincing, as can be seen in Fig. 4.12.

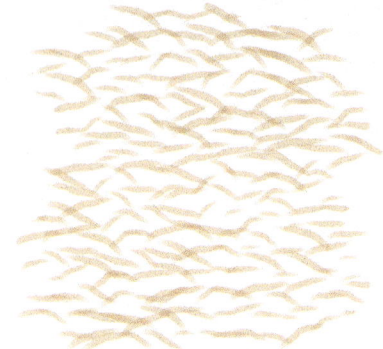

Fig. 4.12 Automatic generation of distribution of shading primitives from examples, as described in [3]. © 2006 Eurographics Association. *Left*: input distribution (example). *Right*: the output sequence of arbitrary size

4.8 Discussion

Today, a skilled NPR user is able to reproduce, more-or-less faithfully, a large variety of traditional artistic shading techniques such as drawing, engraving, stippling, or pen-and-ink illustration. Many powerful concepts and techniques introduced in NPR shading during the last two decades allow to go far beyond simple imitation of traditional artwork. Namely, introducing conceptual separation of drawing primitives from user interaction primitives [4, 5, 28] allows better modularity and clarity of the rendering tools. Programmable stylization introduced in [8, 9] opens the door to meta-stylization. Advanced computer learning techniques introduced by Kalogerakis et al. [14] increase visual appeal of the rendered results.

There is still much work to be done. Almost all the papers described in this chapter use computers as powerful tools always driven by humans. Even in the most advanced cases, rendering quality is learned from artistic examples provided by skilled users. With the tremendous progress in neuroscience (see in [16, 30, 31]) we may hope that one day we shall deeply understand the mechanisms of aesthetical appreciation of depiction and have a computational model for it. Building an efficient computational model for visual cues responsible for perception of synthetic scenes would allow a potential user to predict and control the degree of visual enhancement of the NPR artwork. With such a powerful tool, tomorrow's NPR users will be able to optimize arbitrary synthetic scenes, in such a way as no artist has ever explored in the past.

References

1. Allen, J.R.: Celtic Art in Pagan and Christian Times. Methuen, London (1904)
2. Appel, A.: The notion of quantitative invisibility and the machine rendering of solids. In: Rosenthal, S. (ed.) Proceedings of the 22nd ACM National Conference, 1967, Washington, D.C., USA, pp. 387–393. Thompson, Washington (1967).
3. Barla, P., Breslav, S., Thollot, J., Sillion, F., Markosian, L.: Stroke pattern analysis and synthesis. In: Computer Graphics Forum (Proc. of Eurographics 2006), vol. 25 (2006)

4. Durand, F.: An invitation to discuss computer depiction. In: Proceedings of the 2nd International Symposium on Non-photorealistic Animation and Rendering, pp. 111–124. ACM, Annecy (2002)
5. Durand, F., Ostromoukhov, V., Miller, M., Duranleau, F., Dorsey, J.: Decoupling strokes and high-level attributes for interactive traditional drawing. In: Proc. Eurographics Workshop on Rendering Techniques, pp. 71–82. Springer, London (2001)
6. Elber, G.: Line art rendering via a coverage of isoparametric curves. IEEE Trans. Vis. Comput. Graph. **1**(3), 231–239 (1995). ISSN 1077-2626
7. Elber, G.: Line art illustrations of parametric and implicit forms. IEEE Trans. Vis. Comput. Graph. **4**(1) 71–81 (1998). ISSN 1077-2626
8. Grabli, S., Turquin, E., Durand, F., Sillion, F.X.: Programmable style for NPR line drawing. In: Rendering Techniques 2004 (Eurographics Symposium on Rendering). ACM, New York (2004)
9. Grabli, S., Turquin, E., Durand, F., Sillion, F.X.: Programmable rendering of line drawing from 3D scenes. ACM Trans. Graph. **29**(2), 18 (2010)
10. Hertzmann, A., Zorin, D.: Illustrating smooth surfaces. In: Proc. SIGGRAPH, pp. 517–526. ACM/Addison-Wesley, New York (2000)
11. Hockney, D.: Secret Knowledge (New and Expanded Edition): Rediscovering the Lost Techniques of the Old Masters, expanded edn. Studio (2006)
12. Interrante, V., Fuchs, H., Pizer, S.: Illustrating transparent surfaces with curvature-directed strokes. In: Proc. Visualization, pp. 211–218. IEEE Comput. Soc., Los Alamitos (1996)
13. Jodoin, P.M., Epstein, E., Granger-Piché, M., Ostromoukhov, V.: Hatching by example: a statistical approach. In: Proc. NPAR, pp. 29–36 (2002)
14. Kalogerakis, E., Nowrouzezahrai, D., Breslav, S., Hertzmann, A.: Learning hatching for pen-and-ink illustration of surfaces. ACM Trans. Graph. **31**(1), 1 (2011)
15. Kim, S., Woo, I., Maciejewski, R., Ebert, D.S.: Automated hedcut illustration using isophotes. In: Proceedings of the 10th International Conference on Smart Graphics, pp. 172–183 (2010)
16. Livingstone, M.S.: Vision and Art: The Biology of Seeing. Abrams, New York (2008)
17. Ostromoukhov, V.: Digital facial engraving. In: Proceedings of SIGGRAPH, pp. 417–424 (1999)
18. Ostromoukhov, V., Hersch, R.D.: Multi-color and artistic dithering. In: Proceedings of the 26th Annual Conference on Computer Graphics and Interactive Techniques, pp. 425–432. ACM/Addison-Wesley, New York (1999)
19. Palmer, S.E.: Vision Science: Photons to Phenomenology. MIT Press, Cambridge (1999)
20. Saito, T., Takahashi, T.: Comprehensible rendering of 3-D shapes. SIGGRAPH Comput. Graph. **24**(4), 197–206 (1990)
21. Salisbury, M., Anderson, C., Lischinski, D., Salesin, D.H.: Scale-dependent reproduction of pen-and-ink illustrations. In: Proc. SIGGRAPH, pp. 461–468. ACM, New York (1996)
22. Salisbury, M.P., Anderson, S.E., Barzel, R., Salesin, D.H.: Interactive pen-and-ink illustration. In: Proceedings of SIGGRAPH, pp. 101–108 (1994)
23. Salisbury, M.P., Wong, M.T., Hughes, J.F., Salesin, D.H.: Orientable textures for image-based pen-and-ink illustration. In: Proc. SIGGRAPH, pp. 401–406. ACM/Addison-Wesley, New York (1997)
24. Singh, M., Schaefer, S.: Suggestive hatching. In: Jepp, P., Deussen, O. (eds.) Computational Aesthetics, pp. 25–32. Eurographics, Geneva (2010)
25. Sutherland, I.E.: Sketchpad: a man-machine graphical communication system. In: Johnson, E.C. (ed.) Proc. Spring Joint Computer Conference, vol. 23, pp. 329–346. American Federation of Information Processing Societies, Spartan Books, Baltimore (1963)
26. Thompson, W., Fleming, R., Creem-Regehr, S., Stefanucci, J.K.: Visual Perception from a Computer Graphics Perspective, 1st edn. AK Peters/CRC Press, Wellesley/Boca Raton (2011)
27. Ulichney, R.: Digital Halftoning. MIT Press, Cambridge (1987)
28. Willats, J., Durand, F.: Defining pictorial style: lessons from linguistics and computer graphics. Axiomathes **15**, 319–351 (2005)

29. Winkenbach, G., Salesin, D.H.: Computer-generated pen-and-ink illustration. In: Proceedings of SIGGRAPH, pp. 91–100 (1994)
30. Zeki, S.: Inner Vision: An Exploration of Art and the Brain. Oxford University Press, London (2000)
31. Zeki, S.: Splendors and Miseries of the Brain: Love, Creativity, and the Quest for Human Happiness, 5th edn. Wiley-Blackwell, New York (2009)

Chapter 5
Artistic Stylization by Nonlinear Filtering

Jan Eric Kyprianidis

5.1 Introduction

Digital image processing is a mature field providing a solid foundation for building artistic rendering algorithms. All image-based artistic rendering (IB-AR) approaches utilize image processing operations in some form to extract information or synthesize results. For instance, classical stroke-based rendering utilizes the image gradient for stroke placement. Nevertheless, few of the filters proposed for image processing are suitable in their original form, probably because in image processing, one is often concerned with the restoration and recovery of photorealistic imagery. By contrast, IB-AR generally aims for strong modification and simplification. As a result, researchers have often proposed specialized and adapted forms of existing techniques.

This chapter surveys a selection of nonlinear image processing algorithms that have been found to produce particularly interesting results. These techniques have in common that they perform some kind of edge-preserving simplification, often in combination with edge enhancement. In general, such an operation cannot be achieved by convolution filters, since these are fully determined by their impulse responses (i.e., applying a linear shift-invariant filter is equivalent to a convolution with the point spread function). By contrast, operations that preserve or selectively enhance edges must be guided by local (or even global) decisions based on the input source, leading directly to nonlinear operations that are not shift-invariant. Figure 5.1 illustrates a few examples of the techniques discussed in this chapter.

In contrast to approaches that emulate a specific artistic style, the techniques described here are based on heuristics developed through hands-on experience, showing that certain combinations of filters produce an artistic look. In some cases, the results obtained can be related to traditional styles such as cartoons, pen-and-ink

---

J.E. Kyprianidis (✉)
Hasso-Plattner-Institut, University of Potsdam, Potsdam, Germany
e-mail: kyprianidis@hpi.uni-potsdam.de

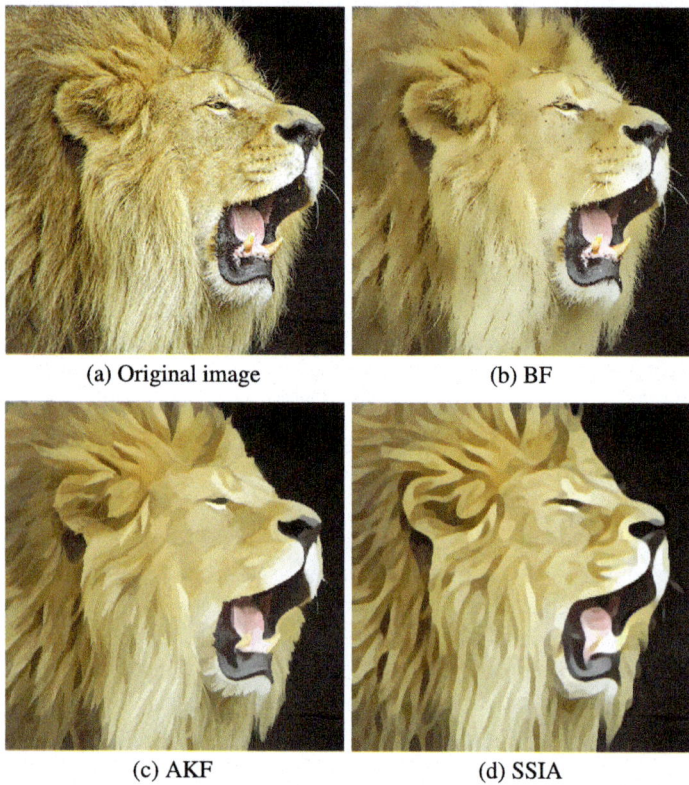

Fig. 5.1 Example showing popular edge-preserving/enhancing smoothing techniques often applied for image abstraction. (**b**) Bilateral filter [52]. (**c**) Anisotropic Kuwahara filter [34]. (**d**) Shape-simplifying image abstraction [24]. Tambako the Jaguar@flickr.com

illustrations, or watercolor paintings. In other cases, however, the connection is less obvious. The artistic look is thereby often achieved or further reinforced by taking the local image structure into account. Directional features and flow-like structures are considered pleasant, harmonic, or at least interesting by most humans [56]. They are also a highly sought after property in many of the traditional art forms, such as paintings and illustrations. Enhancing directional coherence in the image helps to clarify region boundaries and features. As exemplified by Expressionism, it also helps to evoke mood or ideas and even elicit emotional response from the viewer [58]. Particular examples include van Gogh and Munch, who have emphasized these features in their paintings.

Due to the local nature of image processing decisions, parallelization and GPU implementations of image filters are straightforward in most cases and often lead to real-time performance on modern multi-core CPUs and GPUs, making them practical for video processing—and applicable to footage that is otherwise challenging to parse (e.g., water, smoke, fur) using vision methods such as segmentation. This simplicity, however, comes at the expense of style diversity afforded by a higher-level interpretation of content.

The remainder of this chapter is organized as follows. In Sect. 5.2, the bilateral and difference of Gaussians filters are discussed. Together, these provide a powerful approach to the creation of cartoons, which will be discussed in detail. In Sect. 5.3, different variants of the Kuwahara filter are presented. Based on local image statistics, these are highly robust against high contrast noise, and driven by local image flattening, achieve a comparatively consistent level of abstraction across an image. In Sect. 5.4, techniques based on morphological operations are examined. Similar to the Kuwahara filter, these techniques effectively remove small-scale image features, and have been, for instance, successfully used to create watercolor renderings from images and videos. Section 5.5 presents techniques combining diffusion with sharpening. These allow for aggressive simplification while preserving sharp discontinuities. Finally, in Sect. 5.6, a brief overview of techniques operating in the gradient domain is given. Instead of directly operating on the image's gray or color values, these techniques operate on the gradient field of an image.

5.2 Bilateral Filter and Difference of Gaussians

A seminal work in image filtering-based NPR is the work of Winnemöller et al. [60] which, for the first time, presents a fully automatic pipeline for the creation of stylized cartoon renderings from images and video. Their pipeline employs the *bilateral* and *difference of Gaussians* (DoG) filter, and contains several influential ideas that other researchers later built upon. The bilateral filter smoothes low-contrast regions while preserving high-contrast edges, and may, therefore, fail for high-contrast images, where either no abstraction is performed or relevant information is removed because of the parameters chosen. In addition, the bilateral filter also often fails for low-contrast images, where typically too much information is removed. Moreover, iterative application of the bilateral filter may blur edges, resulting in a washed-out look (Fig. 5.1(b)). To some extent, these limitations can be alleviated by overlaying the output of the bilateral filter with outlines (e.g., generated with the DoG filter). Accordingly, the bilateral filter is rarely applied independently. Although the DoG filter can be used independently, preprocessing with the bilateral filter can often reduce artifacts caused by noise in the image. We start with a review of the bilateral and DoG filters, followed by a description the cartoon pipeline built from them.

5.2.1 Bilateral Filter

The *bilateral filter* is a well-known edge-preserving smoothing filter first introduced by Aurich and Weule [4], popularised by Tomasi and Manduchi [52]. A detailed review of the bilateral filter can be found in the survey by Paris et al. [45], which

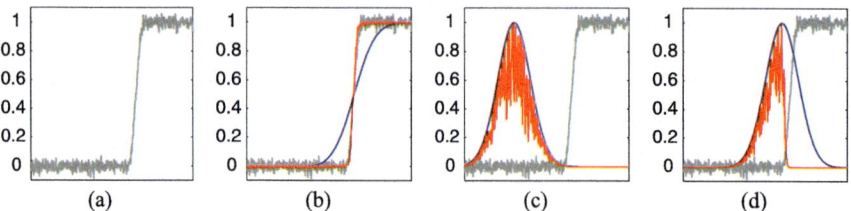

Fig. 5.2 Illustration of the working principle of the bilateral filter. (**a**) Noisy input signal (*gray*). (**b**) Result of the convolution with Gaussian (*blue*) and bilateral (*red*) filter. Note how the Gaussian kernel blurs the signal, while the bilateral filter keeps the sharp transition. In (**c**) and (**d**) the local filter kernel profiles of the Gaussian filter (*blue*) and bilateral filter (*red*) are shown at two different positions. The local filter kernel of the Gaussian filter does not depend on the signal (shift invariance) and is the same in both cases. The bilateral filter adapts its local filter kernel to the signal and thereby limits smoothing across the transition

also discusses various applications. For a given image I and position x_0 the bilateral filter is defined by

$$\frac{\sum_{x\in\Omega(x_0)} I(x) \overbrace{k_d(\|x-x_0\|)}^{\text{domain weight}} \overbrace{k_r(\|f(x)-f(x_0)\|)}^{\text{range weight}}}{\sum_{x\in\Omega(x_0)} k_d(\|x-x_0\|) k_r(\|f(x)-f(x_0)\|)} \quad (5.1)$$

where $\Omega(x_0)$ denotes a sufficiently large neighborhood of x_0, and k_d and k_r are two weighting functions. The *domain weight* given by k_d is based on the spatial distance from the filter origin x_0, whereas the *range weight* given by k_r is based on the distance between the image's values at the corresponding positions. Typically, for both weighting functions a one-dimensional Gaussian

$$G_\sigma(r) = \frac{1}{\sigma\sqrt{2\pi}} \exp\left(-\frac{1}{2\sigma}r^2\right) \quad (5.2)$$

is chosen, but other choices are possible. If k_d is chosen as Gaussian and $k_r \equiv 1$, then the bilateral filter simplifies to the Gaussian filter. The bilateral filter smoothes regions of similar color, while regions with detail are preserved. For instance, if the local neighborhood of a pixel contains an edge, then pixels on the opposite side of the edge receive a low and all others a high weight, resulting in the preservation of the edge (Fig. 5.2).

By using a suitable metric for the computation of the range weight, the bilateral filter extends naturally to color images. For instance, a possible choice is to use the Euclidean metric in RGB color space. Another choice, proposed by Tomasi and Manduchi [52], is using the Euclidean metric in CIELAB color space [62], which is known to correlate with human perception for short distances. Winnemöller et al. [60] and subsequent work adopted this approach.

If domain and range weight are chosen to be Gaussians, increasing the standard deviation of the domain weight generally does not lead to a stronger abstraction effect. Moreover, increasing the range weight results, in most cases, in blurred edges.

(a) Original image (b) 4 iterations (c) 25 iterations

Fig. 5.3 An iterative application of the bilateral filter smoothes the image while preserving edges, achieving a strong simplification effect. Original image courtesy of Philip Greenspun

Instead, to achieve a cartoon-like effect, it is better to apply multiple iterations of the bilateral filter (Fig. 5.3). This was already noted by Tomasi and Manduchi [52], and can be explained theoretically by the connection of bilateral filtering to anisotropic diffusion [5].

A limitation of the bilateral filter for practical applications, especially in the case of real-time processing, is that the direct evaluation of Eq. (5.1) is computationally expensive. For a local neighborhood with radius r the complexity is $O(r^2)$, which means that linear growth of the neighborhood leads to quadratic growth in computational costs. In contrast to the Gaussian filter, the bilateral filter is not separable, since it depends on local image values. Nevertheless, in the context of video compression, Pham and van Vliet [47] were able to show that for small filter sizes a separable implementation of the bilateral filter (Fig. 5.4(b)) can provide reasonable results. Their approach was adopted in the original cartoon pipeline by Winnemöller et al. [60] and was a crucial factor for achieving real-time performance on consumer GPUs at that time. Since then, several other approaches have been developed, such as the bilateral grid [12], approaches that avoid redundant operations by using histograms [48], and recently an approach based on domain transfer and normalized convolution [17].

Of particular interest from the IB-AR perspective are approaches taking local structure of an image into account. Kyprianidis and Döllner [31] proposed a separable implementation of the bilateral filter aligned to the local orientation (Fig. 5.4(c)). The first pass filters in perpendicular direction, while the second pass filters parallel to the local orientation. The adaptation to the local orientation helps to avoid artifacts, and produces more coherent region boundaries. In addition, the filter shape can be adapted to the local image structure, since the parameters for each pass can be controlled individually on a per-pixel basis. For instance, by decreasing the size in the direction of the gradient and increasing it in the direction of the tangent, the overall filter shape becomes elliptic, leading to an enhancement of anisotropic structures. An even stronger enhancement of anisotropic structures can be achieved with the *flow-based bilateral filter* proposed by Kang et al. [26], where the second pass

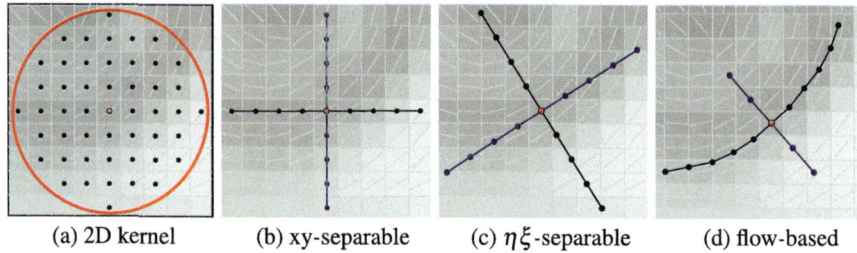

Fig. 5.4 Different variants of the bilateral filter. (**a**) A classical single pass bilateral filter performs a weighted average of a two-dimensional neighborhood. (**b**) Separable implementation with the first pass along the x-axis and second pass along the y-axis. (**c**) Orientation-aligned separable implementation with the first pass perpendicular and the second pass parallel to a vector field derived form the local structure, such as ETF or SST. (**d**) Separable implementation of the flow-based bilateral filter with the first pass perpendicular to the integral curve and the second pass along the integral curve defined by ETF or SST. Created by the author

performs an integration along the integral curves of a vector field given by smoothed tangents (Fig. 5.4(d)), similar to line integral convolution (LIC) [10].

For both approaches, a smooth vector field of high quality representing the local structure is critical (cf., Sect. 6.2.2). The two techniques that are known to produce vector fields of sufficient quality are the *edge tangent flow* (ETF) by Kang et al. [25, 26] and the *smoothed structure tensor* (SST) [31, 33, 34]. The ETF is essentially a bilateral filter, where the range weight has been specifically designed to measure the deviations between two vectors representing an axis. To obtain a reasonably smooth vector field, the ETF must be applied iteratively. The *structure tensor* is a well-known tool in computer vision, and is given by the outer product of the image gradients [9]. Smoothing the structure tensor and then performing an eigenanalysis corresponds to performing a principal component analysis on the gradient vectors. The major eigenvector can thus be interpreted as an averaged gradient and the minor eigenvector as an averaged tangent. In contrast to the EFT, the SST is suitable for speeding up the bilateral filter, since smoothing can be performed using a linear filter, such as a Gaussian filter, and eigenanalysis only involves solving a quadratic equation. Moreover, it is possible to define a coherence measure based on the SST's eigenvalues, which provides information about how anisotropic a local neighborhood is, and which can be used to adapt filters on a per-pixel basis. Local orientation estimation based on the SST fits well into the cartoon pipeline (Fig. 5.7), since the DoG filter, which will be discussed next, can also be significantly improved by adapting it to the local structure.

5.2.2 Difference of Gaussians

Early approaches to edge detection used simple approximations of the image gradient, such as the Prewitt and Sobel filter masks [49], and then thresholded the gradient

5 Artistic Stylization by Nonlinear Filtering

Fig. 5.5 Example showing the output of different edge detection and stylization methods. (**a**) The original image (USC-SIPI image database). (**b**) The globally thresholded gradient magnitude of the Sobel filter. (**c**) Zero-crossing of the Laplacian of Gaussian [40]. (**d**) The output of the Canny edge detector [11]. (**e**) The thresholded DoG as proposed in Winnemöller et al. [60]. (**f**) The thresholded output of the separable implementation of the flow-based DoG [26, 31]. (**g**) The flow-based DoG with XDoG thresholding. The image is pre-processed with a bilateral filter to suppress noise. (**h**) Cartoon-style abstraction generated with bilateral and flow-based DoG filters using the WOG-pipeline

magnitude. However, due to the small size of the filter masks, such approaches are sensitive to noise and fail to detect edges at large scales. The Canny edge detector [11], therefore, combines first order differentials with appropriate smoothing, non-maximum suppression, and hysteresis thresholding. It is one of the most popular edge detectors for applications in computer vision. From an artistic point of view, however, the single pixel-wide edges it creates are typically not attractive and require further processing (Fig. 5.5(d)).

Another popular approach to edge detection based on second derivatives goes back to Marr and Hildreth [40]. For one-dimensional functions, a maximum of the gradient magnitude is equivalent to a zero-crossing in the second derivative. This also generalizes to two dimensions, where the second derivative perpendicular to the zero-crossing has to be considered. However, since this direction is unknown at computation time and would have to be estimated, Marr and Hildreth proposed to use the *Laplacian*

$$\nabla^2 = \frac{\partial^2}{\partial x^2} + \frac{\partial^2}{\partial y^2} \qquad (5.3)$$

which is rotationally invariant. While the Laplacian was known at that time to be useful for sharpening images [18], it has not been used for edge detection due to its high sensitivity to noise. Marr and Hildreth's key insight was to smooth the image before applying the Laplacian. This has two important effects. First, noise is reduced and the differentiation regularized. Second, the bandwidth is restricted, which means that the range of possible scales at which edges can occur is reduced. For the smoothing filter, a two-dimensional Gaussian

$$G_\rho(x) = \frac{1}{2\pi\rho^2} \exp\left(-\frac{\|x\|^2}{2\rho^2}\right) \quad (5.4)$$

was chosen, since it is known that it minimizes uncertainty, which simultaneously measures the spread of a function in the spatial and frequency domains. Since the Laplacian commutes with convolution, it follows that

$$\nabla^2(G_\rho * I) = \left(\nabla^2 G_\rho\right) * I \quad (5.5)$$

Thus, instead of applying smoothing and differentiation in sequence, both operations can be combined into a single operator $\nabla^2 G_\rho$, which can be symbolically computed and is known as the *Laplacian of Gaussian* (*LoG*). Marr and Hildreth, moreover, showed that the LoG operator can be approximated by the difference of two Gaussians

$$D_{\sigma,k}(x) = G_\sigma(x) - G_{k\sigma}(x) \quad (5.6)$$

with $k \approx 1.6$ being a good engineering solution. Results in biological vision, which showed that the ganglion cell receptive fields of cats can be modeled in this way [63], matched this result. This provided motivation for their approach and helped to popularize the technique. To extract edges from a LoG filtered image, the local neighborhood of a pixel is typically examined to detect the zero-crossings. This, however, again results in artistically questionable 1–2 pixel-wide edges (Fig. 5.5(c)) similar to those produced by the Canny edge detector (Fig. 5.5(d)). To achieve an artistically interesting effect, it turns out that simple thresholding works surprisingly well [19, 51, 60], which can be explained as follows. Let I denote a grayscale image. If we wish to generate a two-tone edge image, we essentially have two choices: Either we start with a white image and make certain image regions darker (i.e., set them to black), or we start with a black image and perform highlighting (i.e., set those regions to white). The DoG filter provides exactly this information by describing which high-frequency details have to be added to the low-pass filtered image $G_{k\sigma} * I$ to get

$$G_\sigma * I = G_{k\sigma} * I + D_{\sigma,k} * I \quad (5.7)$$

Hence, the sign of the DoG filter's response describes whether capturing the shape and structure of any nearby edges requires making each pixel darker or brighter than most of its neighbors.

The recently presented *XDoG* filter by Winnemöller [59] further refines the thresholding process by introducing additional parameters, and is defined by

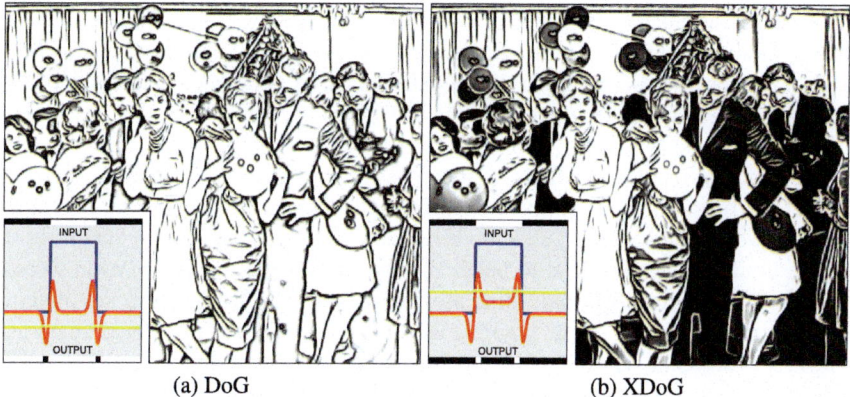

Fig. 5.6 Illustration of the XDoG thresholding scheme for a step edge (*blue*). The output of the DoG and XDoG operator before thresholding is shown in *red*; the threshold ε is indicated by the *yellow line*. (**a**) DoG has no tone mapping effect. Light regions are outlined. (**b**) XDoG allows for a tone mapping effect. Light regions get a black outline, dark regions receive a white outline. In both cases the flow-based variant was used. Original image by X-ray delta one@flickr.com

$$D_{\sigma,k,\tau}(x) = G_\sigma(x) - \tau \cdot G_{k\sigma}(x) \tag{5.8}$$

$$E_{\varepsilon,\varphi}(x) = \begin{cases} 1 & D_{\sigma,k,\tau}(x) > \varepsilon \\ 1 + \tanh(\varphi \cdot (D_{\sigma,k,\tau}(x) - \varepsilon)) & \text{otherwise} \end{cases} \tag{5.9}$$

The parameter σ controls the scale, whereas τ and ε control tone mapping and thresholding. By using tanh and the parameter φ, hard thresholding is avoided, which improves temporal coherence. In Fig. 5.5(e)–(f) and Fig. 5.6, a few examples with different parameter settings are shown. The relationship between the XDoG and the standard DoG can best be seen by rewriting Eq. (5.8) as

$$D_{\sigma,k,\tau}(x) = G_\sigma(x) - \tau \cdot G_{k\sigma}(x) \tag{5.10}$$

$$= (1 - \tau) \cdot G_\sigma(x) + \tau \cdot D_{\sigma,k,\tau}(x) \tag{5.11}$$

which shows that the XDoG approach is equivalent to a weighted average of the blurred image and standard DoG. Unfortunately, adjusting the parameters τ, φ, and ε is difficult, since they depend on each other and must be modified in concert. An alternative, which was proposed in [61], is to normalize the XDoG operator by dividing it by $\tau - 1$.

The XDoG filter is still relatively sensitive to noise. To some extent, ε can be used to reduce sensitivity, but a simple and highly effective approach is to apply 1–2 iterations of the bilateral filter before applying the XDoG filter (Fig. 5.7). An explanation for the high sensitivity can be given by looking at the decomposition of the LoG operator in the direction of the local gradient and tangent. The second derivative in the direction of the gradient contributes to the edge localization, while the one in the tangent direction merely increases the sensitivity to noise. This motivates considering detecting zero-crossings in the second derivative in the direction of the gradient. Such an edge detector was first proposed by Haralick [22], and also the maximum suppression of the Canny edge detector [11] is essentially equivalent to looking for a zero-crossing in the second derivative. A detailed discussion of the relationships between the Laplacian and directional derivatives has been given by Torre and Poggio [53].

The success of second derivative methods for edge detection suggests changing the XDoG filter from an isotropic to a directional operator. However, simply replacing the two-dimensional XDoG with its one-dimensional equivalent in the direction of the gradient does not lead to better results. In fact, the results are even worse. The reason for this is twofold: First, a one-dimensional XDoG is very sensitive to an accurate estimation of the gradient direction, which is typically performed using first order Gaussian derivative operators along the coordinate axes. The scale of these derivatives must be similar to the scale of the XDoG. For instance, if their scale is too large, the estimated gradient direction will, in general, not match the underlying image structure, which limits opportunities for noise suppression. Second, the missing regularization in the tangent direction further increases the sensitivity to noise.

The first work that addressed these issues and provided significantly improved quality over the isotropic DoG is the *flow-based difference of Gaussians* (FDoG) filter by Kang et al. [25]. In this work, the EFT was also initially introduced. It provided Kang et al. with a vector field closely aligned to the underlying image structure, and allowed them to derive an average gradient direction that is less affected by noise. The originally proposed FDoG performs steps along the integral curves of the EFT by using a Euler integration scheme. At each step, a one-dimensional DoG filter in the direction perpendicular to the integral curve is applied, and all these filter responses are accumulated by weighting them using a one-dimensional Gaussian. This accumulation performs regularization in the tangent direction, and shares a similarity with the hysteresis thresholding of the Canny edge detector. A separable implementation that achieves similar quality while being computationally less expensive and simpler to implement was presented by Kyprianidis and Döllner [31] and independently in a follow-up work by Kang et al. [26]. Similar to Fig. 5.4(d), the separable FDoG first performs a one-dimensional DoG, which is then followed by a second pass that performs line integral convolution with a Gaussian kernel. As in the case of the flow-based bilateral filter, the ETF can be replaced by the SST, which leads to a variant of the cartoon pipeline that delivers improved quality at a reasonable computational cost [31, 32]. To further increase the response of the FDoG, Kang et al. [25, 26] proposed to apply the FDoG iteratively by overlaying the previous FDoG response with the input image. While this results in stronger edges, it is also more sensitive to noise, and needs to be used with caution. The FDoG in combination with XDoG thresholding is very versatile. By properly adjusting parameters, a large variety of NPR effects can be created [59, 61].

Kang et al.'s [25] work provided new ideas in the field of IB-AR, and popularized the use of local structure information. It lead to several interesting results of work in areas such as image filtering [24, 26, 31, 33, 34], stippling [27, 50], and texture transfer [37]. Moreover, the flow-based XDoG is used by the ToonPAINT mobile application, which is discussed in Sect. 17.5.

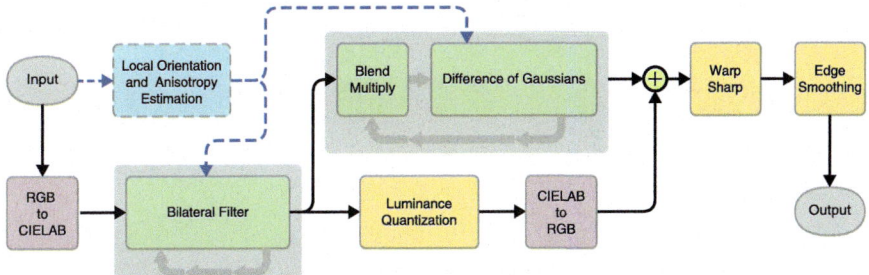

Fig. 5.7 The WOG-pipeline for the creation of a cartoon-like effect in modern generalized form [26, 31, 60]. Processing starts with the conversion of the input to CIELAB color space. Then, the input is iteratively abstracted by using a variant of the bilateral filter. After one or two iterations of the bilateral filter to suppress noise, outlines are extracted from the intermediate result using a variant of the DoG filter. Then more iterations of the bilateral filter are performed, typically up to four, with luminance quantization applied afterwards. DoG edges and the output of the luminance quantization are then composited, followed by an optional sharpening by warping and smoothing of the edges

5.2.3 Cartoon Pipeline

That multiple iterations of the bilateral filter lead to a cartoon-like effect was already noticed by Tomasi and Manduchi [52]. Motivated by this, Fischer et al. [16] applied the bilateral filter in the context of augmented reality to make virtual objects less distinct from the camera stream by applying stylization to the virtual and camera input. However, at that time computing the bilateral filter at full resolution was computationally too expensive. Due to this, Fischer et al. applied the bilateral filter at reduced resolution followed by upsampling, resulting in an inferior result. Winnemöller et al. [60] were faced with the same problem, but applied iteratively the separable implementation of the bilateral filter by Pham and van Vliet [47]. Although this brute force separation is prone to horizontal and vertical artifacts, it provides a reasonable tradeoff in terms of quality and speed, and enabled real-time processing on consumer GPUs of that time. In addition to the bilateral filter, Winnemöller et al. [60] added another processing step performing smooth luminance quantization. The quantization is applied in CIELAB space, with only the luminance channel being modified, creating a strong cartoon-like effect. The quantization is performed using a smooth step function whose steepness is chosen depending on the luminance gradient. This makes the output of the quantization less sensible to small changes in the input and increases temporal coherence when processing video frame-by-frame (cf., Sect. 11.3).

Creating artistic images using the DoG filter was also not new at that time. For instance, Sýkora et al. [51] used the thresholded output of the Laplacian of Gaussian, which is approximated by the DoG filter, to create outlines for colorizing hand-drawn black-and-white cartoons (see also Sect. 14.2 and Sect. 14.5.1), and Gooch et al. [19] used the DoG filter in combination with a model of brightness perception to create human facial illustrations. However, Winnemöller et al. [60] were the first to combine a bilateral and DoG filter into an effective pipeline.

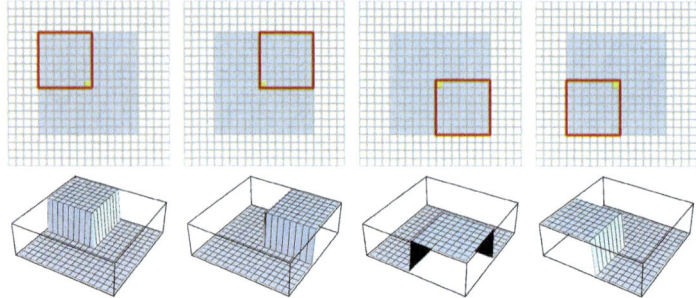

Fig. 5.8 The *top row* shows the four rectangular subregions used by the classical Kuwahara filter. The *bottom row* shows the weighting functions that can be used to describe the subregions—one over a specific subregion, or otherwise zero

A schematic overview of a modern generalized form of the pipeline proposed by Winnemöller et al. [60], hereafter referred to as the *WOG-pipeline*, is shown in Fig. 5.7. Input is typically an image, a frame of a video, or the output of a 3D rendering. In the original pipeline, the local orientation estimation step was not present; this step was added later to adapt the bilateral and DoG filters to the local image structure [25, 26, 31]. Also not present were the iterative application of the DoG filter, which was first proposed in [25], and the final smoothing pass to further reduce aliasing of edges. The introduction of the flow-based DoG filter significantly increased the quality of the produced outlines, and made the warp-based sharpening step of the original pipeline less important. Therefore, this step is typically not present in later work.

5.3 Kuwahara Filter

An interesting class of edge-preserving filters that perform comparatively well on high-contrast images are variants of the Kuwahara filter. Based on local area flattening, these filters properly remove detail in high-contrast regions and protect shape boundaries in low-contrast regions, resulting in a roughly uniform level of abstraction across the image. The *Kuwahara filter* [29] was initially proposed in the mid-1970s as a noise reduction approach in the context of biological image processing. The general idea behind it is to divide the local filter neighborhood into four rectangular subregions that overlap by one pixel (Fig. 5.8). For all subregions the variance, which is the sum of the squared distances to the mean, is computed, and the response of the filter is then defined as the mean of a subregion with minimum variance. As can be seen in Fig. 5.9(a), this avoids averaging between differently colored regions for corners and edges. However, for flat or homogeneous regions the variances of the different subregions are almost equivalent or even the same. A subregion with minimum variance is, therefore, generally not well-defined, and the selection highly unstable, especially in the presence of noise. For small filter sizes the Kuwahara

Fig. 5.9 Comparison of different variants of the Kuwahara filter: (**a**) Classical Kuwahara filter with rectangular subregions; a single subregion is selected. (**b**) Generalized Kuwahara filter with sectors of a disc as subregions; multiple sectors are chosen. (**c**) Anisotropic Kuwahara filter, where the filter shape is derived from the local structure and divided into subregions; multiple filter responses are chosen. Note that the subregions in (**a**), (**b**) and (**c**) are defined to overlap slightly. Redrawn from [34]. © 2009 Blackwell Publishing. Used by permission

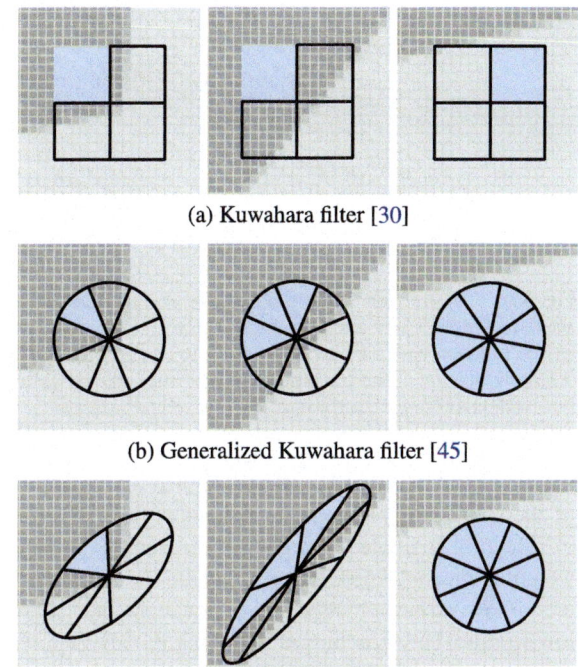

(a) Kuwahara filter [30]

(b) Generalized Kuwahara filter [45]

(c) Anisotropic Kuwahara filter [35]

filter produces reasonable results. However, for IB-AR, comparatively large filter sizes are necessary to achieve an interesting abstraction effect, resulting in clearly noticeable artifacts. These are due to the unstable subregion selection process and the use of rectangular subregions. A more detailed discussion of limitations of the Kuwahara filter can be found in [44].

Several attempts have been made to address the limitations of the Kuwahara filter. The first work that provided an approach suitable for applications in IB-AR is the *generalized Kuwahara filter* by Papari et al. [44], which introduces two important ideas. First, the rectangular subregions are replaced with smooth weighting functions constructed over sectors of a disc in a way that their sum results in a 2D Gaussian. Neighboring weighting functions thereby have to overlap smoothly (Fig. 5.10). Using these weighting functions, for every sector the *weighted mean*

$$m_i(x_0) = \sum_{x \in \Omega(x_0)} w_i(x - x_0) \cdot f(x) \qquad (5.12)$$

and *weighted variance*

$$s^2(x_0) = \sum_{x \in \Omega(x_0)} w_i(x - x_0) \cdot \big(f(x) - m_i(x_0)\big)^2 \qquad (5.13)$$

can be computed. It should be noticed that if the weighting functions are chosen as characteristic functions of the rectangular subregions, as illustrated in Fig. 5.8, then

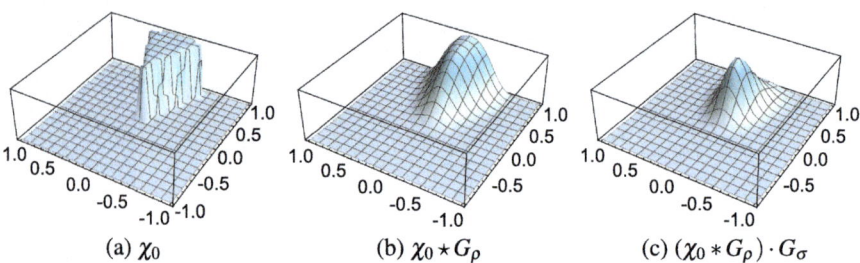

Fig. 5.10 Construction of the weighting functions of the generalized Kuwahara filter: (**a**) Characteristic function χ_0—one over the first sector, or otherwise zero. (**b**) Convolution of the characteristic function with a Gaussian $\chi_0 * G_\rho$ to create smooth transitions between different sectors. (**c**) Multiplication of the smoothed characteristic function with a Gaussian to create a smooth fall-off with increasing distance from the filter center: $(\chi_0 * G_\rho) \cdot G_\sigma$

the weighted mean and variance defined above are exactly the mean and variance of the subregions. Second, a new subregion selection method is defined. Instead of selecting a single subregion, the result is defined as the weighted sum of the weighted means, where the weights are based on the weighted variances, with sectors of low variance receiving a high weight and sectors of high variance receiving a low weight. This is achieved by taking the inverted weighted variance to the power of a user provided parameter q, and given by

$$\sum_{i \in N} m_i \cdot s_i^{-q} \Big/ \sum_{i \in N} s_i^{-q} \qquad (5.14)$$

where N is the number of sectors. In Fig. 5.9(b), the behavior of the generalized Kuwahara filter is illustrated for different local neighborhoods. As can be seen, for corners and edges the filter adapts itself to the neighborhood, thus avoiding blurring across region boundaries. In homogeneous regions, the variances are similar, resulting in similar weights, which makes the filter approximate a Gaussian. In flat and smooth regions, the variances are very small and sensitive to noise, resulting in a poorly approximated Gaussian. To avoid this, a simple solution is to threshold the variances [30].

For highly anisotropic image regions, the flattening effect applied by the generalized Kuwahara filter is typically too aggressive, resulting in blurred anisotropic structures. Moreover, pixels tend to form clusters proportional to the filter size. The *anisotropic Kuwahara filter* by Kyprianidis et al. [34, 35] addresses these issues by replacing the weighting functions defined over sectors of a disc by weighting functions defined over ellipses, as shown in Fig. 5.9(c). By adapting shape, scale, and orientation of these ellipses to the local structure of the input, artifacts are avoided. In addition, directional image features are better preserved and emphasized, resulting in overall sharper edges and the enhancement of anisotropic image features (Fig. 5.1(c)). The local structure is estimated using the SST, where the coherence measure derived from the eigenvalues is used to define the eccentricity of the ellipse. A further modification has been presented in [36], wherein new weighting

5 Artistic Stylization by Nonlinear Filtering

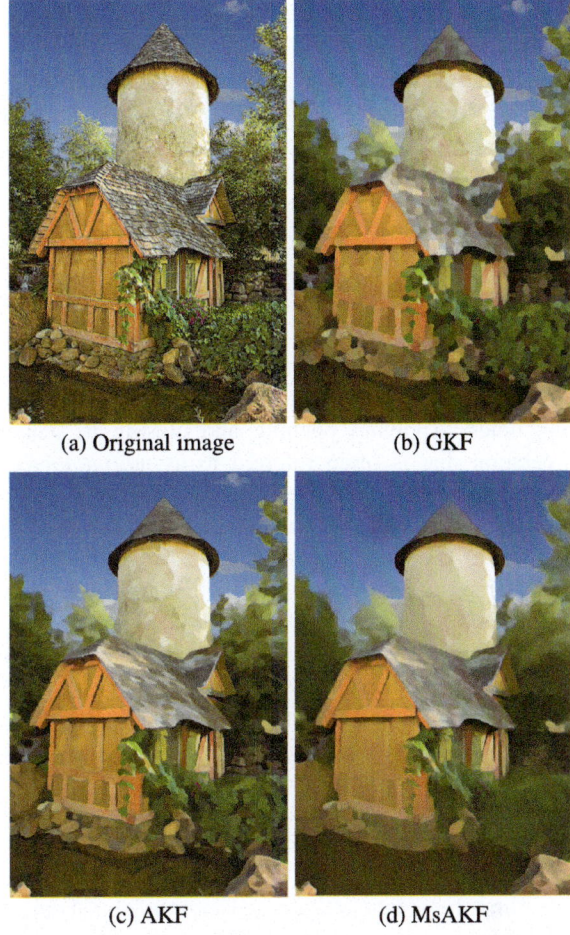

Fig. 5.11 Examples created using different variants of the Kuwahara filter: (**a**) Original image courtesy of chefranden@flickr.com. (**b**) Generalized Kuwahara filter (2 iterations) [44]. (**c**) Anisotropic Kuwahara filter (2 iterations) [34]. (**d**) Multi-scale anisotropic Kuwahara filter [30]

(a) Original image (b) GKF
(c) AKF (d) MsAKF

functions based on polynomials that can be evaluated directly during the filtering process are defined.

The level of abstraction achievable with the generalized and the anisotropic Kuwahara filter is limited by the filter radius. Simply increasing the filter radius is typically not a solution, as it often results in artifacts. Another possibility would be to control the radius adaptively per pixel depending on the local neighborhood, but the computational cost would be very high, as the filter depends quadratically on the radius. The *multi-scale anisotropic Kuwahara filter* by Kyprianidis [30], therefore applies the anisotropic Kuwahara filter at multiple scales. The computations are carried out on an image pyramid, where processing is performed in a coarse-to-fine manner, with intermediate results being propagated up the pyramid. Figure 5.11 shows an example image processed with different variants of the Kuwahara filter.

5.4 Morphological Filters

Mathematical morphology (MM) provides a set-theoretic approach to image analysis and processing. Besides being useful the for extraction of object boundaries, skeletons, and convex hulls, it has been also applied successfully to many pre- and post-processing tasks. A good introduction to the subject, covering aspects of image processing and computer vision, is the tutorial by Haralick et al. [23]. Fundamental operations in MM are *dilation* and *erosion*. From these, a large number of other operators can be derived, most notably *opening*, defined as erosion followed by dilation, and *closing*, defined as dilation followed by erosion. For grayscale images, dilation is equivalent to a maximum filter and erosion corresponds to a minimum filter. Therefore, opening removes light image features by removing peaks, while closing removes dark features by filling holes. Applying opening and closing in sequence results in a smoothing operation that is often referred to as *morphological smoothing*, which, similar to a median filter, quite effectively suppresses salt-and-pepper noise, while being computationally less expensive. In fact, openings and closings are closely related to order-statistics filters. A further in-depth discussion of morphological filters and their relations to other image processing operators can be found in [38, 39].

In Bousseau et al.'s [7, 8] work on watercolor rendering (cf., Sect. 13.3.2.1), morphological smoothing is applied to simplify input images and videos before their heuristically defined rendering approach is applied. In the case of video, a spatio-temporal kernel is used, aligned to the motion trajectory derived from optical flow. Applying opening and then closing generally results in a darkened result. Since watercolor paintings typically have light colors, Bousseau et al. proposed swapping the order of the morphological operators and applying closing followed by opening (Fig. 5.12). Since opening and closing are dual to each other, this is the same as inverting the output of the usual morphological smoothing applied to the inverted image.

Papari and Petkov [43] described another technique, which applied morphological filtering in the context of IB-AR. Motivated by *glass patterns*, and similar to line integral convolution [10], they performed a one-dimensional dilation in the form of a maximum filter over noise along the integral curves defined by a vector field. In contrast to line integral convolution, this technique is more capable of producing thick piece-wise constant coherent lines with sharp edges, resulting in a stronger brush-like effect. Moreover, it can also be applied to color images, by using the location of the first maximum noise value along the integral curve as a look-up position.

Some morphological operators (e.g., with convex polygonal structuring element) can be efficiently implemented by using distance transforms [15]. Criminisi et al. [13] recently demonstrated that edge-sensitive smoothing based on the *generalized geodesic distance transform* (GGDT) can be used for the creation of cartoon-style abstractions. The image is first clustered into a fixed number of colors. Then for every pixel, the probability of the pixel's value belonging to

Fig. 5.12 Mathematical morphology operators. (**a**) Original image courtesy of PDPhoto.org. (**b**) Opening. (**c**) Closing. (**d**) Opening followed by closing. (**e**) Closing followed by opening: The morphological operator chosen by Bousseau et al. [7, 8]

a certain cluster is defined. These probabilities form a soft mask to which the GGDT is applied. The output is then defined as the weighted sum of the cluster's mean values, where the weights are defined based on the corresponding distances.

5.5 PDE-Based Methods

Methods based on *partial differential equations* (PDE) provide a powerful approach to image processing [3]. Interestingly, several local filtering approaches can be interpreted in terms of corresponding PDEs. For example, anisotropic diffusion is closely related to the bilateral filter [5], and PDE formulations for classical morphological processes have been established [55]. There is also a connection between PDEs and the Kuwahara filter. As shown by van den Boomgaard [54], the Kuwahara filter can be interpreted as a PDE with linear diffusion and shock filter terms.

In this section, *shape-simplifying image abstraction* by Kang and Lee [24] will be discussed. This technique applies a diffusion process to simplify the image, followed by shock filtering, which deblurs the image to maintain sharp edges at dis-

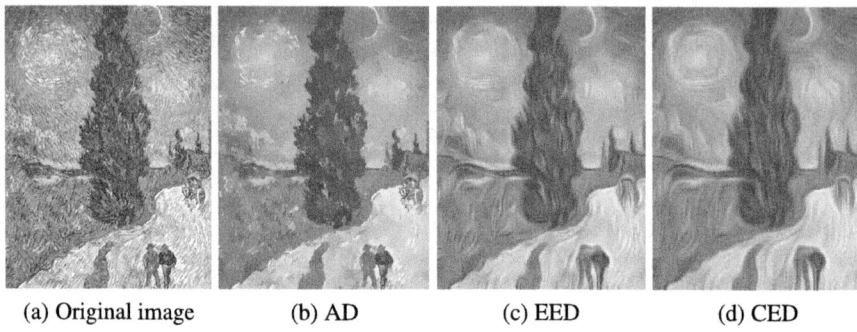

(a) Original image   (b) AD   (c) EED   (d) CED

Fig. 5.13 Examples of different diffusion techniques. (**a**) van Gogh—Road with Cypress and Star. (**b**) Anisotropic diffusion [46]. (**c**) Edge-enhancing diffusion [55]. (**d**) Coherence-enhancing diffusion [55]

continuities. Before discussing it, we briefly review the concepts behind anisotropic diffusion and shock filters.

5.5.1 Anisotropic Diffusion

Let I be a grayscale image, then the solution of the heat equation

$$\frac{\partial u}{\partial t} = \Delta u = \text{div}(\nabla u) \tag{5.15}$$

at a particular time t with initial condition $u(x, 0) = I(x)$ is given by convolution with a two-dimensional Gaussian having standard deviation $\sqrt{2t}$ [55]. To overcome the limitations of isotropic smoothing, Perona and Malik [46] added the regularization term

$$g(s^2) = \frac{1}{1 + \frac{s^2}{\lambda^2}} \quad (\lambda > 0) \tag{5.16}$$

to the heat equation that stops diffusion at the edges:

$$\frac{\partial u}{\partial t} = \text{div}\big(g(|\nabla u|^2)\nabla u\big) \tag{5.17}$$

This is known as *anisotropic diffusion*. Adding such penalization terms is a standard technique often found in PDE-based approaches. For instance, the edge-enhancing and coherence-enhancing diffusion techniques developed by Weickert [56] guide the diffusion using a tensor derived from the SST (Fig. 5.13). More details about anisotropic diffusion and other PDE-based image processing techniques can be found in the books by Weickert [55] and Aubert and Kornprobst [3].

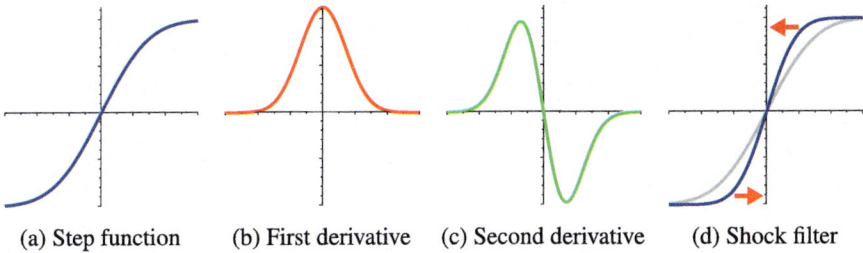

(a) Step function (b) First derivative (c) Second derivative (d) Shock filter

Fig. 5.14 Illustration of shock filtering and mean curvature flow. (**a**) A smooth step edge. (**b**) First derivative of the edge. (**c**) Second derivative of the edge. (**d**) A shock filter applies an dilation where the second derivative is positive and erosion where it is negative

5.5.2 Shock Filter

Osher and Rudin [42] were the first to study *shock filters* in image processing. The classical shock filter evolution equation is given by

$$\frac{\partial u}{\partial t} = -\text{sign}(\mathcal{L}(u))|\nabla u| \tag{5.18}$$

with initial condition $u(x, 0) = I(x)$ and where $\mathcal{L}$ is a suitable detector, such as the Laplacian Δu or the second derivative in direction of the gradient:

$$u_{\xi\xi} = \frac{u_x^2 u_{xx} + 2u_x u_y u_{xy} + u_y^2 u_{yy}}{u_x^2 + u_y^2} \tag{5.19}$$

In the influence zone of a maximum, $\mathcal{L}(u)$ is negative, and therefore a local dilation, with a disc as the structuring element, is performed. Similarly, in the influence zone of a minimum, $\mathcal{L}(u)$ is positive, which results in local erosion. This sharpens the edges at the zero-crossings of Δu, as shown in Fig. 5.14. Shock filters have the attractive property of satisfying a maximum principle, and in contrast to unsharp masking, therefore do not suffer from ringing artifacts.

Instead of the second derivative in the direction of the gradient, also the second derivative in the direction of the major eigenvector of the SST can be used. This was first proposed by Weickert [57] and shares some similarity with the flow-based DoG discussed in Sect. 5.2.2. To achieve an higher robustness against small-scale image details, the input image can be regularized with a Gaussian filter prior to second derivative or SST computation [2]. As demonstrated in Fig. 5.15(b), this provides an aggressive simplification method. Equation (5.18) is typically implemented using a finite difference scheme. Thereby, $\mathcal{L}(u)$ can be approximated using central differences. Discretization of $|\nabla u|$ requires the use of an upwind scheme [3].

Shock filter can also be related to local neighborhood filters. Guichard and Morel [21] showed that the classical Osher–Rudin shock filter, with the Laplacian as the edge detector, corresponds asymptotically to a filter by Kramer and Bruckner [28], which replaces the current gray level value by either the minimum or maximum of the filter region, depending on which is closer to the current value.

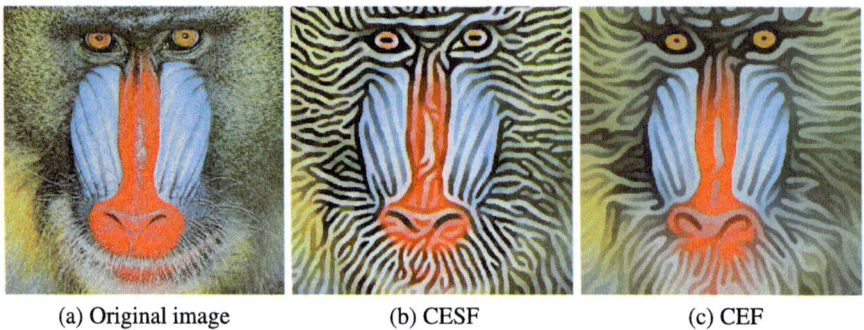

(a) Original image   (b) CESF   (c) CEF

Fig. 5.15 Shock filters in conjunction with regularization provide an aggressive image simplification method. Original image (USC-SIPI image database). (**b**) Weickert's coherence-enhancing shock filter [57]. (**c**) A further refinement, applying curvature-preserving smoothing and shock filtering iteratively [33]

5.5.3 Mean Curvature Flow

Previously, Osher and Rudin [42], as well as Weickert [57], made comments about the artistic look of shock filtered results, but the work of Kang and Lee [24] was the first to apply diffusion in combination with shock filtering for targeting IB-AR. The *mean curvature flow* (MCF) diffusion method was chosen, which evolves isophote curves under curvature speed in normal direction, resulting in simplified isophote curves with regularized geometry. In contrast to other popular edge-preserving smoothing techniques, such as the bilateral or the Kuwahara filter, MCF smoothes not only irrelevant color variations while protecting region boundaries, but also simplifies the shape of those boundaries. The evolution equation of MCF is given by

$$\frac{\partial u}{\partial t} = \kappa |\nabla u| \quad \text{with } \kappa = \frac{u_x^2 u_{xx} - 2u_x u_y u_{xy} + u_y^2 u_{yy}}{(u_x^2 + u_y^2)^{3/2}} \qquad (5.20)$$

denoting the curvature. Equation (5.20) can be implemented using central differences. A better approach, however, is to use a finite difference scheme with harmonic averaging [14].

MCF performs strong simplification of an image, but also creates blurred edges. Therefore, Kang and Lee [24] performed deblurring with a shock filter after some MCF iterations, which helps to keep important edges during the evolution (Fig. 5.16). From an artistic point of view, however, shock filtered MCF is typically still too aggressive, and does not properly protect directional image features (Fig. 5.17). Similar to Eq. (5.17), Kang and Lee therefore constrained the mean curvature flow by using the ETF to penalize diffusion that deviates from the local image structure. The evolution equation is given by

$$\frac{\partial u}{\partial t} = \left((1-r) + r \cdot \left| \left\langle \frac{E}{\|E\|}, \frac{\nabla u^\perp}{\|\nabla u\|} \right\rangle \right| \right) \|\kappa\| \qquad (5.21)$$

5 Artistic Stylization by Nonlinear Filtering

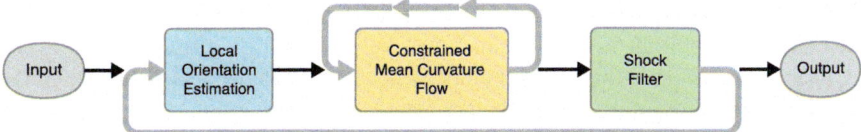

Fig. 5.16 Pipeline for shape-simplifying image abstraction [24]. Processing starts with the estimation of local orientation. Then multiple iterations of constrained mean curvature flow are applied, followed by shock filtering for deblurring. This process is repeated until the desired amount of abstraction has been reached

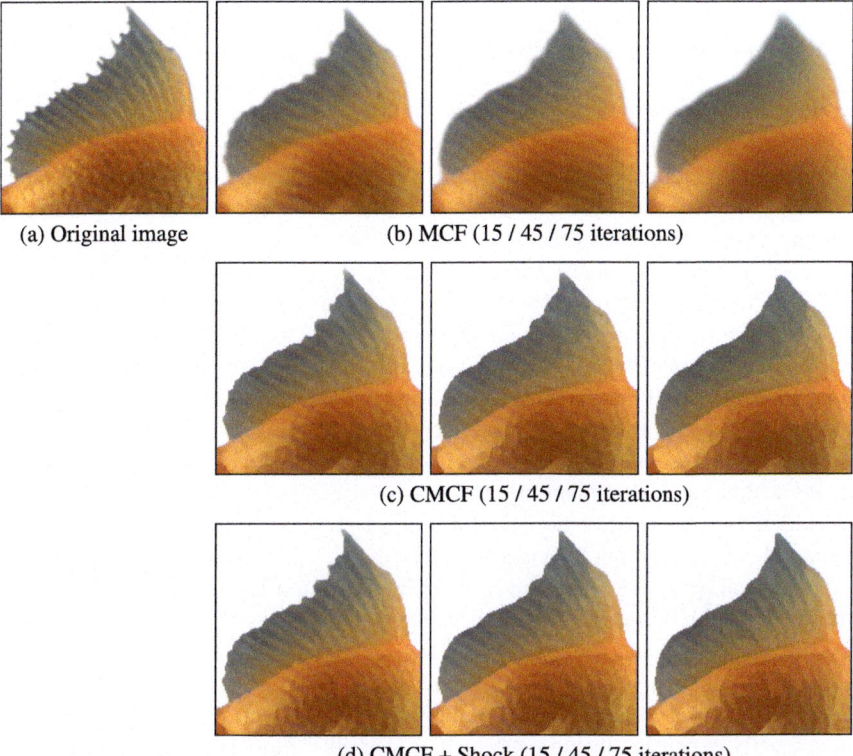

Fig. 5.17 Comparison of mean curvature flow with/without shock filtering and constraint. (**a**) Original image (licensed by Getty images). (**b**) Mean curvature flow. (**c**) Mean curvature flow with shock filtering after 15 iterations. (**d**) Constrained mean curvature flow with shock filtering after 15 iterations. In all cases, a time step of 0.25 was used

where $\langle \cdot, \cdot \rangle$ denotes the per-pixel scalar product of EFT vectors and vectors perpendicular to the image gradients. The control parameter $r \in [0, 1]$ allows for blending between the unconstrained and the constrained MCF. Alternatively, instead of the ETF, the minor eigenvector field of the SST can be used.

MCF, and its constrained variant, contract isophote curves to points [20]. For this reason, important image features must be protected by a user-defined mask. A further limitation is that the technique is not stable against small changes in the input, and therefore not suitable for per-frame video processing. In order to avoid these issues, Kyprianidis and Kang [33] combine curvature-preserving flow-guided smoothing and shock filter-based sharpening orthogonal to the flow, but instead of modeling the process by a PDE, approximations that operate as a local neighborhood filter are used (Fig. 5.15(c)). This makes the technique more stable and particularly suitable for per-frame video processing.

5.6 Gradient Domain Techniques

In recent years, *gradient domain* methods have become very popular in computer vision and computer graphics [1]. The basic idea behind such methods is to construct a gradient field representing the result. However, such constructed fields are rarely conservative, and therefore the result needs to be found as an approximation by solving an optimization problem. In the case of a best-fit in the least squares sense, this corresponds to solving Poisson's equation.

Orzan et al. [41] were the first to apply gradient domain image editing for IBAR. By performing a scale-space analysis, they extracted a multi-scale Canny edge representation with lifetime and best scale information. This representation is then used to define the gradient field, and allows for image operations, such as detail removal and shape abstraction. Moreover, line drawings can be extracted from the multi-scale representation and overlaid with the reconstructed image. A limitation of the technique is that handling contrast is problematic and requires correction. Besides being computationally expensive, this technique is also known not to create temporal coherent output for video.

Bhat et al. [6] have presented a robust optimization framework that allows for the specification of zero-order (pixel values) and first-order (gradient values) constraints over space and time. The resulting optimization problem is solved using a weighted least squares solver. By using temporal constraints, the framework is able to create temporal coherent video output. The framework makes use of several computationally expensive techniques, such as steerable filters and optical flow, and is therefore currently limited to offline processing.

References

1. Agrawal, A., Raskar, R.: Gradient domain manipulation techniques in vision and graphics. In: ICCV Course (2007)
2. Alvarez, L., Mazorra, L.: Signal and image restoration using shock filters and anisotropic diffusion. SIAM J. Numer. Anal. **31**(2), 590–605 (1994). doi:10.1137/0731032
3. Aubert, G., Kornprobst, P.: Mathematical Problems in Image Processing: Partial Differential Equations and the Calculus of Variations. Springer, Berlin (2006)

4. Aurich, V., Weule, J.: Non-linear Gaussian filters performing edge preserving diffusion. In: Proc. DAGM-Symposium, pp. 538–545 (1995)
5. Barash, D., Comaniciu, D.: A common framework for nonlinear diffusion, adaptive smoothing, bilateral filtering and mean shift. Image Vis. Comput. **22**(1), 73–81 (2004)
6. Bhat, P., Zitnick, C.L., Cohen, M.F., Curless, B.: GradientShop: a gradient-domain optimization framework for image and video filtering. ACM Trans. Graph. **29**(2), 10 (2010). doi:10.1145/1731047.1731048
7. Bousseau, A., Kaplan, M., Thollot, J., Sillion, F.X.: Interactive watercolor rendering with temporal coherence and abstraction. In: Proc. NPAR, pp. 141–149 (2006). doi:10.1145/1124728.1124751
8. Bousseau, A., Neyret, F., Thollot, J., Salesin, D.: Video watercolorization using bidirectional texture advection. ACM Trans. Graph. **26**(3), 104 (2007). doi:10.1145/1276377.1276507
9. Brox, T., Boomgaard, R., Lauze, F., Weijer, J., Weickert, J., Mrázek, P., Kornprobst, P.: Adaptive structure tensors and their applications. In: Visualization and Processing of Tensor Fields, pp. 17–47. Springer, Berlin (2006). doi:10.1007/3-540-31272-2_2
10. Cabral, B., Leedom, L.C.: Imaging vector fields using line integral convolution. In: Proc. SIGGRAPH, pp. 263–270 (1993). doi:10.1145/166117.166151
11. Canny, J.F.: A computational approach to edge detection. IEEE Trans. Pattern Anal. Mach. Intell. **8**, 769–798 (1986). doi:10.1109/TPAMI.1986.4767851
12. Chen, J., Paris, S., Durand, F.: Real-time edge-aware image processing with the bilateral grid. ACM Trans. Graph. **26**(3), 103 (2007). doi:10.1145/1276377.1276506
13. Criminisi, A., Sharp, T., Rother, C., Pérez, P.: Geodesic image and video editing. ACM Trans. Graph. **29**(5), 134 (2010). doi:10.1145/1857907.1857910
14. Didas, S., Weickert, J.: Combining curvature motion and edge-preserving denoising. In: Proc. SSVM 2007. LNCS, vol. 4485, pp. 568–579. Springer, Berlin (2007). doi:10.1007/978-3-540-72823-8
15. Fabbri, R., Costa, L.D.F., Torelli, J.C., Bruno, O.M.: 2D Euclidean distance transform algorithms. ACM Comput. Surv. **40**(1), 2 (2008). doi:10.1145/1322432.1322434
16. Fischer, J., Bartz, D., Straber, W.: Stylized augmented reality for improved immersion. In: Proc. VR, pp. 195–202 (2005). doi:10.1109/VR.2005.1492774
17. Gastal, E.S.L., Oliveira, M.M.: Domain transform for edge-aware image and video processing. ACM Trans. Graph. **30**(4), 69 (2011). doi:10.1145/2010324.1964964
18. Gonzalez, R.C., Woods, R.E.: Digital Image Processing, 3rd edn. Prentice Hall, New York (2006)
19. Gooch, B., Reinhard, E., Gooch, A.: Human facial illustrations: Creation and psychophysical evaluation. ACM Trans. Graph. **23**(1), 27–44 (2004). doi:10.1145/966131.966133
20. Grayson, M.A.: The heat equation shrinks embedded plane curves to round points. J. Differ. Geom. **26**(2), 285–314 (1987)
21. Guichard, F., Morel, J.M.: A note on two classical enhancement filters and their associated PDE's. Int. J. Comput. Vis. **52**(2), 153–160 (2003). doi:10.1023/A:1022904124348
22. Haralick, R.M.: Digital step edges from zero crossing of second directional derivatives. IEEE Trans. Pattern Anal. Mach. Intell. **6**(1), 58–68 (1984). doi:10.1109/TPAMI.1984.4767475
23. Haralick, R.M., Sternberg, S.R., Zhuang, X.: Image analysis using mathematical morphology. IEEE Trans. Pattern Anal. Mach. Intell. **9**(4), 532–550 (1987). doi:10.1109/TPAMI.1987.4767941
24. Kang, H., Lee, S.: Shape-simplifying image abstraction. Comput. Graph. Forum **27**(7), 1773–1780 (2008). doi:10.1111/j.1467-8659.2008.01322.x
25. Kang, H., Lee, S., Chui, C.K.: Coherent line drawing. In: Proc. NPAR, pp. 43–50 (2007). doi:10.1145/1274871.1274878
26. Kang, H., Lee, S., Chui, C.K.: Flow-based image abstraction. IEEE Trans. Vis. Comput. Graph. **15**(1), 62–76 (2009). doi:10.1109/TVCG.2008.81
27. Kim, D., Son, M., Lee, Y., Kang, H., Lee, S.: Feature-guided image stippling. Comput. Graph. Forum **27**(4), 1209–1216 (2008). doi:10.1111/j.1467-8659.2008.01259.x

28. Kramer, H.P., Bruckner, J.B.: Iterations of a non-linear transformation for enhancement of digital images. Pattern Recognit. **7**(1–2), 53–58 (1975)
29. Kuwahara, M., Hachimura, K., Ehiu, S., Kinoshita, M.: Processing of ri-angiocardiographic images. In: Digital Processing of Biomedical Images, pp. 187–203. Plenum, New York (1976)
30. Kyprianidis, J.E.: Image and video abstraction by multi-scale anisotropic Kuwahara filtering. In: Proc. NPAR, pp. 55–64 (2011). doi:10.1145/2024676.2024686
31. Kyprianidis, J.E., Döllner, J.: Image abstraction by structure adaptive filtering. In: Proc. EG UK TPCG, pp. 51–58 (2008). doi:10.2312/LocalChapterEvents/TPCG/TPCG08/051-058
32. Kyprianidis, J.E., Döllner, J.: Real-time image abstraction by directed filtering. In: ShaderX7, pp. 285–302. Charles River Media, London (2009)
33. Kyprianidis, J.E., Kang, H.: Image and video abstraction by coherence-enhancing filtering. Comput. Graph. Forum **30**(2), 593–602 (2011). doi:10.1111/j.1467-8659.2011.01882.x
34. Kyprianidis, J.E., Kang, H., Döllner, J.: Image and video abstraction by anisotropic Kuwahara filtering. Comput. Graph. Forum **28**(7), 1955–1963 (2009). doi:10.1111/j.1467-8659.2009.01574.x
35. Kyprianidis, J.E., Kang, H., Döllner, J.: Anisotropic Kuwahara filtering on the GPU. In: GPUPro, pp. 247–264. AK Peters, Wellesley (2010)
36. Kyprianidis, J.E., Semmo, A., Kang, H., Döllner, J.: Anisotropic Kuwahara filtering with polynomial weighting functions. In: Proc. EG UK TPCG, pp. 25–30 (2010)
37. Lee, H., Seo, S., Ryoo, S., Yoon, K.: Directional texture transfer. In: Proc. NPAR, pp. 43–50 (2010). doi:10.1145/1809939.1809945
38. Maragos, P., Schafer, R.: Morphological filters—Part I: Their set-theoretic analysis and relations to linear shift-invariant filters. IEEE Trans. Acoust. Speech Signal Process. **35**(8), 1153–1169 (1987). doi:10.1109/TASSP.1987.1165259
39. Maragos, P., Schafer, R.: Morphological filters—Part II: Their relations to median, order-statistic, and stack filters. IEEE Trans. Acoust. Speech Signal Process. **35**(8), 1170–1184 (1987). doi:10.1109/TASSP.1987.1165254
40. Marr, D., Hildreth, R.C.: Theory of edge detection. Proc. R. Soc. Lond. B, Biol. Sci. **207**, 187–217 (1980)
41. Orzan, A., Bousseau, A., Barla, P., Thollot, J.: Structure-preserving manipulation of photographs. In: Proc. NPAR, pp. 103–110 (2007)
42. Osher, S., Rudin, L.I.: Feature-oriented image enhancement using shock filters. SIAM J. Numer. Anal. **27**(4), 919–940 (1990). doi:10.1137/0727053
43. Papari, G., Petkov, N.: Continuous glass patterns for painterly rendering. IEEE Trans. Image Process. **18**(3), 652–664 (2009). doi:10.1109/TIP.2008.2009800
44. Papari, G., Petkov, N., Campisi, P.: Artistic edge and corner enhancing smoothing. IEEE Trans. Image Process. **16**(10), 2449–2462 (2007). doi:10.1109/TIP.2007.903912
45. Paris, S., Kornprobst, P., Tumblin, J., Durand, F.: Bilateral filtering: theory and applications. Found. Trends Comput. Graph. Vis. **4**(1), 7–73 (2009). doi:10.1561/0600000020
46. Perona, P., Malik, J.: Scale-space and edge detection using anisotropic diffusion. IEEE Trans. Pattern Anal. Mach. Intell. **12**(7), 629–639 (1990). doi:10.1109/34.56205
47. Pham, T.Q., van Vliet, L.J.: Separable bilateral filtering for fast video preprocessing. In: Proc. ICME, pp. 454–457 (2005). doi:10.1109/ICME.2005.1521458
48. Porikli, F.: Constant time O(1) bilateral filtering. In: Proc. CVPR, pp. 1–8 (2008). doi:10.1109/CVPR.2008.4587843
49. Pratt, W.K.: Digital Image Processing, 3rd edn. Wiley, New York (2001). doi:10.1002/0471221325
50. Son, M., Lee, Y., Kang, H., Lee, S.: Structure grid for directional stippling. Graph. Models **73**(3), 74–87 (2011). doi:10.1016/j.gmod.2010.12.001
51. Sýkora, D., Buriánek, J., Žára, J.: Colorization of black-and-white cartoons. Image Vis. Comput. **23**(9), 767–782 (2005). doi:10.1016/j.imavis.2005.05.010
52. Tomasi, C., Manduchi, R.: Bilateral filtering for gray and color images. In: Proc. ICCV, pp. 839–846 (1998). doi:10.1109/ICCV.1998.710815

53. Torre, V., Poggio, T.A.: On edge detection. IEEE Trans. Pattern Anal. Mach. Intell. **8**(2), 147–163 (1986). doi:10.1109/TPAMI.1986.4767769
54. van den Boomgaard, R.: Decomposition of the Kuwahara–Nagao operator in terms of linear smoothing and morphological sharpening. In: Proc. ISMM, pp. 283–292. CSIRO, Collingwood (2002)
55. Weickert, J.: Anisotropic Diffusion in Image Processing. Teubner, Leipzig (1998)
56. Weickert, J.: Coherence-enhancing diffusion of colour images. Image Vis. Comput. **17**(3), 201–212 (1999)
57. Weickert, J.: Coherence-enhancing shock filters. In: DAGM-Symposium, pp. 1–8. Springer, Berlin (2003). doi:10.1007/978-3-540-45243-0_1
58. Wikipedia: Expressionism—Wikipedia, The Free Encyclopedia (2012)
59. Winnemöller, H.: XDoG: Advanced image stylization with eXtended difference-of-Gaussians. In: Proc. NPAR, pp. 147–155 (2011). doi:10.1145/2024676.2024700
60. Winnemöller, H., Olsen, S.C., Gooch, B.: Real-time video abstraction. In: Proc. SIGGRAPH, pp. 1221–1226 (2006). doi:10.1145/1141911.1142018
61. Winnemöller, H., Kyprianidis, J.E., Olsen, S.C.: XDoG: an extended difference-of-Gaussians compendium including advanced image stylization. Comput. Graph. **36**(6), 740–753 (2012). doi:10.1016/j.cag.2012.03.004
62. Wyszecki, G., Stiles, W.S.: Color Science: Concepts and Methods, Quantitative Data and Formulae. Wiley-Interscience, New York (1982)
63. Young, R.A.: The Gaussian derivative model for spatial vision: I. Retinal mechanisms. Spat. Vis. **2**(4), 273–293 (1987). doi:10.1163/156856887X00222

Chapter 6
NPR for Traditional Artistic Genres

Eugene Zhang

6.1 Introduction

Automatic stylization from images and videos has been one of the goals for non-photorealistic rendering (NPR) research since its inception. Such automatic techniques can enable its users, often amateurs, to *automatically stylize* photographs or video clips with the appearance of various traditional forms of arts, such as oil painting, watercolors (western and oriental), or hand-drawn sketches. In this chapter we review algorithms behind these techniques for the aforementioned art forms. Note that each of these algorithms is typically the aggregated work of several research papers. Instead of reviewing all these papers separately in an incremental fashion, we will describe the algorithm as a whole and cite all relevant research.

While the NPR algorithms are often highly dependent on the art form (or media) that they emulate, occasionally one NPR algorithm can be used to generate different art forms, such as oil painting and watercoloring. We will note this as we describe the algorithms.

6.2 Oil Painting

Oil painting is perhaps one of the most well-researched NPR media. In this chapter we review a number of topics such as rendering, brush stroke orientation generation, and multi-style rendering for images and videos.

E. Zhang (✉)
School of Electrical Engineering and Computer Science, Oregon State University, 2111 Kelley Engineering Center, Corvallis, OR 97331, USA
e-mail: zhange@eecs.oregonstate.edu

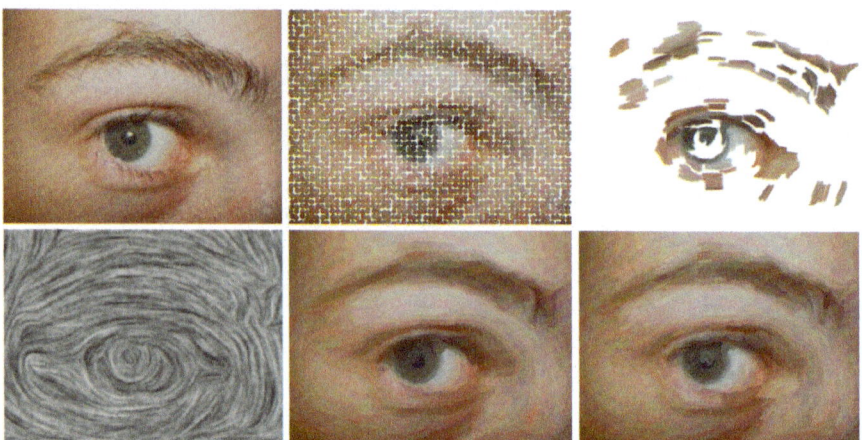

Fig. 6.1 The work flow of Impressionism in the Kayaga et al. [13] system: given the input image (*upper-left*), the edge field is extracted (*lower-left*) and a set of brush stroke seeds (disks) is placed on a jittered 2D grid (*upper-middle*). Advection of the seed image along the field (*lower-left*) results in the first layer rendering (*lower-middle*). From here, places where the painting result contains a large error are detected and an additional layer of brush strokes is generated (*upper-right*), which when composed with the first layer results in the final rendering (*lower-right*)

6.2.1 Rendering

There are a number of approaches to painterly rendering, including *procedural techniques* and *implicit methods*. Procedural techniques are based on explicitly constructing the rendering primitives (brush strokes). Implicit methods do not construct strokes explicitly. Instead, they are based on image processing techniques such as filtering and image composition. Chapter 2 provides an excellent survey on the topic of stroke-based method, while Chap. 5 reviews artistic filters. In this chapter we will focus on implicit methods based on image advection and composition.

Cabral and Leedom [4] make use of line integral convolution to generate vector field visualization. The idea is to take a noise texture and perform iterative image advection and composition. Kagaya et al. [13] adapt this idea to perform high-quality, interactive painterly rendering. We review this framework next.

Given an input image I (see Fig. 6.1 (upper-left)), a set of user-specified style parameters, and an orientation field which can be designed by the user or automatically generated (Fig. 6.1 (lower-left); details see Sect. 6.2.2), the system generates an image of seeds (Fig. 6.1 (upper-middle)). Each seed is a disk whose color is given by the color at the center pixel of the disk from the input image. The seed image is then advected according to the orientation field, which results in a second image in which the disks are displaced and possibly deformed. The displaced seed image is then composited with the original seed image through weighted average. Figure 6.2 illustrates this process with a seed of four disks (a). After one round of image advection and composition, the resulting image (Fig. 6.2(b)) consists of four relatively short brush strokes. The process can be repeated to generate even

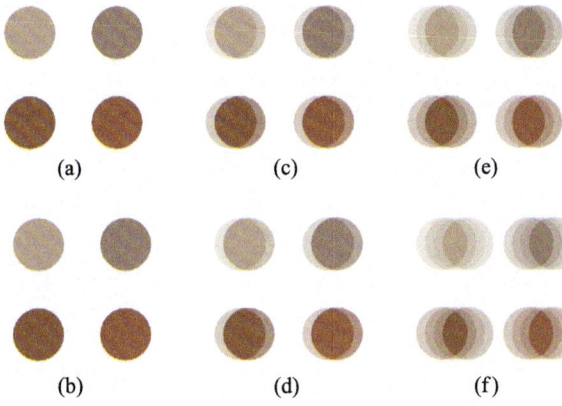

Fig. 6.2 This figure illustrates the process of an implicit renderer [13] which advects a source image (**a**) in the direction of an underlying vector field: (**b**) the image in (**a**) is warped based on V, (**c**) is obtained by combining (**a**) and (**b**), (**d**) the image in (**c**) is again warped according to V, (**e**) is obtained by combining (**a**) and (**d**), and (**f**) is obtained from (**e**) by two more iterations of warping and blending

longer brush strokes (Fig. 6.2(c)). After a number of iterations (based on the desired brush stroke length), the resulting image has the painterly appearance (Fig. 6.1 (lower-middle)). When multiple layers are used, the seed map for the second layer is generated based on the algorithm of Hertzmann [10], which, through the same image advection and composition process, can lead to the painting at the next layer (Fig. 6.1 (upper-right)). Finally, images from different layers are composited in such a way that the color of a pixel in the final rendering is taken from the corresponding pixel from the highest layer for which the pixel is *not* in the background (Fig. 6.1 (lower-right)).

When compositing the seed map with its displacement under the orientation field, it is difficult to decide consistently which color to use, since the same pixel may be covered by two different brush strokes. Randomly making a decision can lead to color bleeding. Since the strokes are not explicitly constructed and it is difficult to maintain a brush stroke ID map, Kayaga et al. [13] use a pre-defined color order to decide which brush is on top. In their implementation they first compare the color intensity, and in case of a tie compare the green channel, the red channel, and finally the blue channel. Experimenting with different color orders and understanding their impact on the painterly results can be an interesting future research topic.

6.2.2 Brush Stroke Orientation: Representation and Generation

In many oil painting styles, one can observe long and curved brush strokes. Who, after seeing van Gogh's masterpiece titled "Starry Night", can forget the sense of restlessness (or liveliness) conveyed by brush strokes that seem to be following a wave in the otherwise motionless dark sky? If and when carefully designed, the underlying wave field, which orients the brush strokes and specifies their trajectories, can convey ideas, stylization, and even illusions (for example the dark sky that seems to move like the waves).

Most existing painterly rendering algorithms focus on controlling aspects of brush strokes such as color, texture, location, spacing, transparency, and width.

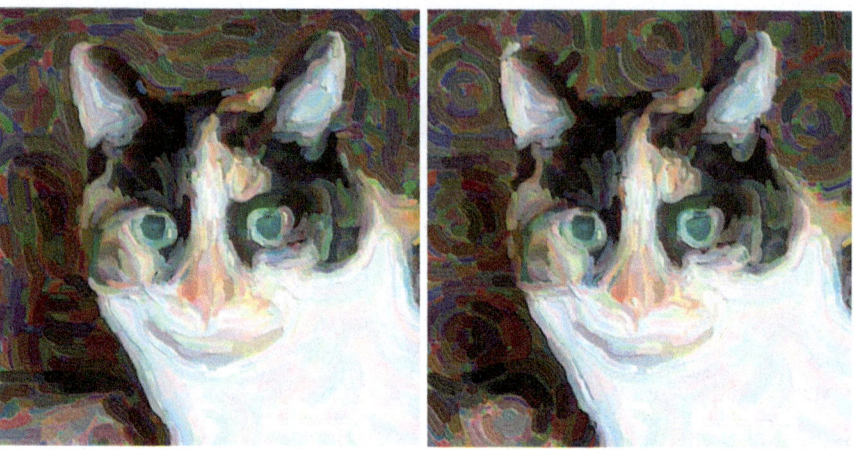

Fig. 6.3 Numeric estimation of the edges in the image leads to rather noisy directions in the background due to relatively uniform color (*left*). Through tensor field design, a number of circular patterns are added to give the background more attention. Image courtesy of [12] © 2011 IEEE

While many of them make use of a directional field to guide brush stroke orientations, the directional field is completely determined from the input image by first extracting the strongest edges in the image and then propagating the edge directions to the rest of the canvas. This treatment can alleviate *color bleeding*, which refers to the phenomenon in which a brush stroke covering two objects of different colors causes the color of one object to be spilled onto the other. However, it is impossible with this approach to create the kind of illusory motion in the "Starry Night" from a photo of a dark sky.

Zhang et al. [20, 21] introduce the problem of *field design*, in which a user specifies the directional field that orients the brush strokes to produce desired visual effects, such as circular patterns in an otherwise featureless background; making the background appear more lively (Fig. 6.3).

Zhang et al. also note the link between a number of visual artifacts in painterly rendering and the *singularities* in the underlying field and propose means to either remove a pair of singularities or move a singularity to a more desirable (perhaps less visible) location. Figure 6.4 provides an example in which by moving a singularity in the underlying field, the artifact in Mona Lisa's forehead was removed.

Initially, Zhang et al. [20] follow the popular approach of treating the directional field as a vector field. Their singularity editing operations (removal and movement) are based on well-known results from Dynamical Systems, such as the Poincaré index and Conley index theory [15]. However, it is difficult to start by modifying a given field, such as the one estimated from the input image using the Sobel filter. This leads to the realization that representing brush stroke orientations as a vector field is inappropriate. Consider an image in which a rectangle in black is drawn over a white canvas (Fig. 6.5: left). Most existing edge detection methods first extract the strong edges, which are the outlines of the black region. Next, the *image gradient* is

Fig. 6.4 Singularities in the tensor field (*left*: *colored dots*) can lead to artifacts in the rendering, such as the one on the left side Mona Lisa's forehead. Through topological editing operations, the singularity that caused the artifact (*yellow dot*) is moved to the corner of her left eye, leading to a more natural result. This figure is a courtesy of [21], © 2007 IEEE

extracted for each pixel on the edges. The image gradient for a pixel is defined as:

$$g(\mathbf{p}) = \left(\frac{\partial I}{\partial X} \quad \frac{\partial I}{\partial Y} \right) \quad (6.1)$$

in which $I = \sqrt{R^2(\mathbf{p}) + G^2(\mathbf{p}) + B^2(\mathbf{p})}$ is the intensity of the pixel $\mathbf{p}$. Note that other functions such as the luminance $0.3R(\mathbf{p}) + 0.59G(\mathbf{p}) + 0.11B(\mathbf{p})$ can be used in place of I. For the example in Fig. 6.5 (left), the image gradient on the left and right sides of the black region is pointing to the opposite side (red arrows). To obtain the directions along the edges, the image gradient is turned counterclockwise by $\frac{\pi}{2}$ everywhere along the edges. This leads to the edge vectors pointing upward along the left side and downward along the right side (green arrows in Fig. 6.5 (middle).

Fig. 6.5 This figure illustrates the need to model brush stroke orientations as line fields (bidirectional) instead of vector fields

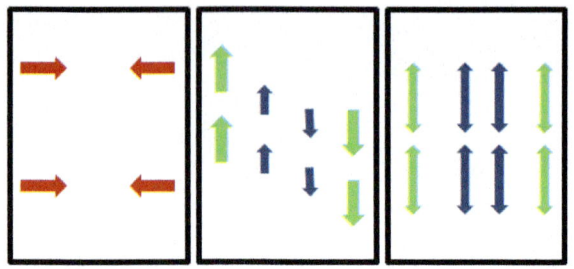

While this is *not* a problem for brush strokes along the silhouette (when tracing a brush stroke one always traces in the forward and backward directions), propagating these directions to the white pixels leads to a line of singularities in the middle of the box (Fig. 6.5 (middle): blue arrows). This is because when extrapolating the directions, arrows in opposite directions cancel each other. This leads to noisy stroke orientations, which can be distracting in the rendered result.

Zhang et al. [21] propose to guide stroke orientations with a *line field*, which associates each pixel with two vectors that point in opposite directions. Mathematically, this can be realized using 2×2 traceless, symmetric tensors. A 2×2 tensor t is a matrix $t = t_{ij}$. It is symmetric if $t_{12} = t_{21}$. It is traceless if $t_{11} + t_{22} = 0$. The set of traceless, symmetric 2×2 tensors can be parameterized as follows:

$$\rho \begin{pmatrix} \cos 2\theta & \sin 2\theta \\ \sin 2\theta & -\cos 2\theta \end{pmatrix} \quad (6.2)$$

where $\rho \geq 0$ is the magnitude of the tensor and $\theta \in [0, \pi)$ is the angle between the *major eigenvector* and the X-axis. A major eigenvector is the eigenvector corresponding to the larger eigenvalue of the matrix. When $\rho = 0$ the matrix has two equal eigenvalues, and their respective eigenvectors cannot be differentiated. This is referred to as a *degenerate tensor*. Note that when v is a major eigenvector, so is $-v$. This ambiguity in the eigenvectors makes tensors an ideal representation for bidirectional vectors that orient the brush strokes. Basically, we wish to construct a tensor field from the image gradient g (Eq. (6.1)) such that the major eigenvectors in the tensor field are perpendicular to g wherever g is not zero.

A tensor field T is a continuous tensor-valued function. A point (pixel) $\mathbf{p}$ is a *singularity* if $T(\mathbf{p}) = 0$. To enforce the previous condition, we need that

$$T(\mathbf{p}) = |g(\mathbf{p})| \begin{pmatrix} \cos 2\theta(\mathbf{p}) & \sin 2\theta(\mathbf{p}) \\ \sin 2\theta(\mathbf{p}) & -\cos 2\theta(\mathbf{p}) \end{pmatrix} \quad (6.3)$$

where $|g(\mathbf{p})|$ and $\theta(\mathbf{p}) - \frac{\pi}{2}$ are the length and the angle of $g(\mathbf{p})$, respectively. This representation has led to smoother directional fields for brush strokes (Fig. 6.6). The left column is based on the vector representation, while the right is based on the tensor representation. Notice that the field is smoother and more natural in the right.

Numerical estimation of the edges from the image, even under the tensor representation, can still have undesirable artifacts due to self-collision in the tensor field. Such self-collisions can be characterized by the singularities in the tensor field

Fig. 6.6 Treating the brush stroke orientations as a tensor field (*right*) leads to smoother results than as a vector field (*left*)

(Fig. 6.4, left). A singularity in the tensor field can be characterized by its *index* which must be a multiple of $\pm\frac{1}{2}$. The first-order singularities are: wedges (with a $\frac{1}{2}$ index), and trisectors (with a $-\frac{1}{2}$ index). In Fig. 6.4 the singularities are colored in yellow if they are wedges and blue if they are trisectors. Notice that the tensor pattern near a wedge is reminiscent of a *U-turn*, while near a trisector it is similar to that a *three-point turn*. Not incidentally, U-turns and three-point turns are the two most fundamental ways to reverse driving directions. (Driving backward is not considered.) Such patterns are impossible in vector fields, which again highlights the fact that tensor fields are more flexible in modeling phenomena in which an orientation is given without a clear forward direction.

Delmarcello and Hesselink show that the total index of a tensor field on a manifold is equal to the *Euler characteristic* of the manifold [9]. Consequently, in order to remove a singularity from the field, another singularity with the opposite tensor index must be removed simultaneously in order to maintain the total tensor index. In other words, a wedge and a trisector must be removed together. This leads to the singularity pair cancellation operation [20, 21]. Alternatively, one can move a singularity to a more desirable location (singularity movement). Zhang et al. [20] provide efficient implementations of singularity pair cancellation and movement for vector fields based on Conley index theory from Dynamical Systems [15], which they adapt to the same topological editing operations for tensor fields based on a bijective map between the set of traceless, symmetric matrices and vectors [21]. For details on this we refer the readers to their work.

Another important use of tensor field design, is to elaborate upon the input image. For example, interesting circular patterns may be added to the painting by modifying the underlying brush stroke orientation field through tensor field design (Fig. 6.3).

6.2.3 Multi-style Painterly Rendering

To date most research in painterly rendering has focused on emulating a particular painting style, such as *Pointillism*, *Impressionism* and *Expressionism*. Little attention has been given to the purpose (semantics) of these styles. For example, what about impressionism that can capture our attention? Kagaya et al. [13] introduce the notion of *multi-style painterly rendering*, in which different parts of the input image are stylized differently, with some artistic goals such as emphasizing or deemphasizing an object, increasing or decreasing contrast between neighboring objects (Fig. 6.7), etc.

In addition, style parameters can also change between frames in a video, leading to a change in emphasis in the objects in the video and the effect of *Rack focus* (Fig. 6.8 (top)). Style parameters can also be changed to create a stress-to-calm effect (Fig. 6.8 (bottom)). These are just some examples of space-time-varying style parameters in painterly rendering.

In the system of [13], the user can take an input image, perform manual segmentation, and then assign style parameters such as brush stroke color, width, length, transparency, and orientation to some objects in the scene. Note that the orientation can be generated automatically or based on tensor field design [21]. Some predefined combinations of style parameters can also be used to reduce the amount of work by the user. Objects that do not receive style assignment will get its style parameters through a process in which style parameters from assigned regions (objects) are propagated to the unsigned regions through the so-called heat diffusion process.

For video processing, the user first extracts a temporally coherent segmentation, and then assigns style parameters to some objects in a set of key frames. We refer to these objects as *assigned objects*, while objects that are not given any style assignment are *unassigned objects*. To ensure that every object in every frame eventually receives a style assignment, Kagaya et al. [13] make use of a two-stage pipeline. In the first stage, the style parameters of an assigned object in a non-key frame are ob-

Fig. 6.7 A comparison between single style (*lower-left*) and multi-style (*lower-right*) rendering for input image of a flower (*upper-left*). Notice that in the multi-style rendering, the stamens are given fine details, the leaves are deemphasized, and the contrast between three regions are made more pronounced

tained by interpolating the style parameters from the proceeding and succeeding key frames for the object. If the non-key frame does not have a proceeding key frame, then its style parameters will be identical to that of its succeeding frame. A similar treatment is made for non-key frames that do not have a succeeding key frame. Note that the proceeding and succeeding key frames are object-dependent. Once all the assigned objects have their styles determined throughout the video, the unassigned objects receive their style parameters in a per-frame fashion. That is, for each frame, the same heat diffusion process described for image style propagation is used.

In addition, optical flows are used to propagate brush strokes from one frame to the next. Moreover, brush stroke orientations are propagated through the optical flow. We refer the reader to [13] for implementation details of their system. Note

Fig. 6.8 *Top*: by using different style parameters on different people (a mother and her daughter) and varying them over time, the effect of Rack focus can be achieved. *Bottom*: by modifying the style parameters in the scene, a stress-to-calm effect can be created

that the ability to perform high-quality image and video segmentation is key to the success of any multi-style rendering system.

6.3 Watercolorization

Watercolor is another form of traditional art that has captured the imaginations of generations around the world. Two styles of watercolors, i.e., oriental and western, are perhaps the most practiced watercolorization. The physical process behind both styles of watercolorization is rather similar. For example, water-soluble pigments of various degrees of dryness and colors are applied onto the paper through hairy brushes. As the water flows on the surface of the paper, the pigment is transported, diluted, and eventually deposited on the paper. In contrast, oil painting is based on a rather different physical process, making use of pigments and a canvas that have rather different physical properties than the watercolor pigments and the paper, respectively. These differences lead to rather different physical appearances between watercolor and oil painting, such as the lighting effects and transparency of the strokes.

Next we will review work on watercolorization by the NPR community.

6.3.1 Physically-Driven Models

One of the major approaches to computer-generated watercolors is by physically emulating the process in which watercolor paintings are generated. This includes both natural processes, such as how water flows, transports pigments on the surface of the paper, and is absorbed by the paper, as well as the processes that have human involvement, such as the ways in which brushes are applied on the paper. Chapter 2 provide details on how brushes are modeled. In the remainder of this section we will focus on how the interaction among water, pigments, and paper is simulated.

There are a number of watercolor effects that are rather unique to watercolor, such as the following [7]:

1. Dry-brush effect: A nearly dry-brush is applied at a proper grazing angle which causes the paint to be only applied to the raised area of the paper.
2. *Edge darkening*: When applying a wet-to-dry brush stroke, the pigments are confined to the interior of the stroke due to the paper and surface tension of the water. Gradually the pigments move towards the boundary of the stroke, causing a darkening edge.
3. *Backruns*: When water moves into a region of wet paint, some pigment will be carried by the water, leading to complex patterns within a stroke.
4. *Granulation and separation of pigments*: The granulation of pigments leads to a grainy texture over the paper.
5. *Flow patterns*: In a wet-in-wet situation, the water flows freely over the surface of the paper.
6. *Glazing*: A thin, pale layer of watercolor is added over existing and already dried layers of watercolor.

Among these effects, glazing is perhaps the most differentiating effect between watercolor painting and painting in other media, such as oil. In watercolor, the mixture of pigments of different colors is optical, instead of physical, leading to a rather luminous effect that is unique to watercolor painting.

To simulate these effects, Curtis et al. [7] devise a three-layer model: the shallow-water layer, the pigment-deposition layer, and the capillary layer, in the order of top to bottom. The water carrying pigments flows on the shallow-water layer. As the water dries up, the pigment is deposited in the pigment-deposition layer. The paper absorbed by the paper flows in the capillary layer, which is used only to model the backrun effect.

In the shallow-water layer, a fluid simulation based on the *shallow-water model* is performed for every newly applied brush stroke to track the movement of the

Fig. 6.9 Computer-generated hatching based on a photo. This figure is a courtesy of [7], © 1997 ACM

water as well as the pigments. A shallow-water model, not to be confused with the shallow-water layer or the fluid simulation therein, is essentially a 2D fluid dynamics model which applies to the case when the largest depth of the waterflow is relatively small compared to the area where the flow covers.

The quantities involved in the fluid simulation in the shallow-water layer include the wet-area mask (whether the point is wet or dry), the 2D velocity and pressure of the water, the concentration of each pigment in the paper, the slope of the rough paper, and the viscosity of the water. Pigments can be transferred within the shallow-water layer.

Between the shallow-water layer and the pigment-deposition layer, pigments can be absorbed by or desorbed from the pigment-deposition layer. The rates of absorption and desorption, which are mutually different, are impacted by the density of and the straining power of the pigments.

Most of the effects such as dry-brush, edge darkening, granulation, flow patterns, and glazing can be achieved with just the shallow-water layer and the pigment-deposition layer. For the backrun effect, which occurs in damp regions where the dominant behavior is the capillary effect, a simulation is run between the shallow-water layer and the capillary layer to produce the desired effect.

The final rendering is produced based on the amount of pigments in the pigment-deposition layer. Curtis et al. [7] assign optical properties to the pigments, including how they interact when co-existing, and make use of the Kubelka–Munk model. Figure 6.9 demonstrates the effectiveness of watercolor simulation with an input image of fruits.

Fig. 6.10 Watercolor painting produced using the method of Bousseau et al. [2]. Copyright of ACM

6.3.2 Other Approaches

Many of the techniques for western watercolorization can be adapted to oriental paintings in terms of the appearance of the strokes. Chu and Tai [5] develop a model for brushes that is better suited for oriental painting. They later [6] describe a physically-motivated framework for the creation of oriental painting. Their framework is similar in spirit to that of Curtis et al. [7]. Xu et al. [19] provide a unified framework for both western and oriental watercolors which again is based on fluid simulation involving water, pigments, and binding materials.

There have been other techniques for creating the appearance of watercolors that are less dependent on physical simulation.

Bousseau et al. [2] first create an abstraction of the image using segmentation [8] (Chap. 7). Each region is assigned a color that best approximates the colors in the region (typically one or multiple objects). This abstracted image is then combined with a texture that provides various watercolor effects, such as the turbulence of the flow, the dispersion of the pigments, and the variation in the paper. This leads to high-quality watercolor effects without performing a computationally expensive fluid simulation (see Fig. 6.10). Bousseau et al. [2, 3] also extend this method to achieve temporally coherent video abstraction and watercolorization. Many of these details can be found in Chap. 13.

Kagaya et al. [13] use a similar approach. However, instead of generating an abstraction of the input image, they create the "colorist wash" style [10] of the input. A colorist wash painting allows each brush stroke to be transparent. (See Chap. 1 for details.)

Fig. 6.11 Example oriental watercolor paintings from user provided contours based on some input images or calligraphy. This figure is a courtesy of [18], © 2010 ACM

6.3.3 Oriental Watercolors

The techniques reviewed are mostly designed to simulate western watercolor paintings.

Oriental painting, also known as Chinese watercolor in China and sumi-e in Japan, is another popular medium that has received much attention from the NPR community. In many ways oriental painting is similar to western watercolor except for the differences in the physical properties of the paper, pigments, and brushes. Another major difference is that many traditional oriental paintings are rather abstract, with only a few strokes to illustrate the main objects in the drawing and are used for calligraphy, whereas in western watercolors the canvas is typically filled with ink from brush strokes. There is also a difference in how brushes are applied as well as how colors are used, leading to a rather different look in the results.

Many of the techniques for western watercolorization can be adapted to oriental paintings in terms of the appearance of the strokes. Chu and Tai [5] develop a model for brushes that is better suited for oriental painting. They later [6] describe a physically-motivated framework for the creation of oriental painting. Their framework is similar in spirit to that of Curtis et al. [7]. Xu et al. [19] provide a unified framework for both western and oriental watercolors which again is based on fluid simulation involving water, pigments, and binding materials.

For oriental painting, it is important to be able to abstract an image with a few strokes which is essential in simulating classical oriental painting (see Fig. 6.11). Xie et al. [18] allow the user to draw a few rough strokes of the input photo that capture the contours of the main objects in the image. Their algorithm then automatically determines the optimal trajectory for these contours and produces strokes based on the optimal trajectories (Fig. 6.11).

6.4 Line Drawing

Pen-and-ink drawing is also a well-researched topic in NPR. In a typical setting, a set of geometric primitives such as points (stipples) and lines (hatches) are used to illustrate objects (see Chap. 3 and Chap. 4 for more details). While these primitives can be in different colors, pen-and-ink drawings are usually monochromatic

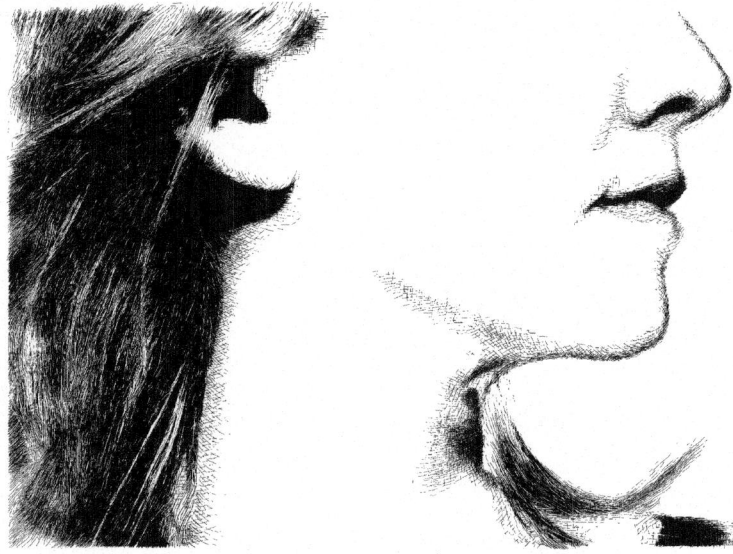

Fig. 6.12 Computer-generated hatching based on a photo. This figure is a courtesy of [17], © 1997 ACM

(typically black) and they are placed against a background (typically white). The locations and densities of these primitives are used to outline the shapes, present the main features in the objects, and convey the shading. In the case of line primitives, the directions of lines can also be used to illustrate geometric features in the shape, such as ridges and valleys. Given the close connection between stippling and halftoning, we will not review computer-based stippling techniques in this chapter and instead focus on line drawings, i.e., the use of straight and curved lines to stylize an image or depict a 3D object.

6.4.1 Streamline Placement

We first review existing approaches to line drawing based on an input image (Fig. 6.12). Like painterly rendering algorithms [10, 13], the edges in the image are extracted and used to generate an orientation field. This field is used to determine the trajectory (shape) of each hatch. Notice that in this sense hatching can be considered as a painting style, in which all the strokes are thin (one pixel wide) and of the same color (black). The latter (all strokes are black) dictates that sufficient space must be given between nearby strokes, or they will not be distinguishable. In addition, due to the loss of color, effects such as shadows and highlights must be reflected in other visual cues. Both issues are addressed using the density (or spacing) of strokes in that brighter regions in the input image receive fewer strokes and darker regions receive more strokes. Inside a region where the brightness in the input image is rather uniform, the spacing between the strokes should also be nearly even. When the minimal spacing in a region is still insufficient to reflect the tone of the region, cross-hatches are introduced, which uses two families of mutually perpendicular strokes to increase the darkness of the region without decreasing the spacing between strokes.

One approach is to compute a set of evenly-spaced streamlines that follow the orientation field. Jobard and Lefer [12] generate a set of evenly-spaced streamlines given a vector field V by placing one streamline at a time. Given the seed of a new streamline, it is tested against all existing streamlines to see whether it is closer to any of them than the spacing requirement. The seed survives only if it passes this test. Then the tracing of the streamline starts from the seed, typically based on numerical methods such as Runge–Kutta. That is, given the current end point of the streamline $\mathbf{p}$, a line segment from $\mathbf{p}$ to $\mathbf{p} + V(\mathbf{p}) * dt$ is added to the streamline. When $dt > 0$ is sufficiently small, the line segment approximates the trajectory at $\mathbf{p}$. Note that in this scheme a streamline (hatch) is represented as a polyline. Let $\mathbf{p}'$ be the new end point. Streamline tracing stops when one of the following criteria is met:

1. $\mathbf{p}'$ is outside the domain.
2. $\mathbf{p}'$ is closer to an existing streamline than the spacing threshold.
3. $\mathbf{p}'$ is closer to a singularity (source, sink, saddle) than a user-specified distance.
4. $\mathbf{p}'$ is closer to existing segments of the same streamline than the spacing threshold, i.e., a loop has been found.

In addition, a maximal length is often imposed on each streamline to ensure that all the streamlines have comparable length.

The same framework can be adapted to tracing a tensor field [1, 21], which, as described earlier, is a more appropriate representation for edges in the image. To build cross-hatching, two families of even-spaced hatches are generated, following the major and minor eigenvectors of the tensor field, respectively. A final rendering can be generated based on the process described in Fig. 6.13. These two families of hatches (streamlines) will be used to generate two images, one following the major eigenvector field, and the other the minor eigenvector field. We refer to these two images as I_1 and I_2, respectively. In addition, an image I_3 based on the outlines of objects in the original image is also generated. Furthermore, a pixel with a value of 1 is white and a value of 0 is black. These three images will then be composited into a single image as follows:

$$I(p) = \begin{cases} 0 & \text{if } I_3(p) = 0 \\ 1 & \text{if in highlight} \\ min(I_1(p), I_2(p)) & \text{if in shadow} \\ I_2(p) & \text{otherwise} \end{cases} \quad (6.4)$$

Notice that in the above one can also choose to always use $I_1(p)$ for single-hatched regions. Another means of generating I_1 and I_2 is to first project the principal directions onto the image plane and trace hyperstreamlines in the image plane. This alternative is view-dependent but typically is fast enough for interactive applications. In contrast, the object-based approach requires much time for pre-processing but is then ready for interactive display, except when the resolution is changed.

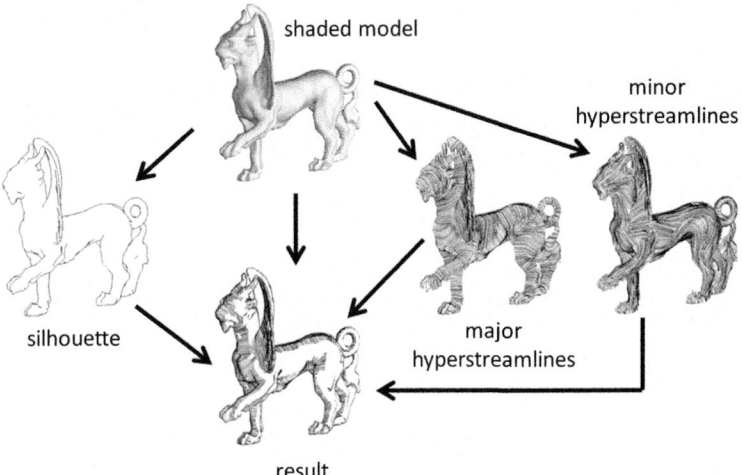

Fig. 6.13 The process of generating a hatch-based drawing from an input image, possibly a rendered 3D model

6.4.1.1 Textures

Generating hatching from evenly-spaced streamlines is computationally expensive. An alternative approach is to place textures that have the appearance of strokes of various level of densities as well as single-hatching and cross-hatching patterns [14]. These textures are then placed at the desired locations on the canvas in the appropriate orientations. This approach is fast, high-quality, and robust against scale variations in the objects in the original image. However, it is important to deal with the discontinuity in the places where patches with different tone or orientation overlap. Fortunately the hatch textures are typically of high frequency. When blended, it is not as easy to see the discontinuity as with rather low-frequency signals.

The original field can be extracted from the image or generated through user design.

6.4.2 Orientation Field Representation for Hatching

Finally, proper representation of hatch orientations is important. Traditionally hatch orientations are treated as the principal directions of the curvature tensor. Hertzmann and Zorin [11] point out that a more proper representation of hatch representation are cross fields, i.e., by not distinguishing between the major and minor principal curvature directions. This has led to the notion of N-way rotational symmetries, where a vector, line, or cross correspond to 1-, 2-, and 4-way rotational symmetries. Cross fields can be used to model corners of a cube with a first-order *singularity*, while such corners cannot be modeled by a tensor field (equivalent to a line field). This leads to smoother hatching directions during initial generation and subsequently modification [14] (Fig. 6.14).

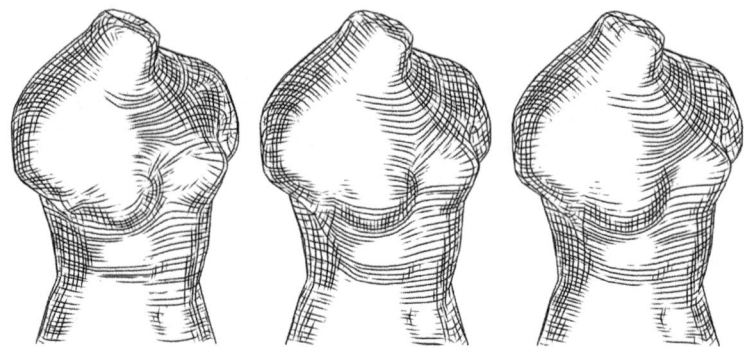

Fig. 6.14 Difference between different hatching orientation representations: (*left*) line field, and (*middle*) cross field. Notice that the features are better represented by the cross representation. Such a representation also enables rotational symmetry field editing, which leads to more natural result (*right*). This figure is a courtesy of [16], © 2007 ACM

6.5 Conclusions

In this chapter we review some existing work in simulating traditional art genres, such as oil painting, watercolorization, oriental painting, as well as hatching. We also discuss some relatively recent development such as orientation field representation as well as multi-style rendering.

For future work, we believe it is important to consider other forms of art that have not received much attention, such as African art and ceramics painting. There are also more modern styles of painting that we are not able to simulate. Understanding the semantics of art, such as the purpose of each style in terms of delivering information or recording emotions and moods, could be another fruitful future research direction.

References

1. Alliez, P., Cohen-Steiner, D., Devillers, O., Lévy, B., Desbrun, M.: Anisotropic polygonal remeshing. ACM Trans. Graph. **22**(3), 485–493 (2003)
2. Bousseau, A., Kaplan, M., Thollot, J., Sillion, F.X.: Interactive watercolor rendering with temporal coherence and abstraction. In: NPAR'06: Proceedings of the 4th International Symposium on Non-photorealistic Animation and Rendering, pp. 141–149 (2006)
3. Bousseau, A., Neyret, F., Thollot, J., Salesin, D.: Video watercolorization using bidirectional texture advection. In: SIGGRAPH'07: ACM SIGGRAPH 2007 Papers, p. 104 (2007)
4. Cabral, B., Leedom, L.C.: Imaging vector fields using line integral convolution. In: SIGGRAPH'93: Proceedings of the 20th Annual Conference on Computer Graphics and Interactive Techniques, pp. 263–270 (1993)
5. Chu, N.S.H., Tai, C.L.: Real-time painting with an expressive virtual Chinese brush. IEEE Comput. Graph. Appl. **24**(5), 76–85 (2004). doi:10.1109/MCG.2004.37
6. Chu, N.S.H., Tai, C.L.: MoXi: real-time ink dispersion in absorbent paper. In: ACM SIGGRAPH 2005 Papers, SIGGRAPH'05, pp. 504–511 (2005). doi:10.1145/1186822.1073221

7. Curtis, C.J., Anderson, S.E., Seims, J.E., Fleischer, K.W., Salesin, D.H.: Computer-generated watercolor. In: Proceedings of the 24th Annual Conference on Computer Graphics and Interactive Techniques, pp. 421–430 (1997). doi:10.1145/258734.258896
8. DeCarlo, D., Santella, A.: Stylization and abstraction of photographs. In: Proceedings of the 29th Annual Conference on Computer Graphics and Interactive Techniques, pp. 769–776 (2002). doi:10.1145/566570.566650
9. Delmarcelle, T., Hesselink, L.: Visualizing second-order tensor fields with hyperstream lines. IEEE Comput. Graph. Appl. **13**(4), 25–33 (1993)
10. Hertzmann, A.: Painterly rendering with curved brush strokes of multiple sizes. In: SIGGRAPH'98: Proceedings of the 25th Annual Conference on Computer Graphics and Interactive Techniques, pp. 453–460 (1998)
11. Hertzmann, A., Zorin, D.: Illustrating smooth surfaces. In: SIGGRAPH'00: Proceedings of the 27th Annual Conference on Computer Graphics and Interactive Techniques, pp. 517–526 (2000)
12. Jobard, B., Lefer, W.: Creating evenly-spaced streamlines of arbitrary density. In: Proc. of 8th Eurographics Workshop on Visualization in Scientific Computing, pp. 45–55 (1997)
13. Kagaya, M., Brendel, W., Deng, Q., Kesterson, T., Todorovic, S., Neill, P.J., Zhang, E.: Video painting with space-time-varying style parameters. IEEE Trans. Vis. Comput. Graph. **17**, 74–87 (2011)
14. Markosian, L., Kowalski, M.A., Goldstein, D., Trychin, S.J., Hughes, J.F., Bourdev, L.D.: Real-time nonphotorealistic rendering. In: Proceedings of the 24th Annual Conference on Computer Graphics and Interactive Techniques. SIGGRAPH '97, pp. 415–420. ACM/Addison-Wesley, New York (1997). ISBN 0-89791-896-7. doi:10.1145/258734.258894
15. Mischaikow, K., Mrozek, M.: Conley index. In: Handbook of Dynamical Systems, vol. 2, pp. 393–460. North-Holland, Amsterdam (2002)
16. Palacios, J., Zhang, E.: Rotational symmetry field design on surfaces. ACM Trans. Graph. **26**(3), 55 (2007)
17. Salisbury, M.P., Wong, M.T., Hughes, J.F., Salesin, D.H.: Orientable textures for image-based pen-and-ink illustration. In: Proceedings of the 24th Annual Conference on Computer Graphics and Interactive Techniques, pp. 401–406 (1997). doi:10.1145/258734.258890
18. Xie, N., Laga, H., Saito, S., Nakajima, M.: IR2s: interactive real photo to Sumi-e. In: Proceedings of the 8th International Symposium on Non-Photorealistic Animation and Rendering, pp. 63–71 (2010). doi:10.1145/1809939.1809947
19. Xu, S., Tan, H., Jiao, X., Lau, F.C.M., Pan, Y.: A generic pigment model for digital painting. Comput. Graph. Forum **26**(3), 609–618 (2007). doi:10.1111/j.1467-8659.2007.01084.x
20. Zhang, E., Mischaikow, K., Turk, G.: Vector field design on surfaces. ACM Trans. Graph. **25**(4), 1294–1326 (2006)
21. Zhang, E., Hays, J., Turk, G.: Interactive tensor field design and visualization on surfaces. IEEE Trans. Vis. Comput. Graph. **13**(1), 94–107 (2007)

Part II
Stylization from Structure

Part II of this book focuses on techniques that rely upon parsing the visual structure from an image to synthesize artwork. In most cases this is performed using a region segmentation algorithm (either automated or user assisted), or in some cases by fitting a model (e.g. of facial structure) to the source image. We also cover techniques for stylizing this region based representation of images. A diverse variety of stylization and shading techniques are included; from gradient diffusion, to packing algorithms for packing regions with paths, tiles, and other rendering primitives.

Region-based color sketch, painting and stained glass rendering. All were produced using segmentation based rendering algorithms described in Chap. 7. Courtesy of Fang Wen

Chapter 7
Region-Based Abstraction

David Mould

7.1 Introduction

In this chapter we discuss image stylizations organized around regions. For the purposes of this chapter, *regions* are contiguous areas of the image plane, often corresponding to semantic divisions of the image content. Individual regions may be quite meaningless, however, with meaning emerging only from the overall arrangement of regions.

We will distinguish regions from *tiles*. Tile shapes usually have little relationship to the image content. Moreover, tiles are generally quite homogeneous in shape and size, while regions can be of arbitrary shape and size, usually varying widely. For example, segmentation of a photo of a forest might produce some tiny regions (corresponding to leaves and branches of the trees) as well as some very large regions (such as the featureless sky). We make an exception to this usage pattern when we discuss stained glass, where we retain the traditional use of the term "tile" to refer to the irregular regions in the glass.

One of the central challenges in image-based stylization is to make the stylized output match up with the viewers' understanding of the semantics of the original image. Image understanding is a vast and active field, but automatic image understanding is not presently possible, nor is it feasible to communicate a detailed understanding of an image from a human to a computer system.

Fortunately, impressive effects can be achieved with only a weak representation of the image semantics. One possible mechanism is *segmentation*, whereby the image is divided into regions in some fashion; the segments are distinct from each other in some way, whether based on color, texture content, or otherwise. Segmentation might be done automatically or with user guidance; semi-automatic methods such as GrabCut [28] are extremely powerful. Manual boundary tracing is less common but examples exist; SnakeToonz [2] uses active contours to assist in tracing boundaries

D. Mould (✉)
Carleton University, Ottawa, Canada
e-mail: mould@scs.carleton.ca

of a photograph, while iR2S [38] has users trace freehand over an input photograph to form region boundaries that are then transformed into strokes.

Automatic segmentation has many disadvantages, mainly arising from the lack of robustness and potentially low quality of segmentation. Automatic methods tend to be brittle: while they may work well for some images, other images can be problematic. The segmentations may not correspond with semantic features; for example, the shading of an object may cause its intensity to vary, producing oversegmentation. Shadows might cause spurious segments to appear. Some features may be inherently difficult to segment: for example, thin features such as tree branches are problematic for the graph cuts algorithm.

An example of an automatic segmentation is shown in Fig. 7.1. We used EDISON, a widely used mean-shift segmentation system, to obtain the middle image and applied morphological smoothing to obtain the rightmost image. Although the smoothing operation has tidied up some oversegmented regions (such as the car's wheel) by removing very small regions, it has also destroyed some structure (such as the palm tree on the upper right) by smoothing complex region boundaries and corners. The windows of the building have also been modified, largely for the worse, as corners have been smoothed and thin areas between windows have been absorbed into the window regions. Nonetheless, overall the filtered regions have simpler shapes, are more uniform in size, and in general are more suitable for subsequent stylization tasks than the original regions were.

Still, smoothing operations cannot in general repair poor initial segmentations of difficult areas such as texture; further, smoothing can be harmful when the actual region boundary is complex, such as that of the palm leaves. The difficulty of automatic segmentation, illustrated in part in the figure, has prompted use of manual intervention in many of the methods discussed in this chapter.

If automatic segmentation can be made to work, however, it is extremely useful. Human time is expensive compared to machine time, so anything we can do to reduce the burden on human artists is helpful. In applications such as animation, we do not want to require each frame to be manually segmented. In real-time applications, such as live video or computer games, we need to maintain a high frame rate and automation is the only possibility. (While none of the methods discussed in this chapter operate at interactive speeds, requiring human intervention would make high frame rates impossible even in principle.)

Many of the methods we discuss occupy a middle ground of *semi-automatic* segmentation, where the detailed work is done automatically but a human user guides the system towards better results, possibly by merging segments or by indicating with broad gestures which portions of the image belong to the foreground instead of the background. Techniques for productivity enhancement of manual segmentation have a long history in image processing, and we will mention a few custom approaches in the remainder of this chapter.

Once a segmentation has been constructed, it can be used in diverse ways to achieve a wide variety of artistic effects. Many historical artworks used segments explicitly, including stained glass, mosaics, and stencils. Others contain visible segments; woodcuts, tilings, and many modern styles of illustration have this property. Some historical artistic styles are reviewed in Sect. 7.1.2.

7 Region-Based Abstraction

Fig. 7.1 Segmentation and morphologically smoothed segments. Original image courtesy of Philip Greenspun

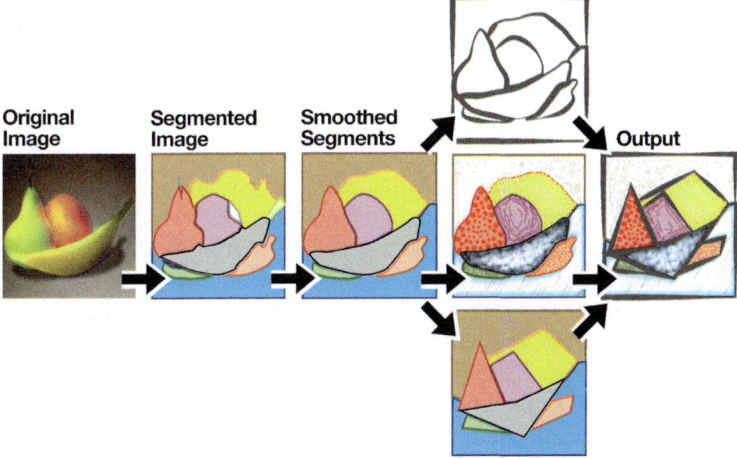

Fig. 7.2 Region-based stylization flowchart

Segmentation has been used as an element of stylization algorithms even where explicit segments are not a key feature of the intended output, as in some abstraction algorithms or some media simulations, such as watercolor. Alternatively, segmentation can be used as a precursor to a further stylization or optimization step, as in Jigsaw Image Mosaics [18] or maze creation [40]; the latter is discussed in detail in Chap. 9. We discuss the general process next.

7.1.1 Generic Process for Region-Based Stylization

A generic process for region-based stylization is depicted in Fig. 7.2. We begin with an input image or video sequence. The image is divided into regions by some means; this might be a fully automated segmentation algorithm, a semi-automatic user-guided segmentation, or a completely manual tracing process. Then, region boundaries are adjusted: perhaps simply smoothed, or perhaps more aggressively modified, with regions being shrunk, simplified, distorted, or abstracted entirely. The resulting regions serve as the basis for a rendering process. Region interiors are populated, perhaps directly with color, texture, and/or geometry, or with other primitives which are rendered separately. At the same time, region boundaries are rendered, again either directly or by populating the boundaries with strokes or other primitives and rendering them. Finally, the aggregate of regions, region boundaries, and ancillary primitives is consolidated into an output image.

For some algorithms, the main burden of the method is on the segmentation, with the region filling process done in a fairly simple way. In other cases, the segmentation is performed mainly to restrict the scope of local operators, and the majority of the work lies in the region filling process. We will see examples of both when we discuss specific algorithms from the research literature; a tour of the literature will form the second half of this chapter.

7.1.2 Regions in Art

Stylized rendering can use regions in an indirect way; for example, as a foundation for a painterly rendering or stippling algorithm. However, regions can also be used directly. Many historical artworks are assembled from discrete physical pieces, visible as regions in the final design.

Among the oldest surviving historical artworks are mosaics: designs made by arranging pieces of stone into abstract patterns or representational forms [12, 21]. *Opus tesselatum*, traditional mosaics where the stones are small cubes (tesserae), have been extensively studied in NPR, beginning with Hausner's work [16]. Hausner's used a manual segmentation of the input image, prohibiting individual tesserae from straddling region boundaries. *Opus vermiculatum*, in which rows of tesserae follow the boundaries of regions, is a historical style which depends even more heavily on an initial segmentation. Finally, *opus sectile* is a historical form which has been relatively little studied in NPR, but where the regions have still greater importance. Opus sectile involved substantially larger pieces of stone than the tesserae: the pieces were cut into representational shapes to form the design more directly. Opus tesselatum and opus sectile are shown in the top row of Fig. 7.3.

Stained glass is another ancient art form that uses physical regions to portray images. Stained glass windows both ancient and modern use large glass tiles, carefully shaped, to depict image content. Sometimes the glass is also painted, but sometimes not, as in the example shown in Fig. 7.3. Because of the need to make the tile arrangement correspond to the image structure, to date segmentation has been used in all image-based techniques for synthetic stained glass.

Many forms of illustration make use of distinct regions. Art nouveau, exemplified by a drawing by Alphonse Mucha in the middle right of Fig. 7.3, often displays uniformly or near-uniformly colored regions with distinct boundaries. Cartoons possess these characteristics as well, as do many styles of modern graphic art. Some historical image reproduction techniques, such as woodcuts or other types of printmaking,

7 Region-Based Abstraction

Fig. 7.3 Regions in art. *Above*: opus vermiculatum; opus sectile. *Middle*: stained glass; art nouveau illustration. *Below*: Ukiyo-e print; jack o'lantern. R. Berteig (medusa); Jim Linwood (angel); Steve Cadman (glass); Alphonse Mucha (advertisement); Danny Choo (ukiyo-e); William Warby (jack o'lantern)

produced images with solid-colored regions. Ukiyo-e, a Japanese artform based on woodblock printing, is depicted in the lower left of Fig. 7.3.

Stencils provide our last example. A stencil is a piece of solid material with carefully shaped holes cut through it so as to form an image. A stencil could be used as a shield through which paint is sprayed, leaving a design in the shape of the holes. Or, light can shine through the holes, as is the case in the illustrated jack o'lantern. For that matter, stencils are available for pumpkin carving, where the holes are copied from the flat stencil onto the pumpkin. Stencil creation algorithms must cope with the double problem of representing an image with few simple shapes plus the physical constraint that the different parts of the stencil must be linked together into a single piece.

7.1.3 Uses of Regions

We will distinguish between two main uses of regions. Regions can be a *source of structure* with which we can organize other primitives: for example, a segment could be a container for paint strokes, enhancing perceived structure by clipping strokes to region boundaries. Alternatively, regions can be *rendering primitives* in their own right. For example, the tiles in a medieval stained glass rendering are the primitives from which the overall image is made. Regions are rendered simply, and the shapes of regions and relationships between regions convey the image content.

7.1.3.1 Regions as Structure

We will first discuss the use of segmentation in NPR as a source of structure. Unstructured stroke-based rendering can sometimes obscure or confuse important edges and features. Segmentation provides structure in two main ways:

- *Contrast.* Regions provide edges which primitives should not cross; region boundaries therefore remain visible in the final image.
- *Coherence.* Regions provide medium-scale, usually semantically meaningful sets of pixels within which information can be aggregated. For example, within a segment, strokes can have similar color and direction.

An early example of regions used to supply contrast is the mosaic creation of Hausner [16]. The user-supplied segmentation is used as a guideline for tile placement: tiles are prevented from straddling region boundaries. Many mosaic creation methods use similar ideas. The region boundaries are emphasized by the tile placement; without this step, the mosaic is likely to be less comprehensible.

An example of regions used to supply coherence comes from the "Artistic Vision" of Gooch et al. [15]. Automatic segmentation provides region shapes, and detailed analysis of region shapes yields local stroke directions. Within a region, stroke directions are aligned, promoting a sense of order in the synthetic output.

7.1.3.2 Regions as Primitives

Another application of segmentation is to use the regions themselves as the primary primitives. In this treatment, the regions themselves are usually quite simply presented, with uniform color or texture in their interiors; the shapes of the regions and the contrasts between adjacent regions reveal the image content. Region shape is potentially emphasized by using a separate rendering process for region boundaries, e.g., drawing the boundaries with heavy black lines.

When using regions as primary primitives, region shape is of foremost importance. For faithful representation of the original image content (e.g., in black and white rendering) a high-quality segmentation is needed. When greater abstraction is the goal, the region shapes may be smoothed or otherwise modified, sometimes quite drastically as in the Arty Shapes of Song et al. [32].

7.2 Algorithmic Building Blocks

Here we briefly discuss some of the algorithms that underlie many of the results in region-based stylization. As we saw in Fig. 7.2, a typical region-based stylization first involves a segmentation into regions, possibly done automatically; the segmentation step is then followed by smoothing of region boundaries. We will discuss each of these elements in turn in this section.

7.2.1 Segmentation

Segmentation is the process of automatically dividing an input image into meaningful regions. Typically, segmentation algorithms seek to assign similar pixels to the same regions, and discontinuities in pixel characteristics mark region boundaries.

The simplest segmentation algorithms separate pixels into regions using thresholding, possibly subsequent to an analysis of intensity histograms to obtain appropriate thresholds. Not including spatial relationships among pixels is a regrettable failing of such methods.

Region growing methods are a class of segmentation algorithms that involve starting with a small region, perhaps a single pixel, and adding pixels on the perimeter one by one as long as the added pixel has properties similar to the region as a whole. Such methods are most effective when enough is known about the input images to craft sufficiently powerful similarity criteria.

For some time, the *mean-shift* algorithm [9] was the favored method for segmentation. The freely available software EDISON was frequently incorporated into the pipeline for published stylization methods. However, despite the effectiveness of mean shift relative to other automatic algorithms, performance relative to the human vision system is lacking. Consequently, the current trend in region-based stylization is to avoid reliance on fully automatic segmentation, and instead to allow user input to disambiguate difficult cases and correct undesired segmentation results. Methods such as GrabCut [28], which have extremely simple interaction mechanisms, are sometimes used; occasionally, custom methods are developed for the stylization task at hand. To improve segmentation performance, an initial oversegmentation into superpixels may be undertaken; a recent robust method for finding superpixels is the *simple linear iterative clustering* method of Achanta et al. [1].

This survey is necessarily brief and segmentation is a large field. Good starting points for further reading include image processing texts such as that of Gonzalez and Woods [14] or that of Sonka et al. [33].

7.2.2 Boundary Smoothing

Handcrafted regions, such as those in the artworks in Fig. 7.3, tend to be bounded by smooth, elegant curves. However, automatic segmentation tends to produce jagged and irregular boundaries. To improve boundary quality, smoothing is often employed.

Two basic options are available for boundary smoothing. The boundaries can be smoothed directly, for example, using filtering operations on a 1D signal. Or, the regions themselves can be modified, usually by using morphological operations. We will discuss these two possibilities in turn.

Smoothing the boundaries can be undertaken in different ways. One smoothing approach is to subsample the boundary and link the points with splines, resulting in a smoother curve. A more explicit approach is to extract sets of boundary curves and apply smoothing operations to each curve separately; an early but thorough treatment of curve smoothing is given by Finkelstein and Salesin [13]. In either case, boundary curves must be extracted and fixed points noted; typically, the corners where three regions meet are treated as fixed. Care must be taken to ensure that the smoothing process does not introduce spurious intersections of boundary curves.

Morphological operators allow interaction with and modification of the regions themselves rather than their boundaries. In region-based stylization, they have been a popular choice for tidying an initial automatic segmentation, by smoothing segment boundaries and removing tiny regions. The latter is a natural side effect of morphological operations, whereas boundary smoothing approaches require a separate stage if tiny regions are to be eliminated.

There are two basic morphological operators: *erosion* and *dilation*. Both operate on a binary image by means of a *structuring element*, a binary mask that controls the shape and size of the morphological change. Informally speaking, erosion has the effect of scrubbing the structuring element like an eraser around the exterior of the region, shrinking it; dilation has the opposite effect, expanding the region boundary by the structuring element.

Erosion and dilation are building blocks for more elaborate operations. An erosion followed by a dilation is called "opening": it has the effect of separating regions which are joined by thin strands, and of eliminating regions smaller than the structuring element. Dilation followed by erosion is called "closing"; it fills in small holes. Both operations also remove small features from region boundaries. When we refer to "morphological smoothing", it is typically an opening or closing operation.

Although erosion and dilation are defined in terms of their effects on binary images, they can be applied to images with multiple regions by applying them to each region, one by one. Dilation can proceed unchanged, but the erosion operator must be modified, for example by relabeling the eroded pixel with the label of the nearest exterior region rather than simply by the opposite binary label. An alternative to incremental erosion is to erode all regions simultaneously, introducing a new "background" label that can then be consumed in a subsequent dilation step.

Boundary smoothing and repair, whether boundary-based or region-based, is generally a necessary part of a region-based stylization process. The remainder of this chapter describes specific stylization methods from the literature; we generally do not mention boundary smoothing operations for each method, but they are often present.

7.3 Review of Specific Works

This section provides a tour through selected research results that employed regions. We divide the literature into work that primarily used regions as containers to be filled with other primitives, work that populated regions with texture, and work that chiefly emphasized region boundaries, especially involving manipulation of the boundaries. Along the way, we touch briefly on stylization of video.

Before beginning the tour proper, we want to single out the work of DeCarlo and Santella [10], who created one of the first examples of region-based abstraction. This work is notable for three main reasons: it introduced the concept of gaze as a lightweight control mechanism for identifying important image regions; it made use of a hierarchy of segmentations; and it produced a novel abstraction mechanism, not specifically designed in imitation of a historical artistic style or medium. Followup work [29] also made use of gaze, serving a painterly abstraction technique.

DeCarlo and Santella's initial groundbreaking system automatically computes segmentations at different scales. A hierarchy is inferred by computing the overlap between regions at different levels, and each region is assigned a single parent, up to the top level where the entire image is a single region. The hierarchy, plus a set of image edges, is precomputed for a given image. After the hierarchy is computed, the segmentations are smoothed by low-pass filtering the segmentation boundary curves, with the curve endpoints (where three or more regions meet) being held fixed.

At runtime, a user examines the image while gaze is tracked. The resulting gaze data create a salience map which is used in rendering. Rendering consists of placing uniformly colored regions plus smoothed edges from an edge detection filter. Textured edges are suppressed by omitting short edges and by requiring that medium-length edges lie on region boundaries. Portions of the image receiving more atten-

Fig. 7.4 Region-based abstraction from DeCarlo and Santella. © 2002 ACM, Inc. Included here by permission

tion are rendered with more detail: more salient areas are depicted using smaller regions, from lower in the hierarchy.

A rendered image is shown in Fig. 7.4. The user mainly looked at the people in the background and at the face of the person in the foreground, resulting in a lesser degree of abstraction for these parts. The body of the foreground figure, the texture on the wall, and the structure of the walls and ceiling have all been abstracted heavily. Also notice how the separately smoothed edges and region boundaries are no longer perfectly aligned, producing a sketchy, handmade impression. The ideas in this paper have had enormous influence on subsequent image-based abstraction techniques, region-based and otherwise.

7.3.1 Filling Regions

In this section, we discuss the coherence-enhancing usage of regions. Regions can be used as an organizational principle, with a single value or signature used to describe the region's contents; the segmentation process is assumed to produce regions with sufficiently uniform properties that this makes sense. The most basic way of using this is to apply a single uniform color to a region; this is widely used, both in cases where regions have high importance, such as the stained glass of Mould [24], and in cases where regions are only incidental, such as the watercolor rendering of Bousseau et al. [3], whose abstraction makes use of a segmentation where the colors are averaged within regions.

One of the most common uses of regions in NPR is as containers to constrain or organize discrete primitives. Among the first to use regions in this way were Deussen et al. [11]; in this work, an input image is manually segmented into regions which are then filled with stipples. These authors articulate a complaint which might be echoed by creators of automatic region-based methods even up to the present day: "segmentation might be done automatically, but our experiences in this direction are not very promising." Once the regions are determined, the average graylevel of each region is measured and an appropriate number of stipples placed, with stipple locations adjusted by relaxation and potentially by further user interaction. The method is described in more detail in Chap. 3.

Following Deussen et al., regions were used as an organizational tool for arranging mosaic tiles by Hausner [16], among others. Mosaics are described more thoroughly in Chap. 10. Image-based mosaic algorithms commonly forbid tiles from crossing region boundaries, and in Hausner's case, tiles are also oriented to follow the boundaries. The segmentation thus structures the tile arrangement, emphasizing the large-scale features even as the tiles' color varies depending on the local image content. The Jigsaw Image Mosaics of Kim and Pellacini depend even more heavily on the regions for image structure: in this work, regions are progressively filled by tiny irregularly shaped tiles, but there is no attempt to match small-scale image detail. Color matching is done at the scale of the region: a region is assigned a color, and tiles with colors matching the region are preferred.

The "Artistic Vision" of Gooch et al. [15] was an early effort to make use of region shape to guide region contents. The initial stages of the algorithm are concerned with obtaining the segmentation. Segmentation of the image was done using a custom flood-fill algorithm based on image tone similarity. The resulting regions were not necessarily well shaped; region shapes were adjusted using, firstly, removal of isolated pixels and small holes, then secondly, morphological operations to adjust region boundaries.

Having obtained a reasonable segmentation, the algorithm then moves to the stroke placement phase. The medial axis of each region is extracted using a distance transform. Next, the medial axes are thinned to produce fragmentary ridges, which are then grouped to form strokes. The ridge grouping strategy ensures that the strokes will approximately travel the length of the region; stroke widths are chosen to match region widths. In short, the overall collection of strokes forms a structure guided by the initial segmentation. The authors note that the quality of the final painting depends on the segmentation: segmentations with smaller regions produce paintings with greater detail, which may be appropriate for applications such as portrait painting. We show a sample result from the system in Fig. 7.5.

As an aside, the distance transform is also used in the Batik stylization of Wyvill et al. [37], seeking to recreate the effect of Batik dyes. In this work, an initial binary segmentation is obtained manually. A distance field stores the distance to the nearest crack or region boundary; cracks begin at points of greatest distance and propagate along the direction in which distance decreases most rapidly, with the direction perturbed by noise. By placing sufficient numbers of cracks, a dense network of cracks is created. The resulting cracking effect is unusual within NPR; an example is shown in Fig. 7.6.

Stroke directions based on region shape is a theme revisited by Li and Huang [19]. In this work, an initial segmentation supplies regions which structure all subsequent computation. For each region, a local direction is calculated: if the region contains little texture, the region orientation itself is used, whereas textured regions use the texture direction, computed by finding the peak in the gradient orientation histogram. The set of region directions provides a global vector field, and

Fig. 7.5 Painterly rendering from Gooch et al. Created by Hua Li using code provided by Bruce Gooch. Used with permission

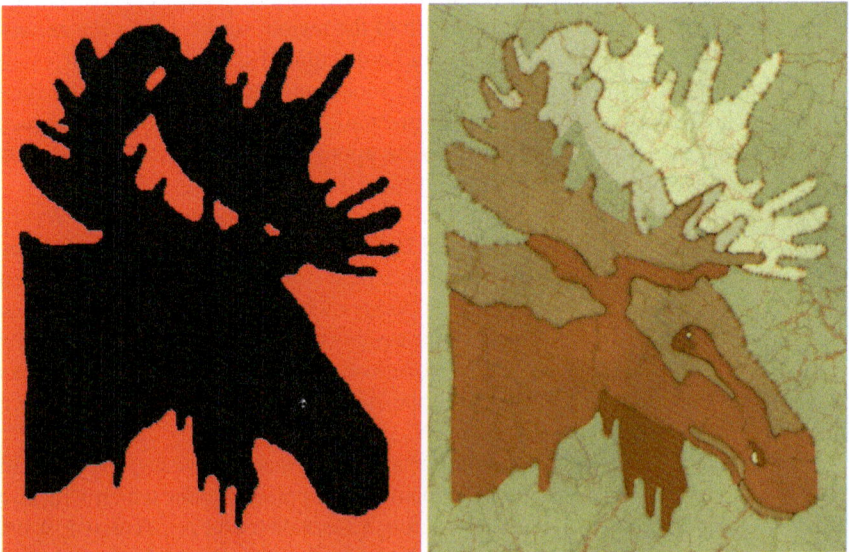

Fig. 7.6 Batik by Wyvill et al. This result was made from six separate binary segmentations, the most prominent of which is shown. © 2004 ACM, Inc. Included here by permission

Fig. 7.7 Pencil rendering (*left*, from Li and Huang) and woodcut rendering (*right*, from Mello et al.). *Right* side: Created by Vincius Mello. Used with permission

the final rendering is done by applying line integral convolution [7] to a white noise field approximating the local image intensity. An example appears in Fig. 7.7; tones are well matched and the line integral convolution imparts a sketchy impression.

The vector field created by Li and Huang can be criticized for its excessive simplicity. A more elaborate vector field is created by Mello et al. [22] in an effort to create woodcut-like images. The visual style of Mello et al.'s virtual woodcuts is contingent on the assumption that stroke directions should be perpendicular to segment boundaries; this intent is realized in the following way.

First, the algorithm applies mean-shift segmentation to obtain regions. Next, the vector field is created: control vectors are placed along region boundaries, oriented perpendicular to the boundary, and on weaker edges within regions. Additional control vectors can be placed by a user, if desired. A full vector field is computed by interpolating the control vectors throughout the image plane. Strokes are then distributed through the image, usually originating at region boundaries, and follow the vector field. The final rendered image consists of both the strokes and the region boundaries. An example appears in Fig. 7.7; the image content is conveyed mainly through region boundaries, with the strokes sometimes adding a sense of surface shape. Just as in many other region-based methods, the effectiveness of the method depends on the quality of the initial segmentation.

7.3.2 Textured Regions

Coherence of color and of orientation are two reasons to segment. Coherence of *texture* is another possibility. We next present some examples where texture matching within regions is the objective.

For emulation of stained glass, it is natural to split the image into regions. Setlur and Wilkinson [30] use mean-shift segmentation to obtain regions which will become stained glass tiles. Region boundaries are smoothed by replacement with Bezier curves, and dilation of region boundaries gives the leading area. To populate region interiors, they use a data-driven approach, matching textures from a glass swatch database with local textures from the image.

Texture matching is also the main concern of Qu et al. [27] in their effort to automatically screen photographs in a black and white manga style. The objective of this work is to convey the color and texture of an original photograph in a black and white image by using different patterns. This is accomplished by first segmenting the image into many different regions, then matching the texture signature within a region to one of the texture signatures of the predefined patterns. For regions where no good-quality match is available, the patterns are selected so as to maintain the same perceptual distance between patterned regions as the original colored regions.

The visible segments present in the results of Qu et al. are sometimes unattractive. Li and Mould [20] present an alternative in which the screening process is unified over the entire image: different screening masks are used for different regions, but individual screening calculations are done over neighborhoods which cross region boundaries. This reduces the dependency on the initial segmentation. Results from segmentation-based screening are shown in Fig. 7.8.

Returning to stained glass, Brooks [5] provided a carefully planned system for stained glass image synthesis. While the method is based on segments, an inevitable feature of stained glass algorithms, Brooks avoided the difficulties of automatic segmentation by providing a user tool for segmentation assistance: a hierarchy of automatic segmentations is computed and a user then creates final regions by selecting, splitting, and merging regions across different levels of the hierarchy. Brooks uses a sophisticated combination of color transfer, texture synthesis, and image warping to create a glassy appearance within regions, and relies on image analogies [17] to compute the leading between glass tiles. Both Setlur and Wilkinson [30] and Brooks made use of example-based techniques for stained glass, and sample results from both are shown in Fig. 7.9.

Brooks's mixed media simulation [6] is unusual in partitioning the image not into semantically meaningful regions, but into regions which contain different levels of detail. In practice, segmentation by detail may separate out semantically meaningful regions anyway, particularly if the input photograph uses a limited depth of field. Also, the system augments the basic detail-based segmentation with a custom face detection system for separating out faces in service of a portraiture style.

7 Region-Based Abstraction

Fig. 7.8 Segmentation-based screening. *Left*: Qu et al; *right*: Li and Mould. Manga image © 2010 ACM, Inc. Included here by permission. *Left* side: Created by Hua Li. Used with permission

Fig. 7.9 Example-based stained glass. *Left*: Setlur and Wilkinson; *right*: Brooks. *Left* image © 2006 CGI. Included here by permission. *Right* image © 2006 IEEE. Included here by permission

Once the segmentation is done, the regions are smoothed using morphological closing. Then, the regions are rendered: a user selects from among available NPR filters (from the GIMP or Photoshop, in the reported work) and applies a different one to each region. Finally, the different regions are fused into a single image using Poisson blending [26]. The results are intriguing and mixing filters produces images which would be very difficult to reproduce with a more conventional approach of treating the image as a whole. An example result appears in Fig. 7.10.

Fig. 7.10 Mixed media image filtering. Created by Stephen Brooks. Used with permission

7.3.3 Video

Stylization of video is a difficult problem, chiefly owing to the requirement of temporal coherence, discussed in Chap. 13. Regions provide a possible mechanism to promote coherence: region boundaries can be moved directly [2]; regions can act as container shapes [31] or canvases [34, 35] so that internal primitives can follow region movement; or 3D regions can be extracted from a video cube [8, 34].

Video segmentation can be undertaken automatically, either frame-by-frame or within a video cube, but flawed segmentations can produce extremely distracting defects in video. Accordingly, manual intervention to repair or initialize segmentations is commonplace. Such intervention can be quite lightweight; for example, SnakeToonz [2] used an average of 4 seconds of user time per frame, mainly concentrated into the minority of frames at the beginning of scene changes. Problems and solutions in video stylization are discussed further in Chap. 13.

7.3.4 Region Boundary Manipulation

In some work, the major goal has been creating region shapes or arrangements of regions which adhere to certain constraints. For example, stencils have the physical constraint that the entire stencil must be a single piece: isolated, "floating" elements are forbidden.

The work of Mould [24] was the first to treat stained glass in NPR. Its main concern was to devise appropriate region shapes, governed to some extent by the content of an input image, but more strongly by consideration of medieval stained glass technology. In medieval times it was not possible to produce large flat sheets of glass (glassblowing was the main manufacturing process) so tiles were small, and thin features could not reliably be cut without the glass breaking. In Mould's filter, an initial mean-shift segmentation was followed by morphological region smoothing, then subdivision of regions to remove isolated regions, split regions at thin features ("bottlenecks"), and subdivide very large regions. Mould also chose to highly

Fig. 7.11 Medieval stained glass by Mould [24]. Original image courtesy of Philip Greenspun

restrict the color palette of the tiles, matching original image colors to a seven-color palette inspired by heraldic tinctures. Perlin noise texture and height-mapped leading, followed by rendering, completed the glass image. An example result from the process is shown in Fig. 7.11. The procedural glass surface is quite striking, and the tiles have been divided into manageable size; however, due to the scale of objects in this image, the stylization has made the image contents difficult to recognize.

Bronson et al. [4] created an automated system for stencil planning. Their system expected polygonal meshes as input, and used toon shading and silhouette finding to craft a binary image; in general, the binary image will consist of some set of disconnected regions, which are then transformed into a single region without holes or islands by constructing a minimum spanning tree over a graph representing the set of regions. Edges in the graph represent bridge strips added to the stencil, linking formerly isolated island regions. Their algorithm was sufficiently successful that they were able to use it to fabricate real stencils to be used in theatrical lighting.

Xu and Kaplan [41] used global optimization to assign black or white colors over a segmentation. This work is notable for allowing communication between regions; as we have seen, oftentimes one of the purposes behind the segmentation is to permit the algorithm to concentrate on one region at a time, performing calculations on different regions independently. This work is discussed in greater detail in Chap. 11. Alternatively, black and white segmentation can be created directly using graph cuts, as in the work of Mould and Grant [25], also discussed in Chap. 11. The graph cuts algorithm has the drawback of providing only two regions; also, the graph cut energy is highly influenced by the length of the cut, so that thin features (with a low

Fig. 7.12 Color sketch rendering from Wen et al. [36]. Created by Fang Wen; copyright Microsoft Research China. Included here by permission

ratio of area to perimeter) are discouraged. Mould and Grant ameliorated the latter problem by combining a base layer from a graph cut with a histogram-based detail layer. In the case that black and white output is desired, the limitation that graph cuts provides only a binary segmentation is not a drawback at all.

Milder boundary adjustment was an element of the work of Wen et al. [36], whose semi-automatic method transforms photographic input into abstracted images emphasizing foreground figures. An initial mean-shift segmentation is manually repaired by merging regions, splitting regions, and redrawing region boundaries as necessary. The user separates the regions into foreground and background; then, the background regions are shrunk by moving the control points of a spline representation of the boundary. Regions are recolored to make the background fade and make the foreground more prominent. An example of the results of the algorithm is shown in Fig. 7.12; notice how the regions are no longer a complete partition of the image plane, but leave some areas uncolored.

A highly effective shape abstraction method was given by Mi et al. [23]. This work did not deal with images per se, but could potentially be included in a region-based abstraction system. The method applies to 2D shapes, which are divided into parts automatically based on considerations of local symmetry. Optionally, a user can help to guide the decomposition. The collection of parts is heuristically assembled into a dependency graph, which provides an order in which parts can be removed: eliminating parts in the order suggested by the dependency graph provides different levels of abstraction of the original shape. The overall abstraction process provides an alternative to blind region smoothing, being able to preserve important features as well as maintaining overall shape until very late in the part removal sequence. An example result appears in Fig. 7.13.

7 Region-Based Abstraction

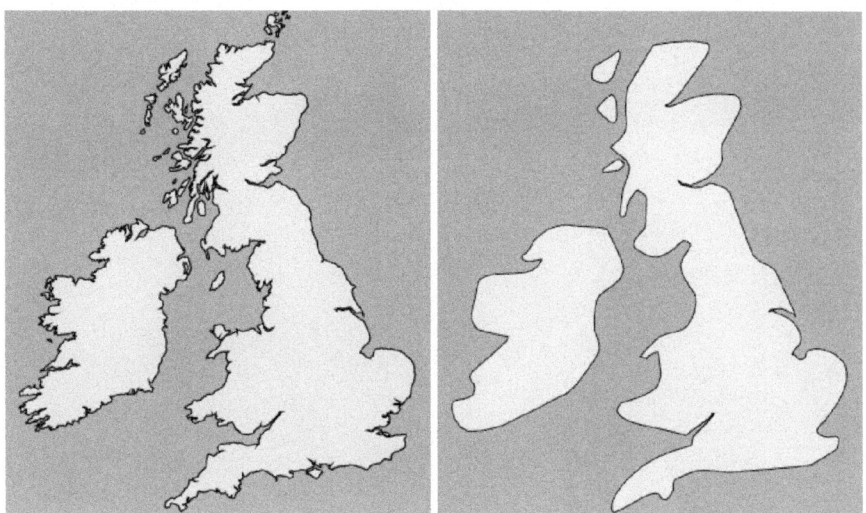

Fig. 7.13 Region abstraction by parts. © 2009 ACM, Inc. Included here by permission

Extreme shape abstraction is one of the contributions of Song et al.'s Arty Shapes [32]. Following a segmentation, each region is matched with a simple shape, such as a circle or triangle. Manual labeling of segmentations of test images provided training data for a classifier, which is then able to classify regions automatically in future images. The use of a classifier here is somewhat inspired, since it is able to encode human judgement to some extent and errors on difficult classification decisions have little effect on the final appearance of the image. Alternatively, the matching step can be omitted, and the same basic shape used for every region: every region could be replaced by a rectangle, for example. The dimensions of the shapes can still vary to match the region.

Once the shape selections are made, the images can be rendered, replacing each region with its corresponding shape, uniformly colored. Sample results are shown in Fig. 7.14. By manipulating the region boundaries, quite extreme abstractions are possible while still preserving some sense of the overall composition of the image.

One example of interactive stylization using regions is the sumi-e rendering of Xie et al. [38, 39]. In this work, users draw stroke outlines, possibly freehand on a blank canvas, but more likely tracing outlines of regions on an input photograph. Each user-created region is filled by a single stroke, mapping scanned stroke textures into the region and applying a final smoothing step to simulate pigment and water dispersion. An example result is shown in Fig. 7.15. By relying heavily on user input, the segmentation well reflects human perception of the scene, and the overall result is extremely successful.

This work is unusual in a number of respects. Unlike most region-based techniques, it allows overlapping regions; while overlapping regions are featured in work that uses hierarchical segmentation, typically the rendered output does not display the overlap, whereas the finished sumi-e strokes overlap considerably. Stroke-based

Fig. 7.14 Arty shapes: massive abstraction of source image in Fig. 7.11. *Left*: superellipses; *right*: rectangles. Created by Yi-Zhe Song. Used with permission

techniques involving regions generally use the regions as a way to organize many strokes, rather than making a one-to-one correspondence between strokes and regions as is the case here. Finally, due to the intended style, regions cover only a small portion of the canvas, rather than partitioning the whole image as is more usual.

7.4 Future Directions

As we saw in the survey, many of the most effective techniques depended on manual intervention to create semantically meaningful segmentations. Automatic segmentation has been less effective. Thus, a goal of future work can be to improve the state of the art of automatic segmentation.

Entirely automated, meaningful segmentation is viewed by some as a pipe dream that will not manifest in the foreseeable future. While we have some sympathy for this view, it does not mean that progress towards the ideal is impossible. For artistic stylization, we need not automatically segment every possible input image; it may suffice to treat only well composed, adequately lit images. Use of information beyond simply color, such as depth or blur, will help inform segmentation of future images. When the intent is to recognize specific details, such as faces, custom algorithms and large databases can be brought to bear on the problem.

7 Region-Based Abstraction

Fig. 7.15 Sumi-e. *Above*: original image and hand-drawn contours; *below*: final result. Created by Xie Ning. Used with permission

Even with a well-developed ability to segment, automatic techniques may not be able to obtain desired results, simply because the desired result is not a function of the image alone but a joint function of the image and a user's intention. Since we cannot read the user's mind, we still need some user guidance to get the desired output. Consequently, interaction schemes remain a future direction, particularly lightweight interactions and fast exploration of different possible outcomes. This is not a new direction; some such techniques have been explored already (and were described in this chapter) but research on interaction techniques certainly will not cease.

Styles depending on regions can be further explored. The various works on image-based stained glass still leave room for further improvement. The region-based abstraction of Song et al.'s "Arty Shapes" points the way towards region shape stylization; more elaborate shape abstractions could be conceived, as well as shape stylizations which occupy a middle ground between abstraction and representation, as in many modern cartoons.

For artistic stylization, segmentation is not an end in itself, but an intermediate representation en route to achieving the desired artistic effect. Consequently, regions will continue to be used opportunistically whenever researchers see value in them.

Acknowledgements Thanks foremost to the various authors of the papers who provided images or source code. We would also like to thank photographers R. Bertieg, Steve Cadman, Danny Choo, Jim Linwood, and William Warby for the images in Fig. 7.3. Thanks to Jordan Miller for the artwork for Fig. 7.2.

References

1. Achanta, R., Shaji, A., Smith, K., Lucchi, A., Fua, P., Süsstrunk, S.: SLIC superpixels. Tech. Rep. EPFL-REPORT-149300, École Polytechnique Fédrale de Lausanne (EPFL) (2010)
2. Agarwala, A.: SnakeToonz: a semi-automatic approach to creating cel animation from video. In: Proceedings of the 2nd International Symposium on Non-Photorealistic Animation and Rendering, NPAR'02, pp. 139–ff (2002). doi:10.1145/508530.508554
3. Bousseau, A., Kaplan, M., Thollot, J., Sillion, F.X.: Interactive watercolor rendering with temporal coherence and abstraction. In: NPAR, pp. 141–149 (2006)
4. Bronson, J., Rheingans, P., Olano, M.: Semi-automatic stencil creation through error minimization. In: Proceedings of the 6th International Symposium on Non-Photorealistic Animation and Rendering, pp. 31–37 (2008). doi:10.1145/1377980.1377989
5. Brooks, S.: Image-based stained glass. IEEE Trans. Vis. Comput. Graph. **12**, 1547–1558 (2006)
6. Brooks, S.: Mixed media painting and portraiture. IEEE Trans. Vis. Comput. Graph. **13**(5), 1041–1054 (2007). doi:10.1109/TVCG.2007.1025
7. Cabral, B., Leedom, L.C.: Imaging vector fields using line integral convolution. In: Proceedings of the 20th Annual Conference on Computer Graphics and Interactive Techniques, pp. 263–270 (1993). doi:10.1145/166117.166151
8. Collomosse, J.P., Rowntree, D., Hall, P.M.: Stroke surfaces: temporally coherent artistic animations from video. IEEE Trans. Vis. Comput. Graph. **11**, 540–549 (2005)
9. Comaniciu, D., Meer, P.: Mean Shift: A robust approach toward feature space analysis. IEEE Trans. Pattern Anal. Mach. Intell. **24**, 603–619 (2002)
10. DeCarlo, D., Santella, A.: Stylization and abstraction of photographs. ACM Trans. Graph. **21**(3), 769–776 (2002). doi:10.1145/566654.566650
11. Deussen, O., Hiller, S., van Overveld, C.W.A.M., Strothotte, T.: Floating Points: A method for computing stipple drawings. Comput. Graph. Forum **19**, 41–50 (2000)
12. Dunbabin, K.: Mosaics of the Greek and Roman World. Cambridge University Press, Cambridge (1999)
13. Finkelstein, A., Salesin, D.H.: Multiresolution curves. In: Proceedings of the 21st Annual Conference on Computer Graphics and Interactive Techniques, pp. 261–268 (1994)
14. Gonzalez, R., Woods, R.: Digital Image Processing. Pearson Prentice Hall, Upper Saddle River (2008)
15. Gooch, B., Coombe, G., Shirley, P.: Artistic Vision: painterly rendering using computer vision techniques. In: Proceedings of the 2nd International Symposium on Non-Photorealistic Animation and Rendering, pp. 83–ff (2002). doi:10.1145/508530.508545
16. Hausner, A.: Simulating decorative mosaics. In: Proceedings of the 28th Annual Conference on Computer Graphics and Interactive Techniques, pp. 573–580 (2001). doi:10.1145/383259.383327
17. Hertzmann, A., Jacobs, C.E., Oliver, N., Curless, B., Salesin, D.H.: Image analogies. In: Proceedings of the 28th Annual Conference on Computer Graphics and Interactive Techniques, pp. 327–340 (2001). doi:10.1145/383259.383295
18. Kim, J., Pellacini, F.: Jigsaw image mosaics. ACM Trans. Graph. **21**(3), 657–664 (2002). doi:10.1145/566654.566633
19. Li, N., Huang, Z.: A feature-based pencil drawing method. In: Proceedings of the 1st International Conference on Computer Graphics and Interactive Techniques in Australasia and South East Asia, pp. 135–ff (2003). doi:10.1145/604471.604498

20. Li, H., Mould, D.: Content-sensitive screening in black and white. In: GRAPP, pp. 166–172 (2011)
21. Ling, R.: Ancient Mosaics. British Museum Press, London (1998)
22. Mello, V.B., Jung, C.R., Walter, M.: Virtual woodcuts from images. In: Proceedings of the 5th International Conference on Computer Graphics and Interactive Techniques in Australia and Southeast Asia, pp. 103–109 (2007). doi:10.1145/1321261.1321280
23. Mi, X., DeCarlo, D., Stone, M.: Abstraction of 2D shapes in terms of parts. In: Proceedings of the 7th International Symposium on Non-Photorealistic Animation and Rendering, pp. 15–24 (2009). doi:10.1145/1572614.1572617
24. Mould, D.: A stained glass image filter. In: Proceedings of the 14th Eurographics Workshop on Rendering, pp. 20–25 (2003)
25. Mould, D., Grant, K.: Stylized black and white images from photographs. In: Proceedings of the 6th International Symposium on Non-Photorealistic Animation and Rendering, pp. 49–58 (2008). doi:10.1145/1377980.1377991
26. Pérez, P., Gangnet, M., Blake, A.: Poisson image editing. ACM Trans. Graph. **22**(3), 313–318 (2003). doi:10.1145/882262.882269
27. Qu, Y., Wong, T.T., Heng, P.A.: Manga colorization. ACM Trans. Graph. **25**(3), 1214–1220 (2006). doi:10.1145/1141911.1142017
28. Rother, C., Kolmogorov, V., Blake, A.: "GrabCut": interactive foreground extraction using iterated graph cuts. ACM Trans. Graph. **23**(3), 309–314 (2004)
29. Santella, A., DeCarlo, D.: Abstracted painterly renderings using eye-tracking data. In: Proceedings of the 2nd International Symposium on Non-Photorealistic Animation and Rendering, pp. 75–82 (2002)
30. Setlur, V., Wilkinson, S.: Automatic stained glass rendering. In: Computer Graphics International, pp. 682–691 (2006)
31. Smith, K., Liu, Y., Klein, A.A.: In: Proceedings of the 2005 ACM SIGGRAPH/Eurographics Symposium on Computer Animation, pp. 201–208 (2005). doi:10.1145/1073368.1073397
32. Song, Y.Z., Rosin, P.L., Hall, P.M., Collomosse, J.P.: Arty shapes. In: Computational Aesthetics, pp. 65–72 (2008)
33. Sonka, M., Hlavac, V., Boyle, R.: Image Processing, Analysis, and Machine Vision. Thomson, Tampa (2007)
34. Wang, J., Thiesson, B., Xu, Y., Cohen, M.F.: Image and video segmentation by anisotropic kernel mean shift. In: ECCV, vol. 2, pp. 238–249 (2004)
35. Wang, J., Xu, Y., Shum, H.Y., Cohen, M.F.: Video tooning. ACM Trans. Graph. **23**(3), 574–583 (2004). doi:10.1145/1015706.1015763
36. Wen, F., Luan, Q., Liang, L., Xu, Y.Q., Shum, H.Y.: Color sketch generation. In: Proceedings of the 4th International Symposium on Non-Photorealistic Animation and Rendering, pp. 47–54 (2006). doi:10.1145/1124728.1124737
37. Wyvill, B., van Overveld, K., Carpendale, S.: Rendering cracks in Batik. In: Proceedings of the 3rd International Symposium on Non-Photorealistic Animation and Rendering, pp. 61–149 (2004). doi:10.1145/987657.987667
38. Xie, N., Laga, H., Saito, S., Nakajima, M.: IR2s: interactive real photo to Sumi-e. In: Proceedings of the 8th International Symposium on Non-Photorealistic Animation and Rendering, pp. 63–71 (2010). doi:10.1145/1809939.1809947
39. Xie, N., Laga, H., Saito, S., Nakajima, M.: Contour-driven Sumi-e rendering of real photos. Comput. Graph. **35**(1), 122–134 (2011)
40. Xu, J., Kaplan, C.S.: Image-guided maze construction. ACM Trans. Graph. **26**(3), 1–9 (2007). 29. doi:10.1145/1276377.1276414
41. Xu, J., Kaplan, C.S.: Artistic thresholding. In: Proceedings of the 6th International Symposium on Non-Photorealistic Animation and Rendering, pp. 39–47 (2008). doi:10.1145/1377980.1377990

Chapter 8
Gradient Art: Creation and Vectorization

Pascal Barla and Adrien Bousseau

8.1 Introduction

Among existing methods employed to create stylized images, drawing is the oldest one. The notion of *style* is complex, though, and goes from the tools and medium used to produce an image, to rules of image composition. The focus of this chapter is on *color gradients*, which form a basic, yet essential part of style in digital drawing.

Examples of color gradients abound in paintings, as well as in illustrations and graphic novels. Although such pictures may make use of very different media such as watercolor, oil paint, acrylic or pencil, they all tend to reproduce gradients in similar respects. Firstly, they are not constrained by physical accuracy: a few smooth gradients are enough to produce a convincing appearance or to elicit a feeling through an abstract composition. Second, they exhibit sharp color discontinuities that may be used to convey occluding edges or to create shading or stylization effects. Compositions made of color gradients may be obtained in different ways: by carefully reproducing the gradients found in a photograph, by freely taking inspiration and then departing from them, or by being directly drawn from scratch. In this chapter, we consider the whole spectrum of techniques to create color gradients in digital images.

Before starting our investigation of computer-aided methods for the drawing of color gradients, let us take a brief look at hand-made paintings and drawings and how they use these gradients. In pure color compositions such as abstract art (see Fig. 8.1a), gradients may convey an abstract sense of motion or lighting. The level of abstraction varies among artists, and for that reason there is no a priori family

---

P. Barla (✉)
Inria Bordeaux, 200 avenue de la Vieille Tour, 33405 Talence Cedex, France
e-mail: pascal.barla@inria.fr

A. Bousseau
Inria Sophia Antipolis, 2004 route des Lucioles, 06902 Sophia Antipolis Cedex, France
e-mail: adrien.bousseau@inria.fr

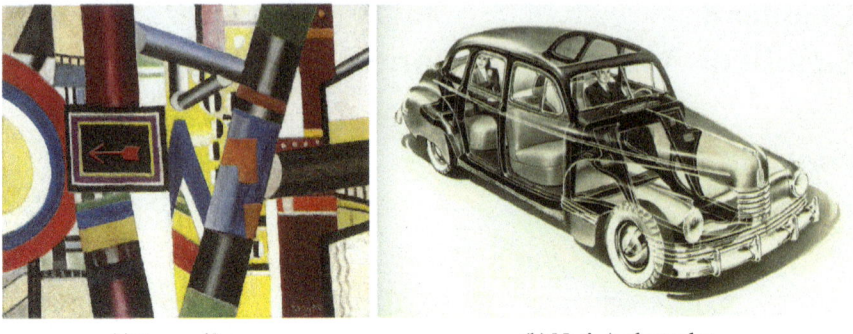

(a) Fernand Leger   (b) Nash Ambassador

Fig. 8.1 Smooth color gradients are ubiquitous in art and illustration. (**a**) Fernand Leger. (**b**) Courtesy of Nash Motors

of gradients that could be made to answer every imaginable artistic needs. Other compositions make use of smooth shading-like gradients to convey characters and objects in a rather iconic style, like in the art of Tamara de Lempicka. Although her style is a lot more figurative, it is still quite far from an accurate reproduction of a real-world image: in particular, shapes and lighting are often drastically simplified. In industrial design, communication imperatives make the use of color gradients more tightly coupled with faithful shape reproduction (see Fig. 8.1b). However, industrial designers often depart from realistic shading to convey shape and materials unambiguously. Even hyper-realistic images make use of color gradients in their own specific way. Although such images look surprisingly similar to photographs, they actually go further than photo-realism by showing details that could not be seen with the naked eye, thus exaggerating the impression of realism.

When it comes to *digital* drawing in general, and color gradients in particular, one is faced with a choice between two alternatives: either use raster or vector graphics.

Raster graphics solutions such as Adobe Photoshop, Corel Painter or Gimp offer by design a more direct analogy with traditional, hand-made paintings and drawings: each drawn brush stroke is recorded in a pixel grid that represents the canvas, and blended in a variety of ways depending on the choice of tool and medium. Tools may tightly simulate their real-world counterparts (e.g., [2]), or they might provide novel types of interaction (e.g., [18]). In both cases, though, users create color gradients by layering multiple strokes. The first issue raised by this layering approach is that the resulting gradient is not easily editable, and artists usually have to re-paint over them when a change is required. A second limitation of raster images is their lack of scalability: the resolution of the pixel grid limits the amount of details that can be drawn.

Vector graphics, on the other hand, offers a more compact representation, resolution independence (allowing scaling of images while retaining sharp edges), and geometric editability. Vector-based images are more easily animated (through keyframe animation of their underlying geometric primitives), and more readily stylized (e.g. through controlled perturbation of geometry). For all of these reasons, vector-based drawing tools, such as Adobe Illustrator, Corel Draw, and Inkscape, continue to enjoy great popularity, as do standardized vector representations, such as Flash and SVG.

However, for all of their benefits, *basic* vector-drawing tools offer limited support for representing complex color gradients, which are integral to many artistic styles. In order to better understand these limitations, let us consider the following two important requirements for any vector-based solution:

1. Accurate manual control should be provided at sharp discontinuities, while a somewhat more automated control (albeit accurate) is preferable in smooth regions. These different levels of control are necessary because small changes of sharp color variations are more noticeable, while smooth color variations are more difficult to draw.
2. Completing a drawing should require as few vector primitives as possible to get to the intended result. Such sparse representations are necessary to endow artists with more direct control of entire parts of the image at once, and limit the amount of user interaction for simple edits.

Basic color gradient tools have huge restrictions regarding both requirements. In a nutshell, they require many primitives to create even simple images, work solely with closed contours, and provide only for very simple interior behaviors. Section 8.2 explains these limitations in detail, and presents the alternative primitives that form the core of this chapter.

Despite considerable improvements in vector-based color gradient primitives, we must say that as of today, there is no single solution that fulfils the above-mentioned requirements unequivocally. This is mainly due to the extent to which each method makes use of a reference raster image. For methods that strive to faithfully convert a photograph to a vector representation—a process known as vectorization—primitives need to stick as much as possible to underlying color variations (req. 1), hence making it hard to provide holistic editing functionalities (req. 2). On the opposite end of the spectrum, methods that let artists create color gradients from scratch—i.e., vector drawing—must at the same time provide control in precise locations (req. 1), and incorporate priors to fill-in smooth regions with few primitives (req. 2). These examples are extreme cases, and a host of intermediate solutions has been proposed in the literature. This is elaborated in greater depth in Sect. 8.3.

An ideal solution would reside in a single tool for both vector drawing and image vectorization: one could start from an image and more or less deviate from it according to the intended message conveyed by the picture, in a style either personal or optimized for legibility for instance. Even if such a method becomes available one day, there will still be a last important point to consider: with more advanced conversion and editing capabilities come more complex rendering requirements. To reach a wide audience, the rendering of vector-based color gradients should be efficient (ideally real-time) and robust (artifact-free). We present in Sect. 8.4 existing rendering solutions and compare their merits.

The gradient primitives, construction techniques, and rendering algorithms presented in the following sections have been used for applications outside of color

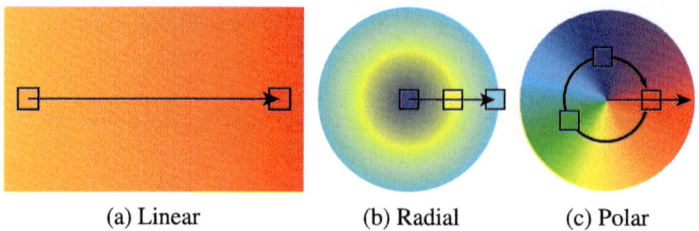

(a) Linear (b) Radial (c) Polar

Fig. 8.2 Examples of elemental gradients and their parameterization and color control points

gradients. One important instance is the (re-)construction of normal and/or depth images (e.g. [14]), which provide for 3D-like shading capabilities. We refer the interested reader to Sects. 14.3.2, 14.3.3 of this book, where it is shown how diffusion-based methods in particular have proven useful for a variety of applications. We have intentionally focused on still 2D graphics; throughout the chapter, we will also mention vector-based 3D methods, but only in contexts where they are of interest to 2D color gradients.

8.2 Gradient Primitives

We start by describing existing gradient primitives, focusing on how they are created and manipulated. We distinguish between three families of primitives: elemental primitives that fill the whole space given a small set of parameters, primitives that rely on meshes to provide more accurate and dense control, and primitives that rely on extremal curves and a propagation process to fill-in space between them.

8.2.1 Elemental Gradients

Elemental gradients are composed of two ingredients: a parametrization of the plane $\mathbb{R}^2 \to [0, 1]$, and a one-dimensional color gradient $[0, 1] \to [0, 1]^4$ that assigns a color and opacity to each parametric value. The types of gradient differ in the way they define the parametrization from two control points. The most common parametrizations are linear, radial and polar, as shown in Fig. 8.2: a linear gradient produces constant colors along directions perpendicular to the line defined by the two control points; a radial gradient produces circles of constant colors centered on the first control point; a polar gradient produces rays of constant colors originating from the first anchor point. In the last case, the 1D gradient should be periodic to avoid color discontinuities. The distance function may be adapted to produce contours of constant colors with different shapes, such as rectangles or stars.

Each gradient is controlled by a pair of 2D control points (at least) for the parametrization, and a series of colors and opacity control values arranged on the

(a) Complex combination of gradients (b) Individual linear gradient

Fig. 8.3 Complex images require the combination of a multitude of elemental gradients. loswl@vecteezy.com. Used under CC Licence

[0, 1] interval. A piecewise-linear interpolation is commonly used to define this 1D color function, although other interpolants such as splines can produce smoother variations. The final 2D color gradient is either assigned to the background, or to the interior of a closed 2D shape.

While the extent of an elemental gradient can be infinite, these primitives are often used to fill-in closed shapes. Figure 8.3(a) shows a complex image created entirely with linear and radial gradients. Figure 8.3(b) highlights how a linear gradient fills a region to produce a convincing reflection. Although this example is compelling, it requires advanced skills and a lot of time to complete a drawing. This is why elemental gradients are most of the time confined to simple compositions.

8.2.2 Gradient Meshes

The main idea of a gradient mesh is to decompose the image plane into a connected set of simple 2D patches $P_i : \mathbb{R}^2 \to [0, 1]^2$, and assign each patch a color based on a *two-dimensional* color gradient $[0, 1]^2 \to [0, 1]^4$. It improves on the elemental gradients in two ways: the mesh structure permits gradient structures to be produced that are a lot more complex; and the use of a 2D elemental gradient for each patch permits a greater variety of smooth color variations to be created.

The original gradient mesh tool is based on quad patches with curved boundaries, as illustrated in Fig. 8.4. RGB colors and tangents are assigned to each vertex of the mesh. Colors are interpolated inside the patch guided by tangents, which allows artists to finely tune color variations inside a patch.

This tool provides a far more advanced control over the structure of the gradients: any kind of curve can be used. However, the grid-like structure constrains the topology of control curves as a whole: users must align the main direction of the quad mesh with the structure of the drawing they want to create in advance, and holes are not easily treated. In practice, two types of grid are commonly employed: Cartesian and angular grids. Their use depends on the structure of the gradient to be drawn, which must often be decided in advance as well.

Alternative representations for gradient meshes have been proposed, such as the triangular patches of Xia et al. [25]. Although in most cases colors are stored at

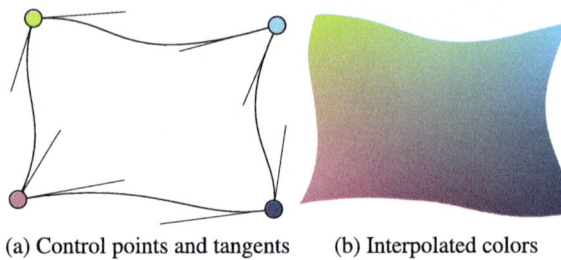

Fig. 8.4 Example of a simple gradient mesh

(a) Control points and tangents

(b) Interpolated colors

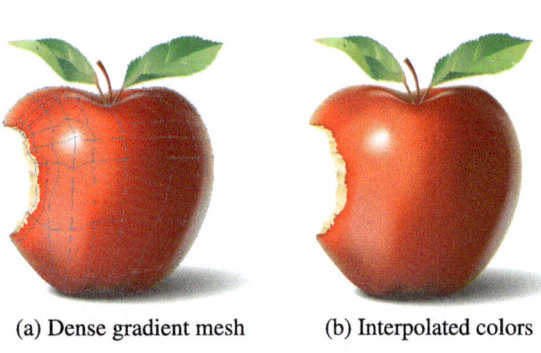

Fig. 8.5 Gradient meshes are well suited to represent the smooth shading and subsurface scattering of organic materials. rcraighead@vecteezy.com. Used under CC Licence

(a) Dense gradient mesh

(b) Interpolated colors

vertices and interpolated over patches [21, 22], some methods store color control points inside the patches [25]. Such representations are more adapted to image vectorization, as will be discussed in Sect. 8.3.

Figure 8.5 shows a Cartesian gradient mesh used to depict an apple. Note how the structure has to be bent around the highlight, and the density of lines increased near silhouettes. Gradient meshes are quite similar in spirit to 3D meshes, with which artists have learnt to represent a shape with the smallest number of patches; except that gradient meshes represent 2D color gradients instead of 3D surfaces.

The use of gradient meshes thus not only provides a gain in accuracy, but also increases the number of control points that must be manipulated by the artist to reach a desired goal, and requires some experience to make the right choice of structure in advance.

8.2.3 Gradient Extrema

The idea of using extrema (i.e. discontinuities) of color gradients to represent images originally comes from the Vision literature. Among the many papers that have stressed their importance, Elder's article [7] has insisted on the ability of edges to encode most of the visual information in an image.

Following this work, Diffusion Curves [19] have been introduced as a vector-drawing primitive entirely based on extremal curves of color gradients. A primitive path consists of a Bézier curve $C_i : [0, 1] \to \mathbb{R}^2$ to which is assigned color control

8 Gradient Art: Creation and Vectorization

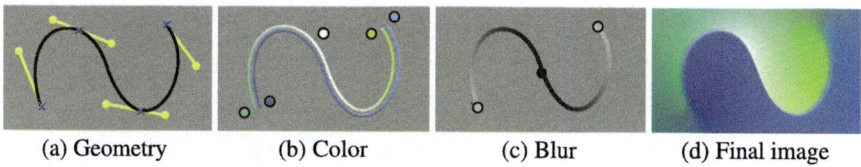

(a) Geometry   (b) Color   (c) Blur   (d) Final image

Fig. 8.6 A Diffusion curve is composed of (**a**) a geometric curve described by a Bézier spline, (**b**) arbitrary colors on either side, linearly interpolated along the curve, (**c**) a blur amount linearly interpolated along the curve. The final image (**d**) is obtained by diffusion and reblurring. Note the complex color distribution and blur variation defined with a handful of controls

points on either side of the curve. Colors are first interpolated along the curve to yield two 1D color gradients $[0, 1] \rightarrow [0, 1]^3$, one for each side of the curve; second, colors are extrapolated to the whole image plane through a propagation process, which mimics heat diffusion in the original approach. The primitive may be augmented with blur control points, located anywhere on the curve. They are also interpolated along the curve to yield a single blur gradient $[0, 1] \rightarrow [0, 1]$, which is then used to control the sharpness of the color transition from one side to the other. This is illustrated in Fig. 8.6.

The main advantage of this primitive compared to others is that it leaves artists free to position extremal curves anywhere they want and to vary their number depending on the amount of detail they wish to depict. Gradient extrema do not have to be closed and nearby curves interact together more than curves that are far apart. They may also intersect, although care should be taken with color assignment in this case: the presence of multiple colors at the location of the intersection will produce visual artifacts. Proper user interfaces remain to be proposed to facilitate color assignment in such configurations. The ability to blur color transitions across curves allows artists to create interesting effects without having to duplicate primitives or to adjust their color control points, as is the case with gradient meshes.

The main limitation of diffusion curves is the lack of control over the propagation of colors. This is the reason why several extensions have been proposed to improve artistic control using directional diffusion and blockers [3, 4], or to produce a smoother color propagation [10]. Jeschke et al. [13] also use diffusion curves to control the parameters of procedural textures, while Hnaidi et al. [11] create height fields by diffusing height from curves that represent ridges and cliffs. Finally, Takayama et al. [24] extend diffusion curves to diffusion surfaces to create volumetric models with 3D color gradients.

Figure 8.7 shows a drawing made using diffusion curves. The complex fold patterns would have been difficult to obtain with a more structured primitive such as a gradient mesh. It is also natural to add more curves to increase details with this approach. On the downside, the method is less localized than gradient meshes: for instance, to obtain the black background colors, it is necessary to assign black colors outside of all contour curves. This is partly solved by the use of Diffusion Barriers [3], but an efficient treatment of occluding contours and layers remains an open research challenge.

(a) Diffusion Curves   (b) Interpolated colors

Fig. 8.7 Diffusion Curves can represent freeform color gradients such as the folds in this stylized cloth

8.3 Construction Techniques

There is an obvious visual gap between the primitives illustrated in Figs. 8.2, 8.4 and 8.6 and the complex drawings obtained with them, shown in Figs. 8.3, 8.5 and 8.7. With enough skill and patience, these latter images may be drawn manually from scratch. However, an often faster solution is to take an input photograph as a reference, either by using the image to guide the drawing process, or by relying on a conversion algorithm that involves no intervention on the part of the artist.

8.3.1 Manual Creation

Elemental gradients are often assigned to their own layer or 2D shape and blended with layers below. With this approach, a lot of blended primitives are required to obtain color gradients that are not directly expressible from available elemental primitives, as shown in Fig. 8.8.

When working with gradient meshes, artists first need to indicate the number of meshes necessary to represent each part of the drawing. Then, as with 3D modeling tools, artists often start with a low resolution and add in details progressively. With a regular quad-based mesh, users can add vertical or horizontal curves, move control points and assign them new colors. Finer meshes are often needed to draw objects with complex topology.

When a reference image is available, the mesh can be aligned with the image features by hand, and vertex colors can be automatically sampled from underlying pixels. A faster solution is to use optimization techniques [21, 22] that optimize the color and position of vertices to best match the input image, as illustrated in Fig. 8.9. Even if these methods are not entirely automatic, they save a lot of time for artists.

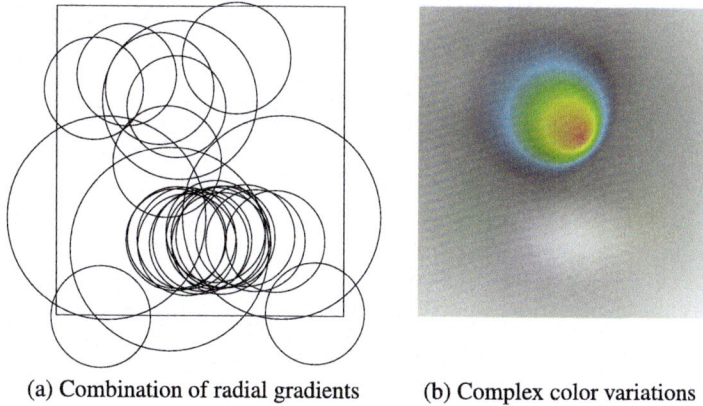

(a) Combination of radial gradients   (b) Complex color variations

Fig. 8.8 Multiple elemental (here radial) gradients (**a**) need to be combined to create more complex color variations (**b**). Courtesy of Inkscape

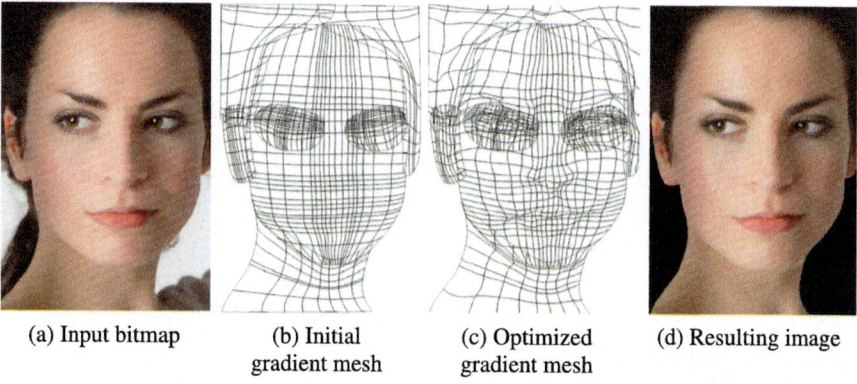

(a) Input bitmap   (b) Initial gradient mesh   (c) Optimized gradient mesh   (d) Resulting image

Fig. 8.9 Starting from a user-defined mesh (**b**), Sun et al. [22] optimize the position and color of the vertices (**c**) to best match an input bitmap (**a**, **d**). © Copyright 2007 ACM

Alternative structures that work with triangular meshes for instance are a lot harder to draw entirely from scratch: the overall structure has to be changed when one wants to add details or move some parts of the structure. This is why such methods have been rather confined to automatic conversion.

When working with gradient extrema such as diffusion curves, a simple strategy consists of first drawing the curves as a line drawing, and then adding or editing colors and blur transitions along each curve. This approach is somewhat similar to the traditional "sketching + coloring" process in traditional drawing. Because of their flexibility, extremal primitives are also well adapted to multi-touch user interfaces [23]. To facilitate color editing, Jeschke et al. [13] propose storing for each pixel a list of the most influential curves and color control points. Users can then specify the color at a pixel to modify the color of the curves accordingly.

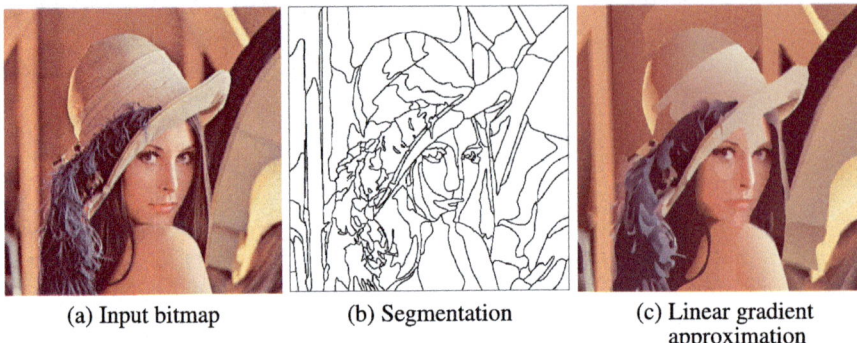

(a) Input bitmap   (b) Segmentation   (c) Linear gradient approximation

Fig. 8.10 The Ardeco system [17] converts an input bitmap into a collection of linear or radial gradients. The algorithms segments the image into regions well approximated by the elemental gradients. © Copyright 2006 Eurographics

When a reference image is available, active contours [15] can be used to snap extremal curves to image locations where the color gradient is strong [19]. To assign color values, two methods have been proposed. A direct solution consists of sampling a dense set of color control points along each side of a curve directly from the image, and then simplifying the set of samples by keeping only the most relevant ones using the Douglas–Pucker algorithm [19]. However, this method still requires many color control points to reach satisfying results. A better solution, proposed by Jeschke et al. [13], consists of finding optimal color control points using a least-squares approach.

8.3.2 Automatic Conversion

The earliest of automatic conversion methods were designed for image compression purposes, and relied on simple triangulations [6]. One of the first techniques that presented vectorization for stylization purposes is the Ardeco system [17] that converts bitmap images into linear or radial gradients. The core of this method is a region segmentation algorithm based on an energy minimization that combines two terms: one term aims at creating compact regions while the other term measures the goodness of fit of elemental color gradients.

As a result, the output of the system is a fully editable collection of 2D shapes with their assigned gradients, as illustrated in Fig. 8.10. The method is particularly efficient at converting images of artwork composed of very smooth gradients and very sharp transitions, hence the name of the system which is reminiscent of the artistic movement of the 1920s.

Although the restriction to elemental color gradients makes further editing straightforward, it also severely restricts the kind of images that can be depicted. Consequently, methods based on gradient meshes specifically tailored to image vec-

8 Gradient Art: Creation and Vectorization

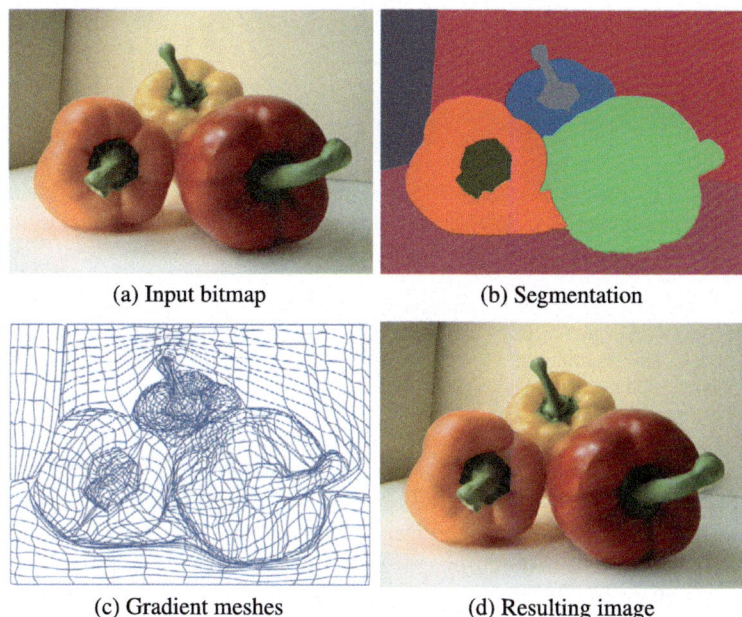

(a) Input bitmap (b) Segmentation

(c) Gradient meshes (d) Resulting image

Fig. 8.11 The method of Lai et al. [16] uses image segmentation to identify the main regions in the image. A gradient mesh is then optimized over each region. © Copyright 2009 ACM

torization [16, 25] have flourished and greatly improved the accuracy of the conversion process. Image segmentation and edge detection algorithms are typically used to identify the important features of the image and guide the mesh creation process, as illustrated in Fig. 8.11.

Such methods produce images that can look remarkably similar to photographs, but are often difficult to edit and stylize due to the complexity of the resulting meshes. On the other hand, mesh-based representations are well suited to image deformations [1].

Edge detection algorithms can also be used to automate the conversion of bitmap images into gradient extrema. Elder and colleagues [7, 8] first proposed converting a bitmap image into a representation based on edges. However, their representation remains in a raster form suitable for image compression and editing. Orzan et al. [19] build upon this approach to vectorize diffusion curves with color and blur control points for stylization purposes. Their method works in two stages: (1) the bitmap image is analyzed at multiple scales to detect not only the most salient color edges, but also their blur which is important to represent out-of-focus objects or soft shadow boundaries; (2) the extracted data are converted to a vector form, in a way similar to methods for color assignment presented in the previous section.

An example is shown in Fig. 8.12. Similar to the Ardeco system, results are easily edited using gradient extrema tools. In addition, gradient extrema are able to reproduce a greater variety of images (even photorealistic ones) with a small number of primitives, which makes their manipulation and editing more flexible than

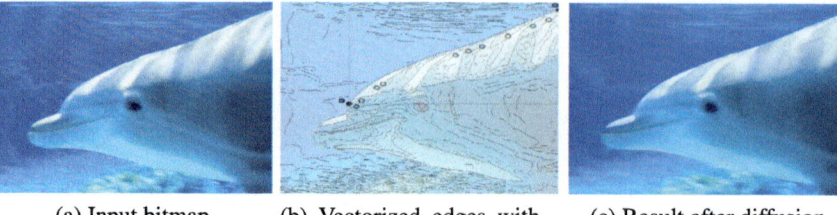

(a) Input bitmap (b) Vectorized edges with estimated color control points (c) Result after diffusion

Fig. 8.12 Automatic conversion of a bitmap image into diffusion curves. The algorithm fits Bezier splines on the image edges (**b**). Colors are sampled along each spline and approximated as polylines in color space. The resulting diffusion curve image closely matches the input bitmap, although details can be lost in textured regions. © Copyright 2008 ACM

with mesh-based representations. However, representations based on gradient extrema reach their limits with textured images. By definition, textures contain a lot of edges, which prevent simple and direct editing. Very little work has been done on the vectorization of textured images with gradient extrema methods. A notable exception is the work of Jeschke et al. [13] that represent textures with procedural noise controlled by diffusion curves. Nevertheless, a challenging direction for future research is to generate the minimal set of extremal curves that vectorizes an image under a given quality threshold. This vectorization problem is related to image compression, although the measure of quality may also be designed to encourage the editability of the set of curves.

8.4 Rendering Algorithms

Independently of the choice of primitive, the creation of an image requires a method to rasterize them into a grid of pixels. We make the distinction between methods that allow the computation of a pixel color from an analytical expression (closed-form methods) and methods that require solving a system of linear equations (optimization-based methods). Closed-form approaches allow the computation of pixels independently while optimization-based methods require computing the entire image at once.

8.4.1 Closed-Form Methods

Elemental gradients and gradient meshes are evaluated with closed-form methods, which makes them straightforward to render. For elemental gradients, rendering consists of a simple evaluation of Cartesian or polar coordinates, followed by a (usually linear) interpolation in the space of the 1D color gradient.

$$I_1(u,v) = vC_1(u) + (1-v)C_3(u)$$
$$I_2(u,v) = uC_2(v) + (1-u)C_4(v)$$
$$P(u,v) = (1-u)(1-v)P_{00}$$
$$+ (1-u)vP_{01}$$
$$+ u(1-v)P_{10}$$
$$+ uvP_{11}$$

$$I(u,v) = I_1(u,v) + I_2(u,v) - P(u,v)$$

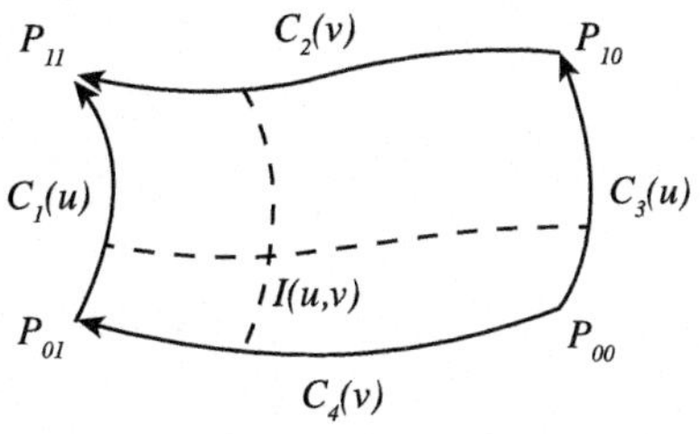

Fig. 8.13 A Coons patch is define by 4 vertices P_{00}, P_{01}, P_{11}, P_{10}, and is bounded by 4 curves $C_1(u)$, $C_2(v)$, $C_3(u)$, $C_4(v)$. The formula is used to interpolate the position and color of $I(u, v)$

For gradient meshes, the first step consists of identifying to which patch P_i a pixel belongs to; then its parametric coordinates must be computed, and colors evaluated via a 2D interpolation.

The last step depends on the type of patch. In the common case of a regular quad mesh, the color at the (u, v) coordinates of a patch is given by surface interpolation. Figure 8.13 provides the equations for the Coons patch to interpolate the position and color at a given coordinate (u, v) [9]. Sun et al. use the Ferguson patch for this purpose [22].

Due to the simplicity of the rendering process, these methods have found a widespread use in graphics applications. They have a limitation specific to rendering though: they do not deal with blurring in closed form. To compensate for this, some applications such as Inkscape rather apply a Gaussian blur in post-processing to produce more complex images.

8.4.2 Optimization-Based Methods

Methods based on gradient extrema define the color image as the solution to a partial-differential equation. The original formulation [19] uses the Laplace equation to enforce color variations in-between curves to be as smooth as possible. Finch et al. [10] propose instead to use the Bi-Laplace equation that provides higher-order smoothness.

The Laplace equation enforces an image to be as constant as possible by minimizing the Laplace operator, which is the sum of the second partial derivatives of the image I:

$$\Delta I(x, y) = \frac{\partial^2 I}{\partial x^2} + \frac{\partial^2 I}{\partial y^2} = 0 \quad (8.1)$$

A Diffusion Curve image is obtained by solving the Laplace equation subject to the color specified along the curves. To do so, Orzan et al. discretize the equation over the image grid using finite differences:

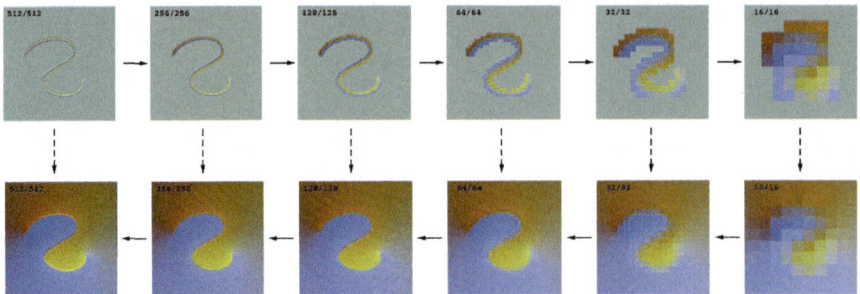

Fig. 8.14 The multigrid algorithm. Color constraints are repeatedly down-sampled (*top row*). A coarse solution is quickly computed at the lowest level, by iteratively diffusing the color constraints. The solution is then upsampled and refined using the finer-scale color constraints (*bottom row*)

$$\Delta I(x, y) = 4I(x, y) - \bigl(I(x-1, y) + I(x+1, y) + I(x, y-1) + I(x, y+1)\bigr)$$
$$= 0$$
$$I(x, y) = C(x, y) \quad \text{if pixel } (x, y) \text{ stores a color value}$$

The resulting sparse linear system of equations can be solved with a direct solver, or using iterative solvers such as Jacobi relaxation that repeatedly update the value at a pixel from the values of neighboring pixels at the previous iteration:

$$I^{k+1}(x, y) = \bigl(I^k(x-1, y) + I^k(x+1, y) + I^k(x, y-1) + I^k(x, y+1)\bigr)/4$$
$$I^{k+1}(x, y) = C(x, y) \quad \text{if pixel } (x, y) \text{ stores a color value}$$

To obtain real-time performances, Orzan et al. [19] adopt a multi-scale approach inspired by the multigrid algorithm [5] that applies Jacobi iterations in a coarse-to-fine scheme. Figure 8.14 illustrates this algorithm. The color constraints are first down-sampled to form a pyramid. A few iterations on the coarsest level of the pyramid is sufficient to solve for the low frequencies of the image. This coarse solution is then repeatedly upsampled and refined to efficiently solve for the finer details in the image. Despite GPU implementations of the multigrid, the time to convergence may still be slow to generate images at high resolution. Jeschke et al. [12] present a faster solution that initializes the color at each pixel with the color of the closest curve, and uses finite differences with variable step size to accelerate the convergence rate of Jacobi iterations.

While the Laplace equation produces a smooth image away from color constraints, it does not enforce smooth derivatives. The resulting image is a membrane interpolant that forms creases, or "tents", along the diffusion curves. Finch et al. [10] provide smooth derivatives using the Bi-Laplace equation:

$$\Delta^2 I(x, y) = \left(\frac{\partial^2 I}{\partial x^2}\right)^2 + 2\left(\frac{\partial^2 I}{\partial xy}\right)^2 + \left(\frac{\partial^2 I}{\partial y^2}\right)^2 = 0 \tag{8.2}$$

Fig. 8.15 Comparison between the solution of the Laplace and Bi-Laplace equations. The Laplace equation produces a membrane interpolant with tent-like artifacts along the curves. The Bi-Laplace produces a thin-plate spline interpolant with higher smoothness

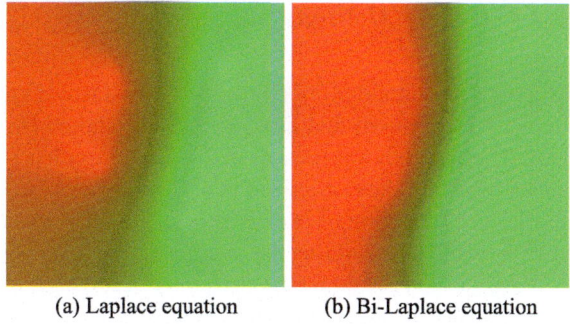

(a) Laplace equation   (b) Bi-Laplace equation

for which the solution is called the "Thin Plate Spline" function, a physical analogy involving the bending of a thin sheet of metal (see Fig. 8.15). Using finite differences over the pixel grid, the discrete equation is expressed as

$$\Delta^2 I(x,y) = 20I(x,y) - 8\big(I(x-1,y) + I(x+1,y) + I(x,y-1) + I(x,y+1)\big)$$
$$+ 2\big(I(x-1,y+1) + I(x+1,y+1) + I(x-1,y-1)$$
$$+ I(x+1,y-1)\big)$$
$$+ I(x-2,y) + I(x+2,y) + I(x,y-2) + I(x,y+2) = 0$$
$$I(x,y) = C(x,y) \quad \text{if pixel } (x,y) \text{ stores a color value}$$

As in Orzan et al. [19], Finch et al. use a multigrid solver to obtain the final color image. However, care must be taken when solving the linear system of equations because the Bi-Laplace problem has a larger condition number than the Laplace problem. A robust computation requires double-precision arithmetic, or damped iterative relaxations where the color of a pixel is only partly updated with the values of its neighbors at each iteration. Figure 8.15 provides a visual comparison between the solutions of the Laplace and Bi-Laplace equations.

These optimization techniques have a number of limitations in practice. When working with multigrid solvers, temporal flickering artifacts can occur when curves are edited because of the rasterization of the curves over a discrete multi-scale pixel grid. Although flickering is greatly reduced by the technique of Jeschke et al. [12], it only works for the original version of diffusion curves: extensions that have been further proposed are not trivial to render with an optimized solver. Moreover, although the thin-plate spline solution is smoother than the membrane solution, it may produce unexpected colors as the thin-plate splines can extrapolate colors while the membrane can only interpolate.

In all cases, important issues remain: the setting of color constraints on each side of a curve is prone to numerical inaccuracies when discretized on a pixel grid, and the blurring across a curve is usually performed by an additional diffusion of the blur values that control the size of a Gaussian blur applied in post-processing.

8.4.3 Hybrid Methods

Most of the limitations of optimization-based solvers presented so far are due to one implicit assumption: that gradient extrema should be rasterized directly in a pixel grid. The methods we present in this section rather use an intermediate representation, which is then rasterized in a second step. Such hybrid methods are suitable for the fast rendering of static vector images, but any modification of the extremal curves requires re-building the intermediate representation.

Pang et al. [20] convert Diffusion Curves into a triangle-mesh representation where colors are linearly interpolated over each triangle. They first apply a constrained triangulation to build a mesh from the curves. The positive Mean-Value Coordinate (pMVC) interpolant is then used as a (closed-form) approximation to color diffusion in order to compute the color at each vertex of the mesh. In a nutshell, positive Mean-Value Coordinates express the interpolated color at a point as a weighted sum of the colors of the curves visible from this point. The main difficulty with this approach is to evaluate visibility efficiently. Pang et al. propose a sorting algorithm that identifies the curve segments visible from each vertex. Similarly, Takayama et al. [24] use the hardware depth buffer to compute visibility of diffusion surfaces over the vertices of a mesh, while Bowers et al. [4] perform ray tracing in a pixel shader to render diffusion curves.

These methods have investigated a promising direction of research for rendering gradient extrema, with the potential practical effect of making these primitives available to a wider audience. However, they are still limited in a number of respects: none of them provides solutions to the Bi-Laplacian, and the approximations necessary for real-time rendering can degrade visual quality. Like previous rendering algorithms, blur is not dealt with directly, and should be added in post-processing.

Therefore, finding a propagation algorithm that combines the advantages of closed-form solutions with the flexibility of gradient extrema primitives remains a challenging research direction.

8.5 Discussion

We have presented vector primitives dedicated to the creation of color gradients, along with methods to construct them and algorithms to render images out of them. As of now, elemental gradients are ubiquitous in vector applications, and since gradient meshes have appeared in Adobe Illustrator, they have acquired support from a large base of users. However, only basic construction methods are available in vector graphics packages, and non-regular meshes are still confined to the vectorization of photographs. Diffusion Curves have appeared in various forms (stand-alone applications, webGL), but the issues raised by rendering algorithms make it hard to run them on all platforms, since they often require advanced GPUs.

Gradient extrema are thus mainly limited regarding rendering, although in some instances it is easier to use gradient meshes because the control over interiors is more direct. On the other hand, gradient meshes are straightforward to render, but often tend to produce too dense representations. This trade-off is reflected by the open scientific challenges we gave hints at throughout the chapter.

There might be a greater challenge though. To understand it, imagine placing the methods we have presented on an axis ranging from those more prone to creation, to those more adapted to conversion. Methods based on gradient extrema will cluster on the creation side, while those based on gradient meshes will rather be packed on the conversion side. In other words, there is a "virgin land" that has not yet been reached, and it might necessitate the invention of yet another kind of primitive, which better accounts for the structure found in images while still being sparse enough to promote direct, intuitive control.

Throughout this chapter we have only considered static images, but another appeal of vector graphics is animation. For instance, rotoscoping methods might make use of patches and curves to track image features from frame to frame and vectorize them. Then least-square optimizations could be employed to assign them colors smoothly in both space and time. Finally, these color gradients could serve as base layers to guide further stylization processes, hence finding their place in stylized rendering pipelines.

References

1. Barrett, W.A., Cheney, A.S.: Object-based image editing. ACM Trans. Graph. **21**(3), 777–784 (2002). doi:10.1145/566654.566651
2. Baxter, W.V., Scheib, V., Lin, M.C.: dAb: interactive haptic painting with 3D virtual brushes. In: SIGGRAPH, pp. 461–468 (2001)
3. Bezerra, H., Eisemann, E., DeCarlo, D., Thollot, J.: Diffusion constraints for vector graphics. In: Proceedings of the International Symposium on Non-Photorealistic Animation and Rendering (NPAR), pp. 35–42 (2010). doi:10.1145/1809939.1809944
4. Bowers, J.C., Leahey, J., Wang, R.: A ray tracing approach to diffusion curves. Comput. Graph. Forum **30**(4), 1345–1352 (2011). doi:10.1111/j.1467-8659.2011.01994.x
5. Briggs, W.L., Henson, V.E., McCormick, S.F.: A Multigrid Tutorial. SIAM, Philadelphia (2000)
6. Demaret, L., Dyn, N., Iske, A.: Image compression by linear splines over adaptive triangulations. Signal Process. **86**(7), 1604–1616 (2006). doi:10.1016/j.sigpro.2005.09.003
7. Elder, J.H.: Are edges incomplete? Int. J. Comput. Vis. **34**(2–3), 97–122 (1999). doi:10.1023/A:1008183703117
8. Elder, J.H., Goldberg, R.M.: Image editing in the contour domain. IEEE Trans. Pattern Anal. Mach. Intell. **23**(3), 291–296 (2001). doi:10.1109/34.910881
9. Farin, G., Hansford, D.: Discrete Coons patches. Comput. Aided Geom. Des. **16**, 691–700 (1999)
10. Finch, M., Snyder, J., Hoppe, H.: Freeform vector graphics with controlled thin-plate splines. ACM Trans. Graph. **30**(6), 166 (2011). doi:10.1145/2070781.2024200
11. Hnaidi, H., Guérin, E., Akkouche, S., Peytavie, A., Galin, E.: Feature based terrain generation using diffusion equation. Comput. Graph. Forum **29**(7), 2179–2186 (2010)
12. Jeschke, S., Cline, D., Wonka, P.: A GPU Laplacian solver for diffusion curves and Poisson image editing. ACM Trans. Graph. **28**, 116 (2009). doi:10.1145/1618452.1618462
13. Jeschke, S., Cline, D., Wonka, P.: Estimating color and texture parameters for vector graphics. Comput. Graph. Forum **30**(2), 523–532 (2011)

14. Johnston, S.F.: Lumo: illumination for cel animation. In: Proceedings of the International Symposium on Non-photorealistic Animation and Rendering (NPAR) (2002). doi:10.1145/508530.508538
15. Kass, M., Witkin, A., Terzopoulos, D.: Snakes: Active contour models. Int. J. Comput. Vis. **1**(4), 321–331 (1988)
16. Lai, Y.K., Hu, S.M., Martin, R.R.: Automatic and topology-preserving gradient mesh generation for image vectorization. ACM Trans. Graph. **28**(3), 85 (2009). doi:10.1145/1531326.1531391
17. Lecot, G., Lévy, B.: ARDECO: Automatic Region DEtection and Conversion. In: 17th Eurographics Symposium on Rendering—EGSR'06, pp. 349–360 (2006)
18. McCann, J., Pollard, N.S.: Real-time gradient-domain painting. ACM Trans. Graph. **27**(3), 93 (2008)
19. Orzan, A., Bousseau, A., Winnemöller, H., Barla, P., Thollot, J., Salesin, D.: Diffusion curves: a vector representation for smooth-shaded images. ACM Trans. Graph. **27**, 92 (2008). doi:10.1145/1360612.1360691
20. Pang, W.M., Qin, J., Cohen, M., Heng, P.A., Choi, K.S.: Fast rendering of diffusion curves with triangles. IEEE Comput. Graph. Appl. **32**(4), 68–78 (2011). doi:10.1109/MCG.2011.86
21. Price, B.L., Barrett, W.A.: Object-based vectorization for interactive image editing. Vis. Comput. **22**(9–11), 661–670 (2006). doi:10.1007/s00371-006-0051-1
22. Sun, J., Liang, L., Wen, F., Shum, H.Y.: Image vectorization using optimized gradient meshes. ACM Trans. Graph. **26**(3), 11 (2007). doi:10.1145/1276377.1276391
23. Sun, Q., Fu, C.W., He, Y.: An interactive multi-touch sketching interface for diffusion curves. In: Proceedings of the 2011 Annual Conference on Human Factors in Computing Systems (CHI), pp. 1611–1614 (2011). doi:10.1145/1978942.1979176
24. Takayama, K., Sorkine, O., Nealen, A., Igarashi, T.: Volumetric modeling with diffusion surfaces. ACM Trans. Graph. **29**, 180 (2010). doi:10.1145/1882261.1866202
25. Xia, T., Liao, B., Yu, Y.: Patch-based image vectorization with automatic curvilinear feature alignment. ACM Trans. Graph. **28**(5), 115 (2009). doi:10.1145/1618452.1618461

Chapter 9
Depiction Using Geometric Constraints

Craig S. Kaplan

9.1 Introduction

An artist creates a drawing by distributing a sequence of marks on an initially empty canvas. Simple marks such as stipple dots and hatching lines can be used to indicate tone, texture, and shape, sometimes all at once. Usually those marks are chosen to be unremarkable as individuals. Only in aggregate do they fulfill their collective destiny and communicate an image.

Novel artistic styles can emerge when the marks that make up a drawing are promoted to a higher level of significance. A well known example in computer graphics is the *image mosaic*, in which a single large image is approximated via a grid of smaller images chosen from a collection. The dual role played by each of the smaller images creates a dynamic tension between the whole and its constituent parts.

In this chapter, I present several related algorithms that achieve a similar tension in the creation of line drawings. In all cases, the low-level geometry of the marks will call attention to itself, and disclose a secondary purpose distinct from the marks' participation in the overall drawing. These algorithms all connect marks together to form long paths. Such drawing styles derive great benefit from computation, because algorithmic approaches can balance between complex geometric constraints on mark placement and global representational goals like halftoning. I will discuss continuous line drawing (Sect. 9.2), in which the marks align into a single closed loop; tree-based drawing (Sect. 9.3), in which marks are arranged into an image-wide branching structure; and mazes (Sect. 9.4), in which paths must also satisfy the complex geometric goal of forming a compelling maze puzzle. As a reflection of the research frontier in this subject, most topics will be seen from two perspectives: a drawing style inspired by standard data structures and algorithms in computational geometry, and a style based on simulation and a metaphor with a physical process.

C.S. Kaplan (✉)
University of Waterloo, 200 University Avenue West, Waterloo, Ontario N2L 3G1, Canada
e-mail: csk@uwaterloo.ca

9.2 Continuous Line Drawing

As previously discussed in Chap. 3, halftoning is the process of approximating a continuous-tone image with information in only two colours (usually black and white). Most traditional and computational halftoning techniques rely on the distribution of a large number of small primitives, which can be disjoint (as in stippling) or overlapping (as in crosshatching). In both cases, the local density of primitives approximates the tone of a source image in the vicinity of those primitives.

We might ask whether there are alternatives to primitives that avoid or overlap one another. One interesting artistic and algorithmic challenge would be to communicate a halftoned image using a single continuous path. We would expect such a path to meander all over the canvas in order to deposit ink wherever it is needed. The path might be made to vary locally in both density and line thickness in order to communicate continuous changes in tone.

This notion has its precedents in traditional art and design, as shown in Fig. 9.1. An ink drawing from 1884 depicts its subject using a single spiral path that varies primarily in thickness, though variations in the shape of the path are also used to communicate texture and three-dimensional form to some extent. More recently, artist and designer J. Eric "Mo" Morales has created a number of line drawings that he calls "labyrinthine projections". His hand-drawn designs typically use a constant-width line with large variations in local spacing to depict tone. Fiona Ross has created several line drawings from simple closed paths, in part to demonstrate visually the hidden complexity of the Jordan Curve Theorem [20]. In all cases, the fact that the path does not intersect itself is an important part of the aesthetic.

In this section, I discuss two computational techniques for creating a halftoned representation of an image from a single, continuous, closed path. The first is based on the fact that solutions to the Euclidean Travelling Salesman Problem cannot be self-intersecting; the second evolves a suitable path incrementally via a physical simulation.

9.2.1 The Travelling Salesman Problem

The *Travelling Salesman Problem* (TSP) is one of the most well known problems in optimization, and its intractability is an important result in complexity theory [6]. Given an arbitrary graph with weighted edges, the TSP asks for the "tour"—the closed path that visits every vertex exactly once—for which the sum of the weights of the path's edges is minimized. In the present context we are particularly interested in the *Euclidean TSP*, in which we are given only a set of "cities" in the plane (i.e., two-dimensional points). We implicitly construct the complete graph with the cities as vertices, taking Euclidean distances between pairs of cities as edge weights. This problem can be shown to be NP-hard in the number of cities; certainly the naïve approach of trying every ordering of the cities does not scale.

For the purposes of constructing line drawings, the deep mathematical intricacies of the TSP are not of direct relevance. Rather, we need just two main facts.

9 Depiction Using Geometric Constraints

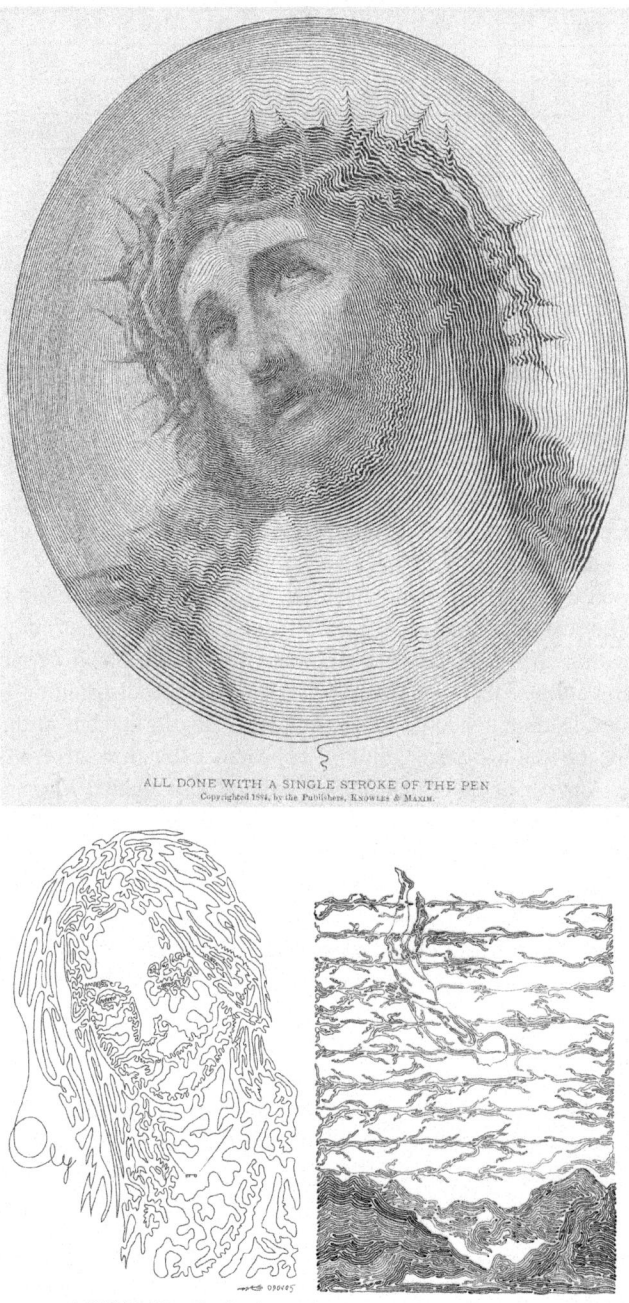

Fig. 9.1 Three hand-drawn examples of continuous line art. *Top*: "All done with a single stroke of the pen", from a 19th century manual on penmanship [19]. *Bottom left*: "Olya" © 2009 J. Eric Morales (ink drawing). *Bottom right*: "When we could be diving for pearls", by Fiona Ross (ink drawing, 2011). Used with permission

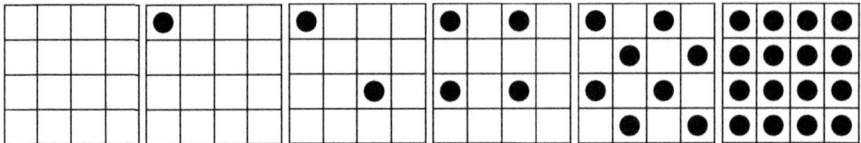

Fig. 9.2 A set of grids for ordered dithering that yield point distributions suitable for TSP art

First, it can be shown that a minimum-cost solution to the Euclidean TSP cannot be self-intersecting.[1] Second, there are efficient heuristic algorithms that produce approximate solutions to the Euclidean TSP. These algorithms cannot necessarily achieve optimality, but they are guaranteed to avoid crossings.

An implementation of continuous line halftoning can now be readily assembled from well understood components. Given an image, we apply any stippling algorithm (see Chap. 3) to obtain a distribution of points. We then use a heuristic TSP solver, such as the Lin–Kernighan heuristic technique in Concorde [2], passing in the stipple locations as cities. The solver outputs an ordering of the cities that can be drawn as a continuous closed path.

Early experiments in so-called "TSP Art" used stratified sampling to distribute points [5]. The image is divided up into cells and points are distributed uniformly at random within each cell, with the number of points in a cell derived from the image's average tone there. This method creates a wide distribution of distances between points, leading to a large variance in edge lengths in the resulting tour. This variance lends the tour a jagged, "crinkly" appearance that distracts from the quality of the result. A superior point distribution method is Weighted Voronoi Stippling, discussed in Sect. 3.2.2. The resulting Poisson-like distribution of stipples interacts favourably with the TSP solver.[2] Of course, the aesthetic character of a TSP tour is not necessarily tied directly to the quality of the underlying point distribution algorithm. For example, while the set of simple ordered dither matrices shown in Fig. 9.2 do not constitute an effective stippling algorithm on their own, they lead to interesting rectilinear designs when combined with the TSP. Examples of TSP drawings created with these point distribution methods are shown in Fig. 9.3.

Even when backed by a high-quality point distribution algorithm such as Weighted Voronoi Stippling, we cannot expect TSP tours to reproduce the tones of an input image with high fidelity. As Secord reports in his thesis [21], Weighted Voronoi Stippling tends to underestimate density, producing stippled drawings that we perceive as lighter than the images on which they are based. As the same time,

---

[1] This fact relies on a proof by contradiction. Assuming that two edges in the tour cross each other, we replace the crossing edges with non-crossing alternatives in a way that is guaranteed to reduce the total tour length.

[2] The evenness of Weighted Voronoi Stippling also tends to produce especially hard Euclidean TSP instances, because there are many possible edges with nearly identical distances. Perhaps for this reason, several stippled drawings are now used as challenges for TSP software; see http://www.tsp.gatech.edu/data/ml/monalisa.html.

9 Depiction Using Geometric Constraints

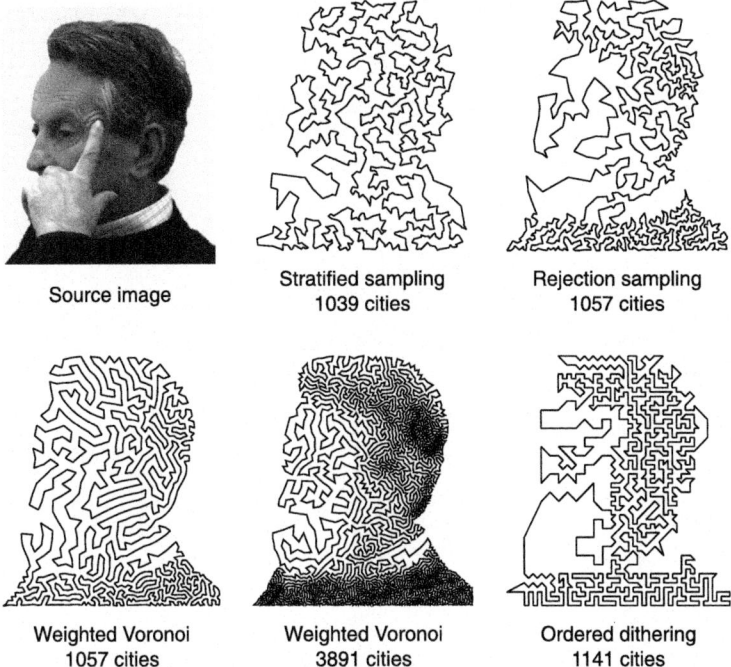

Fig. 9.3 TSP tours constructed from a variety of point distribution algorithms. The source image has been cropped, rescaled, contrast enhanced, and matted using image editing software. Two examples of Weighted Voronoi Stippling are shown with different stipple counts; both are relaxed arrangements of initial distributions created via rejection sampling

the additional ink used to draw the edges of the tour will darken the entire image, effectively lowering the dynamic range of TSP drawings.

One way to mitigate these effects is to boost the contrast of the source image before stippling. (A more thorough solution would be to precompute, analytically or empirically, a tone mapping relationship between stipple densities and perceived tone, and to apply the inverse of that tone mapping curve to the input image.) Stippling algorithms also modulate the radii of stipples in order to compensate for bias in the density distribution; we can use these radii to draw a variable-width TSP tour that better reproduces image tone, as in Fig. 9.4. Figure 9.5 shows a larger example of a TSP Art drawing with a thickened path.

The negative aesthetic impact of joining stipples into a continuous path is most pronounced in areas of an image that are almost but not quite white. Here, an individual stipple may be quite distant from its neighbours. The path must nevertheless pass through this stipple, adding a disproportionate amount of extra ink. The relative isolation of this part of the path also causes it to stand out incorrectly as a salient part of the drawing, rather than an incidental mark used for tone reproduction. This problem is most easily remedied by choosing a brightness threshold and not placing any stipples in image regions brighter than the threshold.

Fig. 9.4 The two Weighted Voronoi-based TSP tours from Fig. 9.3, redrawn with variable weight paths

Fig. 9.5 An example of a TSP Art drawing, based on a photograph courtesy of http://philip.greenspun.com

9.2.2 Evolving Labyrinthine Paths

Lloyd's method (see Sects. 3.2.1 and 10.3), which underlies Weighted Voronoi Stippling, operates as a kind of physical simulation. When a point moves to the centroid of its Voronoi region, that point can be seen as responding to repulsive forces exerted upon it by points in neighbouring regions. Viewed this way, the Voronoi diagram itself provides a convenient optimization, by associating to each point the small number of neighbours whose action upon it must be taken into account. Instead of using a Voronoi diagram as an intermediary and building the TSP tour in a final step, it is also possible to define a physical simulation that applies forces to points more directly, maintaining a simple closed path as it evolves. The technique presented in this section can be regarded as a kind of geometric reaction–diffusion model, one that produces closed loops under the influence of a large set of tunable parameters. In Sect. 9.4.3 I will present a maze generation algorithm based more directly on reaction–diffusion.

Fig. 9.6 An example of a simple curve evolving organically (redrawn from Pedersen and Singh [18])

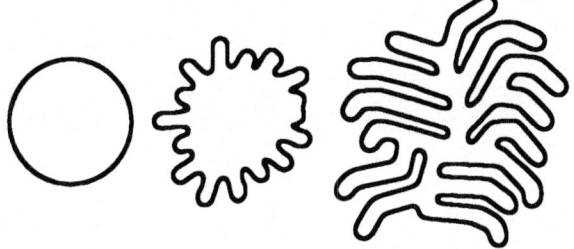

We begin with a non-self-intersecting polygon $P = \{p_1, \ldots, p_n\}$, which will evolve in a physical process to become the final continuous line drawing. The core of this kind of physical simulation is to compute, at each time step, the sum F_{tot} of all the forces acting on a sample point p_i, and to displace p_i by some fraction of that force vector. Specifically, to evolve from time t to time $t + 1$, we set $p_i^{(t+1)} = p_i^t + \Delta t F_{\text{tot}}$. The constant $\Delta t > 0$ controls the speed of the simulation; small values keep the simulation stable, while large values allow it to run more quickly. The goal, then, is to define a family of forces that will guide the simulation to create drawings in the desired style.

The most obvious force required for continuous line drawing is one that pushes the path to achieve a desired spacing. To this end, every edge $p_j p_{j+1}$ will exert an *attraction–repulsion* force on a given sample point p_i. When the point is at some chosen distance d from the edge, the two are at equilibrium and no force is applied. For distances smaller than d the edge exerts a repulsive force on the point, and for larger distances the edge attracts the point. Pedersen and Singh achieve this balance using the Lennard–Jones potential, borrowed from the modelling of Van der Waals forces in chemistry [18]. The total attraction-repulsion force on point p_i, denoted F_{ar}, is computed by summing over all edges $p_j p_{j+1}$.

We wish to coerce P to evolve and grow, not just achieve an equilibrium state with respect to attraction-repulsion forces. To that end we introduce randomness into the simulation by displacing p_i by a randomly generated *Brownian motion* force F_{bm} with normally distributed magnitude and uniformly distributed direction.

Finally, we wish to smooth out any high-frequency kinks introduced by F_{ar} and F_{bm}. We add a *fairing* force F_{f} that aims to minimize curvature. Each point p_i experiences a force that moves it a fraction of the way towards the edge defined by $p_{i-1} p_{i+1}$.

The total force F_{tot} on p_i can then be defined as $\alpha F_{\text{ar}} + \beta F_{\text{bm}} + \gamma F_{\text{f}}$. The weights α, β and γ trade off between the relative importances of these forces; they can also be expressed as functions of the plane in order to vary the trade-off spatially. Figure 9.6 shows the evolution of a simple curve under the influence of low Brownian motion and high attraction-repulsion. Pedersen and Singh also modulate these calculations by a spatially varying length scale that allows the path to achieve different rest distances in different parts of a drawing.

The simulation process can cause the sample points to become distributed non-uniformly around the path, making it difficult to evolve new geometry. Therefore,

Fig. 9.7 An artwork generated from an organic labyrinthine path: "me" by Karan Sher Singh (ink on mylar, 2010). From Karan Singh. Used with permission

after every generation we resample the curve by coalescing short edges and splitting long ones.

Figure 9.7 shows an example of a completed drawing created using this simulation method.

9.2.3 Discussion

TSP Art, introduced in Sect. 9.2.1, betrays a very strong mathematical aesthetic. The connection of these drawings to the legendary Travelling Salesman Problem seems to imbue them with extra significance in the minds of some viewers. But ultimately, it is not clear how important the TSP is in the construction of drawings of this kind. We neither expect nor require an optimal tour; one that is "short enough" and free from intersections always suffices aesthetically. On the other hand, the quality of the underlying city placement seems to have a much larger effect on the perceived quality of the drawing. Yet it is difficult to develop strategies for point distribution that permit any kind of aesthetic control when the resulting points are passed through the black box of a heuristic TSP solver.

The simulation algorithm presented in Sect. 9.2.2 is brimming over with tunable parameters that can drive the simulation to produce curves in a wide range of styles. For this reason, it is a very practical workhorse for generating continuous line drawings.

9.3 Drawing with Trees

Notwithstanding Ross's assertion of the complexity of the Jordan Curve Theorem [20], a continuous closed path is a fairly simple object. A tree, with branches that split unpredictably, is more complex both geometrically and perceptually. This extra complexity is actually a benefit in the context of creating drawings based on images: the ability to spawn branches offers us extra flexibility in the placement of primitives.

In this section I present two techniques for image representation via trees. As with continuous line drawings, one approach uses standard ideas from computational geometry to post-process a point distribution, and the other builds the tree incrementally by making an analogy with a physical process.

9.3.1 Drawing with Minimum Spanning Trees

If the Euclidean TSP provides the natural basis for connecting a set of points into a single closed loop, then the Euclidean Minimum Spanning Tree (MST) is the natural tree structure that connects those points. Like the TSP, the problem of constructing an MST can be formulated on an arbitrary graph with weighted edges: it is the tree formed from the edges of the graph that has the lowest possible total edge weight. The Euclidean MST is the special case based on the complete graph formed from a set of points in the plane, using Euclidean distance as edge weights. In other words, the TSP produces the shortest route that visits every city and returns home; the MST produces the cheapest overall road network that permits travel from any city to any other.

A method for tree-based depiction follows immediately. As with TSP Art, we construct a suitable point distribution, for example via Weighted Voronoi Stippling. We can then build a tree using any of a suite of standard Euclidean MST algorithms [7]. The most obvious are Kruskal's algorithm (connect pairs of points in increasing order of distance until a tree is formed) and Prim's algorithm (grow a tree by repeatedly adding the shortest edge from a vertex in the tree to one not in it). Both of these can be implemented naïvely in quadratic time, which will probably suffice for many practical cases. For better performance, we exploit the fact that an MST can always be extracted from the edges of a Delauney triangulation of the points; the MST can then be constructed in time $O(n \log n)$, the cost of computing the triangulation [8]. See Fig. 9.8 for examples of MST drawings created from the point distributions of Fig. 9.3.

Our visual systems are tuned to detect branching, and so trees create a very different visual impression than closed loops. Nevertheless, the two have similar low-level graphical properties. A tree on n points will have $n - 1$ edges, nearly identical to the n edges in a loop. To a first approximation, we therefore estimate that the two structures will have comparable tone reproduction properties (though the sum of the edge lengths of the TSP tour will typically be higher than that of the MST). As discussed previously, we might derive the curve that maps from point distributions at

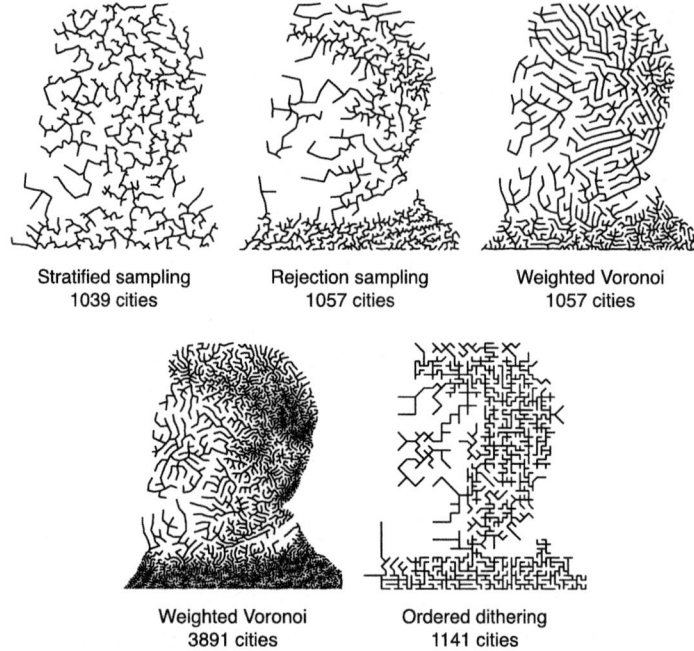

Fig. 9.8 Minimum spanning tree drawings constructed from the same point distributions as those of Fig. 9.3

different densities to output tone, whether analytically or empirically, and use that curve to guide the initial placement of points. It is also possible to associate radii with the stipples in the initial distribution, and vary the widths of the tree edges to interpolate between those radii.

There is a deeper connection between minimum spanning trees and labyrinthine paths. Imagine a minimum spanning tree as a geometric figure in the plane, drawn with infinitesimal lines. The locus of points at some small constant distance from the MST is a closed loop that never intersects itself. There may be an opportunity for a simple, efficient continuous line drawing algorithm based on tracing around the outside of an MST while varying the offset distance in an intelligent way.

9.3.2 Growing a Tree via Path Planning

The MST-based approaches discussed above can be considered continuous, in that the point locations are chosen freely in the plane. There are also tree-drawing algorithms that rely on a discrete raster grid. Here, some of the grid cells are designated as point locations, and the edges that join them must travel through the grid. The resulting edges are typically meandering paths rather than the straight lines of an MST, and the shapes of these paths can therefore be used as an extra channel through which to depict the features of a source image.

Dendritic stylization borrows from the field of path planning in robotics. Given a graph with weights on the edges, a simple path planning task is to compute, for two vertices, the cheapest path connecting those vertices relative to some cost function on edges. A typical solution is to use Dijkstra's algorithm [7], which computes the best paths from a single source to every other vertex in the graph. To create a drawing, we construct a graph in which every pixel in a source image is a vertex, with edges connecting it to its horizontal, vertical and diagonal neighbours. If we set the weight of an edge to be equal to the average brightness of the pixels it connects, then Dijkstra's algorithm will in some sense give us the tree of darkest paths from a source pixel to every other pixel. Drawing those paths will place ink preferentially where the source image is dark.

However, this naïve approach produces unsatisfactory drawings. The problem is that Dijkstra's algorithm incurs a heavy penalty for long paths: a long path consisting entirely of low-cost (i.e., dark) edges might be rejected in favour of a short path with a single high-cost edge, even though the former would be preferable. Long and Mould's solution [16] adopts a modified cost function used for path planning over uneven terrain. We effectively move from an L^1 norm to an L^∞ norm, and measure the cost of a path by its *worst* edge instead of the sum of the edges. By measuring the cost of a path this way, we favour the construction of long, meandering paths that avoid high-cost edges. To support this change, we modify Dijkstra's algorithm to maintain the maximum edge weight seen from the source to every vertex on the frontier of the developing tree.

The edge weights need not be taken directly from the darkness of the source image. For example, we can construct an abstract "importance image" by taking the weighted sum at every pixel of brightness and gradient magnitude (Long and Mould suggest weighting the gradient three times as heavily as brightness). This combination trades off between reproducing tone and depicting edges.

To apply dendritic stylization to an image, we begin by creating a distribution of points via a stippling method, with the stipples restricted to pixel centres. We can stipple the source image directly, or the importance image if desired. We label a central stipple as the source, and use the modified Dijkstra's algorithm to compute paths to all stipple locations. These paths can then be rendered as before, possibly thickened in proportion to importance. As a simple alternative to Dijkstra's algorithm, it is possible to compute a minimum spanning tree of the entire grid and prune it to extract the subtree that connects all the stipple locations. Examples based on Dijkstra's algorithm and MSTs are shown in Fig. 9.9.

9.4 Mazes

Many of the algorithms discussed so far in this chapter produce drawings reminiscent of mazes. Articles on continuous line and tree-based stylization usually note

Fig. 9.9 Two drawings created using dendritic stylization: a drawing of Lena by Long and Mould [16] (*left*) (used with permission), created using a modification of Dijkstra's algorithm; a drawing created from a pruned minimum spanning tree (*right*)

this connection, either in passing or by exploring maze construction in some detail. However, while these drawings might be mazes in a strict mathematical sense, they are unsatisfying because they do not respect the usual aesthetic conventions of maze design. Designers like Christopher Berg create mazes in which every path simultaneously contributes to the representation of an image and participates in the structure of a compelling puzzle [3]. In this section I discuss specialized techniques for constructing path-based drawings that respect principles of effective maze design.

9.4.1 Grid Mazes

The construction and solution of simple mazes based on square grids is a fertile playground in which to explore many core data structures and algorithms in computer science. I use this simplified context to introduce the maze terminology and concepts that will be required in the sequel.

Suppose that we wish to construct a maze based on an $m \times n$ grid of unit squares. By erasing a *wall* (i.e., an edge of the grid), we connect the two cells that border that wall into a short *passage*. If we erase a sufficient number of walls, then every cell will be connected to every other via a set of passages and the maze itself is said to be *connected*. On the other hand, if we keep enough walls in place then there will be no set of passages that connect together into a loop. When we balance between these constraints then the maze is both connected and acyclic, and is called a *perfect maze*. For this discussion we will always seek to construct perfect mazes. While

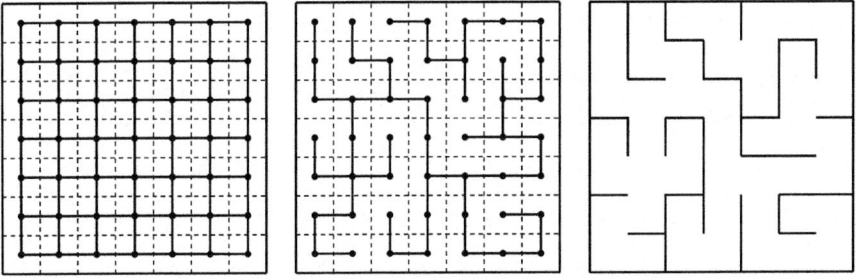

Fig. 9.10 The connection between a cell graph and a perfect grid maze. A cell graph is shown superimposed on a grid on the *left*. In the *middle*, a spanning tree of the cell graph has been computed. The spanning tree determines the walls to remove to construct the perfect maze on the *right*

cycles are a valuable tool in the maze designer's arsenal, they are easy to construct from a perfect maze by erasing edges.

The dual of this wall-erasing process can be regarded as operating on a graph called the *cell graph*, in which the vertices are the cells of the grid. Two vertices representing adjacent grid cells are connected by an edge precisely when the wall between those cells has been removed. Viewed this way, a perfect maze corresponds to a spanning tree of the cell graph. Conversely, any spanning tree algorithm can be used as a maze construction algorithm under this dual relationship, as illustrated in Fig. 9.10. For example, we can run Kruskal's algorithm on a random ordering of the walls of the grid, continuing until we have erased just enough walls to leave behind a perfect maze. Different strategies for assigning "weights" to the walls, and different spanning tree algorithms, can yield mazes with distinct visual characteristics and levels of difficulty.

9.4.2 Mazes from Generalized Cell Graphs

The grid-based construction above can easily be generalized. Any planar subdivision can be treated as a cell graph, with the subdivision's faces as vertices. The construction of a picture maze with a particular style or texture might then be reduced to the problem of constructing a suitable planar subdivision and breaking walls as before. Examination of the work of professional maze designers suggests three maze textures that are particularly important to emulate algorithmically. They are illustrated in Fig. 9.11 and described below.

In a *directional maze*, passages flow preferentially in one direction, or are more generally aligned with a vector field. Given a region of the plane and a vector field defined over that region (perhaps defined by interpolating from a few hand-placed strokes), we can use standard streamline placement algorithms [12] to draw long curves that flow along the vector field, together with a second set of curves in a perpendicular field. These intersecting curves induce a planar subdivision from which

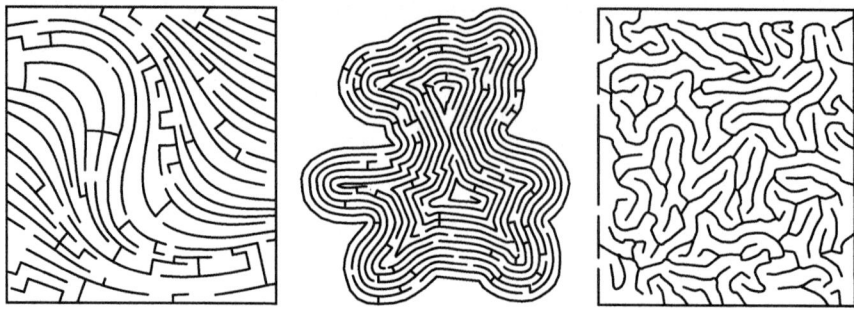

Fig. 9.11 The construction of mazes with different textures, as described by Xu and Kaplan [29]. From *left* to *right*, examples of a directional maze, a spiral maze and a random maze. © 2007 ACM, Inc. Included here by permission

a maze might be constructed. We can assign weights to the edges of the subdivision from two probability distributions, with the perpendicular edges biased to have lower expected weights than the aligned ones. A minimum spanning tree with these weights will tend to break more perpendicular walls, producing passages that flow along the vector field.

On his web page,[3] Berg discusses the importance of *spirals and vortices* as devices that add complexity to a maze. Spirals also have a long tradition as decorative devices in art and ornament. To construct spiral passages within a region, we can fill the region with a sequence of concentric copies of the boundary (computed using the straight skeleton [1], or by simulating the motion of boundary points inward along image gradients [22]). We divide the annuli delineated by these concentric curves with radial lines. The result is another cell graph, in which we preferentially remove the radial walls in order to bias towards concentric passages.

A final important maze style is a *random*, coral-like texture that fills a region evenly and isotropically. The random structure of the simulation-based labyrinths of Sect. 9.2.2 have the right form to some extent, but the wrong topology: we require the branching walls of a maze rather than a single labyrinthine path. But examination of that algorithm suggests that it is not necessarily confined to a single closed loop. Indeed, it is possible to construct a standard grid maze in a region and then "relax" that maze by running the physical labyrinth simulation on its walls.

A given maze might be made up of different regions that rely on a combination of these three styles. To construct a maze from an image, we would then segment that image into regions manually or computationally, and then assign a texture to each region. The pixels of the original image can be incorporated in the construction and rendering process in several places. Gradients can be used to define seed vectors for the vector field in a directional maze. Also, image tone can drive the modulation of both line width and line spacing, in order to allow the walls of the maze to act as halftoning primitives. Figure 9.12 shows an example of a maze in which lines depict multiple distinct textures and tones.

---

[3] http://www.amazeingart.com/.

9 Depiction Using Geometric Constraints

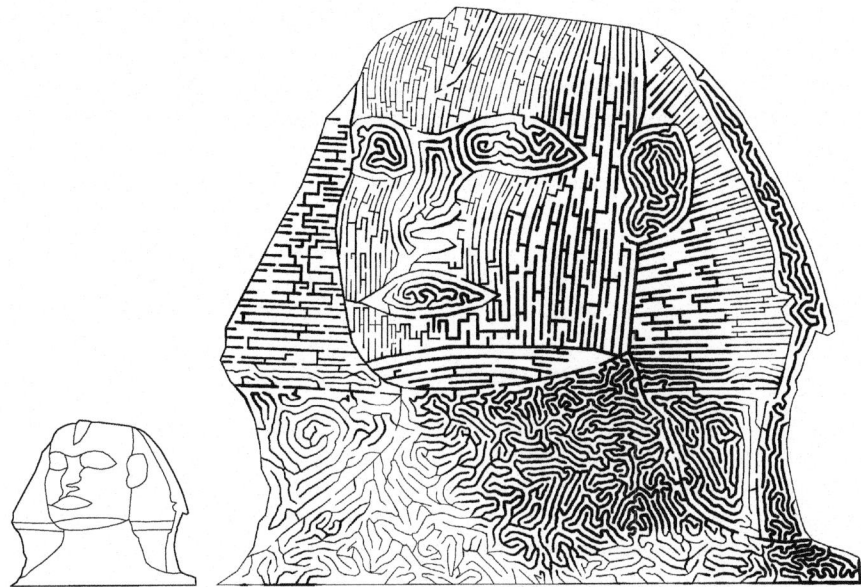

Fig. 9.12 A maze constructed from a photograph of the Sphinx, based on segmenting the photograph by hand and assigning directional, spiral and random textures to different segments. The segmented template is shown on the *left*. Note also that the walls of the maze have been thickened to reproduce tone, using a technique described by Xu and Kaplan [29]

9.4.3 Mazes from Reaction–Diffusion Patterns

Reaction–diffusion refers to a general class of mathematical models that describe the behaviour of two (or more) chemical compounds as they spread out into a space and interact with each other. These models, originally developed by Turing as a basis for explaining morphogenesis, have found wide applicability in both computer graphics and chemistry. Reaction–diffusion models can be tuned to produce a wide variety of visual imagery, including spots, stripes and cellular patterns. A classic computer graphics paper by Turk demonstrates the use of reaction–diffusion to synthesize surface textures [23]. Many people have observed that carefully balanced reaction–diffusion patterns resemble the tangled passages of a random maze. We can make this connection real by using such patterns as the basis for building the walls of real mazes.

One simple means of obtaining reaction–diffusion textures is to use a cellular neural network (CNN), a simple computational model resembling a cellular automaton. In a CNN, each cell in a grid performs a small calculation based on its current contents and the contents of cells in its local neighbourhood. By iteratively updating the contents of the cells in a sequence of generations, we evolve the state of the CNN towards a desired goal.

In particular, let $X = \{X_{ij}\}$ be a grid of scalar values representing the current state of the CNN, and let A be a filter kernel, i.e., a small matrix. We also define

$Y = \{Y_{ij}\}$ to be the "output" of the CNN, a grid of the same dimensions as X. Each Y_{ij} is computed as $f(X_{ij})$ for a given transfer function f. We can now express the rate of change of the elements of X at a given time as $\frac{dX}{dt} = -X + Y * A$, where $Y * A$ denotes the discrete convolution of Y with kernel A.

We can construct a cellular neural network that behaves like a reaction–diffusion model by defining a transfer function $f(x)$ that clamps x to $[-1, 1]$, together with the 5×5 filter kernel

$$A = \begin{bmatrix} -0.25 & -1.0 & -1.5 & -1.0 & -0.25 \\ -1.0 & 2.5 & 7.0 & 2.5 & -1.0 \\ -1.5 & 7.0 & -23.5 & 7.0 & -1.5 \\ -1.0 & 2.5 & 7.0 & 2.5 & -1.0 \\ -0.25 & -1.0 & -1.5 & -1.0 & -0.25 \end{bmatrix}$$

In each iteration of the algorithm we set $X^{(t+1)}$ to be $X^{(t)} + \Delta t \frac{dX}{dt}$, for a constant Δt small enough to keep the simulation stable.

Taking a grid of noise as the initial value of X and iterating for hundreds of generations will produce a random maze-like texture, as shown in Fig. 9.13. We might hope to guide the evolution of the texture by initializing X to the contents of some image I, but that initial impulse can get washed out after many generations. We reinforce the source image by pumping it back into the system with the revised equation $\frac{dX}{dt} = -X + Y * A + I$. As Wan et al. point out [24], we must remap the brightness of the source image to the experimentally derived range $[-0.208, 0176]$, in order to stay within the tolerances for maze-like reaction–diffusion patterns. Figure 9.14 demonstrates the effect of this modification.

After a sufficient number of generations, we use a vectorization algorithm to extract the paths that run along the black regions of the grid, as shown in the bottom right image of Fig. 9.13. These paths, and the connections between them, induce a planar subdivision. However, the subdivision is not yet a (perfect) maze—it may contain isolated regions and cycles. The topological flaws are corrected by adding and removing walls as necessary, yielding a final maze puzzle.

It may seem awkward to derive the geometry of a curvilinear maze from an inherently discrete process. But the technique is robust, and it produces high-quality output, an example of which appears in Fig. 9.15. Furthermore, it has the advantage that many desirable visual properties of mazes can be expressed in terms of simple image processing operations on the source. Simple shapes in the source generate concentric walls that can be used to create a spiral maze. Pixel-level noise leads directly to randomness in the maze. On the other hand, the discrete grid does not adapt well to variable wall spacing. One solution is to run the CNN at variable spatial resolutions. To scale up the wall spacing at a cell X_{ij}, we downsample the grid before convolving with A at that cell.

9.5 Summary

The techniques related in this chapter, and the visual styles they enable, occupy a niche in the world of non-photorealistic rendering. These styles communicate using

9   Depiction Using Geometric Constraints   183

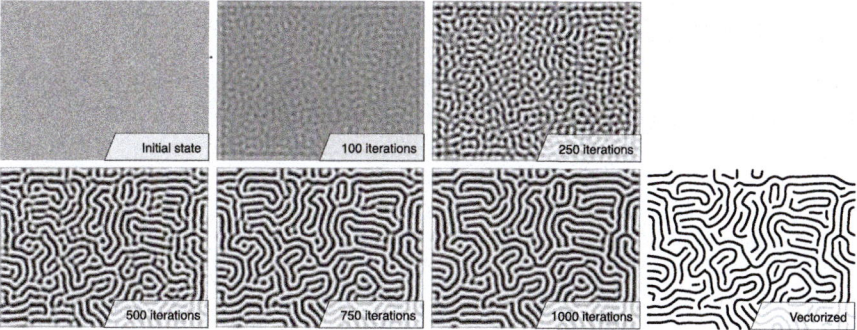

Fig. 9.13 A sequence of generations of a cellular neural network creating a reaction–diffusion texture from a random source image. After the final generation, the texture can be vectorized to extract paths

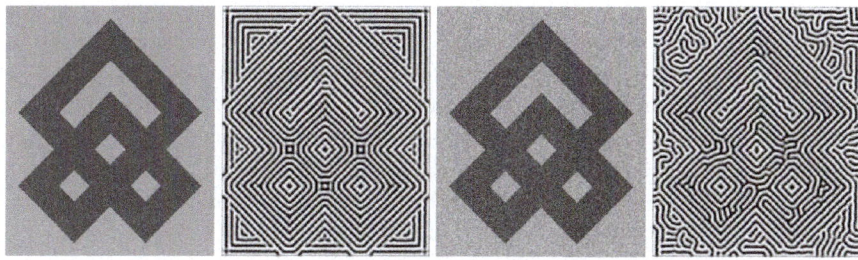

Fig. 9.14 A demonstration of biasing the cellular neural network by repeatedly injecting a source image into the simulation. Each pair of images shows the initial and final states of the grid. The *left* pair uses a rasterized version of a simple vector glyph; the *right* adds noise, producing more random variation far from image edges

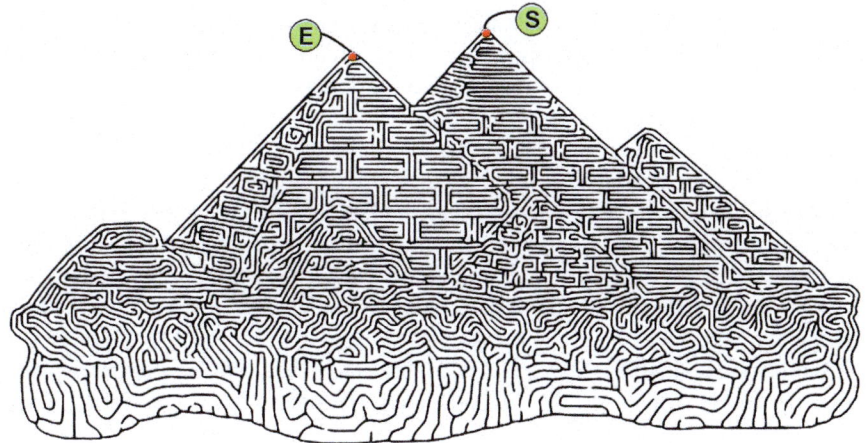

Fig. 9.15 An example of a maze created from reaction–diffusion textures, using the method of Wan et al. [24]. © 2010 IEEE. Included here by permission

a restricted vocabulary of geometric primitives, without assigning colour or texture to the canvas. Whereas primitives in ordinary halftoning algorithms would seek to be assimilated by the human eye as it fuses them into a coherent drawing, here they retain a separate voice in the final artwork. Often, that voice refuses to mask its clear mathematical origins, and the overt geometric structure is essential to the aesthetic character of the resulting artworks. The marriage of line drawing to computational geometry and simulation offers endless opportunities for exploration, and will continue to produce new works of art that bear the mark of a computational aesthetic.

9.6 Notes

TSP Art was first suggested by Bosch and Herman [5], and later refined by Kaplan and Bosch [14] to use Weighted Voronoi Stippling [21]. Bosch has continued to investigate the aesthetic possibilities of TSP Art in a more abstract setting. In particular, by carefully controlling an exact TSP solver he is able to impose constraints on which parts of the plane will be inside and outside the path [4]. He can therefore design TSP tours with meaningful interiors. Somewhat related is the "Constellation" series by contemporary artist Kumi Yamashita.[4] She winds a continuous thread around a set of nails to create a large portrait. Her path reuses individual nails as many times as necessary to achieve a desired tone.

The simulation-based approach to continuous line drawing is due to Pedersen and Singh [18]. Their technique is protected by US Patent 7928983.[5] Their paper includes a method for biasing the path direction to flow along a vector field by scaling the attraction-repulsion forces non-uniformly. They also discuss high-level tools for authoring drawings, the relationship of their work to mazes, and an analogue of their technique that generates labyrinths on surfaces in three dimensions. Recent work by Xing et al. [28] demonstrates similar results on mesh surfaces. Their technique can be interpreted as using Kruskal's algorithm to construct a spanning tree of the dual of the mesh and tracing around it to form a closed curve (as suggested at the end of Sect. 9.3.1), though it is not presented that way.

Inoue and Takahashi introduced the use of minimum spanning trees for line drawing [11]. They used an analytical model to approximate expected tone from sample density, and validated their model experimentally. They also suggested dividing the image plane into two parts and constructing disjoint spanning trees; the dividing line between those trees can play the role of a solution path in a maze. However, because the branches of the trees do not interleave across the path, the division is often plainly visible.

Diffusion-Limited Aggregation (DLA) is a classic algorithm for drawing pixel-level branching structures [25]. In DLA, an initial seed point is chosen in a fixed

---

[4]http://www.kumiyamashita.com/constellation/.
[5]http://www.google.com/patents?id=83rLAQAAEBAJ.

grid. The rest of the grid is then peppered with a set of particles, which proceed to take random walks in the grid. Any particle that comes into contact with a seed freezes in its current position and becomes another seed. The process can be continued until any desired number of particles have aggregated to the seed. The result is an organic branching structure with fractal-like properties. Greenfield experimented with the use of DLA to generate a mosaic of duotone tiles that communicate two images simultaneously [9].

Dendritic stylization is the work of Long and Mould [15, 16]. The second part of their journal article, not discussed in this chapter, extends the drawing algorithm to construct realistic looking trees whose branches embed a hidden image, a visual phenomenon known as *pareidolia*. They model the branching characteristics of different trees, and transfer texture from tree images to enhance realism.

Even the simple world of rectilinear grid mazes offers opportunities for interesting picture generation. *Maze-a-pix* puzzles, by Conceptis,[6] appear to be unadorned grid mazes. But a binary image is revealed by filling in the cells that make up the solution path. On the surface, the construction of a Maze-a-pix puzzle would seem to require the difficult computation of a Hamiltonian path. But a recent paper by Okamoto and Uehara [17] suggests an efficient alternative that will by now be familiar: construct a grid at half the desired resolution, find a spanning tree of the cells, and trace around it (thereby doubling the resolution) to build a Hamiltonian tour.

Xu and Kaplan experimented with a direct, geometric approach to constructing vortices and linking them together into mazes [30]. Their work was concerned with mazes as abstract designs rather than representations of images, and with an inquiry into sources of difficulty in maze solving. A later paper [29], which forms the basis for Sect. 9.4.2, introduces techniques for constructing directional, spiral, and random mazes. They also present an algorithm that can build passages that conform to arbitrary user-specified solution paths. Their algorithm can be used to define solution paths that blend seamlessly with the rest of the maze and that fulfill higher-level semantic goals (such as visiting a given set of regions in a prescribed order).

Wan et al. presented the method for using a cellular neural network to evolve a texture from which a maze may be extracted [24]. They also discuss an interface for "painting" maze generation properties onto an image; for example, a noise brush and a blur brush play the complementary roles of adding and reducing randomness in the resulting maze. Walls and passages can even be painted directly and maintained during the evolution process. Contemporaneous work by Wong and Takahashi [26] combines picture mazes and Maze-a-pix puzzles. They use the direction maze method introduced by Xu and Kaplan, based on a vector field induced by edge tangent flow of a source image [13] as illustrated in Fig. 9.16. They then use a heuristic method to force the solution path to trace out a superimposed bi-level image (though the method of Okamoto and Uehara seems particularly apt here).

Finally, two recent projects are worthy of mention in the context of path-based rendering.

---

[6]http://www.conceptispuzzles.com/index.aspx?uri=puzzle/maze-a-pix.

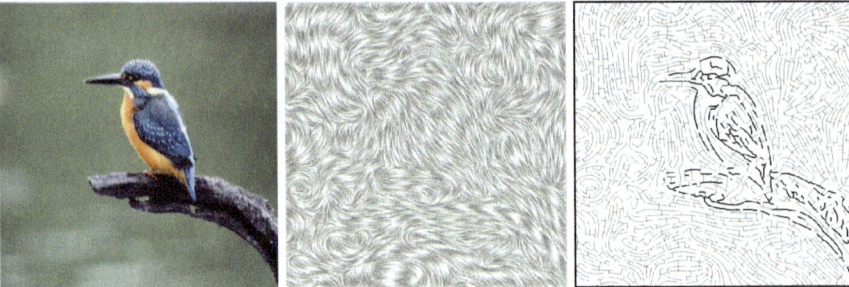

Fig. 9.16 An example of a maze created using the method of Wong and Takahashi [26], showing the source image, vector field, and the resulting maze

In a traditional art context, "continuous line art" usually refers to a form of gesture drawing in which the artist rapidly sketches a figure in one continuous motion, sometimes without even looking at the drawing as it takes form. The result often sacrifices legibility, but gains expressiveness and energy in return. Wong and Takahashi propose a technique for creating gesture drawings from images [27]. They extract vectorized edges from an image and connect them into a continuous path. The results are promising, but they betray the computational nature of the edges used, a common obstacle in high-quality artistic rendering.

Inglis, Inglis and Kaplan explored the tradition of line-based and curve-based Op Art [10], in which families of closely spaced parallel lines in multiple directions are placed on a page in such a way that bends or kinks in the lines communicate a shape via inferred contours. A two-colour image quantized to a square grid can always be depicted as the bends in lines in two directions. They extend their technique to three and four colours by using optimization to minimize undesirable artifacts at the line intersections that coincide with object boundaries in the underlying illustration.

References

1. Aichholzer, O., Aurenhammer, F., Alberts, D., Gärtner, B.: A novel type of skeleton for polygons. J. Univers. Comput. Sci. **1**(12), 752–761 (1995)
2. Applegate, D.L., Bixby, R.E., Chvátal, V., Cook, W.J.: The Traveling Salesman Problem: A Computational Study. Princeton University Press, Princeton (2006)
3. Berg, C.: Amazing Art: Wonders of the Ancient World. Harper Collins, New York (2001)
4. Bosch, R.: Simple-closed-curve sculptures of knots and links. J. Math. Arts **4**(2), 57–71 (2010). doi:10.1080/17513470903459575
5. Bosch, R., Herman, A.: Continuous line drawings via the traveling salesman problem. Oper. Res. Lett. **32**(4), 302–303 (2004). doi:10.1016/j.orl.2003.10.001
6. Cook, W.J.: In Pursuit of the Traveling Salesman: Mathematics at the Limits of Computation. Princeton University Press, Princeton (2011)
7. Cormen, T.H., Leiserson, C.E., Stein, R.L.R.C.: Introduction to Algorithms, 3rd edn. MIT Press, Cambridge (2009)
8. de Berg, M., Cheong, O., van Kreveld, M., Overmars, M.: Computational Geometry: Algorithms and Application, 3rd edn. Springer, Berlin (2010)

9. Greenfield, G.: Composite digital mosaics using duotone tiles. In: Kaplan, C.S., Sarhangi, R. (eds.) Proceedings of Bridges 2009: Mathematics, Music, Art, Architecture, Culture, pp. 155–162. Tarquin Books, Mill Valley (2009)
10. Inglis, T.C., Inglis, S., Kaplan, C.S.: Op Art rendering with lines and curves. Comput. Graph. **36**(6), 607–621 (2012). doi:10.1016/j.cag.2012.03.003
11. Inoue, K., Urahama, K.: Halftoning with minimum spanning trees and its application to maze-like images. Comput. Graph. **33**(5), 638–647 (2009). doi:10.1016/j.cag.2008.09.015
12. Jobard, B., Lefer, W.: Creating evenly-spaced streamlines of arbitrary density. In: Visualization in Scientific Computing'97. Proceedings of the Eurographics Workshop, Boulogne-sur-Mer, France, pp. 43–56. Springer, Berlin (1997)
13. Kang, H., Lee, S., Chui, C.K.: Flow-based image abstraction. IEEE Trans. Vis. Comput. Graph. **15**(1), 62–76 (2009). doi:10.1109/TVCG.2008.81
14. Kaplan, C.S., Bosch, R.: TSP art. In: Bridges 2005: Mathematical Connections in Art, Music and Science, pp. 301–308 (2005)
15. Long, J.: Modeling dendritic structures for artistic effects. Master's thesis, University of Saskatchewan (2007)
16. Long, J., Mould, D.: Dendritic stylization. Vis. Comput. **25**(3), 241–253 (2009)
17. Okamoto, Y., Uehara, R.: How to make a picturesque maze. In: Proceedings of the 21st Annual Canadian Conference on Computational Geometry, pp. 137–140 (2009)
18. Pedersen, H., Singh, K.: Organic labyrinths and mazes. In: Proceedings of the 4th International Symposium on Non-photorealistic Animation and Rendering, NPAR'06, pp. 79–86. ACM, New York (2006). doi:10.1145/1124728.1124742
19. Real Pen Work: Self-Instructor in Penmanship. Knowles & Maxim, Pittsfield (1885). http://www.iampeth.com/books/real_penwork/real_pen_work_index.php
20. Ross, F., Ross, W.T.: The Jordan curve theorem is non-trivial. J. Math. Arts **5**(4), 213–219 (2011). doi:10.1080/17513472.2011.634320
21. Secord, A.: Weighted Voronoi stippling. In: 2nd International Symp. on Non-Realistic Animation and Rendering (NPAR), pp. 37–43. ACM, New York (2002)
22. Sethian, J.A.: Level Set Methods and Fast Marching Methods: Evolving Interfaces in Computational Geometry, Fluid Mechanics, Computer Vision, and Materials Science. Cambridge University Press, Cambridge (1999)
23. Turk, G.: Generating textures for arbitrary surfaces using reaction–diffusion. Comput. Graph. **25**(4), 289–298 (1991)
24. Wan, L., Liu, X., Wong, T.T., Leung, C.S.: Evolving mazes from images. IEEE Trans. Vis. Comput. Graph. **16**(2), 287–297 (2010)
25. Witten, T.A. Jr., Sander, L.M.: Diffusion-limited aggregation, a kinetic critical phenomenon. Phys. Rev. Lett. **47**, 1400–1403 (1981). doi:10.1103/PhysRevLett.47.1400
26. Wong, F.J., Takahashi, S.: Flow-based automatic generation of hybrid picture mazes. Comput. Graph. Forum **28**(7), 1975–1984 (2009). doi:10.1111/j.1467-8659.2009.01576.x
27. Wong, F.J., Takahashi, S.: A graph-based approach to continuous line illustrations with variable levels of detail. Comput. Graph. Forum **30**(7), 1931–1939 (2011). doi:10.1111/j.1467-8659.2011.02040.x
28. Xing, Q., Akleman, E., Taubin, G., Chen, J.: Surface covering curves. In: Cunningham, D., House, D. (eds.) Workshop on Computational Aesthetics, pp. 107–114. Eurographics Association, Annecy (2012). doi:10.2312/COMPAESTH/COMPAESTH12/107-114
29. Xu, J., Kaplan, C.S.: Image-guided maze construction. ACM Trans. Graph. **26**(3), 29 (2007). Proceedings of SIGGRAPH 2007. doi:10.1145/1276377.1276414
30. Xu, J., Kaplan, C.S.: Vortex maze construction. J. Math. Arts **1**(1), 7–20 (2007)

Chapter 10
Artificial Mosaic Generation

Giovanni Puglisi and Sebastiano Battiato

10.1 Introduction

Mosaic is an ancient art form, with first examples going back some 4,000 years or more. Some mosaics can be found in Sumerian ancient manufacts with unusual cone shaped-tesserae of various length [11]. Other mosaics realized in the same period can be also found in some Egyptian and Phoenician manufacts. Later, different colored stones to create patterns have been used in pebble pavements by the 8th century BC. Greek artists improved this art form by using precise geometric patterns and detailed scenes of people and animals (4th century BC). Later, in order to provide extra detail and range of color to the mosaic, small manufactured pieces (tesserae) have been used. By properly using small tesserae with varying shape and color, mosaics can imitate paintings. Examples of the work of Greek artists can be found, for example, at Pompeii. From the 5th century onwards, with the rise of the Byzantine Empire, centered on Byzantium (now Istanbul, Turkey), novel characteristics were exploited. Specifically, these novelties are related to the style (eastern influences) and the usage of glass tesserae called smalti. Different from before, in Byzantine culture one mainly covered walls and ceilings instead of floors like the Roman mosaics. The used smalti allows light to reflect and refract within the glass. In the 8th century, the Moors brought Islamic mosaic into the Iberian peninsula. Their motifs are mainly geometric and mathematical [8]. During Gothic Revival there was influence from medieval themes. Some famous artists like Antonio Salviati and Antoni Gaudì gave new emphasis to the mosaic world in the modern area.

Mosaics, in essence, are images obtained cementing together small colored fragments. Likely, they are the most ancient examples of discrete primitive based im-

---

G. Puglisi (✉) · S. Battiato
University of Catania, Catania, Italy
e-mail: puglisi@dmi.unict.it

S. Battiato
e-mail: battiato@dmi.unict.it

ages. In the digital realm, mosaics are illustrations composed by a collection of small images called "tiles". The tiles tessellate a source image with the purpose of reproducing the original visual information rendered into a new mosaic-like style. The same source image may be translated into many strikingly different mosaics. Factors like tile dataset, constraints on positioning, deformations, and rotations of the tiles are indeed very influent upon the final results.

10.2 Digital Mosaic Generation

The generation of a digital mosaic from a raster image can be formulated as a mathematical optimization problem:

> Given a rectangular region I^2 in the plane $\mathbb{R}^2$, a tile dataset and a set of constraints, find N sites $P_i(x_i, y_i)$ in I^2 and place N tiles, one at each P_i, such that all tiles are disjoint, the area they cover is maximized and the constraints are verified as much as possible.

Taking into account the mosaic generation process four different definitions can be given to solve specific problems:

Crystallization Mosaic Given an image I^2 in the plane $\mathbb{R}^2$ and a set of constraints (i.e., on edge features), find N sites $P_i(x_i, y_i)$ in I^2 and place N tiles, one at each P_i, such that all tiles are disjoint, the area they cover is maximized, each tile is colored by a color which reproduces the image portion covered by the tile. In this case in order to allow a solution the requirements have to be relaxed by asking only that the constraints are verified as much as possible.

Ancient Mosaic Given an image I^2 in the plane $\mathbb{R}^2$ and a vector field $\phi(x, y)$ defined on that region by the influence of the edges of I^2, find N sites $P_i(x_i, y_i)$ in I^2 and place N rectangles, one at each P_i, oriented with sides parallel to $\phi(x_i, y_i)$, such that all rectangles are disjoint, the area they cover is maximized and each tile is colored by a color which reproduces the image portion covered by the tile [14].

Photo-Mosaic Given an image I^2 in the plane $\mathbb{R}^2$, a dataset of small rectangular images and a regular rectangular grid of N cells, find N tile images in the dataset and place them in the grid such that each cell is covered by a tile that "resembles" the image portion covered by the tile.

Puzzle Image Mosaic Given an image I^2 in the plane $\mathbb{R}^2$, a dataset of small irregular images and an irregular grid of N cells, find N tile images in the dataset and place them in the grid such that the tiles are disjoint and each cell is covered by a tile that "resembles" the image portion covered by the tile.

The former two types of mosaics decompose a source image into tiles (with different color, size, and rotation), reconstructing the image by properly painting the tiles (Figs. 10.1, 10.2). The latter two kinds of mosaic are obtained by fitting images

Fig. 10.1 Example of Crystallization Mosaic generated by using [18]

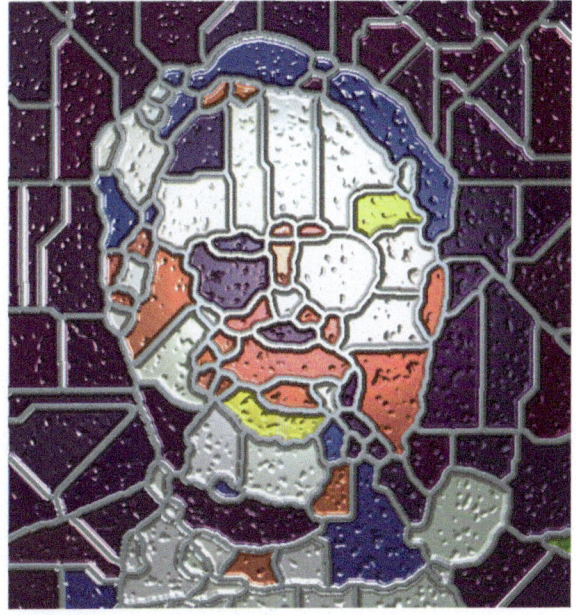

Fig. 10.2 Example of Ancient Mosaic generated by using [5]

from a database to cover an assigned source image. They may hence be grouped together under the denomination of *multi-picture mosaics* (Figs. 10.3, 10.4). Many mosaic techniques may fit in more than a single class and it is likely that other new types of mosaics will appear in the future. A detailed survey is available in [3]. This chapter will review several solutions focusing on Ancient Mosaic generation algorithms.

Fig. 10.3 Example of Image Mosaic generated by using [10]. © 1998 Springer

Fig. 10.4 Example of Puzzle Image Mosaic generated by using [15]. © 2002 ACM

Fig. 10.5 Example of Ancient Mosaic generated by using [14]. © 2007 Eurographics Association

10.3 Artificial Mosaics Resembling Ancient Mosaics

Ancient mosaics are artworks constituted by cementing together small colored tiles. A smart and judicious use of orientation, shape, and size may allow to convey much more information than the uniform or random distribution of N graphic primitives (like pixels, dots, etc.). For example, ancient mosaicists avoided lining up their tiles in rectangular grids, because such grids emphasize only horizontal and vertical lines. Such evidence may distract the observer from seeing the overall picture. To overcome such potential drawback, old masters placed tiles emphasizing the strong edges of the main subject to be represented.

One of the earliest algorithms of artificial mosaic generation was developed by Hausner [14] who also proposed the mathematical formulation of the mosaic problem (see Sect. 10.2). Hausner's technique is an iterative approach in which the user selects important feature edges to be used for mosaic generation. An orientation field is then computed considering the gradient of the Euclidean distance transform from the edges. This field $\phi(x, y)$ follows edge orientation if (x, y) is close to the edge. Tile placing is then performed by using a modified version of the Centroidal Voronoi Diagram (CVD)—see Sect. 3.2.1 for more detail. The CVD, which usually arranges points in regular hexagonal grids, has been adapted to place tiles in curving square grids. This adaption is performed by using the Manhattan distance instead of the Euclidean one. Efficiently computing the CVD is made possible by leveraging the z-buffer algorithm available in many graphics cards. Although this approach is able to produce good results (see Fig. 10.5) the convergence of the iterative algorithm could be a drawback if there is no direct access to the graphic acceleration engine.

Another strategy of artificial mosaic generation has been proposed in [7] and in [2]. The proposed approach tries to emulate mosaicist work making use of directional guidelines and distance transform. First one segments the image by using the Statistical Region Merging algorithm [19] and divide the image into background and foreground regions. Although this step is optional, it enables generation of mosaics that mimic "opus vermiculatum" style. Later, for each pixel the distance transform from the segmented region bounds is evaluated. The gradient matrix and the level line matrix are then computed. Finally, based on the previous steps, tiles are placed. The authors, in order to obtain a high degree of similarity in terms of style with respect to ancient mosaics, also consider tile cutting. Several examples of mosaics generated by using [7] with and without considering tile cutting are shown in Figs. 10.6 and 10.7.

In [20] an interesting framework for stroke-based rendering based on a multi-agent system is proposed. These agents (RenderBots) represent one stroke and during the simulation disseminate themselves in the environment (a source image and possibly additional G-buffer support images such as edge image, luminance image, etc.). The output of the algorithm is created at the end of the simulation when each RenderBot executes its painting function. Different styles can be created by using the same framework: stippling, hatching, painterly rendering, and mosaics. This high degree of flexibility is achieved by using a specific class of RenderBot for each style. Figure 10.8 has been obtained by using the RenderBots algorithm without user interaction. Better results can be achieved by using a manual segmentation.

In [9] a technique that tries to simulate the classic mosaic art form is presented. First, feature curves are extracted from the input image. Later, offset curves are computed and the self-intersecting segments get trimmed off with the guidance of Voronoi diagrams. Finally, tiles are placed along the computed curves without overlapping. Although results are interesting (see Fig. 10.9), this technique requires user interaction in the selection of the edges to be followed.

In [12] an interactive technique able to create visually pleasing ancient mosaics is proposed. The authors, starting from the study of ancient mosaics, derive a set of characteristic features of a generic mosaic. Specifically, they consider the splices among tiles (which should be constant), the variations of colors (tone and luminance), size, and shape of the tiles. Moreover, tiles should be placed along feature lines of the input image and their orientation should vary in a smooth way. To satisfy the above mentioned properties, the authors design a method based on Lloyd's algorithm for CVT (Centroidal Voronoi Tessellation) computation and can be viewed as a smart extension and/or optimization of the technique proposed by Hausner [14]. Instead of considering heuristics to automatically generate the artificial mosaic, they model their solution as an interactive tool. The user can arrange tiles of various shapes and sizes, and control the distribution process by adding additional data such as contour lines and directional information. Moreover, tiles can be sized or shaped to better approximate the master image features. Although this algorithm obtains impressive results it requires user interaction, and therefore depends on the user's aesthetic skill and experience.

Fig. 10.6 Examples of Ancient Mosaic generated by using [7] without performing tile cutting

Fig. 10.7 Examples of Ancient Mosaic generated by using [7] with tile cutting

Fig. 10.8 Examples of Ancient Mosaic generated by using [20] without performing manual segmentation

A novel technique for ancient mosaic generation has been presented in [16] and further refined in [17]. The tile orientation field is generated respecting the strong edges of the underlying image. Moreover orientations are forced to vary smoothly in order to produce pleasing mosaics and reduce the gap between tiles. This field is obtained by using a global optimization approach (α-expansion algorithm) [6]. The packing of the tiles is then performed in two steps. First a set of mosaic layers ($M_1, M_2, \ldots, M_n$) is generated. Starting from a random pixel p each mosaic layer is created with a region growing strategy based on a greedy assumption (the nearby pixel s that does not overlap and with the minimum gap space with respect to p is chosen). Later the mosaic layers are stitched together taking into account gap space minimization, the absence of broken tiles and the crossing of strong edge intensity. This task is performed through the graph cuts algorithm [6]. Several mosaics generated by the aforementioned approach can be seen in Fig. 10.10.

Fig. 10.9 An example of mosaic generated by using [9]. © 2003 Springer

In [4, 5] the authors propose a mosaic generation approach based on Gradient Vector Flow (GVF) [21] computation together with some smart heuristics to drive tile positioning. Edge information is preserved, propagated in the close regions and merged together in a smooth way. Once the orientation field has been computed, several heuristics are employed to follow principal edges and cover, as much as possible, the overall mosaic area. Several examples of mosaics generated by [5] are shown in Fig. 10.11. To obtain mosaics with irregular tiles, the authors extended their approach considering two different strategies of tile cutting: subtractive and shared cut (see Fig. 10.12). The former cuts only the novel tiles, i.e., tiles that are not already present in the mosaic; the latter cuts both novel and already placed tiles. In order to improve the mosaic visualization experience they also developed an application for the 3D mosaic rendering [1]. Each 2D tile becomes a 3D truncated pyramid with its bottom base slightly bigger than the top one; oblique sides increase the effect of depth. By properly modifying the pixels' coordinates adapting them to the 3D virtual environment a planar 3D mosaic is simple obtained. A cement-like background is also used to improve the overall aesthetic effect. Several 3D surfaces can be obtained by simply transforming pixel coordinates. The following surfaces have been considered in their approach: Plane, Dome, Cylinder, and Pyramid. Several examples are shown in Fig. 10.13.

To summarize this section, the keys of any technique aimed at the production of digital ancient mosaics are clearly the tile positioning and orientation. The methods presented in this section use different approaches to solve this problem, obtaining different visual results. Some techniques are based on a CVD approach [9, 12, 14]) whereas other methods [5, 17] compute a vector field by making use of different strategies (i.e., gradient vector flow, graph cuts minimization). Tile positioning is then performed with iterative strategies [9, 12, 14, 17] or reproducing the ancient artisans' style by using a "one-after-one" tile positioning [2, 5, 7]. A different non-deterministic approach is used in [20].

10 Artificial Mosaic Generation

Fig. 10.10 Examples of Ancient Mosaic generated by using [17]

Fig. 10.11 Examples of Ancient Mosaic generated by using [5] without performing tile cutting

10 Artificial Mosaic Generation

Fig. 10.12 Example of Ancient Mosaic generated by using [5] with tile cutting

Fig. 10.13 Examples of Ancient Mosaic generated by using [1]

10.4 Discussions

Designing a technique able to automatically generate a high quality mosaic is a challenging task. As discussed earlier, several design choices influence the final results. It is worth noting that, whenever possible, all results presented here are meant to try to reproduce a mosaic by considering the same underlying structure (e.g., shape and tile size). This section will review in detail some of the aspects related to the orientation, size, and shape of the tiles, providing useful hints for the design of novel automatic mosaic generation approaches.

10.4.1 Tile Orientation

Tile orientation has a strong visual influence on the overall perception of the mosaic. In particular orientation cannot be arbitrary but it is constrained to follow the gestalt choices made by the author of the source picture. Tiles, hence, must follow and emphasize the main orientations chosen by the artist. Some approaches [9, 12, 14] solve this problem with an interactive strategy allowing the user to provide useful hints for the creation of the orientation field. On the contrary other techniques try to automatically generate this field [5, 17].

In order to properly find the correct orientation Battiato et al. [5] make use of the GVF (Gradient Vector Flow) field computation based on [21] algorithm. GVF is a dense force field designed by the authors of [21] in order to solve the classical problems that affect snakes: sensitivity to initialization and poor convergence to boundary concavity. Starting from the gradient of an image, this field is computed through diffusion equations. GVF is a field of vectors $\mathbf{v} = [v, u]$ that minimizes the following energy function:

$$E = \int\int \mu\left(u_x^2 + u_y^2 + v_x^2 + v_y^2\right) + |\nabla f|^2 |\mathbf{v} - \nabla f|^2$$

where the subscripts represent partial derivatives along x and y axes respectively, μ is a regularization parameter and $|\nabla f|$ is the gradient computed from the intensity input image. Due to the formulation described above, GVF field values are close to $|\nabla f|$ values where this quantity is large (the energy E, to be minimized, is dominated by $|\nabla f|^2|\mathbf{v} - \nabla f|^2$) and are slow-varying in homogeneous regions (the energy E is dominated by the sum of the squares of the partial derivatives of the GVF field). An example of the GVF field is shown in Fig. 10.14. This vector field can then be used to effectively drive tile positioning. Edge information is preserved, propagated in the close regions, and merged in a smooth way.

Another approach able to automatically compute the tile orientation field has been proposed in [17]. The authors make use of a global optimization framework based on the graph cuts algorithm. Specifically, the object function has been designed to obtain smooth variations in tile orientations and alignment of the tile with the strong edges. The authors formulate the mosaic generation problem as a labeling one. Tiles have been represented by using two labels (center and orientation). Considering an image I to be mosaicized, let P the set of all pixels belonging to I. For each pixel p they assign a pair (v_p, ϕ_p), where v_p is a binary variable representing

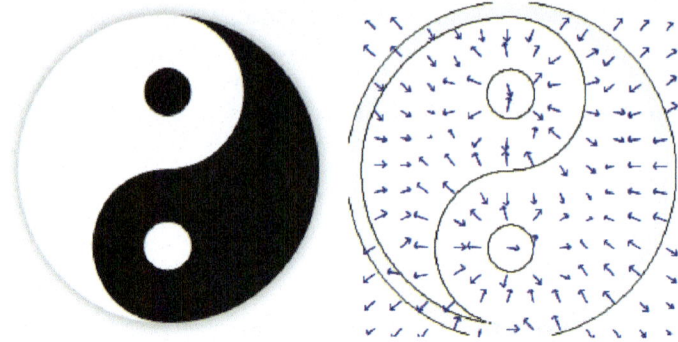

Fig. 10.14 Input image and its corresponding GVF field. Input image and its corresponding GVF field. Source image from http://commons.wikimedia.org/wiki/File:Yin_and_Yang.svg

the visibility of the tile and ϕ_p the related orientation. The energy function has then been formulated as follows:

$$E(v,\phi) = \sum_{p \in P}(1 - v_p) + \sum_{p \in P} v_p D_p(\phi_p) + \sum_{\{p,q\} \in N} V_{pq}(v_p, v_q, \phi_p, \phi_q)$$

The first sum is useful for the gap space minimization. The data term (second sum) measures the alignment of the tiles with respect to the main edges. The smoothness term (third sum) forces neighboring pixels to have similar orientations.

10.4.2 Tile Size

As already discussed before, many parameters influence the final quality of the generated mosaic. It is worth noting that tile size is a crucial parameter, difficult to set without user interaction. Specifically, it depends not only on the dimension of the input images but also on the intrinsic size of the objects contained into it. Considering a specific image, if tile size is not properly set (too big or too small), important details could be lost or the output images could lose the mosaic effect. An example of mosaics generated with increasing tile size is reported in Fig. 10.15.

10.4.3 Tile Shape

Ancient mosaicists could make use of irregular tiles in the mosaic creation. Irregular tiles are suited to follow principal image edges, properly cover the image canvas obtaining hence visually pleasant mosaics. In order to emulate this aspect some approaches introduces different strategies of tile cutting.

Fig. 10.15 Examples of mosaics obtained by using [5] with increasing tile size (from 3 × 3 to 13 × 13 at steps of two pixels)

Di Blasi et al. [7] studied ancient artisans' work and tried to emulate them. Ancient mosaicists outline the shapes of the image they want to obtain, fill the shapes with a set of parallel curves and place the tiles along these curves. Di Blasi et al. [7] compute directional guideline by using a combination of standard filters (Gaussian, Laplacian edge detector, etc.). Starting from the computed directional guideline, making use of the distance transform [13], two novel matrices are computed: gradient matrix and level line matrix. While there are chains of pixels not yet processed in the level line matrix, the algorithm works as follows:

- select a chain;
- starting from an arbitrary pixel on it, follow the chain;
- place new tiles at regular distances along the path (the orientation of the tiles is assigned using the gradient information from matrix).

Fig. 10.16 The novel tile B overlaps a previously placed tile A. Tile B is then cut, removing the overlapping area C

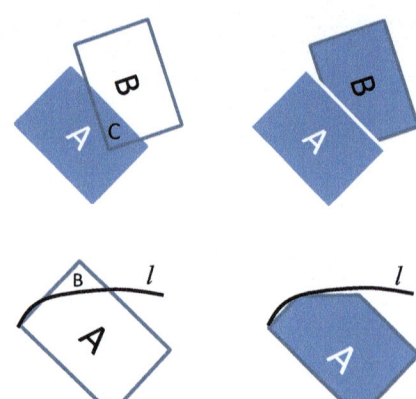

Fig. 10.17 Tile A crosses the border l. Region B is then cut away

In order to improve the aesthetic quality of the final mosaic by also avoiding the overlapping of the tile they adopt the following strategy:

- if the novel tile overlaps a previously placed one, a cut is performed (see Fig. 10.16).
- if a novel tile crosses the border curves it is trimmed against this line (see Fig. 10.17).

The algorithm proposed in [5] has been extended to introduce tile cutting. In particular when the tile to be placed overlaps with some already placed tiles, a series of cutting heuristics is introduced as detailed below. Specifically, two tile cutting strategies have been considered: subtractive and shared cut. The former cuts only the novel tiles, i.e., tiles that are not already present in the mosaic (shared cut actually unions two tiles and can be considered a tile-merging strategy); the latter cuts both novel and already placed tiles. Let $tile_P$ and $tile_N$ be the tiles already placed and to be placed (novel), respectively. Their intersection creates some novel vertices placed on their border. The cutting is performed considering the line connecting these vertices (see Fig. 10.18). As already stated, the cut is performed both on $tile_P$ and $tile_N$. It is worth noting that the shared cut creates convex tiles without irregular parts. However it should be carefully used because it tends to increase the sides of polygons and round shapes. Sometimes the shared cut cannot be used (e.g., further cutting of the placed tiles cannot be done due to the limit specified by the user); in these cases the subtractive cut could be useful. It does not modify the already placed tiles but removes part of the novel tile. As shown in Fig. 10.19 two possible cuts can be considered along the side of the tile already placed. In order to preserve more information and increase the possibility of satisfying all the constraints about tile cutting, the cut removing less area is chosen. It is worth noting that the subtractive cut gives higher importance to the already placed tiles (the orientations of their sides are taken into account in the cutting).

Both shared and subtractive tile cuts depend on a set of thresholds detailed as follows:

- T_P, maximum percentage of total cut area, from an already placed tile.

Fig. 10.18 Shared cut

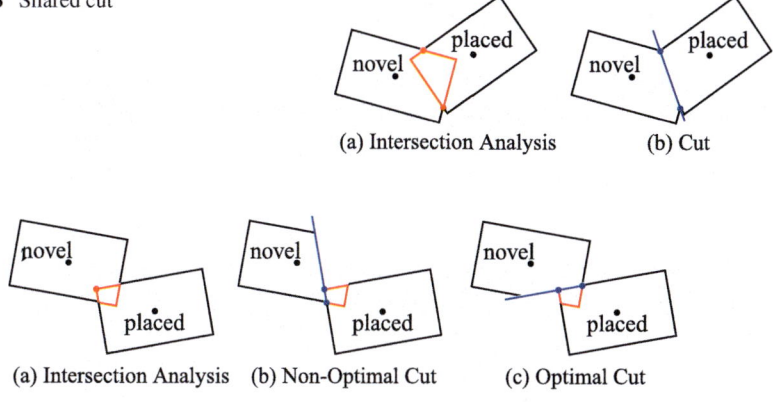

Fig. 10.19 Subtractive cut. If both cuts satisfy the aforementioned constraints, cut (**c**) is chosen. In this way a smaller area is removed from the novel tile

- S_P, maximum percentage of cut area, with a single cut, from an already placed tile; it should be noted that $S_P \leq T_P$.
- T_N, maximum percentage of total cut area, from a novel tile.
- S_N, maximum percentage of cut area, with a single cut, from a novel tile; it should be noted that $S_N \leq T_N$.

Let A_0^N be the original tile area (i.e., the area of the rectangular shape the tile has when it is generated) of the novel tile and A_0^P the area of the already placed tile. Let A_i^N and A_i^P the corresponding tile area after the ith cut.

The tile cutting of a novel tile has to satisfy the following constraints:

$$\frac{A_i^N - A_{i+1}^N}{A_0^N} \leq S_N, \quad i = 1, \ldots, M_N - 1$$

$$\frac{A_0^N - A_{M_N}^N}{A_0^N} \leq T_N$$

where M_N is the overall number of cuts performed on the novel tile. The tile cutting of an already placed tile has to satisfy the following constraints:

$$\frac{A_i^P - A_{i+1}^P}{A_0^P} \leq S_P, \quad i = 1, \ldots, M_P - 1$$

$$\frac{A_0^P - A_{M_P}^P}{A_0^P} \leq T_P$$

where M_P is the overall number of cuts performed on the already placed tile. Notice that there is a subtractive cut if $T_P = 0$ or $S_P = 0$.

10.5 Conclusions

In this chapter we review several approaches for the generation of artificial mosaics. In particular, techniques generating mosaics resembling the ancient ones have been considered. Finally, also some useful discussion of fundamental aspects of artificial mosaic generations such as the choice of tile orientation, size, and shape have been provided.

Acknowledgement We would like to thank the authors of [7, 17] and [20] for providing the original code or the images used in this chapter.

References

1. Battiato, S., Puglisi, G.: 3D ancient mosaics. In: Proceedings of ACM Multimedia Technical Demos (2010)
2. Battiato, S., Di Blasi, G., Farinella, G., Gallo, G.: A novel technique for opus vermiculatum mosaic rendering. In: Proceedings of the 14th International Conference in Central Europe on Computer Graphics, Visualization and Computer Vision (WSCG'06), pp. 133–140 (2006)
3. Battiato, S., Di Blasi, G., Farinella, G.M., Gallo, G.: Digital mosaic frameworks—an overview. Comput. Graph. Forum **26**(4), 794–812 (2007)
4. Battiato, S., Di Blasi, G., Gallo, G., Guarnera, G.C., Puglisi, G.: A novel artificial mosaic generation technique driven by local gradient analysis. In: Proceedings of International Conference on Computational Science (ICCS'08)—Seventh International Workshop on Computer Graphics and Geometric Modeling (CGGM'08), vol. 5102, pp. 76–85 (2008)
5. Battiato, S., Di Blasi, G., Gallo, G., Guarnera, G.C., Puglisi, G.: Artificial mosaics by gradient vector flow. In: Short Proceedings of EUROGRAPHICS (2008)
6. Boykov, Y., Veksler, O., Zabih, R.: Fast approximate energy minimization via graph cuts. IEEE Trans. Pattern Anal. Mach. Intell. **23**(11), 1222–1239 (2001)
7. Di Blasi, G., Gallo, G.: Artificial mosaics. Vis. Comput. **21**(6), 373–383 (2005)
8. Du Sautoy, M.: Symmetry: A Journey into the Patterns of Nature. Harper Collins, New York (2008)
9. Elber, E., Wolberg, G.: Rendering traditional mosaics. Vis. Comput. **19**(1), 67–78 (2003)
10. Finkelstein, A., Range, M.: Image mosaics. In: Proceedings of Raster Imaging & Digital Typography (RIDT), pp. 11–22 (1998)
11. Fiorentini Roncuzzi, I., Fiorentini, E.: Mosaic: Materials, Techniques and History. MWeV (2002)
12. Fritzsche, L., Hellwig, H., Hiller, S., Deussen, O.: Interactive design of authentic looking mosaics using Voronoi structures. In: Proceedings of the 2nd International Symposium on Voronoi Diagrams in Science and Engineering VD 2005 Conference, pp. 1–11 (2005)
13. Haralick, R., Shapiro, L.: Computer and Robot Vision, vol. 1. Addison-Wesley, Reading (1992)
14. Hausner, A.: Simulating decorative mosaics. In: Proceedings of the 28th Annual Conference on Computer Graphics and Interactive Techniques (SIGGRAPH'01), pp. 573–580 (2001)
15. Kim, J., Pellacini, F.: Jigsaw image mosaics. ACM Trans. Graph. **21**(3), 657–664 (2002)
16. Liu, Y., Veksler, O., Juan, O.: Simulating classic mosaics with graph cuts. In: Proceedings of Energy Minimization Methods in Computer Vision and Pattern Recognition, pp. 55–70 (2007)
17. Liu, Y., Veksler, O., Juan, O.: Generating classic mosaics with graph cuts. Comput. Graph. Forum **29**(8), 2387–2399 (2010)

18. Mould, D.: A stained glass image filter. In: Fourteenth Eurographics Workshop on Rendering, pp. 20–25 (2003)
19. Nock, R., Nielsen, F.: Statistical region merging. IEEE Trans. Pattern Anal. Mach. Intell. **26**(11), 1452–1458 (2004)
20. Schlechtweg, S., Germer, T., Strothotte, T.: RenderBots—multi-agent systems for direct image generation. Comput. Graph. Forum **24**(2), 137–148 (2005)
21. Xu, C., Prince, L.: Snakes, shapes, and gradient vector flow. IEEE Trans. Image Process. **7**(3), 359–369 (1998)

Chapter 11
Non-photorealistic Rendering with Reduced Colour Palettes

Yu-Kun Lai and Paul L. Rosin

11.1 Introduction

In fine art the limitations of the media often dictate that the work employs a small number of tones or colours, e.g. pen and ink, woodblock, engraving, posters. However, artists have worked to take advantage of such restrictions, producing masterpieces that prove that "less is more". This chapter describes NPR techniques that also work within the confines of a reduced palette, from the extreme case of binary renderings to those that use a handful of tones or colours.

A reduced palette is also common in popular culture. A good example is the iconic representational style of The Blues Brothers that has spun out of the classic cult film. Mostly dating after the film's release, these graphics have developed a distinctive style (see Fig. 11.1 for one that we have created). They appear to be generated by applying some simple filters to source colour images taken from the original film, with the processing pipeline something like the following: foreground extraction $\rightarrow$ blurring $\rightarrow$ colour to greyscale conversion $\rightarrow$ binary thresholding $\rightarrow$ additional manual correction. Thus, the first four steps perform abstraction, while the last step preserves salient details and ensures that the aesthetic quality is satisfactory.

In fact, the above exemplifies the goals of non-photorealistic rendering with reduced colour palettes and the steps involved. As is normal for image based NPR, geometric abstraction is required to remove the noise and extraneous detail present in captured images. Moreover, as the number of tones/colours decreases and the image's information content is further reduced, ensuring that significant details are preserved becomes even more critical. Thus, the overall goal can be summarised as

Y.-K. Lai (✉) · P.L. Rosin
School of Computer Science and Informatics, Cardiff University, Cardiff, UK
e-mail: Yukun.Lai@cs.cardiff.ac.uk

P.L. Rosin
e-mail: Paul.Rosin@cs.cardiff.ac.uk

Fig. 11.1 An example similar to the abstracted black and white designs produced as spin-offs from The Blues Brothers film. (*Left* image courtesy of Hallenser@flickr.com)

a combination of geometric and photometric abstraction along with detail preservation.

There is a large computer vision literature containing methods for processing images that could be applied to the task of simplifying the geometric and photometric properties of images. However, when applied naïvely they tend not to be effective for producing pleasing "artistic" renderings. For example, when a standard thresholding algorithm [23] is applied to a grey level version of the image in Fig. 11.2(a) the result is unattractive, and moreover contains blotches, speckles, and has lost many significant details (Fig. 11.2(b)). In fact, no single threshold is sufficient to produce a satisfactory result. Detail can be better retained if the global threshold is replaced by a threshold surface created by interpolating local thresholds calculated in subwindows—Fig. 11.2(c). However, a consequence is that noise and other unwanted detail is also increased. Alternatively, Fig. 11.2(d) shows the results of first segmenting [9] the image, and then re-rendering the regions so that each is given a flat colour consisting of the mean colour of that region in the source colour image. Although some details and structures have been captured better, others are lost, and the effect is unattractive. Another segmentation (using graph cuts [3]) shown in Fig. 11.2(e) is more successful, but still contains visual clutter while losing salient details. Using adaptive colour quantisation such as the median cut algorithm [12], the result in Fig. 11.2(f) preserves some details, but is not aesthetically pleasing due to the spurious boundaries caused by quantisation; a subtle change of colour may lead to the pixel being quantised to a different colour.

Whilst describing a range of reduced palette techniques, the scope of this chapter does not cover methods that are focussed on rendering using strokes or other small primitives. Some of these are described in detail elsewhere in this book—stippling and halftoning (Chap. 3), hatching (Chap. 4), pen and ink (Chap. 6), path based rendering (Chap. 9) and mosaicing (Chap. 10)—although other highly specialised techniques such as digital micrography [19], ASCII art [37], etc. are outside the scope of this book. Another related but complementary topic, focussing more on the creative use of regions, is provided in Chap. 7.

Fig. 11.2 Unsuccessful attempts to render images using computer vision algorithms. (**a**) Source colour image (courtesy of Anthony Santella), (**b**) image with global thresholding, (**c**) image with local thresholding, (**d**) segmented image with regions rendered with the mean colour from the corresponding source colour image pixels, (**e**) alternative segmentation, (**f**) image with colour quantisation using median cut (10 colours)

11.2 Binary Palettes

Converting a colour image to black and white is the most extreme version of colour palette reduction. While it is the most challenging case, it is also the most interesting, and can potentially produce the most dramatic stylisation. Although image thresholding has been popular in the image processing community for over 50 years, it is only recently that it has become of significant interest to the NPAR community. To differentiate NPAR methods from traditional thresholding algorithms, Xu and Kaplan [35] coined the term "artistic thresholding" to describe approaches to thresholding that try to preserve the visibility of objects and edges.

Xu and Kaplan's [35] method starts by over-segmenting the input image, to produce small regions (i.e. superpixels), which are connected to form a region adjacency graph. The assignment of black or white labels to the regions will define a binary segmentation of the image. Each region is described by a set of properties: its average colour, area; also the lengths of the shared boundaries between adjacent regions are stored. Several cost functions are then designed to capture specific aspects of a potential labelling: (1) The normalised pixelwise difference between the binary assignment and the intensity of the source image. (2) The difference between the current proportion of black in the segmented image and a target black proportion. (3) Two cost functions are defined to take into account the effectiveness of the labelling of adjacent regions, since adjacent regions with contrasting colours should be assigned opposite black and white labels, while adjacent regions with similar colours should be assigned the same labels. They are computed using both the difference in intensity between the labelled region and the source image pixels and the amount of common region boundary. (4) If the image has been partitioned into a number of high-level components then there is a cost function to encourage a homogeneous distribution of the labels amongst these components. Finally, these individual cost functions are combined as a weighted sum, where the weights can be chosen to produce different artistic effects. The overall cost function is optimised using simulated annealing. Perturbing individual region labels provides too local an effect, and so sub-graphs of size 3–5 vertices are modified by enumerating all label assignments and choosing the one with the lowest cost. A post-processing step tidies up the results, applying mathematical morphology opening and closing operations to remove small regions and increase abstraction. In addition, lines are inserted between adjacent regions if their colour difference is above a threshold. An interesting consequence of the cost function is that segments are sometimes inverted from their natural tone so as to maintain boundaries; see Fig. 11.3(a).

The approach by Mould and Grant [21] initialises their binary rendering using adaptive thresholding (see Fig. 11.2(c)). Next, a cost function is minimised using the graph cut algorithm. Let the intensity at each pixel be I_p, the local mean intensity in the neighbourhood of pixel p be μ_p, and the global variation in image intensity be σ. The basic data term is defined as the distance from the local mean,

$$\frac{1}{2}e^{-(I_p-\mu_p)^2/2\sigma^2}$$

This is later modified by weighting with a penalty function in an attempt to downweight outliers. The smoothness term has a similar form applied to image gradients, and penalises differences in neighbouring intensities. To balance abstraction and preservation of detail, Mould and Grant separate the image into a simplified base

Fig. 11.3 Examples of rendering with a binary palette. (**a**) Xu and Kaplan [35] (courtesy of Craig Kaplan), (**b**) Mould and Grant [21] (courtesy of David Mould), (**c**) Winnemöller [33] (courtesy of Holger Winnemoeller), (**d**) Rosin and Lai [25]

layer and a detail layer. The base layer is generated by applying the graph cut algorithm with the cost function modified to increase the smoothness term and decrease the data term. For the detail layer, as well as determining black and white pixels by adaptive thresholding, a third class is included whose intensities are as yet uncertain (a "don't know" class) if $|I_p - \mu_p| \leq 0.4 \times \sigma$. The known values in the detail layer are refined using graph cuts, and combined with the base layer by a further energy minimisation. The cost function takes its data term values from the detail layer except for those locations with "don't know" labels which use the base layer energies. The smoothness term from the detail layer is reused. This further optimisation is only carried out in the detail region and in a 5-pixels wide band around it. Finally, the result is tidied up by removing small isolated regions; see Fig. 11.3(b).

The Difference of Gaussians (DoG) operator that has been commonly used in computer vision for edge detection has been extended by Winnemöller [33] to produce a filter capable of generating many styles such as pastel, charcoal, hatching, etc. Of relevance to this section is its black and white rendering with both standard black edges and negative white edges. The DoG is modified so that the strength of the inhibitory effect of the larger Gaussian is allowed to vary according to the parameter τ:

$$D_{\sigma,k,\tau}(x) = G_\sigma(x) - \tau \times G_{k\sigma}(x)$$

and the output is further modified by an adjustable thresholding function that allows soft thresholding:

$$T_{\epsilon,\psi}(u) = \begin{cases} 1 & \text{if } u \geq \epsilon, \\ 1 + \tanh(\psi(u - \epsilon)) & \text{otherwise} \end{cases}$$

τ controls the brightness of the result and the strength of the edge emphasis, ψ controls the sharpness of the black/white transitions, and ϵ controls the level below which the adjusted luminance values will approach black. Since τ and ψ are coupled it was found more convenient to reparameterise the filter as

$$S_{\sigma,k,\rho}(x) = (1+\rho)G_\sigma(x) - \rho \times G_{k\sigma}(x)$$

so that the new parameter controls just the strength of the edge sharpening effect. For black and white images a large value of ψ is used. The DoG output contains both minima and maxima, and so increasing their magnitude by setting large values of ρ will encourage negative edges (i.e. white lines on a black background). To improve the spatial coherence of the results, the isotropic DoG filter is replaced by the anisotropic flow-based DoG [14]. See Fig. 11.3(c).

Rosin and Lai's [25] 3-tone method described in the next section can also be adapted to produce binary renderings. In brief, it uses the flow-based DoG to extract both black and white (negative) lines (cf. Winnemöller's [33] approach). The source image is thresholded, and the lines are drawn on top; see Fig. 11.3(d) and Fig. 11.4(b).

Meng et al. [20] described a specialised method to generate paper-cuts restricted to human portraits. These are effectively binary renderings with the extra constraint that the black pixels form a single connected region. They use a simplified version of the hierarchical composition model [36] which represents the face by an AND–OR graph. Nodes in this graph represent facial components (e.g. left eyebrow, right eye, nose); the AND nodes provide the decomposition of the face, while the OR nodes provide alternative instances for facial components. The latter are created by artists who manipulated photographs to extract a set of binary templates for typical mouths, eyes, etc. which form the leaves of the AND–OR graph. Facial features are located in the source image by fitting an active appearance model [7], and local thresholding is applied at each feature's bounding subwindow to produce a set of regions (the "proposal")

$$T' = \{\text{nose}', \text{mouth}', \ldots\}$$

These features are matched using a greedy algorithm to the AND–OR graph to minimise the following cost:

$$d(T_{i,j,\ldots}, T') + \lambda c(T_{i,j,\ldots})$$

where

$$T_{i,j,\ldots} = \{\text{nose}_i, \text{mouth}_j, \ldots\}$$

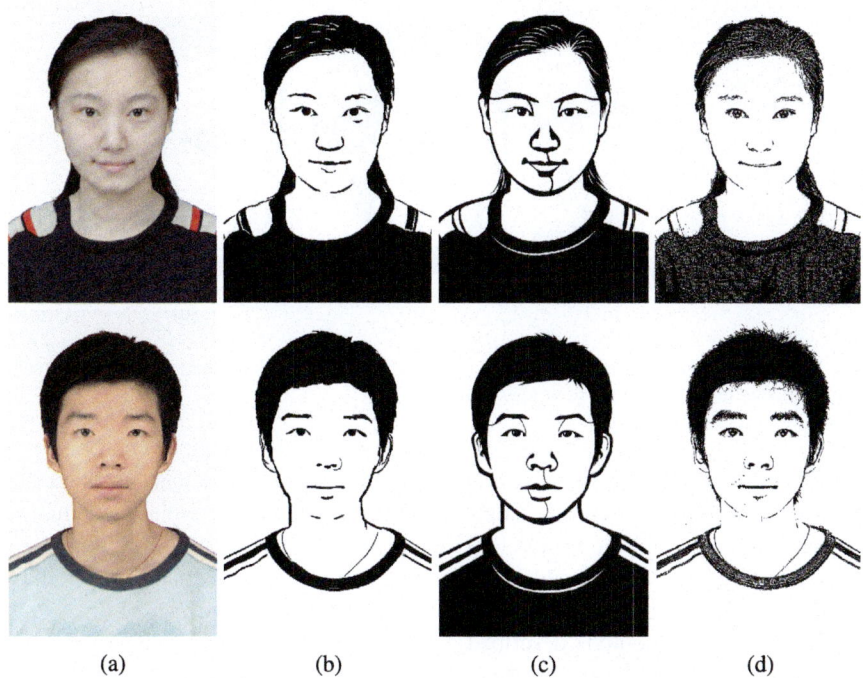

Fig. 11.4 Examples of rendering with a binary palette. (**a**) Source image (courtesy of Mingtian Zhao), (**b**) Rosin and Lai [25], (**c**) Meng et al. [20], (**d**) Gooch et al. [10]

denotes a set of facial component templates from the AND–OR graph that make up a complete face, d is the distance between the template and the proposal, and c is the number of different original paper-cut template that the selected components are taken from. Finally, post-processing is applied to extract the hair and clothing using graph cut segmentation, and enforce connectivity by inserting a few curves; see Fig. 11.4(c).

Another approach that was designed and applied to faces was given by Gooch et al. [10]. They computed brightness according to a model of human perception involving computation of DoGs over multiple scales. A simple global threshold was then applied, typically close to the average brightness, which produced a line-like result. Finally, dark regions were extracted from the source intensity image by performing thresholding at about 3–5 % intensity range. and combined with the lines by a multiplication or logical AND; see Fig. 11.4(d).

Xu and Kaplan [34] describe a specialised stylistic method for rendering images as calligraphic packings in which the black regions are approximated by letters which form one or several words. The method is limited to relatively simple images from which a simple foreground object can be extracted. The foreground is simplified by blurring, and thresholded, to produce the "container region" in which the letters will placed. The positions of the letters are refined using a version of Lloyd's algorithm: at each iteration the container is partitioned into subregions (one for each

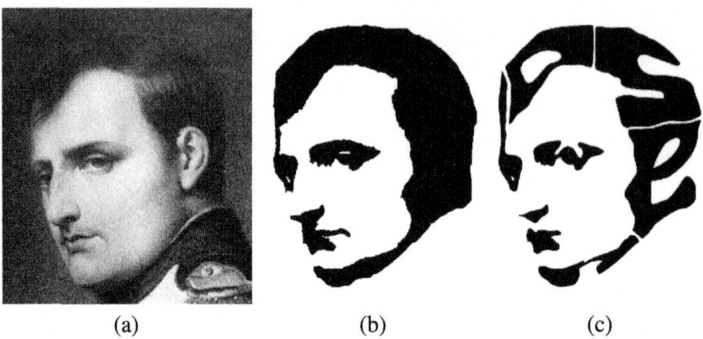

Fig. 11.5 Stages in calligraphic packing: source image, thresholded image, calligraphic packing [34] using text "Lose Win" (courtesy of Jie Xu)

letter), and each letter is moved to its subregion's centroid. The letters are also scaled to fit their subregion. The subregion boundaries are simplified using mathematical morphology, and then the source letter templates are warped to fit their enclosing subregions by warping individual convex subpolygons in such a manner as to maximise the similarity between the subregion and letter shapes; see Fig. 11.5.

Comparing the methods described above for rendering using a binary palette, certain similarities and differences become apparent. The two basic approaches use either filtering or perform segmentation and labelling as part of an optimisation framework. While the former has the advantage of efficiency, the latter is more flexible regarding the terms that can be incorporated into the cost function, and is able to consider more global aspects of the rendering. As outlined in the introduction, a combination of abstraction and detail preservation is necessary to achieve good stylisation, and this is carried out by all the methods. For instance, lines can be extracted from the image or from the region adjacency graph, and inserted into the rendering. In addition to rendering with black regions and/or lines, several approaches take advantage of negative (white) lines to include extra information without increasing the palette. In a similar manner, region tones can also be inverted. Most of the techniques are general purpose, but a model based approach can be advantageous. For instance, in the second row in Fig. 11.4(a) there is low contrast around the woman's chin. This causes the contour to be missed by the general methods, but it can be captured with the facial model.

For binary rendering, one of the issues for most of the methods is to set an appropriate level for some thresholding or segmentation step in their processing pipeline, and this is done either using preset values, dynamically, or manually. This setting is most critical for a binary palette since the limited intensities mean that an error in the setting will tend to have more drastic consequences on the results than for larger palettes. Unfortunately, unless high-level semantics is available (e.g. in the form of a facial model) it is not possible to expect any automatic method to work 100 % reliably, since low level image cues such as gradient, colour, shape etc may at times be misleading.

11.3 Palettes with Fixed Number of Tones

While two tone rendering is probably most interesting as it reduces the palette to an extreme and mimics some artistic forms such as pen-and-ink drawing, introducing a small number of extra tones may be beneficial, e.g. to improve the expressibility. Similar to binary palette rendering, to achieve artistic effect, various abstraction strategies have been proposed to remove extraneous detail, reduce the number of tones and the complexity of shapes. However, the availability of additional tones gives opportunities to preserve more subtle detail and gives more flexibility in determining the choice of tones, shapes of regions etc. without sacrificing recognisability. Different algorithms are needed to handle extra tones properly to achieve a balance of abstraction and recognisability using a combination of techniques. We focus on techniques that produce rendering with a fixed or perceptually fixed number of tones and cover more general rendering with variable number of tones in the next section.

Rosin and Lai [25] proposed an approach that produces a three-tone rendering where the grey background is overlaid with a combination of dark (black) and light (white) tonal blocks and lines. As the mid-tone is grey, both light and dark regions can be well delineated. A multi-level adaptive thresholding [23] is used to extract the dark and light tonal blocks which are then refined by using GrabCut [26] (an iterative graph cut based algorithm). Lines are further extracted to make the image more recognisable. a modified coherent line drawing algorithm by Kang et al. [13] is used. Kang's approach first finds a smooth edge tangent flow following the salient image edges which is then used to produce a local edge-aware kernel, combined with difference-of-Gaussian (DoG) and thresholding to obtain binary edge pixels that are more coherent with dominant edges. To apply this for three-tone rendering, both dark and light lines are extracted by using [13] both on the input image I and its inverse $\bar{I}$. Some further improvements involve using hysteresis thresholding [4] where edgels with intermediate strength are preserved only if there is some path connecting them to strong edgels, and deleting small connected components. These improvements lead to a cleaner edge map with less fragments and noise. Consider four set of pixels: dark lines, light lines, dark blocks and light blocks. Each pixel can belong to none or multiple sets. A quite sophisticated set of rules with all the 2^4 combinations of set membership is introduced. The rationale is to make lines more visible when combined with tonal blocks. So a black line over a white tonal block can be rendered black while a black line over a black tonal block should be rendered differently (e.g. grey) to be distinctive (see Fig. 11.6(d)). They also extended their method to apply the three-tone rendering to an image pyramid with three levels and average the obtained image, leading to a 10-tone rendering (see Fig. 11.6(e)). Compared with binary rendering, the additional tones allow more detail such as highlights and shadows to be preserved. The results preserve more salient details and generally contain less unimportant details than simple thresholding (Fig. 11.6(b), (c)).

Another approach to achieve a fixed number of tones is quantisation and in practice soft quantisation is often used to avoid artefacts which produces perceptually fixed number of tones. Winnemöller et al. [32] proposed an approach for real-time

Fig. 11.6 Examples of rendering using a palette with a fixed number of tones. (**a**) Source image, (**b**) simple thresholding (3 tones), (**c**) simple thresholding (10 tones), (**d**) Rosin and Lai (3 tones) [25], (**e**) Rosin and Lai (pyramid: 10 tones) [25], (**f**) Kyprianidis and Döllner [16], (**g**) Olsen and Gooch [22]. Part **g**: © 2011 ACM, Inc. Included here by permission

image and video abstraction. They first produced a more abstracted image by simplifying the low-saliency regions while enhancing high-saliency features. They enhanced the image contrast by using an extended non-linear filter [2] which in the automatic real-time scenario reduces to the bilateral filter [28] but also allows extra saliency measures as input. This step was followed by an edge enhancement step where a difference-of-Gaussian (DoG) filter is used for edge detection. To produce more stylised images, such as cartoon or paint-like effects, they used an optional colour pseudo-quantisation step to reduce the number of tones. For each channel, q

(typically 8–10) equal-sized bins are chosen. If hard quantisation were used, a maximum of q^3 tones would be produced. To improve the time coherence for videos, their approach was instead a soft quantisation, so the exact number of tones may be more but remains perceptually similar. For each pixel location $\hat{x}$, assume the channel value is $f(\hat{x})$, the nearest bin boundary is q_{nearest}, and Δq is the bin size, the quantised value is calculated as

$$Q(\hat{x}, q, \varphi q) = q_{\text{nearest}} + \frac{\Delta q}{2} \tanh\left(\varphi q \cdot \left(f(\hat{x}) - q_{\text{nearest}}\right)\right)$$

where $\tanh(\cdot)$ is a sigmoid (smooth step) function, φq controls how sharp the step function is. A fixed φq would create transition boundaries in regions with large smooth transitions. An adaptive approach was proposed instead to use larger φq for pixels where the local luminance gradient is large. The soft quantisation improves time coherence and thus reduces flickering in video stylisation.

Kyprianidis and Döllner [16] proposed an approach based on a similar framework, and soft quantisation as in [32] is used to produce a more stylised effect. Before that, the image abstraction is instead obtained by adapting the bilateral filter (for region contrast enhancement) and DoG (for edge enhancement) guided by a smoothed structure tensor. The input image is treated as a mapping $f : (x, y) \in \mathbb{R}^2 \rightarrow (R, G, B) \in \mathbb{R}^3$, where (x, y) is the pixel coordinate and (R, G, B) is the vector comprising three colour components. The directional derivatives (Sobel operators) in x and y directions are: $\frac{\partial f}{\partial x} = (\frac{\partial R}{\partial x} \frac{\partial G}{\partial x} \frac{\partial B}{\partial x})^T$, $\frac{\partial f}{\partial y} = (\frac{\partial R}{\partial y} \frac{\partial G}{\partial y} \frac{\partial B}{\partial y})^T$. Denote the Jacobian matrix $(\frac{\partial f}{\partial x}, \frac{\partial f}{\partial y})$ as J and the structure tensor is computed as

$$(g_{ij}) = J^T J = \begin{pmatrix} \frac{\partial f}{\partial x} \cdot \frac{\partial f}{\partial x} & \frac{\partial f}{\partial x} \cdot \frac{\partial f}{\partial y} \\ \frac{\partial f}{\partial x} \cdot \frac{\partial f}{\partial y} & \frac{\partial f}{\partial y} \cdot \frac{\partial f}{\partial y} \end{pmatrix}$$

$J^T J$ is a symmetric positive semi-definite matrix and assume $\lambda_1 \geq \lambda_2 \geq 0$ are two eigenvalues and v_1 and v_2 are corresponding eigenvectors. v_1 shows the direction with the maximum rate of change and v_2 the minimum. So the direction field derived from v_2 follows the local edge direction. To improve smoothness and reduce discontinuities, a Gaussian smoothing operator on the local structure tensor is applied before eigen decomposition. An example is shown in Fig. 11.6(f). Details as well as the original tones are largely preserved. Region boundaries are generally smooth due to the soft quantisation.

In the settings of image simplification and vectorisation, Olsen and Gooch [22] proposed an approach to produce stylised images with three-tone rendering using soft and hard quantisation. The stylisation helps to reduce the complexity of images and make it effective in vectorisation. Their method worked on greyscale images and started with similar blurring and unsharp masking to suppress low-saliency regions and enhance significant features. The object boundaries were then simplified using line integral convolution guided by a smoothed edge orientation field as in [16]. After that, a piecewise linear intensity remapping is applied to increase the contrast. A soft quantisation approach was then used, similar to [32] but more flexible as the bins do not need to be equal-sized. Assume feature (bin centre) values for all the bins are $\mathbf{b} = (b_1, b_2, \ldots, b_n)$, where n is the number of bins. For an arbitrary intensity value v, it is first clamped to the range of $[b_1, b_n]$. Then assuming for some j, $v \in [b_j, b_{j+1}]$, the width w_j and vertical shift c_j are defined as $w_j := \frac{1}{2}(b_{j+1} - b_j)$ and $c_j := \frac{1}{2}(b_{j+1} - b_j)$ respectively. The soft quantised output p is then defined as

$$p(v, s) := w_j \frac{\text{sig}(\frac{s}{w_j}(v - c_j))}{\text{sig}(s)} + c_j$$

where sig is a sigmoid function. The formula ensures C^0 continuity and since $p'(c_j, s) = \frac{s \times \text{sig}'(0)}{\text{sig}(s)}$, the derivative (sharpness) at the midpoint between two regions is solely determined by the parameter s, regardless of the bin size. As a vectorisation method, the three-tone regions are further traced and boundaries smoothed to obtain a compact representation. An example is shown in Fig. 11.6(g). The result looks more stylised as the region boundaries are smoothed.

From this section we see that to obtain renderings with a fixed number of tones, two general approaches are considered. The fixed number of tones can be a natural result of some generating model, such as combining multiple layers of rendering, mimicking the art forms of e.g. charcoal and chalk. Another general approach is to use (soft) quantisation. Using quantisation alone is usually not sufficient as it can easily mix the salient features with extraneous detail, but it can be an effective way of making the intermediate results more artistically appealing. This technique is typically combined with algorithms such as image filtering that produce smooth but abstracted rendering to produce a cartoon-like flat shading.

11.4 Palettes with Variable Number of Tones

Image rendering with reduced but a variable number of tones is useful to achieve paint-like flat rendering, thus removing the non-essential detail. Segmentation is often used to find regions with homogeneous colours. A simple but widely used strategy is to use a flat colour for each region. A further improvement involves manipulating the tones and regions to enhance the stylisation. For segmentation based stylisation of videos, special attention needs to be paid to ensure temporal coherence. Alternative approaches to achieve fewer tones include image filtering or can be formulated as an energy optimisation problem. An example of a variable number of fixed tones produced by a GIMP cartoon filter plug-in[1] is given in Fig. 11.7(b).

11.4.1 Stylisation Using Segmentation

Segmentation is often used to produce stylised images with flat colours. Examples shown in Fig. 11.2(d), (e) demonstrate that traditional image segmentation techniques may not be ideal for stylisation.

---

[1] Many cartoon effect filters are available for GIMP—we have used CarTOONize by Joe1GK.

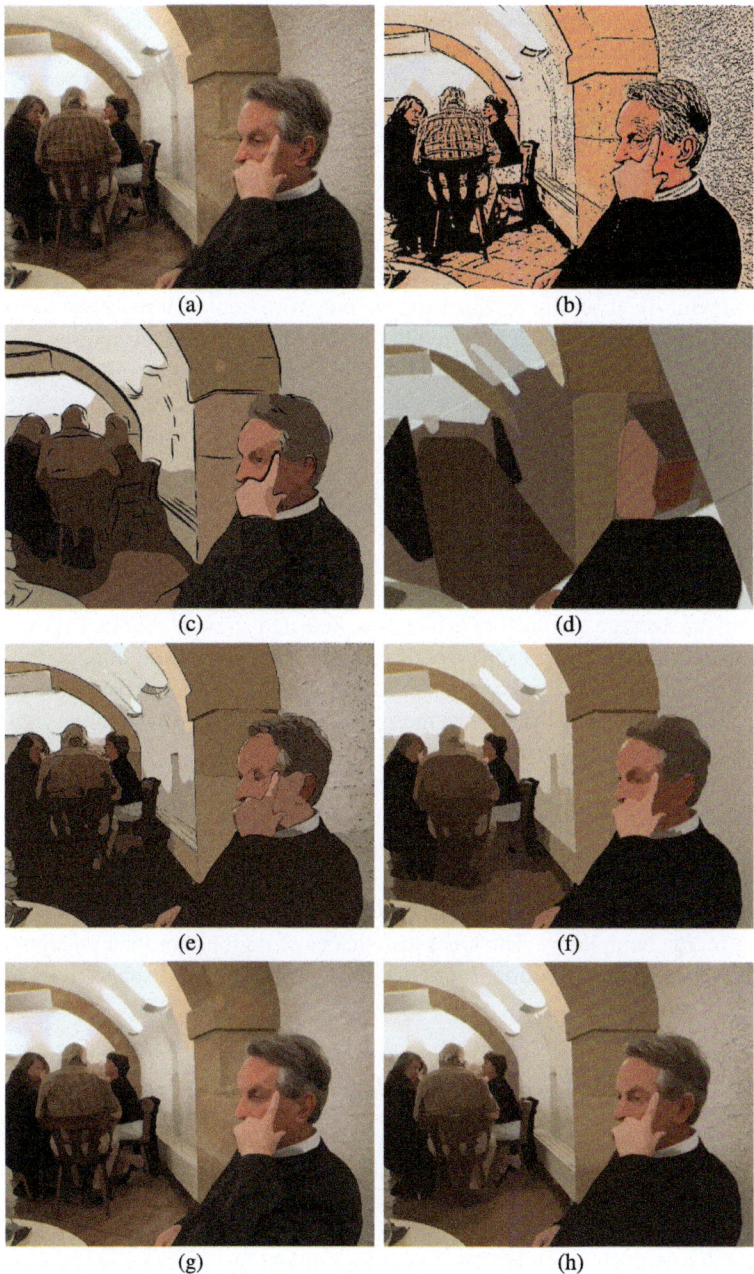

Fig. 11.7 Examples of rendering using a palette with a variable number of tones. (**a**) Source image (courtesy of Anthony Santella), (**b**) result using GIMP cartoon filter, (**c**) DeCarlo et al. [8], (**d**) Song et al. [27] (courtesy of Yi-Zhe Song), (**e**) Zhang et al. [39] (courtesy of Song-Hai Zhang), (**f**) Weickert et al. [30], (**g**) Kyprianidis et al. [17] (courtesy of Jan Eric Kyprianidis), (**h**) Xu et al. [38]. Part **c**: © 2002 ACM, Inc. Included here by permission

DeCarlo and Santella [8] proposed an approach that renders abstracted and stylised images based on eye tracker data such that regions receiving more attention are better preserved. The method starts with a hierarchical image segmentation to build a region hierarchy. The input image is repeatedly down-sampled to form an image pyramid. The image at each resolution is segmented individually using an existing method. Following scale-space theory, the regions at finer scales tend to be included within regions at the coarser scales. A region hierarchy is formed using a bottom-up merging process. Starting from the regions at the finest scale, treat each as a leaf node, proceed up the pyramid until reaching the coarsest level. At each level, a finer region is generally assigned to the parent region with the most significant overlap as long as this does not violate the tree (hierarchical) structure. To render the image in a more abstracted and stylised manner, for areas receiving more attention, more detail needs to be preserved, thus finer regions in the hierarchy should be used. Similarly, coarser regions should be used for areas with less attention. This effectively defines a frontier, a separation of the tree structure determining whether a branch or its children nodes should be used for rendering. Since region boundaries are determined by the finest level segmentation, region boundaries are smoothed by treating them as a curve network and the interior nodes are smoothed using low-pass filtering while keeping the branching nodes fixed. The final rendering is obtained by showing the average colour for each region. Selected smoothed lines are overlaid if the boundary lines belong to the frontier and they are sufficiently long with respect to the fixation. The line thickness is also determined by the length, with longer lines being thicker. An example is shown in Fig. 11.7(c); effective abstraction is obtained, but this also requires eye tracking data as input.

Although a vast literature exists for image and video segmentation, it remains particularly challenging to obtain semantically meaningful regions. An alternative approach is to use some interactive segmentation instead. The work in [31] for colour sketch generation starts from the mean-shift image segmentation [6]. They then designed a user interface to allow users to merge and split regions as well as editing region boundaries. The tones and shapes of regions are then manipulated to further enhance the stylisation. More detail is given in the next subsection.

11.4.2 Tone and Region Manipulation

Whilst it is natural to take the mean colour of a region to achieve abstraction, the results may not be sufficiently stylised. In an effort to learn the artist's experience of choosing appropriate colours, Wen et al. [31] further consider applying learning based colour shift to each region. The training data involve a set of regions from some training images, with their average colour $\mathbf{O}_k$ and artist painting colour $\mathbf{P}_k$, both vectors in a perceptually uniform (hue, chroma, value) colour space. For each region $\mathbf{R}_i$ in the current image with M regions, N candidate colours are obtained from the training set such that the hue is similar (within a difference threshold) and chroma and value are as close as possible. A graph is then built treating each region as a vertex. An edge is created for an adjacent pair of regions or regions with similar colours. Edges between a foreground region and a background region are excluded, making it two separated graphs. Following the artist's experience, different rules are applied for foreground and background regions. The heuristics are then formulated as an energy minimisation problem, considering all the following: For example, background regions tend to have the same colour as the training region with similar colour, area and perimeter. Non-adjacent background regions with similar colour tend to be coloured the same. Foreground regions often have increased chroma and value but also adjacent and homogeneous foreground regions tend to preserve the original chroma and value contrast, etc.

Instead of requiring example pairs of original and artistic colours as training data, Zhang et al. [39] take a reference video or reference colour distribution as input and adjust the region colour from a simple average to follow the style of the reference. HSV colour space is used. The hue is adjusted using mean shift [6] and the saturation and value are adjusted using some linear scaling. Ignoring the pixels with low S and/or V, for the reference video, the following are calculated: the colour histogram for the H channel, the mean μ_S and standard deviation σ_S for the S channel, and the mean μ_V for the V channel. For the current input frame, assuming μ_s, σ_s and μ_v are defined similarly and computed based on the whole frame. (h, s, v) is the average colour of a region being considered, and (h', s', v') is the adjusted colour. h' is obtained by updating h using mean shift for a few iterations:

$$h \Leftarrow \frac{\sum_{c \in N(h)} c D(c)}{\sum_{c \in N(h)} D(c)}$$

where $N(h)$ represents 30° neighbourhood in the reference histogram, and $D(c)$ is the corresponding histogram entry. s' and v' are adjusted to match the overall saturation and value:

$$s' = \mu_S + (s - \mu_s)\frac{\sigma_S}{\sigma_s}, \qquad v' = v\left(\lambda + (1 - \lambda)\frac{\mu_V}{\mu_v}\right)$$

where λ is a parameter balancing the brightness variation between the input and the reference. To improve temporal coherence, the adjusted colour is further blended across time.

The region boundaries may also be manipulated to enhance artistic styles. To simulate artistic sketching, Wen et al. [31] observe that regions do not entirely fill the image and more specifically light pixels close to boundaries are shrunk leaving white blanks to emphasise the shading. For each region, the boundary is first smoothed and then down-sampled to obtain a list of control points. Each control point is then adjusted individually. For a control point P_0, the closest opposite boundary point along the normal direction is denoted as P_1. N points are evenly sampled along $\overline{P_0 P_1}$. A weight is assigned for each point X_k as $W_k = 1 - I_k$ where I_k is the intensity at pixel X_k. This gives more weight to darker pixels. Two centres are then calculated, a geometric centre P_c as the average of all the coordinates X_k and a weighted centre P_w with W_k as the weight. If more dark pixels exist closer to P_1, i.e. $d = \|\overline{P_0 P_w}\| - \|\overline{P_0 P_c}\| > 0$, P_0 is moved by d along the normal direction and otherwise no adjustment is needed for P_0. Self-crossing generated in this process is detected and resolved using heuristics.

Instead of using regions directly obtained from segmentation, the work by Song et al. [27] considers extreme abstraction by replacing each region with some more abstracted shape (see Fig. 11.7(d) for an example). The algorithm starts by segmenting the image into regions using existing methods. Each region can be fitted with various primitives and the following are considered: circles, rectangles, triangles, superellipses and robust convex hull. Specifying the appropriate type of shape primitive is time-consuming as there may exist a large number of regions. Since aesthetics is a subjective judgement, a supervised learning approach is used. Regions in the training set are obtained by segmenting selected images. Each region used in the training set is manually labelled to indicate the ideal primitive type and a feature vector is extracted consisting of the errors between the region and fitted shape of each type. These are fed into a C4.5 decision tree [24]. For a new input image, they first segment the image into two levels of details (by changing the number of regions). Regions are rendered using the flat mean colour. Coarse-level regions are rendered first. Fine-level regions are rendered on top of that if the difference between the fine-level region and pixels underneath are larger than some threshold (measured in L_2 difference in the CIELab colour space). This provides a balance between abstraction (using large regions) and recognisability (using small regions). For regions with the same level of detail, shapes are rendered in descending order of approximation error compared with the regions they represent.

These tone and region manipulation techniques can in principle be combined with other colour palette reduction approaches to produce more stylised rendering.

11.4.3 Temporally Coherent Stylisation Using Segmentation

Segmentation based stylisation can also be used for video rendering. In this case, temporal coherence is essential.

Zhang et al. [39] propose a system for automatic on-line video stylisation. Their approach also uses segmentation and flat colour shading to produce artistic effect. In this case temporal coherence is essential to avoid flickering. To ensure real-time performance on live video streams, the algorithm works on individual frames. The first frame is segmented using some image segmentation algorithm. For each subsequent frame, as edges give important information for regions, the Canny edge detector [4] is used to extract the edge map. To balance abstraction with recognisability, important areas such as human faces need more regions to be well represented. This is accomplished by using a face detector and applying a smaller threshold for edge detection, leading to more detailed edges in these areas. To preserve coherence between frames, segmentation labels are propagated from the previous frame using optical flow. This gives for each source pixel in the previous frame a corresponding target pixel. Not all the pixels in the current frame receive consistent labels from propagation. The target pixel will remain unlabelled if any of the following conditions is true: either the colour difference between the target and source pixels is above some threshold, or the target pixel has none or multiple source pixels associated. The propagated labels are often noisy and a morphological filter is applied to improve the regions by updating the label of a pixel based on its eight connected neighbours: if the current pixel is either unlabelled or consistent with the labels of more than half of its neighbours, it obtains/keeps this label and otherwise it is marked unlabelled. Unlabelled pixels are assigned to adjacent regions if they have consistent colours. The remaining pixels are treated as belonging to new regions and a trapped-ball segmentation is applied. This strategy deals with video shot change as a large number of pixels will be unlabelled and thus a new segmentation applied. An example where this technique is applied to an image is shown in Fig. 11.7(e).

Another technique related to segmentation based stylisation is rotoscoping, used for generating cartoon-like videos. To obtain high-quality temporally coherent regions, user assistance is often needed. Agarwala et al. [1] proposed a system for rotoscoping based on interactive tracking. Users are asked to draw a set of curves for a pair of keyframes. The rotoscoping curves are then interpolated between these frames. The interpolation needs to take into account smoothness of the curve, smooth transition over time, and consistency with underlying image transitions. This is formulated as an energy minimisation problem with five terms (three shape terms and two image terms) and the obtained non-linear least squares problem is solved using the Levenberg–Marquardt (LM) algorithm. Interpolated rotoscoping curves may also be edited if users prefer. Smoothly changing rotoscoping curves allow various rendering styles, including cartoon-like flat shading or brush strokes following the curve evolution.

Wang et al. [29] also propose an interactive system for rotoscoping based video tooning. The user input is similar: the user needs to draw a few curves in keyframes to roughly indicate the semantic regions. Keypoints on these curves are also specified, indicating the correspondences. For time coherence, they instead treat the video as a 3D volume of pixels and a 3D generalisation of the mean-shift algorithm is first applied. The curves drawn by the user are then used to guide the merging of 3D segments. Assume a pair of loops $L(k_1)$ and $L(k_2)$ are specified in frames k_1 and k_2 respectively. $S(k_1)$ and $S(k_2)$ indicate segments that each have the majority of their pixels located within loops $L(k_1)$ and $L(k_2)$ in the corresponding frame respectively. For intermediate frame t, $k_1 < t < k_2$, to produce closed regions, pixels fully surrounded by pixels in $S(k_1) \cup S(k_2)$ are also included and after that segments with the majority of their pixels included form a set $S*$. Within each frame t, $S*$ indicates a mean-shift suggested boundary $L_{ms}(t)$. Simple linear interpolation also produces a boundary $L_s(t)$. An optimisation approach is then used, iteratively deforming $L_s(t)$ to be closer to $L_{ms}(t)$ while preserving smoothness. After mapping keypoints from user drawn curves to the deforming curve using local shape descriptors, the deformation is formulated as an energy minimization with two terms. For two adjacent frames, the first term E_{smooth} measures the change in movement of each control point as well as the vector between adjacent keypoints and thus prefers consistent and stable transitions. The second term simply measures the distance between corresponding control points of $L_S(t)$ and $L_{ms}(t)$. This iterates until the local minimum is reached. In addition to 3D regions, boundaries between them also form 3D edge sheets. When the video is rendered, the 3D regions and edge sheets are intersected with the frame to form a 2D image. The region is rendered in a flat colour and the strength of edges is determined by a few factors such as time in the frame sequence, or the location on the intersected curve and motion.

11.4.4 Abstraction Using Filtering

Filtering, in particular anisotropic filtering, is an effective approach for image abstraction. Although not guaranteed, in practice, certain filters tend to produce stylised rendering with reduced palettes. Detailed discussion about filtering is given in Chap. 5, and in this section we only focus on its application for reduced palette rendering.

Anisotropic diffusion has been studied in the image processing community for a long time. Although it was not directly considered for the application of NPR, such techniques can actually produce reasonable stylisations. An example produced by Weickert et al. [30] is given in Fig. 11.7(f). Assume $f(x)$ represents an image with x represents the coordinate of a pixel. $u(x, t)$ is a filtered image, with t being a scale parameter, conceptually as time. $u(x, t)$ is the solution of the diffusion equation

$$\partial_t u = div\big(g\big(|\nabla u_\sigma|^2\big)\nabla u\big)$$

with the boundary conditions $u(x, 0) = f(x)$, $\partial_n u = 0$ for boundary pixels where n is the normal direction to the boundary. ∇u_σ is the gradient of u after smoothing by a Gaussian kernel with σ being the standard deviation. $g(s)$ is a non-linear function for anisotropic diffusion. If s is close to zero, $g(s)$ is close to 1, and $g(s)$ drops with increasing s. This ensures that diffusion is less likely to cross high gradient pixels which tend to be region boundaries.

More recently, Kyprianidis et al. extend Kuwahaha filter with anisotropic kernels derived from structure tensor, similar to [16] (see Fig. 11.7(g) for an example). Their experiments demonstrate that sufficiently abstracted results are obtained, even without further quantisation. A further improvement [15] has later been proposed to strengthen the abstraction while avoiding some artefacts, by using an image pyramid, and propagates from coarse to fine orientation estimates and filtering results.

11.4.5 Reduced Tone Rendering Using Optimisation

Unlike most segmentation techniques where regions are obtained first, followed by an estimation of the representative colour for each region, it is possible to formulate both region segmentation and colour estimation in a uniform energy minimisation formulation. Xu et al. [38] propose an approach that aims at finding an optimal output image S for an input image I such that S contains as little change as possible while close to I. Assume $\partial_x S_p$ and $\partial_x S_p$ represent the colour difference around pixel p between adjacent pixels in the x and y directions, respectively. The energy to be minimised is represented as

$$E(S) = \sum_p (S_p - I_p)^2 + \lambda C(S)$$

where λ is a weight balancing the two terms. The first term ensures S is as close to I as possible, and $C(S)$ is the count of non-zero elements (a.k.a. L_0 norm) and defined as

$$C(S) = \#\{p \mid |\partial_x S_p| + |\partial_y S_p| \neq 0\}$$

is the number of elements in the set. This formulation naturally leads to a reduced palette rendering as the number of colour changes is minimised. An example of L_0 energy minimisation is given in Fig. 11.7(h). This approach is nicely formulated, however, it is an NP-hard problem to find the global optimum, and therefore in practise only an approximate solution is achieved [38].

While a variety of methods have been proposed for rendering with a variable number of tones, the use of a relatively small number of tones naturally leads to flat-shaded regions. However, these regions may be explicitly calculated or implicitly obtained. Explicit approaches use segmentation to obtain regions and assign an appropriate tone to each region. Although image segmentation has been studied for decades, it is still challenging in practice to obtain aesthetically pleasing rendering for various input images, especially when a smaller number of regions is used. In many cases, additional input is resorted to, such as eye tracking data and user interaction. Unlike the filtering based approaches, when video is stylised, special care needs to be taken to ensure temporal coherence. Approaches proposed involve propagation of segmentation labels along adjacent frames or treating the temporal sequence of 2D frames as a 3D volume. Alternatively, implicit approaches do not calculate regions directly; they are rather by-products of tone reduction process. Image filtering (in particular anisotropic filtering) based approaches cannot guarantee to reduce the number of tones and thus are often combined with (soft) quantisation. However, certain filtering methods can directly obtain sufficient abstraction with perceptually reduced number of tones. Another implicit approach, which is studied more recently, is to formulate the reduced tone rendering as an energy minimisation problem. While obtaining regions explicitly seems to require more effort and is more error prone as inappropriate segmentation may lead to loss of essential detail or distracting region boundaries, these methods naturally have more flexibility in manipulating the regions, by adjusting the tones and/or region boundaries.

11.5 Pre-processing

As part of the image stylisation pipeline it is often useful to apply various pre-processing steps to improve the suitability of the image for rendering. Previous sections have already mentioned the application of filtering to remove noise and perform abstraction. Likewise, there are other pre-processing algorithms that, while they have not necessarily been applied yet in the context of reduced palette rendering, could be usefully incorporated. Examples include: saliency detection to control levels of abstraction [8]; colourimetric correction to provide color constancy which will ensure more consistent and correct palettes; colour harmonisation to produce more attractive palettes [5]; depth estimation to control relighting and other stylisation effects [18]; intrinsic image decomposition to extract shading and reflectance from an image to enable rendering to better capture the underlying scene characteristics, conversion from a colour image to greyscale whilst attempting to preserve the colour contrast in the greyscale image [11].

We demonstrate the effect of the last example in Fig. 11.8. This is especially critical for rendering with a binary palette since limiting the final colours to just black and white means the standard colour to greyscale conversion method (a simple weighted combination of the three colour channels) is prone to missing detail that is more easily retained when a larger palette is available. The conversion that preserves colour contrast (Fig. 11.8(c)) has retained a much higher contrast between the aeroplane and the background foliage compared to the standard colour to greyscale conversion (Fig. 11.8(b)). This subsequently enables the intensity thresholding step in Rosin and Lai's [25] rendering pipeline to achieve a better foreground/background separation (see Fig. 11.8(d), (e)).

11.6 Conclusions

This chapter has described techniques for transforming a colour or grey level image into a reduced palette rendering for artistic effect. Although there is a large variety of techniques and stylisations (see Figs. 11.9, 11.10, 11.11 for more rendering examples), it is evident that there are several common elements in the rendering pipelines. First, some degree of abstraction should be performed, otherwise a pixel-wise recolouring will tend to result in noisy, fragmented and unartistic renderings. Second, detail needs to be preserved or re-inserted, since the reduced palette and the abstraction tends to remove salient features that are necessary to fully recognise important aspects of the image/scene. Third, for arbitrary images determining the palette boundaries is non-trivial, and most algorithms are liable to make errors at least occasionally. Therefore some techniques use a soft thresholding approach which reduces the visual impact of such palette boundary errors, and has a stabilising effect which will increase temporal coherence for video stylisation.

We note that for the different classes of reduced palettes that have been discussed in this chapter, the smaller the palette, the greater the variety in the stylisations. This can be explained by the fact that large palettes enable the renderings to reproduce the original image more faithfully (while still incorporating subtle stylistic differences) than smaller palettes such as the two tone rendering. Since the latter is not aiming for fidelity, it uses relatively extreme stylisation techniques such as region and line tone inversions that are not seen in large palette renderings.

Fig. 11.8 Effects of image pre-processing before stylisation. (**a**) Source image (courtesy of Armchair Aviator@flickr.com), (**b**) standard colour to greyscale conversion, (**c**) colour contrast preserving colour to greyscale conversion [11], (**d**) Rosin and Lai's [25] two tone rendering of (**b**), (**e**) Rosin and Lai's [25] two tone rendering of (**c**)

The results presented in this chapter show that many reduced palette rendering methods are available and capable of achieving effective stylised effects. However, in the literature they tend to be demonstrated on good quality images and systematic evaluation is limited (see Chap. 15 and Chap. 16). Therefore it is not easy to determine the reliability of the techniques, or the effect of applying them to images with varying resolution, foreground/background characteristics, colour/intensity distributions, etc. Nevertheless, even if it is difficult to develop general purpose methods that are guaranteed a 100 % success rate on arbitrary images, this does not exclude

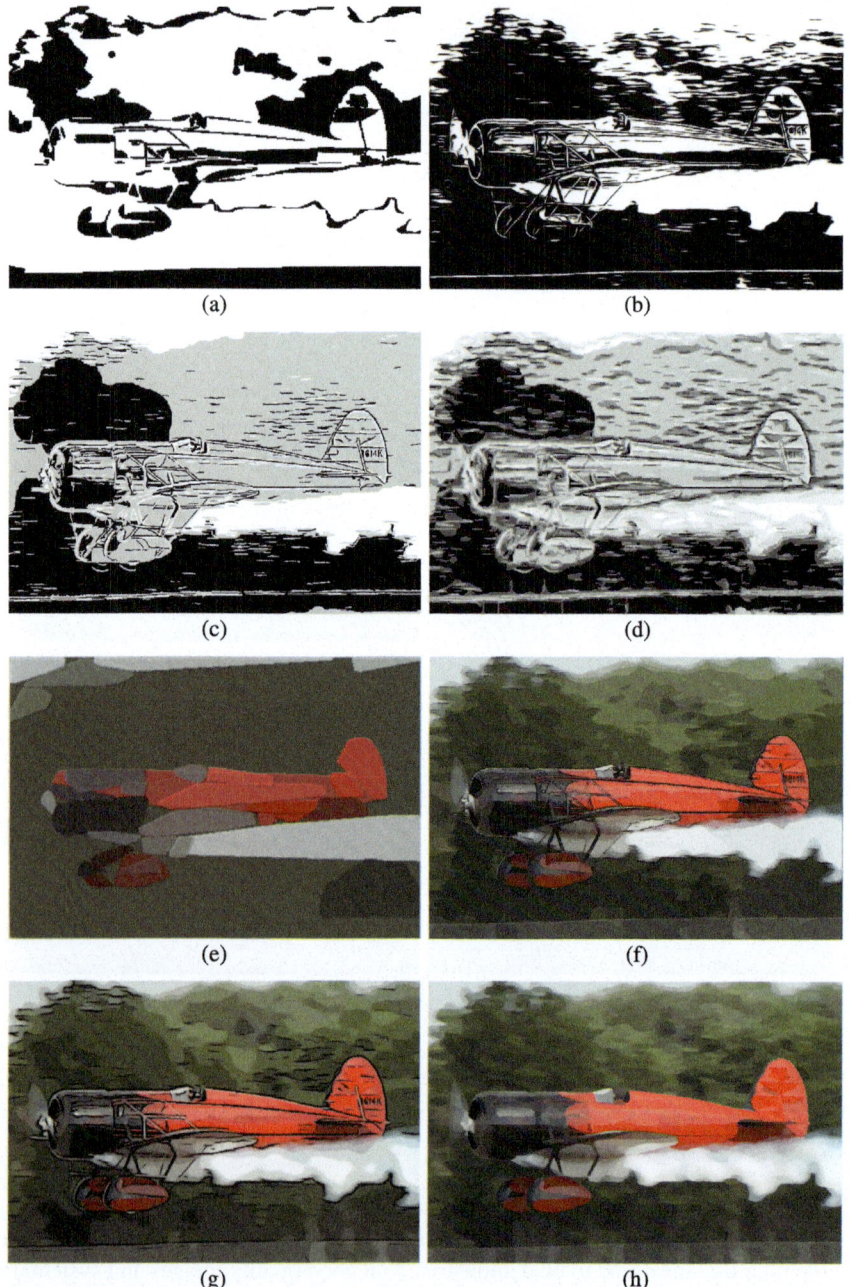

Fig. 11.9 Examples of rendering with various styles. (**a**) Xu and Kaplan [35] (courtesy of Craig Kaplan), (**b**) Winnemöller [33] (courtesy of Holger Winnemoeller), (**c**) Rosin and Lai [25] (3 tones), (**d**) Rosin and Lai [25] (pyramid: 10 tones), (**e**) Song et al. [27] (courtesy of Yi-Zhe Song), (**f**) Zhang et al. [39] (courtesy of Song-Hai Zhang), (**g**) Kyprianidis and Döllner [16] (courtesy of Jan Eric Kyprianidis), (**h**) Kyprianidis et al. [17] (courtesy of Jan Eric Kyprianidis)

Fig. 11.10 Examples of rendering with various styles. (**a**) Source image (courtesy of Philip Greenspun), (**b**) Xu and Kaplan [35] (courtesy of Craig Kaplan), (**c**) Winnemöller [33] (courtesy of Holger Winnemoeller), (**d**) Rosin and Lai [25], (**e**) Zhang et al. [39] (courtesy of Song-Hai Zhang), (**f**) Wen et al. [31] (created by Fang Wen; copyright Microsoft Research China. Included here by permission), (**g**) Song et al. [27] (courtesy of Yi-Zhe Song), (**h**) Kyprianidis et al. [17] (courtesy of Jan Eric Kyprianidis)

them from practical applications if some manual interaction is allowed. For instance, the complete 2006 film 'A Scanner Darkly' was rendered using a reduced palette: regions were rendered with flat colours, and some linear features were included. This stylisation was an extremely time-consuming task since all the keyframes were rotoscoped (i.e. hand-traced on top of the source film). However, the state of the art is now at a stage where a much less user intensive, semi-automatic solution would be possible. An alternative solution to improving performance is to design methods

Fig. 11.11 Examples of rendering with various styles. (**a**) Source image (courtesy of PDPhoto.org), (**b**) Mould and Grant [21] (courtesy of David Mould), (**c**) Winnemöller [33] (courtesy of Holger Winnemoeller), (**d**) Rosin and Lai [25], (**e**) Kyprianidis and Döllner [16] (courtesy of Jan Eric Kyprianidis), (**f**) Song et al. [27] (courtesy of Yi-Zhe Song)

for specialised domains, which are then able to use domain specific knowledge and constraints to overcome limitations in the data (noise, ambiguities, missing data). An example given in this chapter is the paper-cut rendering by Meng et al. [20] that used a facial model.

Until recently rendering using a binary palette was an underdeveloped topic, which may explain the recent surge of interest in developing such techniques. As the reduced palette techniques mature it is likely that there will be a trend to video stylisation, especially since related methods for ensuring temporal coherence have been developed for a variety of other stylisation effects (see Chap. 13). Further directions in the future will be to apply reduced palette rendering to a wider range of data types, such as 3D volumetric data, image plus range data (e.g. the Kinect), stereo image/video pairs, low quality images (e.g. mobile phones), etc.

References

1. Agarwala, A., Hertzmann, A., Salesin, D., Seitz, S.M.: Keyframe-based tracking for rotoscoping and animation. ACM Trans. Graph. **23**(3), 584–591 (2004)
2. Barash, D., Comaniciu, D.: A common framework for nonlinear diffusion, adaptive smoothing, bilateral filtering and mean shift. Image Vis. Comput. **22**(1), 73–81 (2004)
3. Boykov, Y., Kolmogorov, V.: An experimental comparison of min-cut/max-flow algorithms for energy minimisation in vision. IEEE Trans. Pattern Anal. Mach. Intell. **26**(9), 1124–1137 (2004)
4. Canny, J.: A computational approach to edge detection. IEEE Trans. Pattern Anal. Mach. Intell. **8**, 679–698 (1986)
5. Cohen-Or, D., Sorkine, O., Gal, R., Leyvand, T., Xu, Y.Q.: Color harmonization. ACM Trans. Graph. **25**(3), 624–630 (2006)
6. Comaniciu, D., Meer, P.: Mean shift: a robust approach toward feature space analysis. IEEE Trans. Pattern Anal. Mach. Intell. **24**(5), 603–619 (2002)
7. Cootes, T.F., Edwards, G.J., Taylor, C.J.: Active appearance models. IEEE Trans. Pattern Anal. Mach. Intell. **23**(6), 681–685 (2001)
8. DeCarlo, D., Santella, A.: Stylization and abstraction of photographs. ACM Trans. Graph. **21**(3), 769–776 (2002)
9. Felzenszwalb, P.F., Huttenlocher, D.P.: Efficient graph-based image segmentation. Int. J. Comput. Vis. **59**(2), 167–181 (2004)
10. Gooch, B., Reinhard, E., Gooch, A.: Human facial illustrations: creation and psychophysical evaluation. ACM Trans. Graph. **23**(1), 27–44 (2004)
11. Gooch, A.A., Olsen, S.C., Tumblin, J., Gooch, B.: Color2Gray: salience-preserving color removal. ACM Trans. Graph. **24**(3), 634–639 (2005)
12. Heckbert, P.: Color image quantization for frame buffer display. In: Proc. ACM SIGGRAPH, pp. 297–307 (1982)
13. Kang, H., Lee, S., Chui, C.K.: Coherent line drawing. In: ACM Symp. Non-photorealistic Animation and Rendering, pp. 43–50 (2007)
14. Kang, H., Lee, S., Chui, C.K.: Flow-based image abstraction. IEEE Trans. Vis. Comput. Graph. **15**(1), 62–76 (2009)
15. Kyprianidis, J.E.: Image and video abstraction by multi-scale anisotropic Kuwahara filtering. In: Proceedings of the ACM SIGGRAPH/Eurographics Symposium on Non-Photorealistic Animation and Rendering, pp. 55–64 (2011)
16. Kyprianidis, J.E., Döllner, J.: Image abstraction by structure adaptive filtering. In: EG UK Theory and Practice of Computer Graphics, pp. 51–58 (2008)
17. Kyprianidis, J.E., Kang, H., Döllner, J.: Image and video abstraction by anisotropic Kuwahara filtering. Comput. Graph. Forum **28**(7), 1955–1963 (2009)
18. Lopez-Moreno, J., Jimenez, J., Hadap, S., Reinhard, E., Anjyo, K., Gutierrez, D.: Stylized depiction of images based on depth perception. In: ACM Symp. Non-photorealistic Animation and Rendering, pp. 109–118. ACM, New York (2010)

19. Maharik, R., Bessmeltsev, M., Sheffer, A., Shamir, A., Carr, N.: Digital micrography. ACM Trans. Graph. **30**(4), 100 (2011)
20. Meng, M., Zhao, M., Zhu, S.C.: Artistic paper-cut of human portraits. In: 18th Int. Conf. on Multimedia, pp. 931–934 (2010)
21. Mould, D.: A stained glass image filter. In: Eurographics Workshop on Rendering Techniques, pp. 20–25 (2003)
22. Olsen, S.C., Gooch, B.: Image simplification and vectorization. In: ACM Symp. Non-photorealistic Animation and Rendering, pp. 65–74 (2011)
23. Otsu, N.: A threshold selection method from gray-level histograms. IEEE Trans. Syst. Man Cybern. **9**, 62–66 (1979)
24. Quinlan, J.: C4.5: Programs for Machine Learning. Morgan Kaufmann, San Mateo (1993)
25. Rosin, P.L., Lai, Y.K.: Towards artistic minimal rendering. In: ACM Symp. Non-photorealistic Animation and Rendering, pp. 119–127 (2010)
26. Rother, C., Kolmogorov, V., Blake, A.: "GrabCut": interactive foreground extraction using iterated graph cuts. ACM Trans. Graph. **23**(3), 309–314 (2004)
27. Song, Y., Hall, P., Rosin, P.L., Collomosse, J.: Arty shapes. In: Proc. Comp. Aesthetics, pp. 65–73 (2008)
28. Tomasi, C., Manduchi, R.: Bilateral filtering for gray and color images. In: ICCV, pp. 839–846 (1998)
29. Wang, J., Xu, Y., Shum, H.Y., Cohen, M.F.: Video tooning. ACM Trans. Graph. **23**(3), 574–583 (2004)
30. Weickert, J., ter Haar Romeny, B.M., Viergever, M.A.: Efficient and reliable schemes for nonlinear diffusion filtering. IEEE Trans. Image Process. **7**(3), 398–410 (1998)
31. Wen, F., Luan, Q., Liang, L., Xu, Y.Q., Shum, H.Y.: Color sketch generation. In: ACM Symp. Non-photorealistic Animation and Rendering, pp. 47–54 (2006)
32. Winnemöller, H., Olsen, S., Gooch, B.: Real-time video abstraction. ACM Trans. Graph. **25**(3), 1221–1226 (2006)
33. Winnemöller, H., Kyprianidis, J.E., Olsen, S.C.: XDoG: an extended difference-of-Gaussians compendium including advanced image stylization. Comput. Graph. **36**(6), 740–753 (2012)
34. Xu, J., Kaplan, C.S.: Calligraphic packing. In: Graphics Interface 2007, pp. 43–50 (2007)
35. Xu, J., Kaplan, C.S.: Artistic thresholding. In: ACM Symp. Non-photorealistic Animation and Rendering, pp. 39–47 (2008)
36. Xu, Z., Chen, H., Zhu, S.C., Luo, J.: A hierarchical compositional model for face representation and sketching. IEEE Trans. Pattern Anal. Mach. Intell. **30**(6), 955–969 (2008)
37. Xu, X., Zhang, L., Wong, T.T.: Structure-based ASCII art. ACM Trans. Graph. **29**(4), 52:1–52:9 (2010)
38. Xu, L., Lu, C., Xu, Y., Jia, J.: Image smoothing via L_0 gradient minimization. ACM Trans. Graph. **30**(6), 174 (2011)
39. Zhang, S.H., Li, X.Y., Hu, S.M., Martin, R.R.: Online video stream abstraction and stylization. IEEE Trans. Multimed. **13**(6), 1286–1294 (2011)

Chapter 12
Artistic Rendering of Portraits

Mingtian Zhao and Song-Chun Zhu

12.1 Introduction

Portraiture, the artistic representations of the appearances and expressions of human faces, is one of the oldest and most popular genres in visual arts. Generally there are two essential factors to consider in creating a portrait.

- The first factor is face fidelity. A portrait should preserve a certain amount of the original face's information, ensuring that not only can it be recognized as a face picture, but there is also an appropriate level of similarity in the perception of the appearance or character of the person in the portrait to the actual person or to the person shown in a photograph.
- The second factor is the artistic style of the portrait picture, chosen to simulate different media such as sketch, painting, paper-cut, and caricature. These styles/forms provide unique dictionaries of visual elements used to express the various facial structures and appearances.

These two factors vary with different ages and genres of portraiture, revealing its two principles, namely the pursuits of likeness and aesthetic. For example, before the invention of photography in the 19th century, the mainstream artists pursued accurate likeness by studying the structure of bones and muscles beneath the facial skin, practicing their skills on depicting them, developing pigments made from various materials, and even using external tools such as mirrors and pinhole imaging to improve the fidelity. Nowadays, with the popularity of digital cameras, perfect fidelity is easily available, but many modern portrait artists usually depict only rough or even distorted likeness. Instead, they resort to new styles and techniques to evoke

---

M. Zhao (✉) · S.-C. Zhu
University of California, Los Angeles, CA 90095-1554, USA
e-mail: mtzhao@ucla.edu

S.-C. Zhu
e-mail: sczhu@stat.ucla.edu

strong psychological and emotional reactions in the audience, demonstrating the sense of aesthetic.

These two factors/principles also apply to computerized artistic rendering of portraits—the simulation of portraiture on the computer. From an image analysis and synthesis perspective, using W to denote the facial information and Δ to denote the elements to compose an image, a natural image (photograph) $\mathbf{I}_N$ is generated with

$$\mathbf{I}_N = f(W_N; \Delta_N) \qquad (12.1)$$

and in a similar way, an artistic portrait $\mathbf{I}_A$ can be synthesized with

$$\mathbf{I}_A = g(W_A; \Delta_A) \qquad (12.2)$$

where f and g are image generating functions (rendering processes). Interestingly, Eqs. (12.1), (12.2) differ in all their three aspects:

- $W_N \neq W_A$. The facial information W usually contains features such as geometry (2D or 3D), appearance, texture, color, and illumination. To generate a realistic photograph, W_N should usually approximate the truth very closely. In contrast, W_A often only captures part of the information interesting to artistic perception, which is regarded as the essence of a face by many artists.
- $\Delta_N \neq \Delta_A$. In the image analysis and computer vision literature, Δ_N is usually modeled with PCA, wavelets like Gabor bases, image patches, etc. Δ_A, however, is usually a dictionary of graphical elements used in creating artworks, for example, graphite sketches, paint brush strokes, etc.
- $f \neq g$. While f is usually a simple linear combination of the image elements, the portrait rendering process g can be a much more complex process involving content-oriented algorithms for manipulating the sketches, strokes, etc.

In the non-photorealistic rendering (NPR) [7] literature, there are plenty of studies on computerized artistic portrait rendering with different implementations of W_A and $g(\cdot; \Delta_A)$, corresponding to likeness and aesthetic, respectively.

- To preserve the facial fidelity, existing portrait rendering methods adopt different models and data structures to represent selected geometry and appearance features in W_A.
- To simulate different artistic styles, existing methods use different dictionaries of graphical elements, which are maintained in Δ_A, and corresponding compositional algorithms, g.

In the rest of this chapter, we review the latest artistic portrait rendering methods and their respective implementations of the two factors. We organize these methods by the four most studied types of portrait in NPR: sketch, paper-cut, oil-painting, and caricature.

12.2 Sketch

A sketch is a rapidly executed drawing demonstrating the basic shape and appearance features of objects. In this section, we review three types of portrait sketching method. The first two types of sketch depict the boundaries and salient edges/curves in portraits with concise strokes (like stick drawings). The former uses holistic models for the shape of face, and the latter uses part-based models with greater expressive power. The third type of portrait sketch focuses more on the facial surface, including the appearance caused by illumination and shading effects.

12.2.1 Holistic Models

Li and Kobatake [10] made one of the earliest investigations in generating facial sketches from photographs. Their method consists of three steps:

1. Color coordinate transformation, in which an input image is first processed with the saturation component enhanced, and transformed to the YIQ color space. In the YIQ color space, the Y channel represents the luma information, and the I and Q channels represent the chrominance information. They are used for extracting the face area and some facial parts: lips are red so they have relatively large values in Q, the face area with skin color is generally larger in Q and smaller in I than the dark gray background, and black pupils of eyes are usually darker than other parts reflected in Y.
2. Facial components detection. In addition to lips and pupils, facial parts such as eyes, mouth, nose, and chin are located with rough edges detected using the Y channel of the image.
3. Approximation of edges with feature points and feature curves. The method takes advantage of a facial sketch representation with 35 feature points connected by feature curves as shown in Fig. 12.1a, in which spliced second-order polynomials are used for approximating the edges of mouth, eyes, nose, and chin. The 35 feature points are then detected as characteristic points on the curves.

In their follow-up work [11], detailed algorithms of the method were improved by adding a symmetry measure, a novel rectangle filter, a geometric template, and morphological processing, all of which led to more robust detections of the positions and edges of facial parts. Figure 12.1b shows two example facial sketches extracted using the method.

In Li and Tobatake's methods, the two factors introduced in Sect. 12.1 are implemented in a very straight-forward way. The facial information W_A is represented with the shape model shown in Fig. 12.1a, which is extracted from the color and gradient features of the input image. This ensures that the portrait sketch looks similar to the photograph. As for the second factor, Δ_A simply defines a line drawing style, with the feature curves fitted using spliced second-order polynomials.

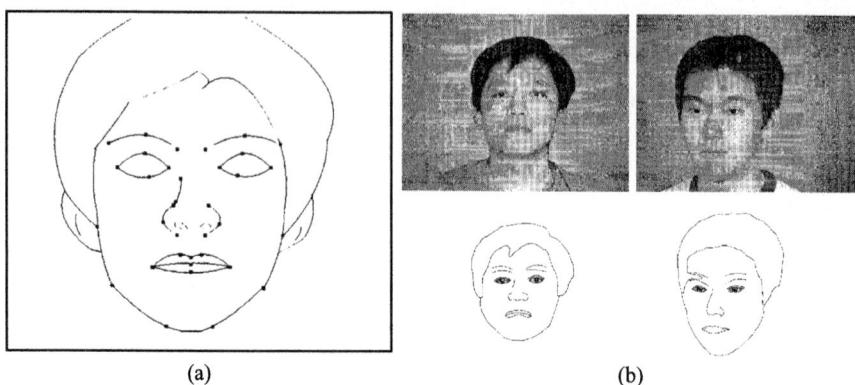

Fig. 12.1 (a) Feature points and feature curves used for extracting facial sketch images by Li and Kobatake [10, 11]. (b) Example results of facial sketch extraction using their method, from [11]. © IEEE

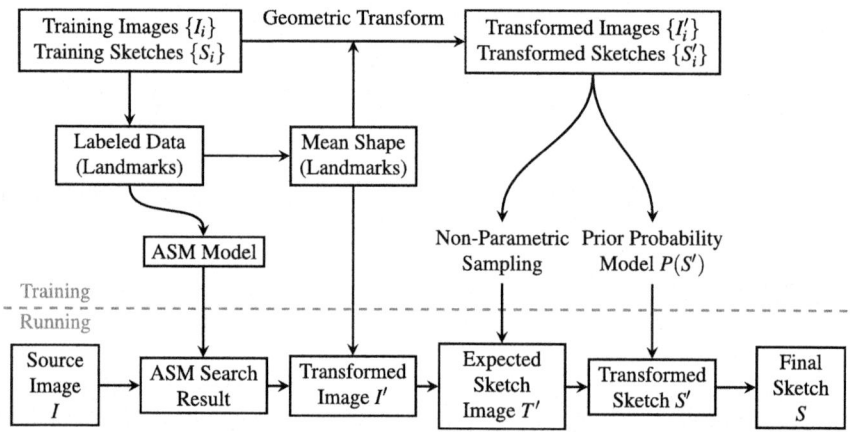

Fig. 12.2 Pipeline of the example-based facial sketch generation system developed by Chen et al. [2]

To further improve the results of Li and Tobatake's method, especially on the aesthetic aspect, many studies have been carried out recently. Chen et al. [2] developed an example-based facial sketch generation system whose pipeline is shown in Fig. 12.2. Observing that the artistic styles of sketches vary among different artists and cannot be easily summarized by precise rules (such as polynomial curves up to a specific order or curvatures of certain degrees), their system refers to a set of training examples for obtaining their styles. Each training example is a pair of a portrait photograph and its corresponding sketch image created by artists. An active shape model (ASM) [5] for the face is also attached to each example, with the landmark points manually labeled for better accuracy.

- In the training phase, a mean shape of face is computed by averaging the ASM landmarks of all training examples. Then a geometric transformation is performed on each training example in order to warp the image and the sketch to match the mean shape. After that, a prior probability model of the sketches is learned to cover three types of curve: those that always appear, those that probably appear but are independent of other curves, and those that depend on other curves.
- At runtime, given an input face photograph, the ASM is first applied to extract the landmark points. Then a geometric transformation is defined between these landmarks and the mean shape. After applying this geometric transformation to warp the input image, non-parametric sampling is used for producing a sketch image for the input, which is then warped back to the original shape using an inverse geometric transformation, producing the final sketch.

Compared to Li and Kobatake's method, Chen et al.'s system improved both W_A and Δ_A. For facial information, W_A, the ASM model provides a more robust way to capture the shape of the face than the model in Fig. 12.1a which relies on local edge detection and curve fitting. For a higher level of aesthetic, the sketches used as graphical elements in the style set Δ_A essentially come from the training examples created by artists, instead of naive polynomial curves, and are encoded within a prior distribution of the sketch curves as we introduced above.

12.2.2 Part-Based Models

A disadvantage of the holistic methods is that the rendered sketches only contain stiff lines and curves, whereas sketches created by artists usually have various curve styles and multiple levels of darkness and thickness for different facial components, as well as the hair. To address this problem, part-based methods were introduced for processing different parts of the face separately in order for greater expressive power. Generally, these part-based models allow richer representations of W_A and larger variety of elements in Δ_A.

12.2.2.1 Flat Model

Chen et al. [3] proposed an example-based composite sketching approach. This approach decomposes the face into semantic parts (as shown in Fig. 12.3) and uses image-based, instead of curve-based, sketches (as shown in Fig. 12.4). Their system also includes a sub-system for hair rendering which contributes greatly to the visual quality of the portrait sketches.

In the composite sketching system of Chen et al., the sketches are split into two layers: a global layer and a local layer. The global layer captures the spatial placement of the facial parts, and the local layer captures how each facial part is depicted. For both layers, features are selected and learned using training image-sketch pairs provided by artists. At runtime, two processing steps are executed:

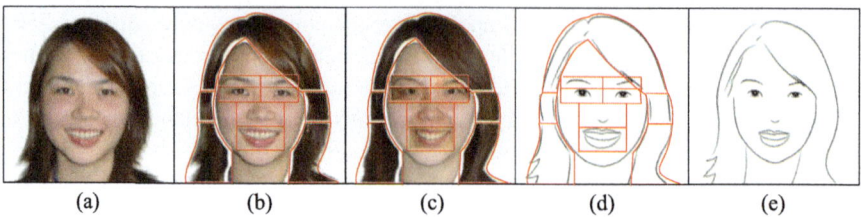

(a) (b) (c) (d) (e)

Fig. 12.3 Portrait sketching using example-based composite sketching [3]. The input image (**a**) is decomposed into facial parts shown in (**b**), then for each part the best match is found in the training examples, as shown in (**c**). Then sketches are drawn for each part in (**d**), which are composed in (**e**) by considering both global and local features. © ACM

Fig. 12.4 Example sketches of facial parts used by Chen et al. [3] for Δ_A. © ACM

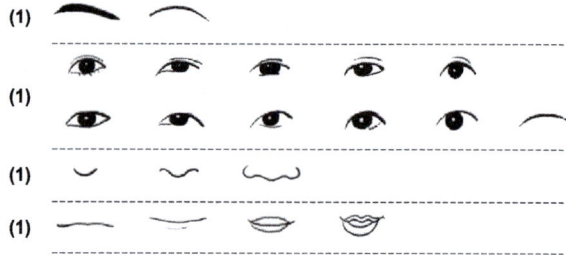

- Local processing. The input image is first decomposed into facial parts using a refined ASM. Then, for each part, the system finds the best match in shape (according to ASM landmarks) from the training examples. After that, the corresponding sketches of the best matches are adopted.
- Global processing. The sketches of the facial parts are composed according to the learned global spatial model, which adjusts the locations, sizes, and orientations of the parts.

The hair rendering sub-system extracts both structural (boundary) and detail (streamline) components in the hair area and fits them with curves. The two types of curve are then rendered using their respective example-based strokes (learned from training examples) to synthesize the hair sketch.

Regarding the two factors we have been discussing in this chapter, the global/local hybrid method of Chen et al. works in a more flexible way for preserving face fidelity in W_A than the global geometric transformation based on ASM used in their early work [2]. For each facial part, the locally best matching sketch is selected and composed into a globally coherent image. But, due to the selection of the best matches instead of a learned local sketch model [2], the system may lose certain degrees of likeness when the number of training examples is small, for example, the locally best matches may not be good enough in terms of similarity. On the aesthetic aspect, however, this method achieves much finer detailed appearances by maintaining image-based sketches instead of stiff curves in Δ_A (as shown in Fig. 12.4) where different facial parts may be sketched using different techniques by artists.

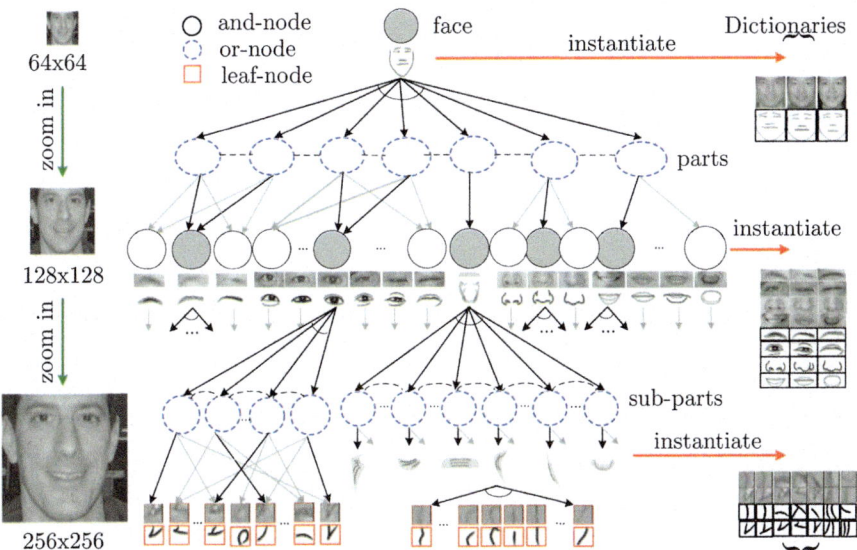

Fig. 12.5 A three-layer And–Or Graph (AOG) representation for face [22]. *Dark arrows* represent the paths for generating an instance from the AOG, by decomposing And-nodes (*solid ellipses*) into sub-components and choosing among alternative types at Or-nodes (*dashed ellipses*). As marked on the *right side*, examples in Δ_N and Δ_A of different scales can be embedded in the AOG. © IEEE

12.2.2.2 Hierarchical Model

Since part-based portrait rendering methods have greater expressive power than global methods, more studies in this direction have been dedicated to better models and algorithms for both global and local processing. A powerful model for organizing the facial components is the hierarchical and compositional And–Or Graph (AOG) [20–22], as shown in Fig. 12.5.

In this AOG, the And-nodes represent decompositions of the face or its parts into sub-components (e.g., decomposing the face into nose, mouth, etc.), and the Or-nodes represent alternative types of a part (e.g., there are multiple ways to sketch a nose, given by either models or examples). On the AOG, complex spatial constraints of the facial parts can be embedded at the And-nodes at multiple levels, for example, by using Markov networks [20]. Also, the photo-sketch similarity measure enforcing the likeness principle can be applied at multiple resolutions (thanks to the hierarchical structure) and optimized by switching at the Or-nodes during rendering.

To create the face AOG, a hierarchical structure is designed by hand with the nodes corresponding to semantic facial parts. Then a set of training sketch examples with their corresponding photographs are collected and manually decomposed corresponding to the structure of the AOG. The decomposed parts are then associated with the nodes in the AOG in order to construct Δ_N and Δ_A for multiple scales in the hierarchy as marked on the right side of Fig. 12.5. Using these Δ_N and Δ_A, models for constraining spatial configurations are learned at the And-nodes,

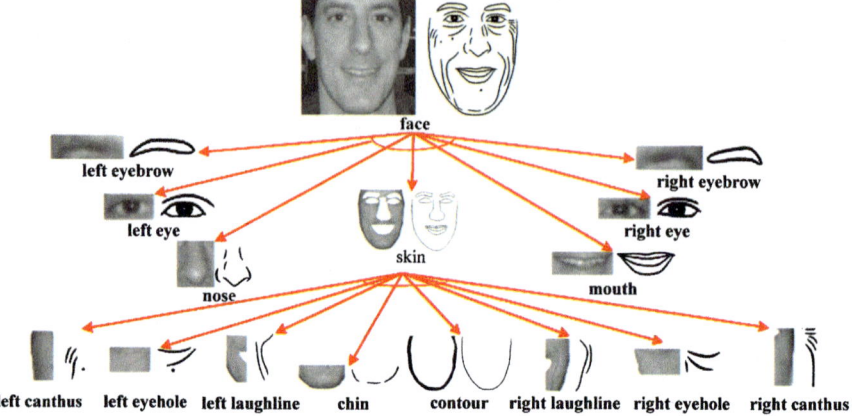

Fig. 12.6 A parse graph instantiated from the AOG in Fig. 12.5 [22]. This process essentially generates a portrait sketch by selecting sketches of different parts and composing them. © IEEE

and switching probabilities are summarized at Or-nodes. Note that if we save all examples in the AOG without merging similar ones, the switching probabilities are uniform.

Generating a portrait sketch from an input photograph is equivalent to instantiating a parse graph from the AOG by decomposing at And-nodes and switching at Or-nodes, as shown in Fig. 12.6. An instance optimizing the probabilities at the And- and Or-nodes, as well as the similarity measures at multiple resolutions, is expected to preserve the fidelity both globally and locally (cf. the global/local hybrid model introduced by Chen et al. [3]).

Compared with the flat model described in the previous section, the hierarchical AOG has two advantages on the aspect of the face fidelity factor.

1. The AOG can encode spatial constraints more efficiently with the And-nodes at multiple levels on the graph. Furthermore, if multiple selections at Or-nodes are clustered and similar ones are merged, the AOG compresses the storage of all training examples, which is important when the training set is large.
2. The hierarchical AOG structure makes it easier to enforce likeness for different facial parts at multiple resolutions, especially when we want different weights for the likenesses at different parts/levels. For example, the likeness of the eyes could be more important than that of the eyebrows, while the appearance of an entire eye might be more important than those of the eyelids at an unnecessarily high resolution. In this sense, the power of the face AOG has yet to be fully developed before comprehensive psychological studies on this topic are carried out.

As for the artistic style factor, Xu et al. [20–22] still used sketch examples created by artists. To improve the visual effects, Min et al. [14] collected more stylish training examples in Δ_A and added two sub-systems for processing the hair and clothes, respectively. Figure 12.7 includes an example generated by their system.

12 Artistic Rendering of Portraits

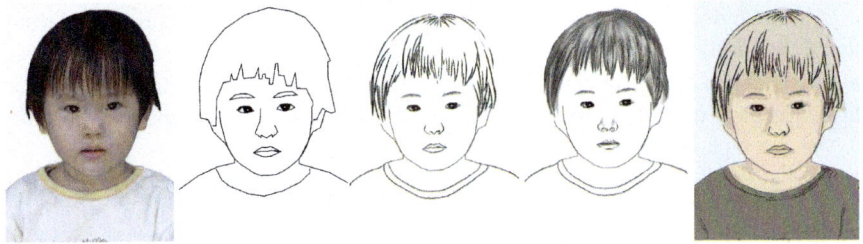

Fig. 12.7 An example portrait sketch generated by the system of Min et al. [14]. © Springer

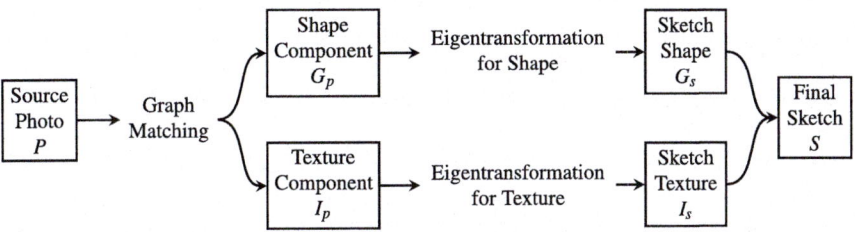

Fig. 12.8 Framework of the portrait sketch system developed by Wang and Tang [19]

12.2.3 Sketching the Facial Surface

In addition to the concise sketching styles discussed in Sects. 12.2.1 and 12.2.2, there is another popular sketching style which pays more attention to the facial surface than the boundaries and salient edges/curves. This style depicts the appearance of facial surface affected by illumination and shading effects. There are a few studies on this type of portrait sketch in the NPR literature.

Wang and Tang [19] proposed an example-based method for synthesizing portrait sketches with surface strokes to depict the facial appearance. Figure 12.8 displays the framework of their method.

In this method, a triangular mesh is attached to the face, whose vertices are located at the fiducial points on the face, for example, the eyeballs, the corners of the mouth, etc. Given a training set containing pairs of portrait photographs and their corresponding sketches created by artists, the fiducial points are located for each image (both photographs and sketches), and the corresponding triangular mesh is constructed for the pair. Then two eigentransformations from photograph to sketch are computed for shape (coordinates of mesh vertices) and texture (grayscale images), respectively. For rendering a given input photograph, its fiducial points and triangular mesh are first computed, and then these are used to warp the image to the mean shape as derived from the training set. This essentially separates the shape component G_p and the texture component I_p, which then pass through their respective eigentransformations we computed before to generate the sketch shape G_s and the sketch texture I_s. After warping I_s back to the original shape of the input, we obtain the final sketch.

Although the two differ in detailed models and algorithms for shape and texture, the global design of the method by Wang and Tang [19] is essentially very similar to that of Chen et al. [3]. They both try to separate the shape and texture information, and each defines certain mapping relationships for both components in order to transfer a photograph into a sketch image.

- For shape, Chen et al. adopted ASM, while Wang and Tang used a triangular mesh.
- For texture, Chen et al. used a non-parametric sketch model dependent on the photograph, while Wang and Tang used an eigentransformation in the image space.

Therefore, the face fidelity and artistic style factors are implemented here in a similar way to the flat model of Chen et al. but with different details. The fidelity is enforced using the triangular mesh attached to the face with shape and texture eigentransformations, and the artistic style is defined by the sketch examples created by artists.

Another interesting work on sketching the facial surface was presented by Tresset and Leymarie [18]. In this work, sketches are drawn randomly as Bézier curves at different densities for each color-clustered region in the segmented face area. In this way, the face fidelity factor is only roughly preserved at a low-resolution level in terms of approximate grayscale levels of different regions and is dropped for most details. Meanwhile, this random sketching process, defined in its style Δ_A, produces a unique appearance which may appear aesthetic to people.

12.3 Paper-Cut

The second portrait genre we review in this chapter is the paper-cut, which is essentially a binary image called a Mooney image in the psychological literature [8]. The binarization process is inhomogeneous for different facial areas, which usually does not correspond strictly to the grayscale levels. While there have been a few studies on the paper-cut in the NPR literature, to the best of our knowledge, the only dedicated portrait paper-cut work is by Meng et al. [13].

The method of Meng et al. adopts the hierarchical AOG face representation introduced in Sect. 12.2.2.2, shown in Fig. 12.9. Its global design is very similar to that of Min et al. [14], except for a few differences in detailed algorithms. Further differentiating the two, sketch examples in the latter are replaced by paper-cut versions in the former, as shown in Fig. 12.10. Meng et al. also used separated sub-systems for the face, the hair and clothes.

Figure 12.11 includes two results generated by the system of Meng et al. The structural information of the face is represented by the AOG model (the fidelity factor), and the style factor and aesthetic rely on the paper-cut examples in Δ_A that were created by artists.

Meng et al. [13] is thus far the only work that studied the trade-off between fidelity and aesthetic in the rendering process. In this work, fidelity is achieved by

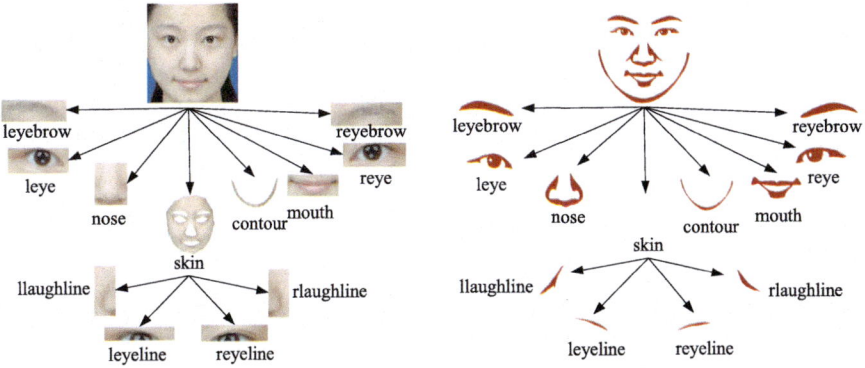

Fig. 12.9 Parse graph of a face image and its corresponding paper-cut [13]

Fig. 12.10 Paper-cut graphical elements in Δ_A for facial parts used in the system of Meng et al. [13]

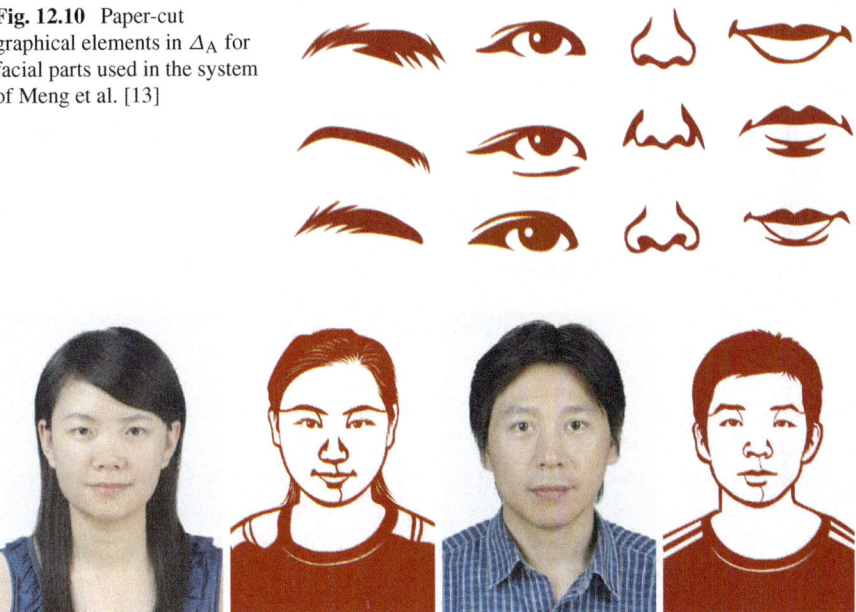

Fig. 12.11 Example paper-cuts generated using the method of Meng et al. [13]

a binary proposal generated from the source image using dynamic thresholding, as shown in Fig. 12.12, and the aesthetic level is controlled by the compatibility level of the facial parts in the template dictionary Δ_A. To obtain a trade-off between the two, a weighted sum of the cost function of each,

$$d + \lambda c \tag{12.3}$$

is measured, where d is the difference between the template image and the binary proposal, and c is the number of template instances that the facial parts are selected

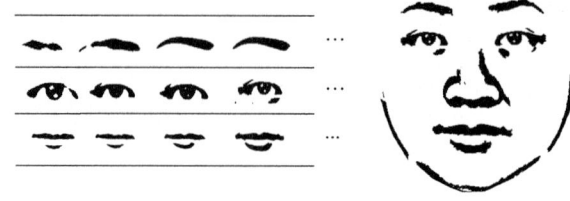

Fig. 12.12 The dynamic thresholding algorithm for computing the binary proposal used by Meng et al. [13]

from, which is a metric of compatibility (assuming parts are more compatible if they are from the same template). By tuning λ it is possible to obtain a continuous spectrum from pursuing only likeness, to considering a weighted combination, then to pursuing only aesthetic.

12.4 Oil-Painting

Besides sketch and paper-cut, another type of visual art in which portraiture plays an important role is oil-painting. Portrait painting has also been studied in the artistic rendering literature.

Zhao and Zhu [24] developed a system for rendering portrait paintings from photographs using active templates. The main idea of this system is similar to many methods introduced above on sketching. However, due to the much more detailed appearance in paintings than in sketches, the algorithms for depicting these details are especially important for both likeness and aesthetic.

The system of Zhao and Zhu has a few crucial components:

- A dictionary of portrait painting templates. Given photographs, artists are asked to paint portraits on a screen with a digitizer, using image-example-based brush strokes as shown in Fig. 12.13. The color statistics (mean and variance), geometry (control points of the backbone curve), and texture (example ID in the brush dictionary [23]) of each stroke used by the artists to compose the portrait are recorded. This gives the complete information about the sequence of brush strokes for each portrait painting, as shown in Fig. 12.14b (only part of the strokes are visualized). A dictionary of these portrait painting examples, along with their corresponding photographs, is constructed as shown in Fig. 12.15. The elements of the dictionary are used as templates later in rendering.
- A representation of the spatial configuration of the face and the brush strokes. For each instance in the dictionary, the shape of the face is captured using an active appearance model (AAM) [6] with 83 landmarks. The positions of these landmarks are put in the same coordinate system as the control points describing the geometry of the brush strokes. Shape matching between two different faces (e.g., an input photograph to paint from and a reference example in the dictionary) are achieved by computing a Thin Plate Spline (TPS) transformation [1] between the coordinate pairs of their AAM landmarks.

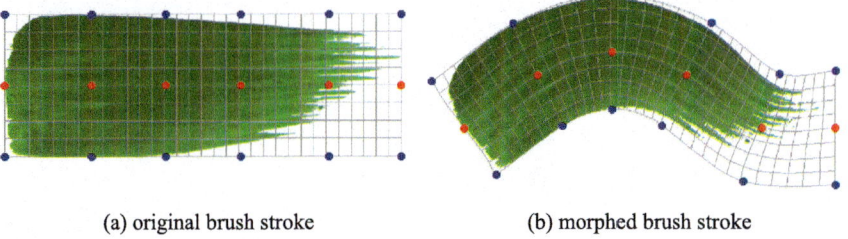

Fig. 12.13 The example-based brush stroke model used by Zhao and Zhu [24]

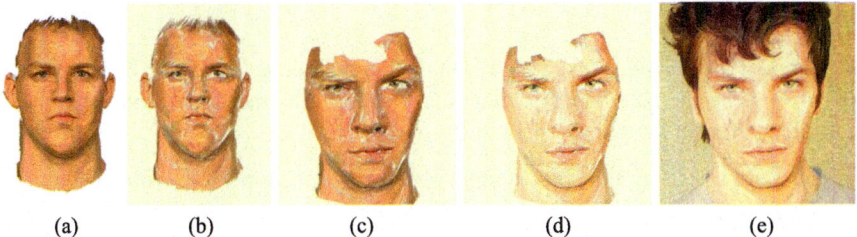

Fig. 12.14 Pipeline of the portrait painting system of Zhao and Zhu [24]. See explanations in text

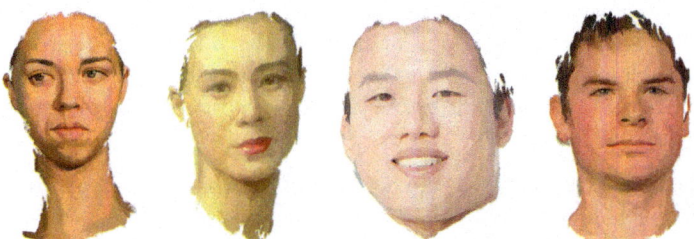

Fig. 12.15 Example portrait painting templates from the dictionary of Zhao and Zhu [24]

- A brush stroke rendering algorithm. Given an input face photograph, in order to synthesize a corresponding portrait painting, we first select a reference example from the dictionary of templates. Then we compute the TPS transformation from the shape of the reference example to that of the input photograph. Afterward, this TPS transformation is applied to the control points of all brush strokes in the reference example, and the output control points with new coordinates defines the new geometry of the strokes for composing the portrait corresponding the input photograph, as shown in Fig. 12.14c. Finally, the color of each brush stroke is transferred to match the color of the target photograph, and the brush strokes are superimposed to compose the result painting image, as shown in Figs. 12.14d, e.

Fig. 12.16 Example results generated using Zhao and Zhu's system [24]

 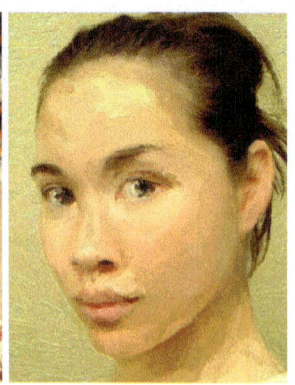

Figure 12.16 displays example results generated using Zhao and Zhu's system. In this system, the face fidelity factor is taken care of by the AAM landmarks and a few algorithms in the portrait painting system:

- Template selection. For a given input photograph, the top-10 best matched examples from the dictionary in terms of both shape and appearance are reported for selection. This avoids using templates differing too much from the target image, which may potentially cause problems in likeness and rendering.
- Shape matching and stroke deformation. Shapes of different faces are matched through the 83 AAM landmark points. Using stroke deformation defined by the matching between landmarks ensures that the strokes are rendered at appropriate positions with correct curvatures to depict the facial surface and parts.
- Stroke color transfer, which maps the colors of all strokes to the target photograph in a coherent way. This contributes crucially to preserving the global appearance of the original photograph.

The artistic style factor and the aesthetic is supported by the portrait painting dictionary, including:

- The sequence of sparse but decisive and colorful strokes which, when put together, convey an impression of 3D structures and vibrant contrasts, and
- The individual textured brush strokes, which deliver elegant oil-painting details with illumination and shading.

12.5 Caricature

Caricature is a very special type of portrait image. It differs from traditional sketch, paper-cut, and painting by manipulating the two factors we study in this chapter. Most caricatures *explicitly* trade a certain degree of fidelity for unique aesthetic effects, for example, by exaggerating features in several parts of the face.

Tominaga et al. [16, 17] developed the PICASSO facial caricaturing system. In the PICASSO system, 445 characteristic points are located on the edges of facial

12 Artistic Rendering of Portraits

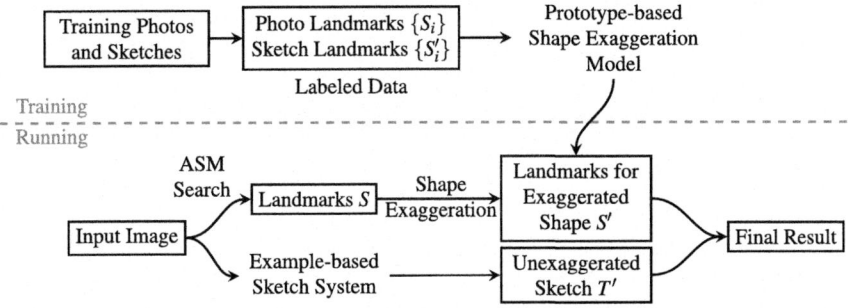

Fig. 12.17 Framework of the example-based caricature generation system of Liang et al. [12]

parts, and various expressions are defined as offsets of these points from a mean face (without expression). The idea of deliberately manipulating the facial shape for caricaturing and further exaggeration is the basis of most later studies on portrait caricatures.

Liang et al. [12], whose framework is shown in Fig. 12.17, extended the sketching method of Chen et al. [2] with exaggeration for generating facial caricatures. In its prototype-based shape exaggeration model, the training examples are analyzed and clustered into a few exaggeration prototypes. Each prototype represents a trend of exaggeration in some facial features, towards which the sketch image is warped using a local linear model at runtime to generate caricatures. The additional exaggeration module extending the system of Chen et al. essentially reduces the level of face fidelity while enhancing features exaggerated in training examples, reflecting a type of aesthetic.

Mo et al. [15] noticed that the exaggeration level should depend not only on the absolute difference from the mean shape, but also the variance level of such differences among examples. This idea enables the comparison between the exaggeration levels of different facial parts, which corresponds better to our perception.

Another interesting work on caricature was presented by Chiang et al. [4], which adds exaggeration upon a mesh-based representation for facial geometry (similar to Wang and Tang [19]) instead of the contour-based ones used by Tominaga et al. [16, 17] and Liang et al. [12]. This enables more details in color and texture in the rendered caricature.

12.6 Summary

In this chapter, by reviewing recent work on artistic rendering of portraits, we have studied its two essential factors, namely, the face fidelity factor supported by certain face representations stored in W_A, and the artistic style chosen to simulate different media with graphical elements and rendering details defined in Δ_A and g, as introduced in Sect. 12.1.

- Fidelity is usually enforced at two different levels. At the local level of details of facial parts, certain similarity measures are adopted between the photograph and the artistic depiction or implicitly applied by defining a mapping/transformation between them. At the global level of the face, certain shape models are adopted, such as ASM, AAM or triangular mesh, to constrain the spatial configuration of the facial parts. Additionally, the And–Or Graph model has been applied to integrate the two or more levels in a single hierarchy.
- The artistic style/format is usually applied by using training-example art pieces or elements created by artists, in addition to some simple rule-based strategies for straightness, smoothness, etc. The unique style of caricature is mainly attributed to the exaggerated features which are also learnable from training examples.

Guided by the two factors, various methods in past studies on artistic rendering of portraits were used to pursue likeness and aesthetic of portraiture.

Despite the progress, a few key questions still remain standing in our way to a systematic theory and solution to the portrait rendering problem:

- How should we select the important information from W_N to be used in W_A? In practice, this means choosing a facial model that captures features essential to artistic perception while ignoring unimportant parts. Also, what is the minimum information needed in W_A to satisfy the likeness principle?
- Is there a principled method for balancing between likeness and aesthetic, or can these two be separated for independent manipulation under certain circumstances? The study of Leopold et al. [9] gives us some hints on this question, indicating that extrapolation against a mean face can preserve a person's identity without confusing with other people in the dataset. This supports the caricature rendering methods based on shape exaggeration which improve the aesthetic without giving up the likeness. Meanwhile, a comprehensive investigation to this problem has yet to be conducted.

Acknowledgements We would like to thank Meng Meng, Jinli Suo and Yaling Yang for discussions and help with the experimental data and figures during studying the likeness and aesthetic principles in portrait rendering, and Amy Morrow for suggestions on the presentation of this chapter. This work has been supported by ONR MURI Grant N000141010933 and DARPA Award FA 8650-11-1-7149.

References

1. Barrodale, I., Skea, D., Berkley, M., Kuwahara, R., Poeckert, R.: Warping digital images using thin plate splines. Pattern Recognit. **26**(2), 375–376 (1993)
2. Chen, H., Xu, Y.Q., Shum, H.Y., Zhu, S.C., Zheng, N.N.: Example-based facial sketch generation with non-parametric sampling. In: Proceedings of ICCV (2001)
3. Chen, H., Liu, Z., Rose, C., Xu, Y., Shum, H.Y., Salesin, D.: Example-based composite sketching of human portraits. In: Proceedings of NPAR (2004)
4. Chiang, P.Y., Liao, W.H., Li, T.Y.: Automatic caricature generation by analyzing facial features. In: Proceedings of ACCV (2004)

5. Cootes, T.F., Taylor, C.J., Cooper, D.H., Graham, J.: Active shape model—their training and application. Comput. Vis. Image Underst. **61**, 38–59 (1995)
6. Cootes, T.F., Edwards, G.J., Taylor, C.J.: Active appearance models. IEEE Trans. Pattern Anal. Mach. Intell. **23**(6), 681–685 (2001)
7. Gooch, A., Gooch, B.: Non-Photorealistic Rendering. AK Peters, Wellesley (2001)
8. Hegdé, J., Thompson, S., Kersten, D.: Identifying faces in two-tone ('Mooney') images: A psychophysical and fMRI study. J. Vis. **7**(9), 624 (2007)
9. Leopold, D.A., O'Toole, A.J., Vetter, T., Blanz, V.: Prototype-referenced shape encoding revealed by high-level aftereffects. Nat. Neurosci. **4**(1), 89–94 (2001)
10. Li, Y., Kobatake, H.: Extraction of facial sketch images and expression transformation based on FACS. In: Proceedings of ICIP (1995)
11. Li, Y., Kobatake, H.: Extraction of facial sketch image based on morphological processing. In: Proceedings of ICIP (1997)
12. Liang, L., Chen, H., Xu, Y.Q., Shum, H.Y.: Example-based caricature generation with exaggeration. In: Proceedings of Pacific Graphics (2002)
13. Meng, M., Zhao, M., Zhu, S.C.: Artistic paper-cut of human portraits. In: Proceedings of ACM MM (2010)
14. Min, F., Suo, J.L., Zhu, S.C., Sang, N.: An automatic portrait system based on and-or graph representation. In: Proceedings of EMMCVPR (2007)
15. Mo, Z., Lewis, J.P., Neumann, U.: Improved automatic caricature by feature normalization and exaggeration. In: SIGGRAPH Sketch (2004)
16. Tominaga, M., Fukuoka, S., Murakami, K., Koshimizu, H.: Facial caricaturing with motion caricaturing in PICASSO system. In: Proceedings of the IEEE/ASME International Conference on Advanced Intelligent Mechatronics (1997)
17. Tominaga, M., Hayashi, J.I., Murakami, K., Koshimizu, H.: Facial caricaturing system PICASSO with emotional motion deformation. In: Proceedings of the 2nd International Conference on Knowledge-Based Intelligent Electronic System (1998)
18. Tresset, P., Leymarie, F.: Generative portrait sketching. In: Proceedings of VSMM (2005)
19. Wang, X., Tang, X.: Face sketch synthesis and recognition. In: Proceedings of ICCV (2003)
20. Xu, Z., Luo, J.: Accurate dynamic sketching of faces from video. In: Proceedings of CVPR (2007)
21. Xu, Z., Chen, H., Zhu, S.C.: A high resolution grammatical model for face representation and sketching. In: Proceedings of CVPR (2005)
22. Xu, Z., Chen, H., Zhu, S.C., Luo, J.: A hierarchical compositional model for face representation and sketching. IEEE Trans. Pattern Anal. Mach. Intell. **30**(6), 955–969 (2008)
23. Zeng, K., Zhao, M., Xiong, C., Zhu, S.C.: From image parsing to painterly rendering. ACM Trans. Graph. **29**(1), 2 (2009)
24. Zhao, M., Zhu, S.C.: Portrait painting using active templates. In: Proceedings of NPAR (2011)

Part III
Stylized Animations

Part III of this book explores the creation of stylized animations from video; either photorealistic video, or existing animations. The first chapter outlines how Computer Vision technology has been applied to the video stylization problem, and how this has enabled the extension of many stroke-based rendering and region-based rendering approaches to video. The second chapter focuses on techniques for analyzing cartoon animations to enable their re-presentation or enhancement in a variety of artistic styles.

Analysis of existing animations to enable their manipulation and re-rendering; described in Sect. 14.4.1. Temporally coherent rotoscoping enabling a cartoon effect; described in Sect. 13.4.1.1

Chapter 13
Temporally Coherent Video Stylization

Pierre Bénard, Joëlle Thollot, and John Collomosse

13.1 Introduction

Artistic Rendering (AR) arguably evolved from semi-automated stroke based rendering (SBR) systems of the early 1990s. SBR is discussed in detail within Chap. 1. In brief, it is the process of compositing primitives (e.g. brush strokes) on to a virtual canvas to create a rendering. Following Willats and Durand [58], we refer to these rendering primitives as "marks". Digital paint systems such as Haeberli's *'paint by numbers'* [24] were among the first to propose such a framework, seeking to partially automate the image stylization process. Marks adopt some attributes (e.g. color, and orientation) from a reference image, whilst user interaction governed other attributes such as scale and compositing order. Soon after, fully automatic algorithms emerged harnessing low-level image processing (e.g. edge filters [26, 40] and moments [50]) in lieu of user interaction. These advances in automation brought with them new algorithms designed *specifically* for video.

This chapter maps the landscape of video stylization algorithms in approximate chronological order of development. We begin by briefly identifying some non-linear filtering methods that, when applied independently to video frames, can produce a coherent rendering output. Chapter 5 explores these techniques in greater detail. We then survey optical flow based methods [40], which, like filters, are very

---

P. Bénard (✉)
University of Toronto, 40 St George Street, Toronto, ON M5S 2E4, Canada
e-mail: Pierre.Benard@laposte.net

J. Thollot
LJK, INRIA, Grenoble University, 655, avenue de l'Europe, 38334 Saint Ismier, France
e-mail: Joelle.Thollot@inria.fr

J. Collomosse
Centre for Vision Speech and Signal Processing, University of Surrey, Guildford, Surrey, GU2 7XH, UK
e-mail: J.Collomosse@surrey.ac.uk

general in the class of video footage that may be processed, but are limited predominantly to painterly styles. These approaches move marks such as strokes or texture fields over time according to a per-frame motion estimate. We then survey early approaches to stylization driven by coherent video segmentation [14, 16, 55]. These approach artistic stylization by treating coherent placement of strokes as a rotoscoping problem, and extend to cartoon-like styles. Finally we survey the recent, interactive techniques that extend this early work to sophisticated rotoscoping and artistic rendering tools.

13.1.1 Temporal Coherence

Barbara Meier developed an early object-space technique for creating painterly animations of 3D scenes [43], and whilst not a video stylization approach *per se* it was the first to consider the important issue of *temporal coherence* in SBR.

Meier's approach to painting was to initialize (seed) marks (in her case, brush strokes) as particles over the 3D surfaces of objects. The particles were projected to 2D during rendering, and brush strokes generated on the image-plane. The motivation to anchor strokes to move with the object arises from Meier's early observations on temporal coherence, and are echoed by many subsequent authors. Painting the scene geometry independently for each frame results in a distracting flicker. Yet, fixing stroke positions in 2D while allowing their attributes (e.g. color) to vary with the underlying video content gives the impression of motion behind frosted glass—the so called *shower door effect*. Meier's proposal was therefore to fix the strokes to the surface of the 3D object; *minimizing flicker* whilst *maximizing the correspondence* between stroke motion and the motion of the underlying object.

Satisfying both criteria for coherence is tractable for 3D rendering where geometry is available, but is non-trivial when painting 2D video. As such, temporal coherence remains a key challenge in video stylization research. Understanding the motion of objects in an unconstrained monocular video feed requires a *robust* and *general* model of scene structure; a long-term goal that continues to elude the Computer Vision community. Moreover, there is no single best model for all video. The model selected to represent the scene's dynamics and visual structure impacts both the *classes of video content that can be processed*, and *the gamut of artistic styles that may be rendered*.

13.1.2 Problem Statement: Coherent Stylization

In order to better describe the problem of temporal coherence in this chapter, we build upon Meier's discussion to propose a definition of temporal coherence. Temporal coherence video requires the concurrent fulfillment of three goals: *spatial quality*, *motion coherence* and *temporal continuity*.

1. *Spatial quality* describes the visual quality of the stylization at each frame. This is a key ingredient in generating computer animations that appear similar to traditional hand-drawn animations. Several properties of the marks must be preserved to produce a convincing appearance. In particular the size and distribution of marks should be independent of the underlying geometry of the scene. As a typical example, the size of the marks should not increase during a zoom, but their spatial density should not change neither. Deformation of the marks should be avoided. Marks should not compress around occlusions for instance.
2. *Motion coherence* is the correlation between the apparent motion flow of the 3D scene and the motion of the marks. A low correlation produces sliding artifacts and gives the impression that the scene is observed through a semi-transparent layer of marks; Meier's *shower door effect* [43].
3. *Temporal continuity* minimizes abrupt changes of the marks from frame to frame. Perceptual studies [47, 60] have shown that human observers are very sensitive to sudden temporal variations such as popping and flickering. The visibility and attributes of the marks should vary smoothly to ensure temporal continuity and fluid animations.

Unfortunately these goals are inherently contradictory and naïve solutions often neglect one or more criteria. For example, the texture advection technique of Bousseau et al. (Sect. 13.3.2.1) can be used to apply the marks over the scene with high motion coherence and temporal continuity, but deformations destroy the spatial quality of the stylization. Keeping the marks static from frame to frame ensures a good spatial quality and temporal continuity but produces a strong shower door effect since the motion of the marks has no correlation with the motion of the scene. Finally, processing each frame independently, similarly to hand-drawn animation, leads to pronounced flickering and popping since the position of the marks varies randomly from frame to frame.

13.2 Temporally Local Filtering

Arguably the most straightforward method to stylize a video is to apply image processing filters independently at each frame. Depending on the type of filter, the resulting video will be more or less coherent in time. Typically filters that incorporate hard thresholds will be less coherent than more continuous filters.

Winnemöller et al. [59] iteratively apply a bilateral filter followed by soft quantization to produce cartoon animations from videos in real-time. Image edges are extracted from the smoothed images with a difference of Gaussian filter. The soft quantization, less sensitive to noise, produces results with higher temporal coherence than traditional hard quantization.

As discussed in Chap. 5, Winnemöller's stylization pipeline has been adapted to incorporate various alternative filters: e.g. Kuwahara based filters [35], combination of Shock filter with diffusion [36], and generalized geodesic distance transform [18] for soft clustering. These filtering approaches are fast to compute as they can be

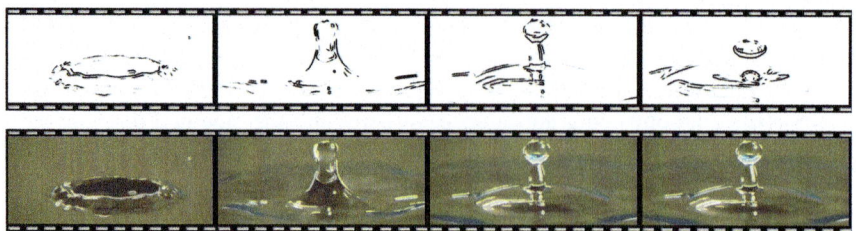

Fig. 13.1 Frames of a water drop video where luminance edges are depicted with *lines* of varying thickness, either drawn in *black* (*top*), or drawn in *white* over the original image (*bottom*), both with a disk footprint. From [52] © 2011 Blackwell Publishing. Included here by permission

implemented on the GPU. However, they are restricted in the gamut of artistic styles that may be produced.

Similarly, Vergne et al. [52] use 2D local differential geometry to extract luminance edges of a video. The feature lines are also implicitly defined, which prevents the use of an explicit parameterization needed for arc-length based effects or for mapping a brush stroke texture. However, they propose to formulate the mark rendering process as a spatially varying convolution that mimics the contact of a brush of a given footprint with the feature line. It allows them to simulate some styles, like thickness variations that remain fully coherent over time (see Fig. 13.1).

This chapter focuses primarily upon video stylization methods that encourage the *temporally coherent placement of marks*. This is achieved by rendering using information propagated from adjacent frames; i.e. frames are not rendered with temporal independence. The remainder of the chapter covers these techniques, and the reader is referred to Chap. 5 for more detailed coverage of the filtering techniques outlined in this section.

13.3 Optical Flow Based Stylization

To make progress beyond independent filtering of frames, temporal correspondence may be established on a per pixel basis using motion estimation. Optical flow algorithms (e.g. [4] and related methods) can be applied to produce such an estimate.

Using this information, local filtering approaches can be extended by defining $2D+t$ filters that smooth the effect of the filter along time as described in Sect. 13.2. Moreover, temporal continuity can be enforced using the optical flow to guide the evolution of the marks along the video. The difficulty is then to ensure the quality of the spatial properties of the marks. Various approaches have been proposed to solve this problem. We classify them in two categories: mark-based (Sect. 13.3.1) and texture-based (Sect. 13.3.2) approaches.

In this section we adopt the notation $\mathscr{I}_t(x, y)$ to denote the RGB video frame at time t, and similarly $I_t(x, y)$ for the grayscale frame. Edge orientation $\Theta_t(x, y)$ and edge strength $|\nabla I_t(x, y)|$ field are so denoted, and computed:

$$\nabla I_t(x, y) = \left(\frac{\delta I_t}{\delta x}^2 + \frac{\delta I_t}{\delta y}^2\right)^{\frac{1}{2}} \quad (13.1)$$

$$\Theta_t(x, y) = \operatorname{atan}\left(\frac{\delta I_t}{\delta y} \bigg/ \frac{\delta I_t}{\delta x}\right) \quad (13.2)$$

13.3.1 Mark-Based Methods

Peter Litwinowicz proposed the first purpose designed algorithm for video stylization in 1997. The essence of the approach is to place marks upon the first video frame, and push (i.e. translate) them over time to match the estimated motion of objects in the video. Marks are moved according to the per-pixel motion estimate derived from the optical flow. As such, Litwinowicz adopts a weak motion model, applicable to very general input footage. However, what optical flow offers in generality, it lacks in robustness. Pixels arising from the same object might be estimated with entirely different motion vectors. Whilst many optical flow algorithms exist, and some enforce local spatial coherence, in practice it is often the case that parts of objects are estimated with incorrect or inconsistent motion. This is especially true for objects with flat texture or weak intensity edges, as these visual cues often drive optical flow estimation algorithms. This can result in the *swimming* of painterly texture, due to motion mismatch between marks and underlying video content. The sequential processing of frames can also cause motion estimation errors to accumulate, contributing to swimming artifacts.

In terms of our criteria for temporal coherence (Sect. 13.1.2), since the marks (e.g. brush strokes) are usually small with respect to object size, their motion remains very close to the original motion field of the depicted scene, providing good *motion coherence*. *Spatial quality* is also preserved by drawing the marks as 2D sprites and by ensuring a adequate density of marks. However as discussed, *temporal continuity* criterion is often violated due to error accumulation and propagation.

Nevertheless, Litwinowicz' algorithm results in aesthetically pleasing renderings in many situations and especially when dealing with highly textured or anisotropic phenomena—where many more recent region-based methods struggle. Fluids, smoke, cloud, and similar phenomena are ideally suited to the generality of the optical flow fields, and the fields may also be manually embellished to produce attractive swirls reminiscent of a Van Gogh. Interactive software implementing this technique won an Oscar for visual effects in the motion picture "What Dreams May Come" (1999), for the creation of painterly landscapes of flowers, sea and sky [23].

13.3.1.1 Impressionist Painterly Rendering

Litwinowicz' [40] algorithm uses a multitude of short rectangular brush strokes as marks, to create a impressionist video effect. A sequence of strokes are created using

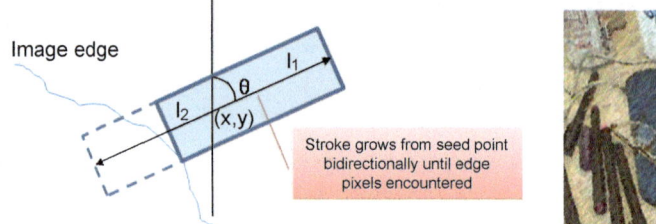 

Fig. 13.2 *Left*: Stroke attributes in Litwinowicz' approach to video stylization [40]. Strokes grow until a strong edge is encountered, thus preserving detail. *Middle*: Source Image. *Right*: Resulting painting. From © 2002 ACM, Inc. Included here by permission

the first frame of video. Pixels within $\mathscr{I}_1$ are sub-sampled in a regular grid (typically every second pixel) yielding a set of N strokes $\mathscr{S}_t = \{s_t^1, \ldots, s_t^N\}$ where each stroke is represented by a tuple $s^i = (x, y, \theta, \mathbf{c})$ encoding each stroke's seed location (x, y), orientation θ, color $\mathbf{c} = \mathscr{I}_1(x, y)$ and length l_1, l_2. Figure 13.2 illustrates the stroke geometry with respect to these parameters. Each stroke is grown iteratively from its seed point (x, y) until a maximum length is reached, or the stroke encounters a strong edge in $|\nabla I_1(.)|$. Strokes do not interact, and a stroke may be grown 'over' another stroke on the canvas. To prevent the appearance of sampling artifacts due to such overlap, the rendering order of strokes in sequence $\mathscr{S}_1$ is randomized—in this first video frame.

The orientation of each stroke is determined in one of two ways, depending on whether $|\nabla I_1(x, y)|$ exceeds a pre-defined threshold. In such cases, the stroke is local to a strong edge and so it is possible to sample a reliable edge orientation $\theta = |\Theta_1(x, y)|$. Otherwise the edge orientation is deemed to be noisy due to a weakly present intensity gradient, and so must be interpolated from nearby strokes that have reliable orientations. The interpolation is performed using a thin-plate spline in Litwinowicz' paper, but in practice any function that smoothly interpolates irregularly spaced samples may be used. In later work by Hays and Essa, for example, radial basis functions are used [25] to fulfil a similar purpose (Sect. 13.3.1.5).

13.3.1.2 Stroke Propagation

Given an optical flow vector field $\mathscr{O}(.)$ mapping pixel locations in $\mathscr{I}_{t-1}$ to $\mathscr{I}_t$, all strokes within $\mathscr{S}_{t-1}$ are updated to yield set $\mathscr{S}_t$ where $s_{t-1}^i(x, y) + \mathscr{O}(x, y) \leftarrow s_t^i(x, y)$. If stroke seed points are shifted outside of the canvas boundaries then those strokes are omitted from $\mathscr{S}_t$. Other stroke attributes within the s_t^i tuple remain constant to inhibit flicker. Note that the rendering order of strokes is randomized only in the first frame, and remains fixed for subsequent frames. This also mitigates against flicker.

The translation process may cause strokes to bunch together, or to become sparsely distributed leaving 'holes' in the painted canvas. A mechanism is therefore

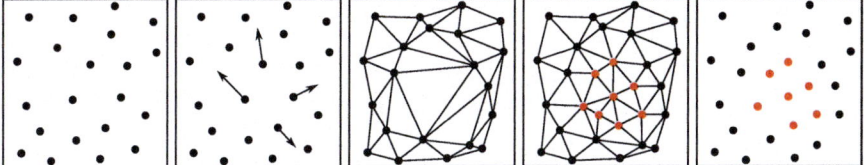

Fig. 13.3 Litwinowicz' mark (stroke) density control algorithm in five steps, from *left* to *right*: (1) Initial stroke positions. (2) Here, four strokes move under optical flow. (3) Delaunay triangulation of the stroke points. (4) *Red points* show new vertices introduced to regularize the density. (5) The updated list of strokes after culling points that violate the closeness test

introduced to measure and regulate stroke density on the canvas (Fig. 13.3). Stroke density is first measured using a Delaunay triangulation of stroke seed points. Using the connected neighborhood of the triangulation it is straightforward to evaluate, for each stroke, the distance to its nearest stroke. Strokes are sorted by this distance. By examining the head and tail of this sorted list one may identify strokes within the most sparsely and densely covered area of the canvas.

Strokes may be culled from $\mathscr{S}_t$ to thin out areas of the canvas with dense stroke coverage. This can be achieved by deleting strokes present in the tail of the list. Strokes may also be inserted into $\mathscr{S}_t$. To do so, new strokes are created from the current frame using the process outlined in Sect. 13.3.1.1. These newly created strokes must be distributed throughout the sequence $\mathscr{S}_t$ to disguise their appearance. A large block of newly created strokes appearing simultaneously becomes visual salient and causes flicker.

13.3.1.3 Dynamic Distributions

Much subsequent work addresses the issue of redistributing marks over time, providing various trade-offs between spatial quality and temporal continuity [25, 27, 51]. The general aim of such a 'Dynamic distribution' is to maintain a uniform spacing between marks (commonly harnessing the Poisson disk distribution for this purpose) while avoiding sudden appearance or disappearance of marks.

Extending the Poisson disk tiling method of Lagae et al. [37], Kopf et al. [34] propose a set of recursive Wang tiles which allows to generate 2D point distributions with blue noise property in real-time and at arbitrary scale. This approach relies on precomputed tiles, handling 2D rigid motions (zooming and panning inside stills). The subdivision mechanism ensures the continuity of the distribution during the zoom, while the recursivity of the scheme enables infinite zoom.

Vanderhaeghe et al. [51] propose a hybrid technique which finds a more balanced trade-off. They compute the distribution in 2D—ensuring blue noise property—but move the points according to the 3D motion of the scene by following the optical flow. At each frame, the distribution is updated to maintain a Poisson-disk criterion. The temporal continuity is enhanced further by (1) fading appearing and disappearing points over subsequent frames; and (2) allowing points in overly dense regions to slide to close under-sampled regions.

To further reduce flickering artifacts, Lin et al. [39] propose to create a damped system between marks adjacent in space and time, and to minimize the energy of this system. They also try to minimize marks insertions and deletions using two passes. Disoccluded regions emerging during the forward pass are not rendered immediately, but deferred until they reach a sufficient size. Then, they are painted and the gaps are completed by backward propagation. Lin's damped spring model is discussed in greater detail in Sect. 13.4.2.3.

The data structures required to manage the attributes and rendering of each individual stroke makes mark-based methods complex to implement and not very well-suited to real-time rendering engines. Nevertheless, Lu et al. [42] proposed a GPU implementation with a simplified stochastic stroke density estimation which runs at interactive framerates but offers fewer guarantees on the point distribution.

To create animated mosaics, Smith et al. [48] and Dalal et al. [19] also rely on the motion flow of the input animation to advect groups of tiles. They propose two policies to spatially localize tiles insertions and deletions at either groups boundaries or groups center. This approach allows coherent group movement and minimizes the flickering of tiles.

13.3.1.4 Frame Differencing for Interactive Painting

The use of general, low-level motion estimation techniques (e.g. optical flow) for video echoes the reliance upon low-level filtering operators by image stylization, circa the 1990s.

Other low-level approaches for painterly video stylization suggested contemporaneously include Hertzmann and Perlin's frame-differencing approach [28]. In their algorithm, the absolute RGB difference between successive video frames was used as a trigger to repaint (or "paint over") regions of the canvas that changed significantly; i.e. due to object motion. A binary mask $M(.)$ was generated using a pixel difference thresholded at an empirically derived value T:

$$M(x, y) = \mathscr{I}_{t-1}(x, y) - \mathscr{I}_t(x, y)| > T \tag{13.3}$$

Strokes seeded at non-zero locations of $M(.)$ are repainted at time t. Flicker is greatly reduced, as only moving areas of the video feed are repainted. Furthermore the computational simplicity of the differencing operation made practical real-time interactive video painting, to create an interactive painterly video experience. This contrasted to optical flow based approaches, which were challenging to compute in real-time due to the limitations in computational power at the time their work was carried out.

A further novelty of Hertzmann and Perlin's interactive painting system was the use of curved brush strokes to stylize video. This work built upon Hertzmann's earlier multi-resolution curved stroke painting algorithm for image stylization (discussed in more detail within Chap. 1). Previously Litwinowicz' approach [40] and similar optical flow based methods [49] had used only short rectangular strokes.

13.3.1.5 Multi-scale Video Stylization with Curved Strokes

Hays and Essa developed a video stylization system fusing the benefits of optical flow, after Litwinowicz [40], with the benefits of coarse-to-fine rendering with curved brush strokes, after Hertzmann [26]. Although experiments exploring this fusion of ideas were briefly reported in [28], this was the first time such a system had been described in detail.

The system of Hays and Essa shares a number of commonalities with Litwinowicz' original pipeline. A set of strokes $\mathscr{C}$ is maintained as before, and propagated forward in time using optical flow. Strokes are also classified as strong, or not, based on local edge strength and interpolation applied to derive stroke orientations from the strong strokes. However, the key to the improved temporal coherence of the approach is the way in which stroke attributes (such as color and orientation) evolve over time. Rather than remaining fixed, or being sampled directly from the video frame, attributes are blended based on their historic values. A particular stroke may have color $\mathbf{c}_{t-1}$ at frame $t-1$, and might sample a color $\mathbf{c}_t$ from the canvas at frame t. The final color of the stroke $\mathbf{c}'_t$ would be a weighted blend of these two colors:

$$\mathbf{c}'_t = \alpha \mathbf{c}_t + (1-\alpha)\mathbf{c}_{t-1} \tag{13.4}$$

Or more generally, all stroke attributes would follow a similar blended update, enforcing a smoothed variation in stroke color, orientation, opacity and any other appearance attributes:

$$\mathbf{s}^i_t \leftarrow \alpha \mathbf{s}^i_t + (1-\alpha)\mathbf{s}^i_{t-1} \tag{13.5}$$

Uniquely, Hays and Essa also propose opacity as an additional mark attribute. When adding or removing strokes to preserve stroke density over time, strokes do not immediately appear or disappear. Rather they are faded in, or out, over a period of several frames. This 'fade-out' greatly enhances temporal coherence and suppresses the 'popping' artifacts that can occur with [40].

Rendering in Hays and Essa's system follows Hertzmann's curved brush stroke pipeline, as described in Chap. 1. To decide where to add strokes, areas of the canvas containing no paint are identified and strokes generated at the coarsest level. Strokes are also added at successfully finer layers, local to edges present at the spatial scale of that layer.

Strokes are deleted if they are moved, by the optical flow process, too far from strong edges existing at a particular spatial scale of the pyramid. This prevents the accumulation of fine-scale strokes that tend to clutter the painting.

13.3.2 Texture-Based Methods

Texture-based approaches are mostly used for continuous textures (canvas, watercolor) or highly structured patterns (hatching). By embedding multiple marks, textures facilitate and accelerate rendering compared to mark-based methods. Textures

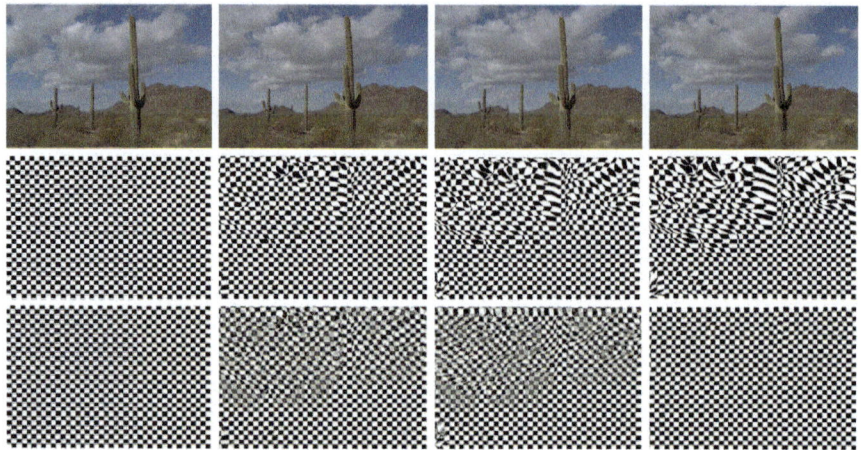

Fig. 13.4 A checkerboard texture (*second row*) advected along the optical flow of a video (*first row*) will rapidly be deformed and lose its spatial properties. Bousseau et al. "Video Watercolorization" propagates one instance of the texture forward and the other one backward in time according to the flow field, and alpha-blends them to minimize the distortion (*third row*). From [11] © 2007 ACM, Inc. Included here by permission

are generally applied over the entire frame. The challenge is then to deform the texture so that it follows the scene motion while preserving the spatial quality of the original pattern.

13.3.2.1 Bi-directional Flow

A criticism of early optical flow techniques is their tendency to accumulate error and propagate it forward in time, causing instability on longer sequences.

Bousseau et al. [11] apply non-rigid deformations to animate a texture according to the optical flow of a video [4]. This approach extends texture advection methods used in vector field visualization [44] by advecting the texture forward and backward in time to follow the motion field. This *bi-directional* advection allows the method to deal with occlusions where the optical flow is ill-defined in the forward direction but well defined in the backward direction.

Rather than placing individual strokes, Bousseau et al. create a watercolor effect by multiplying each video frame $\mathscr{I}_t$ with a global grayscale texture $\mathscr{G}_t$ of identical size to the frame. Pixels in the image and texture field are multiplied place for place to create the stylized frame $\mathscr{I}'_t$:

$$\mathscr{I}'_t = \mathscr{I}_t\big(1 - (1 - \mathscr{I}_t)(\mathscr{G}_t - 0.5)\big) \tag{13.6}$$

where pixels values in both $\mathscr{I}_t$ and $\mathscr{G}_t$ are assumed normalized. This affects a form of alpha-blending of the texture.

The texture in $\mathcal{G}_t$ is a weighted combination of two similarly sized textures, one propagated or "advected" forward in time using the forward flow field, and the other advected back in time. Call these watercolor textures F_t and B_t; their weights are respectively $\omega_f(t)$ and $\omega_b(t)$:

$$\mathcal{G}_t = \omega_f(t) F_t + \omega_b(t) B_t \tag{13.7}$$

Both fields F_t and B_t are generated from some user supplied continuous texture function. Bousseau et al. do not specify a particular texture function but suggest the pixel intensities should have more or less homogeneous spatial distribution, and the texture should exhibit a reasonably a flat frequency distribution.

The texture field is warped under the respective (forward or backward) flow field to render each frame. Over time, the texture will become distorted due to the motion vectors significantly compressing or stretching the texture. This is detected via a set of heuristics, and new textures initialized for advection periodically or as needed. These detection heuristics are outlined in more detail within their paper. Bousseau et al. propose an advanced blending scheme that periodically regenerates the texture to cancel distortions and favor at each pixel the advected texture with the least distortion. Suppose the textures are initialized periodically every τ frames. The weights $\omega_f(t)$ and $\omega_b(t)$ for combining the texture fields F_t and B_t are given as

$$\begin{aligned}\omega_f(t) &= \cos^2\left(\frac{\pi}{2} \frac{t \bmod \tau}{\tau}\right) \\ \omega_b(t) &= \sin^2\left(\frac{\pi}{2} \frac{t \bmod \tau}{\tau}\right)\end{aligned} \tag{13.8}$$

Although the process of advecting a global single texture forward in time is in common use within scientific visualization domain, Bousseau et al. were the first to introduce this approach for video stylization. Flow fields in video exhibit more frequent discontinuities than are typical in scientific visualization, due to object occlusions. The use of bi-directional advection, rather than simply forward advection, was principally motivated by the desired to suppress temporal incoherence caused by such discontinuities. However the bidirectional advection requires the entire animation to be known in advance, which prevents the use of this method for real-time applications. To overcome this limitation, Kass and Pesare [32] propose to filter a white or band-pass noise. Their recursive filter produces a coherent noise with stationary statistics within a frame (high flatness) and high correlations between frames (high motion coherence). This approach is fast enough for real-time application, but is restricted to isotropic procedural noise and it needs depth information to handle occlusions and disocclusions properly.

13.3.2.2 Coherent Shape Abstraction

In order to produce an aesthetically pleasing watercolor effect, Bousseau et al. applied video processing in addition to texture advection, to abstract away some of the visual detail in the scene. This was achieved using morphological operators to remove small-scale details in the frames. Bousseau et al. observed that a binary opening operation (an erosion, following by a dilation) could remove lighter colored objects in the image. The reverse sequence of operations—a binary closure—can remove darker objects. Depending on the scale of the structuring element using in the morphological operations, different scales of object may be abstracted; i.e. removed, or their shapes simplified.

In the Computer Vision literature, the use of morphological scale-space filtering has been well known to produce these kinds of image simplification. For example, the 1D and 2D *image sieves* developed by Bangham et al. in the late 1990s comprise similar morphological operations. Such filtering is particularly effective at image simplification, as angular features such as corners are not 'rounded off' as might result using a linear low-pass filter such as successive Gaussian blurring. Indeed, sieves were applied to color imagery several years earlier in 2003 precisely for the purposes of image stylization [3]. Bousseau et al. were, however, the first to extend the use of such morphological filters to coherently stylize video, filtering in 3D (space–time) rather than on a per frame basis [10].

13.4 Video Segmentation for Stylization

In an effort to improve temporal coherence and explore a wider gamut of styles, researchers in the early-mid 2000s began to apply segmentation algorithms to the video stylization problem.

Segmentation is the process of dividing an image into a set of regions sharing some homogeneity property. The implicit assumption in performing such segmentation is that regions should correspond to objects within the scene. However, in practice the homogeneity criteria used in the segmentation are typically defined at a much lower level (e.g. color or texture). For video segmentation, it is desirable to segment each frame not only with accuracy with respect to such criteria, but also with temporal coherence. The boundaries of regions should remain stable (exhibit minimal change) over time, and spurious regions should not appear and disappear.

The stable mid-level representation provided by video segmentation offers two main advantages over low-level flow-based video stylization:

First, rendering parameters may be applied consistently across objects; a common phenomenon in real artwork. Furthermore, users intervention may be incorporated to selectively stylize particular objects [16, 30].

Second, the motion of rendering marks may be fixed to the reference frame of each region as it moves over time. This ensures motion coherence—one of our key criteria for temporal coherence (Sect. 13.1.2). Rotoscoping and artistic stylization are therefore closely related. Given a coherent video segmentation, one might rotoscope any texture onto the regions for artistic effect, from flat-shaded cartoons to the complex brush stroke patterns of an oil painting. Many image stylization approaches may be applied to video, by considering each region as a stable reference frame upon which to apply the effect [1, 16, 57]. Furthermore, the boundaries of the regions may also be stylized [7, 31, 33].

In essence, a coherent video segmentation enables the coherent parameterization of lines (boundaries) or regions one may wish to stylize. Such a parameterization allows the coherent mapping of textures (or placement of marks) allowing for precise control of a broad range of styles.

13.4.1 Coherent Video Segmentation

Video segmentation is a long-standing research topic in Computer Vision, and a number of robust approaches to coherent video segmentation now exist. However, in the early 2000s, research focused firmly upon image segmentation. Variants of the mean-shift algorithm [17] were very popular. Chapter 7 covers the application of the EDISON variant of mean-shift to a variety of image stylization tasks, spurred by the early work of DeCarlo and Santella [20]. Around 2004 two complementary approaches were simultaneously developed to extend mean-shift to video for the purpose of video stylization. The *Video Tooning* approach of Wang et al.'s [55] adopts an 3D extension of mean-shift to the space–time video cube (x, y, t). Collomosse et al.'s *Stroke Surfaces* approach [14, 16] adopts a 2D plus time $(2D + t)$ approach, creating correspondences between regions in independently segmented, temporally adjacent frames.

13.4.1.1 Video Tooning

Mean-shift is an unsupervised clustering algorithm [21]. It is most often applied to image segmentation by considering each pixel as a point in a 5D space (r, g, b, x, y) encoding color and location. The essence of the algorithm is to identify local modes in this feature space, by shifting a window (kernel) toward more densely populated regions of the space. The resulting modes become regions in the video, with pixels local to each mode being labelled to that region.

Extension of this algorithm to a space–time video cube may be trivially performed by adding a sixth dimension to pixel features, encoding time (r, g, b, x, y, t). Due to differences in the spatial and temporal resolution of video, and the isotropy of typical Mean-shift kernels, this can results in spurious regions manifesting local to movement in the footage. One solution is to add further dimensions to the space, encoding the motion vector (i.e. optical flow) of each pixel however this has the disadvantage of increasing the dimensionality of the feature space, requiring longer videos (i.e. more samples) to cluster effectively. Wang et al.'s contribution was to compensate for the artifacts in a 6D clustering by using an anisotropic kernel during the mean-shift. The scale of the kernel is determined on a per pixel basis by analyzing local variation in color [54].

Fig. 13.5 Video Tooning: (**a**) Space–time mean-shift is used to over-segment the video volume. (**b**) Volume fragments are grouped by the user, and pre-prepared texture applied to create a cartoon rotoscoped effect. (**c**) The interiors and bounding contours of region groups may also be rendered. From [55] © 2004 ACM, Inc. Included here by permission

Fig. 13.6 *Left*: Visualization of the Stroke Surfaces space–time representation [16]. © 2005 IEEE. Included here by permission. *Right*: Two rendering styles generated by rendering the same stroke surface representation [16]

Figure 13.5 provides a representative video segmentation, demonstrating the tendency of space–time mean-shift to over-segment object. In their Video Tooning system, Wang et al. invite users to group space–time volumes into objects using an interactive tool. The resulting regions within each frame may then be rotoscoped with any texture. We discuss a general approach to performing such rotoscoping in Sect. 13.4.2. In the example of Fig. 13.5, a manually created child's drawing is rotoscoped on to each region, and composited upon a drawn background.

13.4.1.2 Stroke Surfaces

Due to memory constraints, a space–time video segmentation is practical only for shorter sequences. Furthermore, such methods are prone to over-segmentation especially of small fast moving video objects, resulting in the representation of objects as many disparate sub-volumes. These can require considerable manual intervention to group. An alternative is to segment regions independently within each video frame, and associate those regions over time (a $2D + t$ approach). Independently segmenting frames often yields different region topologies between frames, and many small noisy regions. However, the larger video objects one typically wishes to rotoscope exhibit greater stability.

The approach of Collomosse et al. is to associate regions at time t with regions at time $t-1$ and $t+1$ using a set of heuristics, e.g. region color, shape, centroid location. These associations form a graph for each region over time, which may be post-processed to remove short cycles and so prune sporadically splitting/merging regions. Only the temporally stable regions remain, forming sub-volumes through the space–time video volume.

At this stage, the space–time volume representation is similar to that of Wang et al. and amenable to rotoscoping (Sect. 13.4.2). However the temporal coherence of the segmented objects is further enhanced in Collomosse et al.'s pipeline through the formation and manipulation of *stroke surfaces*.

A stroke surface is a partitioning surface separating exactly two sub-volumes. Stroke surfaces are fitted via an optimization process adapted from the Active Contour literature; full details are available in [16]. As a single stroke surface describes the space–time interface between two video objects, the coherence of the corresponding region boundary may be smoothed by smoothing the geometry of the stroke surface in the temporal direction. Temporally slicing the surface produces a series of smoothed regions which may be used, as in Wang et al., for rotoscoping.

13.4.1.3 Region Tracking

Both of the above video adaptations of mean-shift above require space–time processing, either for initial segmentation [55] or region association pruning [16]. For online processing (e.g. for streaming video, or to avoid memory overhead) it may be desirable to segment video progressively (on a per-frame basis) based on information propagated forward from prior frames. A number of robust systems have emerged in recent years for tracking a binary matte through video [2], providing single object segmentation suitable for stylizing a single object. However, a progressive segmentation algorithm capable of tracking multiple object labels through video is necessary to perform stylization of the entire scene.

One such approach, recently proposed by Wang et al., harnesses a multi-label extension of the popular graph-cut algorithm to robustly segment video [53]. Wang et al.'s solution is to perform a multi-label graph cut on each frame of video, using information both from the current frame and from prior information propagated forward from previous frames.

Given a segmentation of I_{t-1}, the region map is skeletonized to produce a set of pixels central to each region considered to be labelled with high confidence. These labelled pixels are warped to new positions in I_t, under a dense optical flow fields computed between the two frames. These labels are used to initialize the graph cut on the next frame, alongside models of color and texture that are incrementally learned over time from the labelled image regions.

As discussed in Sect. 13.3.1, dense optical flow fields are often poorly estimated and so this propagation strategy can fail in the longer term. To compensate, Wang

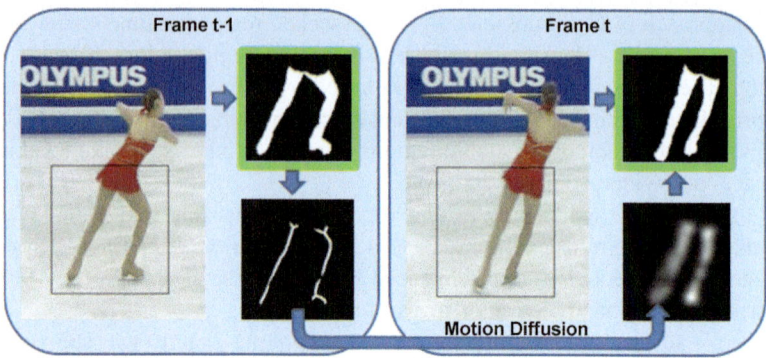

Fig. 13.7 Outline of Wang et al.'s video segmentation algorithm. Multi-label graph cut is applied to each video frame, influenced by region labelings from prior frames. Each labelled region is coded as a binary mask; labels are propagated from prior frames by warping the skeletons of those masked regions via optical flow. The warped skeleton is diffused according to motion estimation confidence and the diffused masks of all regions form a probability density function over labels that is used as a prior in the multi-label graph cut of the next frame

et al. perform a diffusion of each pixel in I_{t-1} over multiple pixels in I_t; each pixel obtains a probability of belonging to a particular region label. In practice this is achieved using a Gaussian distribution centered upon the optical flow-derived location of the point in I_t. The standard deviation (i.e. spread) of the Gaussian is modulated to reflect the confidence in the optical flow estimate, which can in turn be estimated from the diversity of motion vector directions local to the point. Figure 13.7 outlines the process.

13.4.2 Rotoscoping Regions

Once a coherent video segmentation has been produced, marks (such as brush strokes) may be fixed to each region. In all cases it is necessary to first establish correspondence between the boundary of a region across adjacent frames, usually encoded via the control points of a contour. The dense motion field inside the region is then deduced from the motion vectors established between these control points. There are a number methods in the literature to model this dense motion, for example treating the region as follows.

1. A rigid body, e.g. moving under an affine motion model deduced from the control points of the region boundary [16] (Fig. 13.8(a)).
2. A deforming body, with marks adopting motion of the closest control point on the region boundary [1] (Fig. 13.8(b)).
3. A deforming body, with marks moving under a motion model that minimizes discontinuities within the motion field within region, whilst moving with the control points of the region boundary [57] (Fig. 13.8(c)).

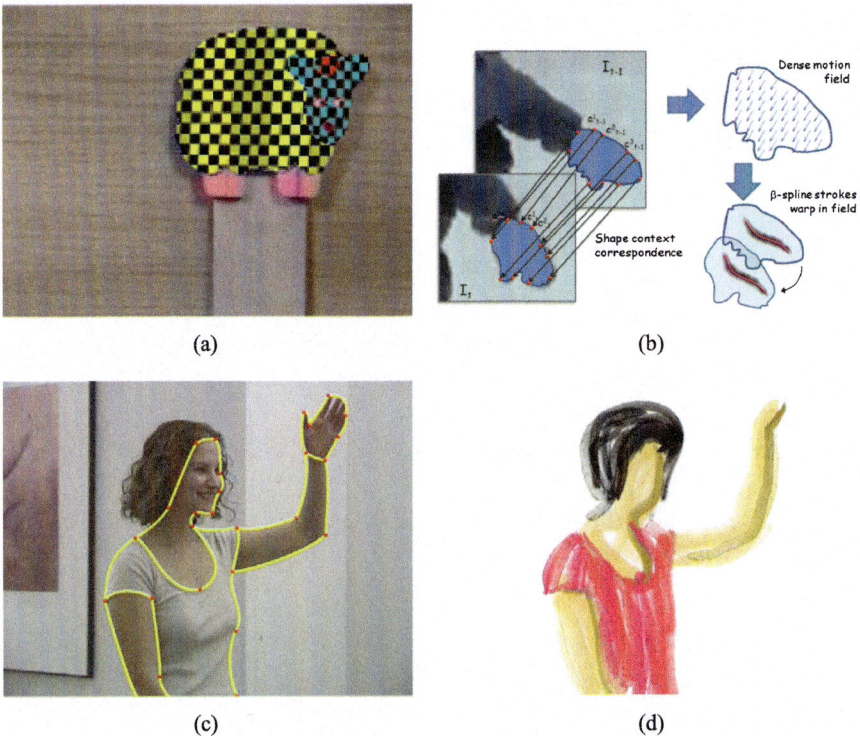

Fig. 13.8 Three region rotoscoping strategies: (**a**) In Stroke Surfaces [16] regions were treated as rigid bodies, mapped using affine transformations. (**c**) Dynamic programming was used by Agarwala et al. [1] to assign points within regions to moving control points on the bounding contour, tracked from (**d**) an initial hand-drawn user contour. (**b**) Wang et al. [57] perform affine registration of regions using shape contexts and then interpolate a dense motion field using Poisson filling. From [16] © 2005 IEEE, [57] © 2011 Elsevier, and [1] © 2004 ACM, Inc. Included here by permission

Although many shape correspondence techniques exist, a robust solution to inter-frame boundary matching is commonly to use Shape Contexts [5]. Suppose using Shape Contexts, or otherwise, we obtain a set of n control points $C' = \{\mathbf{c}'_1, \mathbf{c}'_2, \ldots, \mathbf{c}'_n\}$ at time t, and the corresponding points $C = \{\mathbf{c}_1, \mathbf{c}_2, \ldots, \mathbf{c}_n\}$ at the previous frame $t - 1$. Pixels within the region at time $t - 1$ are written $P_{t-1}\{\mathbf{p}_{1..n}\}$ and we wish to determine their locations $P_t = \{\mathbf{p}'_{1..n}\}$ at time t. We wish to obtain the dense motion field V_{t-1} responsible for this shift:

$$V_{t-1}(\mathbf{p}_i) = \mathbf{p}'_i - \mathbf{p}_i \qquad (13.9)$$

In this chapter we cover one rigid (1) and deforming (3) solution.

13.4.2.1 Rigid motion

If operating under the rigid model we can simply write the ith control point location $\mathbf{c}'_i = \mathbf{A}\mathbf{c}_i$ in homogeneous form, expanded as:

$$\begin{bmatrix} c'_{i,x} \\ c'_{i,y} \\ 1 \end{bmatrix} = \begin{bmatrix} a_1 & a_2 & a_3 \\ a_4 & a_5 & a_6 \\ 0 & 0 & 1 \end{bmatrix} \begin{bmatrix} c_{i,x} \\ c_{i,y} \\ 1 \end{bmatrix} \quad (13.10)$$

The 3×3 affine transformation matrix $\mathbf{A}$ is deduced between C and C' (contain the respective control points in homogeneous form) as a least squares solution:

$$\mathbf{A} = \mathbf{C}'\mathbf{C}^T \left(\mathbf{C}\mathbf{C}^T\right)^{-1} \quad (13.11)$$

The dense vector field (Eq. (13.9)) is created by applying the resulting transformation to all pixels P_{t-1} within the region at $t-1$, i.e. $\mathbf{p}'_i = \mathbf{A}\mathbf{p}_i$.

13.4.2.2 Smooth Deformation

A smooth dense motion field may be extrapolated from control points, for example using a least squares fitting scheme that minimizes the Laplacian of the motion vectors. This is achieved by solving an approximation to Poisson's equation; commonly referred to in Graphics as *Poisson in-filling* after Pérez and Blake's initial application of the technique to texture infilling in 2003 [46].

Recall we wish to deduce a dense motion field $\mathscr{V}_{t-1}(\mathbf{p}_i)$ defining the motion of for all pixels P_{t-1}. However we know only irregularly and sparsely placed points in this field $\mathscr{V}_{t-1}(\mathbf{c}_i) = \mathbf{c}'_i - \mathbf{c}_i$. Call this known, sparse field V and dense field $\mathscr{V}$, dropping the time subscript for brevity.

We seek the dense field $\mathscr{V}_P$ over all pixel values $\Omega \in \Re^2$, such that $\mathscr{V}(c) = V(c), \forall_{c \in C_t}$ and minimizing:

$$\underset{\mathscr{V}}{\text{argmin}} \, \Sigma \Sigma_P (\nabla \mathscr{V} - V)^2 \quad \text{s.t.} \; \mathscr{V}\,|_{\delta P} = V\,|_{\delta P} \quad (13.12)$$

i.e. $\Delta \mathscr{V} = 0$ over P, s.t. $\mathscr{V}\,|_{\delta P} = V\,|_{\delta P}$. This is Poisson's equation and is practically solvable for our discrete field as follows.

The desired $2D$ motion vector field $\mathscr{V}(P)$ is first split into its component scalar fields $\mathscr{V}_x(P)$ and $\mathscr{V}_y(P)$. For each scalar field, e.g. that of the x component, $\mathscr{V}_x(p_i) = v_i$, where $i = [1, n]$ we form the following $n \times n$ linear system using 'known' pixels $V(p) = v_i$ (i.e. at the control points, below denoted $k_i = v_i$) and unknown pixels (i.e. everywhere else):

$$\begin{bmatrix} 1 & 0 & 0 & 0 & 0 & 0 & \cdots & 0 & 0 \\ 0 & 1 & 0 & 0 & 0 & 0 & \cdots & 0 & 0 \\ \vdots & \vdots & \vdots & \vdots & \vdots & \vdots & \vdots & \vdots & \vdots \\ 0 & -1 & \vdots & -1 & 4 & -1 & \cdots & -1 & 0 \\ \vdots & \vdots & \vdots & \vdots & \vdots & \vdots & \vdots & \vdots & \vdots \\ 0 & 0 & 0 & 0 & 0 & 0 & \cdots & 0 & 1 \end{bmatrix} \begin{bmatrix} v_1 \\ v_2 \\ \vdots \\ v_i \\ \vdots \\ v_n \end{bmatrix} = \begin{bmatrix} 0 \\ 0 \\ \vdots \\ k_i \\ \vdots \\ 0 \end{bmatrix} \quad (13.13)$$

The system can be solved efficiently by a sparse linear solver such as LAPACK, yielding values for all v_i and so the dense scalar field—in our example for the x component of $\mathscr{V}(P)$. Repeating this for both x and y components yields the dense motion field $\mathscr{V}(P)$ that may be used to move strokes or other rendering marks within the region as Fig. 13.8 illustrates.

A variety of other smoothness constraints have been explored for region deformation, including thin-plate splines [39] and weighted combinations of control point motion vectors [1].

13.4.2.3 Spring-Based Dampening

Once strokes, or similar marks, have been propagated to their new positions under the chosen deformation model, their position may be further refined. Inaccuracy in the region segmentation, and occlusions, can cause sporadic jumps in stroke position. Lin et al. showed that this can be successfully mitigated by dampening stroke motion using a simple string model [39].

Strokes are connected to their space–time neighbors (i.e. other strokes present within a small space–time range) using springs. Using the notation $S_{i,t}$ to denote the putative position of stroke i at time t—and $S^0_{i,t}$ to denote the initial (i.e. post-deformation) position of the strokes—the energy of the spring system $E(S)$ is given as a weighted sum:

$$E_{\text{system}}(S) = E_1(S) + 2.8 E_2(S) + 1.1 E_3(S) \quad (13.14)$$

In their formulation the first term $E_1(.)$ indicates spatial deviation from the initial position:

$$E_1(S) = \sum_{\forall S_{i,t}} |S_{i,t} - S^0_{i,t}|^2 \quad (13.15)$$

The second term enforces temporal smoothness in position:

$$E_2(S) = \sum_{\forall S_{i,t}} (S_{i,t-1} + 2 S_{i,t} + S_{i,t+1})^2 \quad (13.16)$$

and the third term enforces proximity to neighboring strokes, which are denoted by the set $\mathcal{N}_{i,t}$ for a given stroke $S_{i,t}$:

$$E_3(S) = \sum_{\forall S_{i,t}} \sum_{\forall p \times q \in \mathcal{N}_{i,t}} \delta(p,q)^2 \qquad (13.17)$$

here $\delta(.)$ is a function evaluating smaller for strokes of similar size and spatial position. The system is minimized via an iterative Levenburg–Marquadt optimization over all strokes in the video.

13.4.3 Rotoscoping Boundaries for Stylized Lines

Parameterized lines allow the use of texture mapping to produce dots and dashes or to mimic paint brushes, pencil, ink and other traditional media. The correspondence of region boundaries outlined in Sect. 13.4.2 enables such a parameterization to be established in a temporally coherent fashion. This opens the door to a wide variety of artistic line stylization techniques.

There are two simple policies for texturing a path. The first approach, which we call the *stretching policy* (Fig. 13.9(a)), stretches or compresses the texture so that it fits along the path a fixed number of times. As the length of the path changes, the texture deforms to match the new length. The second approach, called the *tiling policy* (Fig. 13.9(b)), establishes a fixed pixel length for the texture, and tiles the path with as many instances of the texture as can fit. Texture tiles appear or disappear as the length of the path varies.

The two policies are appropriate in different cases. The tiling policy is necessary for textures that should not appear to stretch, such as dotted and dashed lines. Because the tiling policy does not stretch the texture, it is also usually preferred for still images. Under animation, however, the texture appears to slide on or off the ends of the path similarly to the shower door effect (Fig. 13.9(b)). In contrast, the stretching policy produces high motion coherence under animation, but the stroke texture loses its character if the path is stretched or shrunk too far (Fig. 13.9(a)). Kalnins et al. [31] combine these two policies with 1D texture synthesis using Markov random field to reduce repetitions.

The *artmap* method [33] (Fig. 13.9(c)) is an alternative to the simple stretching and tiling policies. This method uses texture pyramid, where each texture has a particular target length in pixels. At each frame, the texture with the target length closest to the current path length is selected and drawn. This mechanism ensures that the brush texture never appears stretched by more than a constant factor (often 2×).

Nevertheless, stretching artifacts still appear when the length of the path extends beyond the length of the largest texture in the artmap. Fading or popping artifacts can also occur during transitions between levels of the texture pyramid. Finally, a major drawback of the artmap method resides in the manual construction of the texture

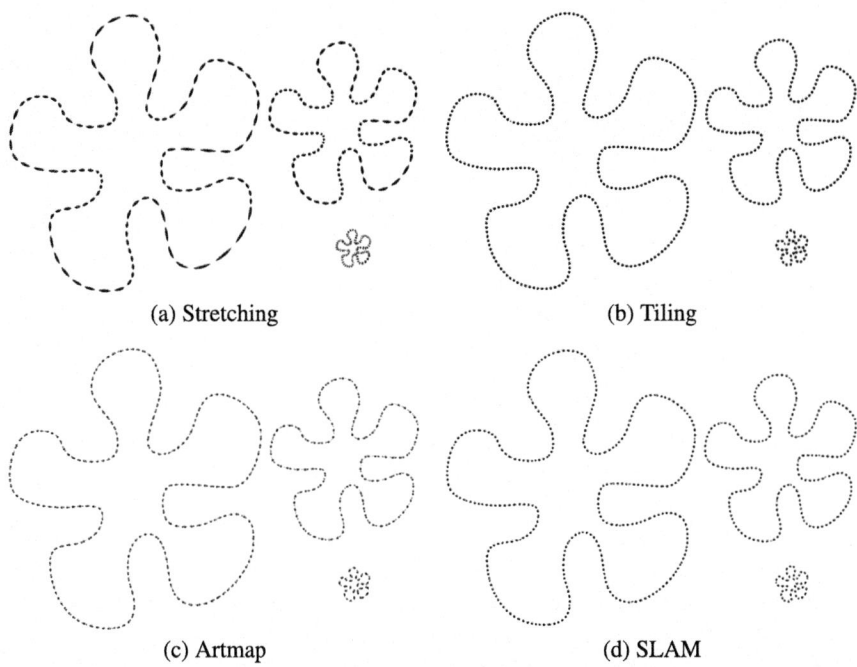

Fig. 13.9 Four strokes texture mapping policies. (**a**) Stretching ensures coherence during motion but deforms the texture. Conversely (**b**) tiling perfectly preserves the pattern, but produces sliding when the path is animated. (**c**) Artmap [33] avoids both problems at the price of fading artifacts because the hand-drawn texture pyramid is usually too sparse. (**d**) Self-Similar Line Artmap [7] solves this problem. From [9] © 2012 Blackwell Publishing. Included here by permission

pyramid. Artists need to draw each level of the pyramid, tacking care of the coherence across levels. As a result, current artmap implementations such as "Styles" in Google SketchUp© use as few as four textures, which accentuates artifacts during transitions.

To reduce transition artifacts and automate the creation process, Bénard et al. [7] propose *Self-Similar Line Artmap* (*SLAM*), an example-based artmap synthesis approach that generates an arbitrarily dense artmap based on a single exemplar. Their synthesis not only guarantees that each artmap level blends seamlessly into the next, but also provides continuous infinite zoom by constructing a self-similar texture pyramid where the last level of the pyramid is included in the first level. The synthesis takes a few minutes as a pre-process and provides good results for many brush textures, although fine details might be lost for very complex patterns.

13.4.4 Painterly Rotoscoping Environments

Early papers recognizing the links between coherent stylization and rotoscoping [16, 55] used the techniques of Sect. 13.4.2 to directly fix marks to regions, enabling those marks to match-move video content.

However recent systems adopt a more indirect approach, harnessing the region correspondence to transform data fields over time that drive the placement of strokes. A popular choice of field is the intensity gradient (equivalently, the edge orientation) field, which typically plays an important role in the placement of individual marks such as strokes [26]. Ensuring coherence in the transformed orientation field ensures coherence in the final rendering.

The advantage in deferring stroke placement until the rendering of individual frames (rather than placing strokes on the first frame, and subsequently moving them) is that more frame-specific information can be taken into account during stylization. This can lead to a broader range of styles as Kagaya et al. demonstrated in their multi-style video painting system [30]. It can also lead to greater control, as when framed in an interactive setting, users can manipulate the fields and parameters used to create particular effects on particular objects. For example, O'Donovan and Hertzmann's AniPaint system enable the rotoscoping of regular curved strokes onto regions, along with "guide strokes" that influence the orientation of further strokes placed on the frame [45]. Kagaya et al.'s multi-style rendering system [30] enables the interactive specification of tensor fields at key frames that are used to form elegant brush strokes in a manner reminiscent of the Line Integral Convolution methods used to create a painterly effect in the filtering approaches of Chap. 5. These key framed fields are smoothly interpolated over time using a space–time extension of the heat diffusion process outlined in Chap. 6, which like the smooth deformation method of Chap. 13.4.2.2, is based upon a Laplacian smoothing constraint.

The incorporation of user interaction into the video stylization pipeline also offers the possibility of correcting the initial automated video segmentations provided by Computer Vision algorithms. These corrections remain inevitable as the general video segmentation problem is far from solved.

13.5 Segmentation for Motion Stylization

Video analysis at the region level enables not only consistent rendering within objects, but also the analysis of object motion. This motion may then be stylized using a variety of motion emphasis cues borrowed from classical animation, such as mark-making (speed-lines, ghosting or 'skinning' lines), deformation and distortion as a function of motion, and alteration of timing. In his influential paper, Lasseter [38] describes many such techniques, introducing them to the Computer Graphics community. However his paper presents no algorithmic solutions to the synthesis of motion cues. Hsu et al. [29] also identify depiction of motion as important, though the former discusses the effect of such cues on perception. Both studies focus only the placement of speed-lines through user-interactive processes.

Automated methods to generate speed-lines in video require camera motion compensation, as the camera typically pans to keep moving objects within frame. This can be approximated by estimating inter-frame homographies. Trailing edges of object may be corresponded over time to yield a set of trails, which having been warped

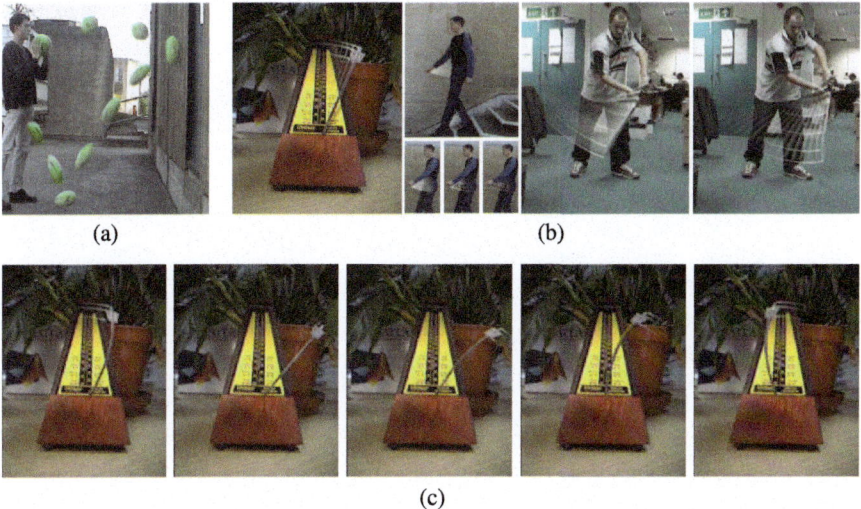

Fig. 13.10 Motion stylization in Video using [15]. (**a**) Squash and Stretch effect with flight and collision emphasis. (**b**) Augmentation of motion using blur and speed-lines. (**c**) Deformation emphasizing inertia. From [15]

to compensate for the camera motion-induced homography, may be smoothed and visualized as speed-lines. A collection of heuristics derived from animation practice were presented in [15] and optimized against to obtain well placed speed-lines. The trailing edges of objects may also be rendered to produce ghosting or 'skinning' effects, which when densely packed can additionally serve as motion blur. The visual nature of speed-lines has also led to their application in motion summarization via reverse story-boarding [22] visualized using a mosaic constructed from the video frames. Chenney et al. [12] presented the earliest work exploring automated deformation of objects to emphasize motion. This work introduced the 'squash and stretch' effect, scaling 3D objects along their trajectories and applying the inverse scale upon surface impact. A similar effect was applied to 2D video in [15], where a nonuniform scaling of the object was performed within a curvilinear basis set established using a cubic spline fitted to the object's trajectory. Other distortions were explored within this basis set including per-pixel warping of the object according to velocity and acceleration; giving rise to the visual effect of emphasizing drag or inertia. Figure 13.10 illustrates the gamut of effects available in this single framework.

A layered approach to deformation was described by Liu et al. [41]. Video frames were segmented into distinctly moving layers, using unsupervised clustering of motion vectors (followed by optional manual correction). The layers were then distorted according to an optical flow estimate of pixels within each layer. Texture infilling algorithms were applied to fill holes, and a priority ordering assigned to layers to resolve conflicts when warped layers overlapped post-deformation. Animators frequently manipulate the timing and trajectory of object motion to emphasize an

Table 13.1 Summary of the trade-offs made by the different families of methods surveyed in this chapter

		Spatial quality	Coherent motion	Temporal continuity	Style variety	Complexity	Footage diversity
Naïve	Static marks	++	−−	++	++	++	++
	Advection	−−	++	++	++	−	++
	Random marks	++	−−	−−	++	++	++
Filtering	Chapter 5	++	++	+	−	++	++
Opt. Flow	Mark-based	++	++	−	+	−	+
	Texture-based	+	++	+	+	−	+
Segmentation	3D (x, y, z)	++	++	+	+	−−	−−
	$2D + t$	++	++	+	+	−−	−

action; for example, a slight move backward prior to a sprint forwards. This effect is referred to as *anticipation* or *snap* in the animation. The automated introduction of snap into video objects was described in [13], learning an articulated model of the moving object e.g. a walking person, by observing the rigidity and inter-occlusion of moving parts in that object. The joint angles parameterizations were manipulated to exhibit a small opposing motion in proportion to the scale of each movement made. A more general motion filtering model based of region deformation, rather than articulated joints, was described in [56].

13.6 Discussion and Conclusion

This chapter illustrates the large amount of work addressing the problem of temporally coherence video stylization, and highlights a number of limitations that represent interesting directions for future research. The requirements implied by temporal coherence are both contradictory and ill-defined, which in our sense is one of the challenges of this field. In order to facilitate the concurrent analysis of existing methods in this chapter, we proposed a formulation of the temporal coherence problem in terms of three goals: spatial quality, motion coherence and temporal continuity. Table 13.1 summarizes the relative trade-offs against these criteria exhibited by the main families of technique surveyed in this chapter. In addition, we compare against three additional criteria which should be considered when selecting appropriate methods. These are the overall complexity of implementation, the variety of styles that may be simulated, and the diversity of footage that may be processed.

Of these criteria it is arguably hardest to precisely define the goal of *spatial quality*. To go further, we are convinced that human perception should play a greater role in evaluating video stylization work (see Chap. 15 for an in-depth survey of evaluation approaches in NPR). Our spatial quality criterion relates to the perception of each frame as being somehow 'hand-made'. Temporal continuity involves *visual attention* which encapsulates explain human visual sensitivity to flicker and 'popping'. Motion coherence could benefit from studies on *motion transparency* to describe more precisely sliding effects. Some studies have been done in the context of 3D scenes animations [6, 8] and could be use as a starting point for evaluating stylized videos. Beyond the evaluation of temporal coherence, these connections could also help drive coherent video stylization algorithms. Quantitative measurements could be deduced from perceptual evaluations, paving the way to the formulation of temporal coherence as a numerical optimization problem. Such a formulation would give users precise control on the different goals of temporal coherence.

The coherent stylization of video footage remains an open challenge. This is primarily because the coherent movement of marks with video content requires the accurate estimation of video content motion. This is currently an unsolved problem in Computer Vision, and is likely to remain so in the near-term. Consequently the more successful solutions, and arguably the more aesthetically compelling output, has resulted from semi-automated solutions that require user interaction. Such system enable both the correction the stylization process, but more fully embrace the user interaction to enable intuitive and flexible control over the stylization process.

Currently video stylization algorithms are caught in a compromise between robustness and generality of style. Low-level motion estimation based on flow can produce a reasonable motion estimation over most general video, but this is frequently noisy because each pixel may potentially be estimated with a different motion vector. Although modern flow estimation algorithms seek to preserve spatial coherence in the motion vector estimates, in practical video it is common to see inconsistent motion estimation within a single object. On the other hand, Mid-level motion estimation based on video segmentation can ensure consistency within objects by virtue of their operation—delimited the boundaries of objects through coherent region identification. However such methods trade this robustness for the inability to deal with objects than cannot be easily delineated such as hair, water, smoke, and so on. The treatment of stylization as a rotoscoping problem in mid-level framework is attractive, as it allows easy generalization of image-based techniques to video, and the creation of aggressively stylized output such as cartoons. This leads to greater style diversity with these techniques, versus flow-based techniques (and non-linear filtering techniques covered in Chap. 5) that have so far been limited to painterly effects. An open challenge in the field is to somehow combine the benefits of these complementary approaches, perhaps by finding a way to fuse both into a common framework to reflect the mix of object types within typical video footage. Regarding region-based video stylization, and rotoscoping more generally, the region deformation models currently considered in the literature (e.g., those of Sect. 13.4.2) are quite basic. Region boundaries may deform naturally, or due to scene occlusion, yet there is no satisfactory method for discriminating between, and reacting to, these different causes of shape change.

Despite these shortcomings, stylized video is featuring increasingly within the creative industries within movies (e.g., "Waking Life", "Sin City", "A Scanner Darkly"), TV productions, advertisements and games. The field should strive to work more closely with the end-users of these techniques. If user interaction and creativity will remain within the stylization work-flow for some time, then collaboration with Creatives and with Human Factors researchers may prove at least as fruitful a research direction as raw algorithmic development, and would prove valuable in evaluating the temporal coherence of algorithms developed.

References

1. Agarwala, A., Hertzmann, A., Salesin, D.H., Seitz, S.M.: Keyframe-based tracking for rotoscoping and animation. ACM Trans. Graph. **23**, 584–591 (2004)
2. Bai, X., Wang, J., Simons, D., Sapiro, G.: Video SnapCut: robust video object cutout using localized classifiers. ACM Trans. Graph. **28**(3), 70 (2009)
3. Bangham, J.A., Gibson, S.E., Harvey, R.: The art of scale-space. In: Proc. BMVC, pp. 569–578 (2003)
4. Beauchemin, S.S., Barron, J.L.: The computation of optical flow. ACM Comput. Surv. **27**(3), 433–466 (1995)
5. Belongie, S., Malik, J., Puzicha, J.: Shape matching and object recognition using shape contexts. IEEE Trans. Pattern Anal. Mach. Intell. **24**(4), 509–522 (2002)
6. Bénard, P., Thollot, J., Sillion, F.: Quality assessment of fractalized NPR textures: a perceptual objective metric. In: Proceedings of the 6th Symposium on Applied Perception in Graphics and Visualization, Chania, Greece, pp. 117–120. ACM, New York (2009)
7. Bénard, P., Cole, F., Golovinskiy, A., Finkelstein, A.: Self-similar texture for coherent line stylization. In: Proceedings of the 8th International Symposium on Non-Photorealistic Animation and Rendering, Annecy, France, p. 91. ACM, New York (2010)
8. Bénard, P., Lagae, A., Vangorp, P., Lefebvre, S., Drettakis, G., Thollot, J.: A dynamic noise primitive for coherent stylization. Comput. Graph. Forum **29**(4), 1497–1506 (2010)
9. Bénard, P., Bousseau, A., Thollot, J.: Temporal coherence for stylized animation. Comput. Graph. Forum **30**(8), 2367–2386 (2012)
10. Bousseau, A., Kaplan, M., Thollot, J., Sillion, F.X.: Interactive watercolor rendering with temporal coherence and abstraction. In: Proc. NPAR, pp. 141–149 (2006)
11. Bousseau, A., Neyret, F., Thollot, J., Salesin, D.: Video watercolorization using bidirectional texture advection. ACM Trans. Graph. **26**(3), 104 (2007)
12. Chenney, S., Pingel, M., Iverson, R., Szymanski, M.: Simulating cartoon style animation. In: Proc. NPAR, pp. 133–138 (2002)
13. Collomosse, J.P., Hall, P.M.: Video motion analysis for the synthesis of dynamic cues and futurist art. Graph. Models **68**(5–6) 402–414 (2006)
14. Collomosse, J., Rowntree, D., Hall, P.M.: Stroke surfaces: a spatio-temporal framework for temporally coherent nonphotorealistic animations. Tech. Rep. CSBU-2003-01, University of Bath, UK (2003). http://opus.bath.ac.uk/16858/
15. Collomosse, J., Rowntree, D., Hall, P.M.: Video analysis for cartoon-style special effects. In: Proc. BMVC, pp. 749–758 (2003)
16. Collomosse, J., Rowntree, D., Hall, P.M.: Stroke surfaces: temporally coherent nonphotorealistic animations from video. IEEE Trans. Vis. Comput. Graph. **11**(5), 540–549 (2005)
17. Comaniciu, D., Meer, P.: Mean shift: a robust approach toward feature space analysis. IEEE Trans. Pattern Anal. Mach. Intell. **24**(5), 603–619 (2002)
18. Criminisi, A., Sharp, T., Rother, C., Pérez, P.: Geodesic image and video editing. ACM Trans. Graph. **29**(5), 134 (2010)
19. Dalal, K., Klein, A.W., Liu, Y., Smith, K.: A spectral approach to NPR packing. In: Proceedings of the 4th International Symposium on Non-photorealistic Animation and Rendering, pp. 71–78. ACM, New York (2006)

20. DeCarlo, D., Santella, A.: Stylization and abstraction of photographs. In: Proc. SIGGRAPH, pp. 769–776 (2002)
21. Fukunaga, K., Hostetler, L.: The estimation of the gradient of a density function, with applications in pattern recognition. IEEE Trans. Inf. Theory **21**, 32–40 (1975)
22. Goldman, D.B., Curless, B., Salesin, D., Seitz, S.M.: Schematic storyboarding for video visualization and editing. ACM Trans. Graph. **25**(3), 862–871 (2006)
23. Green, S., Salesin, D., Schofield, S., Hertzmann, A., Litwinowicz, P., Gooch, A., Curtis, C., Gooch, B.: Non-photorealistic rendering. In: SIGGRAPH Courses (1999)
24. Haeberli, P.: Paint by numbers: abstract image representations. In: Proc. SIGGRAPH, pp. 207–214 (1990)
25. Hays, J., Essa, I.: Image and video based painterly animation. In: Proc. NPAR, pp. 113–120 (2004)
26. Hertzmann, A.: Painterly rendering with curved brush strokes of multiple sizes. In: Proc. SIGGRAPH, pp. 453–460 (1998)
27. Hertzmann, A.: Paint by relaxation. In: Computer Graphics International, pp. 47–54. IEEE Comput. Soc., Hong Kong (2001)
28. Hertzmann, A., Perlin, K.: Painterly rendering for video and interaction. In: Proc. NPAR, pp. 7–12 (2000)
29. Hsu, S.C., Lee, I.H.H., Wiseman, N.E.: Skeletal strokes. In: Proc. UIST, pp. 197–206 (1993). doi:10.1145/168642.168662
30. Kagaya, M., Brendel, W., Deng, Q., Kesterson, T., Todorovic, S., Neill, P.J., Zhang, E.: Video painting with space-time-varying style parameters. IEEE Trans. Vis. Comput. Graph. **17**(1), 74–87 (2011)
31. Kalnins, R.D., Markosian, L., Meier, B.J., Kowalski, M.A., Lee, J.C., Davidson, P.L., Webb, M., Hughes, J.F., Finkelstein, A.: WYSIWYG NPR: drawing strokes directly on 3D models. In: Proceedings of SIGGRAPH 2002, San Antonio, USA, vol. 21, p. 755. ACM, New York (2002)
32. Kass, M., Pesare, D.: Coherent noise for non-photorealistic rendering. ACM Trans. Graph. **30**, 30 (2011)
33. Klein, A.W., Li, W., Kazhdan, M.M., Corrêa, W.T., Finkelstein, A., Funkhouser, T.A.: Non-photorealistic virtual environments. In: Proceedings of SIGGRAPH 2000, New Orleans, USA, pp. 527–534. ACM, New York (2000)
34. Kopf, J., Cohen-Or, D., Deussen, O., Lischinski, D.: Recursive Wang tiles for real-time blue noise. ACM Trans. Graph. **25**(3), 509–518 (2006)
35. Kyprianidis, J.E.: Image and video abstraction by multi-scale anisotropic Kuwahara filtering. In: Proceedings of the ACM SIGGRAPH/Eurographics Symposium on Non-Photorealistic Animation and Rendering, pp. 55–64. ACM, New York (2011)
36. Kyprianidis, J.E., Kang, H.: Image and video abstraction by coherence-enhancing filtering. Comput. Graph. Forum **30**(2), 593–602 (2011)
37. Lagae, A., Dutré, P.: A procedural object distribution function. ACM Trans. Graph. **24**(4), 1442–1461 (2005)
38. Lasseter, J.: Principles of traditional animation applied to 3D computer animation. In: Proc. SIGGRAPH, vol. 21, pp. 35–44 (1987)
39. Lin, L., Zeng, K., Lv, H., Wang, Y., Xu, Y., Zhu, S.C.: Painterly animation using video semantics and feature correspondence. In: Proc. NPAR, pp. 73–80 (2010)
40. Litwinowicz, P.: Processing images and video for an impressionist effect. In: Proceedings of SIGGRAPH, Los Angeles, USA, vol. 97, pp. 407–414. ACM, New York (1997)
41. Liu, C., Torralba, A., Freeman, W., Durand, F., Adelson, E.H.: Motion magnification. ACM Trans. Graph. **24**(3), 519–526 (2005)
42. Lu, J., Sander, P.V., Finkelstein, A.: Interactive painterly stylization of images, videos and 3D animations. In: Proceedings of the 2010 ACM SIGGRAPH Symposium on Interactive 3D Graphics and Games, Washington, USA, vol. 26, pp. 127–134. ACM, New York (2010)
43. Meier, B.J.: Painterly rendering for animation. In: Proc. SIGGRAPH, pp. 477–484 (1996). doi:10.1145/237170.237288. dl.acm.org/citation.cfm?id=237288

44. Neyret, F.: Advected Textures. In: Proceedings of Eurographics/SIGGRAPH Symposium on Computer Animation, pp. 147–153. Eurographics Association, San Diego (2003)
45. O'Donovan, P., Hertzmann, A.: AniPaint: interactive painterly animation from video. IEEE Trans. Vis. Comput. Graph. **18**(3), 475–487 (2012)
46. Perez, P., Gangnet, A., Blake, A.: Poisson image editing. In: Proc. ACM SIGGRAPH, pp. 313–318 (2003)
47. Schwarz, M., Stamminger, M.: On predicting visual popping in dynamic scenes. In: Proceedings of the 6th Symposium on Applied Perception in Graphics and Visualization, Chania, Greece, p. 93. ACM, New York (2009)
48. Smith, K., Liu, Y., Klein, A.: Animosaics. In: Proc. SCA, pp. 201–208 (2005)
49. Szirányi, T., Tóth, Z., Figueiredo, M., Zerubia, J., Jain, A.: Optimization of paintbrush rendering of images by dynamic MCMC methods. In: Proc. EMMCVPR, pp. 201–215 (2001)
50. Treavett, S.M.F., Chen, M.: Statistical techniques for the automated synthesis of non-photorealistic images. In: Proc. EGUK, pp. 201–210 (1997)
51. Vanderhaeghe, D., Barla, P., Thollot, J., Sillion, F.: Dynamic point distribution for stroke-based rendering. In: Proceedings of the 18th Eurographics Symposium on Rendering 2007, pp. 139–146. Eurographics Association, Grenoble (2007)
52. Vergne, R., Vanderhaeghe, D., Chen, J., Barla, P., Granier, X., Schlick, C.: Implicit brushes for stylized line-based rendering. Comput. Graph. Forum **30**, 513–522 (2011)
53. Wang, T., Collomosse, J.: Progressive motion diffusion of labeling priors for coherent video segmentation. IEEE Trans. Multimed. **14**(2), 389–400 (2012)
54. Wang, J., Thiesson, B., Xu, Y., Cohen, M.F.: Image and video segmentation by anisotropic kernel mean shift. In: Proc. ECCV, pp. 238–249 (2004). doi:10.1007/978-3-540-24671-8_19
55. Wang, J., Xu, Y., Shum, H.Y., Cohen, M.F.: Video tooning. ACM Trans. Graph. **23**(3), 574 (2004)
56. Wang, J., Drucker, S.M., Agrawala, M., Cohen, M.F.: The cartoon animation filter. ACM Trans. Graph. **25**(3), 1169–1173 (2006)
57. Wang, T., Collomosse, J., Hu, R., Slatter, D., Greig, D., Cheatle, P.: Stylized ambient displays of digital media collections. Comput. Graph. **35**(1), 54–66 (2011). doi:10.1016/j.cag.2010.11.004
58. Willats, J., Durand, F.: Defining pictorial style: lessons from linguistics and computer graphics. Axiomathes **15**, 319–351 (2005)
59. Winnemöller, H., Olsen, S., Gooch, B.: Real-time video abstraction. In: Proc. SIGGRAPH, pp. 1221–1226 (2006)
60. Yantis, S., Jonides, J.: Abrupt visual onsets and selective attention: evidence from visual search. J. Exp. Psychol. Hum. Percept. Perform. **10**(5), 601–621 (1984)

Chapter 14
Computer-Assisted Repurposing of Existing Animations

Daniel Sýkora and John Dingliana

14.1 Introduction

Paper and pencil are the only tools that a skilled artist needs to create a fascinating world of cartoon animation. With these tools the artist has complete freedom, as there are no limitations apart from the size of the paper and length of the lead. However, this freedom is tempered by the enormous effort and time needed to complete the artwork especially in the case of colorful animation where hundreds of painted drawings are required.

In recent times, computer-assisted 3D animation systems have become very popular as they can save a great deal of manual work. Here, the key advantage is that the system already knows the structure and motion of an animated object, therefore the final artwork is simply created by an automated rendering algorithm without any additional effort. As a result, everything can be easily manipulated and modified. However, the compromise is that the artist loses a part of their freedom and expressivity. Moreover, the creation of fully consistent 3D models can become very tedious when compared to simple 2D drawing.

The aim of this chapter is to present a set of tools that enable ease of modification, manipulation, and rendering similar to 3D animation systems, whilst preserving the expressivity and simplicity of the original hand-drawn animation. To achieve this, it is necessary to infer a part of the structural information hidden in the sequence of hand-drawn images, namely the partitioning into meaningful segments, their topology variations, depth ordering, and correspondences. Since this inference can be very ambiguous and cannot be fully automated, we let the artist provide a couple of rough hints that make this problem tractable.

D. Sýkora (✉)
FEE, DCGI, CTU in Prague, Karlovo nám. 13, 121 35 Praha 2, Czech Republic
e-mail: sykorad@fel.cvut.cz

J. Dingliana
Trinity College Dublin, College Green, Dublin 2, Ireland
e-mail: John.Dingliana@scss.tcd.ie

Fig. 14.1 Interactive segmentation of a hand-drawn image using LazyBrush [33]. The algorithm finds an optimal labelling based on a set of roughly placed positional constraints—scribbles. It automatically handles small gaps in outlines (note the small subaxillary gap), correctly maintains anti-aliasing, and is not sensitive to imprecise placement of scribbles (e.g., the large brown scribble over the plane). Reproduced with kind permission from Blackwell Publishing Ltd. © Anifilm + © EG & Blackwell. Used with permission

The rest of the chapter is organized as follows. First we introduce an interactive tool which enables quick partitioning of the image into a set of meaningful parts, Sect. 14.2. These play a crucial role in the depth assignment and layering framework, Sect. 14.3, which can further help to simplify deformation and retrieval of correspondences between animation frames, Sect. 14.4. Finally, we demonstrate how reconstructed structural information and correspondences can help to solve more complex problems such as auto-painting, example-based synthesis, temporally coherent texture mapping, or 3D-like shading, Sect. 14.5.

14.2 Segmentation

This section presents *LazyBrush*—an interactive tool for segmenting hand-draw images in various drawing styles [33], see Fig. 14.1. It addresses common limitations of area selection tools used in professional ink-and-paint systems (usually called *magic wand* or *bucket fill*). These are typically based on a variant of the flood-fill algorithm which works well for images containing large flat regions separated by continuous outlines. However, hand-drawn images are typically more complex and thus tedious manual corrections are necessary to obtain clean segmentation. Typical problems that can arise when one wants to segment a hand-draw image using flood-fill based tools are depicted in Fig. 14.2. These problems feature even in recent advanced image segmentation [3, 10] and colorization algorithms [20, 27, 30], see Fig. 14.3.

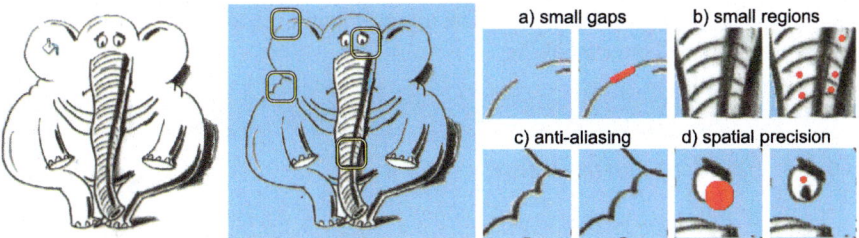

Fig. 14.2 Typical problems of flood-fill based tools when applied to a hand-drawn image: (**a**) small gaps cause leakage, the user has to retrieve them and draw a closure, (**b**) small regions require the user to perform many detailed mouse clicks, (**c**) anti-aliasing is not preserved well due to intensity thresholding mechanisms, the user has to tune the threshold to obtain better results, however, one single value is typically not sufficient for the whole image, (**d**) the user has to move the mouse pointer exactly inside the region of interest. © Anifilm. Used with permission

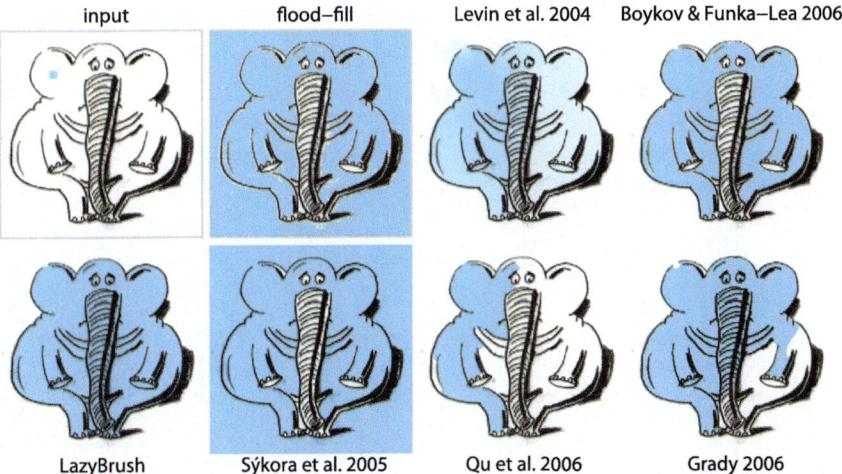

Fig. 14.3 LazyBrush [33] versus flood-fill and modern image segmentation and colorization algorithms: Levin et al. [20] suffers from leakage, Sýkora et al. [30] does not handle small gaps and small regions, Qu et al. [27] get stuck in a local minima, small regions when not arranged in a repetitive hatching pattern need to be handled individually, anti-aliasing is not supported, Grady [10] tends to produce weird boundaries and does not handle anti-aliasing, Boykov and Funka-Lea 2006 [3] have problems with small regions as well as anti-aliasing. Reproduced with kind permission from Blackwell Publishing Ltd. © Anifilm + © EG & Blackwell. Used with permission

LazyBrush uses a popular interaction metaphor called *scribbles*, see Fig. 14.1, which was originally used to perform interactive colorization of gray-scale images [20] and segmentation of photographs [3]. Instead of a single point click inside the region of interest, the user specifies a set of constrained pixels upon which the algorithm resolves the final labelling. Compared to previous approaches [3, 20], LazyBrush scribbles are not necessarily meant to be hard constraints, i.e., the user can overdraw the region of interest. The algorithm will recognize such inaccuracies and try to produce better labelling.

14.2.1 Problem Formulation

Similarly to recent advanced image segmentation and colorization techniques [3, 10, 20, 27] LazyBrush formulates segmentation as an energy minimization problem. It defines a new energy function that is custom tailored to hand-drawn images and thus can overcome issues depicted in Fig. 14.2 and Fig. 14.3.

14.2.1.1 Energy Function

As an input we consider a gray-scale image I consisting of pixels P in a 4-connected neighborhood system N. Each pixel $p \in P$ has an intensity $I_p \in \langle 0, 1 \rangle$. In addition to this, the user marks a subset of pixels using scribbles S. Each scribble $s \in S$ has a specific label ℓ_s taken from a set of possible labels L, see Fig. 14.1 left. The aim is to find an optimal labelling ℓ^*, i.e., the label-to-pixel assignment, see Fig. 14.1 right, that minimizes the following energy:

$$E(\ell) = \sum_{\{p,q\} \in N} V_{p,q}(\ell_p, \ell_q) + \sum_{p \in P} D_p(\ell_p) \quad (14.1)$$

where the *smoothness term* $V_{p,q}$ represents the energy of label discontinuity between two neighbor pixels p and q (i.e., when $\ell_p \neq \ell_q$ otherwise $V_{p,q} = 0$), and *data term* D_p the energy of assigning a label ℓ to a pixel p.

14.2.1.2 Smoothness Term

As the aim is to maintain anti-aliasing, discontinuities between two labels are preferred to appear at pixels p where the intensity I_p is low, i.e., inside dark outlines, see Fig. 14.4(A) left. Therefore we need to set $V_{p,q} \propto I_p$. This is a fundamental difference from standard image segmentation techniques [3, 10] where the aim is to push segment boundaries to pixels with maximal gradient. Such a setting is undesirable in our scenario as it reveals discontinuities at soft edges, Fig. 14.4(A) right.

Next we need to favor compact hole-free regions, see Fig. 14.4(B) left, therefore it is necessary to set $V_{p,q} > 0$, otherwise outlines with zero intensity will not influence the minimum of Eq. (14.1) therefore can easily produce disconnected holes in the final segmentation, Fig. 14.4(B) right. We avoid this by always adding 1 to the smoothness term, i.e., $V_{p,q} = 1 + I_p$. However, when the original image contains long creeks such simple additions can lead to unintended shortcuts, see Fig. 14.4(C) right. To suppress them, discontinuities going through the white pixels should have

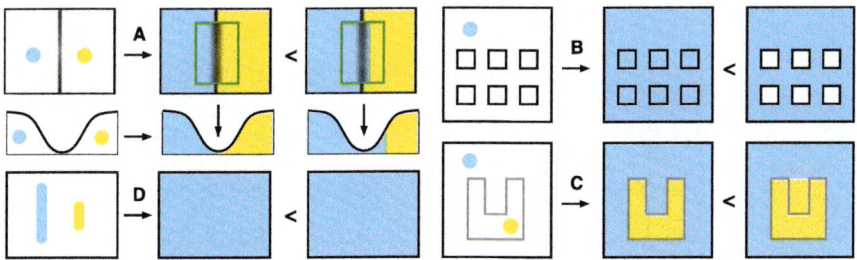

Fig. 14.4 The energy function used in LazyBrush satisfies the following inequalities: (A) a discontinuity inside the outline always has lower energy than a discontinuity on the edge (bottom inset depict intensity profile), (B) length of the discontinuity counts, i.e., compact hole-free regions have lower energy, (C) shortcut through the white areas has higher energy than a discontinuity along a creek even if the contrast of the outline is low, (D) soft scribbles respect rule of majority, i.e., the label of a scribble which occupies the largest area inside a homogeneous region will prevail. Reproduced with kind permission from Blackwell Publishing Ltd.

very high energy K. As the aim is to have overall energy of a shortcut higher than a sum of energies over a long creek, a good estimate for K can be a perimeter of I.

Another source of shortcuts is low contrast between homogeneous areas and outlines visualized by light gray in Fig. 14.4(C). This can happen, e.g., in unprocessed scans of soft pencil drawings. To overcome this, a nonlinear mapping that enhances contrast is required. We use a gamma correction: $V_{p,q} = 1 + K \cdot I_p^\gamma$, with, e.g., $\gamma = 5$. Similar preprocessing of input intensities is required when segmenting grayscale images. In this case outlines need to be emphasized first (e.g., using the negative response of Laplacian-of-Gaussian filter [30], see also Sect. 5.2.2) and then segmentation can be performed using the LazyBrush algorithm (cf. Fig. 14.18, for details see [33]).

To summarize the previous discussion, the smoothness term $V_{p,q}$ is defined as follows:

$$V_{p,q}(\ell_p, \ell_q) = \begin{cases} 1 + K \cdot I_p^\gamma & \text{for } \ell_p \neq \ell_q \\ 0 & \text{otherwise} \end{cases} \quad (14.2)$$

where K is the perimeter of I and $\gamma = 5$.

14.2.1.3 Data Term

In recent image segmentation and colorization algorithms, the data term D_p is usually set to reflect some image-based prior such as intensity [3] or a repetitive hatching pattern [27]. However, repetitive hatching or intensity variations are not typical for hand-made drawings and even if they are present, correspondences between intensity/pattern and a meaningful segment in the image are rare. To address this fact, LazyBrush uses only a user-driven data term. Among other properties, this setting ensures that all label segments are always connected to their initial scribbles. A similar approach is also used in [10], however, here a key difference is that LazyBrush

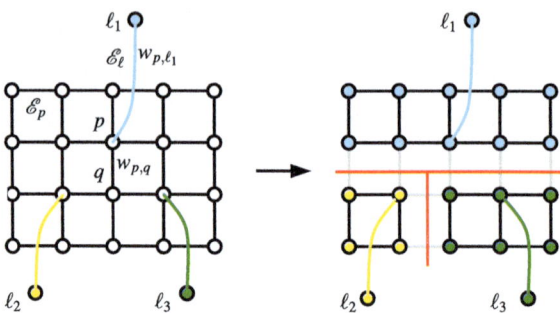

Fig. 14.5 Multiway cut—a basic structure of a graph $\mathscr{G}$ (*left*): pixels P (*white dots*), label terminals L (*color dots*), pixel edges $\mathscr{E}_p$ with weight $w_{p,q}$ (*black lines*), and links to label terminals $\mathscr{E}_\ell$ with weight $w_{p,\ell}$ (*color lines*). The resulting multiway cut and corresponding labelling of pixels (*right*). Reproduced with kind permission from Blackwell Publishing Ltd.

does not necessarily assume that all user-defined scribbles serve as hard constraints. It introduces a new rough positional constraint—*soft scribble*, which preserves the so called *rule of majority*, i.e., within a homogeneous area a label whose scribble occupies the majority of pixels will prevail, see Fig. 14.4(D). In other words, the overall energy Eq. (14.1) should be lower for the left labelling in Fig. 14.4(D) even thought all pixels under the yellow scribble have not received its label. This behavior can be accomplished using the following data term:

$$D_p(\ell_p) = \begin{cases} K & \text{no scribble} \\ 0.95 \cdot K & \text{soft scribble} \\ 0 & \text{hard scribble} \end{cases} \qquad (14.3)$$

where K is the perimeter of the image I (i.e., the energy of a discontinuity at white pixels). For a derivation of this setting and a more detailed discussion about the rule of majority see [33].

14.2.2 Problem Solution

Once the energy function Eq. (14.1) is defined we can proceed to its minimization. Since the value of the smoothness term $V_{p,q}$ depends only on the case where two neighbor pixels have different labels, our energy satisfies the *Potts* model [26]. As shown in [5], minimizing such energy is equivalent to solving a *multiway cut* problem on a certain undirected graph $\mathscr{G} = \{\mathscr{V}, \mathscr{E}\}$ where $\mathscr{V} = \{P, L\}$ is a set of vertices and $\mathscr{E} = \{\mathscr{E}_p, \mathscr{E}_\ell\}$ a set of edges, see Fig. 14.5.

Vertices $\mathscr{V}$ consist of pixels P and terminals L. Each pixel $p \in P$ is connected to its 4 neighbors via edges $\mathscr{E}_p$ having weight equal to smoothness term $w_{p,q} = V_{p,q}$ for the case $\ell_p \neq \ell_q$. There are also auxiliary edges $\mathscr{E}_\ell$ that connect terminals L to marked pixels. Each $\mathscr{E}_\ell$ has a weight $w_{p,\ell} = K - D_p(\ell)$ (hard scribbles have $w_{p,\ell} = K$ and soft $w_{p,\ell} = 0.05 \cdot K$).

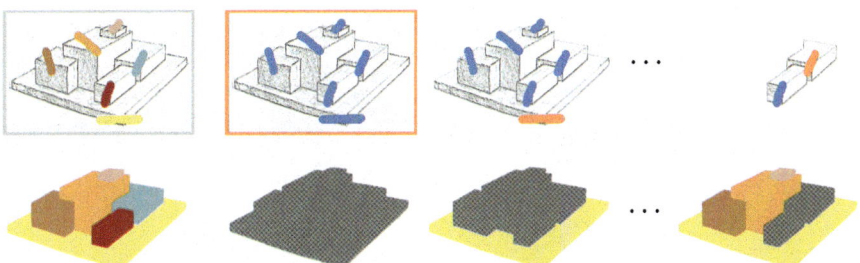

Fig. 14.6 Greedy approximation to multiway cut in progress—computing binary max-flow/min-cut subproblems on gradually reducing graphs (*top*), corresponding mask of already labelled pixels (*bottom*, checkerboard indicates unlabelled pixels). Reproduced with kind permission from Blackwell Publishing Ltd. © Ondřej Sýkora + © EG & Blackwell. Used with permission

A multiway cut with two terminals is equivalent to a max-flow/min-cut problem for which efficient algorithms exist [4, 12]. However, for three or more labels the problem becomes NP-hard [6]. Nevertheless, in practice a simple greedy approximation can quickly deliver a solution which is visually close to the global minimum. It is based on a sequence of binary solutions. The algorithm selects an arbitrary label as a first terminal and all other labels as a second terminal. Then it solves a binary max-flow/min-cut problem and removes a part of the graph associated to the first terminal. The same operation is repeated on a reduced graph with a reduced set of labels until there are only two different labels, see Fig. 14.6.

14.3 Adding Depth

In this section, an extension of the LazyBrush algorithm is presented that enables quick addition of depth information into hand-drawn images [34]. It is motivated by perceptual studies that have tried to understand how humans reconstruct depth from a single image [17, 18]. These studies show that humans typically fail to specify absolute depth values, however, are much more accurate in telling whether some part of the object is occluded by another and vice versa. Therefore the aim is to avoid inputs requiring knowledge of absolute depth and instead use a set of sparse *depth equalities* that are much easier to specify, see Fig. 14.7.

14.3.1 Depth from Depth Inequalities

Supposing that we have already partitioned the input image into a set of meaningful regions, see Fig. 14.8 left, and specified a set of depth inequalities which indicate their relative ordering in depth Fig. 14.8 middle. Such input can be represented as an oriented graph $G(V, E)$ where vertices V correspond to regions (red dots in Fig. 14.8) and oriented edges E represent depth inequalities (green arrows in Fig. 14.8). Now the task is to assign a depth value into each vertex $v \in V$ so

Fig. 14.7 If we ask a human to tell us what are the absolute depths of regions denoted by *question marks* (*left*) they immediately start to think in terms of pairwise above/under relationships (*right*) from which they reconstruct absolute depths. This tedious process can be automated so that the user can directly specify only these pairwise relationships (depth inequalities) and the system will resolve absolute depths automatically. © UPP & DMP. Used with permission

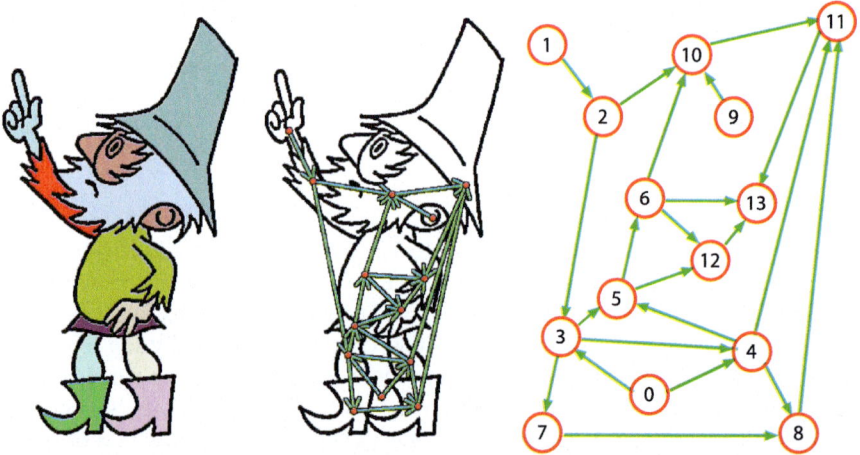

Fig. 14.8 Depth from depth inequalities—a user specifies meaningful segmentation (*left*) and a set of depth inequalities (*middle*). Based on this input, a graph is built (*right*) and its vertices are enumerated according to their topological order. Reproduced with kind permission from Blackwell Publishing Ltd. © UPP & DMP + © EG & Blackwell. Used with permission

that it satisfies all specified depth inequalities E (see the graph in Fig. 14.8 and the resulting depth map in Fig. 14.10).

This task is equivalent to a graph theoretical problem called *topological sorting* [15]. It can be solved by a simple algorithm, the input of which is graph $G(V, E)$, a set of vertices having no incoming edges S, and an empty set L. The algorithm repeats the following steps:

```
while S ≠ ∅ do
    S := S − {n}   and   L := L ∪ {n}
    for ∀m ∈ V having edge e : n → m do
        E := E − {e}
        if m has no other incoming edges then
            S := S ∪ {m}
    endfor
endwhile
if E ≠ ∅ then
    G has at least one oriented cycle else L contains topologically sorted
    nodes.
```

A topologically sorted list of vertices L is returned only if the graph G does not contain oriented loops. This situation can happen when a new depth inequality is added in the wrong direction or when the partitioning of the input image is insufficient. The system will inform the user about this problem and ask them to change the direction or refine the partition of the input image so that the loop is removed. This leads to an interactive process where segmentation and specification of depth inequalities is interchanged until the desired depth assignment is reached.

14.3.2 Outline-to-Region Assignment

The LazyBrush algorithm places segment boundaries inside the outline therefore it is not clear to which segment the outline actually belongs. This knowledge is crucial for applications where a precise extraction of individual parts is necessary. The task is equivalent to the *figure-ground separation* problem [25], which is non-trivial and requires additional semantic knowledge. However, an important part of this knowledge is already encoded in the absolute depth ordering. This information is sufficient to produce good results with only minor artifacts, see Fig. 14.9.

First we need to estimate local thickness of outlines using two distance maps [8]: D^1 computed from the boundaries of regions being expanded, red color in Fig. 14.9(b) and D^2 from all other regions, blue color in Fig. 14.9(b). Pixels where $D^1_p = D^2_p$ form a medial axis from which we can propagate estimates of outline thickness t to all other pixels, Fig. 14.9(c).

This propagation can be understood as a variant of *diffusion curves* [24] (see Sect. 8.2.3) and so can be formulated as a solution to the Laplace equation: $\nabla^2 t = 0$ with the following boundary conditions ($q \in N_p$):

$$\text{Dirichlet: } t_p = 2D^1_p \iff D^1_p = D^2_p$$
$$\text{Neumann: } t'_{pq} = 0 \iff D^1_p = 0 \text{ or } D^2_p = 0$$

This formulation leads to a sparse system of linear equations which is solvable using simple Gauss–Seidel iterations or some more advanced techniques such as [13].

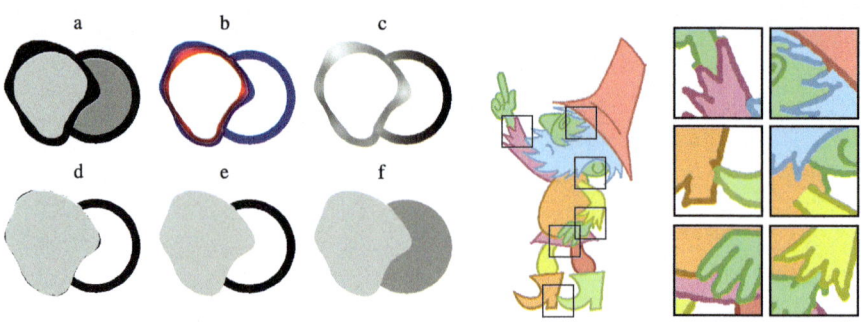

Fig. 14.9 Outline-to-region assignment—a synthetic example (*left*): (**a**) input depth map with dark outlines, (**b**) medial axis obtained using two distance maps computed from the active region (*red*) and all other regions (*blue*), (**c**) propagation of outline thickness from the medial axis to all other outline pixels, (**d**) outline-to-region assignment based on the local estimation of outline thickness, (**e**) filling in small gaps, (**f**) final expanded depth map. A practical example (*right*): several minor artifacts are depicted in selected zoom-ins. Reproduced with kind permission from Blackwell Publishing Ltd. © UPP & DMP + © EG & Blackwell. Used with permission

With the estimation of outline thickness we can expand the region to pixels where $d_p^1 < t_p$, Fig. 14.9(d), and fill in small gaps by removing connected components whose size is below a predefined threshold, Fig. 14.9(e). The expanded region is then removed from the depth map and the same process is applied to all other remaining regions in a front-to-back order to obtain the resulting assignment, Fig. 14.9(f).

14.3.3 Smooth Depth Transitions

When the absolute depths and outline-to-region assignments are known, we can produce smooth depth transitions in areas where depth discontinuities between segments were enforced due to a depth assignment process based on topological sorting (note the depth discontinuity between body and arm in Fig. 14.10).

As we already know where the original depth inequalities were placed, we can use their endpoints to define a set of point constraints $U_\circ$ (see red dots in Fig. 14.10) from which we can smoothly propagate absolute depth values to the rest of the image. Values are taken from $\hat{d}$, which denotes the initial depth map produced by Lazy-Brush and the topological sorting algorithm described in Sect. 14.3.1, see Fig. 14.10 left.

This is again a problem similar to diffusion curves and can be solved using the Laplace equation: $\nabla^2 d = 0$ with the following boundary conditions ($q \in N_p$):

$$\text{Dirichlet: } d_p = \hat{d}_p \iff p \in U_\circ$$
$$\text{Neumann: } d'_{pq} = 0 \iff \hat{d}_p \neq \hat{d}_q \wedge I_p < \tau$$

Fig. 14.10 Enforcing smooth depth transitions—the initial depth map (*left*) produced by Lazy-Brush (Sect. 14.2) and the topological sorting algorithm (Sect. 14.3.1) contains artificial depth discontinuities at pixels where the body and arm connects. This artifact can be removed (*right*) by calculating a smooth transition between the endpoints (*red dots*) of the original depth inequality which was used to specify depth ordering of these two regions (depicted in Fig. 14.8). Reproduced with kind permission from Blackwell Publishing Ltd. © UPP & DMP + © EG & Blackwell. Used with permission

Here Neumann conditions enforce zero derivative only at pixels where the depth discontinuity in the initial depth map $\hat{d}$ is valid, i.e., lies inside the outline (τ is a threshold for the intensity of outlines).

14.4 Deformation

Image deformation tools are invaluable for computer assisted production of hand-drawn cartoon animations since they allow for quick animation prototyping, example-based synthesis and can help to obtain rough correspondences between individual animation frames. Recently the as-rigid-as-possible deformation model [1] has become very popular due to its ability to produce plausible deformations with only little user intervention [11], see Fig. 14.11.

14.4.1 Rigid Square Matching

In this section we describe a simple yet effective algorithm called *rigid square matching* [37], which enables interactive as-rigid-as-possible shape manipulation and can be easily extended to perform fully automatic or supervised image registration [32].

Fig. 14.11 As-rigid-as-possible shape manipulation—the user selects a few control points (*red dots*) on the pre-segmented image (*left*), drags them to a desired location (*middle* and *right*), and the algorithm deforms the image in a way that the rigidity of the original shape is preserved. © UPP & DMP. Used with permission

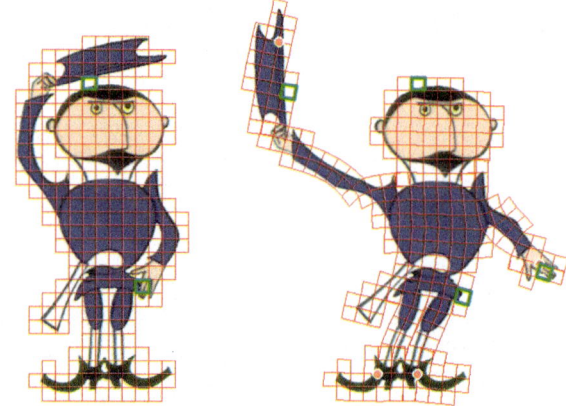

Fig. 14.12 Rigid square matching—the original image is embedded within a square lattice whose connectivity respects the initial segmentation and depth layering provided by the user (*left*). To avoid gluing of disconnected parts during the deformation (*right*) there can exist multiple collocated squares with different connectivity (examples are denoted in *green*). © UPP & DMP. Used with permission

An initial step of the rigid square matching algorithm is to embed the input image into a *control lattice*, see Fig. 14.12, consisting of interconnected squares whose topology respects segmentation and depth layering specified by the user. Each square is assigned a bitmap with corresponding pixels and a depth map to resolve the local layering problem when displaying self-occluded poses, see Fig. 14.11. This solution has an advantage over the triangulation used in [11] as it is much easier to implement and there is no need to approximate shape boundaries using piecewise linear segments.

To avoid gluing due to insufficient resolution of the control lattice, the algorithm allows several collocated squares with different connectivity, green squares in Fig. 14.12. For segments glued together due to occlusion, see hands or boots in Fig. 14.13(a), the user can additionally specify a subset of depth inequalities, blue arrows in Fig. 14.13(a), that will mark corresponding depth discontinuities as tears, Fig. 14.13(b). This modification is important namely for the image registration scenario where it can help to improve the accuracy of the final registration, Fig. 14.13(c).

Fig. 14.13 Introducing tears—a subset of depth inequalities (*blue arrows*) is selected (**a**) to specify tears at corresponding depth discontinuities (**b**). This can help to improve the accuracy of the image registration algorithm (**c**) when a source image (**a**) is registered to a target image (**d**). Reproduced with kind permission from Blackwell Publishing Ltd. © UPP & DMP + © EG & Blackwell. Used with permission

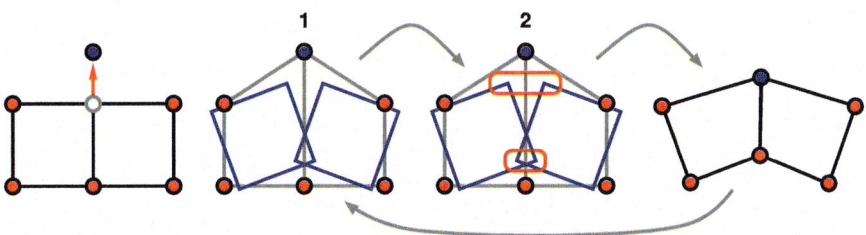

Fig. 14.14 Schematic overview of two simple steps repeated by the rigid square matching algorithm: (1) computation of rigid transformation for each square and (2) moving vertices towards centroid computed from their instances in connected squares

14.4.1.1 Algorithm

When the control lattice is created, the user selects a subset of its vertices called *control points* and moves them to arbitrary locations to define the desired deformation, see Fig. 14.11 and Fig. 14.12. The aim of the rigid square matching algorithm is to move all remaining vertices on the lattice so that deformation of the corresponding squares will be as close as possible to a rigid transformation, i.e., just rotation $\mathbf{R}^*$ and translation $\mathbf{t}^*$. This is accomplished by iterating the following two simple steps, see Fig. 14.14:

1. For each square, compute optimal rigid transformation ($\mathbf{R}^*, \mathbf{t}^*$) and use it to transform its vertices.
2. Move each vertex to the centroid of its transformed instances in all interconnected squares.

Step (1) can be computed as follows:

The aim is to find the optimal rigid transformation ($\mathbf{R}^*, \mathbf{t}^*$) that moves the vertices of the original square $\mathbf{p}_i$ so that the sum of squared distances to the corresponding vertices in the desired pose $\mathbf{q}_i$ is minimized:

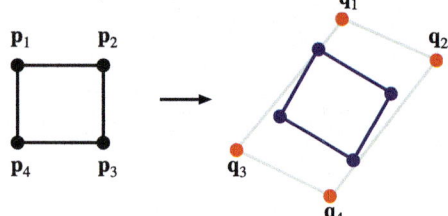

$$(\mathbf{R}^*, \mathbf{t}^*) = \arg\min_{\mathbf{R}, \mathbf{t}} \sum_i |\mathbf{R} \cdot \mathbf{p}_i + \mathbf{t} - \mathbf{q}_i|^2 \qquad (14.4)$$

A simple closed form solution exists to this least square problem in 2D [28]. It can be shown that the optimal rigid transformation ($\mathbf{R}^*, \mathbf{t}^*$) always moves the centroid $\mathbf{p}_c$ of the source vertices to the centroid $\mathbf{q}_c$ of the target vertices. When we align source and target vertices in a way that their centroids are in the origin (i.e., $\hat{\mathbf{p}}_i = \mathbf{p}_i - \mathbf{p}_c$ and $\hat{\mathbf{q}}_i = \mathbf{q}_i - \mathbf{q}_c$) then the optimal rotation $\mathbf{R}^*$ can be computed as follows:

$$\mathbf{R}^* = \frac{1}{\mu} \sum_i \begin{pmatrix} \hat{\mathbf{p}}_i \\ \hat{\mathbf{p}}_i^\perp \end{pmatrix} \begin{pmatrix} \hat{\mathbf{q}}_i^T & \hat{\mathbf{q}}_i^{\perp T} \end{pmatrix} \qquad (14.5)$$

where

$$\mu = \sqrt{\left(\sum_i \hat{\mathbf{q}}_i \hat{\mathbf{p}}_i^T\right)^2 + \left(\sum_i \hat{\mathbf{q}}_i \hat{\mathbf{p}}_i^{\perp T}\right)^2} \qquad (14.6)$$

T denotes transposition, and the operator $\perp$ denotes the perpendicular vector, i.e.: $(x, y)^\perp = (y, -x)$. Once the rotation matrix $\mathbf{R}^*$ is known, the translation vector $\mathbf{t}^*$ can be computed directly:

$$\mathbf{t}^* = \mathbf{q}_c - \mathbf{R}^* \cdot \mathbf{p}_c \qquad (14.7)$$

14.4.2 As-Rigid-As-Possible Image Registration

The knowledge of correspondences between individual hand-drawn animation frames is crucial for many applications described in this chapter. However, obtaining them automatically is a challenging task. The problem is that each animation frame is unique and when compared to a previous frame, it typically undergoes a large amount of free-form deformation and notable change in appearance, see Fig. 14.15.

Popular computer vision techniques based on local similarity (*SIFT keys* [21]) or global context (*shape contexts* [2]) typically fail on such images since they rely on unique local features or stable global configurations, which are common in photographs but rare in hand-drawn images. A more powerful approach—*deformable image registration* based on discrete optimization [9, 29] allows retrieval of correspondences even in the presence of local/global free-form deformation, however, it

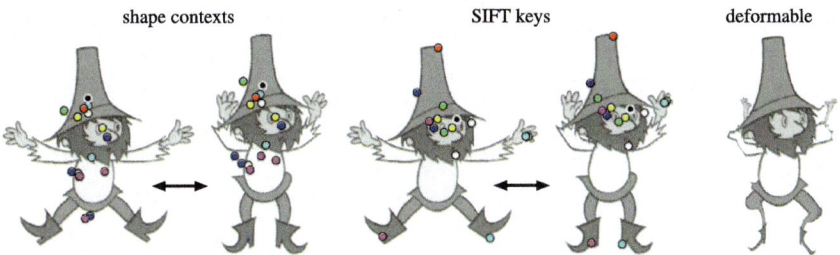

Fig. 14.15 Automatic retrieval of correspondences between two hand-drawn images—SIFT keys [21] or shape contexts [2] fail as there are only a few distinct local features and the global context is not preserved. Deformable image registration [9] cannot handle large displacements. © UPP & DMP. Used with permission

Fig. 14.16 Result of fully automatic as-rigid-as-possible image registration—the aim is to register source and target image with depicted initial overlap, after several push/regularize iterations the source is deformed so that it approximately matches the target (cf. final overlap and deformed source). © UPP & DMP. Used with permission

becomes computationally intractable for larger displacements due to an exponentially increasing state space.

In this section we describe a simple yet effective extension of the rigid square matching algorithm that enables fully automatic or supervised deformable image registration [32]. As the deformation model employed enforces local rigidity and respects the original shape articulation, the algorithm is more robust to larger displacements, see Fig. 14.16. Moreover, due to its iterative nature, it allows the user to inspect the registration process and intervene when necessary.

The algorithm iterates two simple steps until a stable configuration is reached, see Fig. 14.17:

1. **Push** all vertices to locations with minimal visual difference.
2. **Regularize** control lattice using the rigid square matching algorithm.

The aim of the push phase is to find a new location for each vertex on the embedding lattice that minimizes visual difference in its local neighborhood. To do this we can utilize a simple *block matching* algorithm, which guarantees a globally optimal shift within a predefined search area.

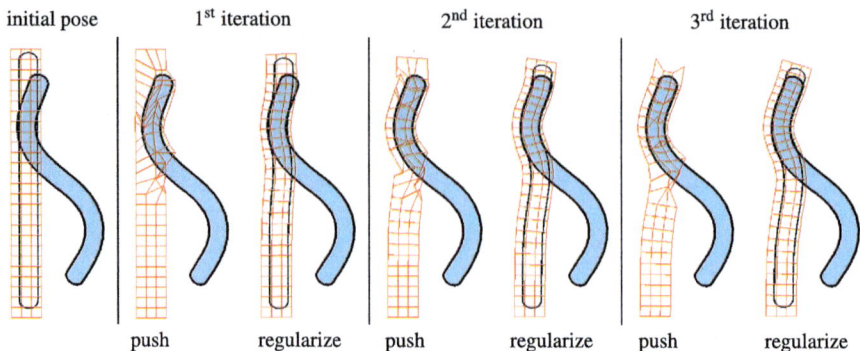

Fig. 14.17 As-rigid-as-possible image registration in progress—in each iteration two steps are executed: first all vertices are pushed towards locations with minimal visual difference (*left*) and then the shape is regularized using the rigid square matching algorithm (*right*). For clarity, the source shape is filled with a transparent color and the control lattice is visualized

Formally, the aim is to find an optimal shift vector $\mathbf{t}^*$ within a local search area M that minimizes the sum of square differences over a neighborhood N, i.e.:

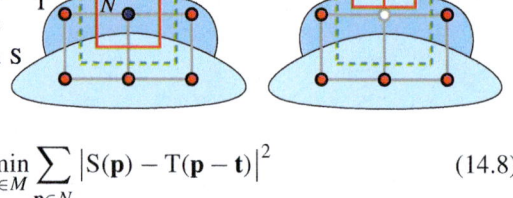

$$\mathbf{t}^* = \arg\min_{\mathbf{t} \in M} \sum_{\mathbf{p} \in N} |S(\mathbf{p}) - T(\mathbf{p} - \mathbf{t})|^2 \qquad (14.8)$$

where S denotes the source and T the target image. Note that in spite of shift optimization, the overall image registration algorithm is not limited to pure translation, since S is slightly deformed during the regularization phase and local neighborhoods of vertices gradually adapt to more complicated deformations, see Fig. 14.17.

In addition to the block matching algorithm the user can also intrude into the push phase by specifying their own positional constraints similarly to the shape manipulation scenario, Fig. 14.11, or just quickly guide the process by simply dragging selected vertices towards desired locations. The key difference from the stand-alone rigid square matching algorithm is that during the push phase *all* vertices are moved (not only those representing user-defined constraints). As can be seen in Fig. 14.17 this leads to temporarily inconsistent configurations, however, in the regularization phase, vertex positions are immediately relaxed by a couple of rigid square matching iterations that enforce local rigidity and make the overall shape consistent.

14.5 Applications

The techniques described in previous sections can now be used as basic building blocks in various practical applications enabling repurposing of existing or creation

Fig. 14.18 Examples of interactive painting (*left*) and colorization (*right*) of hand-drawn images in various drawing styles using the LazyBrush algorithm. Reproduced with kind permission from Blackwell Publishing Ltd. © Lukáš Vlček + © UPP & DMP + © EG & Blackwell. Used with permission

of new hand-drawn cartoon animations with a look that is distinct from traditional techniques.

14.5.1 Painting, Colorization and Texture Mapping

The first straightforward application of segmentation and registration is *painting* and *colorization*, see Fig. 14.18 and also Sect. 17.5. Here desired colors or color components are assigned to the resulting segments and, in each pixel, multiplied/combined with the original gray-scale intensity. The greedy multi-label segmentation algorithm presented in Sect. 14.2.2 is fast enough to enable interactive response when working in PAL resolution.

To avoid repeated specification of scribbles for all animation frames, as-rigid-as-possible image registration, Sect. 14.4.2, can be used to register the first frame to the following frame, transfer the scribbles, and use the LazyBrush algorithm to obtain the segmentation, see Fig. 14.19. As the LazyBrush algorithm is robust to imprecise positioning of scribbles, small mismatches in the registration are allowed. However, for scenes where detailed painting is required (e.g., many small regions with different colors), the user may need to specify additional correction scribbles to keep the segmentation consistent.

Instead of a single color, the user can also specify a texture and make the region filling more visually rich. However, in contrast to a single color there is an additional problem: the texture should follow the motion and/or deformation of its corresponding regions in the subsequent frames to preserve temporal coherency. This can be problematic in hand-drawn animation as it is typically impossible to obtain one-to-one correspondence between individual frames, see Sect. 14.4.2.

Fortunately, as noted in [39] the human visual system tends to focus more on visually salient regions, while devoting significantly less attention to other, less vi-

Fig. 14.19 Auto-painting—color scribbles (**a**) are transferred from already painted (**b**) to yet unpainted frames (**c**) using as-rigid-as-possible image registration algorithm (**d**). LazyBrush is then utilized to compute the final painting (**e**). Reproduced with kind permission from ACM. © Anifilm + © ACM. Used with permission

Fig. 14.20 Texture mapping with approximate temporal coherence—scribbles used to paint the first frame (**a**), textures were applied to selected regions (**b**), texture transfer to a new frame using a deformation field obtained by as-rigid-as-possible image registration algorithm (**c**), final painting of the new frame (**d**), small gaps were filled using extrapolation of texture coordinates. Reproduced with kind permission from ACM. © Anifilm + © ACM. Used with permission

sually important, areas. In hand-drawn animations contours are the salient features. Textures are typically less salient and thus attract considerably less attention [36]. Exploiting this property, an illusion of temporal coherent animation can be created using only rough correspondences obtained by an as-rigid-as-possible image registration algorithm [35], see Fig. 14.20.

14.5.2 Simulation of 3D-Like Effects

In this section we describe techniques which allow artists to simulate 3D-like effects common for computer-generated movies entirely in the 2D domain without the need to reconstruct and render a 3D model, see Fig. 14.23(d). They are based on

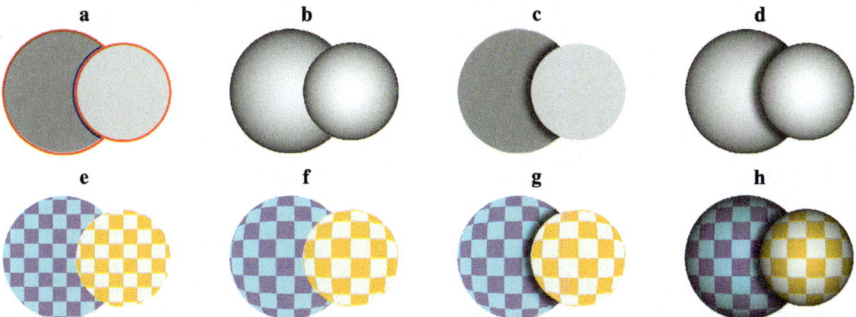

Fig. 14.21 Simulation of 3D-like effects: (**a**) depth map with Dirichlet (*red*) and Neumann (*blue*) boundary conditions, (**b**) Lumo shading, (**c**) simulation of ambient occlusion, (**d**) simulation of ambient occlusion with Lumo shading, (**e**) texture mapping using flat UV coordinates, (**f**) texture rounding based on shading, (**g**) texture rounding with ambient occlusion, (**h**) texture rounding with shading and ambient occlusion

the segmentation and depth obtained using the algorithms described in Sect. 14.2 and Sect. 14.3.

14.5.2.1 Ambient Occlusion

Ambient occlusion is a popular technique that can approximate smooth light attenuation on diffuse surfaces caused by occlusion. Its key advantage is that it can enhance the perception of depth in the image [19]. In our setting with known segmentation and depth order this effect can be simulated by unsharp masking the depth buffer [22] or by simply superimposing a stack of regions with blurred boundaries in a back-to-front order, see Fig. 14.21(c) and Fig. 14.23(c).

14.5.2.2 Shading

Another popular technique that can profit from knowledge of segmentation and depth is *Lumo* [14]. The method approximates the normal field inside a region using the 2D normals computed on its boundaries. The main idea is that on the silhouette of an object the normal component in the viewing direction is always equal to zero, hence the normal is completely specified by its x and y components. Furthermore, the gradient of the image intensity is orthogonal to the silhouette, giving exactly the required normal components. This simple rule holds only when the target shape contains silhouette pixels, i.e., for interior strokes, depth discontinuities should be taken into account. In the original method the user had to trace over the region boundaries and then manually specify an over-under assignment map to produce correct results.

In this section we describe a new formulation of Lumo [35], which exploits algorithms described in this chapter in order to obtain similar results with much less

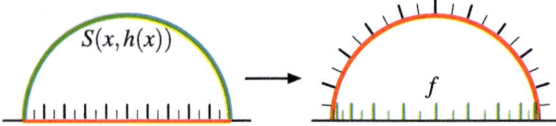

Fig. 14.22 Texture rounding (1D example): linearly interpolated texture coordinates on the surface S and their back projection f to the plane

effort, see Fig. 14.21(b) and Fig. 14.23(c). The formulation is analogous to diffusion curves. The resulting normal field is obtained by solving the Laplace equation $\nabla^2 f = 0$ (where f is either the x or y component of the normal vector n) with the following boundary conditions, see Fig. 14.21(a):

$$\begin{aligned}\text{Dirichlet:} \quad & f_p = d'_{pq} \iff d_p > d_q \\ \text{Neumann:} \quad & f'_{pq} = 0 \iff d_p < d_q\end{aligned} \quad (14.9)$$

where q is a neighboring pixel to p, d'_{pq} is the derivative of the depth map at pixel p in the direction pq and f'_{pq} is the derivative of the normal component (n_x or n_y). This leads to a sparse system of linear equations with two different right hand sides (n_x and n_y). As in the original method n_z is computed using n_x and n_y components via the sphere equation:

$$n_z = \sqrt{1 - n_x^2 - n_y^2} \qquad (14.10)$$

14.5.2.3 Texture Rounding

Values of n_z can be further utilized to simulate a *texture rounding* effect, i.e., when the curvature of the surface generates an area distortion and causes the texture to scale. *Parallax mapping* [16] is typically used to simulate this scaling [38], however, the disadvantage here is that it does not preserve UV coordinates at region boundaries thus produces noticeable texture sliding when used in animation [35]. This artifact can be avoided by interpolating texture coordinates on a virtual 3D surface $S = (x, y, h(x, y))$, where the height h is taken from the z component of the extrapolated normal: $h(x, y) = n_z(x, y)$, see Fig. 14.22.

Such interpolation can be computed directly in 2D by solving the *inhomogeneous Laplace equation*: $\nabla_w^2 f = 0$ where ∇_w^2 is the *Laplace–Beltrami* operator, which measures actual distances on the surface S. This yields another large sparse system of linear equations, now with an irregular Laplacian matrix where the weights w_{ij} between pixels i and j are computed as the inverted length of the edge connecting their corresponding 3D vertices on S:

$$w_{ij} = \frac{1}{\sqrt{1 + (h_i - h_j)^2}} \qquad (14.11)$$

Fig. 14.23 Simulation of 3D-like effects (real example): (**a**) original image with LazyBrush scribbles and depth inequalities, (**b**) depth map, (**c**) ambient occlusion and Lumo shading, (**d**) final composition: original image, textures, ambient occlusion, Lumo shading and texture rounding. Reproduced with kind permission from ACM. © Anifilm + © ACM. Used with permission

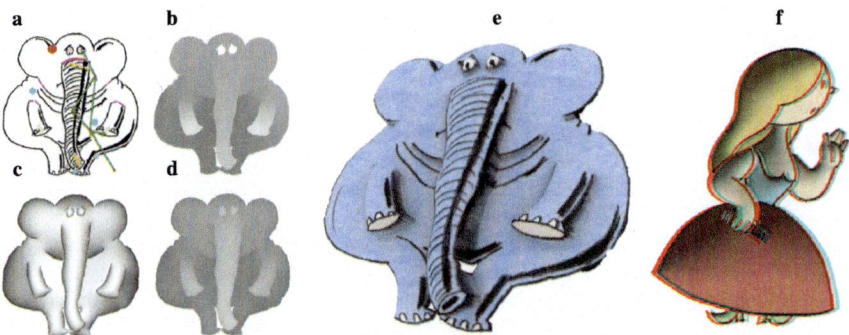

Fig. 14.24 Approximate 3D model and stereo: (**a**) original image with LazyBrush scribbles and depth inequalities, (**b**) depth map, (**c**) Lumo shading, (**d**) depth map after shape-from-shading applied on the Lumo shading, (**e**) approximate 3D mode with texture, (**f**) anaglyph stereo. Reproduced with kind permission from Blackwell Publishing Ltd. © Anifilm + © UPP & DMP + © EG & Blackwell. Used with permission

Solving this inhomogeneous system with Dirichlet boundary conditions and two different right hand sides yields texture coordinates for the surface S projected on the plane, see Fig. 14.21(f) and Fig. 14.23(d).

14.5.2.4 Approximate 3D Model and Stereo

We can further combine the depth map with Lumo shading and apply shape-from-shading [7] to reconstruct an approximation of the 3D surface, see Fig. 14.24(a–e). Such a simple 3D model can be further refined in some modelling tool or rendered from two different viewpoints to obtain stereoscopic images, Fig. 14.24(f).

Fig. 14.25 Local layering—depth inequalities can be used to obtain desired visibility during the interactive shape manipulation (**a**) and fragment composition (**b**), the approach can handle complex self-occlusions (**c**). Reproduced with kind permission from Blackwell Publishing Ltd. (**a**). © Anifilm + © UPP & DMP + © EG & Blackwell. Used with permission

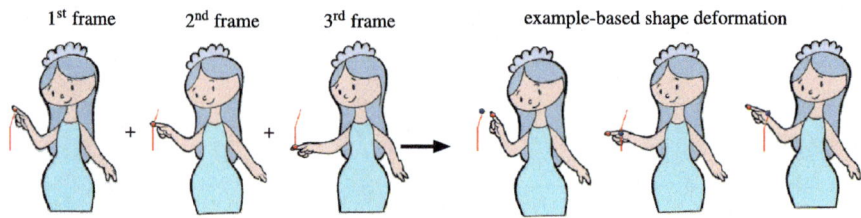

Fig. 14.26 Example-based shape manipulation—by registering several consecutive frames (*left*) a smooth sequence of intermediate frames can be generated. This can be utilized for a synthesis of new poses satisfying a user-given positional constraint (*right*): the current position of the dragged point (*red dot*) is projected (*blue dot*) on its original motion trajectory (*red curve*) to retrieve the corresponding intermediate frame, which is subsequently deformed to match the current position of the dragged control point. Reproduced with kind permission from ACM. © UPP & DMP + © ACM. Used with permission

14.5.3 Shape Manipulation and Example-Based Synthesis

Depth maps generated by the algorithm described in Sect. 14.3 can be used to resolve the visibility of occluded parts during interactive shape manipulation, see Fig. 14.11. The user can freely interact with the shape and modify the visibility on the fly using additional depth inequalities, Fig. 14.25(a). A similar problem arises in systems where the user extracts and composes fragments of images [31]. Here depth inequalities allow quick reordering of regions to obtain correct composition, see Fig. 14.25(b). This operation is also known as *local layering* for which alternative techniques exist [23], however, the approach presented in this chapter is more general as it handles complex self-occlusions, Fig. 14.25(c).

The knowledge of correspondences between consecutive animation frames allows the creation of smooth intermediate transitions, see Fig. 14.26. For this task sub-pixel accurate registration is required. We can use the results of the as-rigid-as-possible image registration, Sect. 14.4.2, as an initial guess for a more precise algorithm with a flexible deformation model, e.g., [9]. Then, intermediate frames can be obtained by interpolating positions of vertices on the control lattice and performing several shape regularization iterations to enforce rigidity. Inside each square, sub-pixel accurate source-target and target-source deformation fields together with pixel blending help to produce the final smooth transition.

The process of inbetweening can be additionally controlled by the user. This extension can be viewed as an example-based shape manipulation which respects the original animation but is more flexible than simple inbetweening. In this scenario, the user can drag a specific vertex on the control lattice and move it to a different location. By projecting this new location on its inbetweening trajectory we can generate the closest transition frame and deform it to match the user-specified constraint, see Fig. 14.26, for details refer to [32].

Acknowledgements This work has been supported by the Marie Curie action ERG, No. PERG07-GA-2010-268216 and partially by the Technology Agency of the Czech Republic under the project TE01010415 (V3C—Visual Computing Competence Center). Hand-drawn images used in this chapter are courtesy of UPP & DMP, Anifilm, Lukáš Vlček, and Ondřej Sýkora.

References

1. Alexa, M., Cohen-Or, D., Levin, D.: As-rigid-as-possible shape interpolation. In: ACM SIGGRAPH Conference Proceedings, pp. 157–164 (2000)
2. Belongie, S., Malik, J., Puzicha, J.: Shape matching and object recognition using shape contexts. IEEE Trans. Pattern Anal. Mach. Intell. **24**(24), 509–522 (2002)
3. Boykov, Y., Funka-Lea, G.: Graph cuts and efficient N-D image segmentation. Int. J. Comput. Vis. **70**(2), 109–131 (2006)
4. Boykov, Y., Kolmogorov, V.: An experimental comparison of min-cut/max-flow algorithms for energy minimization in vision. IEEE Trans. Pattern Anal. Mach. Intell. **26**(9), 1124–1137 (2004)
5. Boykov, Y., Veksler, O., Zabih, R.: Markov random fields with efficient approximations. In: Proceedings of IEEE Conference on Computer Vision and Pattern Recognition, pp. 648–655 (1998)
6. Dahlhaus, E., Johnson, D.S., Papadimitriou, C.H., Seymour, P.D., Yannakakis, M.: The complexity of multiway cuts. In: Proceedings of ACM Symposium on Theory of Computing, pp. 241–251 (1992)
7. Ecker, A., Jepson, A.D.: Polynomial shape from shading. In: Proceedings of IEEE Conference on Computer Vision and Pattern Recognition, pp. 145–152 (2010)
8. Felzenszwalb, P.F., Huttenlocher, D.P.: Distance transforms of sampled functions. Tech. Rep. TR2004-1963, Cornell University (2004)
9. Glocker, B., Komodakis, N., Tziritas, G., Navab, N., Paragios, N.: Dense image registration through MRFs and efficient linear programming. Med. Image Anal. **12**(6), 731–741 (2008)
10. Grady, L.: Random walks for image segmentation. IEEE Trans. Pattern Anal. Mach. Intell. **28**(11), 1768–1783 (2006)
11. Igarashi, T., Moscovich, T., Hughes, J.F.: As-rigid-as-possible shape manipulation. ACM Trans. Graph. **24**(3), 1134–1141 (2005)
12. Jamriška, O., Sýkora, D., Hornung, A.: Cache-efficient graph cuts on structured grids. In: Proceedings of IEEE Conference on Computer Vision and Pattern Recognition, pp. 3673–3680 (2012)
13. Jeschke, S., Cline, D., Wonka, P.: A GPU Laplacian solver for diffusion curves and Poisson image editing. ACM Trans. Graph. **28**(5), 116 (2009)

14. Johnston, S.F.: Lumo: illumination for cel animation. In: Proceedings of International Symposium on Non-photorealistic Animation and Rendering, pp. 45–52 (2002)
15. Kahn, A.B.: Topological sorting of large networks. Commun. ACM **5**(11), 558–562 (1962)
16. Kaneko, T., Takahei, T., Inami, M., Kawakami, N., Yanagida, Y., Maeda, T., Tachi, S.: Detailed shape representation with parallax mapping. In: Proceedings of International Conference on Artificial Reality and Telexistence, pp. 205–208 (2001)
17. Koenderink, J.J.: Pictorial relief. Philos. Trans. R. Soc. Lond. **356**(1740), 1071–1086 (1998)
18. Koenderink, J.J., van Doorn, A.J., Kappers, A.M.L.: Pictorial surface attitude and local depth comparisons. Percept. Psychophys. **58**(2), 163–173 (1996)
19. Langer, M.S., Buelthoff, H.H.: Depth discrimination from shading under diffuse lighting. Perception **29**(6), 649–660 (2000)
20. Levin, A., Lischinski, D., Weiss, Y.: Colorization using optimization. ACM Trans. Graph. **23**(3), 689–694 (2004)
21. Lowe, D.G.: Distinctive image features from scale-invariant keypoints. Int. J. Comput. Vis. **60**(2), 91–110 (2004)
22. Luft, T., Colditz, C., Deussen, O.: Image enhancement by unsharp masking the depth buffer. ACM Trans. Graph. **25**(3), 1206–1213 (2006)
23. McCann, J., Pollard, N.S.: Local layering. ACM Trans. Graph. **28**(3), 84 (2009)
24. Orzan, A., Bousseau, A., Winnemöller, H., Barla, P., Thollot, J., Salesin, D.: Diffusion curves: a vector representation for smooth-shaded images. ACM Trans. Graph. **27**(3), 92 (2008)
25. Pao, H.K., Geiger, D., Rubin, N.: Measuring convexity for figure/ground separation. In: Proceedings of IEEE International Conference on Computer Vision, pp. 948–955 (1999)
26. Potts, R.: Some generalized order-disorder transformation. In: Proceedings of Cambridge Philosophical Society, vol. 48, pp. 106–109 (1952)
27. Qu, Y., Wong, T.T., Heng, P.A.: Manga colorization. ACM Trans. Graph. **25**(3), 1214–1220 (2006)
28. Schaefer, S., McPhail, T., Warren, J.: Image deformation using moving least squares. ACM Trans. Graph. **25**(3), 533–540 (2006)
29. Shekhovtsov, A., Kovtun, I., Hlaváč, V.: Efficient MRF deformation model for non-rigid image matching. Comput. Vis. Image Underst. **112**(1), 91–99 (2008)
30. Sýkora, D., Buriánek, J., Žára, J.: Colorization of black-and-white cartoons. Image Vis. Comput. **23**(9), 767–782 (2005)
31. Sýkora, D., Buriánek, J., Žára, J.: Sketching cartoons by example. In: Proceedings of Eurographics Workshop on Sketch-Based Interfaces and Modeling, pp. 27–34 (2005)
32. Sýkora, D., Dingliana, J., Collins, S.: As-rigid-as-possible image registration for hand-drawn cartoon animations. In: Proceedings of International Symposium on Non-photorealistic Animation and Rendering, pp. 25–33 (2009)
33. Sýkora, D., Dingliana, J., Collins, S.: LazyBrush: flexible painting tool for hand-drawn cartoons. Comput. Graph. Forum **28**(2), 599–608 (2009)
34. Sýkora, D., Sedlacek, D., Jinchao, S., Dingliana, J., Collins, S.: Adding depth to cartoons using sparse depth (in)equalities. Comput. Graph. Forum **29**(2), 615–623 (2010)
35. Sýkora, D., Ben-Chen, M., Čadík, M., Whited, B., Simmons, M.: TexToons: practical texture mapping for hand-drawn cartoon animations. In: Proceedings of International Symposium on Non-photorealistic Animation and Rendering, pp. 75–83 (2011)
36. Walther, D., Koch, C.: Modeling attention to salient proto-objects. Neural Netw. **19**(9), 1395–1407 (2006)
37. Wang, Y., Xu, K., Xiong, Y., Cheng, Z.Q.: 2D shape deformation based on rigid square matching. Comput. Animat. Virtual Worlds **19**(3–4), 411–420 (2008)
38. Winnemöller, H., Orzan, A., Boissieux, L., Thollot, J.: Texture design and draping in 2D images. Comput. Graph. Forum **28**(4), 1091–1099 (2009)
39. Yarbus, A.L.: Eye Movements and Vision. Plenum, New York (1967)

Part IV
Evaluation and Impact of Artistic Stylization

Parts I–III of this book have focused on the techniques that have been developed as the building blocks for creating an NPR pipeline. In Part IV the remaining chapters consider the principles behind the important and difficult task of assessing results from such an NPR system, so as to be able to compare different approaches, and determine the quality of any individual technique. And finally, now that NPR has built up a solid research foundation, this has led to commercial impact and applications, which are reviewed in the last chapter.

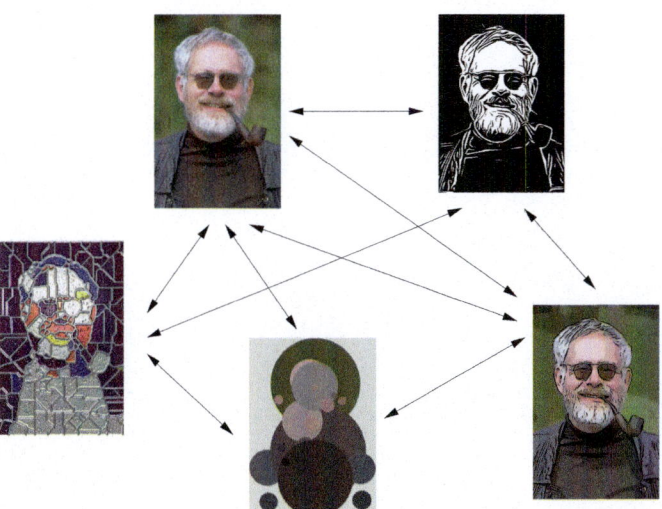

The image in the *top left* is rendered in various styles using algorithms described in Chap. 5, Chap. 7, and Chap. 11. The *arrows* represent the goal of comparing and evaluating renderings. Courtesy of Philip Greenspun

Chapter 15
Evaluating and Validating Non-photorealistic and Illustrative Rendering

Tobias Isenberg

15.1 Introduction

With non-photorealistic, artistic, and illustrative rendering (which is collectively being called NPR in this book) having developed into a mature field over the last two to three decades, researchers have begun to question the validity, usefulness, appropriateness, and acceptance of the large variety of different techniques that have been created [13]. This chapter aims to survey the different evaluation and validation techniques that have been employed within NPR to provide inspiration for future work and to encourage the use of evaluation techniques in the field. For the purpose of this chapter on evaluation, however, we treat the domain of NPR a bit more broadly than only the stylization of images and video as in the rest of this book: we incorporate all NPR approaches in the discussion, including those that use 3D scenes as input as well as methods for illustrative visualization.

To be able to discuss specific NPR evaluation strategies, however, we need to start by thinking about what it is that we want to or need to learn. In fact, there are many different questions one may ask about the field of NPR as a whole or about individual techniques. Hertzmann [26], for example, talks about evaluating human aesthetics and the question of how people respond to NPR, while Salesin [47] mentioned the *NPR Turing test* as one of his seven grand challenges for NPR in 2002 (recently revisited by Gooch et al. [19]): Can we render images using NPR that a normal person is no longer able to distinguish from hand-made ones? While answering these questions is certainly a worthwhile endeavor, the potential for evaluation within NPR is much larger. One may ask, for example, the following questions:

T. Isenberg (✉)
INRIA Saclay, Orsay, France
e-mail: tobias@isenberg.cc

- Why do we want to or need to use NPR in the first place?
- What are appropriate goals for NPR?
- Is a given approach/technique/application accepted by its intended users, does it serve the intended purpose?
- By which mechanism/principle does NPR imagery assist a given goal, and how can we take advantage of such mechanism/principle?
- What do people think about NPR imagery or how do they respond to it?
- What emotions or (potentially) unconscious reactions can/does NPR imagery invoke in viewers?
- How do NPR images compare to hand-made drawings/paintings/illustrations?

Each of these points, in turn, cover a broad range of more specific questions (see also [19, 26, 47]). To be able to discuss NPR evaluation in a more systematic way we, therefore, group these questions roughly into three major areas:

1. the question of providing a general motivation for the use of NPR techniques (Sect. 15.2),
2. the question of understanding how NPR techniques support a specific purpose (Sect. 15.3), and
3. the question of comparing hand-made images with computer-generated (non-photorealistic) ones (Sect. 15.4).

Before we turn to discussing these three main questions, however, we need to briefly touch on study methodologies in general. We do this, in particular, because there is a danger of selecting a wrong study methodology [20, 26] or misinterpreting the results [5, 32]. While a more comprehensive overview of study methodology can be found elsewhere (e.g., [11, 34]), a useful short overview is given by Carpendale [4] for the domain of information visualization but which similarly applies to the study of NPR. Generally, there are two major types of evaluation methodologies that can be employed: *quantitative evaluation* which focuses on hypotheses, measurable variables in controlled experiments, and a statistical analysis of the results and *qualitative evaluation* which tries to gain a richer understanding of the subject matter by taking a more holistic approach and which uses techniques like observation and interviewing [4]. Both general techniques as well as combined approaches can be and have been applied to NPR evaluation, the specific type of methodology depending on the questions that one is asking. For example, the question of what effect a stylized depiction vs. photograph have on learning and recognizing [18] is rightfully studied with a quantitative technique, while the question of what people think about hand-drawn illustrations vs. computer-generated visualizations [30] is better studied with a qualitative approach. We illustrate the various methodologies further in the discussion of the individual techniques below.

15.2 Providing a General Motivation for NPR

While the ability to create images in a specific artistic or illustrative style can be motivation enough for the development and application of NPR techniques, we can also examine people's reactions to seeing NPR visuals to better understand why it makes sense to use NPR in the first place. This insight in the general motivation for the use of NPR can then inform the design of new techniques as well as their practical application.

Such an early example of "assessing the effect of non-photorealistic[ally] rendered images" was presented by Schumann et al. [50] in 1996. They were motivated by the continued use of hand drawing in the domains of architecture and CAD [52] and examined the effect that a sketchy rendering style (as opposed to 'normal' shading and regular CAD plots) has on the communicative goals during the development of architectural designs. To study this effect, the authors started from three hypotheses: (1) that sketched depiction styles are preferred to CAD plots and shaded images for presenting early drafts of architectural designs, (2) that sketches perform better in communicating affective and motivational aspects of an image, while CAD plots and shaded images perform better in cognitive aspects, and (3) that sketches stimulate viewers to participate in an active discussion and development of a design, more than shaded images. To examine these hypotheses, Schumann et al. [50] used a questionnaire-based approach that both asked for quantitative ratings (selection of an image that is preferred for a given task or responses on a 5-point Likert scale) and for qualitative feedback. The questionnaires were sent to 150 architects and architectural students, 54 of which (36 %) returned it. Based on these responses the authors analyzed their three hypotheses.

The results showed that of the people who regularly use CAD tools (67 % of the responses), 53 % would use the NPR sketch to present an early draft, while only 33 % would use a CAD plot for this purpose and only 22 % would use a shaded image. In contrast, only 8 % would use the NPR sketch for a final presentation, while a CAD plot would be used by 50 % and the shaded image by 42 %. These results confirm the first hypothesis and, thus, show that stylistic depictions can be used to indicate the stage of a design process—a fact that has since then been used, for example, in the domain of sketch-based interaction and modeling (e.g., [27, 49]).

To analyze the second hypothesis the participants were asked to assess the impression that the three different images have on them in more detail. The authors used a classification scheme from the psychology literature and asked the participants to rate each image according to criteria from a cognitive group, an affective group, and a motivational group. They found that the NPR sketch was rated significantly higher/better on affective and motivational criteria, while the CAD plot was rated significantly higher/better on cognitive criteria. This result indicates the potential for stylistic depiction to evoke emotion and to stimulate active involvement, a question that was further examined with respect to the third hypothesis.

To analyze this involvement in a design process, the CAD-using participants were asked how they would communicate design changes using either an NPR sketch or a shaded image: (a) using verbal descriptions, (b) using gestures or pointing, (c) by drawing onto a separate sheet of paper, or (d) by drawing into the presented image. The only statistically significant difference that was found between the NPR sketch and the shaded image was that participants are much more likely to draw into the NPR sketch (69 %) than into the shaded image (33 %), confirming the authors' third hypothesis. This means that style of a rendering can have an effect on how willing somebody is to interact with the depiction, and the authors suggest that the stylization leaves more room for interpretation with respect to the exact design.

This effect of stylistic imagery on people—in other words whether and how people are affected by NPR—was also examined by Duke et al. [10] and Halper et al. [21, 22] who describe a motivation for employing NPR styles based higher-level psychological principles. For example, Halper et al. [21, 22] discuss the effect of figure-ground segregation as supported by NPR elements such as silhouettes and feature lines. Their study looked at whether people would rather select objects from an image that were depicted with an abstracting style consisting of cartoon shading and silhouette or objects shown in a more detailed, oil-painting style. Their results suggest that the rendering style had an effect on which objects people selected, with participants tending to select two or more objects depicted in the cartoon-style.

A second evaluation by Halper et al. looked at people's social perception and judgment. They presented participants with simple line drawings of scenes with previously established social connotations about safety and danger, such as a house (typically associated to be safe) and a group of trees (typically considered to be less safe). They then depicted the house in a zig-zaggy and the trees in a rounded style, which changed participants' behavior to no longer associate the house with safety. A simple comparison of the same object rendered in different styles supported these findings, also associating certain (zig-zaggy) line styles with danger.

Finally, Halper et al. examined aspects of environmental psychology and people's participation and interaction in environments. In particular, they studied how the level of detail in a rendering affects people's behavior. They provided images with two paths, one depicted in more, and another in less detail. They found that the amount of detail has an effect on the choice of path people make—participants preferring the more detailed path over the one with less detail.

Based on these and other experiments, Duke et al. [10] explain people's behavior using the concept of *invariant* from perception, which describes a property common to or shared by a range of entities of behavior. Duke et al. argue that the stylistic differences (i.e., NPR styles) and their stylistic invariants lead to specific behavior in the experiments due to latent, implicational knowledge and that this may lead to higher-level cognitive interpretations common across a range of people (affected by their culture and language). This insight can then be used, as suggested by Duke et al., to associate depicted objects with emotions or to guide people's engagement and attention, for example in computer games and virtual environments.

These two aspects—the effect of NPR on emotion and the use of NPR to guide attention—which both form a strong motivation for the use of NPR in practice have been studied in more detail by two other teams of authors. The first aspect, the effect that NPR imagery has on people's emotions, has recently been studied in detail by Mandryk et al. [41] and Mould et al. [44] who looked at how the stylization of photographs changed people's emotional response to the images. They selected 18 images covering a wide range of topics from the IAPS image database (created specifically as affective stimuli and with known emotional content), and examined the emotional response of 42 participants. They measured the emotional response of their participants with respect to an established dimensional scheme of emotion (using a 5 × 3 pictorial scale that allowed participants to analyze and report their emotional state) including the dimensions valence, arousal, dominance, and aesthetics. For that purpose they compared the emotional response of the original images (whose previous rating for affective content was known) with those of the result of five image-based NPR styles and those of two blurred versions.

The result of Mandryk et al.'s [41] and Mould et al.'s [44] analysis was that all NPR techniques significantly shifted their participants' reported experiences of valence (pleasure/positive or displeasure/negative of a feeling) and arousal (energy/activation of a feeling) to the neutral rating, thus reducing the strength of the emotion, but never eliminating the emotion completely. They found that some techniques preserve the emotions better than others, but that the effect might be attributed to the amount of detail that was preserved by a given technique. It is interesting that this muting of emotion to some degree stands in contrast to the observations of Duke et al. [10] and Halper et al. [21, 22], but this effect can probably be explained based on the different types of stylization employed by both evaluations: Mandryk et al. [41] and Mould et al. [44] examined image-based (i.e., mostly space-filling) techniques in which the style's amplitude (as measured in tone or color) is reduced by the NPR technique from the original photograph due to the introduced abstraction, while Duke et al. and Halper et al.'s analysis of emotion (social perception and judgment) was based on line drawings in which the strong emotion (fear) was caused by a high-amplitude zig-zaggy style.

Another recent study adds to these mixed results: Seifi et al. [51] looked at what effect color palettes have on the perception of emotion in painterly rendered faces. They used color palettes designed to enhance certain emotions (joy, surprise, anger, and fear) and examined their effect for still images and animations. Seifi et al. found that sometimes the perceived emotion is emphasized if the palette matches the face's expression, while non-matching palettes dampen the perceived emotion. However, they also report about a general damping effect for some emotions, and that even sometimes the perceived emotion is damped further when the matching palette is used than for non-matching palettes (e.g., fear in the animated scenario).

The second general aspect to be affected in a controlled manner by NPR styles as suggested by Duke et al. [10] and also previously mentioned by Strothotte et al. [52]—the guiding of people's attention—was studied in detail by Santella and DeCarlo [48]. Their goal was, based on eye tracking data, to understand the effectiveness *meaningful abstraction* (i.e., directed removal of detail) with the intent of guiding a person's attention. For that purpose Santella and DeCarlo created four types of abstraction of an input photograph: one using constant abstraction with a high amount of detail, one using constant abstraction with a low amount of detail, one with adaptive abstraction in which the detail points are based on image saliency, and one with adaptive abstraction in which the detail points are based on a person's fixation points for the original photograph. The authors then used their eye tracker to analyze where 74 study participants fixated when looking at one of the five different versions (original and four abstracted versions) of 50 input images (using a between-participants design).

The study results showed that the local treatment of abstraction does have an effect on where people look in an image, the salience-based and fixation-based adaptive abstractions receiving fewer fixation clusters than the other images. The analysis of the distance of the fixation clusters to the detail points also showed that these are smaller for both adaptive abstractions, leading to a concentration of the visual interest. Moreover, the authors also argue that the distance from a detail point to a cluster is consistently smaller for the eye tracking condition than for the salience condition, suggesting that eye tracking points were more closely examined, i.e., that there seems to be less interest in salience points. These results provide evidence for the previously discussed hypothesis that the control of the amount of detail as is possible with NPR styles can be used to guide people's attention.

Related to the use of NPR for guiding attention is also the issue of whether or not the abstraction introduced by NPR techniques has a positive effect on the ability to recognize and to memorize objects. This question was examined by Gooch et al. [16, 18] specifically for face illustrations, but similar to the previous studies their work provides a motivation for NPR in general. In their psychophysical study the authors compare photographs of faces with line illustrations as well as with line-based caricatures of the same faces. Specifically, Gooch et al. used controlled, quantitative experiments to measure the speed and accuracy of participants recognizing known faces and learning new faces, using photographs, computer-generated line illustrations, and caricatures produced with computer support.

In a first experiment, Gooch et al. used images created from face pictures of the 12 most familiar out of 20 possible people (colleagues) and asked their 42 participants to recognize them when presented in a random order. Each participant saw only two types of images, either photographs and illustrations, photographs and caricatures, or illustrations and caricatures. The results of this experiment were that participants were slightly faster in naming photographs than caricatures, with the other combinations not showing a significant effect and with the accuracy for all conditions being high (98 %)—thus without a speed-for-accuracy trade-off.

To examine the learning of the different types of depictions in a second experiment, Gooch et al. created the same types of images for faces that were unknown to 30 different participants. As before, each participant was shown 12 face pictures, but this time a name was associated with each picture and each participant only saw one type of image (i.e., three groups of 10 participants). Then, the image stack was shuffled and the participants were asked to recall the name previously associated to a face as the stack of images was presented one image at a time. If a name was incorrect, then the participant was corrected. This process (including shuffling) was repeated until all names were recalled correctly. The analysis showed that illustrations were learned more than twice as fast as photographs. While caricatures were about $1.5\times$ as fast as photographs, this difference was not statistically significant.

Interestingly, a similar experiment about the ability to recognize and memorize objects using abstractions vs. real photographs was later conducted by Winnemöller et al. [54], using their real-time video abstraction technique as a foundation (Chap. 5). This meant that they could investigate color images as opposed to the black-and-white images used by Gooch et al. [16, 18]. Like Gooch et al., Winnemöller et al. used faces for the recognition task (using celebrity images) but employed arbitrary scenes for the memory task in a memory card game setting. Overall, their results supported the findings by Gooch et al., but in contrast also found that recognition was significantly faster with the abstracted images as opposed to the real photographs. However, this result does not generalize to all NPR depiction styles—Zhao and Zhu [56], for example, showed that objects depicted in both painterly rendering and actual paintings are recognized slower than actual photographs.

In summary, the mentioned studies provide evidence for a number of benefits or effects of stylistic depictions created with NPR techniques, and thus motivate the development of as well as the application of NPR approaches in practice. This includes that they can encourage participation in design discussions [50], that they can assist figure-ground segregation, can carry social connotations, and can steer people's interest [10, 21, 22], that their style has an effect on people's emotions [41, 44], that they can be used to guide people's attention [48], and that they can affect how people recognize and memorize depictions of objects [16, 18, 54].

15.3 Understanding How NPR Supports a Specific Purpose

While the studies discussed in Sect. 15.2 necessarily each use a specific study setting, their findings do provide a motivation for employing NPR styles more generally as we just outlined. However, there have also been a number of evaluations of NPR techniques that, we find, point to more specific usage possibilities because they illustrate how NPR can support a specific purpose or application domain. We first discuss a number of evaluations that examine aspects that relate to human perception of NPR with respect to textures, then examine techniques that support the creation of visualizations using NPR approaches, and finally look at application contexts in the domains of virtual and augmented reality (VR and AR).

15.3.1 Perception of NPR Textures

A large body of NPR work addresses the creation of textures for a variety of application domains. For example, the creation of stippling (dot placement, see Chap. 3) and hatching (line placement) are among the most fundamental NPR techniques, applicable both to the representation of 2D images and the depiction of 3D shapes. Thus it is important to understand how people see and interpret such textures.

To obtain this kind of understanding, Kim et al. [35, 36] looked specifically at the use of textures for the representation of 3D shapes and their impact on people's shape categorization judgments. In this context it is important that a texture supports the perception of 3D shapes, despite them only being depicted as a projection on a 2D image. Specifically, Kim et al. investigated which effect the texture type has on shape perception, using a set of five different types: one-directional hatching, perpendicular cross-hatching, swirly lines, three-directional hatching, and noise; with three additional variations. Based on these types, the authors conducted a controlled study in which they asked their participants to classify surface patches as ellipsoid, cylindrical, saddle-like, or flat as well as to categorize them as convex, concave, both (for saddles), or none (for flat patches). They found that, overall, the texture type does have a significant effect on shape perception, with the perpendicular cross-hatching along the principal directions performing best, confirming a hypothesis formulated earlier [15]. They also found that certain textures and an oblique viewing direction can alleviate problems that arise from orthographic projection.

To examine the situation further, Kim et al. [36] performed a second experiment to concentrate on single-, dual-, and triple-hatching textures. Some of the hatching directions of the new texture set followed the principal directions, while others were turned away from a principal direction by 45 degrees. Using the same experimental procedure as in the first study, Kim et al. found that, surprisingly, the two-directional hatching texture was now outperformed for some shapes by the single-hatching as well as, in particular, the three-directional hatching. The authors speculate that this effect may be due to people inferring non-existent lines from the otherwise regular hatching patterns as well as distances along these non-existent lines to be able to understand and classify the depicted shape as well as or better than with 'normal' two-directional hatching along the principal directions.

While Kim et al. [36] examined the issue of 3D shape classification based on the applied textures, another problem in NPR is the use of textures on 3D shapes for stylized animation. Traditionally, the straightforward process of applying 2D textures to 3D objects led to a number of issues during an animation including popping, sliding, and deformations—leading to the use of 'fractalized' (i.e., self-similar on different levels of scale) NPR textures in such 3D scene animations. Because these fractalized textures are no longer identical to the traditional textures, Bénard et al. [3] conducted an experiment to analyze this perceived change and, based on these results, to derive a quantitative metric for the introduced texture distortion. In the study the authors asked participants to rank pairs of original and fractalized textures (representative of a variety of media replicated by NPR; including, e.g., stippling, hatching, cross-hatching, and paint texture) with respect to how much distortion participants perceived to have been introduced by the fractalization.

The authors statistically analyze the results and find that, between two sets of textures of the same categories, participants seem to have treated them roughly the same way overall. However, it also is apparent that the class of a texture (e.g., "cross-hatching") does not always get classified the same way if different instances of the texture class are used. More interestingly, however, Bénard et al. try to extract a correlation between known image metrics and their empirical results to find a model that is able to predict a potential perceived dissimilarity of the fractalization for a new texture instance. They find that deriving the average co-occurrence error between the local gray-level co-occurrence statistics of the original and the 'fractalized' version of a texture strongly correlates with the distortion perceived with their participants, and thus suggest it could be used to predict such perceived distortion.

Related to the issue of 'fractalized' NPR textures is the general problem of 2D geometric texture synthesis and the degree of perceived visual similarity between two such synthesized textures. AlMeraj et al. [2] conducted two psychophysical experiments to analyze this question, motivated by the fact that geometric texture synthesis as a sub-domain of NPR is itself based on human perception. In their first experiment, they asked participants to interactively generate a larger dot texture based on a small sample, and then asked the participants both quantitative and qualitative questions to understand their strategies. To analyze the answers to the qualitative questions, the authors used an open coding approach, resulting in the ability to compare responses between participants. From this comprehensive analysis AlMeraj et al. extracted a number of causal attributes that motivated participants' generation styles (dominant visual properties perceived, local themes identifies, and recognition of large spatial structures), a number of strategies for generating geometric arrangements (tiling, structured approach, and random approach), and a number of criteria for evaluating similarity (symmetry, apparent shape, repetition, conformity to apparent rules, and accuracy of copied samples).

To understand the quality of the textures participants had synthesized, AlMeraj et al. conducted a second mixed-method study with a new group of participants to avoid bias. In this study participants were again provided with a sample texture, but this time were shown five synthesized textures. These synthesized textures were derived from the previous experiments (180 textures) which were complemented with 36 computer-generated textures, either using a random or a perfect tiling approach. Participants then had to rank the five shown textures according to their similarity to the shown sample, similar to the approach by Bénard et al. [3]. In addition to extracting the list of criteria used by participants, again using a qualitative approach, AlMeraj et al. [2] analyzed the similarities quantitatively, in particular taking the generation strategies (tiling, structured, random) of the first experiment into account. The results show that the textures generated by people using a tiling approach were ranked as "most similar" to the sample textures, likely because participants were able to detect the repeated instances in the larger images. The authors identify an apparent hierarchy in the criteria used for rating similarity: first looking for complete samples, then the identification of themes (small dot arrangements) that are consistently distributed in the synthesized textures, and finally an overall comparison of texture to sample using global mathematical attributes. The overall results are interesting since typically researchers strive for a more structured approach to computer-driven texture synthesis, and also the structured techniques used by participants were also rated higher in AlMeraj et al.'s first study.

15.3.2 Evaluation of Illustrative Visualizations

One specific application area of NPR research is the recently emerged domain of illustrative visualization [45]. In this sub-domain of the general field of visualization it is essential to understand how people see and perceive visuals, thus the evaluation of illustrative visualization plays a particularly important role.

For example, while the previous section examined the evaluation of the perception of NPR textures in general, researchers also have specifically looked at the evaluation of NPR textures in a visualization context. The first approach discussed in this section is closely related to those discussed in Sect. 15.3.1. This evaluation is particularly interesting because it employs an evaluation strategy otherwise typically used in an artistic context: critique sessions. Jackson et al. [31] and Acevedo et al. [1] report on feedback from expert designers/illustration educators on a number of texture-based visualization techniques to represent 2D vector fields and their properties. The critique by experts as an evaluation strategy promises to provide rich qualitative feedback which cannot only suggest which type of technique is better suited for a given purpose but also, in particular, why this is the case. Acevedo et al. [1] also compared the critique-based results by Jackson et al. [31] to those of a previous controlled experiment [38]. They found in their pilot study that the results exhibited the same patterns for both studies, but that the designer critique generally took less time. Both Laidlaw [37] and Keefe et al. [33] describe this critique-based evaluation strategy in the larger context of art-science collaboration, outlining how the evaluation fits into the general visualization design workflow.

In general, NPR and illustrative visualization are both driven by inspiration from artistic practice, leading to a number of artistic visualization techniques. For example, Healey et al. [23, 24] describe a texture-based visualization technique for 2D vector and scalar data that employ techniques from painterly stroke-based rendering [25]. Because the simple inspiration is not sufficient for validating the usefulness of such a technique, they validated their approach using a series of psychophysical experiments. First, they examined whether, in general, people are able to rapidly and accurately identify a group of target brush strokes within a larger stroke set by color or orientation. They found that participants could identify stroke groups better by color than by orientation and that random colors interfere with the identification of orientations. They also concluded that their results indicate that the use of painterly strokes for visualization seems feasible, and thus continued to create one.

Based on these results and also inspired by positive expert feedback, Healey et al. [24] thus conducted a second experiment, this time with their newly created actual 2D visualization of weather data. They examined whether the illustrative visualization could support practical analysis tasks on real-world data and compared their technique to existing (traditional) visualizations. Participants in this controlled experiment were asked to identify which visualization would make it easiest from them to distinguish data aspects such as temperature, precipitation, wind speed, and wind direction; to identify regions in the visualizations with certain combinations of high/low values of the scalar properties, as well as to identify regions with rapid change of temperature. The results of this experiment showed that Healey et al.'s illustrative visualization was as good as or better than the traditional weather visualization for all the tested cases, thus specifically for identifying multi-dimensional patterns in the data (which the study was designed to evaluate).

The techniques examined in Sects. 15.3.1 and 15.3.2 thus far aim primarily at two-dimensional NPR and visualization techniques. The domain of scientific visualization, however, primarily examines spatial datasets that are defined in three dimensions, and illustrative visualization approaches have also been developed for this purpose. Consequently, researchers are interested in validating such techniques, for example in the context of medical visualization. Tietjen et al. [53], for instance, looked at the domain of surgery planning and education and, specifically, at the different visualization of detail and context of the human anatomy. Their hybrid visualization technique combined traditional shading techniques (usually for focus objects) with volumetric rendering and NPR line rendering (for both near-focus and context objects), and the authors were interested in how the use of different visualization techniques for depicting, in particular, context objects would support tasks both for medical practitioners and for laypeople.

To examine these questions, the authors employed a questionnaire-based evaluation methodology and distributed the questionnaires to surgeons and participants without a medical education. Each page of the questionnaire showed two different visualizations, one of which needed to be chosen based on personal preference, questions with respect to the usefulness of the visualization for specific tasks were asked (using Likert-scale ratings), and the visualization particularly suited for surgery education needed to be identified. Using this approach, Tietjen et al. compared one specific visualization (their reference) to all other variants they tested, and also conducted comparisons of some other combinations for cross-validation. Based on this approach, the authors conclude that their technique was considered to be appropriate by most of the participating surgeons, and that these surgeons tend to prefer little context information as long as context is present. Laypeople favored images in which the context was shown with colored silhouettes or with silhouettes combined with additional surface shading.

15.3.3 Perception of NPR in the Context of VR/AR and Immersion

As we have seen in Sects. 15.3.1 and 15.3.2, human perception plays an important role in the evaluation of NPR results. It is particularly important to understand how perception affects viewers if we use NPR in contexts that augment or completely replace the 'normal' reality as we experience it every day—i.e., in fields like virtual and augmented reality (VR and AR). While to date there have not been that many approaches to apply NPR in such a context, there have already been some noteworthy evaluations of VR/AR NPR settings.

An early example was presented by Gooch and Willemsen [17] who tried to answer the question how the perception of space and distances in a VR context if the normal (photorealistic) environment was replaced by an NPR one. Specifically, they created a model of their physical lab environment to be able to create a black-and-white NPR version of it using silhouettes and feature lines (creases). With the help of a tracked head-mounted display (HMD) setup they were then able to present participants with the NPR environment as well as with the real world (no HMD). In Gooch and Willemsen's controlled experiment (within-participants design), the participants were shown a target shape a certain distance away from their position (in either the NPR or real-world condition), were able to look around (turn the head but not move it), and then were asked to walk blind-folded up to the point where they had perceived the object—the distance of which was recorded.

The quantitative analysis of the recorded walked distances showed that, in the NPR condition, participants walked 66 % of the distance to the object, while in the real world they would walk 97 % of the distance on average. While the difference of walked distances in the NPR condition from the real world seems to be an indication for the inappropriateness of using NPR within VR, the authors argue that the observed over-estimation of NPR-VR corresponds well to how people perceive and interact in 'normal/traditional' (i.e., photorealistic) VR environments, thus conclude that NPR-based VR environments are a viable alternative to photorealistic ones.

In fact, when using immersive environments it is not always necessary to decide for either a physical or a virtual world, but it is also possible to combine both in an augmented reality. Such setups add virtual objects to otherwise realistic scenes which are captured through a camera system or see-through glasses. The problem with such setups is that, due to an incomplete knowledge of all environmental influences and the ability to render in a completely photorealistic way, the real and the virtual objects look quite different. To address this discrepancy, people have proposed to use stylized augmented reality which applies stylization to both the real and the virtual parts of the image and thus masks the differences between them. To understand the effectiveness of this approach, Fischer et al. [12] conducted a psychophysical study in which participants were asked to determine if an object shown in a stylized augmented reality setting would be real or virtual.

Based on still images and short video clips (between-participants factor), 18 participants were asked to answer this question for 30 objects (half of which were virtual, the other half real). The results showed that participants were able to correctly determine the type of object in 69 % of the cases in the stylized AR style as opposed to 94 % in a traditional AR style on average, with the results being consistent between the two groups with still images and video clips. Interestingly, it was more difficult to correctly identify physical objects than virtual objects, but this result was not statistically significant. The authors speculate that these results are due to the lack of compelling 3D models which led to a number of rendering errors which made it easier for participants to tell that virtual objects were, in fact, virtual. However, the authors also conclude that their experiment showed stylized AR to be successful in solving the discrepancy problem as it was more difficult to tell objects apart in the stylized condition.

In dynamic 3D environments—such as the mentioned VR/AR settings—it is often also important to correctly and reliably perceive the shape of objects, which may be assisted by NPR means. In fact, one of the defining and seminal NPR publications [46] argues that adding NPR elements (silhouettes and feature lines) to conventionally rendered objects makes them more comprehensible. To examine if such a correlation really exists, Winnemöller et al. [55] present an experimental framework and psychophysical study that examines the usefulness of a number of shape cues in dynamic environments. Specifically, they analyze how shading, contours, texture, and a mix of shading with contours (which Saito and Takahashi [46] suggest makes shapes comprehensible) affect the recognition of rigidly moving objects.

In the actual experiment, the 21 participants were asked to identify those shapes that moved with other shapes across a touch-sensitive display, using a background similar to the moving foreground objects, that shared a certain shape characteristic. The object depictions and backgrounds were chosen such that they only used contours, only used shading, only used one of two textures, or used a combination of shading and textures. The analysis of the task accuracy showed that the use of only shading lead to the best correct recognition rates, before outlines and textures. Interestingly, the combination of shading with outlines did not perform better than just shading, but worse than it (while still being more accurate than just outlines). While it seems to contradict intuition [46] and studies mentioned earlier [10, 21, 22], Winnemöller et al. attribute this effect to participants' feeling that the mixed condition provided too much and, thus, confusing information since also the background shapes were rendered with additional outlines—unlike in the earlier techniques [46] and evaluations [10, 21, 22]. Nevertheless, this example illustrates well that one should not simply base NPR and illustrative rendering design decisions on assumptions but should always validate these assumptions before employing a new technique in a practical application.

15.4 Comparing Hand-Made Images with Computer-Generated Non-photorealistic Rendering

The final major type of evaluation of NPR techniques to be addressed in this discussion is the question of how NPR imagery compares to human-made images or drawings. This question may initially seem quite straightforward; however, it is not as easy to answer as one may think because it is not clear from the question's general phrasing what we mean by "to compare to." While the NPR Turing test [19, 47]—whether a person is able to distinguish a hand-made from a computer-generated image—that was mentioned in the introduction may be one form of the question, there are also several other possible ways to compare the different types of images.

For example, we may be interested in the question of how drawing patterns differ between hand-made examples and computer-generated styles. This is a question about differences that affect the perceived aesthetics of an image as pointed out by Maciejewski et al. [39] specifically for the area of stipple rendering (see Chap. 3). Maciejewski et al. discuss this difference of aesthetics, overall, in the context of intentional dot placement with several high-level considerations (also discussed in detail by Martín et al. [42]) on the side of hand-drawn stippling—as opposed to a mechanistic stipple placement with many more stipple points, according to simple illumination models and simple stipple shapes, and without the mentioned high-level considerations on the side of the computer-generated stippling.

Maciejewski et al. [40] then proceed to evaluate such differences with respect to the distribution of the stipple dots using statistical methods, specifically by examining the gray-scale textures that characterize the two different styles. For this purpose they employ the gray-level co-occurrence matrix (GLCM) as a tool which measures the frequency in which certain gray levels occur in a given spatial relationship. Based on this matrix they then derive three properties: contrast, energy, and correlation which they use to compare textures from hand-drawn and computer-generated stippling. This analysis unveils a number of differences that Maciejewski et al. initially only hypothesized about: for example, the regular artifacts of stippling based on centroidal Voronoi diagrams (which cause undesired correlation across the textures) as well as similarity of hand-drawn stippling to natural textures. The results also show that, while certain computer stippling techniques that incorporate randomness also exhibit strong correlations with hand-drawn stippling, they still can be easily distinguished from hand drawings due to other regularities. Interestingly, Martín et al. [43] later employed the same statistical evaluation technique to analyze a resolution-dependent halftoning-based stippling with randomness applied to stipple locations but with example-based stipple dots (see Chap. 3, also for example images). The analysis showed that Martín et al. were able to create computer-generated stipple textures whose statistical properties were virtually identical to those of hand-drawn stippling. This suggests that using an example-based approach for NPR as opposed to a purely algorithmic technique may be better able to create results that are less distinguishable from their hand-drawn counterparts.

This observation, however, may not apply to all NPR techniques since some of the primitives used in traditional artistic depiction heavily rely on mathematical principles. One of the best examples for such techniques is the creation of sparse line drawings—lines that consist of silhouettes/contours [29] and feature lines. One question that comes up in this context is "where do people draw lines" [6, 7, 9] and how are these lines related to the zoo of lines typically employed in NPR?; another question is "how well do [such] line drawings depict shape" [6, 8].

To answer the first question, Cole et al. [6, 7, 9] conducted a study to compare the line drawings created by artists to depict 3D shapes with NPR-based computer-generated line renderings. For this purpose they conceived an ingenious study setup to satisfy two apparently conflicting constraints: they wanted to (1) allow their participants full freedom in creating line drawings, while (2) at the same time they needed to be able to precisely compare lines created by the artists with lines rendered by NPR algorithms. Cole et al. resolved this conflict by first allowing their participants to draw the 3D shapes freely based on a shaded depiction of the 3D shape, and then in a second step asked them to copy only the drawn lines onto a faint copy of the shaded depiction. This approach resulted in hand-made line drawings that could be compared to computer-generated ones on a pixel basis with a high level of accuracy.

Using this setup, Cole et al. collected input from 29 participating artists or art students, each of whom drew up to twelve 3D shapes, resulting in 208 line drawings in total. To analyze the data, the authors compared the hand-dawn lines both with each other as well as with those lines created by a number of established NPR line techniques including silhouettes/occluding contours, suggestive contours, apparent ridges, image intensity edges, and geometric ridges and valleys.

The analysis showed that artists drew their lines very close to other artists' lines, 75 % of the lines being within 1 mm of lines from all other artists. Silhouettes/occluding contours account for most of these similarities, comprising 57 % of all lines that were drawn. Other categories of lines from computer graphics/NPR that explain lines the participants draw are large gradients in image intensity as well as object-space feature lines. In fact, all object-space NPR line definitions together account for 81 % of the lines drawn by the participants, while each of the category explains some lines that the others do not explain. Overall, the output of all considered line definitions only accounts for 86 % of the hand-drawn lines. Cole et al. speculate that the rest could be explained by looking at other local properties, combinations of the existing line definitions, as well as by some higher-level decisions that have to do with what the artists want to communicate or what they think is implied.

Of course, the difference between hand-drawn and computer-generated sparse line drawings is not only interesting from an aesthetic standpoint but also affects how the respective images can be employed for specific purposes. It is particularly important to understand whether it makes a difference to people to use hand-drawn as opposed to computer-generated illustrations of shapes if the people need to correctly perceive, understand, and interpret the 3D shape of the depicted objects. Therefore, Cole et al. [6, 8] conducted a follow-up study based on the data they acquired in their first study to examine the question of shape depiction and perception. For this purpose they employed the established gauge figure protocol to ask people to estimate the perceived orientation of a surface at many points, based on both hand-drawn and computer-generated sparse line drawings (as well as shaded images for comparison). Due to the first experiment's [6, 7, 9] setup they also had access to the ground truth in form of the 3D shapes that people illustrated or that were used in generating the NPR images.

Their results show that, for about half of the 3D models they used in the study, the line drawings that performed best were almost as good as the shaded images the authors used for comparison. For other models (e.g., those with organic, smooth, or blobby shapes) viewers had not only more problems understanding the shaded image but also were unable to correctly interpret the line drawings. The study also showed that computer-generated line drawings based on differential properties have the potential to be as effective as hand drawings: for all but one shape there was a computer-generated line drawing that caused lower errors in shape perception than the drawings created by an artists. However, the specific type of lines to be used for a good depiction depends on the specific 3D shape as it was not always the same line type that was responsible for the better result.

The question of which specific primitive to use to depict a given shape not only applies to line renderings of 3D shapes but even more so to pixel art, a unique form of expression arising from early computer depiction [14, 28]. Recently, the question of how to generate such pixel representations from images or vector graphics was examined and evaluated [14, 28]. For example, Inglis and Kaplan [28] create pixel art from vector line drawings and evaluated these by comparing hand-created images with their automatic technique. To achieve this comparison, they first asked their participants to create pixel images for given vector input using a Web tool, and in a second stage asked them to compare these images with each other as well as with synthetically generated ones. Specifically, Inglis and Kaplan asked their participants to compare the images with respect to their visual appeal and with respect to their fidelity. The results showed that the Pixelator technique conceived by

Inglis and Kaplan outperformed other computer-generated techniques. The results also showed that, interestingly, people liked Pixelator images better than all groups of human-created images. However, the authors note that this does not mean that Pixelator images outperformed all human-created examples, but instead that their group classification is not a good indicator for how people judge the results. Another interesting result was that images created by people with lots of experience and a high artistic level were not rated very well, likely due to a lot of artistic 'interpretation' rather than a faithful depiction as examined by the authors. Here, an evaluation approach that asks for aesthetic judgment [14] may yield different results.

While studies like the ones discussed in this section so far are able to shed light on quantitatively measurable properties of NPR imagery or the suitability of an NPR algorithm, they cannot provide answers to questions about what happens when people look at such images. For example, how do people understand and assess NPR illustrations in general, what do they think about both hand-drawn and computer-generated images, and does a potential difference mean that they would prefer one over the other? Such questions are not easily answered with the more common quantitative evaluation techniques but require a more qualitative approach.

To examine such questions in the context of hand-drawn and computer-generated pen-and-ink illustrations, Isenberg et al. [30] conduced a qualitative, observational study. Specifically, they used an ethnographic approach to avoid biasing people by asking questions in a certain way since any question inherently biases the person asked. The study methodology they chose is an unconstrained pile sorting task which asks participants to 'sort' the objects they are given into piles, the specific number and size of the piles being determined by the participant. The objects to be sorted in this case were computer-generated and hand-drawn illustrations of three different objects, each printed on a Letter-sized page. They also had three different types of participants: people with illustration/drawing experiences, NPR researchers, and illustration end users (general university students). Each participant was presented with the pile of illustrations with the images in a random order, and then was asked to form the piles. After that part was completed, the participant was asked to explain what characterized each of the piles in order to understand the reasons for grouping images, and only after this were asked a number of questions about preference, potential use context, and also whether some images/piles looked particularly hand-drawn or computer-generated.

The analysis of the results showed that the different types of participants grouped the images in similar ways and that people generally did group by illustration style and amount of detail. More interestingly, none of the participants constructed piles of the images by whether they thought that an image looked particularly hand-drawn or computer-generated. However, participants were generally able to tell one type from the other with only a few (but consistent) exceptions. Nevertheless, this clear difference did not mean that the participants would like one type better than the other; instead participants liked them for different reasons. For example, participants liked the clarity, precision, three-dimensionality, detail, and—ironically—the realism of the NPR images, while they similarly appreciated the artistic appearance and character of the hand-drawn illustrations. Based on these and other insights from the rich qualitative feedback provided by the participants due to the chosen study methodology, Isenberg et al. provide a number of recommendations and guidelines for future NPR research including to know one's goal, to know one's audience, to explore material depiction and non-realistic models, to avoid patterns and regularities, and to pay close attention to marks and tools.

15.5 Conclusion

The various evaluations of NPR styles and techniques that were introduced in this chapter demonstrate that there are numerous questions that one may want to answer about the produced images. One of the most fundamental ones, however, is the question of the goal of a technique and whether this goal is achieved [30]. One of the obvious goals one may potentially want to strive for is to become indistinguishable from hand-made drawings, paintings, or illustrations. We have seen, however, that the NPR Turing test as proposed by Salesin in 2002 [19, 47] has, to date, not successfully been passed, as demonstrated, for instance, by observations by Isenberg et al. [30] or by texture statistics by Maciejewski et al. [40]. Even cases where we as NPR researchers come close (the very few of the NPR images examined by Isenberg et al. [30] that were often thought to be hand-drawn, the stippling distributions examined statistically by Martín et al. [43], or the abstract painterly style of Zhao and Zhu [56]) we can still observe obvious differences, for example on the lack of perceived 'skillfulness' of drawings or the lack of support of higher-level painting/drawing/stippling strategies.

Therefore, the goal of being indistinguishable from artwork is not necessarily the most interesting one for NPR as a field, and thus is also not the most relevant driving force for employing evaluation and validation as part of the research. Instead, the goal of providing general motivations for stylistic rendering as identified in Sect. 15.2, the need for support of specific goals as discussed in Sect. 15.3, or the general question of aesthetic judgments (e.g., in Gerstner et al.'s [14] work) may serve as alternative reasons for evaluating and validating NPR algorithms. Nevertheless, comparing one's results to their hand-made counterparts as reviewed in Sect. 15.4 can also be instructive, but should not only be reduced to an NPR Turing test. In fact, in Chap. 16 of this book Hall and Lehmann look at NPR in the context of traditional artistic depiction and ask the question of how to assess the generated visuals from the perspective of art history. In taking this view, they nicely make the point that an NPR Turing test does not provide any insight on the aesthetic value of the NPR visuals, but that the produced images instead have to be appreciated by people—just like traditional artworks.

Appendix: Data Resources

Some of the datasets used/created in the mentioned studies are available online for further analysis and future studies. For example, the following datasets are available online at the moment of writing (of course, the URLs are always subject to change):

- sparse line drawing comparison by Cole et al. [6, 7, 9];
  → captured registered drawings, models, etc.: http://gfx.cs.princeton.edu/proj/ld3d/
- shape perception based on sparse line drawings by Cole et al. [6, 8];
  → gauge settings: http://gfx.cs.princeton.edu/proj/ld3d/
- evaluation of the pixelization of line art by Inglis and Kaplan [28];
  → user study data: http://sites.google.com/site/tiffanycinglis/generating-pixel-art/generating-pixel-art—outlining
- ethnographic study of illustrations by Isenberg et al. [30];
  → images: http://www.cs.rug.nl/~isenberg/VideosAndDemos/Isenberg2006NPR
- shape perception in dynamic 3D environments by Winnemöller et al. [55];
  → 3D models: http://www.cs.northwestern.edu/~holger/Research/projects.htm

References

1. Acevedo, D., Laidlaw, D., Drury, F.: Using visual design expertise to characterize the effectiveness of 2D scientific visualization methods. In: Proceedings Compendium of IEEE InfoVis and Visualization 2005, pp. 111–112 (2005). doi:10.1109/VIS.2005.109
2. AlMeraj, Z., Kaplan, C.S., Asente, P., Lank, E.: Towards ground truth in geometric textures. In: Proc. NPAR, pp. 17–26. ACM, New York (2011). doi:10.1145/2024676.2024679
3. Bénard, P., Thollot, J., Sillion, F.: Quality assessment of fractalized NPR textures: a perceptual objective metric. In: Proc. APGV, pp. 117–120. ACM, New York (2009). doi:10.1145/1620993.1621016
4. Carpendale, S.: Evaluating information visualizations. In: Information Visualization: Human-Centered Issues and Perspectives. LNCS, vol. 4950, pp. 19–45. Springer, Berlin (2008). doi:10.1007/978-3-540-70956-5_2
5. Cohen, J.: The Earth is round ($p < 0.05$). Am. Psychol. **49**(12), 997–1003 (1994). doi:10.1037/0003-066X.49.12.997
6. Cole, F.: Line drawings of 3D models. Ph.D. thesis, Princeton University (2009)
7. Cole, F., Golovinskiy, A., Limpaecher, A., Barros, H.S., Finkelstein, A., Funkhouser, T., Rusinkiewic, S.: Where do people draw lines? ACM Trans. Graph. **27**(3), 88 (2008). doi:10.1145/1360612.1360687
8. Cole, F., Sanik, K., DeCarlo, D., Finkelstein, A., Funkhouser, T., Rusinkiewicz, S., Singh, M.: How well do line drawings depict shape? ACM Trans. Graph. **28**(3), 28 (2009). doi:10.1145/1531326.1531334
9. Cole, F., Golovinskiy, A., Limpaecher, A., Barros, H.S., Finkelstein, A., Funkhouser, T., Rusinkiewicz, S.: Where do people draw lines? Commun. ACM **55**(1), 107–115 (2012). doi:10.1145/2063176.2063202
10. Duke, D.J., Barnard, P.J., Halper, N., Mellin, M.: Rendering and affect. Comput. Graph. Forum **22**(3), 359–368 (2003). doi:10.1111/1467-8659.00683
11. Field, A., Hole, G.: How to Design and Report Experiments. Sage, London (2003)
12. Fischer, J., Cunningham, D., Bartz, D., Wallraven, C., Bülthoff, H., Straßer, W.: Measuring the discernability of virtual objects in conventional and stylized augmented reality.

In: Proc. EGVE, pp. 53–61. Eurographics Association, Goslar (2006). doi:10.2312/EGVE/EGVE06/053-061
13. Gatzidis, C., Papakonstantinou, S., Brujic-Okretic, V., Baker, S.: Recent advances in the user evaluation methods and studies of non-photorealistic visualisation and rendering techniques. In: Proc. IV, pp. 475–480. IEEE Comput. Soc., Los Alamitos (2008). doi:10.1109/IV.2008.75
14. Gerstner, T., DeCarlo, D., Alexa, M., Finkelstein, A., Gingold, Y., Nealen, A.: Pixelated image abstraction. In: Proc. NPAR, pp. 29–36. Eurographics Association, Goslar (2012). doi:10.2312/PE/NPAR/NPAR12/029-036
15. Girshick, A., Interrante, V., Haker, S., Lemoine, T.: Line direction matters: an argument for the use of principal directions in 3D line drawings. In: Proc. NPAR, pp. 43–52. ACM, New York (2000). doi:10.1145/340916.340922
16. Gooch, B.: Human facial illustrations: creation and evaluation using behavioral studies and functional magnetic resonance imaging. Ph.D. thesis, University of Utah, USA (2003)
17. Gooch, A.A., Willemsen, P.: Evaluating space perception in NPR immersive environments. In: Proc. NPAR, pp. 105–110. ACM, New York (2002). doi:10.1145/508530.508549
18. Gooch, B., Reinhard, E., Gooch, A.A.: Human facial illustrations: creation and psychophysical evaluation. ACM Trans. Graph. 23(1), 27–44 (2004). doi:10.1145/966131.966133
19. Gooch, A.A., Long, J., Ji, L., Estey, A., Gooch, B.S.: Viewing progress in non-photorealistic rendering through Heinlein's lens. In: Proc. NPAR, pp. 165–171. ACM, New York (2010). doi:10.1145/1809939.1809959
20. Greenberg, S., Buxton, B.: Usability evaluation considered harmful (some of the time). In: Proc. CHI, pp. 111–120. ACM, New York (2008). doi:10.1145/1357054.1357074
21. Halper, N., Mellin, M., Herrmann, C.S., Linneweber, V., Strothotte, T.: Psychology and non-photorealistic rendering: the beginning of a beautiful relationship. In: Proc. Mensch & Computer, pp. 277–286. Teubner, Stuttgart (2003)
22. Halper, N., Mellin, M., Herrmann, C.S., Linneweber, V., Strothotte, T.: Towards an understanding of the psychology of non-photorealistic rendering. In: Proc. Workshop Computational Visualistics, Media Informatics and Virtual Communities, pp. 67–78. Deutscher Universitäts, Wiesbaden (2003)
23. Healey, C.G., Enns, J.T.: Perception and painting: a search for effective, engaging visualizations. IEEE Comput. Graph. Appl. 22(2), 10–15 (2002). doi:10.1109/38.988741
24. Healey, C.G., Tateosian, L., Enns, J.T., Remple, M.: Perceptually-based brush strokes for nonphotorealistic visualization. ACM Trans. Graph. 23(1), 64–96 (2004). doi:10.1145/966131.966135
25. Hertzmann, A.: A survey of stroke-based rendering. IEEE Comput. Graph. Appl. 23(4), 70–81 (2003). doi:10.1109/MCG.2003.1210867
26. Hertzmann, A.: Non-photorealistic rendering and the science of art. In: Proc. NPAR, pp. 147–157. ACM, New York (2010). doi:10.1145/1809939.1809957
27. Igarashi, T., Matsuoka, S., Tanaka, H.T.: A sketching interface for 3D freeform design. In: Proc. SIGGRAPH, pp. 409–416. ACM, New York (1999). doi:10.1145/311535.311602
28. Inglis, T.C., Kaplany, C.S.: Pixelating vector line art. In: Proc. NPAR, pp. 21–28. Eurographics Association, Goslar (2012). doi:10.2312/PE/NPAR/NPAR12/021-028
29. Isenberg, T., Freudenberg, B., Halper, N., Schlechtweg, S., Strothotte, T.: A developer's guide to silhouette algorithms for polygonal models. IEEE Comput. Graph. Appl. 23(4), 28–37 (2003). doi:10.1109/MCG.2003.1210862
30. Isenberg, T., Neumann, P., Carpendale, S., Sousa, M.C., Jorge, J.A.: Non-photorealistic rendering in context: an observational study. In: Proc. NPAR, pp. 115–126. ACM, New York (2006). doi:10.1145/1124728.1124747
31. Jackson, C.D., Acevedo, D., Laidlaw, D.H., Drury, F., Vote, E., Keefe, D.: Designer-critiqued comparison of 2D vector visualization methods: a pilot study. In: ACM SIGGRAPH Sketches & Applications. ACM, New York (2003). doi:10.1145/965400.965505
32. Kaptein, M., Robertson, J.: Rethinking statistical analysis methods for CHI. In: Proc. CHI, pp. 1105–1114. ACM, New York (2012). doi:10.1145/2207676.2208557

33. Keefe, D.F., Karelitz, D.B., Vote, E.L., Laidlaw, D.H.: Artistic collaboration in designing VR visualizations. IEEE Comput. Graph. Appl. **25**(2), 18–23 (2005). doi:10.1109/MCG.2005.34
34. Kerlinger, F.N., Lee, H.B.: Foundations of Behavioral Research, 4th edn. Wadsworth Publishing/Thomson Learning, London (2000)
35. Kim, S., Hagh-Shenas, H., Interrante, V.: Conveying shape with texture: an experimental investigation of the impact of texture type on shape categorization judgments. In: Proc. InfoVis, pp. 163–170. IEEE Comput. Soc., Los Alamitos (2003). doi:10.1109/INFVIS.2003.1249022
36. Kim, S., Hagh-Shenas, H., Interrante, V.: Conveying shape with texture: experimental investigation of texture's effects on shape categorization judgments. IEEE Trans. Vis. Comput. Graph. **10**(4), 471–483 (2004). doi:10.1109/TVCG.2004.5
37. Laidlaw, D.H.: Loose, artistic "textures" for visualization. IEEE Comput. Graph. Appl. **21**(2), 6–9 (2001). doi:10.1109/38.909009
38. Laidlaw, D., Kirby, R., Jackson, C., Davidson, J., Miller, T., da Silva, M., Warren, W., Tarr, M.: Comparing 2D vector field visualization methods: a user study. IEEE Trans. Vis. Comput. Graph. **11**(1), 59–70 (2005). doi:10.1109/TVCG.2005.4
39. Maciejewski, R., Isenberg, T., Andrews, W.M., Ebert, D.S., Sousa, M.C.: Aesthetics of hand-drawn vs. computer-generated stippling. In: Proc. CAe, pp. 53–56. Eurographics Association, Goslar (2007). doi:10.2312/COMPAESTH/COMPAESTH07/053-056
40. Maciejewski, R., Isenberg, T., Andrews, W.M., Ebert, D.S., Sousa, M.C., Chen, W.: Measuring stipple aesthetics in hand-drawn and computer-generated images. IEEE Comput. Graph. Appl. **28**(2), 62–74 (2008). doi:10.1109/MCG.2008.35
41. Mandryk, R.L., Mould, D., Li, H.: Evaluation of emotional response to non-photorealistic images. In: Proc. NPAR, pp. 7–16. ACM, New York (2011). doi:10.1145/2024676.2024678
42. Martín, D., Arroyo, G., Luzón, M.V., Isenberg, T.: Example-based stippling using a scale-dependent grayscale process. In: Proc. NPAR, pp. 51–61. ACM, New York (2010). doi:10.1145/1809939.1809946
43. Martín, D., Arroyo, G., Luzón, M.V., Isenberg, T.: Scale-dependent and example-based stippling. Comput. Graph. **35**(1), 160–174 (2011). doi:10.1016/j.cag.2010.11.006
44. Mould, D., Mandryk, R.L., Li, H.: Emotional response and visual attention to non-photorealistic images. Comput. Graph. **36**(5), 658–672 (2012). doi:10.1016/j.cag.2012.03.039
45. Rautek, P., Bruckner, S., Gröller, E., Viola, I.: Illustrative visualization: new technology or useless tautology? Comput. Graph. **42**(3), 4:1–4:8 (2008). doi:10.1145/1408626.1408633
46. Saito, T., Takahashi, T.: Comprehensible rendering of 3-D shapes. Comput. Graph. **24**(3), 197–206 (1990). doi:10.1145/97880.97901
47. Salesin, D.H.: Non-photorealistic animation & rendering: 7 grand challenges. Keynote talk at NPAR (2002)
48. Santella, A., DeCarlo, D.: Visual interest and NPR: an evaluation and manifesto. In: Proc. NPAR, pp. 71–78. ACM, New York (2004). doi:10.1145/987657.987669
49. Schmidt, R., Isenberg, T., Jepp, P., Singh, K., Wyvill, B.: Sketching, scaffolding, and inking: a visual history for interactive 3D modeling. In: Proc. NPAR, pp. 23–32. ACM, New York (2007). doi:10.1145/1274871.1274875
50. Schumann, J., Strothotte, T., Raab, A., Laser, S.: Assessing the effect of non-photorealistic rendered images in CAD. In: Proc. CHI, pp. 35–42. ACM, New York (1996). doi:10.1145/238386.238398
51. Seifi, H., DiPaola, S., Enns, J.: Exploring the effect of color palette in painterly rendered character sequences. In: Proc. CAe, pp. 89–97. Eurographics Association, Goslar (2012). doi:10.2312/COMPAESTH/COMPAESTH12/089-097
52. Strothotte, T., Preim, B., Raab, A., Schumann, J., Forsey, D.R.: How to render frames and influence people. Comput. Graph. Forum **13**(3), 455–466 (1994). doi:10.1111/1467-8659.1330455
53. Tietjen, C., Isenberg, T., Preim, B.: Combining silhouettes, shading, and volume rendering for surgery education and planning. In: Proc. EuroVis, pp. 303–310. Eurographics Association, Goslar (2005). doi:10.2312/VisSym/EuroVis05/303-310

54. Winnemöller, H., Olsen, S.C., Gooch, B.: Real-time video abstraction. ACM Trans. Graph. **25**(3), 1221–1226 (2006). doi:10.1145/1141911.1142018
55. Winnemöller, H., Feng, D., Gooch, B., Suzuki, S.: Using NPR to evaluate perceptual shape cues in dynamic environments. In: Proc. NPAR, pp. 85–92. ACM, New York (2007). doi:10.1145/1274871.1274885
56. Zhao, M., Zhu, S.C.: Sisley the abstract painter. In: Proc. NPAR, pp. 99–107. ACM, New York (2010). doi:10.1145/1809939.1809951

Chapter 16
Don't Measure—Appreciate! NPR Seen Through the Prism of Art History

Peter Hall and Ann-Sophie Lehmann

16.1 Introduction

The question of how to judge NPR images and video is often raised, both within and without the field. The argument from outside is that NPR papers cannot be properly assessed, because there is no objective measure of quality; some even imply that NPR is somehow of lesser value for it. We do not accept the argument and reject the implication. Indeed in this book Isenberg ably argues that NPR images not only can be assessed but should be assessed. Importantly, he points out that the purpose of the NPR image (e.g. scientific visualisation) should have an impact upon the method of assessment (see Chap. 15). We focus on that class of NPR images which have the primary purpose of "being art" and consider how to judge these images based on methods used in Art History.

The problem of assessing NPR is relevant across the whole field, but is most pertinent for NPR pieces (images and video) that have been produced automatically. After all, an artist using a computer to produce art should rightly compete with artists using traditional media. Therefore it is algorithms for automatic NPR we focus upon, but to obtain a more rounded and robust view we do include interactive NPR too.

One answer, a seemingly obvious answer, to the question of evaluating NPR is "use the Turing Test". There are many variants, but all of them ask whether a human has produced a piece or not. We argue that the Turing test is not suit-

---

P. Hall (✉)
Department of Computer Science, University of Bath, Bath, UK
e-mail: pmh@cs.bath.ac.uk

A.-S. Lehmann
Department of Media and Culture Studies, University of Utrecht, Utrecht, The Netherlands
e-mail: a.s.lehmann@uu.nl

able for us because its aim is to identify the maker, not to evaluate the output: we are not interested in assessing forgery. For similar reasons we argue against experiments that claim to measure NPR value in some objective way. There is no reliable objective measure, instead NPR, like all art must be *appreciated*. This means its value derives first from the rest of NPR, and second from the culture in which NPR as whole sits. It is hardly a surprise to find a Western researcher producing NPR that resembles the Western tradition, and an Eastern researcher producing NPR that resembles the Eastern tradition [44]. The algorithms each produces can be assessed on equal terms, but evaluating the output may be more problematic because each of us inherits a cultural bias that we may not be aware of.

Consider this: suppose alien life were to make contact with humans here on Earth. It is a fair bet that creatures advanced enough to reach us would have a highly developed culture. The question is: would we recognise it as art? We would know it is not made by humans, so the Turing test is clearly of no relevance. The general problem is one of learning to appreciate art, be it from another planet, from another era or continent, or—as in our case—as made by a computer.

Given that NPR is analogous to human produced art it is relevant to look to Art History to help us *appreciate* its value. The question of why an art work is good or not, and whether art can be judged in such terms at all, has usually been easy to answer in relation to individual art works, yet difficult to clarify when it comes to developing general objective criteria. To develop such criteria has nonetheless been an on-going enterprise in the history of art, ever since Giorgio Vasari founded the discipline of Art History in the sixteenth century and Georg Wilhelm Friedrich Hegel argued in the nineteenth century that art moves towards the expression of perfection [22]. Yet since Modernism contradicted dominant teleological models that advocated an aesthetic development towards a particular standard, Art Historians and Art Philosophers have eschewed attempts to define aesthetic value in an objective sense. That is, however, no barrier to a discourse which evaluates works of art as being great, mediocre, or poor, within the realm of a particular school, style or period [30].

This chapter continues by first arguing in more detail against tests and experiment as a way to solve the problem of evaluating NPR. Next we identify norms used when assessing NPR, in particular the internal norms that might be used by a typical reviewer of an NPR paper, and we also point to external cultural references that assist us when understanding the place of NPR as a whole in the history of art. In this way we identify both an internal scale by which individual contributions can be appreciated, and we begin to calibrate that scale against wider alternatives. We conclude that at least some knowledge of Art History is required to satisfactorily appreciate NPR.

Before continuing we wish to note that NPR is a very active field, and we have been able to cite only a small fraction of the work; there is a great deal of excellent work we have been unable to refer to in this chapter.

16.2 The Unsuitability of the Turing Test and the Impossibility of Absolute Aesthetic Measure

It is not uncommon to hear the Turing test advanced as a solution to the problem of judging the aesthetic value of NPR pictures, for example [6, 73, 82], and specifically in NPR [64]. In this section we argue against both the Turing test and alternatives.

Our argument for the ineligibility of the Turing test is this: the issue at hand is the *aesthetic value* of an image, not whether a human or computer made it. In other words we are not asking "is it made by a human or machine?" but "is it justifiably a good picture?" We want a framework for assessing NPR, not a measure of the deceptive potential of a machine. This is a simple argument, but it is worth exploring a little more.

Before continuing, we should narrow our understanding of *aesthetic value* and in particular differentiate it from *aesthetic quality*. Aesthetic quality has a wide meaning, but essentially possesses a subjective character. Without reference to any agreed definition we can recognise the individual aesthetic qualities in the joy of a summer's day, the exhilaration of winning at sports, and the warmth of a lover's touch. The degree of feeling in each case is the aesthetic measure or, as we call it the "aesthetic value", of that particular quality.

We are concerned with the visual aesthetics of pictures. In keeping with the range of aesthetic quality, there are many distinct flavours of visual aesthetic. Different cultures throughout history and across the world have produced, and continue to produce, distinctive forms of visual art. Indeed, cultures are in part delimited by their sense of aesthetic quality, as expressed in pictures. Therefore we must appreciate art, including NPR, relative to the cultural norms in which it was produced. It follows that there is more than one measure of *visual aesthetic value*. Nonetheless we can point to 'good', 'bad' and 'indifferent' examples within each cultural tradition, implying distinct but congruent scales. A corollary is the impossibility of assessing the aesthetic value of an NPR piece without reference to not just to other NPR pieces (so setting an internal scale) but also with reference to the wider culture in which the pieces sit (so calibrating the NPR scale against other scales).

We are not alone in rejecting the Turing Test as a valid aesthetic measure. Pease and Colton [61] give a detailed account of why the Turing test is not suitable for assessing creativity in general. Like us they point to differences in cultural heritage, but they make additional points too, including that the knowledge of the agent making a piece of art is important when assessing that piece—information that the Turing test deliberately excludes.

The question of measuring aesthetic value is much older than the Turing test it dates back to Antiquity and the notion of ideal proportions in humans, buildings, and nature, as well as the fascination with overarching principles guiding beauty, such as the number π. These discussions always concern issues of regularity and the ideal relation between the parts of a whole. For example, there is Pliny's famous account of the painter Zeuxis, who in looking for a model among the maidens of Croton for a painting of the most beautiful woman—Helena—ended up combining the most beautiful part of five maidens, as no individual human being could embody perfect beauty alone. This anecdote would shape art theory for centuries after.

In the early twentieth century, the philosopher Birkoff defined aesthetic measure as the ratio of 'orderliness' over 'complexity' [5]. Psychologists have used this to propose a specific measure for colour harmony [55], later tested experimentally [33], and the relation between beauty and truth in scientific experiment continues to be discussed [74]. Birkoff's measure has rarely been used in computational environments but did influence a study into the layout of graphical windows [57]. More recently, colour harmony has been studied [40] using a fuzzy logic framework. The measure has also influenced a study that concludes the aesthetic value of a scientific visualisation impacts upon understanding [26]. Whether both 'orderliness' and 'complexity' can be defined and measured in images and in video is an interesting open question. A particular issue arises because they do not seem to be independent and both relate to entropy: a system that is well ordered is not complex—it has low entropy; conversely a complex system is (almost by definition) is not well ordered and has high entropy.

We find the argument that aesthetic value has an explanation rooted in our evolutionary history to be appealing. If this is the case, then our sense of aesthetics should be embodied within image statistics. This argument has led to studies using photographs of natural scenes [9, 24], and of art [32]. Other studies show that natural scenes and paintings exhibit similar statistical properties, in particular the Fourier spectrum for photographs is about $(1/f)^{1.2}$ for natural scenes, which compares to $(1/f)^{1.4}$ for artwork [31, 75]. Sparseness of information has been found to be a useful cue [25] as is local contrast [27] which is consistent with an evolutionary explanation of beauty—although aesthetic value and beauty are not necessarily synonymous.

Whether such studies will lead to a measurable quantity that generalizes over all images is an open question, after all it has proven elusive for centuries. This is because quantifying the aesthetic value of an image is not possible based on the image alone. Rather, aesthetic value is intimately connected with the meaning of a picture. For example, knowing that Picasso's Guernica is a comment on the Spanish Civil war will affect the aesthetic value one ascribes to it.

With these ideas in mind we turn away from the Turing test, Birkoff's measure, and even image statistics as means of making progress when assessing the aesthetic value of an NPR picture. Similarly we are cautious of claims that eye-tracking data can be used to evaluate NPR images [65], not only because the attribute of aesthetic value lies beyond the picture itself but also because many pictures of high aesthetic value have no detail to focus upon (e.g., Rothko), while others are a myriad of detail (e.g., Pollock).

Instead we opt to assess the NPR in the same way that all art is assessed, which is to gauge it against the wider cultural background of existing art. In doing so we must take care, because human and computer aesthetic scales may not be coincident. Hence the problem of assessing NPR becomes similar to that faced by Art Historians when assessing any new movement in art. Our effort to establish assessment guidelines is not intended to revive the discussion as to whether computers can generate art, but instead points to the relation NPR undoubtedly has with forms of visual, artistic expression [79].

16.3 Understanding NPR as Art

Our central claim that NPR should be assessed and understood—that is, appreciated—as art. Within the wide range of cultural image production we can consider NPR as a particular sub-genre of computer generated imagery; a point of view justified by the fact that NPR has its own recognisable norms. Currently, these norms are latent—that is they have not been explicitly articulated, but they exist nonetheless, otherwise consistent refereeing would be impossible. It is not at all obvious that these norms are uniformly agreed in all of their parts, but there is sufficient accord for NPR to be a recognisable sub-genre (hence characterisable by some set of norms). These norms not only help us delimit the field, but also to set up an internal scale. By comparing these norms with others from other fields we move towards calibrating the NPR internal scale against its wider cultural background.

16.3.1 Internal Norms

NPR's most defining norm is certainly the "Non-" that divides NPR from photorealism, the initial driving force in the development of computer graphics. Although the name and the inherent opposition of different kinds of realism has often been criticised, and different names have been proposed [67], it seems to best describe the tenet of the genre as being to create convincing, effective and scientifically valid images in other ways than complete visual verisimilitude, thereby employing the whole wide range of mediated visual expressions that are not bound to the photographic mechanism/technology. It has rightfully been argued that photo-realistic rendering and NPR both are equal members of the family of computer depiction [20, 23]. Yet the distinction is kept intact as images remain to be judged against the two overarching principles of photographic documentation of the visual world on the one hand and its pictorial representation on the other (notwithstanding the on-going hybridization of these principles [52]).

While photorealist rendering only has one defining medium to be judged against, NPR has many. It is this many-headed hydra that makes NPR interesting, yet difficult to assess. Its initial indistinctness therefore affords the affinity to existing, pictorial styles and hints at the immense project that NPR is: while an (ideal) image-machine that can generate photorealistic renderings is imaginable, an image-machine that cannot only generate all known pictorial styles but also new pictorial styles, may be a utopian project [66].

Art History offers an appropriate model for the assessment of a multitude of different styles because it developed criteria based on resemblance, style as well as originality long before the invention of photography. Photography, in its early days perceived in art historical terms as the "brush of nature", only briefly and in part served as a foil to judge art against. Mainly, by claiming visual realism as 'good', it stimulated painting to develop a new diversity of styles moving beyond the mimetic representation of the visual world [28, 29]: without photography it is questionable whether Cubism would ever have been, for example. NPR therefore is essentially connected to art historical principles of aesthetic evaluation.

This connection predicts the second norm of NPR: the fact that many NPR authors claim relationship between their NPR and some or other school of art: the output their algorithms produce is said to be like that of some or other school or artist. Not all authors of NPR algorithms make such a claim explicit, but even amongst those who are silent on the issue a likeness to some school remains. This provides us with an obvious link to wider culture, and invites us to make direct comparison between particular pieces on NPR and pieces produced by humans—but only in the sense of calibrating the cultural progression of NPR. (The Turing Test is appropriate only if an author claims that their algorithm is capable of forgery, most claim a likeness.) However, we should be careful to note that the styles of artists within a school offer considerable variation, and even a single artist varies over their lifetime. These matters complicate comparison between NPR and schools, and lead us to treat claims of likeness (explicit or otherwise) with caution. Even so, linking NPR to existing art is inevitable, and this link is a norm of NPR.

Closely related to the third norm of emulating pictorial style is the norm of emulating media: is it not possible to emulate oil painting without emulating oil paint. Success in this norm is much easier to asses, at least if we adopt a narrow point of view that judges the visual similarity between a synthetic and real medium. Whether NPR will ever develop its own unique medium or media is an interesting open question.

A fourth norm is the elimination of direct human input to create artistic images. Arguably, it is this norm that leads some to argue for some objective measure of success. We recognise that not all NPR shares this aim, some NPR algorithms aim to make it easier for human artists to create art, sometimes by the provision of synthetic media, other times smart tools. In this paper we are thinking almost exclusively on fully automated NPR, because it is there that the relevant issues have their sharpest profile.

A fifth norm is that algorithms should be as simple and as elegant as possible, particularly for automated NPR. This norm is inherited from the wider contexts of Computer Science and Mathematics. Additionally, it corresponds to Art Historians using knowledge about how a piece was made when coming to understand the aesthetic value of a piece. In some sense, the art of NPR is designing simple and elegant algorithms that produce output of high aesthetic value.

The final norm is novelty. In the case of human produced art this means finding a new way to express or communicate. Within NPR, novelty usually has a more restricted definition: it is the algorithm that must be novel when compared to relevant literature. This restricted view provides some evidence that NPR is not sufficiently mature for novelty to be judged more widely. We do not see this as a criticism, but as a challenge.

A sixth norm is "prettiness", or a "wow factor", although this is rarely stated, at least within NPR. Wider Computer Graphics, on the other hand is not quite so bashful: the idea that output should "look good" (that is, look like a photograph) is acknowledged as the driving force. NPR seems to have inherited the "look good" criterion but modified it away from using the photograph as a foil to using schools and artists. We argue that this is a norm that should not be used for NPR, for at least two reasons: first it is culturally specific, e.g. animation in Eastern Europe is very different from animation in the USA, so that, unless researchers and reviewers are cognisant of their own cultural bias, the "look good" criterion is a distorting prism. Second, and most important, even with a given tradition, art does not have to look good to qualify as great art, as we illustrate in the next subsection.

We would not be surprised if reviewers of NPR submissions make use of the above norms when arriving at a judgement regarding acceptance of a paper, indeed we would be surprised if these norms were not used. To be clear, we are not claiming these are the only issues used by reviewers—clarity of writing is not included in the above list but is a factor when assessing papers, for example. However, the norms correspond to large degree to the taxonomy of NPR that is used when assessing the aesthetic value of the NPR output—it is, after all, impossible to ignore the algorithm. These norms are useful in assessing NPR internally, that is in relation to itself. However, as mentioned already, NPR should be assessed against a wider cultural context if is to be more roundly understood.

16.3.2 Cross Cultural Comparisons

Internal norms help us give an initial assessment of individual NPR pieces with respect to the rest of NPR. However, the progress in NPR as a whole can be assessed only by referencing it to art as a whole: if NPR is ever to claim artistic merit, then it must be judged in an equivalent way.

Art is much more than producing pretty objects. Of course it is true that art can be beautiful, but "prettiness" *per se* is no criteria at all by which to judge any work of art. We have already mentioned Guernica: the painting is impossible to appreciate without recognising that it represents the bombing of unarmed civilians—hardly a pretty subject—hardly a pretty painting. Many of Goya's paintings are difficult to look at, unpleasant even, explicitly depicting, as they do, the horrors of war. The work of Joseph Beuys, made from fat and fur, is all the more compelling when one realizes the artist survived in fat and fur after being shot down as a fighter pilot. The photographs of Dorothea Lange depicting social deprivation in America in the 1930s are not mantle-piece objects. Yet all of these artists produce work of the highest aesthetic value; art is not imprisoned by "looking good".

Art as practised by humans draws upon every conceivable experience, and appreciating any piece demands the viewer draws from that same well. Unfortunately the depth and breadth of the pooled, common experience is vastly wider and deeper than that of any particular individual, or even that of any particular culture. Thus, a viewer versed in the Western tradition may find it difficult to appreciate Oriental art, for example; and vice versa. It takes effort and education and some humility to overcome these barriers.

By comparison, NPR is very limited in its scope. Most of NPR sets out to imitate art that already exists. More exactly, NPR sets out to imitate the appearance of art that already exists. Even there it is limited because the appearance is nearly always limited to output on a screen; much of the power of a Van Gogh, for example comes from paint so thickly applied it holds the passion of its maker. That passion is completely drained out when the work is presented flat, on a postcard or on a computer screen.

So far as we can tell, NPR is judged by the six norms explained above, especially on "looking good", meaning similarity—assumed or claimed—to existing (culturally specific) genres; and by the elegance and novelty of the algorithm. None of the six norms reference the wider issues of concern to art, and because of that we cannot accept the full weight of Hertzman's argument [38] that NPR has explanatory power with regard to art. For example, NPR does not aim to comment on social issues but art often does, and since such a commentary is essential for art appreciation NPR is the poorer for being mute. However, Hertzmann may be correct in that NPR may help to understand perceptual elements, such as why the patterns used by Van Gogh are so appealing, or how Cezanne composes his paintings. Some Art Historians argue that pictures possess a grammar [69]; NPR might be of assistance there.

When compared to the rest of art, NPR is very much found to be wanting. Works of NPR cannot currently be assessed in exactly the same way as works of art produced by humans. This is not to deny the area as a subject of study. On the contrary, acknowledging the scale and the nature of the NPR project is, we claim, the best way to drive the field. Moreover, remarkable progress has already been made, progress we now explore a little. We will find that there are three basic questions NPR algorithms must address, and that progress to date has answered one very well, partially answered the second, but barely considered the third.

16.4 The How, Where, and What of NPR

In this section we will discuss the technical issues that face NPR in general, which we name 'how', 'where', and 'what'. These issues can be used not only to broadly classify NPR algorithms but to chart the progress of NPR against art in general.

There are three basic issues that any picture maker (human or computer) must address: how to make marks at all, where to make marks, and what to depict. *How* to make marks means deciding on media such a oil paint or pencil, as well as a particular rendering styles such as cross-hatch, impasto, palette knife, including also the choice of no perceptible mark. Having chosen how to make marks, the maker must next chose *where* to place marks on the image plane. At its most basic, marks could be placed at the edges of an object, or inside it. Support for this pair of issues comes from [83], who separates *projective system* from the *denotational system* when discussing art. He argues that schools of art are delineated by the class of projection (from 3D to 2D) they use, rather than the marks they make. This dualism is of course directly tied to the question of whether the image is figurative and therefore refers to an object in the world, or if it is abstract and so refrains from an iconic relation to the visual world. In the following, we discuss images of the former kind, with various gradations of abstraction, but always with some relation to the visible world. A human artist may not be conscious of solving 'how' and 'where'; but must solve them nonetheless. NPR algorithms are forced to explicitly solve these problems.

The third issue is *what* to depict. Humans will typically be primarily concerned with the semantic meaning of the picture; and presumably come equipped with a rich and complex internal representation capable of supporting pictures of the highest aesthetic value. This is currently beyond the scope of NPR: finding an equivalent is the grand challenge for the field.

16.4.1 How: Mark Making and Media Emulation

Any picture is an accumulation of marks: whether interactive or automatic, all approaches to NPR require an agent (human or computer) to make marks. The easiest way to make a mark using a computer is to distribute uniform colour around a point, line, or area. This approach yields marks that are flat and consistent—characteristics that are almost unique to early computer generated art. However, many people dislike such marks because it is difficult to be expressive with them, and in the early history of computer graphics they have described them as cold and unemotional (for some excellent examples see the SIGGRAPH documentary *The Story of Computer Graphics*, 1999). The response of the NPR has been to engage in research to emulate traditional artistic media.

Variations in media have long existed, with early interactive systems leading the way both in two dimensions from image [34] and in three dimensions by painting on models [36]. Media emulation has now become a staple of NPR. In fact, the affordance to simulate all artistic materials—from oil paint to charcoal, pen and ink, pastel, clay etc.—may be regarded as a distinctive material quality of NPR [49].

In fact, it was only in the early days, that Computer Graphics had a "typical" appearance because it could not yet render specific material qualities in detail (accordingly, it was often compared to plastic, which also is often like, but not quite like, a material it imitates). Emulation involved modelling the application device (brush, pencil, etc.) the pigment, be it liquid or solid, and the receiving surface. Just as photorealism models the interaction of light with matter, so media emulation models physical media and their application devices. Hairy Brushes is one early example [72], followed by many others including physical simulations of brush hairs [48]. However, the transfer of paint from brush to surface depends on more than the physics of brushes; it depends too on the bi-directional flow of physical paint [16]. Today, many of the traditional media have been emulated, not limited to oil paint [4], watercolour [16], pencil [71], charcoal [53], pen-and-ink [18], wood-engraving [59], copper-plate [50] and mixed-media [8]. This is a non-exhaustive list as a full list would occupy several pages, but NPR has made a few interesting omissions, including tempera and fresco.

Not all mark making requires brushes, pencils or such like. Mosaics use small coloured have been studied within NPR [21]. Larger scale cut from photographs showing different views of the same object have been used to simulate Cubist-like NPR [12]. Collage is a related genre in that it requires pieces cut from many pictures, but each of a different object. Automated collage has recently been addressed within NPR; Huang et al. [41] describe a sophisticated system for cut-and-paste from Internet images to produce Arcimboldo-like pictures.

16.4.2 Where: A Salient Question for NPR

We argue that where to place marks is more important than what marks are made. We have already noted that Willats [83] correlated schools of art with a projective rather than a denotational system. It is true that the nature of marks often defines the personal style of an artist (connoisseurship works that way). However, in an NPR context the location of a mark is the most important factor in the production of aesthetic value. We can conduct a thought experiment in which the marks making up a picture are all replaced with marks of another type: would we expect the aesthetic value of the picture to change? Our answer is 'yes', because although marks are important, the change would not be so much as if the same marks were moved to non-salient positions, for example.

Placing marks is a very difficult problem. It is hardly controversial and no accident that the highest quality NPR comes from interactive systems, in which the responsibility of *where* to place marks is passed to the user. Many interactive systems are now very sophisticated [68]. At its most complex, deciding where to place a mark depends upon the semantic meaning of the object that mark is related to, and to all other marks in the picture. Possibly apocryphal, Cezanne is reputed to have remarked to Ambroise Vollard that he could not possibly change one stroke on the hand of his portrait, for then he needed to change all others. For automated NPR, the 'where' question is a significant one.

In terms of 3D models, automation began in the early 1990s [63] that used edge maps computed by differentiating depth maps. More recently locating marks often comes down to deciding which parts of a model are salient, at least from a given point of view [7, 62], including when these change in time [78]. However, the focus of our attention is image based NPR.

When working from images, early attempts at automatically choosing mark locations depended upon edge detection [51] or local variance [76]. Both of these are *low level* operations, meaning they make only weak assumptions about image content and so are applicable to many input images. The output of these and similar algorithms is often related to the Impressionist school [51]. It remains one of the most extensively studied approaches to producing NPR. Innovations include a coarse-to-fine placement of edge-approximating strokes rather than simple blobs of paint [37] and more recently the use of filters based on structure tensors [47] or edge-aware Laplacian pyramids [60].

However, edge detection maps look very different from human sketches, even when made from the same photographic source. In fact, the difference is measurable using precision-recall plots [54]. Typically humans make many fewer marks than computers, and place marks judiciously—so that the content of the picture is efficiently depicted. In any case, it is interesting to observe that many artists, typified by Cezanne, tried to move away from painting edges at all. However, even Cezanne failed to completely remove edges. Nonetheless, edge detection and other low-level approaches to answering the 'where' question tend to treat all detections with equal weight, whereas artists will usually give greater weight to some edges rather than others. We call this *differential emphasis*, and reaching for it has been a driver of NPR. Interestingly, NPR rarely considers marks that become invisible by over-painting, as is the case in oil paintings by Jan van Eyck or the Photorealists.

The easiest way to pursue differential emphasis in NPR is to make use of salience maps. A salience map highlights areas that are supposed to be important to understand an image. The production of salience maps without explicit reference to any image content has been discussed in the Computer Vision literature for some time, Itti, Koch and Niebur provide a well known example [43]. Salience was recognised as useful to NPR from around 2002. DeCarlo and Santella [17] use eye-track data; they assumed that peoples' gaze dwells on important image regions for longer than it does less important regions. They build a hierarchical description of an image, which is rendered from top to bottom to maintain details. Such an interactive approach is of limited value to automatic NPR because it provides no model of salience that can be used generally. Recently a model that predicts where humans look has appeared [45], and it has been used to emulate the results of DeCarlo and Santella [17]. However, excellent results can be achieved in other ways. Bangham et al. [3] build a hierarchical image description, based on morphological operations centred on intensity extrema, which those authors assume to be salient. Collomosse and Hall [11] defined salience via rarity, the idea being that salient image regions are uncommon in a given picture; hence they assumed that salience is a global property in that the whole image must be taken into account. The same authors used their definition of salience maps to define an objective function that guided a genetic search that lay down brush strokes in an optimal way: to "smudge out" unwanted detail while maintaining acuity where necessary [13].

Despite these efforts the problem of salience has yet to be definitely solved. A general solution will, to borrow from probability, almost for sure have to be conditioned on task: the question to ask is *is this image element salient, given this image, and given this task?* For example: is this segmented region salient, given the task is to paint a portrait of Ambroise Vollard? An answer clearly requires identification of the region in question: an eye will be painted differently from a tree in the background, and a scar on one person may identify them but be removed for someone else. Knowledge of the subject should be used, where it is available. The down side is that using prior knowledge limits the scope of things that can be rendered. For example DiPaola [19] produces excellent portraits, but at the cost of specialising in portraiture. DiPaloa writes that "... *In general, artistic methodology attempts the following: from the photograph or live sitter, the painting must 'simplify, compose and leave out what's irrelevant, emphasizing what's important'. Since human painters have knowledge of the source imagery, we are limiting this approach to portraiture and therefore take advantage of portrait and facial knowledge in the NPR process.*"

It remains the case that even if salience maps improve the "look good" criterion (should be accept that measure), the outputs will still fall short of the highest aesthetic value witnessed in human art. Hence we are irrevocably drawn towards the dual subjects of abstraction and meaning, from which art derives so much of its power.

16.4.3 What: Steps Towards Abstraction and Meaning

Salience is helpful, maybe even necessary, for automated NPR, but is not sufficient. Moreover, we should not confine ourselves to thinking about brushes or pencils but instead consider all forms of picture making, such as mosaics, paper cut-outs, marquetry, etc. Such methods may require a different definition of salience to those currently in use. Projective systems too should be accounted for—in art, the rules of linear perspective are honoured more in their breach than their observance.

Artists, young and old, good or bad, in all parts of the world and throughout history are characterised by the projective systems they use [83]. Many of these defy simple mathematical modelling, in particular, Willats includes composition in his definition of projective systems, but composition is rarely researched in NPR.

The need for artistic projection in NPR has been recognised for some time now [1]. An array of non-linear camera models are now available to NPR, which allows users to create pictures with more than one focal point; sometimes with finitely many, other times with an infinite number. Most of these cameras are designed to operate on 3D models; RYAN [10] is one such example that combines projections from a finite number of linear cameras into a unified whole. The General Linear Camera (GLC) differs in that being a single camera capable of non-linear projection [84] GLCs are specified by a user defining three vectors, which deforms a plane into a bilinear surface; whereas every linear camera has a plane of points it cannot image–those points are zero homogeneous depth, called *points at infinity*. GLCs possess a bilinear surface of points at infinity. The RTcam (Rational Tensor Camera) is more general still [35], they have tri-quadratic surfaces of such points, and is designed to operate over photographic input.

Before moving on to abstraction, it is worth mentioning real-world non-linear cameras. These comprise fish-eye lens, strip cameras on satellites, and many forms of mirror. In practice no real camera is perfectly linear, but defects in lens and/or mirrors show up as artefacts such as pin-cushion distortion. Artist David Hockney suggests that many artists, such as Vermeer, made use of the equivalent of cameras in their day (e.g., camera obscurer) which were non-linear, either because of imperfections or because of the need to re-focus on different parts of a real-world scene [39]. It is interesting to reflect on whether any such imperfections might be recovered from paintings.

Perhaps the easiest way to move toward abstraction is image segmentation. The aim of segmentation is to partition an image into semantic regions such as "face" and "tree"—a problem that not only remains open within Computer Vision but also is arguably the most difficult of all problems in that field. Helpfully for NPR, segmentation can be hierarchical, so that an eye is segmented as a part within a face. We have already seen that heuristics such as eye-tracking and image morphology can be used to build salience maps. However, Computer Vision does furnish us with a battery of alternative techniques that are beginning to match human performance.

Voronoi regions are a popular choice in NPR research, typically defined via morphology to make renderings similar to stained glass [56]. Similar segmentation techniques, coupled with some interaction, lie behind the sketches produced by [81]. Scale-space hierarchies have also been exploited by the NPR literature to abstract images, see [58] for example. Others make use of hierarchical segmentations, such as N-cuts coupled with shape classification to produce paper cuts image that shadow Matisse and others [70].

Motion may also be segmented with positive results on NPR output. The early methods of painting video would paint strokes in frame one, and then use optical flow to push those strokes across frames [51]. Unfortunately, this leads to 'flicker', which is caused by a combination of several effects: optical flow is not defined in the interior of regions of uniform colour; it is noisy, it is interrupted by occlusion, and so on. Segmenting the video as a spatio-temporal volume is a first step to solving this issue [15, 80] because the eigenframe of segments (which are assumed to correspond to objects) act as object-centric reference frames in which to place strokes. Furthermore, tracking objects throughout a video sequences yields a trajectory that can be used to create typical cartoon effects such as streak-lines, squash-and-stretch, and anticipation [14].

There is little work in NPR beyond segmentation; *The Painting Fool* is a rare exception, see e.g. [46]. The Painting Fool is a computer program, but is perhaps better understood as a research programme investigating artificial intelligence and creativity.[1] It is one of the few computer programs to have exhibited in real galleries.

16.4.4 NPR As Perceptually Acceptable Photorealism

At first glance *NPR as Photorealism* is an oxymoron, but closer inspection reveals this is not the case, at least photorealism as perceived is a potential output of NPR.

Consider a feature film that requires some special effect. A good example appears in *The Mummy* comedy adventure in which a sand storm—raised by the power-hungry, newly resurrected mummy—is sent to devour the heroes and heroines. The

---

[1] http://www.thepaintingfool.com/index.html.

face of the mummy gapes out of the storm wall, all built of moving sand. The motion cannot be real, but the visual appearance has to convince the viewer that the storm is real. This is not normally called NPR, and if NPR related only to rendering appearance then it should not be; yet if we allow NPR to refer to motions too, then it is NPR.

The question of photo-retouching is similar. It has long been common practice for artists to 'retouch' photographs, especially in advertising, to add highlights to a car, to remove skin blemishes from a model, or to replace objects altogether. This practice continues, but now using a computer instead of an airbrush. Since a photograph is the source, it is undeniable that retouching moves the image away from veridical photorealism and into what might be called *perceptually acceptable photorealism*. Whether this shift is sufficient such that the output can be declared as examples of NPR is a question that depends on the tightness of the definition of NPR. Since that definition is not tight at all, it is arguable that NPR includes examples of images that look photorealistic, but which cannot be photographs.

Additionally animation and film often combine different modes of visual styles—for instance photorealism, cartoon-style and impressionist pastel style—into new hybrids of NPR, which may even constitute the most original style in NPR to date. The result can be described as functional realism, i.e. a style geared towards creating particular effects for and in the viewer [23]. Film studios and advertising houses engage with this form of NPR on an everyday basis. To a large degree it is the singular most successful branch of NPR. It is true that is relies almost exclusively on human input, but it does suggest that NPR, understood in its most general sense, has a bright future.

16.5 Conclusion

We have considered the question *how should NPR be evaluated*? More exactly, how should NPR be evaluated, when 'art' is its 'task'. It is a question that arises very often, both within and without the NPR community of researchers.

We agree with [38] that NPR cannot be assessed by experiments, and in particular agree with Pease and Colton [61] that the Turing test is not a valid prescription for NPR. We disagree that NPR has an explanatory power regarding art [38], instead it seems the other way around: art informs NPR. We argue that NPR cannot be evaluated in any objective measurable way, rather it is to be appreciated by reference first to internal norms, thereby distinguishing a scale from 'bad, to 'good' for comparable work; and second to external norms that give reference to a wider cultural background. The second set of norms are mutable in that they depend on culture, on the intention of the artists, and so on; it is for this reason a single objective definition of aesthetic value has evaded both historians and philosophers of art, and it is likely to evade NPR too.

When NPR is compared to a wider culture we see it focuses on technical matters, such as *how* to make a mark and (more complex) *where* to mark. Addressing the issue of *what* to make marks about is in its infancy in NPR, but is undoubtedly the central question asked by human artists. To be clear, technique is important to humans and to art history, but only in so far as it produces art of high aesthetic value—in this case judged by cultural norms that at present are beyond the reach of NPR.

NPR research is likely to progress in the mid-term by attending to thorny issues such as object identity and function, and in the longer term by the integration of deeper cultural knowledge into its output. It has yet to find its own distinctive style; the high-water mark for NPR at this moment is—arguably—Perceptually Acceptable Photorealism because that appears so often in photographs, films etc.

Finally, and pragmatically, we argue that NPR might widen its internal norms to include terms of reference that more closely resemble those used by art historians. We suggest 8 points to consider:

1. When choosing a certain artistic school be aware of the historical background and the artists. For example, the emergence of Impressionism depended two developments: (1) Leaving the studio and the academy as a restrictive environment that had adapted a photorealistic style where the invisibility of the brush stroke was the highest ideal and (2) painting outside, trying to capture natural lightning phenomena directly with paint and without preliminary sketches, thereby developing a quicker, literally patchy manner of painting.
2. Within schools, individual artists' styles vary greatly, so that claims such as 'this paper provides an algorithm that produces art in the style of the Impressionists' needs significant qualification to have real meaning.
3. Individual artists' style varies in time (early and late style, the most famous being Picasso); again qualification is needed to be precise.
4. Materials afford certain processes and movements (brush *strokes*, pen and ink *hatching*). It could be that breaching these rules leads to non-physical media unique to NPR.
5. Media is more than physics! Materials have a distinct impact on style. Get familiar with material accordances, i.e. get the stuff and try it out in order to understand behaviour of oil paint, pastel, tempera, etc. NPR may develop new ways to apply media.
6. Art is not an accident: study, record, analyse artists' movements at work to understand salient choices.
7. Do not work from reproductions, but from the originals if at all possible. For instance, to understand why and how Claude Monet's representation of water, clouds or leaves works so well, one must view his work 'in the flesh'. Only originals allow perception of the surface structure, impasto, and texture of pictures and their materials. More than that, the originals often have a real and compelling power that can never be reproduced on a computer screen or printed on paper: maybe NPR should use media more often than it does [77].
8. Familiarity with basic principles of Art History will help when assessing NPR. Texts relate directly to the problems NPR face include Rudolf Arnheim [2], Ernst H. Gombrich [28, 29], and John Hyman [42].

NPR is in its infancy, and will no doubt flourish in the coming years. We predict it will move to become accepted as an art form in its own right. We suggest NPR should be appreciated in that way.

References

1. Agrawala, M., Zorin, D., Munzner, T.: Artistic multiprojection rendering. In: Peroche, B., Rushmeier, H.E. (eds.) Proceedings of the Eurographics Workshop on Rendering 2000, Brno, Czech Republic, June 2000, pp. 125–136. Springer, Berlin (2000). doi:10.1145/647652.732127
2. Arnhiem, R.: Art and Visual Perception: A Psychology of the Creative Eye, 2nd edn. University of California Press, Berkeley (1974)
3. Bangham, J.A., Gibson, S.E., Harvey, R.: The art of scale-space. In: British Machine Vision Conference (2003)
4. Baxter, W., Wendt, J., Lin, M.C.: IMPaSTo: a realistic, interactive model for paint. In: Hertzmann, A., Kaplan, C. (eds.) Proceedings of the Third International Symposium on Non-Photorealistic Animation and Rendering (NPAR 2004), pp. 45–56 (2004). doi:10.1145/987657.987665
5. Birkoff, G.: Aesthetic Measure. Harvard University Press, Harvard (1933)
6. Boden, M.: The Turing test and artistic creativity. Kybernetes **39**(3), 409–413 (2010)
7. Breslav, S., Szerszen, K., Markosian, L., Barla, P., Thollot, J.: Dynamic 2D patterns for shading 3D scenes. ACM Trans. Graph. **26**(3), 20 (2007). doi:10.1145/1275808.1276402
8. Brooks, S.: Mixed media painting and portraiture. IEEE Trans. Vis. Comput. Graph. **13**(5), 1041–10,540 (2007). doi:10.1109/TVCG.2007.1025
9. Burton, G.J., Moorhead, I.R.: Color and spatial structure in natural scenes. Appl. Opt. **26**(1), 157 (1987). doi:10.1364/AO.26.000157
10. Coleman, P., Singh, K.R.: Rendering your animation nonlinearly projected. In: Hertzmann, A., Kaplan, C. (eds.) Proceedings of the Third International Symposium on Non-Photorealistic Animation and Rendering (NPAR 2004), Annecy, pp. 129–138. ACM, New York (2004). doi:10.1145/987657.987678
11. Collomosse, J.P., Hall, P.M.: Painterly rendering using image salience. In: EGUK '02: Proceedings of the 20th UK Conference on Eurographics, p. 122. IEEE Comput. Soc., Los Alamitos (2002)
12. Collomosse, J.P., Hall, P.M.: Cubist style rendering from photographs. IEEE Trans. Vis. Comput. Graph. **4**(9), 443–453 (2003). doi:10.1109/TVCG.2003.1260739
13. Collomosse, J.P., Hall, P.M.: Genetic paint: a search for salient paintings. In: Proceedings of EvoMUSART (LNCS). Lecture Notes in Computer Science, vol. 3449, pp. 437–447. Springer, Berlin (2005). doi:10.1007/978-3-540-32003-6_44
14. Collomosse, J.P., Rowntree, D., Hall, P.M.: Video analysis for cartoon-style special effects. In: Proceedings 14th British Machine Vision Conference (BMVC), vol. 2, pp. 749–758 (2003)
15. Collomosse, J.P., Rowntree, D., Hall, P.M.: Stroke surfaces: temporally coherent non-photorealistic animations from video. IEEE Trans. Vis. Comput. Graph. **11**(5), 540–549 (2005). doi:10.1109/TVCG.2005.85
16. Curtis, C.J., Anderson, S.E., Seims, J.E., Fleischer, K.W., Salesin, D.H.: Computer-generated watercolor. In: Whitted, T. (ed.) Proceedings of ACM SIGGRAPH, vol. 97, pp. 421–430 (1997). doi:10.1145/258734.258896
17. DeCarlo, D., Santella, A.: Stylization and abstraction of photographs. ACM Trans. Graph. **21**(3), 769–776 (2002). doi:10.1145/566654.566650
18. Deussen, O., Strothotte, T.: Computer-generated pen-and-ink illustration of trees. In: Proceedings of ACM SIGGRAPH 2000, New Orleans, LA, July 23–28, 2000, pp. 23–28 (2000). doi:10.1145/344779.344792

19. DiPaola, S.: Painterly rendered portraits from photographs using a knowledge-based approach. Proc. SPIE **6492**, 33–43 (2007). doi:10.1117/12.706594
20. Durand, F.: An invitation to discuss computer depiction. In: Finkelstein, A. (ed.) Proceedings of the Second International Symposium on Non-Photorealistic Animation and Rendering (NPAR 2002), pp. 111–124. ACM, New York (2002). doi:10.1145/508530.508550
21. Elber, G., Wolberg, G.: Rendering traditional mosaics. Vis. Comput. **19**(1), 67–78 (2003). doi:10.1007/s00371-002-0175-x
22. Fernie, E.: Art History and Its Methods: A Critical Anthology. Phaidon, Oxford (2011)
23. Ferwerda, J.A.: Three varieties of realism in computer graphics. In: Rogowitz, B.E., Pappas, T.N. (eds.) Proceedings of Human Vision and Electronic Imaging VIII, Santa Clara, California, USA, January 21, 2003. SPIE Proceedings Series, vol. 5007, pp. 290–297. SPIE/IS&T, Springfield (2003). doi:10.1117/12.473899
24. Field, D.: Relations between the statistics of natural images and the response profiles of cortical cells. J. Opt. Soc. Am. A **4**, 2379–2394 (1987)
25. Field, D.: What is the goal of sensory coding? Neural Comput. **6**, 559–601 (1994)
26. Filonik, D., Baur, D.: Measuring aesthetics for information visualization. In: International Conference on Information Visualization, pp. 579–584 (2009)
27. Frazor, R., Geisler, W.: Local luminance contrast in natural images. Vis. Res. **46**, 1585–1598 (2006)
28. Gombrich, E.: Art and Illusion: A Study in the Psychology of the Pictorial Representation. Phaidon, Oxford (1983)
29. Gombrich, E.: The Story of Art. Phaidon, Oxford (1995)
30. Gombrich, E.H.: The claims of excellence. In: Gombrich, E. (ed.) Reflections on the History of Art, pp. 179–185. Phaidon, Oxford (1987)
31. Graham, D., Field, D.: Statistical regularities of art image and natural scenes: spectra, sparseness and nonlinearities. Spat. Vis. **21**, 149–164 (2007)
32. Graham, D., Field, D.: Variations in intensity statistics for representational and abstract art from the Eastern and Western hemispheres. Perception **37**, 1341–1352 (2008)
33. Granger, G.: Aesthetic measure applied to color harmony: an experimental test. J. Gen. Psychol. **52**(2), 205–212 (1955)
34. Haeberli, P.E.: Paint by numbers: abstract image representations. Comput. Graph. **24**(4) 207–214 (1990)
35. Hall, P.M., Collomosse, J.P., Song, Y.Z., Shen, P., Li, C.: RTcams: a new perspective on non-photorealistic rendering from photographs. IEEE Trans. Vis. Comput. Graph. **13**(5), 966–979 (2007). doi:10.1109/TVCG.2007.1047
36. Hanrahan, P., Haeberli, P.: Direct WYSIWYG painting and texturing on 3D shapes. Comput. Graph. **24**(3), 215–223 (1990). doi:10.1145/97880.97903
37. Hertzmann, A.: Painterly rendering with curved brush strokes of multiple sizes. In: Cohen, M. (ed.) SIGGRAPH '98: Proceedings of the 25th Annual Conference on Computer Graphics and Interactive Techniques, pp. 453–460. ACM/ACM SIGGRAPH, New York (1998). doi:10.1145/280814.280951
38. Hertzmann, A.: Non-photorealistic rendering and the science of art. In: Collomosse, J., McGuire, M. (eds.) Proceedings of the Eighth International Symposium on Non-Photorealistic Animation and Rendering (NPAR 2010), Annecy, France, June 7–10, 2010, pp. 147–157. ACM, New York (2010). doi:10.1145/1809939.1809957
39. Hockney, D.: Secret Knowledge: Rediscovering the Lost Techniques of the Old Masters. Thames and Hudson, London (2001)
40. Hsiao, S.W., Chiu, F.Y., Hsu, H.Y.: A computer-assisted colour selection system based on aesthetic measure for colour harmony and fuzzy logic theory. Color Res. Appl. **33**, 411–423 (2008)
41. Huang, H., Zhang, L., Zhang, H.C.: Arcimboldo-like collage using internet images. ACM Trans. Graph. **30**(6), 155 (2011). doi:10.1145/2070781.2024189
42. Hyman, J.: The Objective Eye: Color, Form, and Reality in the Theory of Art. University of Chicago, Chicago (2006)

43. Itti, L., Koch, C., Niebur, E.: A model of saliency based visual attention for rapid scene analysis. IEEE Trans. Pattern Anal. Mach. Intell. **20**(11), 1254–1259 (1998)
44. Jones, B.: Computer imagery: imitation and representation of realities. Leonardo. Supplemental Issue 31–38 (1989)
45. Judd, T., Ehinger, K., Durand, F., Torralba, A.: Learning to predict where humans look. In: IEEE International Conference on Computer Vision (ICCV) (2009)
46. Kreczkowska, A., El-Hage, J., Colton, S., Clark, S.: Automated collage generation with intent. In: International Joint Conference on Computational Creativity (2010)
47. Kyprianidis, J.E., Kang, H.: Image and video abstraction by coherence-enhancing filtering. Comput. Graph. Forum **30**(2), 593–602 (2011)
48. Lee, J.: Physically-based modeling of brush painting. In: Computer Networks and ISDN Systems, pp. 1571–1756 (1997)
49. Lehmann, A.: Taking the lid off the Utah teapot. Towards a material analysis of computer graphics. Z. Medien Kult.-forsch. **1**, 157–172 (2012)
50. Leister, W.: Computer generated copper plates. Comput. Graph. Forum **13**(1), 69–77 (1994). doi:10.1111/1467-8659.1310069
51. Litwinowicz, P.: Processing images and video for an impressionist effect. In: Whitted, T. (ed.) Proceedings of ACM SIGGRAPH 97, Los Angeles, CA, August 3–8, 1997, pp. 407–414. ACM, New York (1997). doi:10.1145/258734.258893
52. Manovich, L.: Image future. Animation **1**(1), 25–44 (2006)
53. Markosian, L., Kowalski, M.A., Trychin, S.J., Bourdev, L.D., Goldstein, D., Hughes, J.F.: Real-time nonphotorealistic rendering. In: Proceedings of ACM SIGGRAPH 97, pp. 415–420 (1997). doi:10.1145/258734.258894
54. Martin, D.R., Fowlkes, C.C., Malik, J.: Learning to detect natural image boundaries using local brightness, color, and texture cues. IEEE Trans. Pattern Anal. Mach. Intell. **26**(5), 530–549 (2004). doi:10.1109/TPAMI.2004.1273918
55. Moon, P., Spencer, D.E.: Aesthetic measure applied to color harmony. J. Opt. Soc. Am. **34**(4), 234–242 (1944)
56. Mould, D.: A stained glass image filter. In: Eurographics Symposium on Rendering: 14th Eurographics Workshop on Rendering, pp. 20–25 (2003)
57. Ngo, D.C.L., Samsudin, A., Abdullah, R.: Aesthetic measures for assessing graphic screens. J. Inf. Sci. Eng. **16**(1), 97–116 (2000)
58. Orzan, A., Bousseau, A., Barla, P., Thollot, J.: Structure-preserving manipulation of photographs. In: Agrawala, M., Deussen, O. (eds.) NPAR '07: Proceedings of the 5th International Symposium on Non-photorealistic Animation and Rendering, pp. 103–110. ACM, New York (2007). doi:10.1145/1274871.1274888
59. Ostromoukhov, V.: Digital facial engraving. In: Proceedings of ACM SIGGRAPH 99, Los Angeles, CA, August 8–13, 1999, pp. 417–424 (1999). doi:10.1145/311535.311604
60. Paris, S., Hasinoff, S.W., Kautz, J.: Local Laplacian filters: edge-aware image processing with a Laplacian pyramid. ACM Trans. Graph. **30**(4), 68 (2011). doi:10.1145/2010324.1964963
61. Pease, A., Colton, S.: On impact and evaluation in computational creativity: a discussion of the Turing test and an alternative proposal. In: AISB Symposium on AI and Philosophy (2011)
62. Rusinkiewicz, S., Cole, F., DeCarlo, D., Finkelstein, A.: Line drawings from 3D models. In: ACM SIGGRAPH 2008 Classes, vol. 39, pp. 1–356 (2008). doi:10.1145/1401132.1401188
63. Saito, T., Takahashi, T.: Comprehensible rendering of 3-D shapes. Comput. Graph. **24**(3), 197–206 (1990). doi:10.1145/97880.97901
64. Salesin, D.: Non-photorealistic animation and rendering: 7 grand challenges. In: Keynote talk at NPAR (2002)
65. Santella, A., DeCarlo, D.: Visual interest and NPR: an evaluation and manifesto. In: Hertzmann, A., Kaplan, C. (eds.) Proceedings of the Third International Symposium on Non-

Photorealistic Animation and Rendering (NPAR 2004), Annecy, France, June 7–9, 2004, pp. 71–78. ACM, New York (2004). doi:10.1145/987657.987669
66. Schelske, A.: Zur Sozialität des nicht-fotorealistischen Renderings. Eine zu kurze, soziologische Skizze für zeitgenössische Bildmaschinen. Image: J. Interdiscip. Image Sci. **6**, 47–58 (2007)
67. Schirra, J.R.J., Scholz, M.: Abstraction versus realism: not the real question. In: Strothotte, T., Deussen, O. (eds.) Computer Visualization—Graphics, Abstraction, and Interactivity, pp. 379–401. Springer, Berlin (1998)
68. Schwarz, M., Isenberg, T., Mason, K., Carpendale, S.: Modeling with rendering primitives: an interactive non-photorealistic canvas. In: Proc. NPAR, pp. 15–22 (2007). doi:10.1145/1274871.1274874
69. Smith, P.: Pictorial grammar: Chomsky, John Willats, and the rules of representation. Art Hist. 562–593 (2011)
70. Song, Y., Hall, P., Rosin, P.L., Collomosse, J.: Arty shapes. In: Proc. Comp. Aesthetics, pp. 65–73 (2008)
71. Sousa, M.C., Buchanan, J.W.: Computer-generated graphite pencil rendering of 3D polygonal models. Comput. Graph. Forum **18**(3), 195–207 (1999). doi:10.1111/1467-8659.00340
72. Strassmann, S.H.: Hairy brushes. Comput. Graph. **20**(4), 225–232 (1986). doi:10.1145/15922.15911
73. Strothotte, T., Schlechtweg, S.: Non-Photorealistic Computer Graphics: Modeling, Rendering, and Animation. Morgan Kaufmann, San Mateo (2002)
74. Tauber, A.: The Elusive Synthesis Aesthetics and Science. Kluwer Academic, Dordrecht (1996)
75. Tolhurst, D., Tadmor, Y., Chao, T.: The amplitude spectra of natural images. Ophthalmic Physiol. Opt. **12**, 229–232 (1992)
76. Treavett, S.M.F., Chen, M.: Statistical techniques for the automatic generation of non-photorealistic images. In: Proceedings of the 15th Eurographics UK Conference (1997)
77. Tresset, P., Leymarie, F.: Generative portrait sketching. In: Proceedings of VSMM (2005)
78. Umenhoffer, T., Szécsi, L., Szirmay-Kalos, L.: Hatching for motion picture production. Comput. Graph. Forum **30**(2), 533–542 (2011)
79. Verlaek, P.: Non-photorealistic rendering as epistemic images. In: Workshop on Abstract Images in Art and Science (2009)
80. Wang, J., Xu, Y., Shum, H.Y., Cohen, M.F.: Video tooning. ACM Trans. Graph. **23**(3), 574–583 (2004). doi:10.1145/1015706.1015763
81. Wen, F., Luan, Q., Liang, L., Xu, Y.Q., Shum, H.Y.: Color sketch generation. In: DeCarlo, D., Markosian, L. (eds.) Proceedings of the Fourth International Symposium on Non-Photorealistic Animation and Rendering (NPAR 2006), Annecy, France, June 5–7, 2006, pp. 47–54. ACM, New York (2006). doi:10.1145/1124728.1124737
82. Wiggins, G.: A preliminary framework for description, analysis and comparison of creative systems. Knowl.-Based Syst. **19**(7), 449–458 (2006)
83. Willats, J.: Art and Representation: New Principles in the Analysis of Pictures. Princeton University Press, Princeton (1997)
84. Yu, J., McMillan, L.: A framework for multiperspective rendering. In: Keller, A., Jensen, H.W. (eds.) Rendering Techniques 2004, Proceedings of Eurographics Symposium on Rendering 2004, pp. 61–68. Eurographics Association, Annecy (2004)

Chapter 17
NPR in the Wild

Holger Winnemöller

17.1 Introduction

In this chapter, we take a look at applications of NPR in the real world. This survey is neither intended to be comprehensive in scope nor in technical detail (for background on specific techniques, please consult the paper references at the end of this chapter). Instead, we focus on representative techniques and applications of various NPR approaches that have found use in production software and entertainment.

To further focus our attention, we shall use a somewhat more restrictive definition of NPR than might be applied elsewhere in this book. Specifically, we shall define NPR as "*computer-enabled synthesis and tools for Art creation and reproduction*". That is, we include systems and tools that enable digital synthesis and creation of traditional artistic styles, but we exclude examples that are clearly non-realistic, yet are not obviously linked to any particular traditional art style (such as the movie "*Tron*", 1982, which makes heavy use of non-realistic visual effects and computer graphics, but does not represent an established artistic style).

The chapter starts with a historical review of artistic styles that were invented or refined as answers to certain production challenges, particularly print reproduction. While modern printing techniques obviate the need for traditional reproduction methods, their artistic merits have prompted NPR researchers to revive them in the digital age. Next, uses of NPR for entertainment, namely movies and games, are discussed, followed by visualization and presentation applications. Finally, a case study focusing on design considerations covers an example of NPR on mobile devices. The chapter closes with some forward looking suggestions to further increase the impact of NPR, particularly to reach a larger audience of artistically untrained users.

H. Winnemöller (✉)
Adobe Systems, Inc., Seattle, USA
e-mail: hwinnemo@adobe.com

17.2 Production Tools

NPR has found use in Art and other production environments in a number of ways. For example, there are *art creation tools*, such as the digital paint brushes discussed in Chap. 2. These art creation tools mimic tools in the real world (e.g. a painter's brush), but often add some unique digital affordances, such as undo, copy/paste, scaling, etc. In many cases, art creation tools straddle the border between NPR and realistic techniques, as they commonly rely on highly realistic, physically based simulations, or approximations thereof.

Another production use of NPR is automatic or user-assisted *style reproduction*. While an artist could be employed to create an artifact manually using an art creation tool, it may sometimes be cheaper, more convenient, and less time consuming to replicate an artistic style using an NPR system. For example, creating a cartoon animation commonly requires between 12–24 individually painted frames per second of the final movie. Automatically converting a live-action video or 3D animation into a cartoon style [27, 34, 50] can significantly save on artists' time and thereby lower production costs.

Finally, there are NPR *assistive technologies*, which help in the style-specific production process, but which are not necessarily contributing to the stylization itself. Examples of such technologies include tweening for animations (Chap. 14), cartoon-optimized flood-filling [45], and animation motion capture and retargeting [7].

17.2.1 Artistic Styles in Printing

Several media reproduction techniques, such as *woodcut, engraving, stamping*, and *stippling* are of particular interest to this section, as they were themselves conceived primarily as answers to production problems, but have since then been recognized as artistic styles in their own right, and subsequently been subject of several NPR investigations.

Before the invention of printing processes like woodblock printing (xylography), movable type, and the Gutenberg printing press, production and copying of written materials was a fully manual process, performed by skilled scribes and artists. Images, illustrations, and visual decorations were drawn and copied by hand. As printing techniques revolutionized the dissemination of information, new methods had to be found to replicate the accompanying figures and images. One of the oldest samples of Eastern woodcut printing dates back to 220 A.D., with variations of the technique being discovered and re-discovered throughout antiquity.

The basic building block of all so-called *relief printing* techniques is the 'relief matrix'. For woodcut, this is simply a level piece of wood. Areas that are intended to appear as 'white' are chiseled or scraped away. The remaining parts appear as 'black' by applying dark ink onto the wood surface and pressing or stamping the wood onto cloth, parchment, or paper (see Fig. 17.1a). It is easy to see how the

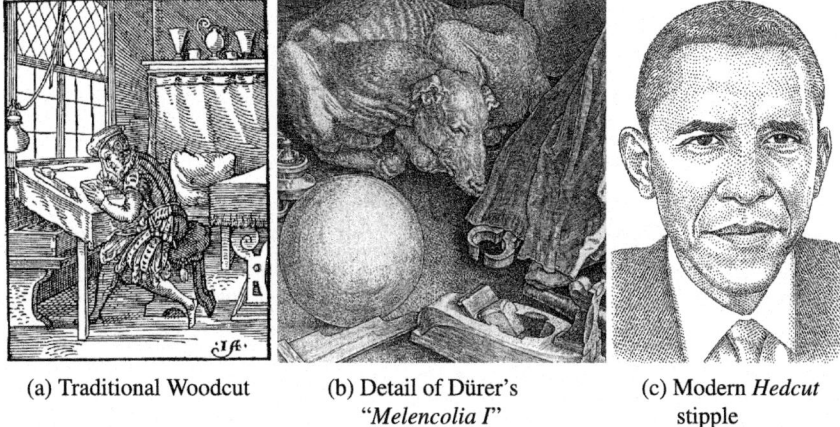

(a) Traditional Woodcut (b) Detail of Dürer's (c) Modern *Hedcut*
                          "Melencolia I"   stipple

Fig. 17.1 *Art (Re)production:* (**a**) Woodcut of a block-cutter by Jost Amman (1568), (**b**) detail of Dürer's engraving *"Melencolia I"* (1514). Note the combined use of hatching and stippling, the masterful texture of numerous materials, and the orientation of marks along surface features. (**c**) Modern Hedcut stipple by Kevin Sprouls, creator of the WSJ portrait style. (**c**) Copyright © 2012 Kevin Sprouls, used with permission

characters comprising text could be chiseled into wood and replicated this way. Even simple images akin to line drawings were reasonably straightforward to achieve in woodcut. However, more intricate or lifelike images proved to be more challenging, because the complexity of shape and particularly shading was difficult to express in terms of simple presence or absence of ink.

As a solution, printmakers adopted artistic techniques to approximate continuous tone (grayscale) images with dot and hatching patterns of a single color. In *stippling*, dark dots of varying size and spacing are placed on a light background. When viewed from a sufficiently large distance, the individual dots are fused into a continuous tone by the human perceptual system. For *hatching* or cross-hatching, lines (parallel or intersecting, respectively) of varying thickness and spacing are used to achieve a similar effect. Both hatching and especially stippling have found extensive use in printing, engraving, etching, tattooing, and scrimshaw. Common-day examples of these techniques include newspaper printing, currency design, and technical illustrations (particularly biology).

The manual creation of high-quality stippling images or engravings requires significant artistic training and, even then, is a time-consuming and laborious process. As such, various NPR works have addressed the need to simplify or automate these production processes. Woodcut-like images are addressed in the work of Mello et al. [31] and Winnemöller et al. [51]. Mizuno et al. [33] have presented a system to virtually model, carve, and print with digital woodblocks.[1] Igarashi and Igarashi [18] developed a method to allow novice users (even children) to produce

---

[1] As such, their work is closer related to physical modeling and simulation than NPR.

physically realizable stencils from 2D drawings. A system for digital facial engraving has been presented by Ostromokhov [35] (Chap. 4).

17.2.2 Stippling—The Story of a Virtuous Cycle

An interesting example for its interplay between art and production is stippling.[2] Technically, hatching and cross-hatching predate stippling both in terms of art use and in printmaking, possibly due to hatching requiring fewer marks (lines) and therefore being faster to produce. A noteworthy aspect of hatching marks is that they are commonly aligned along directions of principal curvature on the perceived surfaces of a drawing. As such, hatching lines suggest surface shape not only by simulating shading, but also by visually encoding important geometric properties of a surface. In artistic use, stippling is often used to depict soft surfaces, such as faces, cloth, or sand, while hatching is used to depict rougher or textured surfaces, such as wood, rocks, or wallpaper. It is common to intermix both techniques within the same work of art (Fig. 17.1b).

Use of these techniques in printmaking followed the same chronological order, with hatching being employed in early woodcuts, while stippling became more common only in later printing methods, such as etching and Mezzotint. Both stippling and hatching served as inspiration for a printing technique called *halftoning*, which allows photographs to be reproduced by automatically mapping them onto one or more[3] screens, which are then applied similar to other relief printing techniques. Commonly, halftone screens consist of grids of regularly spaced dots, where the size of each dot correlates to the darkness of the photograph at the position of the dot. Halftone printing became commercially successful in the late 1800s and, in its modern digital form, is still used in print production and computer printers today. Despite their historical origins, halftoning and the related *dithering* are not generally considered artistic techniques, as they follow fairly simple, deterministic algorithms.

One of the few newspapers that used to frown upon the extensive use of photographic reproduction was the Wall Street Journal (WSJ). One of its past editors, Fred Taylor, has been quoted as ascribing to a "*one word is worth a thousand pictures*" policy. It was felt that the liberal use of photographs would detract from the journalistic quality of the articles. This attitude changed in 1979 after freelance artist Kevin Sprouls approached the WSJ presenting a stipple and hatching-based portrait style, which was later to become a popular visual trademark for the journal. This style, today referred to as *Hedcut stippling*, was reminiscent of traditional engravings and deemed distinctive and formal enough to reflect the journal's aesthetic sensibility. As an added advantage, the Hedcut drawings were often more *legible* than simple halftone prints of the same size (see Fig. 17.1c).

---

[2]For technical details on stippling, refer to Chap. 3.

[3]Multiple screens, commonly rotated relative to one another and with slightly varying grid spacing, are used to reproduce color photographs.

The Hedcut style is qualitatively different from standard NPR stippling approaches [43] in that its stipples are aligned to follow surface features, such as contours or principal curvature, similar to the manual hatching and stippling techniques, described above. Ostromokhov [35] addressed this issue for digital engraving by allowing a user to specify local parametric grids along which the engraving directions would follow. Several recent works have proposed automatic solutions to the Hedcut challenge [25, 44]. As such, it would not be surprising if the online version of the WSJ would leverage NPR Hedcut techniques to augment their articles in the future, for example to aid in projects like their interactive Lego Hedcut [8].

17.3 Entertainment

Both the movie and computer games industries have embraced NPR as a valuable technical resource and differentiator. For movies (particularly animated ones), commonly requiring anywhere between 12–24 individually crafted frames per second, NPR is an invaluable tool to reduce production costs and increase throughput.

For computer games, the motivation for employing NPR techniques is somewhat different. Early computer games were by necessity more abstract than realistic, mainly because computer graphics at the time were too limited to render complex models or realistic looking lighting and environmental effects. As computer graphics matured and graphics hardware became more powerful, game companies competed with each other by offering ever more realistic effects, such as motion blur, depth-of-field, soft shadows, ambient occlusion, and sub-surface scattering. Eventually, a saturation point was reached, where additional realism was ever more difficult to achieve while the resulting visual improvements became increasingly subtle. Confounding this issue was the fact that yearly hardware advances were outpacing game development, which could easily take between 3–5 years. Game studios were thus facing a moving target and kept having to adjust their rendering engines throughout development.

At that point, several game studios started turning to stylistic differentiation to lock-in a visual style (thereby decoupling their rendering pipeline from the realism "arms race") and setting their product apart in the marketplace. Some games that make heavy use of NPR rendering include *XIII* (Ubisoft, 2003), *Prince of Persia* (Ubisoft, 2008), and *Borderlands* (Gearbox Software/2K Games, 2009), amongst others. It should be noted that other forms of stylization can also be found in realism-focused gaming titles. These include cinematographic techniques, such as tracking and panning cameras in the *Need for Speed* series (Electronic Arts), or the 'bullet-time' effect in the *Max Payne* titles (Remedy Entertainment).

17.3.1 Cartooning

In both film and games, the overwhelmingly prevalent NPR style is *cartoon*. The reason for this is historically different for both mediums, but based on the same premise of simplified imagery and easily achievable temporal coherence. For example, manually painting 12 oil paintings for each second of an animation is prohibitively expensive. Instead, animators adopted the simplified shapes and colors of cartoons, which were more manageable to mass produce. For games, temporal coherence is a bigger concern than the visual complexity of an individual frame. Specifically, stylistic elements (such as brush strokes, outlines, hatching) in one frame should be correlated to the corresponding elements in the following frame, lest they produce distracting flickering. Cartoons (in the most basic form) are visually simple, relying only on intrinsic information of a scene (such as positions of lights, objects and viewer, and objects' 3D shape and material properties). No extrinsic properties (e.g. random perturbations, or surface marks, brush splats and hatching strokes) need to be correlated between frames of an animation, thereby guaranteeing temporal coherence on a per-frame basis. That is, temporal coherence can be trivially achieved by applying the same algorithm to each frame individually, without considering temporally neighboring frames. This is particularly relevant for games, where the actions of players are unpredictable and the status of future frames cannot be anticipated.

Given the prevalence of the cartoon style in entertainment applications, it is worthwhile briefly recapturing the relevant NPR literature.

Early Beginnings In 1990 Saito and Takahashi [41] presented a system based on geometry-buffers (G-buffers) to visually enhance geometric features of 3D models. A *G-buffer* is a raster-buffer, like the RGBA color buffer, but instead of colors it stores geometric values (e.g. surface view-depth or normals) at each pixel location. Using several G-buffers, Saito and Takahashi computed silhouettes, creases, and contour lines via simple image processing operations. At the time, the G-buffer approach was somewhat impractical due to the high cost of memory modules and the limited CPU power to perform interactive image processing.[4] As a result, most following works computed geometric features directly on 3D data. However, as it turns out, the G-buffer approach maps elegantly onto modern programmable graphics hardware, so that Saito and Takahashi's approach, over two decades later, forms the basis for ink-lines in cartoon rendering for most state-of-the art computer games (for an example, see Fig. 17.2).

Interactive Rendering Given the hardware limitations of the time, researchers turned to geometric solutions and rendering tricks to implement cartoon rendering at interactive rates. In 1997, Markosian et al. [30] described a probabilistic feature-line detection scheme based on a modification of Appel's hidden line algorithm [3], which allowed for quality trade-offs to enable real-time performance. In 1999, several authors proposed real-time capable edge-feature algorithms [14, 39, 52].

---

[4]Consumer GPUs only became available in the late 1990s and were limited to a fixed function pipeline. General GPU accelerated image processing operations via fragment shaders were introduced in the OpenGL 2.0 specification, in late 2004.

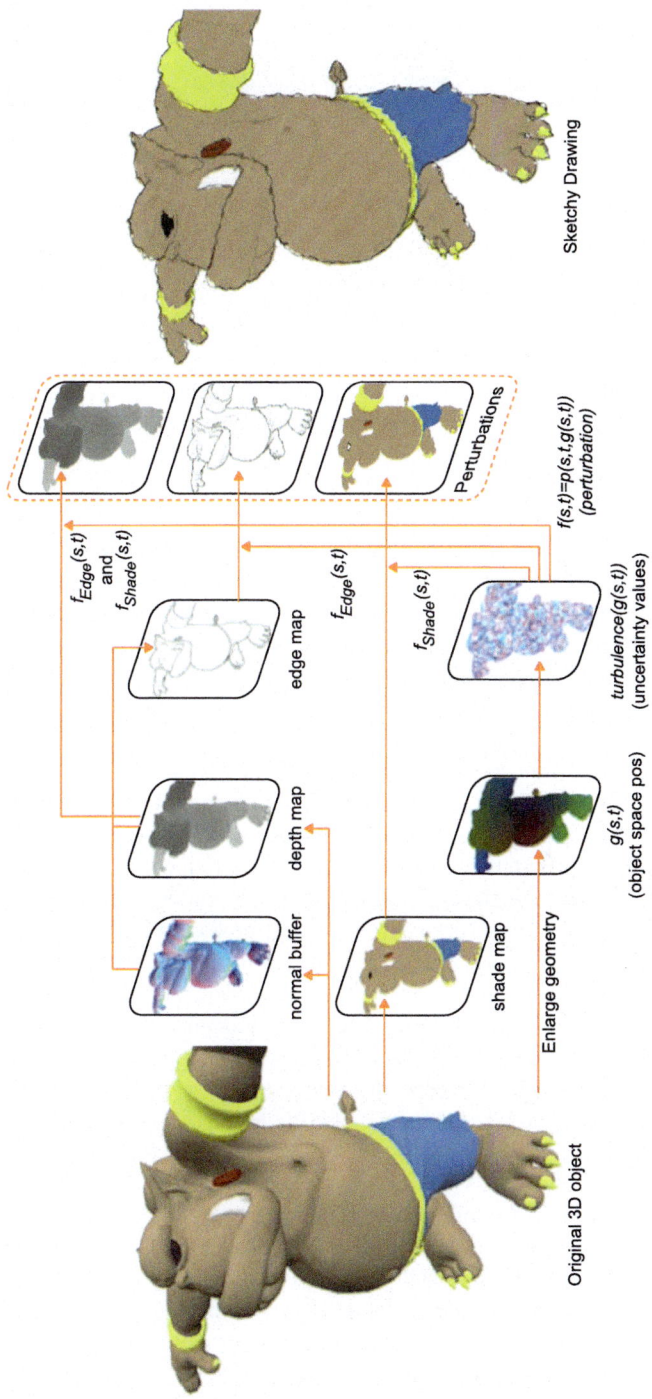

Fig. 17.2 *Cartoon Rendering:* Modern cartoon rendering pipeline, based on G-buffers. Copyright © 2004 Nienhaus and Döllner [34], used with permission

Fig. 17.3 *Cartoon Shading:*
(**a**, *left*-to-*right*) Diffuse shading only, specular shading only, combined diffuse + specular shading;
(**b**, *left*-to-*right*) physically based specular highlight, parametric squaring of highlight, division of highlight, moving highlight.
(**b**) Copyright © 2006 Anjyo et al. [2], used with permission

(a) Diffuse and Specular Cartoon shading [49]

(b) Advanced Cartoon Highlights [1]

Cartoon Shading A year later, Lake et al. [27] presented a full-fledged interactive cartoon rendering approach, including cartoon shading in addition to inklines. To produce the banded multi-tone shading of traditional cartoons, Lake et al. modified the Gouraud shading model [15] via discretized tone-mapping. Instead of Gouraurd's continuous shading, all values below a given threshold value were mapped to one shading tone, while those value above the threshold were mapped to another. Practically, Lake et al. implemented this scheme via texture mapping of a 1D texture, where the texture co-ordinate at each vertex was computed on the CPU using Gouraud's shading model. Texture co-ordinate interpolation across each triangle, along with nearest-neighbor texture lookup ensured that shading boundaries could move smoothly over surfaces and remain crisp without blurring.

Style Extensions At this point, the technical challenges of real-time standard cartoon rendering seemed all but solved, and researchers turned to stylistic extensions and variations. As Lake et al.'s approach only addressed ambient and diffuse shading, Winnemöller and Bangay [49] extended this work to include a specular component (Fig. 17.3a). Based on several heuristics, they proposed an approximation acceleration scheme for sorting surface triangles into front-and back-facing, allowing them to compute a view-dependent specular light contribution with negligible computational overhead. By extending the 1D texture-based cartoon lighting approach to 2D, and encoding the specular mapping in the second dimension, they demonstrated a number of material effects with varying specular and even stylistic behavior. A few years later, Barla et al. used the same approach in their X-Toon system [4], and they were now able to take advantage of GPU-accelerated programmable vertex and fragment shaders.

Randomness In a parallel thread of research, several authors addressed the issue of *randomness* [17, 22, 30, 34]. Up to this point, computer-generated cartoons were directly tied to the underlying model geometry, resulting in a perfect, almost clinical look. In contrast, sketches and cartoon drafts of real artists often exhibit irregular line-widths, crooked and wiggly strokes, and other natural artifacts. Markosian et al. [30] simulated hand-drawn uncertainty by randomly perturbing silhouettes and other features lines and by texturing them with scanned, hand-drawn strokes.

Kalnins et al. [22] took this concept of data-driven randomness a step further and allowed users to directly draw strokes onto models and feature lines. Similar strokes were then applied, by example, to all other feature lines in a scene. This allowed for an unprecedented degree of personalization (capturing actual strokes from a user) coupled with convenience (automatically learning and applying a stroke style).

Consistency One issue with the above randomness approaches was that they treated inking lines separately from fills, resulting in randomized outlines being misaligned with fills, which themselves still perfectly matched the underlying geometry. Nienhaus and Döllner [34] solved this problem by reverting back to a G-buffer based approach and ensuring that the exact same distortions were applied to all buffers responsible for outlines and fills (Fig. 17.2). Specifically, undistorted outlines and fills were rendered using G-buffers and a color buffer. Additionally, a random perturbation map was computed, based on Perlin noise.[5] This noise map was then used to distort the outlines, fills, and depth-map in a model and scene-consistent manner.[6]

Image-based Cartooning Up to this point, the focus of this section has been exclusively on cartoon rendering based on 3D geometry, rather than image or video-based cartooning. The reason for this is that it is the primary use of cartooning in the industry. Despite their obviously stylized appearances, even the movies "*Waking Life*" (2001) or "*A Scanner Darkly*" (2008) did not employ automatic cartooning techniques. Instead, rotoscoping was applied by a large number of artists and custom software was used to interpolate (*tween*) the rotoscoped shapes—altogether a very labor intensive and expensive procedure. For completeness, the interested reader may consult the following references regarding image-based cartooning [12, 14, 23, 26, 50]. In addition, Sect. 17.5 describes a commercial image-based cartooning application.

17.3.2 Entertainment Applications

Equipped with the above overview of cartooning techniques, we now look at examples of some of these techniques in the real world.

17.3.2.1 Movies

In general, computer graphics animations are more cost effective to produce than hand-drawn or stop-motion animations of similar complexity. For this reason, many

---

[5]Random and pseudo-random artifacts are a popular NPR mechanism to simulate natural uncertainty or manual jitter. But since such randomness is extrinsic to the scene, special care must be taken to ensure temporal coherence during animation. Consequently, a number of works are dedicated to this topic [5, 6, 24].

[6]For pseudo-code of their implementation, refer to NVidia's "*GPU Gems 2*" [37], which is also available online.

traditionally animated TV series have moved to digital animation in recent years, including *"Bob the Builder"* and *"Thomas the Tank Engine"* (both by UK-based HIT Entertainment). Critics of this development argue that the look-and-feel of CG animations lacks the liveliness and warmth of manual animations.

As a compromise, some animation studios have opted to manually draw the main characters of a show, but to use computer-generated animations for backgrounds and set elements. For example, Matt Groening's *Futurama* series regularly employs 3D-based cartoon rendering for the main space-ship, the headquarter building (Planet Express), planets, and many other objects undergoing complex 3D rotations (as these motions are the hardest to animate manually). Several challenges exist in seamlessly compositing cartoon rendered scene elements with hand-drawn animations, for example matching lighting (shading) between both types of elements. According to Scott Vanzo of Rough Draft Studios,[7] the shading of hand-drawn characters in Futurama was intentionally kept simple, and highlights and shadows were often placed more for compositional reasons, rather than to portray accurate lighting interactions. To achieve the same look for 3D elements, the animators would lock a light source to an object, thereby synchronizing their movements and minimizing sweeping motions of shadows and highlights across the object's surface.

A more configurable solution to the same problem was developed by the Japanese OLM Inc. for the production of the Pokémon movies and other *anime* series. While specular and other lighting effects had been adopted to cartoon rendering [4, 49], they were still essentially physically based and therefore unable to produce the almost iconic specular highlights used by many anime artists. In 2003, Anjyo et al. [1] offered a solution in the form of a specialized highlight shader, capable of producing split-and-square anime highlights. Three years later, Anjyo et al. [2] improved upon this prior work by allowing a user to adjust the shape, size, orientation, and position of stylized cartoon highlights via direct through-the-lens manipulation. That is, a user could move and adjust highlights in the actual rendered image via simple mouse interactions. Another three years later, Todo et al. [46] added another extension to the system to allow for art-directed tweaking of shading-extent and orientations. In addition to publishing this research and improving workflows for their in-house animators and art directors, OLM made several of their tools freely available as plugins for a variety of third-party software.[8]

In some animation styles, most notably many of Disney's movies, hand-drawn cel animations are composited on top of painted backgrounds. Since the same background image can be used for an entire scene, it is feasible to create a much more elaborate painting than for the animated foreground elements. Background painting artists have developed remarkable techniques to imply changes in perspective and camera angle while panning over the background image [9, 38, 53], but these techniques are still limited by the static nature of the backdrops. To overcome this limitation, thereby creating backgrounds with more depth and dynamics while retaining

---

[7]http://www.gotfuturama.com/Information/Articles/3dani.dhtml.

[8]http://www.olm.co.jp/rd/technology/tools/?lang=en.

(a) Studio Photograph   (b) Final Look

Fig. 17.4 *Painted World:* Painterly rendering in *"What Dreams May Come"* (1998). (**a**) Photograph showing studio set with background blue screen. (**b**) The same scene with painterly rendering and compositing effects added. Copyright © Universal Pictures. All rights reserved. Used with permission

the painterly aesthetic, Disney developed *Deep Canvas* [11]. With Deep Canvas, background artists can paint brush-strokes directly onto 3D scene geometry. In contrast to the simple planar canvas used for traditional backgrounds, 3D backgrounds require artists to cover all surfaces visible during an animation. However, once this is completed, the scene can be rendered from many novel viewpoints and still retain a painterly look-and-feel. Deep Canvas was first used in Disney's *Tarzan* (1999) and went on to earn its creators a Technical Achievement award from the Academy of Motion Picture Arts and Sciences in 2003. Various systems have been developed over the years to simplify a diverse range of cel animation challenges, including shadows [36], shading [20], and texturing [10] (see also Chap. 14).

Painterly Rendering   Despite its prevalence, the cartoon style is not the only artistic style used in movie production. In fact, one of the first uses of NPR in a feature-length movie were the "painted world" sequences of the movie *What Dreams May Come* (1998). In the movie, Robin William's character creates his own afterlife world in the likeness of an impressionist painting. The director's vision was for the world to look both dynamic and alive, yet painted.

To achieve this effect, the decision was made to create a painterly rendering system (MotionPaint) driven by live action footage (see Fig. 17.4). This system was derived from work of Litwinowicz [28] as the first painterly rendering approach to automatically move brush strokes across the screen based on the optical flow field of the input video. While Litwinowicz's system eliminated the need to painstakingly repaint every frame by hand, the overall workflow was still far from automatic. Optical flow methods are imperfect even today, and were much less sophisticated in 1998. To augment the optical flow from the video input, the production team also captured laser range scans of the landscape where the live action footage was filmed, to create a rough 3D model of the scene. This, together with markers placed in the scene, allowed the team to track the camera within the environment and align the 3D model with the film footage.

The captured scene itself was then processed in several stages where different types of brush stroke and distribution pattern were applied to the sky, the mountains, and even different classes of flowers. Part of Litwinowicz's contribution was the ability for art directors to locally specify parameters for distribution and rendering of brush strokes, and for the optical flow to spatially push these parameters through the scene. This reduced the required manual input from specifying such parameters on every frame to specifying them only once, followed by occasional corrections. One might therefore argue that the main importance of Litwinowicz's work was not so much an improvement in painterly rendering (which was largely based on Haeberli's *Paint by Numbers* system [16]), but an improvement in temporal coherence of painterly rendering on video sequences and the mechanisms by which art directors could specify parameters within these sequences. In large part due to the "painted world" scenes, the movie received an Academy Award for Visual Effects.

17.3.2.2 Games

Even with all the advances made in geometry-based cartoon rendering, discussed in Sect. 17.3.1 and employed in several movie titles, modern cartoon rendering for games is more related to the very early *comprehensible rendering* work by Saito and Takahashi [41] than most of the techniques we listed thereafter. The main reason for this is rendering speed, which is paramount for interactive gameplay. Many of the advanced cartoon rendering techniques described above require visibility computations for edges and triangles of an object. For complex scenes with hundreds of objects, such computations can quickly become intractable. Additionally, the rendering cost for such an approach scales with the number of objects in a scene, so care has to be taken to not overload a scene. In contrast, a G-buffer based approach, like that of Saito and Takahashi, only depends on the number of pixels on the screen, which stays constant and is therefore much easier to budget for in terms of computing resources.

Modern cartoon rendering for games makes extensive use of programmable graphics hardware (GPUs). Commonly, each frame is first rendered into three buffers: The color buffer (with ambient lighting only, but including textures), the depth buffer (which encodes the screen distance of the nearest surface underneath a pixel), and the normal buffer (which encodes the normal at the corresponding surface location). Figure 17.2 illustrates this approach. The depth buffer is used to detect sudden changes in depth, which typically occur at object boundaries (silhouettes). Additional features lines, such as valleys, ridges, creases [19], suggestive contours [13], and apparent ridges [21] may be computed by using combined depth and normal buffers. These feature lines are generally detected by evaluating the first or second order differentials with finite differences, or by convolution with appropriate feature kernels (such as the Sobel kernel). A practical issue is that the width of detected feature lines then depends on the size of the kernel and cannot easily be adjusted (morphological operations can be applied to this end, but require an additional rendering pass).

Simple diffuse cartoon lighting can be easily computed using one or more lightsources and a normal map. The initial color buffer is then composited with the feature lines and cartoon lighting to achieve the final cartoon effect. This basic approach, with minor modifications, is used in popular cartoon-style game titles such as *XIII* (Ubisoft, 2003), *Prince of Persia* (Ubisoft, 2008), and *Borderlands* (Gearbox Software/2K Games, 2009).[9] It should be noted that cartoon rendering is but one of several methods to achieve stylistic differentiation. Several games, including Borderlands, Prince of Persia, and *Battlefield Heroes* (Easy Studios/Electronic Arts, 2009) additionally employ hand-painted textures to achieve a unique visual style. Such textures may be applied to static background objects (scenery) as well as actors, and quite often differ in visual style between foreground and background elements to direct the player's attention. Other means of non-realistic game stylization include custom palettes (e.g. black-and-white, super-saturated, desaturated), exaggerated geometry (caricatures and prototypical body types, faces, weapons, and vehicles), and non-realistic motion (bounce-and-stretch, super-human speed or agility).

17.4 Visualization & Presentation

Another use of NPR, in addition to production and entertainment, is the visualization of data or ideas. Traditional architectural designs, for example, may evolve from rough initial sketches to miniature-scale cardboard models, each presentation style focusing on the most critical aspect of the current design stage. First, sketches and blue-prints may focus primarily on the spatial layout of walls and rooms, whereas later design concepts could include specific furniture layout and even wall-art. The challenge for the architect is to provide just enough information and context for the client to make an informed decision, while at the same time avoiding superfluous specifics that could distract the client and cloud or even inhibit the decision making process.

In an empirical study involving 54 architects, Schumann et al. [42] compared the standard output of a CAD software with a smooth-shaded version ("realistic") and an interactive sketch-renderer for several architectural scenes. While the first two presentation modes precisely followed the underlying geometry, the sketching mode employed randomness, abstraction, and stylized textures to simulate a handcrafted look. Schumann et al. found that the stylized rendering was preferred in the early phases of the design, as it was visually more engaging than the precise

---

[9]*Team Fortress 2* (Valve, 2007) also uses stylized shading, but opts for a more customized look based on early 20th century commercial illustration, in addition to heavily exaggerated characters and carefully crafted color palettes [32].

renditions. Moreover, a sketchy look suggested to viewers that the design was not final and therefore fostered more discussion and design exploration than either of the more realistic visualizations.

Modern NPR techniques allow architects and designers to leverage CAD software for convenient design creation and modification, yet produce the hand-crafted look of traditional sketches, which have proven beneficial in the communication and exploration of early ideation. In addition, with automatic NPR algorithms it is trivial to produce numerous custom views in a variety of styles, which would be impractical or costly to produce by hand.

17.4.1 Examples

Piranesi The *Piranesi* system (Informatix Inc.), based on work by Richens and Schofield [40], is one of the first commercial systems that made NPR techniques available for architects to stylize their CAD drawings. While initially intended to be a fully automatic painterly system, the decision was made early on to not focus on any one particular artistic style, but rather to offer the user the control to manually combine a host of effects and filters, thereby creating their own personal look.

A technique used by architects and interior designers to visually enhance their CAD designs is to print them out using conventional plotters and then manually redrawing, coloring, and beautifying them (commonly using watercolors or felt-tip pens). This mode of drawing over CAD data is the guiding principle of Piranesi and makes the system look much like a painting program—however, one with smarter tools than conventional painting software. The reason for this is that Piranesi adds some additional input channels to the standard RGBA canvas, specifically a per-pixel depth buffer and material buffer, both derived from the CAD model and current camera view. Any stylization tool offered in Piranesi has access to these additional channels to perform automatic or smart interactions. For example, an edge-brush can use discontinuities in the depth-buffer to paint silhouettes. Other brushes can differentiate the depth-buffer data to compute surface normals or even curvature, and apply special effects based on these. For example, the normal of a surface can be used to apply lighting effects without requiring a traditional renderer. Principal curvature could be used to infer hatching directions. Deformation brushes may have a different effect depending on what material they are painted on. The output of particular brushes can further be processed by filtering operations. For example, the perfectly straight lines of an edge-detection brush may be randomly perturbed to yield a sketch-like appearance. As an interactive system, Piranesi is not a one-click solution. Rather, it allows skilled users to combine a variety of NPR techniques into a uniquely personal style which highlights semantically important aspects of their CAD design (Fig. 17.5a).

PaletteCAD Another product, *PaletteCAD* (PaletteCAD GmbH) focuses on craftsmen and interior designers. Unlike Piranesi, which ingests output from a CAD

(a) Piranesi   (b) Defaults   (c) PaletteCAD

Fig. 17.5 *Presentation:* (**a**) Architectural illustration using Piranesi; (**b**) default presentation of example scenes; (**c**) automatic watercolor rendering of interior scene by PaletteCAD. (**a**), (**b**, *top*) Default scene Copyright © 2012 Informatic Inc Japan; (**b**, *bottom*), (**c**) Copyright © 2012 Palette CAD GmbH

program, PaletteCAD integrates both CAD development and presentation modules. PaletteCAD's NPR rendering modes emphasize ease-of-use over creative expression. As a result, the product offers several pre-defined, high-quality NPR rendering modes, including black-and-white edge lines, sketchy felt-tip rendering, and watercolor rendering (Fig. 17.5b). The latter is based on the work by Luft et al. [29], which uses an ambient occlusion buffer to modulate and mask two watercolor layers, one for details including colors and textures in lit parts of the scene, and one with complementary coloring for unlit scene parts. A third layer, consisting of contours and hatching for shadowed and dark regions, is combined with the other two layers to complete the rendering. The final result leverages artistic theory of opposing colors, has a convincingly hand-crafted look, yet retains some of the complex lighting effects simulated by the ambient occlusion computation. The watercolor rendition is easily more visually compelling than a simple Gouraud shaded version, but it also stands out when compared with a photorealistic, raytraced version—and in marketing, teasing a second look from a potential customer can mean the difference between a window shopper and a client. For this reason PaletteCAD also offers *PaletteSketch*, a fully automatic drawing system, which renders the output of PaletteCAD one brush stroke and pencil line at a time. The effect for the observer is one of a watercolor painting being performed as if by hand, emphasized by the current painting tool being animated across the screen. Drawn in by this animation, a customer is likely going to engage significantly longer with the display than they might otherwise.

SketchUp Due to Google's widespread impact and its low entry cost, *SketchUp* (@Last, Google, Trimble) is probably the most widely used 3D modeling package to-date. Since the focus of SketchUp is simple and intuitive modeling, rather than sophisticated rendering (which can be achieved by importing SketchUp models into third party rendering software) SketchUp natively produces mainly stylized output. To this end, SketchUp offers a simple local shading model with optional hard shadows. Edges are rendered as black lines by default, but can be customized for increased stylistic variability. Specifically, edges may be extended to produce artificial overshoot, exterior edges may be emphasized over interior edges (profile), and edges may be jittered or textured to suggest a hand-drawn quality. Using SketchUp's *Style Builder*, edges can be further customized by allowing the user to manually draw or scan line textures.

17.5 A Case Study: Mobile NPR

Turning NPR research into end-user facing products is challenging for many reasons. A research prototype may only produce quality results for well-lit images, it may take many minutes to compute a single image, and it may have a large number of technical parameters that need to be tuned by an individual with expert knowledge of the underlying technology. In this section, we discuss the productization of a research system. The reader should note that each technology transfer is different, yet, many of the issues raised in the following text are common productization challenges.

17.5.1 Cartooning with ToonPAINT

ToonPAINT (ToonFX LLC) is a creative mobile application that turns images into cartoons. The underlying NPR technology for this software is based on Winnemöller et al.'s "Real-time Video Abstraction" [50] and extensions by Kyprianidis and Döllner [26]. In the former work, Winnemöller et al. presented a graph-based filter processing framework, which simplified colors via bilateral filtering and pseudo-quantization of the luminance channel, while image shapes were enhanced via Difference-of-Gaussian (DoG) edge detection. The entire system was implemented on the GPU and allowed for real-time processing of streaming video. The work of Kyprianidis and Döllner modified this framework to reduce noise and generate cleaner ink lines by guiding image processing operations along the source image's structure tensor.

Opportunities & Challenges   Adapting this cartooning framework to a mobile platform in 2010 offered many opportunities and challenges. In terms of opportunities, mobile platforms, including mobile phones and tablet devices, allow for successful publishing of so-called one-trick ponies. That is, unlike desktop software, which is traditionally expected to be powerful and feature-packed, mobile apps may be very small and specialized. Consequently, mobile apps may be produced relatively quickly and for lower cost than many larger desktop titles. Additionally, mobile platforms offer sensors and input modalities, such as accelerometers, location services, and touch-screen capabilities, which are generally not present on desktop computers, but which may be used to enhance human–computer interaction.

One major mobile challenge is the reduced processing power of mobile devices, which is a direct consequence of the requirements for low power consumption and

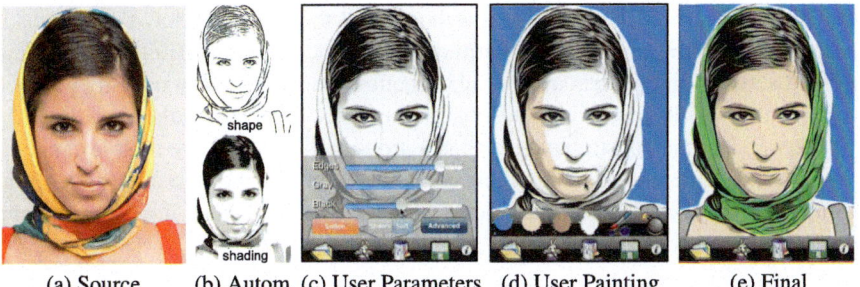

(a) Source (b) Autom. (c) User Parameters (d) User Painting (e) Final

Fig. 17.6 *ToonPAINT:* (**a**) Input photograph; (**b**) XDoG [48] edge detection is used for automatic shape and shading representations; (**c**) user adjustable defaults for edges, mid-tones, and shadows; (**d**) The user paints roughly with manually selected colors; (**d**) the final image is a blend of source image features and the user's imagination. Source © Maryse Casol. Screenshots courtesy Toon-FX, LLC. Used with permission

prolonged battery life. As a rule-of-thumb, the state-of-the-art processing power of mobile devices is roughly similar to the equivalent desktop performance of 3–5 years ago. This is in stark contrast with the image capturing capabilities of mobile devices, which rival those of mid-level dedicated cameras, at least in terms of resolution. The result is a performance mismatch where images of desktop-typical sizes need to be processed on mobile devices, but with much reduced processing resources.

The Audience The makers of ToonPAINT attacked these challenges on a fundamental level by designing a user experience that would at once reduce processing requirements and increase user engagement with the product. Several decisions were made early on in the product design stage: The product should be aimed at users with limited artistic skills (non-professionals) thereby widening the potential user-base. At the same time, the user experience should be more engaging than a mere one-click (fully automatic) algorithm, thereby keeping the users interested and locked-in.

Most instructional art books focus on technical issues that budding artists find challenging, namely the accurate depiction of shape and shading. Coloring, on the other hand, may be crude, employ a limited palette, or even be non-existent, without detracting from the overall sense of expressiveness and creativity of the final image. ToonPAINT's basic workflow was designed around this insight: Using NPR techniques, ToonPAINT represents shapes using flow-DoG based edge-lines and several levels of shading with a multi-adjustable XDoG [48] (Fig. 17.6b). Coloring, while possible to compute fully automatically [50], is left for the user to apply (Fig. 17.6d). Given the automatically pre-computed edge+duo-tone rendition, the user's task reduces to a simple coloring exercise, similar to those in a children's coloring book.

Presets and Robustness Given the image's pre-processing results, the user is presented with an initial output, based on the software's default settings (Fig. 17.6c), exhibiting dark ('inked') outlines, as well as a mid-tone and a shadow-tone for shading. Productization of an NPR algorithm in general, and the feasibility of offering default settings and presets in particular, require the algorithm to robustly produce high-quality results for a wide range of input images, especially if these images may be taken in less than desirable lighting situations, with inexpensive mobile cameras, and by non-professional photographers. Being aware of the possible input variations (lighting levels, noise, etc.) helps to design an NPR implementation around these potential pitfalls.[10]

Outcomes Omitting the automatic coloring component from ToonPAINT addressed many of the above-mentioned issues all at once: Computational steps and storage for color smoothing and quantization could be saved. A high-quality NPR algorithm with robust default settings ensured aesthetically pleasing results, even in black-and-white. The manual coloring process utilized the touch-screen capabilities of the mobile device, thereby providing for a more 'tactile' and fun interaction with the product. Most importantly, comments from those users that provided feedback on their experience via ToonPAINT, blogs, and creative forums made it clear that the simple act of finger-painting a few colors onto the pre-fabricated edge + tone rendition instilled in them a strong sense of ownership and achievement. They felt like they had '*created*' the resulting image (Fig. 17.6e), often neglecting the fact that a lot of work had been done for them by the software.

17.6 Discussion—NPR and *Casual Creativity*

As discussed throughout this chapter, NPR has had a considerable impact in production, entertainment, and specific design and presentation scenarios. However, these applications areas are almost exclusively limited to professional use. Even in movies and games, the end-user is a mere passive consumer of stylized NPR imagery. I believe that there is an important insight to be gained from the above ToonPAINT case study in terms of making NPR research relevant to a broader, non-professional user base.

As noted in the introduction of this chapter, NPR techniques can be roughly categorized as *art creation* tools, *style reproduction* systems, and *assistive technologies*. Traditionally, much of academic NPR research is dedicated to the class of automatic style reproduction systems. Yet, very few true artists find use for those works, because they generally do not seek an automated solution. Instead, they want fine control not only of the final end product, but also of the creative process along the

---

[10]Of course, the maxim "garbage-in → garbage-out" still applies. In general, most NPR algorithms work better with higher contrast images than with lower contrast images. As such, a tone-mapping or normalization pre-processing stage can be used to improve the input to many NPR algorithms. Similarly, bilateral filtering or similar edge-preserving smoothing operations may be used to reduce sensor and other noise before further NPR processing is applied (see also Chap. 5).

way. In essence, they want to express their creativity through artistic means, and while digital *art creation tools* are a convenient way of achieving this, fully automatic *style reproduction systems* often take away too much control. The same is actually true for many non-artists, however they lack the technical skills to produce high-quality artworks unassisted. Encoding an artistic style within an automatic algorithm allows non-artists to transform a photograph into a more interesting looking artifact, which is undoubtedly a desirable goal in itself. However, a fully automatic one-click solution does not engage the user in the creative process and denies them a sense of personal achievement.

In academia, fully automatic solutions are often considered superior to those requiring user-input, as if a semi-automatic approach is by definition incomplete until total automation is achieved. I would argue that putting the user *"into the loop"* may bring significant advantages. For one, a user can often provide perceptual or semantic input that significantly improves the results of an algorithm. Secondly, the user can add creativity to an NPR work, which, in my opinion, is currently beyond the reach of any existing algorithm.[11] Lastly, involving the user in the creative process empowers them to explore their creativity, which they might otherwise feel too daunted to attempt.

17.6.1 A Challenge: User-Centric NPR

The above endorsement of *user-assisted* NPR approaches comes with several practical caveats, and should not be treated as a catch-all for avoiding challenging research questions. If possible, there should be a graduation in user-involvement. An algorithm should be autonomous enough to produce decent results even without user-input. This is important for multiple reasons. A non-artist may be intimidated by the blank page and even an artist may have *"painter's block"*. A reasonable default result can achieve a minimal amount of initial momentum to kick-start the creation process in those situations.

However, it should be possible to integrate user-input into the algorithm to improve the results or to override default behavior. Particularly for professional art creation, directability is of vital importance; for example, to move a shadow or highlight in an otherwise physically lit environment. Importantly, user interactions should be limited as much as possible to engaging and creative tasks, rather than repetitive or tedious ones, where the human is a mere stand-in for imperfect computer vision. Examples of such systems already exist. One of these, Winkenbach and Salesin's much cited Pen-and-Ink approach [47] automatically produces detailed, high-quality illustrations from 3D data. However, the user may manually specify visual emphasis regions, which are then fully rendered, while other regions are intentionally left blank or only *indicated*.

---

[11] Some may find this statement objectionable. For alternative views, the interested reader may search the web for *"Computational Creativity"*.

Overall, NPR researchers might put more emphasis on *assisting* art creation, rather than *automating* it. We should aim to aid users in their creative endeavors, not to disengage them from the process. This requires a conscious consideration for the intended end-user of an NPR system. A well-designed NPR algorithm can achieve a multitude of goals with respect to non-professional user involvement. In an automated form, it can inspire the user to partake in the creative process. In a semi-automated form, it can act as 'training wheels', ensuring a quality result by automating difficult aspects while fostering 'safe' experimentation and learning. In the future, smart algorithms may be able to monitor a user's technical learning progress and back off gracefully until a user has mastered a technique fully unassisted.

References

1. Anjyo, K.i., Hiramitsu, K.: Stylized highlights for cartoon rendering and animation. IEEE Comput. Graph. Appl. **23**(4), 54–61 (2003)
2. Anjyo, K.i., Wemler, S., Baxter, W.: Tweakable light and shade for cartoon animation. In: Proceedings of the 4th International Symposium on Non-photorealistic Animation and Rendering, NPAR '06, pp. 133–139. ACM, New York (2006)
3. Appel, A.: The notion of quantitative invisibility and the machine rendering of solids. In: Proceedings of the 1967 22nd National Conference, ACM '67, pp. 387–393. ACM, New York (1967)
4. Barla, P., Thollot, J., Markosian, L.: X-toon: an extended toon shader. In: Proceedings of the 4th International Symposium on Non-photorealistic Animation and Rendering, NPAR '06, pp. 127–132. ACM, New York (2006)
5. Bénard, P., Bousseau, A., Thollot, J.: Dynamic solid textures for real-time coherent stylization. In: Proceedings of the 2009 Symposium on Interactive 3D Graphics and Games, I3D '09, pp. 121–127. ACM, New York (2009)
6. Bénard, P., Lagae, A., Vangorp, P., Lefebvre, S., Drettakis, G., Thollot, J.: A dynamic noise primitive for coherent stylization. Comput. Graph. Forum **29**(4), 1497–1506 (2010)
7. Bregler, C., Loeb, L., Chuang, E., Deshpande, H.: Turning to the masters: motion capturing cartoons. In: Proceedings of the 29th Annual Conference on Computer Graphics and Interactive Techniques, SIGGRAPH '02, pp. 399–407. ACM, New York (2002)
8. Chen, M.: For some grown-ups, playing with legos is a serious business (2011). http://goo.gl/vFUX4
9. Coleman, P., Singh, K.: Ryan: rendering your animation nonlinearly projected. In: Proceedings of the 3rd International Symposium on Non-photorealistic Animation and Rendering, NPAR '04, pp. 129–156. ACM, New York (2004)
10. Corrêa, W.T., Jensen, R.J., Thayer, C.E., Finkelstein, A.: Texture mapping for cel animation. In: Proceedings of the 25th Annual Conference on Computer Graphics and Interactive Techniques, SIGGRAPH '98, pp. 435–446. ACM, New York (1998)
11. Daniels, E.: Deep canvas in Disney's Tarzan. In: ACM SIGGRAPH 99 Conference Abstracts and Applications, SIGGRAPH '99, p. 200. ACM, New York (1999)
12. DeCarlo, D., Santella, A.: Stylization and abstraction of photographs. ACM Trans. Graph. **21**(3), 769–776 (2002)
13. DeCarlo, D., Finkelstein, A., Rusinkiewicz, S., Santella, A.: Suggestive contours for conveying shape. ACM Trans. Graph. **22**(3), 848–855 (2003)
14. Gooch, B., Sloan, P.P.J., Gooch, A., Shirley, P., Riesenfeld, R.: Interactive technical illustration. In: Proceedings of the 1999 Symposium on Interactive 3D Graphics, I3D '99, pp. 31–38. ACM, New York (1999)

15. Gouraud, H.: Continuous shading of curved surfaces. IEEE Trans. Comput. **20**(6), 623–629 (1971)
16. Haeberli, P.: Paint by numbers: abstract image representations. In: Proceedings of the 17th Annual Conference on Computer Graphics and Interactive Techniques, SIGGRAPH '90, pp. 207–214. ACM, New York (1990)
17. Ho, S.N., Komiya, R.: Real time loose and sketchy rendering in hardware. In: Proceedings of the 20th Spring Conference on Computer Graphics, SCCG '04, pp. 83–88. ACM, New York (2004)
18. Igarashi, Y., Igarashi, T.H.: A drawing editor for designing stencils. IEEE Comput. Graph. Appl. **30**, 8–14 (2010)
19. Interrante, V., Fuchs, H., Pizer, S.: Enhancing transparent skin surfaces with ridge and valley lines. In: Proceedings of the 6th Conference on Visualization '95 (VIS '95), p. 52. IEEE Comput. Soc., Los Alamitos (1995)
20. Johnston, S.F.: Lumo: illumination for cel animation. In: Proceedings of the 2nd International Symposium on Non-photorealistic Animation and Rendering, NPAR '02, pp. 45–ff. ACM, New York (2002)
21. Judd, T., Durand, F., Adelson, E.: Apparent ridges for line drawing. ACM Trans. Graph. **26**(3), 19 (2007)
22. Kalnins, R.D., Markosian, L., Meier, B.J., Kowalski, M.A., Lee, J.C., Davidson, P.L., Webb, M., Hughes, J.F., Finkelstein, A.: WYSIWYG NPR: drawing strokes directly on 3D models. ACM Trans. Graph. **21**(3), 755–762 (2002)
23. Kang, H., Lee, S., Chui, C.: Flow-based image abstraction. IEEE Trans. Vis. Comput. Graph. **15**(1), 62–76 (2009)
24. Kass, M., Pesare, D.: Coherent noise for non-photorealistic rendering. ACM Trans. Graph. **30**(4), 30 (2011)
25. Kim, D., Son, M., Lee, Y., Kang, H., Lee, S.: Feature-guided image stippling. Comput. Graph. Forum **27**(4), 1209–1216 (2008)
26. Kyprianidis, J.E., Döllner, J.: Image abstraction by structure adaptive filtering. In: Proc. EG UK Theory and Practice of Computer Graphics, pp. 51–58 (2008)
27. Lake, A., Marshall, C., Harris, M., Blackstein, M.: Stylized rendering techniques for scalable real-time 3D animation. In: Proceedings of the 1st International Symposium on Non-photorealistic Animation and Rendering, NPAR '00, pp. 13–20. ACM, New York (2000)
28. Litwinowicz, P.: Processing images and video for an impressionist effect. In: Proceedings of the 24th Annual Conference on Computer Graphics and Interactive Techniques, SIGGRAPH '97, pp. 407–414. ACM/Addison-Wesley, New York/Reading (1997)
29. Luft, T., Kobs, F., Zinser, W., Deussen, O.: Watercolor illustrations of CAD data. In: International Symposium on Computational Aesthetics in Graphics, Visualization, and Imaging, pp. 57–63. Eurographics Association, Geneva (2008)
30. Markosian, L., Kowalski, M.A., Goldstein, D., Trychin, S.J., Hughes, J.F., Bourdev, L.D.: Real-time nonphotorealistic rendering. In: Proceedings of the 24th Annual Conference on Computer Graphics and Interactive Techniques, SIGGRAPH '97, pp. 415–420. ACM/Addison-Wesley, New York/Reading (1997)
31. Mello, V.B., Jung, C.R., Walter, M.: Virtual woodcuts from images. In: Proceedings of the 5th International Conference on Computer Graphics and Interactive Techniques in Australia and Southeast Asia, GRAPHITE '07, pp. 103–109. ACM, New York (2007)
32. Mitchell, J., Francke, M., Eng, D.: Illustrative rendering in Team Fortress 2. In: Proceedings of the 5th International Symposium on Non-photorealistic Animation and Rendering, NPAR '07, pp. 71–76. ACM, New York (2007)
33. Mizuno, S., Okada, M., Toriwaki, J.: An interactive designing system with virtual sculpting and virtual woodcut printing. Comput. Graph. Forum **18**(3), 183–194 (1999)
34. Nienhaus, M., Döllner, J.: Sketchy drawings. In: Proceedings of the 3rd International Conference on Computer Graphics, Virtual Reality, Visualisation and Interaction in Africa, AFRIGRAPH '04, pp. 73–81. ACM, New York (2004)

35. Ostromoukhov, V.: Digital facial engraving. In: Proceedings of the 26th Annual Conference on Computer Graphics and Interactive Techniques, SIGGRAPH '99, pp. 417–424. ACM/Addison-Wesley, New York/Reading (1999)
36. Petrović, L., Fujito, B., Williams, L., Finkelstein, A.: Shadows for cel animation. In: Proceedings of the 27th Annual Conference on Computer Graphics and Interactive Techniques, SIGGRAPH '00, pp. 511–516. ACM/Addison-Wesley, New York/Reading (2000)
37. Pharr, M., Fernando, R.: GPU Gems 2: Programming Techniques for High-Performance Graphics and General-Purpose Computation (GPU Gems). Addison-Wesley Professional, Reading (2005)
38. Popescu, V., Rosen, P., Adamo-Villani, N.: The graph camera. ACM Trans. Graph. **28**(5), 158 (2009)
39. Raskar, R., Cohen, M.: Image precision silhouette edges. In: Proceedings of the 1999 Symposium on Interactive 3D Graphics, I3D '99, pp. 135–140. ACM, New York (1999)
40. Richens, P.: The Piranesi system for interactive rendering. In: Proceedings of the Eighth International Conference on Computer Aided Architectural Design Futures, pp. 381–398. Kluwer Academic, Dordrecht (1999)
41. Saito, T., Takahashi, T.: Comprehensible rendering of 3-D shapes. SIGGRAPH Comput. Graph. **24**(4), 197–206 (1990)
42. Schumann, J., Strothotte, T., Laser, S., Raab, A.: Assessing the effect of non-photorealistic rendered images in CAD. In: Proceedings of the SIGCHI Conference on Human Factors in Computing Systems: Common Ground, CHI '96, pp. 35–41. ACM, New York (1996)
43. Secord, A.: Weighted Voronoi stippling. In: Proceedings of the 2nd International Symposium on Non-photorealistic Animation and Rendering, NPAR '02, pp. 37–43. ACM, New York (2002)
44. Son, M., Lee, Y., Kang, H., Lee, S.: Structure grid for directional stippling. Graph. Models **73**(3), 74–87 (2011)
45. Sýkora, D., Dingliana, J., Collins, S.: LazyBrush: flexible painting tool for hand-drawn cartoons. Comput. Graph. Forum **28**(2), 599–608 (2009)
46. Todo, H., Anjyo, K., Igarashi, T.: Stylized lighting for cartoon shader. Comput. Animat. Virtual Worlds **20**(2–3), 143–152 (2009)
47. Winkenbach, G., Salesin, D.H.: Computer-generated pen-and-ink illustration. In: Proc. of ACM SIGGRAPH, vol. 94, pp. 91–100 (1994)
48. Winnemöller, H.: XDoG: advanced image stylization with eXtended difference-of-Gaussians. In: Proceedings of the ACM SIGGRAPH/Eurographics Symposium on Non-Photorealistic Animation and Rendering, NPAR '11, pp. 147–156. ACM, New York (2011)
49. Winnemöller, H., Bangay, S.: Geometric approximations towards free specular comic shading. Comput. Graph. Forum **21**(3), 309–316 (2002)
50. Winnemöller, H., Olsen, S.C., Gooch, B.: Real-time video abstraction. ACM Trans. Graph. **25**(3), 1221–1226 (2006)
51. Winnemöller, H., Kyprianidis, J.E., Olsen, S.C.: XDoG: an eXtended difference-of-Gaussians compendium including advanced image stylization. Comput. Graph. **36**(6), 740–753 (2012)
52. Woo, M., Neider, J., Davis, T., Shreiner, D.: OpenGL PRogramming GUide: THe OFficial Guide to LEarning OpenGL, Version 1.2, 3rd edn. Addison-Wesley Longman, Reading (1999)
53. Wood, D.N., Finkelstein, A., Hughes, J.F., Thayer, C.E., Salesin, D.H.: Multiperspective panoramas for cel animation. In: Proceedings of the 24th Annual Conference on Computer Graphics and Interactive Techniques, SIGGRAPH '97, pp. 243–250. ACM/Addison-Wesley, New York/Reading (1997)

ERRATUM

Erratum to: Artistic Rendering of Portraits

Mingtian Zhao and Song-Chun Zhu

Erratum to: P. Rosin, J. Collomosse (eds.), *Image and Video-Based Artistic Stylisation*,
Computational Imaging and Vision 42, pp. 237–253
DOI 10.1007/978-1-4471-4519-6_12,
© Springer-Verlag London 2013

In Fig. 12.11, the two source photographs are incorrect. The correct figure should be:

Fig. 12.11 Example paper-cuts generated using the method of Meng et al. [13]

The online version of the original chapter can be found at doi:10.1007/978-1-4471-4519-6_12.

M. Zhao (✉) · S.-C. Zhu
University of California, Los Angeles, CA 90095-1554, USA
e-mail: mtzhao@ucla.edu

S.-C. Zhu
e-mail: sczhu@stat.ucla.edu

References

1. Abdel-Malek, K., Blackmore, D., Joy, K.: Swept volumes: foundations, perspectives, and applications. Int. J. Shape Model. **12**(1), 87–127 (2006)
2. Acevedo, D., Laidlaw, D., Drury, F.: Using visual design expertise to characterize the effectiveness of 2D scientific visualization methods. In: Proceedings Compendium of IEEE InfoVis and Visualization 2005, pp. 111–112 (2005)
3. Achanta, R., Shaji, A., Smith, K., Lucchi, A., Fua, P., Süsstrunk, S.: SLIC superpixels. Technical report EPFL-REPORT-149300, École Polytechnique Fédrale de Lausanne (EPFL) (2010)
4. Adobe: Illustrator (2012). http://www.adobe.com/illustrator
5. Adobe: Photoshop (2012). http://www.adobe.com/photoshop
6. Agarwala, A.: SnakeToonz: a semi-automatic approach to creating cel animation from video. In: Proc. NPAR, pp. 139–163 (2002)
7. Agarwala, A., Hertzmann, A., Salesin, D.H., Seitz, S.M.: Keyframe-based tracking for rotoscoping and animation. ACM Trans. Graph. **23**(3), 584–591 (2004)
8. Agrawal, A., Raskar, R.: Gradient domain manipulation techniques in vision and graphics. In: ICCV Course (2007)
9. Agrawala, M., Zorin, D., Munzner, T.: Artistic multiprojection rendering. In: Peroche, B., Rushmeier, H.E. (eds.) Proc. EG Workshop on Rendering, pp. 125–136 (2000)
10. Aichholzer, O., Aurenhammer, F., Alberts, D., Gärtner, B.: A novel type of skeleton for polygons. J. Univers. Comput. Sci. **1**(12), 752–761 (1995)
11. Alexa, M., Cohen-Or, D., Levin, D.: As-rigid-as-possible shape interpolation. In: Proc. SIGGRAPH, pp. 157–164 (2000)
12. Allen, J.R.: Celtic Art in Pagan and Christian Times. Studio Limited (1993)
13. Alliez, P., Cohen-Steiner, D., Devillers, O., Lévy, B., Desbrun, M.: Anisotropic polygonal remeshing. ACM Trans. Graph. **22**(3), 485–493 (2003)
14. AlMeraj, Z., Kaplan, C.S., Asente, P., Lank, E.: Towards ground truth in geometric textures. In: Proc. NPAR, pp. 17–26 (2011)
15. Alvarez, L., Mazorra, L.: Signal and image restoration using shock filters and anisotropic diffusion. SIAM J. Numer. Anal. **31**(2), 590–605 (1994)
16. Anjyo, K.-i., Hiramitsu, K.: Stylized highlights for cartoon rendering and animation. IEEE Comput. Graph. Appl. **23**(4), 54–61 (2003)
17. Anjyo, K.-i., Wemler, S., Baxter, W.: Tweakable light and shade for cartoon animation. In: Proc. NPAR, pp. 133–139 (2006)
18. Appel, A.: The notion of quantitative invisibility and the machine rendering of solids. In: Rosenthal, S. (ed.) Proc. ACM '67, pp. 387–393 (1967)
19. Applegate, D.L., Bixby, R.E., Chvátal, V., Cook, W.J.: The Traveling Salesman Problem: A Computational Study. Princeton University Press, Princeton (2006)

20. Armstrong, J.: Composite Bezier curves (2006). http://www.algorithmist.net/composite.html
21. Arnhiem, R.: Art and Visual Perception: A Psychology of the Creative Eye, 2nd edn. University of California Press, Berkeley (1974)
22. Ambient design. ArtRage (2012). http://www.artrage.com
23. Aubert, G., Kornprobst, P.: Mathematical Problems in Image Processing: Partial Differential Equations and the Calculus of Variations. Springer, Berlin (2006)
24. Aurich, V., Weule, J.: Non-linear Gaussian filters performing edge preserving diffusion. In: Proc. DAGM-Symposium, pp. 538–545 (1995)
25. Bai, B., Wong, K.-W., Zhang, Y.: An efficient physically-based model for Chinese brush. In: Proceedings of the Int. Conf. on Frontiers in Algorithmics, pp. 261–270 (2007)
26. Bai, X., Wang, J., Simons, D., Sapiro, G.: Video SnapCut: robust video object cutout using localized classifiers. ACM Trans. Graph. **28**(3), 1–11 (2009)
27. Bangham, J.A., Gibson, S.E., Harvey, R.: The art of scale-space. In: Proc. BMVC, pp. 569–578 (2003)
28. Baraff, D., Witkin, A.: Physically based modeling: principles and practice. In: SIGGRAPH Courses (1997)
29. Barash, D., Comaniciu, D.: A common framework for nonlinear diffusion, adaptive smoothing, bilateral filtering and mean shift. Image Vis. Comput. **22**(1), 73–81 (2004)
30. Barla, P., Breslav, S., Thollot, J., Sillion, F., Markosian, L.: Stroke pattern analysis and synthesis. In: Computer Graphics Forum, vol. 25, pp. 663–671 (2006)
31. Barla, P., Thollot, J., Markosian, L.: X-toon: an extended toon shader. In: Proc. NPAR, pp. 127–132 (2006)
32. Barrett, W.A., Cheney, A.S.: Object-based image editing. ACM Trans. Graph. **21**(3), 777–784 (2002)
33. Barrodale, I., Skea, D., Berkley, M., Kuwahara, R., Poeckert, R.: Warping digital images using thin plate splines. Pattern Recognit. **26**(2), 375–376 (1993)
34. Battiato, S., Di Blasi, G., Farinella, G.M., Gallo, G.: A novel technique for opus vermiculatum mosaic rendering. In: Proc. WSCG, pp. 133–140 (2006)
35. Battiato, S., Di Blasi, G., Farinella, G.M., Gallo, G.: Digital mosaic frameworks—an overview. Comput. Graph. Forum **26**(4), 794–812 (2007)
36. Battiato, S., Di Blasi, G., Gallo, G., Guarnera, G.C., Puglisi, G.: A novel artificial mosaic generation technique driven by local gradient analysis. In: Proc. International Workshop on Computer Graphics and Geometric Modeling (CGGM'08), vol. 5102, pp. 76–85 (2008)
37. Battiato, S., Di Blasi, G., Gallo, G., Guarnera, G.C., Puglisi, G.: Artificial mosaics by gradient vector flow. In: Short Proceedings of Eurographics (2008)
38. Baxter, W., Govindaraju, N.: Simple data-driven modeling of brushes. In: Proc. SIGGRAPH Symposium on Interactive 3D Graphics and Games, pp. 135–142 (2010)
39. Baxter, W., Lin, M.: A versatile interactive 3D brush model. In: Proc. Pacific Graphics, pp. 319–328 (2004)
40. Baxter, W.V., Scheib, V., Lin, M.C.: DAB: interactive haptic painting with 3D virtual brushes. In: Proc. SIGGRAPH, pp. 461–468 (2001)
41. Baxter, W., Wendt, J., Lin, M.C.: IMPaSTo: a realistic, interactive model for paint. In: Proc. NPAR, pp. 45–56 (2004)
42. Beauchemin, S.S., Barron, J.L.: The computation of optical flow. ACM Comput. Surv. **27**(3), 433–466 (1995)
43. Beeson, C.: Animation in the "Dawn" demo. In: Fernando, R. (ed.) GPU Gems, pp. 223–233. Addison-Wesley Professional, Reading (2004)
44. Belongie, S., Malik, J., Puzicha, J.: Shape matching and object recognition using shape contexts. IEEE Trans. Pattern Anal. Mach. Intell. **24**(4), 509–522 (2002)
45. Bénard, P., Bousseau, A., Thollot, J.: Dynamic solid textures for real-time coherent stylization. In: Proc. SIGGRAPH Symposium on Interactive 3D Graphics and Games, pp. 121–127 (2009)
46. Bénard, P., Thollot, J., Sillion, F.: Quality assessment of fractalized NPR textures: a perceptual objective metric. In: Proc. APGV, pp. 117–120 (2009)

47. Bénard, P., Cole, F., Golovinskiy, A., Finkelstein, A.: Self-similar texture for coherent line stylization. In: Proc. NPAR, pp. 91–97 (2010)
48. Bénard, P., Lagae, A., Vangorp, P., Lefebvre, S., Drettakis, G., Thollot, J.: A dynamic noise primitive for coherent stylization. Comput. Graph. Forum **29**(4), 1497–1506 (2010)
49. Bénard, P., Bousseau, A., Thollot, J.: Temporal coherence for stylized animation. Comput. Graph. Forum **30**(8), 2367–2386 (2012)
50. Berg, C.: Amazing Art: Wonders of the Ancient World. Harper Collins, New York (2001)
51. Bezerra, H., Eisemann, E., DeCarlo, D., Thollot, J.: Diffusion constraints for vector graphics. In: Proc. NPAR, pp. 35–42 (2010)
52. Bhat, P., Zitnick, C.L., Cohen, M.F., Curless, B.: GradientShop: a gradient-domain optimization framework for image and video filtering. ACM Trans. Graph. **29**(2), 10 (2010)
53. Birkoff, G.: Aesthetic Measure. Harvard University Press, Harvard (1933)
54. Boden, M.A.: The Turing test and artistic creativity. Kybernetes **39**(3), 409–413 (2010)
55. Boeing, A.: Physics Abstraction Layer (2009). http://pal.sourceforge.net
56. Boeing, A., Bräunl, T.: Evaluation of real-time physics simulation systems. In: Proc. GRAPHITE, pp. 281–288 (2007)
57. Bosch, R.: Simple-closed-curve sculptures of knots and links. J. Math. Arts **4**(2), 57–71 (2010)
58. Bosch, R., Herman, A.: Continuous line drawings via the traveling salesman problem. Oper. Res. Lett. **32**(4), 302–303 (2004)
59. Bousseau, A., Kaplan, M., Thollot, J., Sillion, F.X.: Interactive watercolor rendering with temporal coherence and abstraction. In: Proc. NPAR, pp. 141–149 (2006)
60. Bousseau, A., Neyret, F., Thollot, J., Salesin, D.: Video watercolorization using bidirectional texture advection. ACM Trans. Graph. **26**(3), 104 (2007)
61. Bowers, J.C., Leahey, J., Wang, R.: A ray tracing approach to diffusion curves. Comput. Graph. Forum **30**(4), 1345–1352 (2011)
62. Boykov, Y., Funka-Lea, G.: Graph cuts and efficient {N-D} image segmentation. Int. J. Comput. Vis. **70**(2), 109–131 (2006)
63. Boykov, Y., Kolmogorov, V.: An experimental comparison of min-cut/max-flow algorithms for energy minimisation in vision. IEEE Trans. Pattern Anal. Mach. Intell. **26**(9), 1124–1137 (2004)
64. Boykov, Y., Veksler, O., Zabih, R.: Markov random fields with efficient approximations. In: Proc. CVPR, pp. 648–655 (1998)
65. Boykov, Y., Veksler, O., Zabih, R.: Fast approximate energy minimization via graph cuts. IEEE Trans. Pattern Anal. Mach. Intell. **23**(11), 1222–1239 (2001)
66. Bregler, C., Loeb, L., Chuang, E., Deshpande, H.: Turning to the masters: motion capturing cartoons. ACM Trans. Graph., **21**(3), 399–407 (2002)
67. Breslav, S., Szerszen, K., Markosian, L., Barla, P., Thollot, J.: Dynamic 2D patterns for shading 3D scenes. ACM Trans. Graph. **26**(3), 20 (2007)
68. Briggs, W.L., Henson, V.E., McCormick, S.F.: A Multigrid Tutorial. SIAM, Philadelphia (2000)
69. Bronson, J., Rheingans, P., Olano, M.: Semi-Automatic stencil creation through error minimization. In: Proc. NPAR, pp. 31–37 (2008)
70. Brooks, S.: Image-based stained glass. IEEE Trans. Vis. Comput. Graph. **12**(6), 1547–1558 (2006)
71. Brooks, S.: Mixed media painting and portraiture. IEEE Trans. Vis. Comput. Graph. **13**(5), 1041–1054 (2007)
72. Brox, T., Boomgaard, R., Lauze, F., Weijer, J., Weickert, J., Mrázek, P., Kornprobst, P.: Adaptive structure tensors and their applications. In: Visualization and Processing of Tensor Fields, pp. 17–47. Springer, Berlin (2006)
73. Burton, G.J., Moorhead, I.R.: Color and spatial structure in natural scenes. Appl. Opt. **26**(1), 157 (1987)
74. Cabral, B., Leedom, L.C.: Imaging vector fields using line integral convolution. In: Proc. SIGGRAPH, pp. 263–270 (1993)

75. Canny, J.F.: A computational approach to edge detection. IEEE Trans. Pattern Anal. Mach. Intell. **8**, 769–798 (1986)
76. Carpendale, S.: Evaluating information visualizations. In: Information Visualization: Human-Centered Issues and Perspectives, vol. 4950, pp. 19–45. Springer, Berlin (2008)
77. Chen, M.: For some grown-ups, playing with legos is a serious business (2011). http://online.wsj.com/article/SB10001424052970203503204577038164225658328.html
78. Chen, H., Xu, Y.-Q., Shum, H.-Y., Zhu, S.-C., Zheng, N.-N.: Example-based facial sketch generation with non-parametric sampling. In: Proc. ICCV, pp. 433–438 (2001)
79. Chen, H., Liu, Z., Rose, C., Xu, Y., Shum, H.-Y., Salesin, D.: Example-based composite sketching of human portraits. In: Proc. NPAR, pp. 95–153 (2004)
80. Chen, J., Paris, S., Durand, F.: Real-time edge-aware image processing with the bilateral grid. ACM Trans. Graph. **26**(3), 103 (2007)
81. Chenney, S., Pingel, M., Iverson, R., Szymanski, M.: Simulating cartoon style animation. In: Proc. NPAR, pp. 133–138 (2002)
82. Chiang, P.-Y., Liao, W.-H., Li, T.-Y.: Automatic caricature generation by analyzing facial features. In: Proc. ACCV, pp. 808–821 (2004)
83. Chu, S.H.: Making digital painting organic. PhD thesis, Hong Kong University of Science and Technology (2007)
84. Chu, N., Tai, C.-L.: Real-time painting with an expressive virtual Chinese brush. IEEE Comput. Graph. Appl. **24**(5), 76–85 (2004)
85. Chu, N.S.-H., Tai, C.-L.: MoXi. ACM Trans. Graph. **24**, 504–511 (2005)
86. Chu, N., Baxter, W., Wei, L.-Y., Govindaraju, N.: Detail-preserving paint modeling for 3D brushes. In: Proc. NPAR, pp. 27–34 (2010)
87. Cohen, J.: The Earth is round ($p < 0.05$). Am. Psychol. **49**(12), 997–1003 (1994)
88. Cohen-Or, D., Sorkine, O., Gal, R., Leyvand, T., Xu, Y.-Q.: Color harmonization. ACM Trans. Graph. **25**(3), 624–630 (2006)
89. Cole, F.: Line drawings of 3D models. PhD thesis, Princeton University (2009)
90. Cole, F., Golovinskiy, A., Limpaecher, A., Barros, H.S., Finkelstein, A., Funkhouser, T., Rusinkiewicz, S.: Where do people draw lines? ACM Trans. Graph. **27**(3), 88 (2008)
91. Cole, F., Sanik, K., DeCarlo, D., Finkelstein, A., Funkhouser, T., Rusinkiewicz, S., Singh, M.: How well do line drawings depict shape? ACM Trans. Graph. **28**(3), 28 (2009)
92. Cole, F., Golovinskiy, A., Limpaecher, A., Barros, H.S., Finkelstein, A., Funkhouser, T., Rusinkiewicz, S.: Where do people draw lines? Commun. ACM **55**(1), 107–115 (2012)
93. Coleman, P., Singh, K.: RYAN: rendering your animation nonlinearly projected. In: Proc. NPAR, pp. 129–138 (2004)
94. Collomosse, J.P., Hall, P.M.: Painterly rendering using image salience. In: Proc. EGUK, pp. 122–128 (2002)
95. Collomosse, J.P., Hall, P.M.: Cubist style rendering from photographs. IEEE Trans. Vis. Comput. Graph. **4**(9), 443–453 (2003)
96. Collomosse, J.P., Hall, P.M.: Genetic paint: a search for salient paintings. In: Proc. Evo-MUSART, vol. 3449, pp. 437–447 (2005)
97. Collomosse, J.P., Hall, P.M.: Video motion analysis for the synthesis of dynamic cues and futurist art. Graph. Models **5**(68), 402–414 (2006)
98. Collomosse, J., Rowntree, D., Hall, P.M.: Video analysis for cartoon-style special effects. In: Proc. BMVC, pp. 749–758 (2003)
99. Collomosse, J.P., Rowntree, D., Hall, P.M.: Stroke surfaces: a spatio-temporal framework for temporally coherent nonphotorealistic animations. Technical report CSBU-2003-01, University of Bath, UK (2003)
100. Collomosse, J., Rowntree, D., Hall, P.M.: Stroke surfaces: temporally coherent nonphotorealistic animations from video. IEEE Trans. Vis. Comput. Graph. **11**(5), 540–549 (2005)
101. Comaniciu, D., Meer, P.: Mean shift: a robust approach toward feature space analysis. IEEE Trans. Pattern Anal. Mach. Intell. **24**(5), 603–619 (2002)

References

102. Cook, W.J.: In: Pursuit of the Traveling Salesman: Mathematics at the Limits of Computation. Princeton University Press, Princeton (2011)
103. Cootes, T.F., Taylor, C.J., Cooper, D.H., Graham, J.: Active shape model—their training and application. Comput. Vis. Image Underst. **61**, 38–59 (1995)
104. Cootes, T.F., Edwards, G.J., Taylor, C.J.: Active appearance models. IEEE Trans. Pattern Anal. Mach. Intell. **23**(6), 681–685 (2001)
105. Corel: Painter (2012). http://www.corel.com/painter
106. Cormen, T.H., Leiserson, C.E., Stein, R.L.R.C.: Introduction to Algorithms, 3rd edn. MIT Press, Cambridge (2009)
107. Corrêa, W.T., Jensen, R.J., Thayer, C.E., Finkelstein, A.: Texture mapping for cel animation. In: Proc. SIGGRAPH, pp. 435–446. ACM, New York (1998)
108. Coumans, E.: Bullet Physics Library (2010). http://www.bulletphysics.org/
109. Criminisi, A., Sharp, T., Rother, C., Pérez, P.: Geodesic image and video editing. ACM Trans. Graph. **29**(5), 134 (2010)
110. Curtis, C.J., Anderson, S.E., Seims, J.E., Fleischer, K.W., Salesin, D.H.: Computer-generated watercolor. In: Whitted, T. (ed.) Proc. SIGGRAPH, pp. 421–430 (1997)
111. Dahlhaus, E., Johnson, D.S., Papadimitriou, C.H., Seymour, P.D., Yannakakis, M.: The complexity of multiway cuts. In: Proceedings of ACM Symposium on Theory of Computing, pp. 241–251 (1992)
112. Dalal, K., Klein, A.W., Liu, Y., Smith, K.: A spectral approach to NPR packing. In: Proc. NPAR, pp. 71–78 (2006)
113. Daniels, E.: Deep canvas in Disney's Tarzan. In: SIGGRAPH Conference Abstracts and Applications, p. 200 (1999)
114. de Berg, M., Cheong, O., van Kreveld, M., Overmars, M.: Computational Geometry: Algorithms and Application, 3rd edn. Springer, Berlin (2010)
115. DeCarlo, D., Santella, A.: Stylization and abstraction of photographs. In: Proc. SIGGRAPH, pp. 769–776 (2002)
116. DeCarlo, D., Finkelstein, A., Rusinkiewicz, S., Santella, A.: Suggestive contours for conveying shape. ACM Trans. Graph. **22**(3), 848–855 (2003)
117. Delmarcelle, T., Hesselink, L.: Visualizing second-order tensor fields with hyperstream lines. IEEE Comput. Graph. Appl. **13**(4), 25–33 (1993)
118. Demaret, L., Dyn, N., Iske, A.: Image compression by linear splines over adaptive triangulations. Signal Process. **86**(7), 1604–1616 (2006)
119. Deussen, O., Strothotte, T.: Computer-generated pen-and-ink illustration of trees. In: Proc. SIGGRAPH, pp. 13–18 (2000)
120. Deussen, O., Hiller, S., van Overveld, K., Strothotte, T.: Floating points: a method for computing stipple drawings. Comput. Graph. Forum **19**(4), 40–51 (2000)
121. Di Blasi, G., Gallo, G.: Artificial mosaics. Vis. Comput. **21**(6), 373–383 (2005)
122. Didas, S., Weickert, J.: Combining curvature motion and edge-preserving denoising. In: Proc. SSVM 2007, vol. 4485, pp. 568–579 (2007)
123. DiPaola, S.: Painterly rendered portraits from photographs using a knowledge-based approach. Proc. SPIE **6492**, 33–43 (2007)
124. DiVerdi, S., Krishnaswamy, A., Hadap, S.: Industrial-strength painting with a virtual bristle brush. In: Proceedings of the ACM Symposium on Virtual Reality Software and Technology, pp. 119–126 (2010)
125. Du Sautoy, M.: Symmetry: A Journey into the Patterns of Nature. Harper Collins, New York (2008)
126. Du, Q., Faber, V., Gunzburger, M.: Centroidal Voronoi tessellations. SIAM Rev. **41**(4), 637–676 (1999)
127. Duke, D.J., Barnard, P.J., Halper, N., Mellin, M.: Rendering and affect. Comput. Graph. Forum **22**(3), 359–368 (2003)
128. Dunbabin, K.: Mosaics of the Greek and Roman World. Cambridge University Press, Cambridge (1999)
129. Durand, F.: An invitation to discuss computer depiction. In: Proc. NPAR, pp. 111–124 (2002)

130. Durand, F., Ostromoukhov, V., Miller, M., Duranleau, F., Dorsey, J.: Decoupling strokes and high-level attributes for interactive traditional drawing. In: Proc. EG Workshop on Rendering Techniques, pp. 71–82 (2001)
131. Eastman, P.: Art of Illusion (2012). http://www.artofillusion.org
132. Ecker, A., Jepson, A.D.: Polynomial shape from shading. In: Proc. CVPR, pp. 145–152 (2010)
133. Elber, G.: Line art rendering via a coverage of isoparametric curves. IEEE Trans. Vis. Comput. Graph. **1**(3), 231–239 (1995)
134. Elber, G.: Line art illustrations of parametric and implicit forms. IEEE Trans. Vis. Comput. Graph. **4**(1), 71–81 (1998)
135. Elber, G., Wolberg, G.: Rendering traditional mosaics. Vis. Comput. **19**(1), 67–78 (2003)
136. Elder, J.H.: Are edges incomplete? Int. J. Comput. Vis. **34**(2–3), 97–122 (1999)
137. Elder, J.H., Goldberg, R.M.: Image editing in the contour domain. IEEE Trans. Pattern Anal. Mach. Intell. **23**(3), 291–296 (2001)
138. Fabbri, R., Costa, L.D.F., Torelli, J.C., Bruno, O.M.: 2D Euclidean distance transform algorithms. ACM Comput. Surv. **40**(1), 2 (2008)
139. Farin, G.: Curves and Surfaces for CAGD: A Practical Guide, 5th edn. Morgan Kaufmann, San Mateo (2002)
140. Farin, G., Hansford, D.: Discrete Coons patches. Comput. Aided Geom. Des. **16**(7), 691–700 (1999)
141. Felzenszwalb, P.F., Huttenlocher, D.P.: Distance transforms of sampled functions. Technical report TR2004-1963, Cornell University (2004)
142. Felzenszwalb, P.F., Huttenlocher, D.P.: Efficient graph-based image segmentation. Int. J. Comput. Vis. **59**(2), 167–181 (2004)
143. Fernie, E.: Art History and Its Methods: A Critical Anthology. Phaidon, Oxford (2011)
144. Ferwerda, J.A.: Three varieties of realism in computer graphics. In: Rogowitz, B.E., Pappas, T.N. (eds.) Proceedings of Human Vision and Electronic Imaging VIII, vol. 5007, pp. 290–297 (2003)
145. Field, D.: Relations between the statistics of natural images and the response profiles of cortical cells. J. Opt. Soc. Am. A **4**, 2379–2394 (1987)
146. Field, D.: What is the goal of sensory coding. Neural Comput. **6**, 559–601 (1994)
147. Field, A., Hole, G.: How to Design and Report Experiments. Sage, London (2003)
148. Filonik, D., Baur, D.: Measuring aesthetics for information visualization. In: International Conference on Information Visualization, pp. 579–584 (2009)
149. Finch, M., Snyder, J., Hoppe, H.: Freeform vector graphics with controlled thin-plate splines. ACM Trans. Graph. **30**(6), 166 (2011)
150. Finkelstein, A., Range, M.: Image mosaics. In: Proceedings of Raster Imaging & Digital Typography (RIDT), pp. 11–22 (1998)
151. Finkelstein, A., Salesin, D.H.: Multiresolution curves. In: Proc. SIGGRAPH, pp. 261–268 (1994)
152. Fiorentini Roncuzzi, I., Fiorentini, E.: Mosaic: Materials, Techniques and History. MWeV (2002)
153. Fischer, J., Bartz, D., Straber, W.: Stylized augmented reality for improved immersion. In: Proc. VR, pp. 195–202 (2005)
154. Fischer, J., Cunningham, D., Bartz, D., Wallraven, C., Bülthoff, H., Straßer, W.: Measuring the discernability of virtual objects in conventional and stylized augmented reality. In: Proc. EGVE, pp. 53–61 (2006)
155. Floyd, R., Steinberg, L.: An adaptive algorithm for spatial grey scale. Proc. Soc. Inf. Disp. **17**(2), 75–77 (1976)
156. Frazor, R., Geisler, W.: Local luminance contrast in natural images. Vis. Res. **46**, 1585–1598 (2006)
157. Fritzsche, L.-P., Hellwig, H., Hiller, S., Deussen, O.: Interactive design of authentic looking mosaics using Voronoi structures. In: Proc. 2nd International Symposium on Voronoi Diagrams in Science and Engineering 2005, pp. 1–11 (2005)

158. Fukunaga, K., Hostetler, L.: The estimation of the gradient of a density function, with applications in pattern recognition. IEEE Trans. Inf. Theory **21**, 32–40 (1975)
159. Gastal, E.S.L., Oliveira, M.M.: Domain transform for edge-aware image and video processing. ACM Trans. Graph. **30**(4), 69 (2011)
160. Gatzidis, C., Papakonstantinou, S., Brujic-Okretic, V., Baker, S.: Recent advances in the user evaluation methods and studies of non-photorealistic visualisation and rendering techniques. In: Proc. IV, pp. 475–480 (2008)
161. Gersho, A.: Asymptotically optimal block quantization. IEEE Trans. Inf. Theory **25**(4), 373–380 (1979)
162. Gerstner, T., DeCarlo, D., Alexa, M., Finkelstein, A., Gingold, Y., Nealen, A.: Pixelated image abstraction. In: Proc. NPAR, pp. 29–36 (2012)
163. Girshick, A., Interrante, V., Haker, S., Lemoine, T.: Line direction matters: an argument for the use of principal directions in 3D line drawings. In: Proc. NPAR, pp. 43–52. ACM, New York (2000)
164. Glocker, B., Komodakis, N., Tziritas, G., Navab, N., Paragios, N.: Dense image registration through MRFs and efficient linear programming. Med. Image Anal. **12**(6), 731–741 (2008)
165. Goldman, D.B., Curless, B., Salesin, D., Seitz, S.M.: Schematic storyboarding for video visualization and editing. ACM Trans. Graph. **25**(3), 862–871 (2006)
166. Gombrich, E.H.: Art and Illusion: A Study in the Psychology of the Pictorial Representation. Phaidon, Oxford (1983)
167. Gombrich, E.H.: The claims of excellence. In: Gombrich, E.H. (ed.) Reflections on the History of Art, pp. 179–185. Phaidon, Oxford (1987)
168. Gombrich, E.H.: The Story of Art. Phaidon, Oxford (1995)
169. Gonzalez, R.C., Woods, R.E.: Digital Image Processing, 3rd edn. Pearson Prentice Hall, Upper Saddle River (2008)
170. Gooch, B.: Human facial illustrations: creation and evaluation using behavioral studies and functional magnetic resonance imaging. PhD thesis, University of Utah, USA (2003)
171. Gooch, B., Gooch, A.: Non-photorealistic Rendering. AK Peters, Wellesley (2001)
172. Gooch, A.A., Willemsen, P.: Evaluating space perception in NPR immersive environments. In: Proc. NPAR, pp. 105–110 (2002)
173. Gooch, B., Sloan, P.-P.J., Gooch, A., Shirley, P., Riesenfeld, R.: Interactive technical illustration. In: Proc. I3D, pp. 31–38 (1999)
174. Gooch, B., Coombe, G., Shirley, P.: Artistic vision: painterly rendering using computer vision techniques. In: Proc. NPAR, pp. 83–90 (2002)
175. Gooch, B., Reinhard, E., Gooch, A.A.: Human facial illustrations: creation and psychophysical evaluation. ACM Trans. Graph. **23**(1), 27–44 (2004)
176. Gooch, A.A., Olsen, S.C., Tumblin, J., Gooch, B.: Color2Gray: salience-preserving color removal. ACM Trans. Graph. **24**(3), 634–639 (2005)
177. Gooch, A.A., Long, J., Ji, L., Estey, A., Gooch, B.S.: Viewing progress in non-photorealistic rendering through Heinlein's lens. In: Proc. NPAR, pp. 165–171. ACM, New York (2010)
178. Gouraud, H.: Continuous shading of curved surfaces. IEEE Trans. Comput. **20**(6), 623–629 (1971)
179. Grabli, S., Turquin, E., Durand, F., Sillion, F.X.: Programmable style for NPR line drawing. In: Proc. EG Symposium on Rendering, pp. 18:1–18:20 (2004)
180. Grabli, S., Turquin, E., Durand, F., Sillion, F.X.: Programmable rendering of line drawing from 3D scenes. ACM Trans. Graph. **29**(2), 18 (2010)
181. Grady, L.: Random walks for image segmentation. IEEE Trans. Pattern Anal. Mach. Intell. **28**(11), 1768–1783 (2006)
182. Graham, D.J., Field, D.: Statistical regularities of art image and natural scenes: spectra, sparseness and nonlinearities. Spat. Vis. **21**, 149–164 (2007)
183. Graham, D.J., Field, D.: Variations in intensity statistics for representational and abstract art from the eastern and western hemispheres. Perception **37**, 1341–1352 (2008)
184. Granger, G.W.: Aesthetic measure applied to color harmony: an experimental test. J. Gen. Psychol. **52**(2), 205–212 (1955)

185. Grayson, M.A.: The heat equation shrinks embedded plane curves to round points. J. Differ. Geom. **26**(2), 285–314 (1987)
186. Green, S., Salesin, D., Schofield, S., Hertzmann, A., Litwinowicz, P., Gooch, A., Curtis, C., Gooch, B.: Non-photorealistic rendering. In: SIGGRAPH Courses (1999)
187. Greenberg, S., Buxton, B.: Usability evaluation considered harmful (some of the time). In: Proc. CHI, pp. 111–120. ACM, New York, (2008)
188. Greenfield, G.: Composite digital mosaics using Duotone tiles. In: Kaplan, C.S., Sarhangi, R. (eds.) Bridges 2009: Mathematics, Music, Art, Architecture, Culture, pp. 155–162 (2009)
189. Guichard, F., Morel, J.M.: A note on two classical enhancement filters and their associated PDE's. Int. J. Comput. Vis. **52**(2), 153–160 (2003)
190. Haeberli, P.: Paint by numbers: abstract image representations. In: Proc. SIGGRAPH, pp. 207–214 (1990)
191. Hall, P.M., Collomosse, J.P., Song, Y.-Z., Shen, P., Li, C.: RTcams: a new perspective on nonphotorealistic rendering from photographs. IEEE Trans. Vis. Comput. Graph. **13**(5), 966–979 (2007)
192. Halper, N., Mellin, M., Herrmann, C.S., Linneweber, V., Strothotte, T.: Psychology and non-photorealistic rendering: the beginning of a beautiful relationship. In: Proc. Mensch & Computer, pp. 277–286 (2003)
193. Halper, N., Mellin, M., Herrmann, C.S., Linneweber, V., Strothotte, T.: Towards an understanding of the psychology of non-photorealistic rendering. In: Proc. Workshop Computational Visualistics, Media Informatics and Virtual Communities, pp. 67–78 (2003)
194. Hanrahan, P., Haeberli, P.: Direct WYSIWYG painting and texturing on 3D shapes. Comput. Graph. **24**(4), 215–223 (1990)
195. Haralick, R.M.: Digital step edges from zero crossing of second directional derivatives. IEEE Trans. Pattern Anal. Mach. Intell. **6**(1), 58–68 (1984)
196. Haralick, R.M., Shapiro, L.G.: Computer and Robot Vision, vol. 1. Addison-Wesley, Reading (1992)
197. Haralick, R.M., Sternberg, S.R., Zhuang, X.: Image analysis using mathematical morphology. IEEE Trans. Pattern Anal. Mach. Intell. **9**(4), 532–550 (1987)
198. Hausner, A.: Simulating decorative mosaics. In: Proc. SIGGRAPH, pp. 573–580 (2001)
199. Hays, J., Essa, I.: Image and video based painterly animation. In: Proc. NPAR, pp. 113–120 (2004)
200. Healey, C.G., Enns, J.T.: Perception and painting: a search for effective, engaging visualizations. IEEE Comput. Graph. Appl. **22**(2), 10–15 (2002)
201. Healey, C.G., Tateosian, L., Enns, J.T., Remple, M.: Perceptually-based brush strokes for nonphotorealistic visualization. ACM Trans. Graph. **23**(1), 64–96 (2004)
202. Heckbert, P.: Color image quantization for frame buffer display. In: Proc. ACM SIGGRAPH, pp. 297–307 (1982)
203. Hegdé, J., Thompson, S., Kersten, D.: Identifying faces in two-tone ('mooney') images: a psychophysical and fMRI study. J. Vis. **7**(9), 642 (2007)
204. Hertzmann, A.: Painterly rendering with curved brush strokes of multiple sizes. In: Proc. SIGGRAPH, pp. 453–460 (1998)
205. Hertzmann, A.: Paint by relaxation. In: Computer Graphics International, pp. 47–54 (2001)
206. Hertzmann, A.: Fast paint texture. In: Proc. NPAR, pp. 91–96 (2002)
207. Hertzmann, A.: A survey of stroke-based rendering. IEEE Comput. Graph. Appl. **23**, 70–81 (2003)
208. Hertzmann, A.: Non-photorealistic rendering and the science of art. In: Proc. NPAR, pp. 147–157 (2010)
209. Hertzmann, A., Perlin, K.: Painterly rendering for video and interaction. In: Proc. NPAR, pp. 7–12 (2000)
210. Hertzmann, A., Zorin, D.: Illustrating smooth surfaces. In: Proc. SIGGRAPH, pp. 517–526 (2000)
211. Hertzmann, A., Jacobs, C.E., Oliver, N., Curless, B., Salesin, D.H.: Image analogies. In: Proc. SIGGRAPH, pp. 327–340 (2001)

212. Hnaidi, H., Guérin, E., Akkouche, S., Peytavie, A., Galin, E.: Feature based terrain generation using diffusion equation. Comput. Graph. Forum **29**(7), 2179–2186 (2010)
213. Ho, S.N., Komiya, R.: Real time loose and sketchy rendering in hardware. In: Proc. SCCG, pp. 83–88 (2004)
214. Hockney, D.: Secret Knowledge (New and Expanded Edition): Rediscovering the Lost Techniques of the Old Masters. Studio, London (2006). Expanded edition
215. Hsiao, S.-W., Chiu, F.-Y., Hsu, H.-Y.: A computer-assisted colour selection system based on aesthetic measure for colour harmony and fuzzy logic theory. Color Res. Appl. **33**, 411–423 (2008)
216. Hsu, S.C., Lee, I.H.H., Wiseman, N.E.: Skeletal strokes. In: Proc. UIST, pp. 197–206 (1993)
217. Huang, H., Fu, T.-N., Li, C.-F.: Painterly rendering with content-dependent natural paint strokes. Vis. Comput. **27**(9), 861–871 (2011)
218. Huang, H., Zhang, L., Zhang, H.-C.: Arcimboldo-like collage using internet images. ACM Trans. Graph. **30**(6), 155 (2011)
219. Hyman, J.: The Objective Eye: Color, Form, and Reality in the Theory of Art. University of Chicago, Chicago (2006)
220. Igarashi, Y., Igarashi, T.: Holly: a drawing editor for designing stencils. IEEE Comput. Graph. Appl. **30**, 8–14 (2010)
221. Igarashi, T., Matsuoka, S., Tanaka, H.: Teddy: a sketching interface for 3D freeform design. In: Proc. SIGGRAPH, pp. 409–416 (1999)
222. Igarashi, T., Moscovich, T., Hughes, J.F.: As-rigid-as-possible shape manipulation. ACM Trans. Graph. **24**(3), 1134–1141 (2005)
223. Inglis, T.C., Kaplany, C.S.: Pixelating vector line art. In: Proc. NPAR, pp. 21–28 (2012)
224. Inglis, T.C., Inglis, S., Kaplan, C.S.: Op art rendering with lines and curves. Comput. Graph. **36**(6), 607–621 (2012)
225. Inoue, K., Urahama, K.: Halftoning with minimum spanning trees and its application to maze-like images. Comput. Graph. **33**(5), 638–647 (2009)
226. Interrante, V., Fuchs, H., Pizer, S.: Enhancing transparent skin surfaces with ridge and valley lines. In: Proc. Visualization, pp. 52–59 (1995)
227. Interrante, V., Fuchs, H., Pizer, S.: Illustrating transparent surfaces with curvature-directed strokes. In: Proc. Visualization, pp. 211–218 (1996)
228. Isenberg, T., Freudenberg, B., Halper, N., Schlechtweg, S., Strothotte, T.: A developer's guide to silhouette algorithms for polygonal models. IEEE Comput. Graph. Appl. **23**(4), 28–37 (2003)
229. Isenberg, T., Neumann, P., Carpendale, S., Sousa, M.C., Jorge, J.A.: Non-photorealistic rendering in context: an observational study. In: Proc. NPAR, pp. 115–126 (2006)
230. Itti, L., Koch, C., Niebur, E.: A model of saliency based visual attention for rapid scene analysis. IEEE Transactions on Pattern Analysis and Machine Intelligence, 1254–1259 (1998)
231. Jackson, C.D., Acevedo, D., Laidlaw, D.H., Drury, F., Vote, E., Keefe, D.: Designer-critiqued comparison of 2D vector visualization methods: a pilot study. In: SIGGRAPH Sketches & Applications. ACM, New York (2003)
232. Jamriška, O., Sýkora, D., Hornung, A.: Cache-efficient graph cuts on structured grids. In: Proc. CVPR, pp. 3673–3680 (2012)
233. Jeschke, S., Cline, D., Wonka, P.: A GPU Laplacian solver for diffusion curves and Poisson image editing. ACM Trans. Graph. **28**(5), 116 (2009)
234. Jeschke, S., Cline, D., Wonka, P.: Estimating color and texture parameters for vector graphics. Comput. Graph. Forum **30**(2), 523–532 (2011)
235. Jobard, B., Lefer, W.: Creating evenly-spaced streamlines of arbitrary density. In: Proc. Visualization in Scientific Computing, pp. 43–56 (1997)
236. Jodoin, P.-M., Epstein, E., Granger-Piché, M., Ostromoukhov, V.: Hatching by example: a statistical approach. In: Proc. NPAR, pp. 29–36 (2002)
237. Johnston, S.F.: Lumo: illumination for cel animation. In: Proc. NPAR, pp. 45–52 (2002)
238. Jones, B.: Computer imagery: imitation and representation of realities. Leonardo 31–38 (1989). Computer Art in Context Supplemental Issue

239. Judd, T., Durand, F., Adelson, E.: Apparent ridges for line drawing. ACM Trans. Graph. **26**(3), 19 (2007)
240. Judd, T., Ehinger, K., Durand, F., Torralba, A.: Learning to predict where humans look. In: IEEE International Conference on Computer Vision (ICCV), pp. 2106–2113 (2009)
241. Kagaya, M., Brendel, W., Deng, Q., Kesterson, T., Todorovic, S., Neill, P.J., Zhang, E.: Video painting with space-time-varying style parameters. IEEE Trans. Vis. Comput. Graph. **17**(1), 74–87 (2011)
242. Kahn, A.B.: Topological sorting of large networks. Commun. ACM **5**(11), 558–562 (1962)
243. Kalnins, R.D., Markosian, L., Meier, B.J., Kowalski, M.A., Lee, J.C., Davidson, P.L., Webb, M., Hughes, J.F., Finkelstein, A.: WYSIWYG NPR: drawing strokes directly on 3D models. In: Proc. SIGGRAPH, vol. 21, p. 755 (2002)
244. Kalogerakis, E., Nowrouzezahrai, D., Breslav, S., Hertzmann, A.: Learning hatching for pen-and-ink illustration of surfaces. ACM Trans. Graph. **31**(1), 1 (2011)
245. Kaneko, T., Takahei, T., Inami, M., Kawakami, N., Yanagida, Y., Maeda, T., Tachi, S.: Detailed shape representation with parallax mapping. In: Proceedings of International Conference on Artificial Reality and Telexistence, pp. 205–208 (2001)
246. Kang, H., Lee, S.: Shape-simplifying image abstraction. Comput. Graph. Forum **27**(7), 1773–1780 (2008)
247. Kang, H., Lee, S., Chui, C.K.: Coherent line drawing. In: Proc. NPAR, New York, pp. 43–50 (2007)
248. Kang, H., Lee, S., Chui, C.K.: Flow-based image abstraction. IEEE Trans. Vis. Comput. Graph. **15**(1), 62–76 (2009)
249. Kaplan, C.S., Bosch, R.: TSP art. In: Bridges 2005: Mathematical Connections in Art, Music and Science, pp. 301–308 (2005)
250. Kaptein, M., Robertson, J.: Rethinking statistical analysis methods for CHI. In: Proc. CHI, pp. 1105–1114 (2012)
251. Kass, M., Pesare, D.: Coherent noise for non-photorealistic rendering. ACM Trans. Graph. **30**(4), 30 (2011)
252. Kass, M., Witkin, A., Terzopoulos, D.: Snakes: active contour models. Int. J. Comput. Vis. **1**(4), 321–331 (1988)
253. Kavan, L., Sloan, P.-P., O'Sullivan, C.: Fast and efficient skinning of animated meshes. Comput. Graph. Forum **29**(2), 327–336 (2010)
254. Keefe, D.F., Karelitz, D.B., Vote, E.L., Laidlaw, D.H.: Artistic collaboration in designing VR visualizations. IEEE Comput. Graph. Appl. **25**(2), 18–23 (2005)
255. Kerlinger, F.N., Lee, H.B.: Foundations of Behavioral Research, 4th edn. Wadsworth/Thomson Learning, Belmont (2000)
256. Kim, J., Pellacini, F.: Jigsaw image mosaics. ACM Trans. Graph. **21**(3), 657–664 (2002)
257. Kim, S., Hagh-Shenas, H., Interrante, V.: Conveying shape with texture: an experimental investigation of the impact of texture type on shape categorization judgments. In: Proc. InfoVis, pp. 163–170 (2003)
258. Kim, S., Hagh-Shenas, H., Interrante, V.: Conveying shape with texture: experimental investigation of texture's effects on shape categorization judgments. IEEE Trans. Vis. Comput. Graph. **10**(4), 471–483 (2004)
259. Kim, D., Son, M., Lee, Y., Kang, H., Lee, S.: Feature-guided image stippling. Comput. Graph. Forum **27**(4), 1209–1216 (2008)
260. Kim, S., Maciejewski, R., Isenberg, T., Andrews, W., Chen, W., Sousa, M.C., Ebert, D.S.: Stippling by example. In: Proc. NPAR, pp. 41–50 (2009)
261. Kim, S., Woo, I., Maciejewski, R., Ebert, D.S.: Automated hedcut illustration using isophotes. In: Smart Graphics, pp. 172–183 (2010)
262. Klein, A.W., Li, W., Kazhdan, M.M., Corrêa, W.T., Finkelstein, A., Funkhouser, T.A.: Non-photorealistic virtual environments. In: Proc. SIGGRAPH, pp. 527–534 (2000)
263. Koenderink, J.J.: Pictorial relief. Philos. Trans. R. Soc. Lond. **356**(1740), 1071–1086 (1998)
264. Koenderink, J.J., van Doorn, A.J., Kappers, A.M.L.: Pictorial surface attitude and local depth comparisons. Percept. Psychophys. **58**(2), 163–173 (1996)

265. Kopf, J., Cohen-Or, D., Deussen, O., Lischinski, D.: Recursive Wang tiles for real-time blue noise. ACM Trans. Graph. **25**(3), 509–518 (2006)
266. Kramer, H.P., Bruckner, J.B.: Iterations of a non-linear transformation for enhancement of digital images. Pattern Recognit. **7**(1–2), 53–58 (1975)
267. Kreczkowska, A., El-Hage, J., Colton, S., Clark, S.: Automated collage generation with intent. In: International Joint Conference on Computational Creativity (2010)
268. Kuwahara, M., Hachimura, K., Ehiu, S., Kinoshita, M.: Processing of ri-angiocardiographic images. In: Digital Processing of Biomedical Images, pp. 187–203. Plenum, New York (1976)
269. Kyprianidis, J.E.: Image and video abstraction by multi-scale anisotropic Kuwahara filtering. In: Proc. NPAR, pp. 55–64 (2011)
270. Kyprianidis, J.E., Döllner, J.: Image abstraction by structure adaptive filtering. In: Proc. EG UK TPCG, pp. 51–58 (2008)
271. Kyprianidis, J.E., Döllner, J.: Real-time image abstraction by directed filtering. In: ShaderX7, pp. 285–302. Charles River Media, London (2009)
272. Kyprianidis, J.E., Kang, H.: Image and video abstraction by coherence-enhancing filtering. Comput. Graph. Forum **30**(2), 593–602 (2011)
273. Kyprianidis, J.E., Kang, H., Döllner, J.: Image and video abstraction by anisotropic Kuwahara filtering. Comput. Graph. Forum **28**(7), 1955–1963 (2009)
274. Kyprianidis, J.E., Kang, H., Döllner, J.: Anisotropic Kuwahara filtering on the GPU. In: GPUPro, pp. 247–264 (2010)
275. Kyprianidis, J.E., Semmo, A., Kang, H., Döllner, J.: Anisotropic Kuwahara filtering with polynomial weighting functions. In: Proc. EG UK TPCG, pp. 25–30 (2010)
276. Lagae, A., Dutré, P.: A procedural object distribution function. ACM Trans. Graph. **24**(4), 1442–1461 (2005)
277. Lai, Y.-K., Hu, S.-M., Martin, R.R.: Automatic and topology-preserving gradient mesh generation for image vectorization. ACM Trans. Graph. **28**(3), 85 (2009)
278. Laidlaw, D.H.: Loose, artistic "textures" for visualization. IEEE Comput. Graph. Appl. **21**(2), 6–9 (2001)
279. Laidlaw, D.H., Kirby, R.M., Jackson, C.D., Davidson, J.S., Miller, T.S., da Silva, M., Warren, W.H., Tarr, M.J.: Comparing 2D vector field visualization methods: a user study. IEEE Trans. Vis. Comput. Graph. **11**(1), 59–70 (2005)
280. Lake, A., Marshall, C., Harris, M., Blackstein, M.: Stylized rendering techniques for scalable real-time 3D animation. In: Proc. NPAR, pp. 13–20 (2000)
281. Lam, D.: Tokamak physics engine (2010). http://www.tokamakphysics.com
282. Langer, M.S., Buelthoff, H.H.: Depth discrimination from shading under diffuse lighting. Perception **29**(6), 649–660 (2000)
283. Lasseter, J.: Principles of traditional animation applied to 3D computer animation. In: Proc. SIGGRAPH, vol. 21, pp. 35–44 (1987)
284. Lecot, G., Lévy, B.: ARDECO: Automatic Region DEtection and Conversion. In: Proc. EGSR, pp. 349–360 (2006)
285. Lee, J.: Physically-based modeling of brush painting. In: Computer Networks and ISDN systems, pp. 1571–1756 (1997)
286. Lee, H., Lee, C.H., Yoon, K.: Motion based painterly rendering. Comput. Graph. Forum **28**(4), 1207–1215 (2009)
287. Lee, H., Seo, S., Ryoo, S., Yoon, K.: Directional texture transfer. In: Proc. NPAR, pp. 43–50 (2010)
288. Lehmann, A.: Taking the lid off the Utah teapot. Towards a material analysis of computer graphics. Z. Med. Kult.-forsch. **1**, 157–172 (2012)
289. Leister, W.: Computer generated Copper plates. Comput. Graph. Forum **13**(1), 69–77 (1994)
290. Leopold, D.A., O'Toole, A.J., Vetter, T., Blanz, V.: Prototype-referenced shape encoding revealed by high-level aftereffects. Nat. Neurosci. **4**, 89–94 (2001)
291. Levin, A., Lischinski, D., Weiss, Y.: Colorization using optimization. ACM Trans. Graph. **23**(3), 689–694 (2004)

292. Lewis, J.P., Cordner, M., Fong, N.: Pose space deformation: a unified approach to shape interpolation and skeleton-driven deformation. In: Proc. SIGGRAPH, pp. 165–172 (2000)
293. Li, N., Huang, Z.: A feature-based pencil drawing method. In: Proc. GRAPHITE, pp. 135–140 (2003)
294. Li, Y., Kobatake, H.: Extraction of facial sketch images and expression transformation based on FACS. In: Proc. ICIP, pp. 520–523 (1995)
295. Li, Y., Kobatake, H.: Extraction of facial sketch image based on morphological processing. In: Proc. ICIP, pp. 316–319 (1997)
296. Li, H., Mould, D.: Content-sensitive screening in black and white. In: Proc. GRAPP, pp. 166–172 (2011)
297. Liang, L., Chen, H., Xu, Y.-Q., Shum, H.-Y.: Example-based caricature generation with exaggeration. In: Proc. Pacific Graphics, pp. 386–393 (2002)
298. Lin, L., Zeng, K., Lv, H., Wang, Y., Xu, Y., Zhu, S.-C.: Painterly animation using video semantics and feature correspondence. In: Proc. NPAR, pp. 73–80 (2010)
299. Ling, R.: Ancient Mosaics. British Museum Press, London (1998)
300. Litwinowicz, P.: Processing images and video for an impressionist effect. In: Proc. SIGGRAPH, pp. 407–414 (1997)
301. Liu, C., Torralba, A., Freeman, W., Durand, F., Adelson, E.H.: Motion magnification. ACM Trans. Graph. **24**(3), 519–526 (2005)
302. Liu, Y., Veksler, O., Juan, O.: Simulating classic mosaics with graph cuts. In: Proc. Energy Minimization Methods in Computer Vision and Pattern Recognition, pp. 55–70 (2007)
303. Liu, Y., Veksler, O., Juan, O.: Generating classic mosaics with graph cuts. Comput. Graph. Forum **29**(8), 2387–2399 (2010)
304. Livingstone, M.S.: Vision and Art: The Biology of Seeing. Abrams, New York (2008)
305. Lloyd, S.P.: Least squares quantization in PCM. IEEE Trans. Inf. Theory **28**(2), 129–137 (1982)
306. Long, J.: Modeling dendritic structures for artistic effects. Master's thesis, University of Saskatchewan (2007)
307. Long, J., Mould, D.: Dendritic stylization. Vis. Comput. **25**(3), 241–253 (2009)
308. Lopez-Moreno, J., Jimenez, J., Hadap, S., Reinhard, E., Anjyo, K., Gutierrez, D.: Stylized depiction of images based on depth perception. In: Proc. NPAR, pp. 109–118 (2010)
309. Lowe, D.G.: Distinctive image features from scale-invariant keypoints. Int. J. Comput. Vis. **60**(2), 91–110 (2004)
310. Lu, T.K., Huang, Z.: A GPU-based method for real-time simulation of Eastern painting. In: Proc. GRAPHITE, pp. 111–118 (2007)
311. Lu, J., Sander, P.V., Finkelstein, A.: Interactive painterly stylization of images, videos and 3D animations. In: Proc. SIGGRAPH Symposium on Interactive 3D Graphics and Games, vol. 26, pp. 127–134 (2010)
312. Luft, T., Colditz, C., Deussen, O.: Image enhancement by unsharp masking the depth buffer. ACM Trans. Graph. **25**(3), 1206–1213 (2006)
313. Luft, T., Kobs, F., Zinser, W., Deussen, O.: Watercolor illustrations of CAD data. In: Proc. CAe, pp. 57–63 (2008)
314. Luo, W.C., Liu, P.C., Ouhyoung, M.: Exaggeration of facial features in caricaturing. In: Proceedings of International Computer Symposium (2002)
315. Maciejewski, R., Isenberg, T., Andrews, W.M., Ebert, D.S., Sousa, M.C.: Aesthetics of hand-drawn vs. computer-generated stippling. In: Proc. CAe, Goslar, Germany, pp. 53–56 (2007)
316. Maciejewski, R., Isenberg, T., Andrews, W.M., Ebert, D.S., Sousa, M.C., Chen, W.: Measuring stipple aesthetics in hand-drawn and computer-generated images. IEEE Comput. Graph. Appl. **28**(2), 62–74 (2008)
317. Maharik, R., Bessmeltsev, M., Sheffer, A., Shamir, A., Carr, N.: Digital micrography. ACM Trans. Graph. **30**(4), 100 (2011)
318. Mandryk, R.L., Mould, D., Li, H.: Evaluation of emotional response to non-photorealistic images. In: Proc. NPAR, pp. 7–16 (2011)
319. Manovich, L.: Image future. Animation **1**(1), 25–44 (2006)

320. Maragos, P., Schafer, R.: Morphological filters–Part I: their set-theoretic analysis and relations to linear shift-invariant filters. IEEE Trans. Acoust. Speech Signal Process. **35**(8), 1153–1169 (1987)
321. Maragos, P., Schafer, R.: Morphological filters–Part II: their relations to median, order-statistic, and stack filters. IEEE Trans. Acoust. Speech Signal Process. **35**(8), 1170–1184 (1987)
322. Markosian, L., Kowalski, M.A., Trychin, S.J., Bourdev, L.D., Goldstein, D., Hughes, J.F.: Real-time nonphotorealistic rendering. In: Proc. SIGGRAPH, pp. 415–420 (1997)
323. Marr, D., Hildreth, R.C.: Theory of edge detection. Proc. R. Soc. Lond. B, Biol. Sci. **207**, 187–217 (1980)
324. Martin, D.R., Fowlkes, C.C., Malik, J.: Learning to detect natural image boundaries using local brightness, color, and texture cues. IEEE Trans. Pattern Anal. Mach. Intell. **26**(5), 530–549 (2004)
325. Martín, D., Arroyo, G., Luzón, M.V., Isenberg, T.: Example-based stippling using a scale-dependent grayscale process. In: Proc. NPAR, pp. 51–61 (2010)
326. Martín, D., Arroyo, G., Luzón, M.V., Isenberg, T.: Scale-dependent and example-based stippling. Comput. Graph. **35**(1), 160–174 (2011)
327. McCann, J., Pollard, N.S.: Real-time gradient-domain painting. ACM Trans. Graph. **27**(3), 93 (2008)
328. McCann, J., Pollard, N.S.: Local layering. ACM Trans. Graph. **28**(3), 84 (2009)
329. Meier, B.J.: Painterly rendering for animation. In: Proc. SIGGRAPH, pp. 477–484 (1996)
330. Mello, V.B., Jung, C.R., Walter, M.: Virtual woodcuts from images. In: Proc. GRAPHITE, pp. 103–109 (2007)
331. Meng, M., Zhao, M., Zhu, S.-C.: Artistic paper-cut of human portraits. In: Proc. International Conference on Multimedia, p. 931 (2010)
332. Mi, X., Xu, J., Tang, M., Dong, J.: The droplet virtual brush for Chinese calligraphic character modeling. In: Proceedings of the IEEE Workshop on Applications of Computer Vision, pp. 330–334 (2002)
333. Mi, X., DeCarlo, D., Stone, M.: Abstraction of 2D shapes in terms of parts. In: Proc. NPAR, pp. 15–24 (2009)
334. Min, F., Suo, J.-L., Zhu, S.-C., Sang, N.: An automatic portrait system based on and–or graph representation. In: Proc. EMMCVPR, pp. 184–197 (2007)
335. Mischaikow, K., Mrozek, M.: Conley index. In: Handbook of Dynamical Systems, vol. 2, pp. 393–460. North-Holland, Amsterdam (2002)
336. Mitchell, J., Francke, M., Eng, D.: Illustrative rendering in team fortress 2. In: Proc. NPAR, pp. 71–76 (2007)
337. Mizuno, S., Okada, M., Toriwaki, J.: An interactive designing system with virtual sculpting and virtual woodcut printing. Comput. Graph. Forum **18**(3), 183–194 (1999)
338. Mo, Z., Lewis, J.P., Neumann, U.: Improved automatic caricature by feature normalization and exaggeration. In: SIGGRAPH Sketch (2004)
339. Moon, P., Spencer, D.E.: Aesthetic measure applied to color harmony. J. Opt. Soc. Am. **34**(4), 234–242 (1944)
340. Mould, D.: A stained glass image filter. In: Eurographics Symposium on Rendering: 14th Eurographics Workshop on Rendering, pp. 20–25 (2003)
341. Mould, D.: Stipple placement using distance in a weighted graph. In: Proc. CAe, pp. 45–52 (2007)
342. Mould, D., Grant, K.: Stylized black and white images from photographs. In: Proc. NPAR, pp. 49–58 (2008)
343. Mould, D., Mandryk, R.L., Li, H.: Emotional response and visual attention to non-photorealistic images. Comput. Graph. **36**(5), 658–672 (2012)
344. Newman, D.J.: The hexagon theorem. IEEE Trans. Inf. Theory **28**(2), 137–138 (1982)
345. Neyret, F.: Advected textures. In: Proc. SCA, pp. 147–153 (2003)
346. Ngo, D.C.L., Samsudin, A., Abdullah, R.: Aesthetic measures for assessing graphic screens. J. Inf. Sci. Eng. **16**(1), 97–116 (2000)

347. Nienhaus, M., Döllner, J.: Sketchy drawings. In: Proc. AFRIGRAPH, pp. 73–81 (2004)
348. Nock, R., Nielsen, F.: Statistical region merging. IEEE Trans. Pattern Anal. Mach. Intell. **26**(11), 1452–1458 (2004)
349. Obaid, M., Mukundan, R., Billinghurst, M.: Rendering and animating expressive caricatures. In: Proc. ICCSIT, pp. 401–406 (2010)
350. O'Donovan, P., Hertzmann, A.: AniPaint: interactive painterly animation from video. IEEE Trans. Vis. Comput. Graph. **18**(3), 475–487 (2012)
351. Okabe, Y., Saito, S., Nakajima, M.: Paintbrush rendering of lines using HMMs. In: Proc. GRAPHITE, pp. 91–98 (2005)
352. Okamoto, Y., Uehara, R.: How to make a picturesque maze. In: Proceedings of the 21st Annual Canadian Conference on Computational Geometry, pp. 137–140 (2009)
353. Olsen, S.C., Gooch, B.: Image simplification and vectorization. In: Proc. NPAR, pp. 65–74 (2011)
354. Orzan, A., Bousseau, A., Barla, P., Thollot, J.: Structure-preserving manipulation of photographs. In: Proc. NPAR, pp. 103–110 (2007)
355. Orzan, A., Bousseau, A., Winnemöller, H., Barla, P., Thollot, J., Salesin, D.: Diffusion curves: a vector representation for smooth-shaded images. ACM Trans. Graph. **27**(3), 92 (2008)
356. Osher, S., Rudin, L.I.: Feature-oriented image enhancement using shock filters. SIAM J. Numer. Anal. **27**(4), 919–940 (1990)
357. Ostromoukhov, V.: Digital facial engraving. In: Proc. SIGGRAPH, pp. 417–424 (1999)
358. Ostromoukhov, V., Hersch, R.D.: Multi-color and artistic dithering. In: Proc. SIGGRAPH, pp. 425–432 (1999)
359. Otsu, N.: A threshold selection method from gray-level histograms. IEEE Trans. Syst. Man Cybern. **9**, 62–66 (1979)
360. Palacios, J., Zhang, E.: Rotational symmetry field design on surfaces. ACM Trans. Graph. **26**(3), 55 (2007)
361. Palmer, S.E.: Vision Science: Photons to Phenomenology. MIT Press, Cambridge (1999)
362. Pang, W.-M., Qin, J., Cohen, M., Heng, P.-A., Choi, K.-S.: Fast rendering of diffusion curves with triangles. IEEE Comput. Graph. Appl. **32**(4), 68–78 (2012)
363. Pao, H.-K., Geiger, D., Rubin, N.: Measuring convexity for figure/ground separation. In: Proc. ICCV, pp. 948–955 (1999)
364. Papari, G., Petkov, N.: Continuous glass patterns for painterly rendering. IEEE Trans. Image Process. **18**(3), 652–664 (2009)
365. Papari, G., Petkov, N., Campisi, P.: Artistic edge and corner enhancing smoothing. IEEE Trans. Image Process. **16**(10), 2449–2462 (2007)
366. Paris, S., Kornprobst, P., Tumblin, J., Durand, F.: Bilateral filtering: theory and applications. Found. Trends Comput. Graph. Vis. **4**(1), 7–73 (2009)
367. Paris, S., Hasinoff, S.W., Kautz, J.: Local Laplacian filters. ACM Trans. Graph. **30**(4), 68 (2011)
368. Pease, A., Colton, S.: On impact and evaluation in computational creativity: a discussion of the Turing test and an alternative proposal. In: AISB Symposium on AI and Philosophy (2011)
369. Pedersen, H., Singh, K.: Organic labyrinths and mazes. In: Proc. NPAR, pp. 79–86 (2006)
370. Pérez, P., Gangnet, M., Blake, A.: Poisson image editing. ACM Trans. Graph. **22**(3), 313–318 (2003)
371. Perona, P., Malik, J.: Scale-space and edge detection using anisotropic diffusion. IEEE Trans. Pattern Anal. Mach. Intell. **12**(7), 629–639 (1990)
372. Petrović, L., Fujito, B., Williams, L., Finkelstein, A.: Shadows for cel animation. In: Proc. SIGGRAPH, pp. 511–516 (2000)
373. Pham, T.Q., van Vliet, L.J.: Separable bilateral filtering for fast video preprocessing. In: Proc. ICME, pp. 454–457 (2005)
374. Pharr, M., Fernando, R.: GPU Gems 2: Programming Techniques for High-Performance Graphics and General-Purpose Computation. Addison-Wesley Professional, Reading (2005)

375. Popescu, V., Rosen, P., Adamo-Villani, N.: The graph camera. ACM Trans. Graph. **28**(5), 158 (2009)
376. Porikli, F.: Constant time $O(1)$ bilateral filtering. In: Proc. CVPR, pp. 1–8 (2008)
377. Potts, R.: Some generalized order-disorder transformation. In: Proceedings of Cambridge Philosophical Society, vol. 48, pp. 106–109 (1952)
378. Pratt, W.K.: Digital Image Processing, 3rd edn. Wiley, New York (2001)
379. Praun, E., Hoppe, H., Webb, M., Finkelstein, A.: Real-time hatching. In: Proc. SIGGRAPH, pp. 581–586. ACM, New York (2001)
380. Price, B.L., Barrett, W.A.: Object-based vectorization for interactive image editing. Vis. Comput. **22**(9–11), 661–670 (2006)
381. Pudet, T.: Real time fitting of hand-sketched pressure brushstrokes. Comput. Graph. Forum **13**(3), 205–220 (1994)
382. Qu, Y., Wong, T.-T., Heng, P.-A.: Manga colorization. ACM Trans. Graph. **25**(3), 1214–1220 (2006)
383. Quinlan, J.R.: C4.5: Programs for Machine Learning. Morgan Kaufmann, San Mateo (1993)
384. Raskar, R., Cohen, M.: Image precision silhouette edges. In: Proc. I3D, pp. 135–140 (1999)
385. Rautek, P., Bruckner, S., Gröller, E., Viola, I.: Illustrative visualization: new technology or useless tautology?. Comput. Graph. **42**(3), 4 (2008)
386. Real Pen Work: Self-Instructor in Penmanship. Knowles and Maxim (1885)
387. Richens, P.: The Piranesi system for interactive rendering. In: Proceedings of the Eighth International Conference on Computer Aided Architectural Design Futures, pp. 381–398 (1999)
388. Rosin, P.L., Lai, Y.-K.: Towards artistic minimal rendering. In: Proc. NPAR, pp. 119–127 (2010)
389. Ross, F., Ross, W.T.: The Jordan curve theorem is non-trivial. J. Math. Arts **5**(4), 213–219 (2011)
390. Rother, C., Kolmogorov, V., Blake, A.: "GrabCut": interactive foreground extraction using iterated graph cuts. ACM Trans. Graph. **23**(3), 309–314 (2004)
391. Rusinkiewicz, S., Cole, F., DeCarlo, D., Finkelstein, A.: Line drawings from 3D models. In: SIGGRAPH Classes, pp. 39:1–39:356 (2008)
392. Saito, S., Nakajima, M.: 3D physics-based brush model for painting. In: Proc. SIGGRAPH, p. 226 (1999)
393. Saito, T., Takahashi, T.: Comprehensible rendering of 3-D shapes. Comput. Graph. **24**(4), 197–206 (1990)
394. Salesin, D.: Non-photorealistic animation and rendering: 7 grand challenges. In: Keynote talk at NPAR (2002)
395. Salisbury, M.P., Anderson, S.E., Barzel, R., Salesin, D.H.: Interactive pen-and-ink illustration. In: Proc. SIGGRAPH, pp. 101–108 (1994)
396. Salisbury, M., Anderson, C., Lischinski, D., Salesin, D.H.: Scale-dependent reproduction of pen-and-ink illustrations. In: Proc. SIGGRAPH, pp. 461–468 (1996)
397. Salisbury, M.P., Wong, M.T., Hughes, J.F., Salesin, D.H.: Orientable textures for image-based pen-and-ink illustration. In: Proc. SIGGRAPH, pp. 401–406 (1997)
398. Santella, A., DeCarlo, D.: Abstracted painterly renderings using eye-tracking data. In: Proc. NPAR, pp. 75–82 (2002)
399. Santella, A., DeCarlo, D.: Visual interest and NPR: an evaluation and manifesto. In: Proc. NPAR, pp. 71–78 (2004)
400. Schaefer, S., McPhail, T., Warren, J.: Image deformation using moving least squares. ACM Trans. Graph. **25**(3), 533–540 (2006)
401. Schelske, A.: Zur Sozialität des nicht-fotorealistischen Renderings. Eine zu kurze, soziologische Skizze für zeitgenössische Bildmaschinen. Image: J. Interdiscip. Image Sci. **6**, 47–58 (2007)
402. Schirra, J.R.J., Scholz, M.: Abstraction versus realism: not the real question. In: Computer Visualization—Graphics, Abstraction, and Interactivity, pp. 379–401. Springer, Berlin (1998)

403. Schlechtweg, S., Germer, T., Strothotte, T.: RenderBots—multi-agent systems for direct image generation. Comput. Graph. Forum **24**(2), 137–148 (2005)
404. Schmidt, R., Isenberg, T., Jepp, P., Singh, K., Wyvill, B.: Sketching, scaffolding, and inking: a visual history for interactive 3D modeling. In: Proc. NPAR, pp. 23–32 (2007)
405. Schumann, J., Strothotte, T., Raab, A., Laser, S.: Assessing the effect of non-photorealistic rendered images in CAD. In: Proc. CHI, pp. 35–42 (1996)
406. Schwarz, M., Stamminger, M.: On predicting visual popping in dynamic scenes. In: Proc. APGV, pp. 93–100 (2009)
407. Schwarz, M., Isenberg, T., Mason, K., Carpendale, S.: Modeling with rendering primitives: an interactive non-photorealistic canvas. In: Proc. NPAR, pp. 15–22 (2007)
408. Secord, A.: Weighted Voronoi stippling. In: Proc. NPAR, pp. 37–43 (2002)
409. Seifi, H., DiPaola, S., Enns, J.T.: Exploring the effect of color palette in painterly rendered character sequences. In: Proc. CAe, pp. 89–97 (2012)
410. Sethian, J.A.: Level Set Methods and Fast Marching Methods: Evolving Interfaces in Computational Geometry, Fluid Mechanics, Computer Vision, and Materials Science. Cambridge University Press, Cambridge (1999)
411. Setlur, V., Wilkinson, S.: Automatic stained glass rendering. In: Computer Graphics International, pp. 682–691 (2006)
412. Shekhovtsov, A., Kovtun, I., Hlaváč, V.: Efficient MRF deformation model for non-rigid image matching. Comput. Vis. Image Underst. **112**(1), 91–99 (2008)
413. Shiraishi, M., Yamaguchi, Y.: An algorithm for automatic painterly rendering based on local source image approximation. In: Proc. NPAR, pp. 53–58 (2000)
414. Shugrina, M., Betke, M., Collomosse, J.P.: Empathic painting: interactive stylization through observed emotional state. In: Proc. NPAR, pp. 87–96 (2006)
415. Singh, M., Schaefer, S.: Suggestive hatching. In: Proc. CAe, pp. 25–32 (2010)
416. Smith, J.M.: Recent developments in numerical integration. J. Dyn. Syst. Meas. Control **96**(1), 61–70 (1974)
417. Smith, A.R.: Digital paint systems: an anecdotal and historical overview. IEEE Ann. Hist. Comput. **23**, 4–30 (2001)
418. Smith, R.: Open Dynamics Engine (2007). http://www.ode.org
419. Smith, P.: Pictorial Grammar: Chomsky, John Willats, and the Rules of Representation. Art Hist. 562–593 (2011)
420. Smith, K., Liu, Y., Klein, A.: Animosaics. In: Proc. SCA, pp. 201–208 (2005)
421. Son, M., Lee, Y., Kang, H., Lee, S.: Structure grid for directional stippling. Graph. Models **73**(3), 74–87 (2011)
422. Song, Y., Hall, P.M., Rosin, P.L., Collomosse, J.: Arty shapes. In: Proc. CAe, pp. 65–72 (2008)
423. Sonka, M., Hlavac, V., Boyle, R.: Image Processing, Analysis, and Machine Vision. Thomson, Tampa (2007)
424. Sousa, M.C., Buchanan, J.W.: Computer-generated graphite pencil rendering of 3D polygonal models. Proc. Eurographics **18**(3), 195–207 (1999)
425. Stoer, J., Bulirsch, R.: Introduction to Numerical Analysis. Springer, Berlin (1980)
426. Strassmann, S.H.: Hairy brushes. Comput. Graph. **20**(4), 225–232 (1986)
427. Strothotte, T., Schlechtweg, S.: Non-Photorealistic Computer Graphics: Modeling, Rendering, and Animation. Morgan Kaufmann, San Mateo (2002)
428. Strothotte, T., Preim, B., Raab, A., Schumann, J., Forsey, D.R.: How to render frames and influence people. Comput. Graph. Forum **13**(3), 455–466 (1994)
429. Sun, J., Liang, L., Wen, F., Shum, H.-Y.: Image vectorization using optimized gradient meshes. ACM Trans. Graph. **26**(3), 11 (2007)
430. Sun, Q., Fu, C.-W., He, Y.: An interactive multi-touch sketching interface for diffusion curves. In: Proc. CHI, pp. 1611–1614 (2011)
431. Sutherland, I.E.: Sketchpad: a man-machine graphical communication system. In: Proc. Spring Joint Computer Conference, vol. 23, pp. 329–346 (1963)

References

432. Sýkora, D., Buriánek, J., Žára, J.: Colorization of black-and-white cartoons. Image Vis. Comput. **23**(9), 767–782 (2005)
433. Sýkora, D., Buriánek, J., Žára, J.: Sketching cartoons by example. In: Proc. SBIM, pp. 27–34 (2005)
434. Sýkora, D., Dingliana, J., Collins, S.: As-rigid-as-possible image registration for hand-drawn cartoon animations. In: Proc. NPAR, pp. 25–33 (2009)
435. Sýkora, D., Dingliana, J., Collins, S.: LazyBrush: flexible painting tool for hand-drawn cartoons. Comput. Graph. Forum **28**(2), 599–608 (2009)
436. Sýkora, D., Sedlacek, D., Jinchao, S., Dingliana, J., Collins, S.: Adding depth to cartoons using sparse depth (in)equalities. Comput. Graph. Forum **29**(2), 615–623 (2010)
437. Sýkora, D., Ben-Chen, M., Čadík, M., Whited, B., Simmons, M.: TexToons: practical texture mapping for hand-drawn cartoon animations. In: Proc. NPAR, pp. 75–83 (2011)
438. Szirányi, T., Tóth, Z., Figueiredo, M., Zerubia, J., Jain, A.: Optimization of paintbrush rendering of images by dynamic MCMC methods. In: Proc. EMMCVPR, pp. 201–215 (2001)
439. Takayama, K., Sorkine, O., Nealen, A., Igarashi, T.: Volumetric modeling with diffusion surfaces. ACM Trans. Graph. **29**(6), 180 (2010)
440. Tauber, A.: The Elusive Synthesis Aesthetics and Science. Kluwer Academic, Dordrecht (1996)
441. Thompson, W., Fleming, R., Creem-Regehr, S., Stefanucci, J.K.: Visual Perception from a Computer Graphics Perspective, 1st edn. AK Peters, Wellesley (2011)
442. Tietjen, C., Isenberg, T., Preim, B.: Combining silhouettes, shading, and volume rendering for surgery education and planning. In: Proc. EuroVis, pp. 303–310 (2005)
443. Todo, H., Anjyo, K., Igarashi, T.: Stylized lighting for cartoon shader. Comput. Animat. Virtual Worlds **20**(2–3), 143–152 (2009)
444. Tolhurst, D., Tadmor, Y., Chao, T.: The amplitude spectra of natural images. Ophthalmic Physiol. Opt. **12**, 229–232 (1992)
445. Tomasi, C., Manduchi, R.: Bilateral filtering for gray and color images. In: Proc. ICCV, pp. 839–846 (1998)
446. Tominaga, M., Fukuoka, S., Murakami, K., Koshimizu, H.: Facial caricaturing with motion caricaturing in PICASSO system. In: Proceedings of the IEEE/ASME International Conference on Advanced Intelligent Mechatronics, p. 30 (1997)
447. Tominaga, M., Hayashi, J.-I., Murakami, K., Koshimizu, H.: Facial caricaturing system PICASSO with emotional motion deformation. In: Proceedings of the 2nd International Conference on Knowledge-Based Intelligent Electronic System, pp. 205–214 (1998)
448. Torre, V., Poggio, T.A.: On edge detection. IEEE Trans. Pattern Anal. Mach. Intell. **8**(2), 147–163 (1986)
449. Treavett, S.M.F., Chen, M.: Statistical techniques for the automated synthesis of non-photorealistic images. In: Proc. EGUK, pp. 201–210 (1997)
450. Tresset, P., Leymarie, F.F.: Generative portrait sketching. In: Proc. VSMM, pp. 739–748 (2005)
451. Turk, G.: Generating textures for arbitrary surfaces using reaction-diffusion. In: Proc. SIGGRAPH, pp. 289–298 (1991)
452. Ulichney, R.: Digital Halftoning. MIT Press, Cambridge (1987)
453. Umenhoffer, T., Szécsi, L., Szirmay-Kalos, L.: Hatching for motion picture production. Comput. Graph. Forum **30**(2), 533–542 (2011)
454. van den Boomgaard, R.: Decomposition of the Kuwahara–Nagao operator in terms of linear smoothing and morphological sharpening. In: Proc. ISMM, pp. 283–292 (2002)
455. Van Laerhoven, T., Van Reeth, F.: Brush up your painting skills: realistic brush design for interactive painting applications. Vis. Comput. **23**(9), 763–771 (2007)
456. Vanderhaeghe, D., Barla, P., Thollot, J., Sillion, F.: Dynamic point distribution for stroke-based rendering. In: Proc. EG Symposium on Rendering, pp. 139–146 (2007)
457. Vandoren, P., Van Laerhoven, T., Claesen, L., Taelman, J., Raymaekers, C., Van Reeth, F.: IntuPaint: bridging the gap between physical and digital painting. In: IEEE International Workshop on Horizontal Interactive Human Computer Systems, pp. 65–72 (2008)

458. Vandoren, P., Claesen, L., Van Laerhoven, T., Taelman, J., Van Reeth, F.: FluidPaint: an interactive digital painting system using real wet brushes. In: Proceedings of the IEEE International Workshop on Tabletops and Interactive Surfaces, pp. 53–56 (2009)
459. Vergne, R., Vanderhaeghe, D., Chen, J., Barla, P., Granier, X., Schlick, C.: Implicit brushes for stylized line-based rendering. Comput. Graph. Forum **30**, 513–522 (2011)
460. Verlaek, P.: Non-photorealistic renderings as epistemic images. In: Workshop on Abstract Images in Art and Science (2009)
461. Walther, D., Koch, C.: Modeling attention to salient proto-objects. Neural Netw. **19**(9), 1395–1407 (2006)
462. Wan, L., Liu, X., Wong, T.-T., Leung, C.-S.: Evolving mazes from images. IEEE Trans. Vis. Comput. Graph. **16**(2), 287–297 (2010)
463. Wang, T., Collomosse, J.: Progressive motion diffusion of labeling priors for coherent video segmentation. IEEE Trans. Multimed. **14**(2), 389–400 (2012)
464. Wang, X., Tang, X.: Face sketch synthesis and recognition. In: Proc. ICCV, pp. 687–694 (2003)
465. Wang, J., Thiesson, B., Xu, Y., Cohen, M.F.: Image and video segmentation by anisotropic kernel mean shift. In: Proc. ECCV, pp. 238–249 (2004)
466. Wang, J., Xu, Y., Shum, H.-Y., Cohen, M.F.: Video tooning. ACM Trans. Graph. **23**(3), 574–583 (2004)
467. Wang, J., Drucker, S.M., Agrawala, M., Cohen, M.F.: The cartoon animation filter. ACM Trans. Graph. **25**(3), 1169–1173 (2006)
468. Wang, Y., Xu, K., Xiong, Y., Cheng, Z.-Q.: 2D shape deformation based on rigid square matching. Comput. Animat. Virtual Worlds **19**(3–4), 411–420 (2008)
469. Wang, T., Collomosse, J., Hu, R., Slatter, D., Greig, D., Cheatle, P.: Stylized ambient displays of digital media collections. Comput. Graph. **35**(1), 54–66 (2011)
470. Weickert, J.: Anisotropic Diffusion in Image Processing. Teubner, Leipzig (1998)
471. Weickert, J.: Coherence-enhancing diffusion of colour images. Image Vis. Comput. **17**(3), 201–212 (1999)
472. Weickert, J.: Coherence-enhancing shock filters. In: DAGM-Symposium, pp. 1–8 (2003)
473. Weickert, J., ter Haar Romeny, B.M., Viergever, M.A.: Efficient and reliable schemes for nonlinear diffusion filtering. IEEE Trans. Image Process. **7**(3), 398–410 (1998)
474. Wen, F., Luan, Q., Liang, L., Xu, Y.-Q., Shum, H.-Y.: Color sketch generation. In: Proc. NPAR, pp. 47–54 (2006)
475. Wiggins, G.A.: A preliminary framework for description, analysis and comparison of creative systems. Knowl.-Based Syst. **19**(7), 458–499 (2006)
476. Willats, J.: Art and Representation: New Principles in the Analysis of Pictures. Princeton University Press, Princeton (1997)
477. Willats, J., Durand, F.: Defining pictorial style: lessons from linguistics and computer graphics. Axiomathes **15**, 319–351 (2005)
478. Winkenbach, G.A., Salesin, D.H.: Computer-generated pen-and-ink illustration. In: Proc. SIGGRAPH, pp. 91–100 (1994)
479. Winnemöller, H., Bangay, S.: Geometric approximations towards free specular comic shading. Comput. Graph. Forum **21**(3), 309–316 (2002)
480. Winnemöller, H., Olsen, S.C., Gooch, B.: Real-time video abstraction. ACM Trans. Graph. **25**(3), 1221–1226 (2006)
481. Winnemöller, H., Feng, D., Gooch, B., Suzuki, S.: Using NPR to evaluate perceptual shape cues in dynamic environments. In: Proc. NPAR, pp. 85–92 (2007)
482. Winnemöller, H., Orzan, A., Boissieux, L., Thollot, J.: Texture design and draping in 2D images. Comput. Graph. Forum **28**(4), 1091–1099 (2009)
483. Winnemöller, H., Kyprianidis, J.E., Olsen, S.C.: XDoG: an extended difference-of-Gaussians compendium including advanced image stylization. Comput. Graph. **36**(6), 740–753 (2012)
484. Witten, T.A. Jr., Sander, L.M.: Diffusion-limited aggregation, a kinetic critical phenomenon. Phys. Rev. Lett. **47**(19), 1400–1403 (1981)

485. Wong, F.J., Takahashi, S.: Flow-based automatic generation of hybrid picture mazes. Comput. Graph. Forum **28**(7), 1975–1984 (2009)
486. Wong, F.J., Takahashi, S.: A graph-based approach to continuous line illustrations with variable levels of detail. Comput. Graph. Forum **30**(7), 1931–1939 (2011)
487. Woo, M., Neider, J., Davis, T., Shreiner, D.: OpenGL Programming Guide: The Official Guide to Learning OpenGL, Version 1.2, 3rd edn. Addison-Wesley, Reading (1999)
488. Wood, D.N., Finkelstein, A., Hughes, J.F., Thayer, C.E., Salesin, D.H.: Multiperspective panoramas for cel animation. In: Proc. SIGGRAPH, pp. 243–250 (1997)
489. Wyszecki, G., Stiles, W.S.: Color Science: Concepts and Methods, Quantitative Data and Formulae. Wiley-Interscience, New York (1982)
490. Wyvill, B., van Overveld, K., Carpendale, S.: Rendering cracks in batik. In: Proc. NPAR, pp. 61–149 (2004)
491. Xia, T., Liao, B., Yu, Y.: Patch-based image vectorization with automatic curvilinear feature alignment. ACM Trans. Graph. **28**(5), 115 (2009)
492. Xie, N., Laga, H., Saito, S., Nakajima, M.: IR2s: interactive real photo to Sumi-e. In: Proc. NPAR, pp. 63–71 (2010)
493. Xie, N., Laga, H., Saito, S., Nakajima, M.: Contour-driven Sumi-e rendering of real photos. Comput. Graph. **35**(1), 122–134 (2011)
494. Xing, Q., Akleman, E., Taubin, G., Chen, J.: Surface covering curves. In: Workshop on Computational Aesthetics, pp. 107–114 (2012)
495. Xu, J., Kaplan, C.S.: Calligraphic packing. In: Proc. Graphics Interface, pp. 43–50 (2007)
496. Xu, J., Kaplan, C.S.: Image-guided maze construction. ACM Trans. Graph. **26**(3), 29 (2007)
497. Xu, J., Kaplan, C.S.: Vortex maze construction. J. Math. Arts **1**(1), 7–20 (2007)
498. Xu, J., Kaplan, C.S.: Artistic thresholding. In: Proc. NPAR, pp. 39–47 (2008)
499. Xu, Z., Luo, J.: Accurate dynamic sketching of faces from video. In: Proc. CVPR (2007)
500. Xu, C., Prince, L.: Snakes, shapes, and gradient vector flow. IEEE Trans. Image Process. **7**(3), 359–369 (1998)
501. Xu, S., Tang, M., Lau, F., Pan, Y.: Virtual hairy brush for painterly rendering. Graph. Models **66**(5), 263–302 (2004)
502. Xu, Z., Chen, H., Zhu, S.-C.: A high resolution grammatical model for face representation and sketching. In: Proc. CVPR, pp. 470–477 (2005)
503. Xu, S., Tan, H., Jiao, X., Lau, F.C.M., Pan, Y.: A generic pigment model for digital painting. Comput. Graph. Forum **26**(3), 609–618 (2007)
504. Xu, Z., Chen, H., Zhu, S.C., Luo, J.: A hierarchical compositional model for face representation and sketching. IEEE Trans. Pattern Anal. Mach. Intell. **30**(6), 955–969 (2008)
505. Xu, X., Zhang, L., Wong, T.-T.: Structure-based ASCII art. ACM Trans. Graph. **29**(4), 52 (2010)
506. Xu, L., Lu, C., Xu, Y., Jia, J.: Image smoothing via L_0 gradient minimization. ACM Trans. Graph. **30**(6), 174 (2011)
507. Yantis, S., Jonides, J.: Abrupt visual onsets and selective attention: evidence from visual search. J. Exp. Psychol. Hum. Percept. Perform. **10**(5), 601–621 (1984)
508. Yarbus, A.L.: Eye Movements and Vision. Plenum, New York (1967)
509. Young, R.A.: The Gaussian derivative model for spatial vision: I. Retinal mechanisms. Spat. Vis. **2**(4), 273–293 (1987)
510. Yu, J., McMillan, L.: A framework for multiperspective rendering. In: Proc. EG Symposium on Rendering, pp. 61–68 (2004)
511. Zeki, S.: Inner Vision: An Exploration of Art and the Brain. Oxford University Press, London (2000)
512. Zeki, S.: Splendors and Miseries of the Brain: Love, Creativity, and the Quest for Human Happiness, 5th edn. Wiley-Blackwell, New York (2009)
513. Zeng, K., Zhao, M., Xiong, C., Zhu, S.-C.: From image parsing to painterly rendering. ACM Trans. Graph. **29**(1), 2 (2009)
514. Zhang, E., Mischaikow, K., Turk, G.: Vector field design on surfaces. ACM Trans. Graph. **25**(4), 1294–1326 (2006)

515. Zhang, E., Hays, J., Turk, G.: Interactive tensor field design and visualization on surfaces. IEEE Trans. Vis. Comput. Graph. **13**(1), 94–107 (2007)
516. Zhang, S.-H., Li, X.-Y., Hu, S.-M., Martin, R.R.: Online video stream abstraction and stylization. IEEE Trans. Multimed. **13**(6), 1286–1294 (2011)
517. Zhao, M., Zhu, S.-C.: Sisley the abstract painter. In: Proc. NPAR, pp. 99–107 (2010)
518. Zhao, M., Zhu, S.-C.: Customizing painterly rendering styles using stroke processes. In: Proc. NPAR, pp. 137–146 (2011)
519. Zhao, M., Zhu, S.-C.: Portrait painting using active templates. In: Proc. NPAR, pp. 117–124 (2011)

Index

A
Active appearance model, 248, 252
Active shape model, 240, 242, 246, 252
Active template, 248
Ancient Mosaic, 190
Ancient Mosaics, 193
And–or graph, 243, 244, 246, 252
Anisotropic diffusion, 94
Architecture, 365

B
Bézier curve, 246
Bilateral filter, 79
  flow-based, 81
  orientation-aligned, 81
  xy-separable, 81

C
CAD, 365, 366
Cartoon, 357
  backgrounds, 362
  coherence, 361
  extended shading, 360, 362
  image-based, 361
  interactive rendering, 358
  shading, 360
  ToonPAINT, 368
Cartoon pipeline, 88
CEF, *see* coherence-enhancing filtering
Characteristic point, *see* feature point
Closing, 92
Coherence-enhancing filtering, 98
Color space
  chrominance, 239
  luma, 239
  YIQ, 239
Computer games, 357, 364
Crystallization Mosaic, 190

D
Deblurring, 96
Difference of Gaussians, 84
  flow-based, 86
  XDoG, 84
Dijkstra's algorithm, 58
Dilation, 92
Distance transforms, 92
DoG, *see* difference of Gaussians

E
Edge enhancement, 77
Edge tangent flow, 82
Edge-preserving filtering, 77
Eigen transform, 245, 246
Entertainment, 357
Erosion, 92
ETF, *see* edge tangent flow
Evaluation, 311, 333
  critique, 320
  ethnographic, 326
  methodologies, 312
  NPR Turing test, 311, 323, 327, 333, 335, 346
  observational study, 326
  psychophysical study, 316, 319, 320, 322
  qualitative, 312, 319, 320, 326
  quantitative, 312
  questions to ask, 311, 327
Exaggeration, 250, 252
Example-based, 241, 242, 245, 252

F
FDoG, *see* flow-based DoG
Feature point, 239
Fiducial point, *see* feature point

G

G-Buffers, 358, 364
Gabor wavelet, 238
Geodesic distance transform, 92
GGDT, *see* geodesic distance transform
Glass patterns, 92
GPU, 358, 364
Gradient domain, 98
Grand challenges of NPR, 311

H

Halftoning, 356
  digital, 45
  dithering, 49
  error diffusion, 47
  Floyd–Steinberg error diffusion, 47
  screening, 45, 49, 60
  threshold quantization, 46
Hatching, 103, 355, 356
Hedcut, 356
Hierarchical, 243, 246, 252
Holistic, 239

I

IB-AR, 77
Image analysis and synthesis, 238
Image and video processing, 103
Integral convolution, 92

K

Kuwahara filter
  anisotropic, 90
  classical, 88
  generalized, 89
  multi-scale, 91
  polynomial, 90

L

Landmark point, *see* feature point
Landmark points, *see* feature points
Laplacian of Gaussian, 84
LIC, *see* line integral convolution
Line integral convolution, 82, 86
LoG, *see* Laplacian of Gaussian

M

Mathematical morphology, 92
  closing, 92
  dilation, 92
  erosion, 92
  opening, 92
Maximum principle, 95
MCF, *see* mean curvature flow
  constrained, 97

Mean curvature flow, 96
  constrained, 96
Mesh, 245, 246, 252
MM, *see* mathematical morphology
Mooney image, 246
Morphological smoothing, 92
Mosaic, 55
Movies
  animations, 361
  Futurama, 362
  Pokémon, 362
  What Dreams May Come, 363
Multi-style painter rendering, 103

N

Non-photorealistic rendering, 103
Nonlinear filter, 77
NPR, 238, 245, 246
  art creation tools, 354
  assistive technologies, 354
  automation, 371
  caricature, 250
  casual creativity, 370
  in the wild, 353
  oil-painting, 248
  paper-cut, 246
  restrictive definition, 353
  sketch, 239
  style reproduction, 354
  user-assisted, 371
  visualization, 365
NPR Turing test, 311, 323, 327, 333, 335, 346

O

Opening, 92
Oriental painting, 103

P

Painterly rendering, 103, 363
Parse graph, 244
Part-based, 239, 241
Partial differential equation, 93
PCA, 238
PDE, *see* partial differential equation
Photo Mosaic, 190
Poisson's equation, 98
Portraiture, 237
  computerized simulation, 238
Principles of portraiture
  aesthetic, 237, 239, 242, 244, 246, 250, 252
  likeness, 237, 239, 242–244, 246, 250, 252
  trade-off, 246, 250–252

Printing, 354, 356
Production, 354
Puzzle Image Mosaic, 190

R
Randomness, 361

S
Scientific illustration, 49, 60, 319
    data-driven, 60
Scientific visualization, 333
    illustrative visualization, 60, 311, 319
Semantic, 241
Shock filter, 95, 96
Smoothed structure tensor, 82
Software
    Deep Canvas, 363
    Mobile, 368
    MotionPaint, 363
    PaletteCAD, 367
    Piranesi, 366
    SketchUp, 367
    ToonPAINT, 368
SST, *see* smoothed structure tensor
Stippling, 49, 355, 356
    arbitrary objects, 53
    centroidal Voronoi tessellation, 50
    example-based, 56
    example-based distributions, 56
    example-based stipple dots, 56, 57
    hedcut, 356
    hedcut illustrations, 58
    high-level processing, 58
    Lloyd's method, 50
    scale-dependent, 57
    structure-aware, 58
    Voronoi tessellation, 50
    weighted centroidal Voronoi tessellation, 51

T
Temporal coherence, 358, 361, 363
Thin plate spline, 248
Turing test, 311, 323, 327, 333, 335, 346

U
Unsharp masking, 95

V
Vector and tensor field design, 103

W
Wall Street Journal, 356
Watercolor, 92
Watercolorization, 103
Weighted least squares, 98
WOG pipeline, 88
Woodcut, 355

X
XDoG, 84

The manufacturer's authorised representative in the EU is Springer Nature Customer Service Centre GmbH, Europaplatz 3, 69115 Heidelberg, Germany. If you have any concerns regarding our products, please contact ProductSafety@springernature.com

Printed and bound by CPI Group (UK) Ltd, Croydon, CR0 4YY
23/03/2026
02076654-0001